MODERN POLITICAL ECONOMY

MODERN POLITICAL ECONOMY

An Introduction to Economics

Richard B. McKenzie

Department of Economics
Clemson University

Gordon Tullock

Center for Study of Public Choice
Virginia Polytechnic Institute and State University

McGraw-Hill Book Company

New York St. Louis San Francisco Auckland Bogotá
Düsseldorf Johannesburg London Madrid Mexico
Montreal New Delhi Panama Paris São Paulo
Singapore Sydney Tokyo Toronto

For

Susan, John, and David McKenzie

This book was set in Helvetica by Progressive Typographers.
The editors were J. S. Dietrich, Marjorie Singer,
and J. W. Maisel; the designer was Joan E. O'Connor;
the production supervisor was Dennis J. Conroy.
The drawings were done by J & R Services, Inc.
Von Hoffmann Press, Inc., was printer and binder.

MODERN POLITICAL ECONOMY: An Introduction to Economics

1234567890 VHVH 78321098

Library of Congress Cataloging in Publication Data

McKenzie, Richard B
Modern political economy.

Includes bibliographies and index.
1. Economics. I. Tullock, Gordon, joint author.
II. Title.
HB171.M28 330 77-13320
ISBN 0-07-045159-1

Contents

Part Three Social Order and the Market for Goods and Services

Part Five Social Order and the Market for Labor

Part Six The Extended World Market

To the Instructor

Our aim in writing this book is simply to introduce students to the fascinating and rewarding method of economic inquiry; but we have carried out that purpose in ways different from those used by other books currently available.

We do not include topics such as the history of the labor movement or the oligopolist's kinked demand curve usually found in most texts designed for beginning students. On the other hand, we consider many subjects usually given little or no attention in an economics course. Our discussions of group behavior and politics may appear at first glance to be out of place. However, these topics are juxtaposed with an analysis of the market system and governmental processes in the expectation that the student will acquire a deeper and firmer understanding of the social interaction of individuals. By means of new subject matter and subtle differences in emphasis and format, we make a partial departure from most other introductory economics texts.

Differences, whether subtle or dramatic, do not necessarily make a book "better." They are not compelling reasons for change, and change for the sake of change is not our purpose. But we feel that students gain greater understanding from the method used in the book. In order that you may understand the basis of the book, we would like to explain what the method is.

THE TRADE-OFF BETWEEN THEORY AND APPLICATION

The foundation of economics is the body of theory familiar to all economists. It gives structure to economic knowledge and largely defines the method of economic analysis. If students are to acquire an understanding of what economics is about, they must be introduced to at least a portion of this theoretical understructure. There is no debate here. Having accepted this premise, however, professors and authors of textbooks both face critical choices concerning how much theory is appropriate for beginning students. Adding theoretical refinements to a course makes it more inclusive of the understructure. At the same time, some of the refinements are quite technical and may have only limited usefulness to students who do not intend to become practicing economists themselves. Moveover, the addition of refinements requires that time and student attention (both resources in limited supply) be directed away from repeated emphasis on basic theories. The opportunity to apply the theories to a wide range of political, economic, and social issues will then be limited. In short, the economic problem—the problem of choice—emerges as we decide how we should teach students about that very problem.

Many popular introductory economics texts are encyclopedic in nature: they contain a smattering of almost all theories taught at the intermediate level. Many of the theories are repeated once again in graduate courses on the assumption that they have not yet been learned. In developing their texts, authors trade off elaboration of the subleties of basic theories and the application of those theories for treatment of refinements. By market approval in the past, the trade-off which favors theories has been very successful. We do not wish to detract from this approach; we mean to suggest only that there is another way which, if tried, can be just as successful. In writing this book, we have deliberately made the trade the other way. We have identified a relatively small number of concepts, principles, and models which dominate economic research. We have developed them in detail and have repeatedly emphasized their relevance to economic inquiry through application to social issues. Accordingly, we have traded theoretical refinements for what we believe will be deeper understanding and appreciation of a limited number of analytical tools.

In making this trade, we have taken the position that students can learn as much or more if the number of theoretical refinements is reduced, a point supported by research. In our view, this conclusion is altogether reasonable. Theory is the "engine of analysis," but it is also only a skeleton representation of the world the students know. No apologies are necessary here; it is the way science is transmitted. However, without amplification it is easy for beginning students to conclude that theory has no implications beyond a skeleton form; or, worse yet, that theory is a caricature of the world as they experience it. Through repeated emphasis and application to problems, both familiar and unfamiliar to the immediate circumstances of students, the power and validity of theory are defined: a kind of "flesh" is added to the skeleton. We contend that this approach not only makes the learning process more efficient but also induces more student effort.

THE STRUCTURE OF THE BOOK

Almost all students enter their first course with limited and, in some ways, defective images of the world about them. As Kenneth Boulding has put it, "All learning involves the reconstruction of images," from those presumed to be wrong to those presumed to be right.* The task of the teacher and author is to guide the student through the process of reconstructing incorrect images and reinforcing correct ones. How that process proceeds hinges on the idea the teacher has about the images the students hold when they enter class. The approach and structure of this book is therefore dependent on the instructor's perception of the student's starting point. In the

* Kenneth E. Boulding, "Some Observations on the Learning of Economics," *American Economic Review: Papers and Proceedings*, 65 (May 1975), p. 428.

instructor's view, beginning students' intellectual vision is still largely restricted by their immediate world. Most students know about buying and selling, but their grasp of any concept as abstract as the market is imperfect. Their ability to appraise the workings of the market, except in terms of how it may affect them directly, is also imperfect. The basic problem in guiding students to understand any phenomenon as broad as a market is that they have probably not learned how to abstract from the wealth of information that confronts them on a daily basis; they have not acquired a very precise or efficient framework for analysis of policy issues. Succinctly, students are very familiar with normative analysis but may be only as familiar with positive analysis as they are with the term itself.

The first four chapters of the text are therefore devoted to the development of a limited framework for economic analysis. Because it is so central to almost everything an economist does, we begin with a full exposition of the economist's notion of rationality. This in turn leads directly to discussion of the basic concepts of demand and cost. At every turn we show how this basic model of behavior can be used by students to explain events and circumstances which are immediate to their own frame of reference. Accordingly, we use as examples problems which all students confront in allocating their time between studying and leisure activities. We consider the choice which the smoker faces between years of life and the pleasure gained from smoking. Recognizing that new images can be formed only after old images have been disturbed, we draw attention to the choice the government faces everytime it considers making a highway safer; and we then address such questions as "Is life priceless?" At every possible point, we start with the familiar, but our intent is to help the student attain a greater comprehension of the more distant world of policy issues. We make the implied intellectual jump gradually and only after the student has acquired confidence in the use of basic analytical tools.

Economics is more than a study of principles of individual behavior, the focus of the first four chapters. It is also a means of understanding why and how people interact in a social setting. Further, it is a means by which a social scientist can step back from immediate and narrow policy issues and consider the somewhat artistic problem of structuring and restructuring a given social system made up of independently motivated individuals. Having established the rudiments of an analytical framework, we begin a study of social systems in Chapter 5. First, we reconstruct a state of anarchy, or "Hobbesian jungle," and then proceed with discussion of the development of a social contract, indicating why it will emerge, what are the probable ingredients in the contract, and what is its tenuous nature. By developing the concept of property rights (all explored in the context of several concrete examples), we give the student some insight into why private property exists and why a realignment of property rights may occur from time to time. The emphasis, however, is on how excessive realignments in any direction can have unforeseen consequence.

The problem of structuring social order can be viewed in several ways. As a matter of expository convenience, social order in this text is viewed as an admixture of four "social organizers": (1) voluntary cooperation through group association, (2) government, (3) market exchanges, and (4) violence. Because the economic literature in the area of violence is underdeveloped at this writing (but is beginning to take shape as an important subdiscipline), we make only passing comments about the importance and relevance of crime, war, terrorism, and revolution. In Chapter 6 we explore the characteristics of small and large groups with the aim of demonstrating the importance of groups in structuring social order and satisfying individual and collective wants. We emphasize, however, the limitations of collective behavior through purely voluntary associations of people. We demonstrate that the cost of a group pursuing the common interest of its members can escalate as the group becomes larger; and that beyond some critical group size, the cost can become so great that a voluntary association of people may no longer be able to accomplish goals which are in the common interest of all its members. This general rule is also applicable to the establishment of ethical and behavioral rules; moral considerations are therefore partially set in an economic context and are viewed as an integral component of social structure.

Societies are very large groups. If the common societal objective of raising collective and individual welfares cannot be achieved through *voluntary* group means, how can it be? We examine two means: government and the market. With the analysis of groups as background, we begin an investigation of the market processes in Chapter 7. In that and the following chapters, our objective is to demonstrate how, given the benefits of voluntary association, the market can expand collective and individual welfares. The market is seen as one alternative system which provides private incentives for individuals to work in the interest of the society: It is a means of organizing *large* groups and bringing people in groups out of what may otherwise be a latent state. As is traditional in all introductory textbooks, the efficiency characteristics of competitive markets are explored before we consider the disruptive effects of monopoly power. Because we are very much concerned with students being able to use what they learn, the models of market behavior are developed in the context of real-world examples which, for the most part, involve governmental policy issues.

The market system has its own deficiencies and limitations, as do all the other social organizers. For this reason, before closing our discussion of the market per se, we deal in Chapters 11, 12, and 13 with the major issues surrounding the public debates on price controls, regulation of industry, and consumer protection. For students who are ardent proponents of regulation and consumer protection measures, because this is the side of the debate often given the most attention by the media, the strength of the case against *some* forms of regulation and consumer protection may come as a surprise. In the chapter on regulation, we go beyond other textbooks by including an account of the economic theory of regulation which has been developed over the last decade.

THE RELEVANCE OF POLITICS IN AN ECONOMICS TEXT

Throughout the first half of the book, we concede the defects of the market system. By the same token, we repeatedly stress that the efficiency or desirability of any social organizer must ultimately be judged in terms of its realistic alternatives—not some ideal, such as perfect competition, which may be constructed for theoretical inquiry. This means, of course, that the workings of the market system must be compared with the workings of government, that alternative which in recent decades has risen in relative importance in the areas of total domestic expenditure, control of the economy, and distribution of income.

A fundamental message of any study of the market system is that growth in public welfare is a serendipity emerging from the private pursuits of self-interested (if not "greedy") entrepreneurs who care very little about the public welfare. It is all too tempting to compare this essential message with a vision of the public welfare being pursued directly by public-spirited, socially conscious politicians and government bureaucrats. The comparison is unfair in the sense that there is no a priori reason to assume that people who run for public office or work for government have any more superior motivation than people who work in a private industry. Given this comparison, it is understandable why government intervention in the market is seen by many people as the solution for all market-produced social ills.

Beginning with Chapter 21, we introduce students to the developing field of the economics of politics, or as it is frequently called, public choice. We develop the theory of the public sector using the same motivational assumptions employed in discussing people's behavior in the private sector. We assume, in effect, that politicians and government workers are rational people, who like their counterparts in the private sectors have social concerns and charitable feelings but also pursue definite private interests. We explore the weaknesses of the democratic-bureaucratic processes in an effort to show how the government may achieve less than optimal results. Once this point is made, we are in a position to compare the relative efficiency of the market and government as social organizers and to give the student some insight into the problems of "properly" aligning the public and private spheres.

Macroeconomics is considered in this text as one of many dimensions of government behavior; macroeconomic policy is considered to be the outgrowth of the same political and bureaucratic processes as any other governmental policy. Too often in economics we treat economic policy as an issue on which economists (and their students) have been called to advise a "benevolent dictator." We have implicitly assumed that with the construction of good policy, good men will do good things.

We fully develop for the student an analytical framework for evaluating monetary and fiscal policies of the government. However, we have shied away from displaying an undue reverence for the Keynesian and monetarist models of the macroeconomy, because these models have in recent years come under increasing attack and the student should be alerted to the fact that macroeconomic models are ways by which different groups of economists formulate their own prescriptions for solving the problems of inflation and unemployment. They are not necessarily revealed truth. Furthermore, rather than focus only on the question of what government policy *should* carry out with regard to the federal budget and the national income level, we are concerned in this text with the more positive question of what kind of policy we should expect to emerge from the democratic governmental sector that we discussed in earlier chapters. In this way, we try to give the student an understanding of why government may often adopt policies which are at odds with economic theory.

With these modest changes in direction, we believe that a student's first course in economics can be more interesting and relevant.

ACKNOWLEDGMENTS

It is impossible to undertake a project of this magnitude without the help of many people. Accordingly, we are indebted to Paula Koch, Eva McClain, and Mary Ann McKenzie; and to Joyce Rhymer for clerical and editorial assistance, to Dinah Lanning, who did an exquisite job typing the second and final drafts of the manuscript, and to Stephen Dietrich and Marjorie Singer who expertly and graciously guided the project from contract to the printing press. We are also indebted to many of our colleagues across the country for their advice: Marvin Brams, Jack Brashear, James Buchanan, Paul Combs, Jeane-Pierre Courbois, Roger Faith, Dennis Gerrity, Grace Havnaer, Barry Keating, Mary Ann Keating, Allan Mandelstamm, Dolores Martin, Roland McKean, Stephen Millsaps, Mancur Olson, Dennis O'Toole, Robert Spann, Robert Staaf, Nicolaus Tideman, and E. G. West. We are especially grateful to the following persons for their detailed comments on various drafts of the manuscript: Larry A. Daellenbach, University of Wisconsin, La Crosse; Robert F. Hebert, Auburn University; Hugh Peters, Sacramento City College; Jerry Petr, University of Nebraska, Lincoln; Leonard M. Rodney, Allegheny County Community College; Allen R. Sanderson, College of William and Mary; Marvin Snowbarger, San Jose State University; Robert D. Tollison, Texas A&M University; Donald J. Yankovic, University of Toledo.

Common Sense Economics has kindly given us permission to reprint in Chapter 8 an article which was published in slightly different form in the Spring 1977 issue of that journal.

Richard B. McKenzie
Gordon Tullock

Course Designs

TWO-SEMESTER COURSES

Modern Political Economy is basically designed to be used in a two-semester (or three-quarter) introductory course in economics which emphasizes microeconomics in the first semester and macroeconomics in the second semester. When the textbook is used this way, the chapters can be followed sequentially, and all of the book can be covered within the normal academic year. The first seventeen chapters can be covered in the first semester and the remaining chapters in the second semester. We start with simple but basic concepts in the first few chapters and gradually add to their complexity as additional chapters are covered. In the next several pages, we illustrate how the text can be divided for courses of various lengths.

We recognize that many professors teach their principles courses with macroeconomics in the first semester and microeconomics in the second. We also illustrate in the following pages how the book can be divided for such courses. All in all, the book provides professors with the flexibility they need to design alternative course sequences which emphasize theory in the first part of the course and policy issues at the end.

COURSE OUTLINE FOR YEAR-LONG COURSE WITH MACROECONOMICS IN THE FIRST SEMESTER AND MICROECONOMICS IN THE SECOND SEMESTER

First Semester

1 Economics: A Way of Understanding Social Order
2 The Framework of Economic Analysis
3 The Law of Demand: A Pervasive Rule of Human Behavior
4 Supply and the Importance of Cost in Guiding Human Behavior
5 The Emergence of Social Order: Defining Behavioral Limits
6 The Logic of Group Behavior
18 The Importance and Scope of Government
19 The Bases of Government Action
21 The Economics of the Democratic Process
22 The Political Economy of Bureaucracy
23 The Macroeconomy and Measurements of General Economic Activity
24 The Meaning and Creation of Money
25 The Federal Reserve's Control of the Money Stock and the Causes of Inflation and Deflation
26 The Costs and Benefits of Inflation
27 The Meaning and Causes of Unemployment
28 The New Economics of Unemployment and the National Income Level: An Introduction
29 The "New Economics": A Refinement of the Basic Model
30 The "New Economics" and Government Policy
31 The "Monetarists'" View of Unemployment and Inflation

Second Semester

(Review of Chapters 1 to 4)
7 The Competitive Market: Many Buyers and Many Sellers
8 The Competitive Market: Applications to the World around Us
9 The Government and the Market for Food
10 Private Control of the Market through Monopoly Power
11 Public Control of the Market through Price Ceilings
12 The Regulation Jungle
13 Consumer Protection: A Question of Who Should Be Responsible
14 The Absence of Power in the Labor Market
15 The Presence of Power in the Labor Market
20 Government and the Distribution of Income
16 International Trade and the Extended World Market
17 International Finance: The Lubricant of Trade
32 National Economic Planning

ONE-SEMESTER COURSES

Although the book is basically designed for the year-long introductory course in economics, it can also be used for one-semester introductory courses and for courses in contemporary economic problems. The following outlines illustrate possible approaches for one-semester courses.

A BALANCED ONE-SEMESTER COURSE

1 Economics: A Way of Understanding Social Order
2 The Framework of Economic Analysis
3 The Law of Demand: A Pervasive Rule of Human Behavior
4 Supply and the Importance of Cost in Guiding Human Behavior

5 The Emergence of Social Order: Defining Behavioral Limits
6 The Logic of Group Behavior
7 The Competitive Market: Many Buyers and Many Sellers
10 Private Control of the Market through Monopoly Power
11 Public Control of the Market through Price Ceilings (or Chapters 12 or 13)
14 The Absence of Power in the Labor Market
15 The Presence of Power in the Labor Market
19 The Bases of Government Action
21 The Economics of the Democratic Process
23 The Macroeconomy and Measurements of General Economic Activity
24 The Meaning and Creation of Money
25 The Federal Reserve's Control of the Money Stock and the Cause of Inflation and Deflation
27 The Meaning and Causes of Unemployment
28 The New Economics of Unemployment and the National Income Level: An Introduction
30 The "New Economics" and Government Policy (circular flow sections only)
32 National Economic Planning (if time permits)

COURSE IN CONTEMPORARY ECONOMIC PROBLEMS

(Review Chapters 1 through 4)
5 The Emergence of Social Order: Defining Behavioral Limits
6 The Logic of Group Behavior
7 The Competitive Market: Many Buyers and Many Sellers

(Review Chapter 10)
11 Public Control of the Market through Price Ceilings
12 The Regulation Jungle
13 Consumer Protection: A Question of Who Should Be Responsible
19 The Bases of Government Action
20 Government and the Distribution of Income
21 The Economics of the Democratic Process
22 The Political Economy of Bureaucracy
26 The Costs and Benefits of Inflation
27 The Meaning and Causes of Unemployment
30 The "New Economics" and Government Policy
31 The "Monetarists'" View of Unemployment and Inflation
32 National Economic Planning

To the Student

This book has been written with you in mind. We understand that economics can be abstract and, at times, difficult—problems that cannot be completely overcome. However, there are several features about the book which we think will make it appealing to you. First and foremost, all our discussions of economic principles are in the context of examples and policy issues with which you are likely to be familiar. For instance, we discuss cost, an important concept in economics, as it relates to the purchase of an economy-size box of detergent or a can of orange juice, to the purchase of a home, or to the decision of whether or not a person should put money in a parking meter. We also raise the issue of whether crime pays, which is another way of asking if the typical criminal can cover the costs he or she incurs in the "criminal industry." Before you are finished with this book you will also have explored the public debates surrounding such policy issues as whether or not prices and wages should be controlled by government, whether or not industry should be regulated by government, and whether or not consumers should be protected from producers by government. You will be confronted with the issue of what causes inflation and unemployment and what, if anything, can be done about it. We conclude the book with an analysis of the pros and cons of national economic planning, which is a major policy issue you may hear a great deal about in the near future. Why have we emphasized examples and policy issues to the extent that we have? We simply believe that you will learn more principles of economics if you are constantly shown how those principles can be used in understanding government policy.

We have also tried to ease the problems you confront in studying. At the start of each chapter, we have provided a chapter preview which highlights the central question addressed in the chapter, the major objectives of the chapter, and the major conclusions to be drawn from the discussion. At the start, you are also alerted to the key terms introduced in the chapter. This information, we believe, will make the chapter more readable and understandable; it will also give you a quick review of the chapter. At the end of each chapter, there are several questions which you may want to answer and a selection of readings which will reinforce the major points of the chapter. Rather than ask questions which require for answers only a reiteration of points made in the chapter, we ask questions which we think are challenging—ones that require application of basic principles developed in the chapter to new situations. If you are able to answer these questions, we think that you will be prepared for almost any test your professor can design. To help you master new terms and concepts, a complete glossary has been added at the end of the book that includes text page numbers where a discussion of the term can be found. All in all, we have tried to devise a textbook in economics which is readable and interesting. We think that the most important thing you will learn is that economics is a valuable course of study, regardless of your major. We would be most pleased to hear your personal reaction to the book.

Richard B. McKenzie
Gordon Tullock

Part One
Principles of Individual Behavior

. . . The general principles which regulate our conduct in business are identical with those which regulate our deliberations, our selections between alternatives, and our decisions, in all other branches of life. And this is why we not only may, but must take our ordinary experiences as the starting point for approaching economic problems.

Philip Wicksteed

Philip H. Wicksteed, *The Common Sense of Political Economy* [New York: Augustus M. Kelley, Publisher, 1967 (originally published 1927)], vol. 1, p. 3.

Economics is primarily concerned with people's behavior in a social setting like that which exists in a business firm or market. In order to understand people's social behavior, however, we must first develop principles by which *individuals*, as opposed to *groups*, behave. The purpose of the first four chapters is to develop the basic principles of individual behavior upon which economic analysis is founded. Accordingly, we explain the important concepts of *cost*, *supply*, and *demand* and show how these concepts are relevant to discussions of individual and social behavior.

1

Economics: A Way of Understanding Social Order

We are all doing it; very few of us understand why we are doing it.

Goethe

PREVIEW OF CHAPTER

Central question

What is economics all about?

Major objectives

1 To stimulate interest in the study of economics
2 To indicate the broad boundaries of economics as a discipline and the difficulty of capturing the dimensions of the discipline in a short definition
3 To point out the benefits and limitations of theory as a means of social inquiry

Major conclusions

1 Although there are several ways of defining economics, it is viewed in this text as an *approach* to the study of human behavior or as a method of analysis with several characteristics which will be explained in following chapters.
2 The study of economics is founded upon the assertion that people live in an imperfect world and that they are always capable of envisioning ways to improve their lot.

3 Social phenomena are extremely complex. Theory is the method economists use to simplify the real world and to organize thought in such a way that meaningful conclusions can be deduced.

Important terms or concepts

- Social order
- Markets
- Theory
- Positive economics
- Normative economics

R. A. Radford, an American, was captured and imprisoned during the Second World War. After being released and returning to his homeland, he could have concentrated on writing about the difficulties he and so many others encountered while imprisoned. Individual liberties had been highly restricted, and he and his fellow prisoners experienced considerable degradation. In a prison, life is so constrained that any social organization of the prisoners may appear to be the consequence of the captors' actions. Radford, however, saw something else happening. He has written a vivid account of how a market for goods and services (i.e., a system of exchanges) emerged within the camps and of how the prisoners' welfare was consequently enhanced.[1] This happened even though there were few opportunities for prisoners to produce the things they wanted.

Periodically, the Red Cross distributed to the prisoners rations of cigarettes, toiletries, chocolate, and other amenities. It attempted to distribute the supplies according to a criterion which it considered equitable, which meant in this case that they were distributed equally among all persons. But, he writes, "Very soon after capture people realized that it was both undesirable and unnecessary, in view of the limited size and the equality of supplies, to give away or to accept gifts of cigarettes or food. 'Goodwill' developed into trading as a more equitable means of maximizing individual satisfaction."[2]

As the weeks went by, trade expanded and the prices of goods became progressively more stable. There were those who would have liked to receive better terms (i.e., higher prices) for the items they had to trade. However, there was a problem for them. People who wanted to trade soap had to compete with others who wanted to do the same thing. The "prices" at which people were willing to buy and sell were posted on each bungalow's "Exchange and Mart notice boards." Shops began to emerge and middlemen began to take advantage of any discrepancies in prices offered by the different sellers, making it difficult for anyone to "overcharge." There was a priest, among others, who found that he could exchange, for example, a pack of cigarettes for a pound of cheese in one bungalow, take the cheese to a second and trade it for, say, one and a half packs of cigarettes, and, therefore, return to his own bungalow with more cigarettes than he had begun with. In this way, although he was acting in his interest, he provided the people in the second bungalow with something they wanted—more cheese than they would otherwise have had. The different "prices" for cheese existed partly because the prisoners in the different bungalows had different desires for cigarettes and cheese, and partly because not all prisoners were permitted to interact freely. In learning about and exploiting the discrepancy in prices, the

[1] R. A. Radford, "The Economic Organization of a P.O.W. Camp," *Economica,* November 1945, pp. 189–201.

[2] Ibid., p. 190.

priest moved the camp's store of cheese from the first bungalow, where it was worth less, to the second bungalow, where it was worth more, and *all* persons involved in the trades benefited from what the priest did.

There were also "entrepreneurs" in the camp who, with a stock of cigarettes they had saved, bought up the troops' rations when they were issued and sold them shortly before the issuance of new rations at, of course, higher prices. These "entrepreneurs" were pursuing their own private interests; however, they, like the priest, provided a service to the other prisoners: they bought the rations at a time when the other prisoners wanted to get rid of them and wanted cigarettes, and they sold them at a time when the other prisoners wanted the rations more and cigarettes less. The difference between the "low" price at which the entrepreneurs bought and the "high" price at which they sold provided the entrepreneurs with the incentive they needed to make the trades, to hold onto the rations, and to assume the risk that the price of the rations might not in fact rise.

Radford noticed also that the troops began to use cigarettes in lieu of money as a means of carrying on exchanges. Even prices were quoted in terms of cigarettes. Certain brands were favored over others; and, as he expected, only the less desired brands were actually used in trade; the better brands were not used as money. The general acceptability of cigarettes facilitated the exchange process. The person who wanted soap no longer had to search out those few who might exchange their soap for the jam which he had to offer; he could buy the soap with the cigarettes. Even the nonsmokers began to accept cigarettes in trade for the things they had to sell. On the day the Red Cross distributed new supplies of cigarettes, the prices of other goods in terms of cigarettes rose, adjusting to the influx of new "money." After nights of nearby bombing, when the nervous prisoners would smoke up their holdings of cigarettes, the cigarette price of other goods fell.

Radford saw a form of *social order* (i.e., the way in which the interactions of people are organized) emerge in the most unlikely of environments. He recognized the deficiencies in the prisoners' lives. At the same time, he was able to detect and understand how their lives were eased a little by the spontaneous, voluntary, and completely undirected efforts of the imprisoned individuals. From this introductory example of life in a prisoner-of-war camp, you have already considered the kind of society that Adam Smith outlined in his classic work *The Wealth of Nations,* written more than 200 years ago. Adam Smith is considered to be the founding father of the study of economics because he examined how markets like the one in the POW camps arise and how they contribute to improving the welfare of people, and because he offered so many insights into the relationship between the governmental and private sectors in society.

In this book we will examine society and social order in much the same way and will make many of the same points that Adam Smith and so many other economists have made through the years. Our concern throughout the pages of this book will be with explaining the way society is organized and with making suggestions as to how that organization can be changed for the benefit of all people. The study of economics, therefore, has one overriding goal: to offer the student *understanding* of the society of which we all are a part. However, we must never forget that the social (as opposed to the physical) world is made up of individuals and that all "societal actions" are the consequence of the behavior of individuals. In the remainder of this chapter, and in Chapters 2 through 4, we will develop principles of *individual* behavior which are basic to the economic analysis which follows in this book. To do this properly, we begin by considering the unique position of the first two persons on earth. We then explain the role, necessity, and limitations of theory in social inquiry.

PARADISE LOST

Adam and Eve were very special people. They were special not only because they were the first human beings on earth (someone had to be first), but because of the circumstances of their initial existence. Whether you accept or reject the story of creation, its symbolic meaning is obvious. Adam and Eve's existence was idyllic; they were able to live in a pristine state in which "wants" literally had no meaning. The existence of want or desire means that something is lacking or that a better state can be envisioned; but the first couple's every wish could be readily fulfilled by the abundance which surrounded them. And it is because of this that we, being so far removed, can only wonder what "existence" must have meant to them.

Before the serpent, Adam and Eve did not have to be concerned with the logic of their own conduct because there was no reason to ponder the question of how their existence could be improved. Aside from the "tree of knowledge of good and evil," there was no basis for conflict and no need for methods to resolve conflict. In contrast, our contemporary society relies on many institutional arrangements such as cooperative associations, markets, or government which evolved to satisfy the needs of great numbers of people. Initially, Adam and Eve had no need which could not be filled, and these institutions were not required. Their existence was indeed simple!

It was only after they were evicted from the Garden that unfilled wants began to take on the meaning which we understand today. The new definition of "existence" which emerged has more than a theological dimension. Adam and Eve were thrown into a complex, far from perfect world, only too aware of their limited capacities to cope with what they found.

From that fateful day, people, regardless of their position in time, space, or class, have been aware of the imperfections of their existence and have been able to conceive of things which are lacking and of a state which is better than the one they are in. From this basic motivation, people have attempted over the ages, individually and collectively, to devise means of rendering their existence more pleasant. If men and women could be perfectly content with their station in life, they would (figuratively) never have left the Garden of Eden. However, the study of people and their social behavior is grounded in the assertion that *they have left*, and

Economics is fundamentally about their plight to improve their lot. How they have gone about accomplishing that end and why and to what extent they have succeeded in accomplishing that end are the pivotal questions which lie at the heart of the study of economics.

ECONOMICS AND HUMAN BEHAVIOR

Many beginning students of economics have a limited view of the discipline. They tend to associate economics with a small portion of human experiences, such as man's pursuit of material wealth, with money and taxes, or with commercial or industrial life. Critics are prone to think of economists as being oblivious to the aesthetical, ethical, and humanistic dimensions of man's experience. The criticism is not altogether unjustified because many economists have, from time to time, narrowly focused their attention and research efforts on people's commercial endeavors. This is all changing rather rapidly as economists expand their areas of concern and apply the laws of economics to the full spectrum of human activities. Still, with the current public view of the discipline, it is not surprising that people question its relevance and viability.

We have said that we will focus on the human struggle to improve one's lot. But our examination is not limited simply to the attainment of material goals. True, most of what we say will apply to people's pursuit of material gain, but it will be just as relevant to their aesthetic and humanistic goals. There is no reason why one's appreciation of a poem or a sunset cannot legitimately be the subject of our inquiry. Interestingly, in this text we will not suggest what people should or should not want; we will merely assume that people have "wants." This assumption will provide us with a logic for human behavior, with an understanding of the benefits and limitations of the institutions through which individual and collective goals are pursued, and with an appreciation for what has and also what has not been accomplished with the institutions which have been used.

Economics and Social Order

Our discussions will be far-ranging. Our emphasis will be on *understanding social order.* We define *social order* as how people interact in various ways to obtain what they want. We start by developing principles of individual behavior, but our intent is to show how these principles are applicable to people's social behavior in the context of groups. As most might expect of an economics text, we will be focusing a considerable amount of our attention on the *market.* The *market* is any arrangement by which people exchange goods and services. These goods and services may be material, such as cars and toys, and money might be involved. However, we conceive of the market in much broader terms. The exchange can be merely an exchange of kindnesses—smiles, if you like. One student can help another with an accounting problem in exchange for similar help in English. A family can ask another couple over for dinner in exchange for an evening of good conversation. Neighbors can keep watch over each other's houses while each is away, implying an exchange in similar services.

However, the market, although it may be dominant in human experience, is only one of several means by which people interact, and the efficiency, acceptability, and viability of any one method of social organization like the market must, realistically speaking, be judged in terms of its alternatives. Consequently, we will be delving into the political arena and talking about the benefits and limitations of government and democratic institutions as an alternative means of organizing people's social behavior. Much of human behavior is organized totally outside of any direct exchange relationship. People attempt to achieve common objectives by voluntarily working together in small groups like families and clubs, and they obey, in varying degrees, a host of informally adopted behavioral rules or ethics. These rules guide our interpersonal behavior when market exchanges or the coercive power of political action would be infeasible or simply too expensive. (We do not not use the political process to determine who goes through doors first because of the expense of governmentally enforcing such laws.) Laws and commonly accepted behavioral rules also create the realms in which exchanges and political relationships can occur, and they act as restraints to the kinds and intensity of behavior in the market and in politics. As we will see, all methods of social organization have their benefits and limitations, and the effectiveness of each will have a bearing on how extensively it is used in society.

The Challenge of Social Philosophy

To analyze a social situation, we must be able to learn from the bits and pieces of our everyday experience, but at the same time be able to detach ourselves from this experience and take a broad view of human organization. The ultimate challenge of social philosophy (of which economics is a part) is to understand the alternatives for social policy, to create new ones when that is called for, and to propose by some clearly established evaluation procedure the appropriate mix of those alternatives. To say that our task is ambitious is an understatement of the first magnitude. It is a task which will certainly tax our capacities to communicate effectively. In this book we will not prescribe the appropriate mix; we will, on the other hand, attempt to clarify the issues and to devise the tools which you need to evaluate the alternatives and to make more informed judgments about how the organization of society can be improved.

THE REALM OF ECONOMICS

Jacob Viner, who wrote about and taught economics in the first half of this century, once defined economics as what economists do. In one respect, because nothing is said about what an economist is, the definition fails to say very much that is useful. It fails to limit the boundaries of the discipline and in that way to distinguish economics from other disciplines. On the other hand, it does indicate the inevitable exasperation which economists have felt over the years when attempting to say what they are about. No doubt, relying on this definition, you will experience some difficulty in explaining to your friends the nature of this course. Actually, there is no reason to become disturbed at this point; any concise definition of a discipline is likely to be unsatisfactory, since disciplines are, by their nature, elaborate models of behavior designed to give and sway with the punches of their development. One is not likely to comprehend the boundaries of a discipline until he has sampled a good deal of what people in the field actually do. This book is intended to provide an introductory sample. In a sense, therefore, the definition, "what economists do," is a call for patience.

Be that as it may, a preliminary statement about the nature of economics can show how we perceive the discipline, explain how we will proceed through the book, and may provide a point of reference to which all else that is discussed can be tied. An examination of the topics included in studies by economists will indicate the diversity of "what economists do." Economists have tried to describe the workings of markets, methods of trade, and patterns in commercial and industrial life; but there is also considerable analysis in economic studies on poverty and wealth; on racial, sexual, and religious discrimination; and on politics, bureaucracy, crime, law, and revolution. There is an economics of group interaction generally and of family and marital problems more specifically. Economists can be found working on the problems of inflation, unemployment, and international money problems, as is conventional; but they are also engaged in the study of health care for the very young as well as the elderly, housing for the disadvantaged, committee structures, criminal justice systems, ethics, voting rules, and the legislative process. Indeed, when one samples modern economics discussion, it is difficult to disagree with Robert Mundel:

> Economics seems to apply to every nook and cranny of human experience. It is an aspect of all conscious action. Whenever decisions are made, the law of economy is called into play. Whenever alternatives exist, life takes on an economic aspect. It has always been so.[3]

There are very few problems which social scientists from other disciplines tackle which economists are not trying to solve in one way or another. Recognizing the divergence of economists' interests, what is the unifying factor? What ties it all together and sets the work of the economist apart from that of other social scientists? How is it that we can look at social discussion and say with reasonable accuracy that it is or is not the work of an economist?

In our view,

> the unifying factor is the approach which economists take toward the study of human behavior. They have a distinguishing set of presuppositions about human behavior—a different image of behavior—leading to a different mode of analysis and to conclusions which complement and, at times, appear to conflict with those of other social scientists investigating the same problem.

A purpose of this book is to lay out that approach, to develop commonly accepted principles of economic analysis, and to demonstrate how principles can be used and how useful they have been in solving problems which span the spectrum of human experience. In that way you may acquire a certain set of mental skills and, to paraphrase Goethe, "you may not only be doing it, but you may understand why."

We have titled this book *Modern Political Economy* for a special reason. This book primarily involves a study of economic principles; however, as we have indicated, it is much more than that. It involves an in-depth study of how public policies affect the market system; but, in addition, it involves a study of how economic prin-

[3] Robert A. Mundel, *Man and Economics* (New York: McGraw-Hill Book Company, 1968), p. v.

ciples can be used to understand the political affairs of men and to explain why certain types of public policies can be expected to emerge from democratic organizations like Congress and state legislatures. In short, our interest is with how politics and economics are interrelated, and the phrase *political economy*, although a little ominous-sounding, reflects that interest and capsules the direction this book will take.

DEVELOPING AND USING THEORIES

In the previous section of this chapter, we said that many activities in the realm of human experience can, to one extent or another, be considered in the study of economics. But how do we do this? Life in the real world is complex and provides us with far too many bits of information about relationships between people and between people and the physical environment. An individual student is swamped and bewildered by all he or she sees, hears, or confronts in other ways. There is simply no way an individual student can comprehend all this.

So we begin with full recognition of our limitations and seek a means by which we can approach understanding within these limits. *Theory*—that is, models of how the world is put together—is a means by which science attempts to work within our intellectual limitations.

A theory is a set of abstractions about the real world; it encompasses a limited set of relationships which the scientist hopes will bring the amount of information which he considers within the range of his abilities.

He cannot cope with the entirety of what he senses; so he must resign himself to a second-best position, which is to consider a portion of the real world.

There is a definite, understandable concern among many students about the theoretical approach. They often consider it "abstract," "unreal," and "irrelevant." There is a tendency for students to look upon the theoretician as the proverbial ostrich with his head buried in the sand. Indeed, economics, like other sciences, is abstract; but it is not abstract in the sense that the models employed are vague, that they in some way lack concreteness. Good models are laid out with a good deal of precision. Rather, science is abstract in the sense that the relationships that are considered have been *abstracted from* the full complexity of the real world. Presumably, the relationships considered are those which the scientist feels are the outstanding features of the problem under consideration. Trying to deal with the world in its entirety will lead virtually nowhere; abstractions enable the scientist to move forward and say something. As economist Kenneth Boulding has written,

> It is the principal business of social sciences, indeed to develop those abstractions which are most useful and which give us the most significant information. It is a very fundamental principle indeed that knowledge is always gained by the orderly loss of information, that is, by condensing and abstracting and indexing the great buzzing confusion of information that comes from the world around us into a form which we can appreciate and comprehend.[4]

If the market appears confusing to you, take heart; your problem may be that you are trying to handle too much information, not too little, and/or that you have a very inefficient model through which to interpret the information you have. Also, you may not have acquired that "artistic quality," which comes only after considerable study, to abstract in a meaningful way, to realize the confining nature of one's abstractions, and to know when to adjust one's thinking when conditions call for it.

In a sense, the process of abstracting makes the models that emerge "unreal"; models are not fully descriptive of the real world and, as indicated, are not meant to be so. Furthermore, we must not only abstract, but quite often we must make as-

[4] Kenneth E. Boulding, *Economics as a Science* (New York: McGraw-Hill Book Company, 1970), p. 2.

sumptions about relationships which ease the difficulty of carrying forward the analysis. These are referred to as "simplifying assumptions." For example, we fully recognize that no one eats only oranges and bananas; but we may make this assumption when constructing a model for two reasons. First, it makes the discussion easier, and, second, the essential deductions we make are applicable in a more realistic world of many goods. In our discussion of the POW camp, we focused on just a few activities of the prisoners, and yet we were able to see the workings of a market system.

Throughout the book, we will assume that people are "rational" in a very precise sense (to be developed in Chapter 2), and we may develop the analysis *as if* there can never be, conceptually or otherwise, deviations from our assumption. Although we realize man is not unfailingly rational, we proceed as if he is because this approach enables us to understand more about human behavior than any alternative approach which tries to encompass all possible foundations for behavior. In economics, as we will see, trade-offs are everywhere; and even at this level of discussion, when we are talking simply about how we intend to approach the subject, we find ourselves making trade-offs. We trade completeness and realism for understanding that may not come in any other way. Efficiency in the "production" of knowledge requires this.

The purpose of theory construction is not to incorporate within the theory a complete and realistic description of the real world. However, a good theory should incorporate enough real values to simulate "real life." Therefore, each theory must be judged in terms of what it is intended to accomplish, which is to provide an explanation for what we observe in our experiences and to provide us with a basis for making reasonably accurate predictions for future experiences. Consequently, in response to the criticism that a theory employed in this text is "unreal" our reply must be: "Does it accomplish what it was intended to do? Is our theory able to explain what is observed? And, does it provide a better basis for prediction than alternative theories?" The answer to these questions is often a matter of judgment,

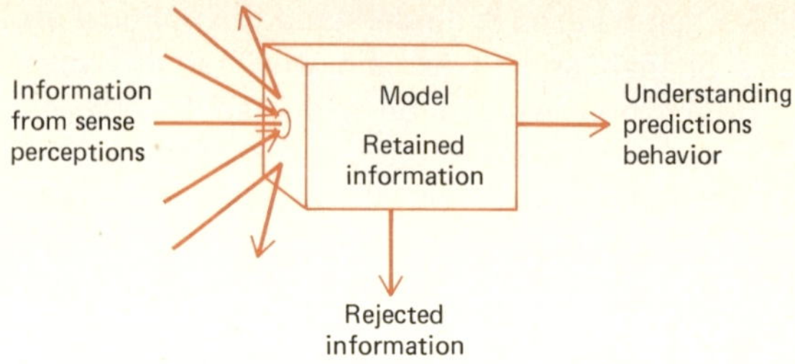

With the aid of a theoretical model of the world about us, we are able to interpret information that we receive through our senses. Just how we interpret the information determines how we understand the world about us, affects our predictions about future events and is, thereby, influential in determining how we behave with regard to future information.

FIG. 1 · 1

and for this reason the process of science involves continuous debate over the appropriateness of competing theories.

The process of developing and using economic theories is fraught with pitfalls and difficulties. As the alert reader may have detected, in that process there are substantial opportunities for errors. For purposes of illustration, we can picture the mind as a box, as in Figure 1·1. To generate "understanding," "explanation," and "prediction," there must be some model or theory of the world in that box; otherwise, all the information which comes to us will be nothing but a mass of confusion. There will be no meaning, no way of interpreting our experiences. Be that as it is, our purpose is to provide you with an *economic* model or theory of behavior and social interaction; and the purpose of the model is to provide you with a means by which you can sift through all the information that you confront and pick out that information which can give meaning to your thought processes. Some information will never be considered because the model you possess predetermines, within limits, that it is irrelevant. Therefore, the information is not admitted to the mental process and does not have a chance of affecting how you think, what you think, or how you behave. Even after information is admitted, it may be found to be insufficiently relevant and may be rejected.

As much as you may like to think to the contrary, you are going through this process of abstracting at this moment. There are, wherever you are, many bits of information which you are presently ignoring because you have deemed them to be irrelevant to your present purpose, which is, presumably, trying to read this book. (Without looking, do you know the number of this page?) The theorist does essentially the same thing in the process of theorizing. He ignores some information, as indicated by the bent arrows in the figure, which does not make it through the opening in the "mental box." Once the information is admitted, a weight must be attached to it to indicate the probability of the information being important and its relative value to whatever is under study. Remember, we live in an uncertain world, and even the scientist must recognize that some of the information he considers may eventually prove to be irrelevant. At the same time, we stress that this process makes the prospect of error not only a possibility but a probability. Because of the model used, the economist, for instance, may ignore some information which, if he did consider it, would prove to be quite relevant to an understanding; and the economist may consider and assimilate into his thinking information which in conjunction with his theory may lead to misleading conclusions, misunderstandings, and predictions which miss the mark. We can only try to develop a means by which these errors can be minimized and leave the door open for advancements in theory.

THE POSITIVE-NORMATIVE DISTINCTION

Economic theorizing is often categorized into two forms, *positive economics* and *normative economics*. Milton Friedman, a Nobel laureate who taught economics at the University of Chicago, described positive economics as follows:

> Positive economics is in principle independent of any particular ethical or normative judgments. As [John Neville] Keynes says, it deals with "what is," not with "ought to be." Its task is to provide a system of generalizations that can be used to make correct predictions about the consequences of any change in circumstances. Its performance is to be judged by the precision, scope and conformity with experience of the predictions it yields. In short, positive economics is, or can be, an "objective" science, in precisely the same sense as any other physical science.[5]

Normative economics is generally distinguished from positive economics in the sense that it deals with what ought to be. Imagine an unsatisfactory condition in society, such as substandard housing among migrant workers. The central problem facing normative economics is to develop means by which one can determine what he or she truly thinks *ought to be;* it is a problem of searching through one's own preferences, or feelings, which may not be clearly defined, with the object of making a value judgment. This may mean that after much thought the individual concludes that migrants' standard of living should be raised through required improvements in housing which are to be made available by employers. Being able to define one's preferences is not always easy; and there may be a science to making such determinations. The point which we are attempting to highlight here is that in normative economics there is an analytical jump from recognition of the problem to a prescription for it.

Positive economics, being the science of *what is*, fills in the analytical gap between recognition of the problem and the prescription for it. It attempts to deal with the consequences of alternative proposals for dealing with, for example, substandard migrant housing and pay. The positive economist directs his attention to the consequence(s) of requiring employers to provide better housing. The direction of one's attention is away from one's own preferences and is on "consequences" or "effects." The relevant question is, "What can we realistically expect in this or that circumstance, *given people's* values?" not "What should they value?" The positive economist's val-

[5] Milton Friedman, *Essays in Positive Economics* (Chicago: The University of Chicago Press, 1953), p. 4.

ues are held suspended while prescribed procedures are applied to an analysis of what will be. In this way the positive economist's analysis is as "value free" as is possible.

In this book *positive economic analysis* is equated with *economic analysis.* However, we hasten to add that subjective evaluations inevitably become entangled in the analytical process; in actuality, economic analysis is not so antiseptic, or value-free, as the above argument may suggest. The inquiry *itself* by which consequences are determined may follow highly rigid rules of analysis, i.e., may be value-free. But the economist must inevitably choose what problems will be investigated and how they will be investigated—he will decide what information to consider and what to ignore. Although one might like to think that these matters can be settled easily by objective criteria, subjective evaluations most certainly creep into the decision-making process. The investigator's judgment may be affected by the professional rewards that may be offered for delving into various problems, or it may depend on what the economist thinks are the problems of greatest concern to some relevant segment of the public or on presuppositions about what he thinks is important from an ethical standpoint.

For example, how one approaches the study of the relationship between the market and government is invariably colored by one's view of the importance of individual freedom, that is, concerning whether or not people *should* have the opportunity to choose. One's procedures may be influenced by what the scientific community expects in terms of the standards and methods of research. This will determine just how much attention one can give to any particular subject and how many other subjects will be ignored. The increase in scientific research on energy and environmental problems is a reflection of the greater "importance" which the nonscientific and scientific communities attach to the solution of these problems.

In the quotation, Friedman suggests that the performance of positive economics is "to be judged by the precision, scope, and conformity with experience of the predictions it yields." One may get the impression that this process is quite straightforward—that no judgmental factors are involved: the economist makes predictions and those predictions are refuted or corroborated by the evidence collected. However, it is indeed rare that the data used in social investigation are perfectly suited for testing a hypothesis. Most of the time a "proxy variable," one that comes *close* to representing the true variable, is employed. This means that the results of the test must be *judged* in terms of the *appropriateness* of the proxy variable. For example, an economic theory might predict that student effort will increase if the rewards from study go up. To test this, the economist may have to use the number of hours studied as a proxy variable for the amount of effort. If the number of hours does not change when the rewards are increased, has the theory been refuted? It is quite possible that it has not; the "intensity" of study effort may have increased, implying an increase in overall effort which is not being revealed by the number of hours the student studies. There is the question of whether or not the theory has been refuted by the evidence or whether the evidence has been proven to be a poor proxy for test of the hypothesis. Further, quite often any hypothesis, particularly if it is controversial, will be subjected to a number of tests, and the results of these tests are not likely to support the hypothesis 100 percent of the time. This may reflect differences in the "quality" of the investigation. At what point is the theory to be accepted or rejected, even tentatively? In such instances, judgments enter the scientific inquiry, and scientific inquiry may incorporate an element of persuasion. The impurity of the positivist's position must be recognized, but it is an ideal to which all can aspire.[6]

[6] The subject of implicit values in scientific investigation and the development of science has been studied by Thomas S. Kuhn, *The Structure of Scientific Revolutions* (Chicago: The University of Chicago Press, 1970), and Paul T. Heyne, "The Abuse of the Positive-Normative Distinction by Economists," paper delivered at the meeting of the Southern Economics Association, November 1974. For the student who wishes to be challenged, both of these works should prove stimulating.

SUMMARY AND EXTENSIONS

In summary, economics is a discipline that can best be described as a way of studying human behavior in the context of social interaction. The methods used by economists are founded upon a set of presuppositions about human behavior and they are based on a substantial body of theory designed to answer positive rather than normative questions. A major purpose of this book is to develop in detail the analytical tools employed by economists and, in that way, to show how economists study human behavior.

The areas of human experience studied by economists are expanding because the laws and theories of traditional economics are being applied to new areas of human experience. Using theories to analyze problems involves difficulties, to which we must always be alert, but it is our best hope of acquiring the understanding we seek.

We now turn to a detailed development of that approach. We start (in Chapters 2 through 4) with the development of principles of individual behavior; we do this simply because we view group behavior as a consequence of individual actions. We therefore argue that the behavior of individuals must be understood before we can broach the subject of people acting in groups and in the context of a "market," the conventional domain of economics. We begin a study of the social interaction of people in Chapter 5. That discussion is broadened in Chapter 6 with the development of an economic theory of group behavior which is later applied to the study of markets for goods and services and labor and to people acting within the confines of the democratic processes. First, however, we must lay the foundation.

QUESTIONS TO PONDER

1 Rations were, as Radford indicated, distributed in the prison camp equally by the Red Cross. Why did this result in trade within and among the bungalows?

2 The priest in Radford's prison camp was able to trade cigarettes for cheese and then cheese for cigarettes in such a way that he ended up with more cigarettes than he started out with. Does this mean that someone else in the prison camp lost out by the priest's activities? Why was the priest able to make such deals and end up better off? What did the priest's activities do to the price of cheese in the different bungalows?

3 Theories may be defective, but yet economists, knowing this, may continue to use them. Why?

4 An introductory economics text can introduce the student to more complex theories than this book will. What are the trade-offs implied in dealing with more complex theories? Why does your professor not employ much more difficult thoeries in class than he or she does?

5 The authors have suggested in the chapter that values can influence scientific inquiry. In what ways is this true? In what ways can "positive" economic analysis affect one's assessment of policy?

RECOMMENDED READINGS

Boulding, Kenneth E.: *Beyond Economics: Essays on Society, Religion, and Ethics* (Ann Arbor, Mich.: The University of Michigan Press, 1970), especially the first essay.

———: *Economics as a Science* (New York: McGraw-Hill Book Company, 1970) especially chap. 1.

Fish, Mary: "Prisoner Inmates as Clandestine Businessmen," in Gordon Tullock, ed., *Frontiers of Economics*, (Blacksburg, Va.: University Publications, Inc., 1976), pp. 43–58.

Knight, Frank H.: "Social Science," *On the History and Method of Economics* (Chicago: The University of Chicago Press, 1956), pp. 121–134.

Mundel, Robert A.: *Man and Economics* (New York: McGraw-Hill Book Company, 1968), chap. 1.

Peterson, Harold: "The Wizard Who Oversimplified: A Fable," in Harry G. Johnson and Burton A. Weisbrod, *The Daily Economist* (Englewood Cliffs, N.J.: Prentice-Hall, Inc., 1973), pp. 1–2.

Radford, R. A.: "The Economic Organization of a Prisoner of War Camp," *Economica*, November 1945, pp. 189–201.

Wicksteed, Philip H.: *The Common Sense of Political Economy* (New York: Augustus M. Kelley, Publisher, 1967), vol. 1, Introduction, pp. 1–9.

2

The Framework of Economic Analysis

Man acts because he is dissatisfied with the state of affairs as it prevails in the absence of his intervention. Man acts because he lacks the power to render conditions fully satisfactory and must resort to appropriate means in order to render them less unsatisfactory.

Ludwig von Mises[1]

PREVIEW OF CHAPTER

Central question

What is the method of analysis used in economics?

Major objectives

1 To outline the basis of economic analysis
2 To explain the concept of *rational behavior*
3 To show how rational behavior can be used to explain our own actions and the actions of people in business, politics, and government service

Major conclusions

1 A cornerstone of economic analysis is a concept known as *rational behavior*. Briefly, rational behavior means that a person knows, within limits, what he wants, is capable of ordering those things which he wants from least preferred to most preferred, and will choose to do those things which will maximize his satisfaction.

[1] Ludwig von Mises, *The Ultimate Foundations of Economic Science: An Essay on Method* (Princeton, N.J.: D. Van Nostrand Co., Inc., 1962), pp. 2–3.

2 The concept of rational behavior implies that the individual is constantly beset with choices to make, and a choice situation always implies that some alternative must be forgone if an action is taken. Since *cost* is defined as the most highly valued alternative forgone, a cost is always incurred in a choice situation.

3 The rational person—whether a consumer, a business person, a politician, or a bureaucrat—will do those things for which the *expected* benefits exceed the *expected* costs.

4 A person's actions will be affected by the nature of the good (whether it is a *private* or *public good*), the time at which benefits are received and costs incurred, and the uncertainty which may exist over the exact size of the benefits and costs.

Important terms and concepts

Rational behavior	Maximizing utility
Utility	Cost-benefit analysis
Cost	Present value
Opportunity cost	Private good
Money cost	Public good
Expected costs	Irrational behavior
Expected benefits	

Economics professors rarely require their beginning students to write a paper analyzing a particular economic situation in the first few weeks of class. In preparing their courses professors recognize that students must first be introduced to and understand the basic concepts of economics and the method used in economic inquiry. In fact, *meaning* implies some *means* through which a problem can be investigated and understood. It requires that the student adopt a point of view or some means of organizing the information which he perceives and can gather. Without this point of view, very little can be understood. This was one of the central points of Chapter 1.

The purpose of this chapter and Chapters 3 and 4 is to outline the system (or means) of inquiry used in economics, so that you will have the tools for understanding problems that are introduced throughout the remainder of the text. A part of this system of inquiry is the economist's notion of *rational behavior,* which we mentioned in Chapter 1. In that first chapter we asserted that people are capable of envisioning alternative ways of improving their position in life. In this chapter we proceed to develop a theory of *how* people will choose from among the alternative courses of action which they envision; and, as we will see, the concept of rationality is at the foundation of how people make choices. It can help us understand many of our own personal actions and the actions of people in business, politics, and government service. The concept of rationality and the behavioral postulates which are further developed in Chapters 3 and 4 comprise the foundations of economic science.

RATIONALITY: A BASIS FOR EXPLORING HUMAN BEHAVIOR

Our analysis begins with reasonable *assumptions* about human behavior because theories must rest on assumptions. Although economic analysis depends heavily upon deductive logic, logic cannot extend backward indefinitely. There must, at some point, be an assertion or axiom about behavior which is not the product of logical deduction. This assertion can be neither proven nor disproven; it is simply a statement which must more or less be taken for granted. Because it seems true and is commonly acknowledged as being true, we can use it as a basis for theorizing.

The Acting Person

The starting assertion in economics is that *the individual acts with a purpose:* in the words of von Mises, "Man acts because he is dissatisfied with the state of affairs as it prevails in the absence of his intervention."[2] In less formal terms, man *acts* to satisfy his wants which are *consciously* perceived; his behavior, in short, is to a degree *interdirected* as opposed to being totally *controlled* by external forces. There is no way that we can "prove" the truth of this assertion. However, economists feel that the assumption that man seeks to satisfy ever-expanding wants is a true picture of the way individuals behave. We cannot satisfy *all* our wants because there is no end to our ability to perceive new ones; the imperfect world of the present thereby restricts our behavior to a second-best position of doing the best that we can, that is, of "maximizing our satisfaction." Since *utility* is a synonym for satisfaction, economists often talk of people seeking to "maximize their utility."

The economist views the *individual* (as opposed to the *group*) as the one who does the "acting." It is the individual who attempts to render his state "less unsatisfactory." It is the individual who possesses wants and desires and looks for *means* to fulfill them. Group action is the consequence of the actions of the individuals who make up the group. Social values of a small group of people or of society have meaning to the extent that they reflect values held collectively by individuals. Economists take it as a given fact that group action cannot be distinguished from the actions of individuals. It is because of this point of view that we look to the *individual's* motivation for action in order to understand group interaction. On the other hand, an individual's behavior can be affected by the size and structure of the group of which he or she is a part. In fact, recognition of these influences is one of the economist's main contributions to understanding social behavior. When we talk of a competitive market, we are actually talking about the influence which a number of competitors has on the behavior of any one member and, therefore, all like members.

[2] Ibid.

Rational Behavior

First, we assume that man acts to satisfy his wants. Second, the economist assumes that the individual acts *rationally*. The economist's notion of rational behavior can be summed up with three propositions:

First, rational behavior means that the individual has a preference, which is another way of saying that the individual identifies, within limits, what he or she wants.

Second, the individual is capable of consistently ordering his or her wants from most preferred to least preferred.

And, third, the individual will choose from within this ordering in such a way as to maximize his or her satisfaction.

Not being able to fully satisfy all personal wants, the individual is always in a position in which he will choose more of what he wants rather than less. Further, he will always choose less rather than more of what he does *not* want. In short, the rational individual always stands ready to further his or her own interests.

For some readers, these basic assertions will appear obvious and acceptable. At the same time, what we have said will cause concern among others. This may be because some other theoretical basis for behavior may seem more convincing or because there may be some misunderstanding about what we mean by "rational behavior." In later sections of this chapter we will indicate the ways in which the concept of rational behavior has been misinterpreted, but for now we need to reflect on the logical consequences of our definition of rational behavior.

RATIONAL DECISIONS IN A CONSTRAINED ENVIRONMENT

Several important ideas flow directly from the economist's presumption of rational behavior which can be summarized succinctly here. First, the individual makes *choices* from among an array of alternative options. Second, in each choice situation, a person must always forgo doing one or more things when doing something else. Since *cost* is the most highly valued alternative forgone, all rational behavior involves a cost. Third, in striving to maximize his or her welfare, the individual will do those things for which the benefits exceed the costs. Each of these ideas is developed in detail in this section.

Choice

We assume that the individual has the capacity to evaluate the available alternatives and is able to select the alternative that maximizes his utility. This assumes, of course, that an array of alternatives actually exists. The individual's range of choices is limited by external forces—but external forces do not determine behavior in the sense that the individual is forced to accept one alternative over another. For example, you, the student, find yourself in a certain social and physical environment and possess certain physical and mental abilities; these environmental and personal factors influence the options which are open to you. For instance, you may have neither the money, the time, nor the "stomach" to study to become a surgeon. Or you may have established a career goal which dictates that you will not have the opportunity to take many of the courses listed in your college catalog. Your range of choices may not be wide, but the point is that choices do exist. You could be doing any one of several things with the time you are spending

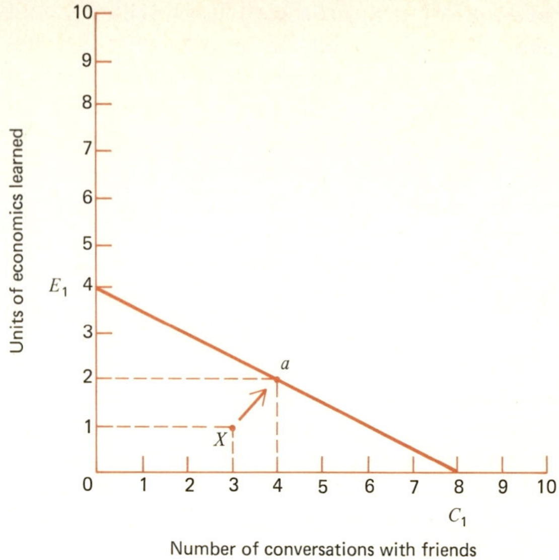

FIG. 2·1 With a given amount of time and other resources, you can "produce" any combination of units of economics learned and conversations with friends along the constraint E_1C_1. Which combination you choose will be a matter of your preferences for the two "goods." You will not stay at X, because by moving from X to a you can have more conversations and learn more economics, which will increase your utility level.

reading this; and you have the capacity to define what these several alternatives are. You could be studying some other subject or going out on a date (or attempting to find a date); you could have chosen to go shopping or engage in intramural sports or simply jog around the block. The fact that you may not be capable of playing varsity sports does not alter the existence of choices for you. In other words, although your choices are limited, constrained—you are not completely free to do as you please—it is still possible for you to choose; and, given your options, you must choose.

There is nothing in the economic definition of rational behavior which suggests that the individual is completely free to do as he wishes. Whenever we talk about individual choices, we are actually talking about *constrained* choices.[3]

To be more precise, let us assume that you have a test tomorrow in economics and that there are two and *only* two things which you can do within the next 12 hours: you can study economics or you can have conversations with friends. These two alternatives are represented in Figure 2 · 1 on the vertical and horizontal axes, respectively. You have only so much time, so much energy, and other resources which you can use to "produce" these activities. Assuming you want to pass your economics test and want to maintain your friendships, both activities yield benefits and are therefore "goods." Conceivably, but improbably, you could use the time available to do nothing more than study economics. However, during the next 12 hours there is only so much you can learn about economics. In our example, the maximum you can learn is placed at four units of economics, or E_1. At the other extreme, you could do nothing but have friendly conversations (assuming, of course, that someone will talk with you!); but, again, there is a limit here—eight conversations in our example, or C_1.

Both of these extremes are likely to be unacceptable to you; this is so because most people consume a combination of goods, and we have made the "simplifying assumption" that the two goods represent all goods. You know that there are intermediate combinations of conversations and economics study open to you. You can, if you are at C_1, adjust your time allotment so that you gradually increase the number of hours spent on economics and move up toward E_1. In short, there are a number of options available to you represented by the straight line E_1C_1 (often called the "production possibilities" or "transformation curve") and the area underneath it. If you consider both of these activities to be "goods," you will choose some combination on E_1C_1, such as a, two units of economics learned and four conversations. You may like to have more friendly conversations and at the same time learn more economics, but that is above the line E_1C_1 and beyond your capabilities (a choice not available to you because of your time and resource constraint). If you move into the interior of the set of available opportunities (say point X), you will be learning less economics and/or having fewer conversations than you are capable of having. And you will not then be maximizing your welfare or utility; by moving from X toward a on E_1C_1, you can have more of both of these activities which give you pleasure. Which combination you actually choose on E_1C_1 depends upon your preferences. Certainly, the goal (constraint) of passing or doing well on the test will influence how you allocate your time.

Changes in environment or physical limitations can affect the available opportunities you have and, consequently, the actual choice you make. For example, if you were to become more intelligent, your aptitude for learning economics would rise. You might then be able to learn, at the extreme, eight units of economics, in which case your whole set of opportunities could expand outward. The interesting part is that even if your *ability* to converse remained the same, your greater aptitude in economics would enable you to increase the number and length of your conversations. Your new set of opportunities would be E_2C_1 in Figure 2 · 2. (Your maximum number of economics units learned has risen because of the increase in your aptitude; your ability to converse has at the limit remained unchanged, C_1.) You can choose any combination along this new curve or within the area below it. It is possible that you will decide to converse the same number of times, four, and increase the number of units in economics learned, moving to combination c. On the other hand, any combination along E_2C_1 is open to you. You can move to a combination like b, in which case you would be learning more economics, three units instead of two, but you would also be engaging more friends in conversations. You will be able to do this because an increase in your ability to learn economics means that you can learn the same amount of economics in *less* time. You may use a part of the extra time to apply to

[3] This is one of those assumptions that we mentioned in Chap. 1 we would make to simplify the analysis. Given the limited argument we have in mind, it does not affect what we have to say. Our only purpose is to illustrate what we mean by a range of choices.

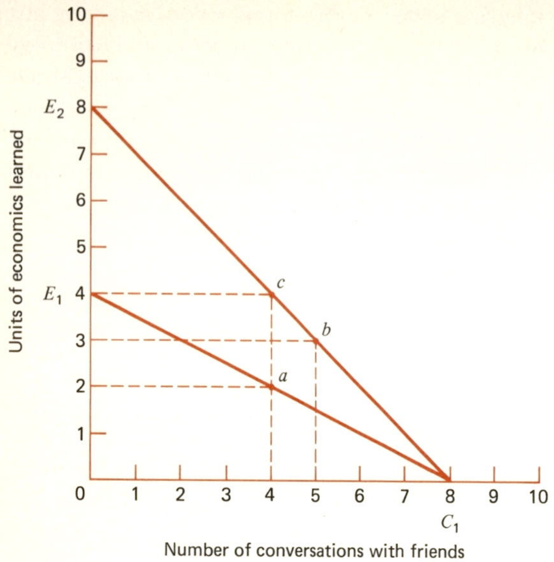

FIG. 2·2 The curve E_1C_1 is the same as the curve in Fig. 2·1. This graph shows the effect of a change in the constraints which face you as a student. Assuming that your aptitude for learning economics increases while your ability to engage in conversations remains constant, the constraint curve which you face shifts from E_1C_1 to E_2C_1. You can increase the amount of economics learned and/or the number of conversations you undertake.

the study of economics, but you may also use a portion to increase the number of conversations in which you engage. *The important point is that, as we stressed earlier, you are able to choose from a range of opportunities; the option you take is not predetermined.*

Cost

Continuing with our assumption that choices exist, we can go on to say that the existence of choices, in and of itself, implies that some alternative must be forgone when one alternative is taken. If A and B represent the relevant opportunities and A is taken, then, at least for that point in time, B must be forgone.

Cost is the value the individual places on the most favored alternative not taken when a choice is made.

and so it can be said that in the presence of choice—a situation in which all alternatives cannot be taken—a cost *must* be incurred.

Notice that cost is a concept which is independent of money; money is a *means* of measuring cost. Generally, we measure cost in terms of money because it reduces all costs to one common denominator. However, *money is not the equivalent of cost.* The shoes which you are wearing may have cost you $25 (i.e., the *money cost*), but the *real* cost (also called *opportunity cost*) is what you could have purchased instead. You could have bought 100 soft drinks, or you could have deposited your $25 in a savings account because you planned to buy something in the future or you could have placed it there merely for precautionary purposes. All of these uses are legitimate alternatives to using the funds for shoes. The point is that the most favored option not taken is the cost of the shoes, whether it be the future good that could have been purchased or the security that could have been "bought" by having the funds in savings.

Looked at this way, so long as you have alternative uses for your time and other resources, there is no such thing as a "free lunch"; nothing can be free if other opportunities are available. One of the goals of this textbook is to help you recognize this very simple principle and to search for costs which may not be obvious. There is a cost to writing a poem, to reading this book, to watching a sunset, to extending a common courtesy if only as small as holding open the door for someone else. In all these examples, money is not usually involved; however, people can use their time to do other things: they have had to forgo some other opportunity. The person may be better off by incurring the cost, but still a cost is incurred.

Cost is not incurred only when behavior is so restricted that there is only one thing which can be done and nothing is forgone. But these instances are difficult to imagine. Cases of life or death, in which death is not really considered to be a viable option, are ones which come most readily to mind. The person to be hanged at sunrise in the town square has no choice; he falls when the hatch is released. He does not act (or else he would get out of there!) but rather is the victim of action (the choice behavior of someone else).

Maximizing Satisfaction

Given the economist's concept of rational behavior, the individual will do those things for which the benefits of whatever is to be done exceed the costs. Another way of saying this is that the individual will maximize his satisfaction: by doing those things, consuming those goods, or producing those goods and services for which the benefits exceed the benefits of the most favored opportunity not taken. In this restatement of the maximizing principle, as it is called, we focus attention on cost as an explanatory factor. With regard to Figure 2 · 1, the student could have moved from combination a toward C_1; that is, he could have "produced" and "consumed" more conversations. However, in order to do that he must forgo units of economics learned; and since the student chose a to begin with, we must assume that he preferred a to any other combination between a and C_1. That is, the student must have received greater pleasure from learning the last unit of economics than would have been received from additional conversation.

To consider the influence which a change in cost has on behavior, suppose someone agrees to play checkers with you, but then receives an offer for a job which will pay him several hundred dollars and last for the duration of your planned contest. Would you expect the contest to occur at the scheduled time? Most likely not. The offer will change your opponent's opportunities in such a way that it makes what would otherwise have been a rational act (to play checkers with you) an irrational one. The *cost* of playing checkers will have risen by several hundred dollars, and this cost exceeds the benefits of most checkers games, particularly since some of those benefits can be recouped by rescheduling the game. Are not games, conversations, and other aspects of interpersonal relationships things which people value? Should we not expect people to behave in at least a similar way with regard to their relationships with others as they do with other more "normal goods"? In some limited manner, people weigh the costs of their actions against the benefits of them. At least, that is what we assume they do. When people make these kinds of calculations, they are engaging in what economists call "cost-benefit" analysis.

Illustrations of Cost-Benefit Analysis

In the economist's way of thinking, much (but certainly not all) of our behavior is based on cost-benefit analysis, as several examples will show. Why do you go to class when you do? The obvious answer is that at the time you decided whether or not to attend class you expected the benefits of attending class to exceed the costs. "What about classes I dislike?" you ask. The principle still applies. There may be no intrinsic benefits from a particular course; but you may believe (or fear) that if you do not go, you will miss information which can be useful on examinations. The benefits of attending class come in the form of receiving a higher grade or in keeping your grade from falling. In addition, given the constraints of having committed yourself to university living, your options on Tuesday morning at 10:00 a.m. may be such that the cost of going is very slight.

Americans are known for the amount of waste they pile up. Our "gross national garbage" is estimated as having a higher value than the gross output of many countries in the world. We throw away much that people in other countries would gladly take as gifts. Why do we waste so much? Morally, waste may be reprehensible and irresponsible, but in a certain context it may be the result of rational behavior. People who waste may find wasting beneficial in a limited personal sense. Wrappings on food products are thrown away, "wasted"; at the same time, they add convenience and freshness to what we buy. In terms of the individual's narrow-choice calculus, the benefits of the wrapping can exceed the costs, particularly if the individual can throw the wrapping on the ground, leaving it for someone else to dispose of. Someone else then incurs a portion of the cost of consuming the good. To illustrate further, Johnny Carson, on the "Tonight" television show, occasionally breaks a pencil or tosses it over his shoulder. These "bits of business," to use a show business term, add "flavor" to Carson's image, which, in turn, contributes to the high level of his ratings. However, although most pencils are probably picked up and saved, some are surely lost—"wasted." To Johnny Carson, the benefits of the waste exceed the costs. To Carlos Ramirez in Bolivia, who would like those pencils, the waste is not beneficial.

Even when considering questions of life and death, we cannot escape the choice component of people's behavior; that is, people choose between alternatives, weighing the expected benefits against expected costs. Many who smoke are fully aware that smoking can cause cancer or in other ways reduce the length of one's life. Many people who smoke ask themselves how much life—how many years, months, hours—they can expect to give up in order to continue smoking. True, many handle the dilemma by deciding that they will be among those who will go unscathed by smoking. In this sense they "rationalize" away the dangers (costs) of smoking. However, as is evident by the number of smokers, many people choose to smoke in spite of the cost (length of life lost) in order to receive what they consider to be the greater benefits of the satisfaction obtained from continued smoking.

Is life priceless? The answer depends upon moral considerations and upon what life and what cost must be paid to preserve it. Several million animals—dogs, opossums, squirrels, and birds—are killed on the highways each year. Most of us make some effort to avoid killing these animals. We swerve to miss a doe that has strayed onto the road, and we put up warning signs of deer crossings. However, there is some level of effort, some cost, which we obviously do not bear. We say "obviously" because many animal deaths could be avoided. If nothing else, we could drive less, but this would mean incurring a significant cost. Even when considering human lives, we are often unwilling to bear the costs necessary to preserve them. People avoid giving help to victims of violent crime, and doctors pass by highway accidents where their services, if rendered, could save lives. Revolutions are founded on the willingness of some people to sacrifice lives—others' and their own—for the achievement of some goal; the expected benefits, presumably, exceed the costs.

In the spring of 1975, the United States merchant ship, *Mayaguez,* was captured in international waters by Cambodian gunboats. The United States responded with military action and rescued the 55 crewmen of the *Mayaguez,* but, in the process, 18 military men were killed and 55 wounded. Politicians and newspaper columnists immediately began to debate the issue of whether or not the "rescue was worth the cost." Although President Ford obviously thought the benefits of the rescue operation justified the cost, others disagreed, revealing the truly subjective or personal nature of cost-benefit analysis.

TIME, UNCERTAINTY, AND RATIONALITY

When an individual acts, not all costs will necessarily be incurred immediately and not all benefits will necessarily be immediately received. The decision to have a child is an example of how present decisions affect the future flow of costs and benefits. A college-educated couple's first child can cost its parents something in excess of $150,000 in terms of 1976 prices from birth through college.[4] Irrespective of the actual figures, the costs will be incurred over a relatively long period of time. The prospective parents do not have to make the full payment immediately. By stringing out the payments—that is, by not making one lump-sum payment of $150,000 now—the money can be kept, for example, in a savings account, accumulating interest. Granted, most new parents do not have that kind of money; by stringing out the payments on their child, they

[4] This estimate is based on a study done several years ago and adjusted for inflation: Ritchie H. Reed and Susan McIntosh, "Costs of Children," in Elliott R. Morss and Ritchie H. Reed (eds.), *Economic Aspects of Population Change: The Commission on Population Growth and the American Future* (Washington: U.S. Government Printing Office, 1972), p. 345.

do not have to borrow $150,000 and make interest payments on it. Either way, $150,000 spent today is actually a much greater cost than $150,000 spent over a period of, say, 20 years. To the $150,000 lump-sum payment we must add the interest that could have been earned with the money in the bank; or, we must add the interest payments that would have to be made on a loan of $150,000. In order to make rational choices, people must compare future costs on an equal footing with costs incurred today: they must appropriately reduce costs incurred in the future to determine what they are worth in today's terms. The value of future costs in today's terms is a concept known as *present value*. How much future costs should be reduced—or *discounted*, as the process is called—depends, as indicated above, on the rate of interest on money saved or on money that is borrowed.

When benefits are received in the future, they also must, if they are to be compared with alternatives that have present benefits only, be appropriately discounted. If you had a choice between receiving $10,000 now and $10,000 one year from now, you would take $10,000 today. You could, if nothing else, save the money in a bank for the interest return; you could also avoid the effects which inflation has on the value of the funds received in the future. Therefore, in order to entice you to choose an alternative with *future* benefits rather than one costing the same with *present* benefits, the raw benefits of the future option have to be greater. How much greater depends upon how you subjectively discount (reduce) the value of the future benefits.[5]

If there is any risk or uncertainty over actually receiving the benefits or incurring the cost of a particular action, the benefits and costs must be further adjusted so that the uncertain outcomes can be compared on an equal basis with outcomes that are certain. Without such adjustments, what may be a perfectly rational act may appear to be quite irrational. For example, criminal behavior is often considered to be irrational behavior. This may be one's reaction if only the raw costs and raw benefits are compared. A burglar may expect to net $1500 from the sale of stolen property from one "job." If caught, prosecuted, and convicted, he may spend a year in jail. If his annual income from a legitimate job is $10,000, the monetary cost of burglarizing a home will be his lost income, $10,000. This is his cost only *if* he is caught, prosecuted, convicted, and sentenced for that burglary. However, given the imperfect effectiveness of the police, the possible inability or reluctance of prosecutors to prosecute, and the prevalence of suspended sentences, the probability of even an inept burglar spending a year in jail may be as low as 10 percent. (This is not an unreasonably low figure.[6]) To estimate in a rough way the expected cost of a typical burglary, the raw cost of $10,000, in this example, can be multiplied by 0.10. The reason this is done is as follows: If the burglar is sent to jail for one out of every ten burglaries, the cost of any one burglary will average out to $1000 ($10,000 × 0.10), which is less than the benefits received, $1500. Although considered morally reprehensible, the criminal act can be (but does not necessarily need to be) grounded in the same decision process which has led you to read this book.

Many people subscribe to the notion that "crime doesn't pay" and conclude, as a result, that criminals are irrational. To suggest an answer to the question of whether or not crime pays, William E. Cobb studied cases of burglary and grand

[5] For the purpose of developing rough estimates of the *present value* of future costs, economists use some rate of interest that will have to be paid on any lump-sum cost payment. The mathematical formula for computing the present value of future cost (or benefits) received one year from now is

$$PV = \frac{1}{1+r} \text{ future costs (or benefits)}$$

where PV is present value and r is the rate of interest.

[6] Gregory Krohm "concluded that the chance of an 'adult' (seventeen or older) burglar being sent to prison for *any single offense* is .0024. . . . For juveniles . . . , the risk was much lower, .0015." "The Pecuniary Incentives of Property Crime," in Simon Rottenberg, ed., *The Economics of Crime and Punishment* (Washington: American Enterprise Institute for Public Policy Research, 1973), p. 33.

larceny in Norfolk, Virginia.[7] For a criminal who committed his first crime and was caught in the act, crime did not actually pay; but Cobb found that the typical criminal, convicted the average number of times and sentenced for the average number of years, would more than triple his lifetime income from a regular salaried job. This was true even after discounting the number of years that the typical criminal was incarcerated. The study was duplicated in Minnesota and the results were not quite as dramatic;[8] this study revealed that the typical criminal doubled his lifetime income. Both of these studies were done among criminals who had been caught at least once; there are many criminals who are never caught. Crime pays handsomely for them.

The same logical process can be applied to your life as a student. When you sign up for courses, you usually have only a very rough idea of how difficult and time-consuming the course will be and what benefits can be received from it. In other words, you are rarely *certain* of what the costs and benefits will be. To make your decision, you will have to discount the raw costs and benefits by the probability of their being realized. It is on the basis of such *expected* values that rational decisions are based. The important point is that uncertainties are pervasive in human experience, and economic analysis must account for this.

RATIONALITY AND THE NATURE OF GOODS: PRIVATE VERSUS PUBLIC GOODS

Economists are inclined to draw a conceptual distinction between two categories of goods: *private goods* and *public goods*. Almost all goods contain a blend of public and private characteristics, but we need to make the distinction clear.

A (pure) private good is a good the benefits of which are exclusively received by the person who has possession of it.

A reasonably good example of a private good is a chocolate bar. For the most part, only the person eating the bar of candy receives any significant pleasure from it.

On the other end of the continuum is the public good.

It is a good the benefits of which are shared by the relevant group if the good is provided or consumed by any one person.

The essence of the (pure) public good is that no one within the relevant group can be excluded from receiving benefits if the good is provided. The classic example, used in almost all discussions of public goods, is national defense. If national defense is provided, all in the country can share benefits which provision of defense may bring. There is vritually no way that a person, if he belongs to the group, can be excluded from the benefits resulting from the presence of the military.[9]

Despite the possible imperfections in our practical examples, making a distinction between public and private goods can still help clarify the difference between the individual's incentive to provide and consume private goods and to provide and consumc public goods. In the case of the private good, the benefits are received solely by the individual; his choice problem is simply one of determining whether or not the private benefits received are greater than the private costs that must be paid. If the perceived benefits (satisfaction) from the candy bar are greater than the perceived costs (money cost, excess calories, etc.), the individual will buy it; otherwise, he is excluded from its consumption.

The same may be true of the public good; if the benefits received by any one individual within the group are greater than the costs of the public good, the individual will be willing to provide the good. The benefits received by others are a kind of by-product (sometimes called a "spillover")

[7] William E. Cobb, "Theft and the Two Hypotheses," in Simon Rottenberg, ed., *The Economics of Crime and Punishment* (Washington: American Enterprise Institute for Public Policy Research, 1973), pp. 19–30.

[8] David L. Johnson, "An Analysis of the Costs and Benefits for Criminals in Theft" (Economics Department, St. Cloud State College, St. Cloud, Minn., May 1974). (Mimeographed.)

[9] By using the phrase "virtually no way" we are suggesting that there might be a way, but it is very costly to use.

from one individual's behavior. For example, a fisherman may place several buoys in the channels he plans to use to remind himself of hidden obstacles in the water; once they are provided, all other boat owners can gain the same benefits as the fisherman. They all know where the channel is shallow, and no one can be effectively excluded from receiving the benefits of this knowledge.

The problem with the provision of a public good comes when the costs of the good to any one person exceed the benefits received by any one person. The collective value placed on national defense by the people of a country can exceed the cost, *but the cost can exceed the benefits to any one individual.* In such an instance, an individual alone will be unwilling to provide the good (*his* costs exceed the benefits received). Since this is true for any one person, it can be true for all persons. The people's behavior may appear to be totally irrational: the people in the group would like to have the public good, but the consequence of individual rational behavior results in the group not having it. Everyone may be waiting for everyone else to make a move and provide the good.

Environmental quality is a form of public good; the people in the relevant group share in the benefits of its provision. If there are unpleasant sights around your college campus (e.g., places where smokers throw their butts, and weeds that are left to grow), everyone would probably feel better off if these places were cleaned up. However, a cost must be incurred in order for a voluntary cleanup to occur. Each person realizes that to clean up a small portion of the trash will change the environment very little; to clean up a large portion may take more time and effort than the person wishes to expend. If people are organized, the collective value which the group places on seeing the eyesore eliminated can be greater than the costs. However, the organization must develop from the initiative of someone, and, again, some one individual bears the cost of organizing people, in terms of time and effort. Those costs may exceed the benefits which one person receives from improving the environment; and, as so often happens, the eyesore remains.

Of course, environmental improvements can be made via individual action. Many of us hold onto our soft-drink cups until we find a trash can, providing a public good (less trash on the ground) and incurring a slight cost in the process. In such cases, the costs are less than the benefits. We also observe Boy Scout troops and other groups out picking up litter, but the line of logic of the public good just outlined may go a long way toward explaining why there are so many instances in which public goods are not provided, whereas private goods—ones which can be sold in the market—are provided in large quantities and varieties.

Concern over the quality of the environment reached a peak in the early 1970s with a march on Washington and a large rally on the grounds of the Washington Monument. Almost everyone there was interested in a cleaner environment, i.e., a public good. When the rally was over, however, the grounds looked like a picnic area for social reprobates; the grounds were covered with litter. Why did this happen? Why did not each participant attempt to clean up the garbage even if it was not his own? Can we assume that many people attending the rally were not sincere, that they were out for a lark that afternoon and hypocritical in their display of interest in environmental quality? Perhaps this was true for some; but, on the other hand, the logic of the public good may explain the behavior of most: there was insufficient incentive for even these people, who were very concerned about the environment, to produce the public good of cleaning up their own litter. Each may have hoped that someone else would pick up the trash. This tendency of individuals to try to "free-ride" can increase as the proportion of the total cost which a person is willing to pay goes down. As an example, you and we *may* agree that we ought to have a strong military force, such as we now have; however, the contribution which you and we are willing to make toward that end is, for all practical purposes, an insignificant portion of the total Pentagon budget. Under such circumstances the rational person can determine that withdrawing his contribution will not significantly (or discernibly) affect the amount of the public good which is provided. The impact of any one person's paying taxes will have an indiscernible effect on the size and strength of the military. This is why many persons attempt to avoid making any contribution—that is, to free-ride it. Each year around the middle of April many people find themselves behaving in this way; they take every opportunity they can, sometimes even dishonest opportunities, to minimize their contribution (i.e., tax payment) to the provision of public goods. In groups of much smaller size, the individual's contribution to the whole is much greater (or, the probability of one person's contribution being detectable increases). Therefore, we would expect that for public goods which span a large part of the population, some form of forced government taxation will be necessary. More will be said on this later.

In reference to public goods, benefits need not extend to the *entire* population of a country, such as is the case with national defense. Police protection is a public good which is generally restricted to a specific geographic location. The restrictions in a housing development, dealing with such things as lot size and type of home, can be a public good for the residents of the development in the sense that such restrictions may add to the market value of their homes. In such instances where the scope of the benefits is limited, exclusion is possible. People can be excluded from the group unless they make some contribution to the provision of the public good. Students pay the university, which in turn pays the faculty member who gives the lecture; if students do not pay, they can be excluded from class. The residents of a housing development can be forced to sign a contract which legally binds them to abide by the restriction. In fact, clubs are means through which limited-scope public goods can be provided by small groups; unless payment is made in the form of dues, membership is not allowed.

WHAT RATIONAL BEHAVIOR DOES *NOT* MEAN

There is perhaps nothing about the economist's approach to the study of social issues that is more bothersome to people unfamiliar with economics than the concept of rational behavior. Most of the difficulties which this concept creates arise out of a misunderstanding of exactly what rationality means. In order to minimize any confusion which may be lingering in the reader's mind, we will try to deal with the objections we hear when using rational behavior as a basis for analysis.

1 The individual does many things which do not work out to his benefit. A person speeds and ends up in the hospital; the student cheats, gets caught, and is expelled from school. Numerous other examples can be cited.

There is nothing in our construction of rational behavior which precludes people from making mistakes. We cannot control future events; we can only predict with some probability what the future holds. By assuming the individual is rational, we are not assuming that he has perfect knowledge; there is every reason to believe that he will incur some costs in seeking information on which he can base his choices. As a sheer matter of probabilities, he will make mistakes. On the other hand, the individual will base his choices on what he *expects* to happen, not what does happen. A mistake can affect only future choices, not past choices.

2 Rational behavior implies that a person is totally self-centered or that he does only those things which are of direct personal benefit.

Altruism can be a part of rational behavior; a person can "want" to be of service to others. There is nothing in the economist's concept of rational behavior which denies this. Most of us receive pleasure from seeing others happy, not least of all when others' happiness is a result of what we do. Further, we do not mean to suggest that all altruism must spring from rational cost-and-benefit calculations. Immanuel Kant, an eighteenth-century philosopher, put great stress on the importance of the *act* itself, independent of any rationally evaluated gains. We grant that much behavior is not rational behavior. To the extent that it is not, our discussion and predictions will miss the mark. There is no reason why we should attempt to preclude the explorations of other bases for discussion of human behavior. In this book our purpose is to show only what can be done with rationality as *one* basis for exploring behavior. Other approaches may complement what economics can contribute.

3 People are subject to psychological quirks, hang-ups, habits, and impulsive behavior; surely, such behavior cannot be considered rational.

Human behavior must be carried out within the constraints of our physical make-up. Like our intelligence, our inclination to psychological aberrations and our impulsive behavior are a part of the constraints within which we must make our choices. These conditions only add an element of imprecision to our ability to make rational choices and will contribute to our mistakes.

Much of what appears to be impulsive or habitual behavior, on the other hand, may be the product of some prior rational choice processes. The mind in its frailty can handle only so much information and can make only so many decisions. Consequently, we may attempt to economize on our time for making decisions by reducing some behavior to habit, or by making it a part of our subconscious. Smoking appears to be totally impulsive, and, indeed, there is a physical addiction which restricts the range of the smoker's choices. The smoker pulls a cigarette from his pack "without thinking." Why does he do this? Perhaps because he has reasoned at some prior point that it will be too costly to contemplate the pros and cons of smoking each and every time he wants a cigarette. By allowing smoking to be more or less automatic, the smoker probably increases the number of cigarettes smoked daily. However, he saves the cost (or tedium) of having to make the decision each and every time he smokes.

If the costs and benefits change, what appears to be an impulsive act may become a conscious act. For example, suppose you smoke "impulsively." Would you not consider changing your behavior if a very *large* friend said that he planned to follow you around and hit you on the head with a bat every time you "impulsively" pulled a cigarette from your pocket? This is an extreme example, but is it not possible that much of what is considered to be irrational behavior is actually grounded on rational choice processes?

We do not mean to define *irrational* behavior away. By defining rational behavior we give conceptual life to its opposite, *irrational behavior. Irrational behavior is inconsistent behavior or behavior which is clearly not in the best interest of the individual, and the individual knows this at the time.* By admitting the existence of irrational behavior, we are reiterating a point made in Chapter 1. We should not expect a perfect theory; the most that we can expect out of any approach is that it will do a better job of doing what it is intended to do, to explain and predict, than its competitors. The economic theory which we discuss in this text has a reasonably good track record in this respect; otherwise, we should advise you to spend your time elsewhere.

4 Rational behavior implies that people know what they want, that they know which alternatives are available, and that they know how to act on this information. However, this places considerable demand on one's ability to obtain and assimilate information. People cannot assimilate the information needed to make rational choices.

People do lack information, and they could make better choices if they had better, more complete information or if information were not often so hard to obtain. To the extent that they have less than perfect information, they will make mistakes when they make choices. However, the concept of rationality we have developed does not require perfect information. People make choices on the basis of the information they have and can *rationally* acquire. The success or failure of people's choices must be measured within these boundaries.

5 People do not necessarily maximize; many people do not perform to the maximum of their abilities.

"Lounging around" can be a good in an individual's preference ordering, and by consuming it the individual can be maximizing his welfare. Criticism of rationality along these lines tends to reflect a normative basis for judging behavior. If an observer equates rational behavior with what he considers "good" behavior to be, it is very easy to demonstrate that much behavior is "irrational." In the economist's way of looking at the concept, it is the values of the *actor,* not the values of the *observer* (or social critic), which determine the rationality of an act.

DIFFERENCES IN POINT OF VIEW: RATIONALITY VERSUS BEHAVIORAL DETERMINISTS

Different social scientists start with different sets of axioms about behavior, and the economist's way of looking at human behavior can be put into perspective by considering an alternate, albeit extreme, view.[10] The view of behavioralists, social determinists, or environmental behavioralists (all designations referring to essentially the same point of view) is that a person's behavior is *determined,* not simply influenced, by his genetic make-up and the environmental and social forces which have operated and are operating on him. A person does not consciously *act* upon the environment; he merely responds to changes in it. He behaves like a puppet; if a string is pulled (a stimulus received), an arm or leg moves, depending on the string, and it moves in a predetermined way: he does not "think," "choose," or "want." A behavioralist would say that you are presently reading this book, not by choice, but because of the forces which have come to bear on you. Essentially, you have been programmed to read this book at this time. The decision (or responsibility for your behavior) is not yours; it was determined by a multiplicity of forces which have caused you to do it.

We have in the course of this chapter based our discussion on the assumption that a *preference,* independent of social, genetic, and environmental forces, can at least be conceptualized and used for theoretical purposes. We cannot prove that this is the case; neither can the contrary be proved. It may very well be that the preference which we exhibit today is indeed the product of all the forces that are said to determine behavior. If this is so, our theory is also essentially deterministic. We have already conceded that a person's opportunity set (that is, his range of choice) is determined by such forces. If the preference is also determined, the actual "choice" taken along the outer boundary is *determined,* and no real choice is involved.

As odd as it seems, this concession does not bother us—and should not bother any economist. When behavioralists talk about all genetic and external forces determining behavior, they are talking about literally innumerable forces or variables. But this number of variables far exceeds the number the mind, even with the help of computers, can handle in any meaningful way. Many of these forces may have only an incidental effect on behavior, particularly those far removed in time and space. The economist's concept of a preference may be nothing more than a useful theoretical construct which condenses these forces, to quote Kenneth Boulding again, "into a form which we can appreciate and comprehend."[11]

Furthermore, the concept of the preference permits us to think in terms of the individual making trade-offs and in terms of how changes in the social and physical environment affect these trade-offs. For example, being given the information that Harry's ability to learn economics has increased, a person taking the strict behavioralist's view may overlook the prospects of the change affecting the relationship between Harry's ability to learn economics and his ability to have enjoyable conversations with friends (as we described in Figure 2 · 2). The researcher may simply look for the effects being realized in terms of Harry's performance in economics. As a matter of fact, this type of myopia (with no pejorative connotations intended) has led some educators to conclude that many of the changes they have made in the classroom over the years have had no appreciable

[10] This theoretical position is most prominently espoused by B. F. Skinner. For example, see B. F. Skinner, *Beyond Dignity and Freedom* (New York: Bantam/Vintage Books, 1972); and *About Behavioralism* (New York: Alfred A. Knopf, Inc., 1974).

[11] Kenneth E. Boulding, *Economics as a Science* (New York: McGraw-Hill Book Company, 1970), p. 2.

effect on the performance of students in a variety of situations. The changes in techniques may in fact have been ineffective; however, most of these studies have been done without an investigation of what the students may have been doing with their time before and after the change. Innovations in education such as teacher education and the use of such new technology as program study guides and audiovisual equipment may have increased the *efficiency* with which students learn. However, by rearranging how they divide their time among alternative activities, students can take the benefits of these changes by putting forth less effort, with the result that any change in student performance is barely detectable. Finally, the deterministic view of behavior never leads the social scientist to discussion of a relationship which economists call the "law of demand." It is to the development of this concept that we turn in Chapter 3.

SUMMARY AND EXTENSIONS

Rational behavior is a pivotal concept in the economist's study of human behavior. Essentially, rational behavior means that the individual has alternatives, can order his or her alternatives on the basis of preference, and is able to act consistently on the basis of this preference. We have concluded in this chapter that an individual who behaves rationally will always do those things for which the expected benefits exceed the expected costs.

The traditional study of economics has centered on the activities of business firms, and much of this book will be devoted to exploring people's behavior in a business and market setting. We, however, will go one step further and consider the behavior of bureaucrats in government service and of voters and politicians in the context of the democratic process. In applying economic theory to business and to the nontraditional areas of bureaucracy and politics, we will carry with us our assumption of rational behavior. That is, we will assume that business people, voters, politicians, and bureaucrats can be expected to maximize their well-being in the sense that all of us do in our everyday lives. The main difference between the observed behavior of, for example, business people and our behavior in our everyday lives should be the product of differences in our preferences and in the institutional setting (i.e., constraints) under which we behave. The behavior can be fundamentally the same: all of us seek to maximize our individual welfares. But the choice ranges of different people in different situations and, therefore, the actual choices made are likely to be different. Because they determine the constraints under which people must act, we will investigate the institutional characteristics of the markets, democracy, and government bureaucracy. Such investigations will help us to see why people behave the way they do—why and under what circumstances profit maximization of businesses will and will not be "socially beneficial" and why government bureaucracies may fail to achieve all that they are established to achieve.

In all our inquiries throughout this book, we will heed the advice of Philip Wicksteed, who has written,

> . . . the general principles which regulate our conduct in business [and politics] are identical with those which regulate our deliberations, our selections

between alternatives, and our decisions in all other branches of life. This is why we not only may, but must take our ordinary experiences as the starting point for approaching economic problems.[12]

However, our forays into nontraditional areas of social inquiry should not be construed to mean that the rules of rational behavior apply universally to *all* behavior. In some areas of human experience, other axioms may be more appropriate than the axioms which make up the concept of rational behavior. By concentrating so heavily on *rational man,* as we do in this book, we do not mean to rule out the existence of *moral man,* that dimension of our character which causes us to adhere to ethical principles regardless of the costs and benefits of the immediate situation. It is incumbent upon the economist–social scientist to be mindful of this prospect.

Furthermore, we must not forget the thoughts poignantly articulated several decades ago by economist Frank Knight:

> The problem of life is to utilize resources "economically," to make them go as far as possible in the production of the desired results. The general theory of economics is therefore simply the rationale of life.—In so far as it has any rationale! The first question in regard to scientific economics is this question of how far life is rational, how far its problems reduce to the form of using given means to achieve given ends. Now this, we shall contend, is not very far; the scientific view of life is a limited and partial view; life is at bottom an exploration in the field of values, an attempt to discover values, rather than on the basis of knowledge of them to produce and enjoy them to the greatest possible extent. We strive to "know ourselves," to find out our real wants, more than to get what we want. This fact sets a first and most sweeping limitation to the conception of economics as a science.[13]

On the other hand, as we indicated in Chapter 1, the process of scientific analysis requires that we take a point of view as a means of efficiently understanding what we observe; without a point of view nothing can be understood. We can glean what we can from the point of view of rational behavior without going to the extreme of believing that it is the only means of understanding or that it can explain all or even most human experience. *In the final analysis, a theory is intended to bridle thinking, not to shackle it or to allow it to run off untamed by reason.*

QUESTIONS TO PONDER

1 What are the costs of taking a course in economics? What are the benefits? (You may be inclined to say there are none, but, obviously, there is at least one or you would not be taking the course now.)

[12] Philip Wicksteed, *Common Sense of Political Economy* (New York: Augustus M. Kelley, Publisher, 1967), vol. 1, p. 3.

[13] Frank H. Knight, "The Limitations of Scientific Methods in Economics," in *The Ethics of Competition and Other Essays* (New York: Harper and Brothers, Publishers, 1935), p. 105.

2 What are the costs and benefits of engaging someone else in a conversation? Does rational behavior fully explain the lengths and types of conversations we have?

3 There is a theory of behavior which suggests that behavior is *determined* by external (environmental and genetic) forces. Would the concept of cost be absent from this theory?

4 Cite some examples of irrational behavior.

5 Would the behavior of someone under the influence of drugs be considered irrational?

6 Under what circumstances would suicide be considered irrational behavior?

7 If a professor's lecture can be considered a *public good* within the context of the classroom, as suggested in this chapter, why may students disagree as to what the lecture should be about and how it should be presented?

RECOMMENDED READINGS

Alchian, Armen A., and William R. Allen: *Exchange and Production: Theory in Use* (Belmont, Calif.: Wadsworth Publishing Company, Inc., 1969), chap. 2.

Johnson, Harry G.: "The Economics of Student Protest," and W. J. Baumol and W. G. Bowen, "On the Performing Arts: The Anatomy of Their Economic Problems," in Harry G. Johnson and Burton A. Weisbrod, eds., *The Daily Economist* (Englewood Cliffs, N.J.: Prentice-Hall, Inc., 1973), pp. 3–14.

McKenzie, Richard B., and Gordon Tullock: *The New World of Economics: Explorations into Human Experience* (Homewood, Ill.: Richard D. Irwin, Inc., 1975), chaps. 2, 3, and 4.

Olson, Mancur: "Economics, Sociology and the Best of All Possible Worlds," *The Public Interest*, Summer 1968, pp. 96–118.

3

The Law of Demand: A Pervasive Rule of Human Behavior

It is not the province of economics to determine the value of life in "hendonic units" or any other units, but to work out, on the basis of the general principles of conduct and the fundamental facts of social situation, the laws which determine prices of commodities and the direction of the social economic process. It is therefore not quantities, nor even intensities, of satisfaction with which we are concerned . . ., or any other absolute magnitude whatever, but the purely relative judgment of comparative significance of alternatives open to choice.

Frank Knight[1]

PREVIEW OF CHAPTER

Central question

What is the law of demand, and how can the principle be used to explain and predict human behavior?

Major objectives

1. To explore how the rational person will organize his purchases in order to maximize his utility
2. To derive the law of demand (or just demand) from the concept of rational behavior

[1] Frank H. Knight, *Risk, Uncertainty, and Profit* [Chicago: The University of Chicago Press, 1971 (originally published 1921)], pp. 71–72.

3 To develop the concept of "elasticity of demand"
4 To show how the concepts of demand and elasticity of demand can be used to explain and predict people's behavior

Major conclusions

1 The rational person will have maximized his utility after fully allocating his income and when his enjoyment of the last unit of each good consumed is equal.
2 The quantity that people will buy of a good or service varies inversely with the price. That is, if the price goes down, the quantity people will buy goes up, and vice versa. This relationship is the law of demand, and it is applicable to a wide range of human activities.
3 Consumers' responsiveness to a price change is different for different goods and services. Their responsiveness is called the "elasticity of demand." Because the quantity people buy can decrease by a "small" or "large" amount when the price increases, total consumer expenditures can rise or fall.

Important terms and concepts

Law of demand (or just demand)	Increase in demand
Marginal utility	Decrease in demand
Demand curve	Normal good
Market demand curve	Luxury good
Elasticity of demand	Inferior good
Elastic demand	Public good demand curve
Inelastic demand	

People adjust to changes in some conditions with a reasonable degree of predictability. When urban department stores announce lower prices for their founder's day sales, customers pour through their doors; the lower the prices, the larger the crowd. People collectively cut back on the number and length of their trips when the price of gasoline goes up—they also tend to buy smaller cars. Students who stray from the sidewalks to the shortcuts across campus malls on sunny days stick to the concrete when the weather is damp and the ground is muddy from the rain. Teachers who independently raise their course requirements and grading standards expect and generally find their enrollments falling as students adjust to these changes. Small children tend to shy away from doing those things for which they have been recently spanked. When lines for movie tickets become long, some people change their minds and go elsewhere for their entertainment. These are common experiences; on an intuitive level you will find them entirely reasonable. Going one step beyond intuition, the economist finds such responses to be the expected consequence of rational behavior; that is, people who attempt to maximize their utility can be expected to respond in the ways indicated. All these responses can be described by a concept called the *law of demand.* Because this concept is so important to the economist's study of human behavior, we will devote this chapter to its development.

FREE CHOICE AND THE LAW OF DEMAND

The assumptions about rational behavior developed in Chapter 2 provide us with a basis for *explaining* past behavior. People do those things for which the benefits exceed the costs; they avoid doing those things for which the opposite is true. Although in ways insightful, such statements do not, however, allow us to *predict future behavior*. *The law of demand*—which, succinctly put, means people will buy more if the price falls—provides us with a basis for *predicting* changes in behavior. This *law* is, as we will see, a logical consequence of our assumption of rationality.

The alert reader may sense an inconsistency at this point and a brief explanation is warranted. The problem may be expressed this way: rational behavior is based on the existence of *choices*. In order for choices to be *real* or *viable*, they must be *free;* that is, they cannot be predetermined or predicted. If one can predict an individual's choices, he must not have been free to choose in the first place. This criticism is well taken. However, from the start of our development of the concept of rationality, we have stated that the individual's choices are constrained by time, genetic factors, and other physical and social factors which restrict his opportunities. In other words, in our system, choice is constrained—it is not completely free. There are limits to the range of choices open to a person. Therefore, if predictions require the existence of constraints, these exist in the economist's notion of rational behavior.

Furthermore, we are unable to specify with precision the individual's every move, that is, his every choice. We are unable to say anything about what Joe Schwartz wants or to what degree he wants the things he does. Before the economist can employ the law of demand he must be told, or must be able to assume, what Joe wants. Given this, we are capable only of indicating the *directional movement* of his behavior; we cannot say, on theoretical grounds alone, how fast or how much Joe's behavior will change.

RATIONALITY AND CONSUMPTION PATTERNS

The essence of the economist's notion of rational behavior can be summed up in this phrase: "More of those goods and services which the individual wants is preferred to less." This implies that the individual will fully use his income in either consumption or saving. Furthermore, the individual will be maximizing his utility (or satisfaction). In order to accomplish this end, he must abide by some rule of behavior; he must have some means of knowing when this end has been achieved.

The individual places a value on each unit of each good or service he consumes, and the value of any one unit of a good is dependent upon the number of units consumed to that point. For example, you may be planning to consume two hot dogs and two Cokes for your next meal; you may expect to pay the same price for each unit of both goods, but there is no reason for us to assume that you place equal value on each hot dog and Coke. Physically, each hot dog may be almost alike, but the value of the last one you eat will usually be influenced by the fact that you have already eaten one. The rule you follow in determining the variety and quantities of goods and services which you consume is actually very simple. If the prices of the goods are the same, you will allocate your income in such a way that the *marginal utility* of the *last* unit of each good will be equal.

Marginal utility is the additional satisfaction received from one additional unit of a good consumed.

This condition can be stated in the following formula:

$$MU_c = MU_h$$

where MU_c = marginal utility of Coke
MU_h = marginal utility of hot dogs

It means simply that if you are rational, your enjoyment of the last Coke will equal your enjoyment of the last hot dog. This equality of marginal utilities is often referred to as *consumer equilibrium*, indicating the consumer is in a stable state or, in other words, has no reason to change his consumption pattern unless conditions change.

To illustrate the meaning of equilibrium, suppose for simplicity that there are only two goods which you can buy, Coke and hot dogs. Further, suppose that each costs the same amount, $1, and that you will fully spend your income. How much your total income is and how many units of Coke or hot dogs you purchase is unimportant here; we just assume that you purchase some combination of these two goods. Finally, suppose that the *marginal utility* from the last Coke consumed is equal to 20 utils[2] and the last hot dog purchased nets a marginal utility of 10 utils. You obviously have not maximized your utility by arranging your purchase this way. The marginal utilities of the goods are not equal:

$$MU_c > MU_h$$

In other words, you could have purchased one less hot dog and used the $1 saved to buy an additional Coke. In doing this, you would have given up 10 utils of satisfaction from the hot dog, but you would have been able to acquire 20 utils of satisfaction from an additional Coke. Your total utility would have risen on balance by 10 utils (20 utils minus 10 utils). You can continue to adjust your purchases of Coke and hot dogs until their marginal utilities are equal. Equality will be attained if the value of each additional Coke consumed diminishes and if the value of each hot dog given up increases: if $MU_c > MU_h$ to start with and MU_c falls while MU_h rises, $MU_c = MU_h$ can result. Because people are observed buying and consuming a combination of goods like Coke and hot dogs, we can assume that equality of marginal utilities is either achieved or closely approximated.

Generally, Coke and hot dogs are not sold at the same price. To this extent, the previous analysis is unrealistic. If we drop the condition of equal prices, the marginal condition for utility maximization becomes considerably more realistic and useful:

[2] A *util* is the economist's name for a unit of satisfaction. We have no earthly idea what "a unit of satisfaction" is, but it provides us with a measure we need for making our point. The reader can assume that a person does get some satisfaction from each unit of a good consumed and that he can in some quantitative and/or qualitative sense compare that satisfaction with the satisfaction received from another good.

$$\frac{MU_c}{P_c} = \frac{MU_h}{P_h}$$

where MU_c = marginal utility of Coke
MU_h = marginal utility of hot dogs
P_c = price of Coke
P_h = price of hot dogs

In the first example the prices of the goods were the same and equal to $1. When the prices are the same, the denominator can be dropped with no harm done to the equality. However, if the prices differ, the denominator must be retained explicitly. The person must allocate his money in such a way that the last penny spent on each commodity yields the same additional satisfaction.

Suppose a Coke costs $0.50 and the price of a hot dog is twice that, $1. If you make hot dogs and Coke your lunch and if the marginal utility for the last Coke and hot dog are the same, 15 utils, you are not at the highest possible level of satisfaction. MU_c/P_c (or 15 utils/$0.50) exceeds MU_h/P_h (or 15 utils/$1). You can improve your welfare by buying fewer hot dogs and increasing your consumption of Coke. If you give up a hot dog, you will save a dollar and you can use that dollar to buy two Cokes. You lose 15 utils by giving up the last hot dog, something you prefer not to do; but, on the other hand, you regain that loss with the first Coke purchased, and the purchase of the second Coke will permit you to go beyond your previous level of satisfaction.

Therefore, if you are rational, you will adjust your purchases until the ratios are equal. As more Coke is consumed, the relative value of each additional Coke will probably diminish until equality in the ratio is attained. For example, if the last Coke gives you 10 utils of satisfaction and the last hot dog gives you 20 utils, you cannot readjust your purchases and increase your satisfaction. By giving up a hot dog, you save $1 and lose 20 utils of satisfaction. By buying two Cokes, you can at best recoup your loss of 20 utils. And since the value of the second additional Coke may very well be below 10 utils, the additional satisfaction from the adjustment may actually be less than what you lose by giving up the hot dog.

We have talked in terms of buying *whole* units

of Cokes and hot dogs; however, what we have said applies to other kinds of choices. For instance, the concept of marginal utility is involved in choosing to move from a 12-ounce can to a 16-ounce can of Coke and from a regular-size hot dog to one a foot long. The discussion could also be developed in terms of adding cole slaw and chili to the hot dog. The pivotal question which the consumer faces in allocating his funds is whether or not the marginal utility of the additional quantity consumed is greater or less than the utility of alternative goods which can be purchased for the same amount of money.

The discussion to this point appears abstract and the expected behavior, that of an automaton; however, you behave in similar ways. Imagine walking into a snack bar somewhere on campus. If your income is unlimited, you have no choice problem; but given a $3 allotment for lunch, your first reaction may be to look at the menu and weigh off the marginal values of the various things you can buy. You are probably so accustomed to making decisions of this sort that you are almost unaware of the act of weighing off alternatives. But do you not find yourself mentally asking whether or not spending an extra $0.20 for a large Coke rather than a small one is *worth* more to you than having lettuce and tomato on your hamburger, or if the lettuce and tomato are worth more than a package of peanuts you could buy instead? Do you not try to come as close as you can to having the last penny or dime spent on Coke yield as much satisfaction as you could receive if the money had been spent on other things? If you realize you have made a mistake after you begin eating, do you not make an effort to correct your mistake in the future? If not, what makes you settle quite often on a small Coke instead of a large one? Why don't you buy all Coke for lunch?[3]

[3] At times, for example, after a noon workout, you may choose to have only a drink for lunch. In such cases, is your behavior inconsistent with the behavior described above? The answer is no. The reason that you "drank your lunch" was that, at the time, given the extent of your thirst and your limited funds, the marginal value of each unit of drink exceeded the marginal value of the first unit of something to eat. Therefore, it would have been irrational for you to move from Coke to French fries.

Granted, in most instances we do not make our choices with such conscious precision. We usually are not able to bring about a perfect *equality* of the ratios; the specific prices and values which we attribute to various units may not permit equality, but *our efforts in such cases are directed at coming as close to equality as possible.* For example, consider Table 3 · 1, which contains a *hypothetical* schedule of the marginal utility for each Coke and hot dog consumed and the prospects if $3 is to be spent on lunch. As you spend your first dollar, you are most likely to spend it on a hot dog. You can acquire 30 utils of satisfaction there, but by buying even two Cokes you can receive only 19 utils (10 + 9). After you have spent your first dollar on a hot dog, you can then buy two Cokes, since the satisfaction from two Cokes will be 19 utils as opposed to 15 utils which can be acquired from the next hot dog. But you can spend your last dollar on the second hot dog. (Why?) Your lunch would be a plate of two hot dogs and two Cokes. If we had used an example with more than two available goods, your lunch may have been more varied (we have been trying to keep the analysis simple).

Note, however, that you have not, by consuming the above combination, achieved equality in the ratio of each marginal utility to its price. The ratios would be:

$$\frac{9 \text{ utils}}{\$0.50} > \frac{15 \text{ utils}}{\$1}$$

The reason for the lingering inequality is not that you would not prefer to attain equality, but that the goods come in units which are not divisible. If you could buy "sips" of Coke and "bites" of hot dogs, you would attempt to buy more Coke and

TABLE 3 · 1

Unit Consumed	Marginal Utility of Cokes ($0.50)	Marginal Utility of Hot Dogs ($1)
First	10 utils	30 utils
Second	9 utils	15 utils
Third	3 utils	12 utils

less hot dog. However, these options have been eliminated partly because of the difficulty (i.e., cost) the store would experience in trying to sell these goods in smaller units. These types of problems rarely bother the analysis because the analysis is based on the assumption that the individual will move *toward* equality, not that he will achieve it.

CHANGES IN PRICE AND THE CONCEPT OF DEMAND

Suppose the price of Cokes rises to $0.75 and the price of hot dogs falls to $0.75. With a budget of $3 you can buy two hot dogs and two Cokes, as before. However, the equality (or approximate equality) of the ratios will be upset. You would be inclined to reduce your consumption of Coke and move toward greater consumption of hot dogs. In fact, your utility-maximizing combination (the one that best satisfies your preferences) would then be one Coke and three hot dogs. If you stay with the old combination (two Cokes and two hot dogs), your total utility will be 64 utils (45 from hot dogs and 19 from Coke). If you move to the new combination, your total utility will rise to 67 utils (57 from hot dogs and 10 from Coke). There is no other combination of Coke and hot dogs which will give you a greater level of satisfaction. (Try to find one.)

The importance of what was said in the preceding paragraph needs to be emphasized. *If the price of hot dogs goes down relative to Coke, a person, acting rationally, will buy more of them. If the price of Coke rises, relative to hot dogs, a person will buy less Coke.* If we reverse the price movements, we will get opposite movements in the individual's purchases. These deductions form the basis of what economists call the

law of demand: that is, everything else held constant, the quantity consumed will vary inversely with the price. This means that if the relative price of a good falls and there are no offsetting forces, the individual will buy more of the good; one will buy less if the price goes up.

All of this falls out of an assumption of rational behavior and the fact that, when the price changes, a person has substitutes to which he can move from one good to another. As we mentioned earlier, we cannot say exactly how many Cokes and hot dogs will be purchased when the consumer is in equilibrium, that is, when he is maximizing his satisfaction. This all depends on the individual's preferences, which in turn depend on a number of factors (how much he likes hot dogs, whether or not he's on a diet, and how concerned he may be with the nutritional deficiencies of such a lunch). But we can predict the directional movement of the response to a change in the price. Figure 3 · 1 depicts quantity of Coke purchased at different prices. The inverse relationship between price and quantity is depicted by the downward sloping curve; if the price falls from $1 to $0.75 in the graph, the quantity the consumer is willing to buy increases from 2 to 3. The opposite behavioral response occurs if the price is raised. Because such a curve describes the concept of

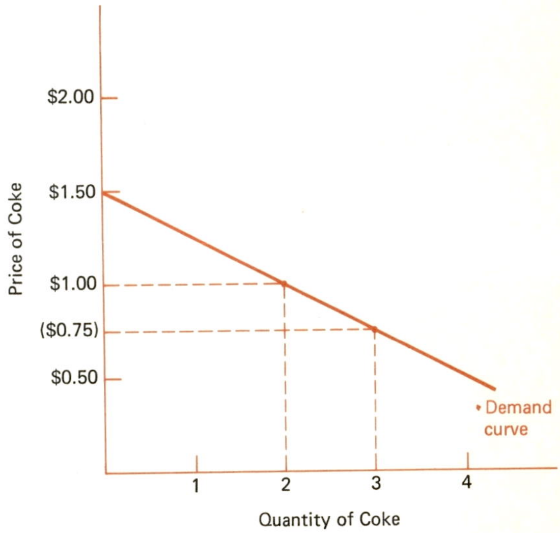

FIG. 3 · 1 The Law of Demand can be described as a downward sloping curve such as the one in this graph. This curve shows that as the price falls, consumers buy a larger quantity of Cokes, and vice versa.

demand, it is appropriately called the *demand curve* or simply the *demand*.

DEMAND AND HUMAN BEHAVIOR

We normally think of the law of demand as applying to market goods and services such as Coke, hot dogs, movies, and football games. However, before we can discuss and draw conclusions about the market system, we must remember that our law of demand was derived from very general postulates about human behavior. All we have said is that the individual has wants and that he attempts to maximize the attainment of his wants. The individual's wants are not restricted to "ordinary" goods and services; the concept of demand is, therefore, a pervasive rule of human behavior: given these wants, he will buy or in other ways seek more of the good if the price is lowered. This goes for anything which the individual wants and the attainment of which is manifested in behavior.

People "want" a wide variety of "material" goods and services, but they also want many things which are aesthetic. A person who wants to see the sunset in the evening must act (*behave*) accordingly. Such people have a *demand* for seeing sunsets which can be characterized by the same downward sloping curve that we have drawn for Coke. No explicit monetary payment may be required in order for them to see the sunset, but the *price* of something is not money. Price is a *concept;* price is what a person has to give up for each unit of goods, services, or anything else purchased, obtained, or consumed. The essence of consumption is not the manner in which satisfaction is obtained, but the fact that it is obtained. If the person who loves to watch sunsets has alternative opportunities, he must bear a price for watching a sunset; he gives up (or exchanges) something for the opportunity. The price may be equal to the "opportunity cost" of the individual's time, or the price can be the added cost and trouble of obtaining a house which will permit his viewing the sunset. The individual, given this price, should be willing to seek some optimum number of minutes per day watching the sunset and should be expected to vary the length of watching inversely with the price that may be only implicitly charged.

HUMAN BEHAVIOR AND MARGINAL UTILITY

People have a demand for friends and companionship. These wants can be treated in much the same way as a person's wants for Coke and hot dogs. The maximizing condition developed earlier can easily be extended to include "friendship" as a good, in which case it would be

$$\frac{MU_c}{P_c} = \frac{MU_h}{P_h} = \frac{MU_f}{P_f}$$

Where MU_f is the marginal utility of the last unit of friendship consumed and P_f is the implicit price of that friendship. The price of friendship may include the time and trouble involved in making and keeping friends: the little kindnesses offered, the emotional turmoil that can come from becoming involved in someone else's troubles, and the demands which one's friend may make on those around. (Some people require a form of respect from those around them, deserved or undeserved.) If a friend significantly raises his implicit price, you may have to break off your relationship. It is not at all uncommon to overhear someone saying something to this effect: "If this is the price I must pay for his friendship, I'll just have to lose it." Divorce can result when one partner demands or expects too much of the other—the price that is charged is too great for the other to continue the relationship. The implication of these unfortunate situations is that if the price had been lowered, the relationship would have been continued.

THE MARKET DEMAND FOR PRIVATE GOODS

The concept of demand has been discussed thus far solely in terms of the individual's behavior; however, our objective in this book is to go beyond the behavior of the individual and talk about the interaction of many people in a social environment. To do this we need some way of *aggregating* (that is, summing up) the preferences

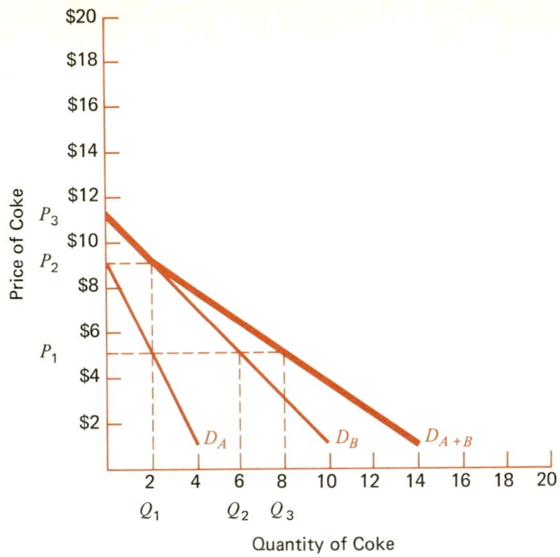

FIG. 3 · 2 The market demand curve D_{A+B} is derived by summing the quantities which individuals A and B are willing to buy at each and every price.

of people who interact in what we loosely call "society" or the "market." The *market demand* for a good or service is the economist's way of aggregating individual demand for private goods.

Simply stated, the market demand for Coke is the horizontal summation of the number of Cokes each person is willing and able to buy at each price. To illustrate how the market demand for a good is derived, we can talk in terms of two individuals who differ in their demand for Coke. In Figure 3 · 2, we have indicated the demand of person A as D_A, which is below the demand of person B, D_B. To determine how many cokes both of these people will demand at each price, all we need do is to add together the number which each will purchase individually at each price. At a price of P_3, neither A nor B is willing to buy any Coke, and, consequently, the market demand must begin at or below P_3. At P_2, A is still unwilling to buy his first Coke; however, B is willing to buy as many as Q_1. The "market" quantity demanded is, therefore, equal to Q_1. If the price falls to P_1, A then wants as many as Q_1 Cokes and B, given his greater demand, wants much more, Q_2. The two quantities combined equal Q_3. We can continue to drop the price, add the quantities that each buys at each price, and obtain a series of quantities demanded by both which lie on the outer, darker curve D_{A+B} which is the market demand for Coke. The way in which the market demand curve is derived is shown in Table 3 · 2.

This is a very simple example, since only two individuals are considered, but it is useful in illustrating the way in which a market demand encompassing many people can be derived. As more people demand Coke, the shape of the market demand curve becomes less steep and farther out to the right. This is because the quantity which all people in the market demand at each price becomes greater with the greater number of people.

We stress that this is the way a market demand for a *private good* is derived. A private good, as you may recall, is one the benefits of which are received by the individual; the good is not consumed *jointly* or *simultaneously* by others who may be in the social environment. Since each person in the market has his own Coke to consume, the problem is one of determining how many units all people in the market will want at each price. As we will see in a later section, the method employed in deriving the demand for a *public good* is dramatically different. For now, however, you should recognize that the market demand curve has the same *general* shape as the demand curve of each individual; that is, it slopes downward.

ELASTICITY: THE RESPONSIVENESS OF CONSUMERS TO A PRICE CHANGE

In the media and in general conversations, we often hear statements such as, "An increase in the price of prescription drugs will *not* affect people's use of them." The same is often heard with regard to people's use of medical services, gasoline, public parks, and salt. The same basic thesis is

TABLE 3·2 CONSTRUCTION OF A MARKET DEMAND CURVE

Price of Coke (1)	Quantity Demanded by A (D_A) (2)	Quantity Demanded by B (D_B) (3)	Market Demand: Quantity Demanded by Both A and B (D_{A+B}) (4)
$11	0	0	0
10	0	1	1.0
9	0	2	2.0
8	0.5	3	3.5
7	1.0	4	5.0
6	1.5	5	6.5
5	2.0	6	8.0
4	2.5	7	9.5
3	3.0	8	11.0
2	3.5	9	12.5
1	4.0	10	14.0

Note: The market demand curve in Fig. 3-2 (the heavy line) is obtained by plotting the quantities in column (4) against their respective prices in column (1).

implicit in some of the discussion surrounding the problem of population growth: present birthrates are established, and then an extrapolation of the trend is made into the future, resulting in a prediction of population growth. At the same time, certain conclusions are drawn concerning the increased demands which this growth will place on world resources, making the resources more scarce than they already are. If the point is made that the "price" of having a child will rise as resources become increasingly scarce, the reaction may still be that such price changes will have *no* effect on population growth. Perhaps the basis for such a contention is the belief that people do not behave rationally with regard to their child-bearing decisions and will not consider the price (or cost) of children. So much of the discussion surrounding publicly provided health care is couched in terms of the subsidized price having no effect on people's behavior; people would use only that amount of care which they "need," or so the argument goes.

Although economists recognize the possibility that there may be goods and services which do not conform to the law of demand, their first assumption, until proven to the contrary, is that the law of demand will hold. When people argue that a price change will have no effect, what we suspect they usually mean is that the price change will have only a *slight* effect. The law of demand states that a price change will have an inverse effect on the quantity that consumers will purchase of any good; it does not specify by how much consumers will change their buying habits when the price changes. Indeed, a subtle but sophisticated point in economic inquiry is that consumers will respond in differing amounts to changes in the price of any given good: for example, as a whole, college students will usually respond less to a 10-cent increase in the price of Coke than people in a low-income neighborhood.

In other words, we have to this point argued that the market demand curve for a good will be downward sloping. The actual demand for Coke in a particular market may look like D_1 or D_2 in Figure 3 · 3. At a price of P_1 the same quantity is consumed under both demand situations. However, if the price is raised to P_2, the response of consumers is substantially greater, with a demand curve shaped more like D_1 than D_2. With a demand of D_1, consumers reduce their purchases to Q_1; whereas with a demand described by D_2, consumers reduce their consumption only to Q_2.

To talk with more clarity about the consumer

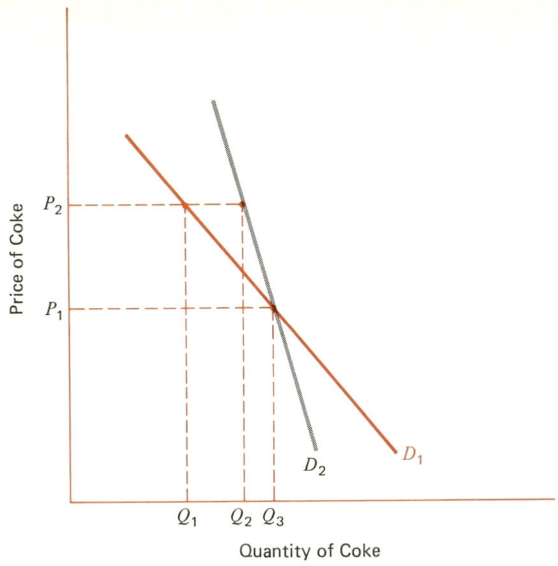

FIG. 3 · 3 The two demand curves, D_1 and D_2, are representative of demands with different "elasticities." D_1 is more "elastic" than D_2 in the sense that consumers are more responsive to a price change.

reaction to price change, economists have developed the concept of the *price elasticity of demand*. The price elasticity of demand is, in general terms, *the responsiveness of consumers to a change in the price*. When we talk about demand being *elastic*, we are suggesting that consumers are relatively sensitive (or responsive) to price changes. A demand curve like D_1 may be characterized as "elastic." If we suggest that demand is *inelastic*, we mean that people, although they may change the quantity they purchase somewhat, are relatively insensitive to price changes; that is, if demand is inelastic, consumers respond very little to price changes, as is true for a demand curve like D_2 in Figure 3 · 3.

This definition of the concept of elasticity of demand is practical but imprecise. What do we mean by "relatively sensitive or insensitive" to price changes? Under what circumstances is consumer response sensitive or insensitive? The economist is able to add precision to the definition of "elastic" or "inelastic demand" in two basic ways. The first way is to examine the effect which a change in price will have on total consumer expenditures; the second is through the development of "elasticity coefficients" or values for levels of elasticity. We deal with each of these methods of defining elastic and inelastic demands separately.

Analyzing Total Consumer Expenditures.

An increase in the price of a particular product can cause the consumers to buy less. Whether total consumer expenditures rise or fall depends upon the *extent* of consumer response. The common assumption is that a business will always raise the price of its good if it has no viable competitors. Although this is quite often the case, it is not always the optimum policy. For example, if a firm sells 50 units of its product for \$1, its revenue is \$50 (50 × \$1). If it raises its price to \$1.50 and sells 40 units, its revenue (or consumer expenditures) rise to \$60 (40 × \$1.50). However, if the consumer is highly sensitive (or responsive) to a price change for this particular good, the 50-cent price increase may lower the quantity sold to 30 units, in which case total consumer expenditures on this product will fall to \$45 (\$1.50 × 30). The opposite can be just as true. If the firm establishes a price of \$1.50 and then lowers it to \$1, the quantity sold can rise, but consumer expenditures will either rise or fall, depending again upon consumer response.

Economists distinguish among "elastic," "inelastic," and "unitary elastic" demands in the following way:

Elastic Demand. Demand is said to be "elastic"

- a When total consumer expenditures rise when the price falls or
- b When total consumer expenditures fall when the price rises.

Inelastic Demand. Demand is said to be "inelastic"

- a When total consumer expenditures rise when the price rises or
- b When total consumer expenditures fall when the price falls.

Unitary Elastic. Demand is said to be "unitary

elastic" when total consumer expenditures do not change with either a decrease or an increase in price. (If the price goes from $1 to $1.50 and the quantity purchased drops from 50 to 33⅓ units, expenditures will still be $50.)

Therefore, by examining changes in total consumer expenditures, economists can get a truer picture of the demand for any good in the market.

Determining Elasticity Coefficients

Although we have established some refinements in our definition of elasticity, our criteria are still imprecise in the sense that they do not allow us to distinguish different degrees of elasticity or inelasticity. One method economists use to make such distinctions is through calculation of the "elasticity coefficient of demand." The elasticity coefficient (E_d) is the ratio of the percentage change in the quantity demanded to the percentage change in the price, or

$$E_d = \frac{\text{percentage change in quantity}}{\text{percentage change in price}}$$

where d reminds us that we are talking about the elasticity of demand. If the percentage change in quantity is greater than the percentage change in price, the elasticity coefficient is greater than 1; when this is the case, the demand is said to be elastic. When the opposite is true—that is, when the percentage change in price is greater than the percentage change in quantity—the elasticity coefficient is less than 1. Economists characterize such demands as inelastic. When the percentage changes in the price and in the quantity are the same, the elasticity coefficient is equal to 1 and the demand is, understandably, referred to as "unitary elastic." These definitions of elasticity of demand are summarized below:

Elastic Demand: $E_d > 1$
Inelastic Demand: $E_d < 1$
Unitary Elastic: $E_d = 1$

With these definitions, economists can more accurately characterize one demand curve as being more elastic or inelastic than another demand curve. For instance, a demand with an elasticity coefficient of 1.75 is more elastic than a demand with an elasticity coefficient of 1.55. By the same token, a coefficent of .25 indicates a more inelastic demand than a demand which has a coefficient of .78.

Although useful for some purposes, the precision which these definitions provide may hide the difficulties which economists have in calculating elasticity coefficients. In the real world the variables which influence how much consumers want of any product are constantly changing and influencing people's purchases. In such a complex real-world setting, it is very difficult to separate out the effects of a price change from all the other forces operating in the marketplace. Small differences in calculated elasticity coefficients may simply reflect the imperfections of statistical analysis and not a true difference in the responsiveness of consumers to a price change.

Applications

The elasticity of demand is particularly important to entrepreneurs selling something; whether or not they raise or lower their price will depend on the elasticity of demand and the cost of production, as an example will illustrate. A firm which lowers its price and sells more incurs greater production costs because it is producing more units; however, if it is facing an elastic demand for its product, its revenues *can* go up by more than its costs, resulting in an increase in profits. During the 1950s and 1960s, the American Telephone and Telegraph Company (AT & T) repeatedly lowered its prices on long-distance calls. In order to justify incurring the expense of servicing the additional calls, it had to reason that the demand for long-distance calls was elastic—sufficiently elastic to more than cover AT & T's additional costs. Many electric power companies requested rate reductions during most of the same two decades because they, too, calculated that their demand was sufficiently elastic to justify such action.

Student organizations responsible for holding dances and pop-artist concerts must try to establish the appropriate admission price. If at a meeting a motion is placed on the floor that the price of a concert be set at $10 and no mention is made of the possibility that the relevant group of consumers has a downward sloping demand, and if no one questions whether or not some other price would be appropriate, tickets may be left unsold. It is quite possible, but not certain, that setting a lower price, say $7, will result in higher student attendance and, at the same time, increase the profit for the club coffers. The costs of putting on the dance may vary little with the number of people who attend. Even if costs rise (for extra workers and more programs) with a greater number of students attending the concert, revenues can rise by a greater amount, making the price reduction desirable.

Government must be concerned about the elasticity of demand for the things which it taxes. It is entirely possible for a state government to increase by too great an amount the excise tax it applies to some good, such as diamond rings, and end up with smaller tax revenues. The higher tax rate causes the final price of the product to be higher, and this, in turn, can cause a negative consumer response (fewer units sold). The higher tax rate multiplied by the smaller quantity sold can mean that the total tax revenues collected go down. Suppose that a government imposes a $1 excise tax on each unit of some good sold, and that 100 units are sold at the going market price. The tax revenues will be $100 ($1 × 100). Suppose that the tax rate is raised to $1.50 per unit and the quantity sold falls to 50; the revenue will fall to $75.

One source of the financial difficulties of large cities is that they have, in the past, incorrectly estimated the elasticity of their residents' demand for living within the city boundaries. A major reason, and there are others, for the migration from city to suburbs and other outlying areas has been to escape rising tax rates. The movement of people out to the suburbs will have an effect on the demand for property within the city and, thereby, on the value of the property. If the assessed value of property is related to its market value, the assessed value (in real terms) can fall and the total property tax collection can fall. Further, by moving just outside a city's boundaries, people can secure many of the benefits the city provides without actually paying for them. Governments, if they are interested in what happens to their revenues, must be careful about their tax policies. Indeed, citizen response is a concern in most legislative or city council debates on tax issues. This discussion helps explain why governments usually impose heavy excise taxes on such goods as cigarettes and liquor, the demands for which *tend* to be inelastic.

THE MAJOR DETERMINANTS OF THE ELASTICITY OF DEMAND

People can respond to a price increase of a particular good if they have substitutes to which they can move. If orange juice is the only beverage you can buy, you will simply be stuck buying whatever quantity of orange juice your income will permit. You will not be able to substitute such drinks as water, wine, and soft drinks.

However, for most goods and services there are substitutes; and if we are in equilibrium, the marginal values of the last unit of each substitute must be (approximately) the same (remember: $MU_c/P_c = MU_h/P_h$), meaning that a person can move to other goods with little lost in the way of satisfaction. The number, variety, and similarity of these substitutes are major determinants of the elasticity of demand for any good. If there are a large number and variety of substitutes, the person is likely to be able to purchase many goods which will yield him approximately the same value as the choice forgone. The similarity of the substitutes, in terms of how well they are able to satisfy the same basic want, also determines how little or much a person will lose by moving to other goods in the event of a price increase. When we talk of "necessities," we are often talking about things which have no "close" substitutes.

There are many substitutes for orange juice—Coke, wine, prune juice, etc.; therefore, we would expect its demand to be more elastic than the demand for something like salt. There are fewer viable alternatives to salt, and its demand is relatively inelastic. Even salt has synthetic substitutes. Physiologically, all of us need some minimum amount of salt to survive. However, most of us consume much more than this minimum, and we can easily give up some of this "extra" if the price of salt rises. The extra salt may add "extra taste." That extra benefit, which is psychological, can be partially recouped by buying other things.

A competitor is, by definition, one among many producers selling essentially the same goods or closely related goods. There are, in other words, other sources for the good which any one sells. For this reason, we would expect the demand faced by a single competitor selling something like cabbage to be more elastic than the demand faced by someone or some organization, like the Pentagon or a power company, which has few competitors. Competitors provide alternative sources for a good. If a seller raises his price, he must deal with the possibility that his customers will move to his competitors. Consumers can move not only to other goods, but to someone else who may be producing the *same* good. In this event the demand for the product category must be distinguished from the demand for *the product* produced by a particular manufacturer. The demand for the product category represents what consumers will purchase if everyone producing the good raises his or her prices; in this case consumers have only the option of moving to other goods. Their options are fewer than if one competitor raises his price. Therefore, the producers of any one good, acting independently, face a demand which is generally more elastic than the demand for the good itself. In many competitive situations, the individual firm is unable to raise the price at all without fear of losing all (or practically all) its customers. This is because the buyers can move elsewhere.

A good example of such a competitor is the Kansas wheat farmer. He can withhold his wheat from the market if he does not like the current market price, but that is all he can do. If a Kansas wheat farmer tries to charge more than the current market price, he is unlikely to sell his wheat. In a highly competitive situation each competitor is a price taker; he merely reacts to the "market" as if it were a part of "nature," like the force of gravity. In a highly competitive market it is a force to be dealt with and not casually manipulated.

Consumption requires time, and, accordingly, some time period must underlie the construction of any demand curve. In a very short time period, say a day, the demand for a good is quite inelastic. If the price of the good is raised, consumers may not be immediately aware of possible substitutes for the good; and, as a result, consumers can respond very little to the price increase. However, given more time to seek out alternatives, the response can be greater, and the demand constructed with this longer time horizon will be more elastic. To illustrate, in 1974 the Arab countries more than tripled the price of their exported crude oil; this enabled domestic producers to also raise their prices. Consumers had established ways of driving and living. They drove big, gas-guzzling cars, and their homes in the suburbs were often far from their work. United States auto makers were not tooled up to mass-produce the mini-compacts. However, given a longer period of time, new alternative modes of transportation will become available, from both domestic and foreign producers. Alternative sources of energy will be found, and people will alter their life styles. Many will learn to walk and ride bicycles. All these changes, which, by the way, have happened to one degree or another, have given the consumer a chance to respond more to the price increase of gasoline. The long-term demand curve has been much more elastic than the short-term curve.

CHANGES IN THE POSITION OF THE DEMAND CURVE

How much of a good people are willing to buy is determined by many variables, and these different variables apply to different goods. The amount of ice cream and the number of golf balls people are willing to buy are dependent upon the weather (very few golf balls are sold at the North Pole); the number of cribs bought is dependent upon the birthrate. Almost all goods are affected in one way or another by (1) consumers' income levels, (2) the prices of other goods, (3) expectations about future prices and incomes, and (4) that catch-all

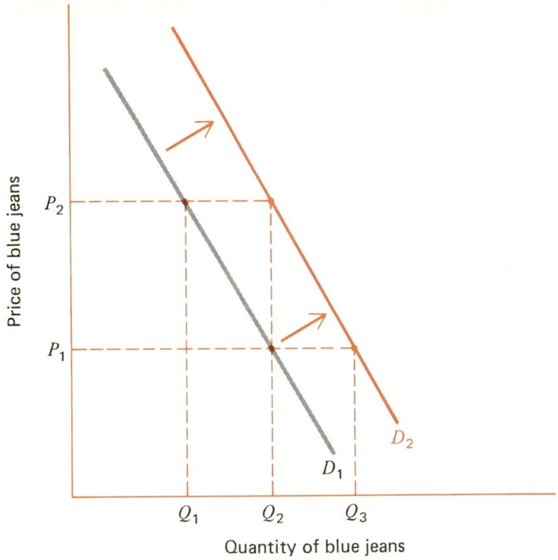

FIG. 3 · 4 The upward shift from D_1 to D_2 equals an *increase* in consumers' demand for blue jeans. This shift means that consumers are now willing to buy a larger quantity at the same price or are willing to pay a higher price for the same quantity.

variable which economists call "tastes" or "preferences." All these variables (and those which they represent) work to determine the position of the demand curve. If the variables change, so will the demand curve.

For example, if people's preference for blue jeans increases, the change should be reflected in an outward movement in the demand curve, as from D_1 to D_2 in Figure 3 · 4. During the early 1960s, college students would go to considerable trouble to avoid wearing blue jeans; jeans were just not in style, except for work purposes. But during the late 1960s tastes changed, and wearing jeans, and faded ones at that, became chic. Such a change in taste, by definition, means that people are willing to buy more of the good at the going market price. If the price is P_1, the quantity demanded increases from Q_2 to Q_3 with the shift in the demand curve. A change in tastes can also mean that people are willing to buy more jeans at each and every price. At P_2 they are willing to buy Q_2 instead of Q_1. From this we can infer not only that consumers are willing to buy more at each price, but that they are willing to pay a higher price for any given quantity. In Figure 3 · 4 an increase in demand means that consumers are now willing to pay as much as P_2 for Q_2 pairs of jeans; they once were willing to pay only as much as P_1. If the consumers' tastes *decrease* rather than increase, the demand curve moves downward to the left as in Figure 3 · 5, implying that consumers are willing to buy a smaller number of blue jeans at P_1 or are willing to pay a lower price for Q_2 jeans.

Regardless of whether or not demand decreases or increases, the curve should remain downward sloping, as in Figure 3 · 1. As we have said, if *everything else remains constant,* people will buy more of the good at a lower price than at a higher one. This qualification is unrealistic, since markets are generally in a state of flux; all vari-

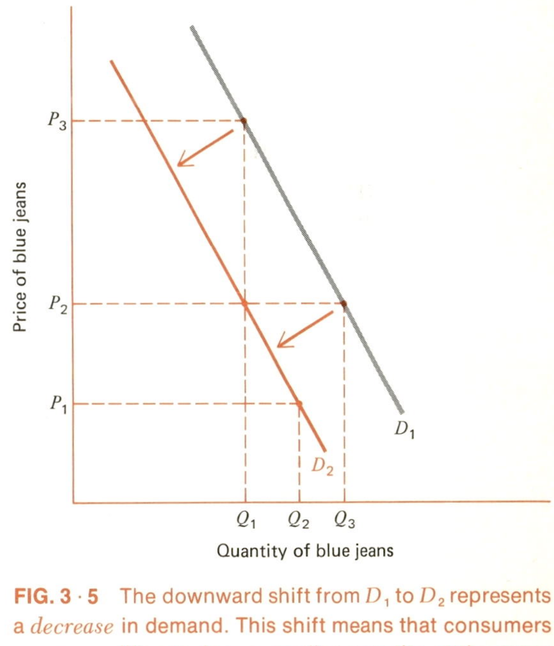

FIG. 3 · 5 The downward shift from D_1 to D_2 represents a *decrease* in demand. This shift means that consumers are now willing to buy a smaller quantity at the same price or are willing to pay a lower price for the same quantity.

ables just do not stay put to allow the price of the good to change by itself. The phrase "everything else remains constant" is useful only for purposes of exposition; it enables us to establish the position of the demand curve and to talk clearly about what is meant by the law of demand. It also enables us to talk about the specific effects of specific changes in market conditions. However, the law of demand tells us that even if conditions change at the same time that price decreases, people will buy more because of the decrease in price than they would otherwise buy. For example, in Figure 3·5, the demand for blue jeans has decreased because people's willingness to buy blue jeans has decreased. However, a price reduction from P_2 to P_1 partially offsets the effects of the preference change: people buy more jeans (Q_2) than they would have purchased if the price had not fallen (Q_1). In the net, the consumers buy fewer jeans than they once did (Q_2 as opposed to Q_3), but the law of demand still holds: *the consumers have increased their consumption over what it would otherwise have been.* The curve in the graph is still downward sloping, which is the only assertion the law of demand makes.

A change in people's income will affect their ability and willingness to buy different goods. Obviously, an increase in income will affect the demand for different goods in different ways. If the demand for a good rises with income, it is called a *normal good.* If the demand for a good rises at a greater rate than people's income rises, it is called a *luxury good.* If, on the other hand, the demand for a good falls as incomes rise, it is called an *inferior good.* Most goods are normal goods—their demands rise with incomes; however, a few goods, like beans, may be inferior goods. People with very low incomes may rely on beans as a staple in their diets or as a "filler" in their meal. If their incomes rise, they may substitute, at least to some degree, meat and other higher-priced foods for the beans which once dominated their diets. Therefore, when their incomes rise, their demand for beans falls.

Economists can predict with a fairly high degree of confidence the directional movement of people's consumption if prices change. However, there is nothing in this theory which will allow us to say, with the same confidence, what will happen to the demand for a particular good (that is, whether it will decrease or increase) if income changes. This is because the individual must determine for himself whether or not a particular good is a normal or an inferior good. The question of whether or not a good is a normal or an inferior good is answered differently by different people in different markets. Beans may be an inferior good among one group of people and a normal good among others. To indicate the problem more clearly, how do you think a change in income affects the demands for "low"-, "medium"-, and "high"-quality liquor? You may have some intuitive notion about the effect, but we doubt you are as confident about your prediction as you are about the effects of a price decrease. As it happens, during the recession of 1974–75 the demands for both low- and high-quality liquor went up. The demand for medium-priced liquor went down. The reporter of this bit of news reasoned that some people switched in part to high-quality liquor to give the impression to their friends that the recession was not affecting them. Others, trying to maintain their overall level of liquor consumption in the face of a decrease in income, switched to a lower quality.

The effects which changes in the price of other goods have on the demand for, say, ice cream depends on the relationship between ice cream and the other commodities; the effects depend on whether or not ice cream and some other good are independent, substitutes, or complements in consumption. For example, a drop in the price of babies' rattles may not affect the demand for ice cream; babies' rattles constitute a very small portion of most people's budgets and carry such a low price anyway that even a substantial percentage reduction in price may not be felt by the family's ice cream consumers. The two goods are therefore independent of one another in consumption. On the other hand, a drop in the price of ice milk can definitely reduce the demand for ice cream as some ice cream eaters switch to ice milk. This is possible because ice cream and ice milk are reasonably close substitutes. Indeed, products are considered substitutes for each other if, when the *price* of one product goes up, the *demand* for the other product goes up.

If A and B are substitutes, the price of A does not have to rise above B before the demand for B is affected. To illustrate, the price of sirloin steak may be $3 per pound and the price of hamburger, $1 per pound. The gap in the price reflects the fact that the consumer believes these two meats are of different quality. If the price of hamburger rises to $2 per pound while sirloin remains constant, many buyers will increase their demand for steak. The reason is that the perceived difference in quality is now greater than the difference in price, causing a movement in consumer buying patterns; the demand for steak rises, as in Figure 3 · 4.

Complementary products are goods which are consumed jointly, such as razors and razor blades, oil and oil filters, and, an extreme example, the left and right shoes. If the price of one complement rises, the cost of using both complementary goods rises, and the demand for both will decrease. (Remember, the demand curve for the joint use of complements is downward sloping.) To illustrate, an increase in the price of razor blades will induce some people to switch to electric razors, causing a decrease in the demand for the safety razors.

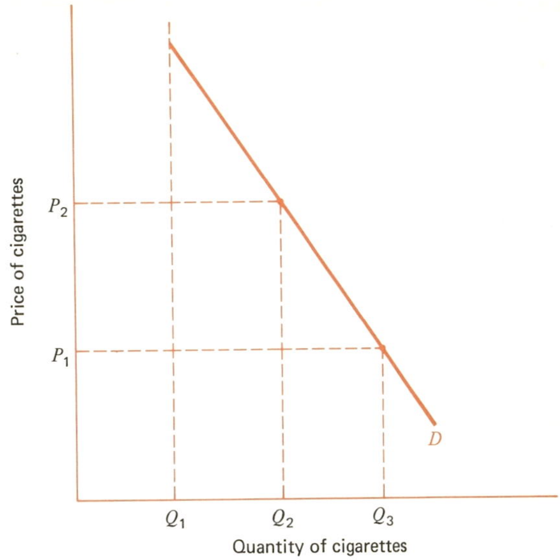

FIG. 3 · 6 When there are "irrational consumers" in the market, the market demand will be equal to the amount purchased by the irrational consumers, Q_1, which does not vary with the price, plus the amount purchased by the rational consumers, which does vary with the price. The total market demand is positioned as D_1. The total quantity purchased by *all* consumers still varies inversely with the price.

THE LAW OF DEMAND AND IRRATIONALITY

So far, demand has been discussed entirely in terms of rational behavior. However, as we indicated in Chapter 2, not all consumer behavior is necessarily rational. In spite of some irrational behavior, the predictions arising from the law of demand are viable as long as there are some people in the market who respond to price. To illustrate, many people buy cigarettes because they are addicted to them. See Q_1 in Figure 3 · 6. Because they do not consider price as a part of their purchase decision, this quantity cannot be expected to vary (except to the extent that it affects the purchasing power of their total income) with price changes. If, however, some cigarette smokers do take the price into consideration when they buy, their demand for cigarettes will take on the normal downward slope. If we add the demand of those who act "irrationally" to the demand of those who act "rationally," the total market demand curve will still be downward sloping, as in the position of D in Figure 3 · 6. At a price of P_1, Q_1 will be bought by "irrational consumers" and $Q_3 - Q_1$ will be bought by "rational consumers." If the price rises to P_2, the total quantity falls to Q_2; but the drop in quantity purchased is a result of the response of rational consumers.

The analysis can be extended to impulsive behavior. There are people who respond more or less impulsively to the packaging of and display gimmicks for various supermarket items. They do not stop to seriously consider price and do not respond to changes in price. Their demand may not be downward sloping. However, as long as some people check prices and resist advertising techniques, the total demand for the supermarket's goods will be downward sloping. Supermarket managers, therefore, must operate on the assumption that changes in price will affect the quantity demanded. The fact that there are people who behave irrationally will tend to reduce the elasticity of the demand, but it does not invalidate the concept.[4]

THE DEMAND FOR PUBLIC GOODS

The development of a community's demand for a *public good* is substantially different from the previous construction of the demand for a private good. The individual has a downward sloping demand for public goods—national defense, environmental quality, etc. (see Chapter 2); however, if a unit of a public good is provided, all within the relevant group can receive benefits from it. This is not true of a private good; a unit of a private good benefits only the person who possesses it. Consequently, the *community's* demand for a public good must be obtained by vertically adding up the values (as measured by the price) which all within the group place on each unit. The reason for this is simply that all can benefit from each unit; and the relevant question is what is the total value which all within the group place on all units. This is why we vertically add each unit, to find the total value.

To illustrate in the simplest possible terms, consider a community made up of only two people. There is some good, like police protection, from which both can receive benefits simultaneously. Suppose, however, that individual B has a greater demand for police protection than A. This condition is illustrated in Figure 3 · 7. For the first unit

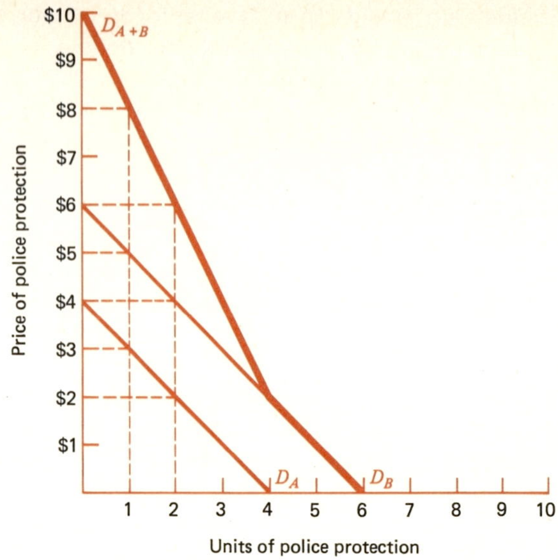

FIG. 3 · 7 The public good demand curve, D_{A+B}, is equal to the vertical summation of the demands of the individuals A and B. The curves are added vertically because both individuals A and B can simultaneously benefit from each unit of police protection provided.

of police protection, A is willing to pay as much as $3, which is an indication of the relative value he places on that unit. B, on the other hand, is willing to pay more, $5 in this example. Both can benefit from the first unit of police protection, and the collective value attached to this unit is $8 ($3 + $5). Since each individual's demand curve is downward sloping, the relative value attached to each unit declines as the quantity is increased. For the second unit, A is willing to pay $2 and B, $4. Collectively, they are willing to pay as much as $6. For the fourth unit, A is unwilling to pay anything; however, B is still willing to pay as much as $2. From that point on, the collective value of police protection is simply equal to the value which B places on the good.

The prices which A and B are willing to pay for each unit are shown and added together in Table 3 · 3. If we plot the collective value which A and B place on each unit (P_{A+B} in the table) against the

[4] Economist Gary Becker has demonstrated rather convincingly that an assumption of rational behavior is actually unnecessary to obtain a downward sloping demand curve. He argues that the curve can emerge from completely random behavior on the part of consumers. For this reason alone, economists cannot say with complete conviction that the fact that people buy more at lower prices *demonstrates* that people are in fact rational. It may demonstrate that they act randomly. See Gary S. Becker, *Economic Theory* (New York: Alfred A. Knopf, Inc., 1972), pp. 19–23.

TABLE 3·3 CONSTRUCTION OF A PUBLIC GOODS DEMAND CURVE

Units of Police Protection (1)	Price A Is Willing to Pay for Each Unit (D_A) (2)	Price B Is Willing to Pay for Each Unit (D_B) (3)	Public Goods Demand: Price A and B Are Willing to Pay for Each Unit When They Act Collectively (D_{A+B}) (4)
0.5	$3.50	$5.50	$9
1	3	5	8
2	2	4	6
3	1	3	4
4	0	2	2
5	0	1	1
6	0	0	0

Note: The public goods demand curve in Fig. 3-7 (the darker line) is obtained by plotting the prices that *A* and *B* are collectively willing to pay for each unit in column (4) against their respective units in column (1).

quantity, we will obtain a demand curve represented by the darker line in Figure 3·7. This curve represents the demand for a public good or service. It represents what the people in the community are willing to pay in total (if they have to) for each unit of police protection. We talk in terms of the collective value of the community because all people can share in the benefits of the good or service if it is provided.

Public officials may be unable to obtain a very accurate picture of the public's demand for a service like police protection. When people vote for representatives or in a referendum, they vote for or against or yes or no. Their votes are only a crude indication of the *intensity* of their preferences for the public good. This is so because all votes count the same. The politicians are forced to try to sense the mood of the people, and in doing that they may provide many people with an opportunity to misrepresent their true demand for the good, that is, how much they are willing to pay. More will be said on this in later chapters. The important point to understand at this juncture is the difference in the construction of the demand for public and private goods.

A FINAL NOTE ON RELATIVE AND ABSOLUTE VALUES

The basic argument which underlies the concept of demand allows us to say a good deal about behavior, but there is much which cannot be determined by the concept. We know that if the price falls, the rational person will buy more. We know also that he will allocate his income in such a way that

$$\frac{MU_b}{P_b} = \frac{MU_h}{P_h}$$

where the abbreviations have the same designation as they had in a prior section. Further, we know that the ratio of prices (P_h/P_b) indicates the relative marginal utilities of the goods. This is because the above ratios can be rearranged to

$$\frac{P_h}{P_b} = \frac{MU_h}{MU_b}$$

That is, if the price of a hot dog is $2 and the price of a Coke is $1, we know that the marginal utility of the last hot dog is twice that of the Coke. If the price of hot dogs is twice that of Coke, in order for the above ratios to be equal, MU_h must be twice MU_b. For this reason, *economists can say that relative prices indicate relative marginal values.*

However, the argument that underlies the concept of demand does not indicate anything about the absolute value of any given good to different people. In other words, in order for the ratios to be equal, the marginal utility of hot dogs and Coke can be 20 and 10 utils, respectively, or they can be 30 and 15 utils, respectively. For that matter, absolute marginal utilities are not only difficult to conceive but also irrelevant to the argument. At the theoretical level, the level at which we are operating, there is no way for us to say which individual, A or B, prefers Coke "more." They both may have to pay the same price for Coke and hot dogs; but in order for them to be in consumer equilibrium, the only necessary condition is that their marginal ratios be equal. Either one of the following cases, shown in the table at the right, can satisfy this condition.

In each case, A and B are in equilibrium. However in case I, B places a higher util rating on Coke and hot dogs than A. In case II, the opposite is true:

	Hot Dogs	Coke
Case I		
Individual A	$\frac{\text{20 utils}}{\$2}$	$\frac{\text{10 utils}}{\$1}$
Individual B	$\frac{\text{30 utils}}{\$2}$	$\frac{\text{15 utils}}{\$1}$
Case II		
Individual A	$\frac{\text{50 utils}}{\$2}$	$\frac{\text{25 utils}}{\$1}$
Individual B	$\frac{\text{40 utils}}{\$2}$	$\frac{\text{20 utils}}{\$1}$

A places a higher util rating on both goods than B. For this reason, economists shy away from making what they call "interpersonal utility comparisons" or, in common English, judgments on who likes what most. This is not to say that such judgments cannot be made, but they require that we step outside the boundaries of economic science.

SUMMARY AND EXTENSIONS

The purpose of this chapter has been to develop the concept of demand. It is *not* just what people would like to have or are willing to pay for; it is *not* conceived as the quantity that consumers are willing to buy at a given price. Rather, demand is conceived as a functional relationship; to be more specific, it is the assumed inverse relationship between price and quantity. It is a series of price-quantity combinations which can be depicted by a downward sloping curve.

Economists do not have complete confidence in all applications of the law of demand—that is, economists will admit to exceptions. However, they consider the relationship between price and quantity to be so firmly established, from both a theoretical and an empirical point of view, that they refer to it as a "law." The burden of proof is generally considered to be on the shoulders of those who wish to dispute the statement that more will be purchased at a lower price. In the real world, when the price of a good goes down, it is possible that the quantity purchased can be observed to fall; however, if this is the case, the economist assumes that something else has changed to more than offset the positive effects of the price decrease on demand.

The major points of the chapter can be summarized as follows:

1 The quantity purchased will vary inversely with the price.

2 The location of the demand curve can be altered by many different forces. These forces may vary from one good to another, but three broad categories of forces are applicable to the markets for almost all goods: consumer incomes,

prices of other goods (complements and substitutes), and consumer preferences.

3 Consumer responsiveness, called the *elasticity of demand,* is different for different goods.

4 The market demand for a private good is obtained by horizontally summing the individual's demand curves, whereas the collective demand for a public good is found by vertically summing the values which people place on each unit.

5 Within the bounds of scientific inquiry, our knowledge of rational behavior says nothing about the relative satisfaction which different people obtain from different goods. As we quoted Frank Knight at the head of this chapter, "It is . . . not quantities, nor even intensities, of satisfaction with which we are concerned . . ., or any other absolute magnitude whatever, but the purely relative judgment of comparative significance of alternatives open to choice."[5]

QUESTIONS TO PONDER

1 What role does the law of demand play in economic analysis?

2 If the price of jeans rises and the quantity sold goes up, is the demand curve upward sloping?

3 If the economy is in the midst of a 15 percent rate of inflation (that is, prices of most goods are rising by an average of 15 percent per year) and the price of gasoline rises at a rate of 10 percent per year, what is happening to the real or relative price of gasoline? What do you expect to happen to the quantity of gasoline used? Why?

4 Suppose that a firm raises its price from $4 to $7 and the quantity sold goes from 250 to 200 units. Is the demand elastic or inelastic?

5 Why does an economist equate relative price with relative marginal value?

6 If the price on the pump remains constant, for example, because of government price controls but people begin waiting in line for gasoline, what happens to the price of gasoline? What should happen to gasoline use?

7 If the number of campus security officers is increased and they are instructed to increase the number of tickets given for parking in the wrong places, what will happen to the number of parking violations? Why? What may be necessary to eliminate all parking violations? Why may this option not be taken?

8 The government has been in the business of subsidizing flood insurance since 1973. What does this do to the price of flood insurance? What will happen to the value of property lost during floods? Why?

9 If the price of ballpoint pens falls, will the *demand* change? What will happen to the demand for pencils? To the demand for paper?

RECOMMENDED READINGS

Boulding, Kenneth E.: "Economics as a Behavioral Science," in *Economics as a Science* (New York: McGraw-Hill Book Company, 1970), pp. 53–75.

[5] Frank H. Knight, *Risk, Uncertainty, and Profit* (Chicago: The University of Chicago Press, 1971), p. 72.

Fels, Rendigs, and Robert G. Uhler: "The Price of Sin" and "Ticket Scalping," in *Casebook of Economic Problems and Policies: Practice in Thinking* (New York: West Publishing Co., 1975), cases 5 and 6.

Manne, Henry G.: "The Parable of the Parking Lots," in Royall Brandis and Steven R. Cox, eds., *Current Economic Problems: A Book of Readings* (Homewood, Ill.: Richard D. Irwin, Inc., 1972), pp. 103–107.

McKenzie, Richard B., and Gordon Tullock: *The New World of Economics: Explorations into Human Experience* (Homewood, Ill.: Richard D. Irwin, Inc., 1975), chaps. 2–4.

4

Supply and the Importance of Cost in Guiding Human Behavior

The economist's stock in trade—his tools—lies in his ability to and proclivity to think about all questions in terms of alternatives. *The truth judgment of the moralist, which says that something is either wholly right or wholly wrong, is foreign to him. The win-lose, yes-no discussion of politics is not within his purview. He does not recognize the either-or, the all-or-nothing, situation as his own. His is not the world of the mutually exclusive. Instead, his is the world of adjustment, or coordinated conflict, of mutual gain.*

James Buchanan[1]

PREVIEW OF CHAPTER

Central question

How does cost affect and limit behavior?

Major objectives

1 To review basic points relating to cost that were developed in Chapter 2
2 To develop the concepts of *marginal cost* and *marginal cost curve* and to show that the marginal cost curve is the individual's supply curve

[1] James M. Buchanan, "Economics and Its Scientific Neighbors," in Sherman Roy Krupp, ed., *The Structure of Economic Science: Essays on Methodology* (Englewood Cliffs, N.J.: Prentice-Hall, Inc., 1966), p. 168.

3 To show how the concepts of *supply* and *demand* can be used to explain the limits of and changes in people's behavior

Major conclusions

1 The *marginal cost* of producing additional units of a good will tend to rise as production is extended.
2 The *supply curve* of a producer tends to be upward sloping.
3 A person will increase his production of a good so long as the marginal benefit of the additional units is greater than the marginal cost and will extend production up to the point where the marginal cost of the last unit produced equals the marginal benefit of it.
4 *Sunk costs* are irrelevant to a choice situation.

Important terms and concepts

Explicit costs
Implicit costs
Marginal cost
Law of diminishing returns
Supply (and supply curve)
Sunk costs
Market supply curve

Cost is pervasive in human action. We are constantly beset with the problems involved in making choices, and choice implies that when something is done, something else must be left undone. As we studied in Chapter 2, cost is the most highly valued opportunity which a person gives up in a choice situation. For this reason economists use the term *opportunity cost* to indicate with more precision what cost actually is. Money is a *means* of measuring cost but is not cost itself.[2]

Although unrecognized as such, cost pervades much of our everyday conversation and thinking processes. When we say, "This course is difficult" or "The sermon was quite long," we are indicating the cost of these activities. In other words, "The sermon was very costly in terms of the picnic that was planned and shortened by the extended sermon." Although we may, at times, be indicating our absolute limitations when we say, "I can't afford a vacation this year," "This research paper is impossible to write," or "Being a friend of his is not worth it," more often than not we are suggesting that the cost of whatever is involved is too great to justify the benefits. Most people who say they "can't afford a vacation" are unwilling to make the necessary sacrifices (i.e., bear the necessary cost). Most students who find research papers "impossible" are unwilling to put forth the effort (i.e., the cost), whether small or very great, to write a minimally acceptable paper.

The purpose of this chapter is to explore further the meaning of cost and its relevance to human behavior. We begin by developing the concepts of *explicit* and *implicit cost* and showing how recognition of the different cost components of a choice situation can explain people's behavior in business and in their everyday lives. We then proceed to develop the concepts of *marginal cost* and *supply* and to show how they, in conjunction with the concept of demand studied in Chapter 3, can help us understand the limits of people's behavior in such activities as oil painting, developing friendships, and preventing accidents. These everyday-type examples will enable us to develop principles which are applicable to the study of businesses and markets, to which we turn in later chapters.

Inevitably, some points relating to cost made in

[2] When using money as a means of measuring cost (i.e., the lamp costs $30), economists frequently use the term *money cost*.

Chapter 2 will be reviewed and extended in this chapter. There is a cost to this repetition; however, there are benefits in a small number of "varied reiterations." By taking this tack we obviously think that the benefits of the repetition will exceed the cost. In the final analysis, you will have to be the judge of this, because that is the subjective nature of cost. If you are interested in learning economics, you will have to make that judgment in terms of the alternative ways the material can be developed.

EXPLICIT AND IMPLICIT COST

Not all costs in choice situations are completely obvious, and one of the skills of the economist is that of uncovering any hidden costs. Generally, obvious costs are out-of-the-pocket expenditures. The money price a person pays for this book is an example of an obvious cost; it is what an economist calls an *explicit cost* of taking an introductory course in economics.

Implicit costs are "hidden," unobvious costs. A student has to spend time going to class and studying and may run the risk of receiving a failing grade or being confronted with material which may disturb prior beliefs. There is an implicit cost to reading this page; it is the value of what you could have done instead. These costs may go unnoticed because they are not out-of-the-pocket expenditures; however, implicit costs may loom much larger in one's total cost calculations than the explicit costs which are recognized. To illustrate, suppose a student takes five courses a semester and the average tuition cost for any one course is $200. This may be viewed as *the* cost of the typical course. However, this calculation ignores the implicit costs. In order to take the course, the student will have to attend classes about 45 times and may have to spend twice that amount of time going to and from class, completing class assignments, and studying for examinations. The total number of hours spent on any one semester course can be 135 (45 hours in class plus 90 hours in traveling, studying, and so forth). The student can spend his time doing other things; he can, for instance, work. If the student values his time at $3 per hour (a possible reflection of the wage rate he could have received working), his time cost, measured in money terms, will be $405 (135 hours × $3). In addition, the course may cause the student some anxiety which he would prefer to avoid. What the student would be willing to pay to avoid anxiety is an indication of his "anxiety (psychic or risk) cost." If he is willing to pay $10 to avoid anxiety, the total cost of taking the course is $635:

Explicit costs		
Tuition	$200	
Books	20	
Total explicit cost		$220
Implicit costs		
Time	$405	
Anxiety	10	
Total implicit cost		$415
Total cost of a course		$635

A significant portion of the calculated total cost is the opportunity value (or cost) of one's time. The value varies from one individual to another. For students who are unable to find work or who lack confidence that they can find work, the opportunity cost can be quite small, and, consequently, so can the cost of taking a course. This is a significant reason why many students are in college. The difference in opportunity time cost can certainly go a long way toward explaining why a large majority of college students are young; generally speaking, their time cost is lower than the time cost of older adults. Regardless, for the typical student, the cost of a one-semester course in economics can be the equivalent of a rather nice television set!

In many universities and colleges, faculty members are required to have their students evaluate their teaching methods and the course's content. These evaluations are frequently used as a means of determining faculty raises and promotions. If all one considers is the explicit costs, that is, the out-of-the-pocket expenditures on paper, printing, and computerizing the results, the cost of the evaluation process may appear trivial. There are, however, other costs; and as we can easily demonstrate, these explicit costs in this example are only a small portion of the total.

Assuming that tuition is $200 per course per semester, the tuition cost of an hour of class time is $4.44 ($200 ÷ 45 class hours). Many of the evaluation forms in use are quite extensive and can take as much as a half-hour of class time to distribute, fill out, and collect. If the student has to fill one out in all 10 of his classes, he will spend approximately 5 class-hours a year evaluating his professors. The tuition cost for this is about $22.20 ($4.44 × 5). If there are 5000 students in school, this implicit, often overlooked, cost amounts to $111,000! The cost of a student evaluation process for modern "megaversities" can be five to seven times as great. This does not include the hours which students and faculty spend devising the forms and analyzing the data, and we have not considered that many faculty members dismiss class after they give out the forms, adding to the tuition cost of the evaluation process—perhaps doubling it. The purpose of instructor evaluation is to raise the efficiency of the teaching-learning process, and student evaluations may contribute to this end. However, when the full cost is considered, do the efficiency benefits received justify the cost? That is the question which university administrators must consider.

COST AND ITS EFFECTS ON BEHAVIOR

In this section we attempt to illustrate through several examples how explicit and implicit costs can affect and explain people's behavior. Not all the examples will seem very important, and, indeed, in a cosmic sense, they are not. However, our purpose is to understand the economist's way of looking at problems and to help anyone evaluate any series of choices with more precision. One of the best ways of accomplishing this end is to consider initially the problems of our everyday experience to which we can all relate. As Philip Wicksteed wrote, ". . . The general principles which regulate our conduct in business are identical with those which regulate our deliberations, our selections between alternatives, and our decisions, in all other branches of life. And this is why we not only may, but must take our ordinary experiences as the starting point for approaching economic problems."[3]

The Parking Meter: Whether or Not to Put Another Nickel In

While preparing to write this chapter, one of the authors, McKenzie, took a break and drove to the student center for a soft drink. He could have walked the half-mile to the center but did not because, like so many students, his time cost, at the time, was higher than the cost of driving. He parked, and as he was about to put a nickel in the meter, he noticed that the meter for the empty space beside his car had more time left than the amount of time he was about to buy with the nickel. McKenzie could have moved his car and saved the nickel, but he didn't. The reason he did not was that the *cost* of getting back in his car (which entailed walking back to it and opening the door), starting the car, moving the car, and getting out again was greater than the benefit of saving a nickel. Furthermore, McKenzie is known for being a little tight-fisted with money and did not want to reinforce this part of his image with those who were with him (this would have meant a "reputation cost").

McKenzie's decision not to move the car was dependent upon his assessment of the costs and benefits when he noticed the meter with the time left on it. If the costs or benefits had been different, he could have been persuaded to change his mind. For example, if he had noticed the other meter before he had turned off the engine, the cost of moving the car would have been less; all he would have had to do was pull into the vacant space. Furthermore, if the meter had required a dollar in change, you can be sure he would have moved the car. The money saved would have justified the cost of moving the car, at least for McKenzie; for others, this may not be true. (Shortly after McKenzie went for a break, Tullock was in a similar situation, but he took the time to move his car. You can draw your own conclusions about

[3] Philip H. Wicksteed, *The Common Sense of Political Economy*, (New York: Augustus M. Kelley, Publisher, 1967), vol. 1, p. 3.

the relative value of McKenzie's and Tullock's time.)

Supermarket Price Cuts

Every week supermarkets run large ads in local newspapers, indicating the specials of the week. They have sales, but not on everything. There are several reasons for their not extending the list of sale items, the most general of which is that the longer list cannot be justified in terms of additional customers attracted into the store. More specifically, the store managers reason that many customers can be attracted to the store by a special on sirloin steak. Managers know that, once in the store, the customers will have to incur a travel cost to buy other grocery items in other stores. Even though peanut butter may be on sale elsewhere, the sale price plus the travel cost can be greater than the regular price of the peanut butter in the store where the steak is on sale. Further, once in the store, customers can be persuaded, through displays and packaging, to buy many other goods, particularly the toiletries, which typically have the highest markups. This does not mean that supermarket chains make huge profits. The grocery industry is reasonably competitive, and supermarket chains generally do not rank very high among corporations in terms of profitability; but the argument does suggest that stores may be able to recoup some of their lost revenues on sale items through higher prices on other goods.

Shoppers could plan to make the rounds of the grocery stores when their sales are announced, and many do. These are, however, people who typically value their time at a relatively low figure and have cheap modes of transportation. It just makes very little sense for a person who values his time at $5 an hour to spend an hour trying to save a dollar or two. Even the cost of gas alone can make the cost of moving from one store to another prohibitively high. Many people do not even know of sales in stores other than the one they shop in. The reason is that there is a cost to acquiring information on the sales, and the shopper may rationally figure that the expected benefits in terms of lower food costs are not sufficiently great to justify incurring the information cost. Consequently, many shoppers, but by no means all, enter the market "rationally ignorant."

Cost and the Economy-Size Box of Tide

Many people literally live from hand to mouth. They have only sufficient funds to buy what they can eat or use during a very short period of time; they are unable, because of their financial constraints, to buy in large quantities. However, many who can afford it still do not take advantage of the available opportunities to save by buying in large quantities.[4] A shopper can generally get more soap per penny by purchasing the largest-size box of Tide than by buying a number of smaller boxes. Does this demonstrate that people are not out to maximize? Of course not! The economy size of anything is a distinctly different commodity from the smaller boxes, and as such, there may be hidden costs associated with the larger-size boxes of detergent. First, if the individual (such as a college student) is without transportation, the larger box is more difficult to carry from store to home; in other words, there is a transportation cost. Second, the larger box requires much more space to store, and this space may have alternative uses, as it surely does in most dormitory rooms and small apartments—another hidden cost. Third, when a person buys a larger box, he spends more at that particular time, and this money, depending upon the size of the box and the rate of use, can be tied up for a long period of time. The money not spent on detergent can be used for other purchases which yield immediate satisfaction; alternatively, the funds can be saved and generate an interest income and, thereby, future command over goods. When all these implicit costs are added into the cost of the largest-size box of soap, the purchase may not look so inexpensive. For the family that has ample storage

[4] The larger sizes do not always carry with them a saving even on a per-ounce basis.

facilities and uses a lot of detergent, the economy-size box of Tide can in fact be that.

Frozen Orange Juice: Large or Small Cans

Frozen orange juice may be less expensive per ounce in large cans than in a collection of 6-ounce cans; however, many continue to buy the smaller cans. The reason may be ignorance or thoughtlessness, which are present in almost all areas of human experience, and we may well realize that most shoppers never take the time to figure out the price of items on a per-ounce basis. However, some people buy the smaller cans knowing that the cost of orange juice in small cans is greater. According to home economists, when a pitcher of orange juice is uncovered, vitamin C can escape into the atmosphere. For a small family or a single person, a large pitcher of orange juice made from a large can will be uncovered many times before it is finished, and the larger the quantity of orange juice, the more times it will be uncovered and the more vitamin C will escape. The result is that a person can consume more vitamin C per penny by buying a carton of smaller cans than by buying an equal amount of juice in a larger can, unless, of course, one wants to drink it all in one sitting.

Implicit Costs and Business Operations

Unless a business takes account of its implicit costs, it can experience an *economic loss*. Suppose a firm has sales of $200,000 and expenses paid to others—the mortgage company, suppliers, and employees—of $175,000 (explicit costs). The proprietor may figure his "book profit" at $25,000. However, his *economic profit*, that

Sales	$200,000
Expenses	175,000
Profit	$ 25,000

which remains after deducting *all* costs, may be much lower than this. The proprietor may have invested $100,000 in the firm's land, building, equipment, and working capital. He may be working for the business, and his salary may not be considered as a bookkeeping expense. If he had invested $100,000 in safe (or reasonably safe) government bonds at a rate of interest of 6 percent, and if he had worked as a manager for another business at $20,000 a year, the implicit costs of his business total $26,000, which, added to the explicit cost, runs the total cost to $201,000. The proprietor may tell others that he made a profit of $25,000, but that is his "book profit." He made no economic profit; in fact, he had an economic loss of $1000.

Costs of Homeowners versus Renters

Homeowners frequently ignore the implicit cost of the down payment on their houses. Their housing costs are typically given in terms of the mortgage, tax, and insurance payments. For instance, a homeowner who has a $45,000 house and a mortgage of $35,000 at 7 percent may tell others that his housing costs him $242 a month. However, he has omitted the interest payment he could have earned on the $10,000 down payment he has made on the house if he had taken this sum and invested it. At 5 percent in a savings account, $10,000 will earn $41.66 a month in interest. Without adding anything for risk cost, his housing payment should be given at $283.66. As the price of the house goes up and the owner's equity in the house rises, his effective house payment also rises.

People who buy mobile homes may overlook the (implicit) depreciation cost (or the loss in the home's value over time). During the first year of ownership, a mobile home can depreciate as much as 20 percent and during every year thereafter, 5 percent. These costs must be computed into the cost of this kind of housing if it is to be compared on an equal footing with the cost of conventional homes or with the cost of apartment living.

MARGINAL COST AND MARGINAL COST CURVE

Thus far, we have considered cost as a fundamental component of decision making; the rational person must weigh the cost of doing something against the benefits and then come to a decision. He or she will undertake to consume or do something if the benefits of that choice exceed the costs. The question which remains to be explored in more detail is, How much of a given good will an individual produce and consume? How does cost operate to *limit* behavior? To tackle these questions the concept of *marginal cost* must be explained. Succinctly,

marginal cost is the additional cost incurred from producing one additional unit of a good, activity, or service.

Marginal cost is the cost incurred in your reading an *additional* page, making an *additional* friend, giving an *additional* gift, or going an *additional* mile. It is the cost of any one unit separate from the cost of all other units.

Marginal Cost and Rational Behavior

The marginal cost of each unit of a good, activity, or service can be the same, or it can vary as more units are produced. For example, imagine that Jan Smith wants to give 10 gifts of candy to her friends. In a sense, Jan is "producing" gifts by procuring boxes of candy. If she can buy as many boxes as she likes at $5, the marginal cost of each and every unit is the same, $5. The marginal cost is *constant* over the range of "production."

However, marginal cost can vary with the level of output for two reasons. The first explanation relies on rational behavior. This time suppose Jan has decided to give her friends a product of her artistic skill. To do this she will have to produce a number of small paintings within a period of a day, and, generally speaking, there are a number of different activities that make up Jan's day which she can choose to forgo. There are many recreational opportunities she can choose to give up, or she may choose to give up work or study. She will, behaving rationally, choose to give up that activity she would otherwise have taken which has the *least* value to her. In other words, in order to make enough time to finish one painting she will give up straightening her room before she gives up eating dinner, assuming dinner is more important *to her*. The marginal cost of the first painting is, therefore, as low as it can be. To produce the second painting, Jan must give up what she considers the next least valuable opportunity. As more paintings are produced, Jan will have to forgo progressively more valuable alternatives, indicating that the marginal cost of paintings rises as output does. If the marginal cost of each successive painting is plotted against the quantity produced, the resulting curve on a graph will be upward sloping, as is the one in Figure 4·1. The marginal cost (MC) of the first unit is MC_1, the marginal cost of the second is MC_2, and so forth. The marginal cost of the paintings is unequal and rises as a greater number of paintings is done.

Although the marginal cost curve is generally assumed to be upward sloping, like the one in Figure 4·1, this need not be the case. It is conceivable that Jan has a number of alternative activities

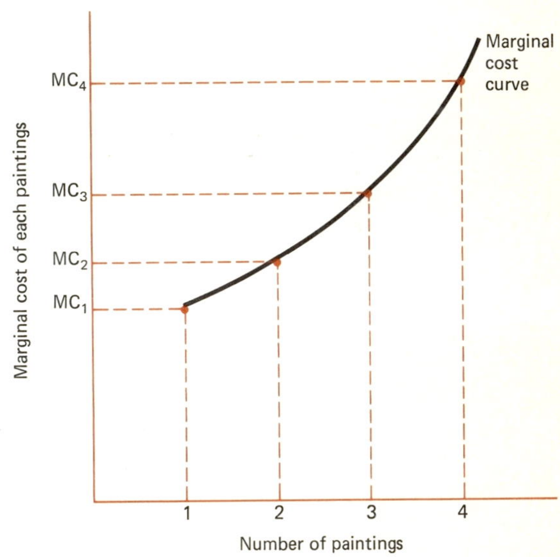

FIG. 4·1 In order to do the paintings, Jan must give up opportunities which are progressively more valuable. Therefore, the *marginal cost* of paintings rises as a larger number are produced. The plotting of the marginal costs of the paintings forms the *marginal cost curve*.

which she can forgo and on which she places equal value. In this case, the marginal cost will be constant, and the marginal cost curve will be a horizontal line—at least, within the relevant range of her ability and desire to paint.

Marginal Cost and the Law of Diminishing Returns

The second explanation for possible changes in marginal cost involves a technological relationship known in economics as the *law of diminishing (marginal) returns*. Simply put, this means:

If successive units of a resource like labor (or fertilizer or anything else) are applied to a fixed quantity of another resource like land, there will be a point in the production process beyond which the *additional* output from each unit of labor applied begins to diminish.

It stands to reason that if beyond some point less output is received for each unit of labor, more labor is required to produce the *same* increase in output. The result: Beyond some point the marginal cost of additional units of output rises.

The law of diminishing returns is a very general statement about the production of anything, but the meaning of the law is most easily grasped in the context of agricultural production. Assume that you are producing tomatoes on an acre of land (the fixed resource), but that the quantity of labor can be varied. The planting of tomato plants is divided into four tasks: digging the holes, pouring water in the holes, putting the plants in the holes, and covering them up. If you try to do all four tasks, you will find yourself spending much time changing tools: putting down the hoe and picking up the bucket to pour water in the holes, putting down the bucket, etc. If a friend helps with the work, the tasks can be divided, the two workers can specialize, and less time can be wasted changing tools. The time which would otherwise have been spent changing tools can be applied to planting tomatoes. More tomatoes can be planted in a given amount of time and more can be harvested. The output may expand at a greater rate than the labor force. That is, the first laborer, by himself, may be able to plant 100 plants in an hour; the first and the second worker may be able to plant 250 tomato plants in an hour. In this event, the marginal cost of planting each of the additional 150 plants can be lower than planting the first 100. As more laborers are, up to a certain point, added, the tasks can be further divided and greater efficiency can be gained; the marginal cost can continue to fall for a period as production expands in this way.

However, there is some point beyond which additional laborers will not contribute as much to production as the previous laborers, and at that point the marginal cost of getting plants into the ground can begin to rise. This is true if for no other reason than that so many workers can be put on the acre that they start bumping into one another and trampling the plants already in the ground, making the process less efficient.

Diminishing returns are a *technological* fact of life. If diminishing returns were not experienced at some point, more and more labor could be applied to agricultural production on an acre of land, the output would expand proportionately, and the world's food supply could be grown on one acre of land! For that matter, the world's food supply could be grown in a flower box. In short, we assume that diminishing returns do set in *at some point*. The point at which they emerge varies from one production process to another. Once they do set in, the marginal cost curve will begin to slope upward to the right, like the curve in Figure 4·1.

A simple table, depicting bushels of tomatoes harvested by successive employees, may be helpful to clarify what is meant by the law of diminishing returns. We assume that each employee is paid $5 for his labor and that production is carried out on a one-acre tract of land. In Table 4·1 the first employee, working alone, can produce a quarter of a bushel of tomatoes; if two workers are used, a complete bushel can be produced; and so forth. See the first two columns of Table 4·1.

The third column shows the amount which each *additional* employee adds to total production.

TABLE 4·1

Number of Employees Used in Tomato Production (1)	Total Number of Bushels of Tomatoes Harvested (2)	Contribution of Each Employee to the Production of Tomatoes (i.e., Marginal Product) (3)		Number of Employees Required to Produce Each Additional Bushel (4)	Marginal Cost of Each Bushel of Tomatoes Figured at $5 Per Employee Used (5)
1	0.25	0.25	(1st bushel)	2	$10
2	1.00	0.75			
3	2.00	1.00	(2d bushel)	1	$ 5
	Point at Which Diminishing Marginal Returns Emerge				
4	2.60	0.60	(3d bushel)	2	$10
5	3.00	0.40			
6	3.30	0.30	(4th bushel)	5	$25
7	3.55	0.25			
8	3.75	0.20			
9	3.90	0.15			
10	4.00	0.10			

The first employee contributes 0.25 (one quarter) of a bushel; this is what economists call the *marginal product* (which is the additional output produced by an additional worker). By adding the second employee, an additional 0.75 of a bushel is harvested. The third contributes 1 bushel; the fourth, 0.60, and so on down the column. The important point of the table is revealed in the last two columns. It takes a total of two employees to produce the first complete bushel; and it takes, perhaps because of the benefits of specialization, only one additional employee to add the second bushel. However, beyond that point, diminishing returns emerge. Each additional employee begins to contribute less, meaning that it takes more employees to increase total output by one bushel. It takes two employees to produce the third bushel, and five employees to produce the fourth. If the table were extended, each bushel beyond the fourth would require a progressively larger number of employees.

If all employees are paid the same amount, $5, for their labor, the marginal cost of a bushel of tomatoes declines from $10 to $5 for the first and second bushels, respectively; but, as can be seen in the last column, marginal cost then rises from $5 to $10 for the third bushel and to $25 for the fourth. Diminishing returns (or increasing marginal costs) begin to emerge with the addition of the fourth employee. The marginal cost of each unit (column 5) plotted against the number of bushels harvested yields a curve like the one in Figure 4·2. Although the curve may be downward sloping at first, economists generally agree that for the purposes of most discussions, the relevant segment of the full marginal cost curve is the upward sloping segment from a point like *a* in Figure 4·2.[5] As we will also see, that portion of the

[5] For an explanation of why the relevant portion of the marginal cost curve is the upward sloping segment (above *a* in Fig. 4·2), see the appendix to this chapter.

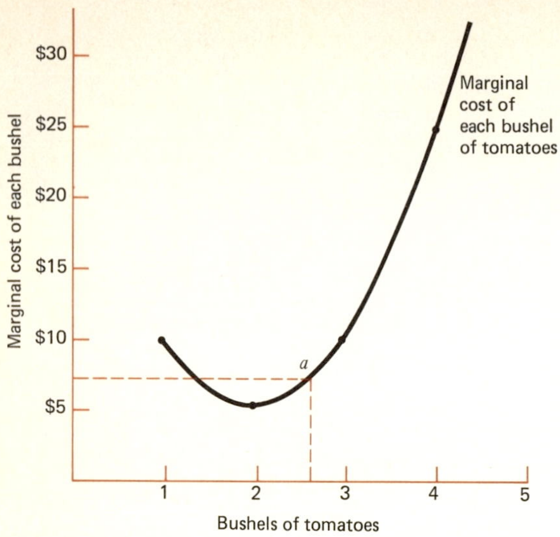

FIG. 4·2 As production expands with the addition of workers, the benefits from specialization of labor can cause the marginal cost to fall at first. However, given the *law of diminishing returns,* marginal cost will eventually rise.

marginal cost curve is also the firm's or individual's *supply curve: it indicates the units of a good that will be produced at each price.*

Diminishing returns *can* set in immediately as production begins, in which case the marginal cost curve will be upward sloping from the production of the first bushel. However, the point of Table 4·1 is that there is no requirement in the "law" that they emerge immediately. At first, there may be constant or increasing marginal returns, meaning constant or decreasing marginal costs. Economists normally assume, for good reason, that marginal cost normally increases when firms expand production with additional laborers and no increase in plant and equipment; even if it does not, the assumption does little harm to the analysis *in most instances.* In fact, an assumption of constant marginal cost will often simplify the analysis, and this assumption will be employed when it is appropriate to do so. However, at times the prospect of decreasing marginal costs will have to be dealt with.[6] For the time being, an assumption of increasing marginal costs will underlie much of the analysis which follows.

CHANGES IN THE MARGINAL COST CURVE

The marginal cost curve in Figure 4·2 represents a given structure of costs incurred in providing units of a good like tomatoes. If the cost incurred to produce each item changes, the curve will shift. For example, if the opportunities which a person gives up to produce tomatoes diminish in value, the marginal costs of producing successive units will, by definition, diminish. The marginal cost curve, MC_1, shifts downward to the right to MC_2 in Figure 4·3. The cost of the first bushel of tomatoes was once measured at $1; and now, because the individual values his alternative activities less, the marginal cost of the bushel falls to $0.25. The cost of the second bushel falls from $1.75 to $1, as does the marginal cost of every other unit.

The land that is used for tomato production has alternative uses. If one of those alternative uses is the production of watermelons, any profit one could make by growing watermelons is part of the implicit cost of producing the tomatoes. If the price and, thereby, the profitability of producing watermelons fall, the *cost* of producing tomatoes on the acre also falls: the marginal cost curve shifts from MC_1 to MC_2.

A downward shift in the curve can also result from an increase in the efficiency of tomato production. A technological innovation may be introduced in the truck farming business which

[6] For example, many argue that electric power is produced under conditions of declining marginal costs. That is, generating facilities can be expanded considerably with lower costs for each additional unit: increasing marginal costs may eventually emerge, but only after the demands of consumers for electric power are met. As we will see (and do not be disturbed if you fail to understand the argument at this point), the argument raises the issues of whether or not competition is viable in the electric power industry and whether or not electricity should be produced under the auspices of a government-protected monopoly. At any rate, when these issues arise, as they do in the study of government regulation of industry (Chap. 12), the implications of a downward sloping marginal cost curve will be considered.

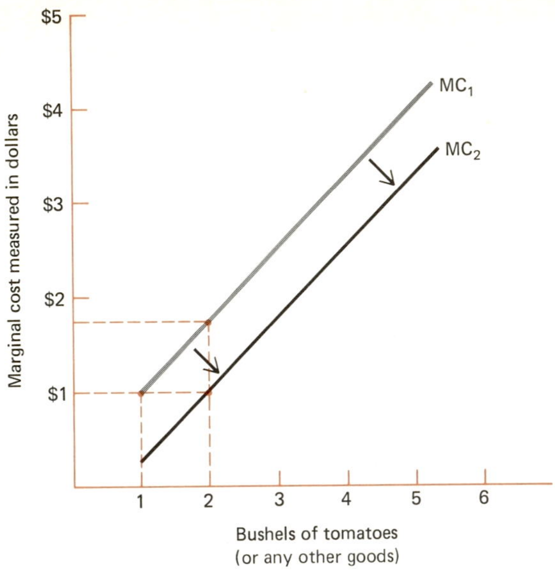

FIG. 4·3 The downward shift in the *marginal cost curve* reflects the assumed *decrease* in the cost of producing tomatoes. Since the marginal cost curve is the *supply curve,* this shift also represents an *increase* in the supply curve.

enables each worker to harvest more tomatoes in a given period of time. If more tomatoes can be grown with the same (or fewer) resources, the cost of harvesting tomatoes falls.[7] The marginal cost of each tomato falls and the curve shifts as in Figure 4·3.

If the price of resources used in tomato production rises or if the efficiency of producing tomatoes, for some reason, drops, the marginal cost of each unit will rise and the marginal cost curve will shift upward to the left. In our example in Figure 4·4, the marginal cost of the first unit rises from $1 to $2, and the marginal cost of the second bushel rises from $1.75 to $3.50. The marginal cost of the other units also rises. We have deliberately avoided drawing MC_1 parallel to MC_2. This is to emphasize that when the effects of cost changes occur, the effects need not be felt equally or proportionately over all units of the good produced.

[7] Assume a worker can harvest 1 bushel of tomatoes in 1 hour and is paid $5 an hour. If his productivity doubles to 2 bushels an hour, the cost of 1 bushel falls to $2.50, assuming the wage rate remains constant.

THE LIMITS OF BEHAVIOR

Applying the law of demand, represented by the demand curve (Chapter 3) and the marginal cost curve together, we can make more precise statements about rational human behavior. Consider again the example of Jan Smith, who paints pictures. What she does with the pictures is of no consequence to the development of the example; she can hang them on the wall, give them away, or store them in a closet. What is important is that she wants to paint. How many paintings will she paint? From Chapter 2 we know that her demand curve for her own paintings is downward sloping, regardless of the use she makes of them; her de-

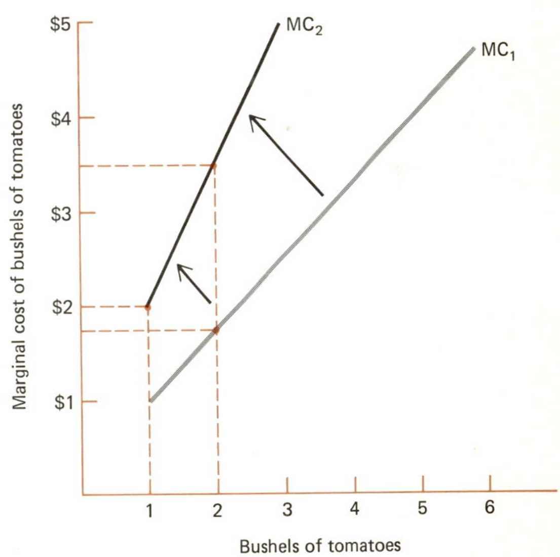

FIG. 4·4 The upward shift in the *marginal cost curve* reflects the assumed *increase* in the cost of producing tomatoes. This shift also represents a *decrease* in the *supply curve.*

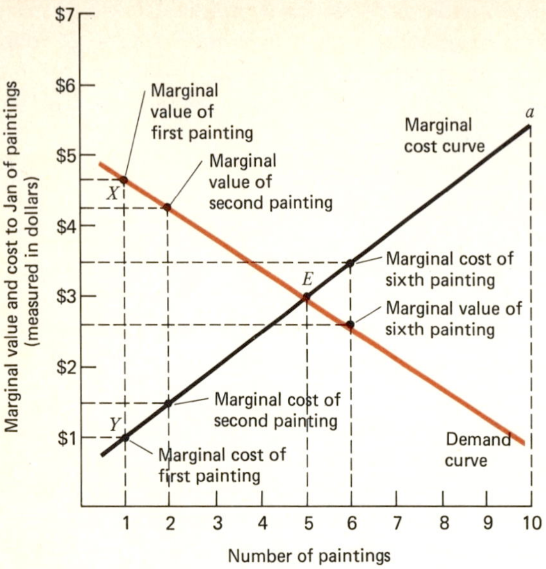

FIG. 4·5 For each painting up to five, Jan gets more benefits from doing the painting than each costs her. On the other hand, the cost of each painting beyond five is greater than the benefits she receives. Therefore, Jan will limit her paintings to five.

mand for her own paintings is depicted in Figure 4·5. Assuming that the cost of painting each additional picture increases, Jan will confront a marginal cost curve like the curve in Figure 4·5.[8] Since she is not selling her paintings, Jan is not likely to place a money value on them, and there is no special reason why she should. We use money prices here and in the graph to illustrate what we mean by the difference between marginal benefit and cost. Again, remember that money figures we use are not themselves values; they are a means of showing relative values.

Given the positions of the curve, Jan will paint up to five pictures. As illustrated by her demand curve, Jan places a relative value of $4.67, measured in monetary terms, on the first painting (point X on Figure 4·5). However, the marginal cost, meaning the value of the opportunities forgone in order to do the painting, is measured at $1 (point Y on Figure 4·5). In other words, Jan will get $3.67 more value out of using her time, energy, and other resources to paint the picture than she can receive from her best alternative. The marginal benefit from the first painting exceeds the marginal cost.

The same holds for the second painting. Although the marginal cost of the second is greater and its marginal value is less than those of the first, Jan still gains by using her time and resources painting it. The marginal value of the second picture to Jan is $4.25 and the marginal cost is about $1.50. The same condition is true for the third and fourth paintings; she will be better off painting them than by engaging in her most highly valued alternative activity. The fifth painting is a matter of indifference to Jan; the marginal value of it is equal to the marginal cost, and we cannot say whether or not the fifth picture will be painted (point E). We can argue that, given circumstances, Jan will move as close as she can to the intersection of the two curves. Five paintings is the *limit* toward which she will move; it is the optimum number of paintings.

She will not paint the sixth picture—at least during the period of time in which the marginal cost and demand curves are applicable. As indicated in the graph, the sixth painting will actually cost Jan more than she receives in benefits; the marginal cost is approximately $3.50 and the marginal benefit, indicated by the demand curve, is about $2.60. Therefore, Jan will go as far as five paintings, but no further.

The Limits of Friendship

The same line of analysis can be applied to people's behavior in acquiring friends. Most people want friends, but not all people have as many as they would like. In other words, many people would receive some benefit from having additional friends or from increasing the "depth" of the friendships that they have. The enjoyment of life can frequently be measured in part by the

[8] In this example, the points on our curve fall in a straight line. This is not a necessary condition for the analysis, however.

strengths and breadth of our human associations. If this is true, why then do people not make more friends? There are many people who, because of mental, physical, or environmental constraints, are incapable of making additional friends. Additionally, however, we suspect that there is a rational limit to the development of friendships just as there is a limit in other areas of human experience. People talk about the difficulty of acquiring and maintaining friends. What they mean is that the cost of additional friends is too great for the benefits received. To acquire additional friends a person's dress and habits may have to be changed; one's willingness to do things for others may have to increase; and, in general, one must be willing to forgo other opportunities. There is a limit, however, to how many of these types of changes a person is willing to make, and this, in turn, sets a limit on the depth and breadth of a person's friendships, on your friendships.

In terms of Figure 4·5 and given the demand and cost structure which we now assume applies to friendship, an individual will acquire friends up to the point where the demand and marginal cost curves intersect. Beyond that point, additional friends, although they may have value to the individual, will actually cost more than they are worth! This statement may seem insensitive, calculating, and cold; but if it is not true, why doesn't the normal healthy individual who enjoys the fellowship of others have several hundred deep, lasting friendships? One would have to spend all one's time and energy in the development and maintenance of friends. To do this one must pass up many other opportunities. If one places little or no value on these alternative opportunities, to devote oneself to friends is entirely rational. Most people, however, have needs and desires which drive them to spend their resources in additional ways. Granted, each of us does not know with precision how valuable or how costly additional friends may be, but this means only that we must base our decisions on the *expected* costs and benefits of acquiring friends. To the degree that we lack information about the costs and benefits of making friends, our behavior will be less than perfect. But that does not destroy the essence of the foregoing argument.

The Limits of Accident Prevention

All of us would prefer to avoid accidents rather than be the victim of them. We therefore have a demand for accident prevention, which, by the way, should have a downward sloping demand curve like all other demand curves. If there is a cost to preventing accidents, will we try to prevent all accidents? The answer, fortunately or unfortunately, is not very likely. The reason is that the cost of preventing an accident may rise above the cost incurred from being a victim. If the cost of *ensuring* that you will never stumble on your stairs is $100 and the only injury you expect to suffer if and when you stumble is a bruised knee, would you spend $100 in accident prevention? Clearly, we do (most of) those things which we *know* will prevent death, even if the costs are very high. The benefits of preventing certain death are, for most of us, quite high; but having said that, there is no reason to follow with a statement that we will incur the necessary costs to prevent *all* accidents.

Suppose that the demand and marginal cost curves in Figure 4·5 apply to accident prevention and that Al Rosa can expect to have 10 accidents during some specified period of time. If he prevents all accidents, the value of the last accident prevented, as indicated by his demand for accident prevention, equals $1. (At 10 on the horizontal axis go up to the demand curve and then read the value on the vertical axis.) The marginal cost of preventing the last accident is much greater—approximately $5.40 to gain $1 in value. Since this would make no sense to the rational person, and we assume Al is rational, he will not try to prevent that accident. As a matter of fact, he will only try, in this example, to prevent five accidents. The marginal cost of the sixth through ninth accidents prevented, like the tenth, will exceed the marginal benefits. Al would try to prevent all accidents only if his demand for accident prevention is sufficiently great for it to intersect the marginal cost curve at *a* in Figure 4·5. This is unlikely, since the marginal cost of preventing accidents may well escalate as more and more accidents are prevented. (If prevention of *all* accidents is physically impossible, the marginal cost curve will become vertical before 10 accidents.)

In other words, some accidents occur because they are simply unavoidable; however, other accidents may be avoidable in the sense that measures *can* be taken to prevent them. Rational behavior, on the other hand, may dictate that they be allowed to happen; the individual can be better off by incurring the costs associated with the accidents than by incurring the greater costs associated with trying to avoid the accidents.

THE EFFECTS OF CHANGES IN DEMAND ON BEHAVIOR

The rational person will operate at the intersection of the marginal cost and demand curves. If demand is originally at D_1 and marginal cost is MC_1 in Figure 4·6, the individual will produce and consume Q_1 units of the good, activity, or service. However, if demand rises to D_2, the marginal value of units between Q_1 and Q_2 becomes greater than the marginal cost of providing them; the individual will, therefore, move up the marginal cost curve to a production and consumption level of Q_2. Referring back to the examples used over the last few pages, with an increase in demand the optimum level (from the perspective of the individual's welfare) of paintings, friends, and accidents increases.

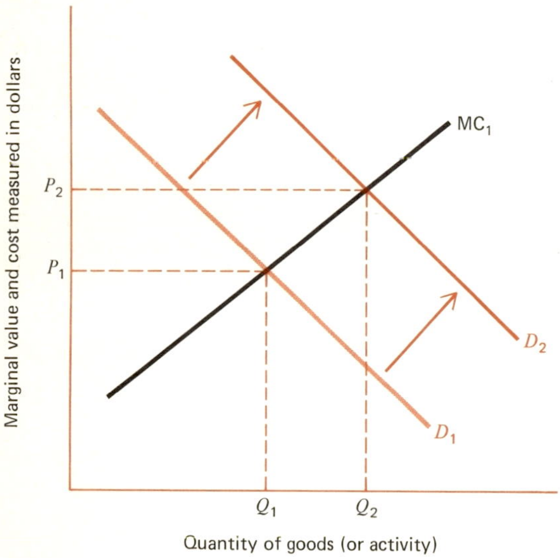

FIG. 4·6 Given the marginal cost curve MC_1, the rational person will produce and consume Q_1 units of the good when the demand curve is D_1. However, when the demand rises, the rational person will increase the quantity consumed to Q_2.

If the demand is viewed as moving up gradually, rather than with the sudden jump implied above, the individual will expand production, moving along the marginal cost curve. The individual will supply more, as indicated by the marginal cost curve. For this reason, economists refer to the individual's marginal cost curve as his *supply curve:* as we said earlier, the supply curve indicates the units of a good that will be produced at each price. It represents the path which will be followed by the individual as production is expanded in response to an increase or decrease in demand.

We have been discussing how an individual will react to an increase in his own demand for what he produces. Now we turn to a discussion of how the individual will behave when selling the good at a price in the market. The price received is equal to the marginal benefit of each unit produced. (One can use the revenue received to buy things which give one pleasure.) If the market price of the good is P_1 in Figure 4·6, the individual (or firm) incurring the marginal cost will still produce (or offer on the market) Q_1 units. The market price (P_1) will be greater than the marginal cost incurred in producing each unit from zero production up to Q_1. From zero to Q_1 the producer is better off producing and selling units in the market than in using the resources in production of some other activity. Beyond Q_1 units produced, the marginal cost of each additional unit will be greater than the market price of P_1. If, on the other hand, the market price rises to P_2, the individual will find that the marginal benefits from the increased price now received are greater than the marginal cost of all units up to Q_2. In other words, as the price rises, the quantity produced by any one (rational) individual or firm will rise likewise. If we plot all possible prices against the quantities the individual is willing to produce at *each* price, we will have a curve like the marginal cost curve. Again, that curve will be the producer's supply curve. It illustrates how much the producer is willing to produce at each price. In other words, the producer who is selling the good on the market for a *constant price*[9] will act (produce) in the same way as if he were producing a good for himself. The production plans will be based on the marginal cost curve.

THE IRRELEVANCE OF SUNK COSTS

Suppose a small airline company buys a plane for $1 million. The plane will last for 10 years, after which it has no value as scrap. For the purposes of initial discussion, suppose also that, once purchased, the plane has no resale value. Although the owners originally thought the plane would be profitable, they determine within the first few months of operations that they can expect to receive $200,000 in revenues for each of the 10 years of service. However, the plane will cost them $160,000 each year in operating costs (i.e., pilot's salary, fuel bills, and repair expenses). Should the plane be operated?

Many readers may conclude the plane should not be operated. They compute the total annual cost at $260,000 ($160,000 in operating costs plus $100,000 per year in depreciation), and this figure exceeds the expected revenues of $200,000. However, a little reflection on the implication of not operating the plane will reveal that the depreciation cost is actually irrelevant to the question. The plane has already been purchased; the $1 million has been spent. If the plane is not operated, the company will have lost $1 million at the end of 10 years. If, on the other hand, the plane is operated, the company will receive annually $40,000 more in revenue than it incurs in operating expenses. At the end of 10 years the net loss will be $600,000 instead of $1,000,000.

[9] This qualification will become important in later discussions. If the individual producer is able to manipulate the price in the sense of being able to choose the price at which he will sell, the marginal cost curve will not be the supply curve, and the following conclusion does not hold.

The decision to buy the plane in the first place was obviously a bad one; if the buyers had that choice to make again, they certainly would not buy the plane. However, as the old adage goes, "bygones are bygones"; and at the point where the question of whether or not to operate the plane is posed, past mistakes and associated costs are just not relevant. This brings us to a very elementary but important point:

the only costs which are relevant to choice are those which will actually be incurred because of the decision.

Those costs which are incurred because of past choices—which economists call *sunk costs*—are irrelevant to present choices. They should be ignored or else they may misguide current choice behavior.

If the plane can be resold, which was not the case in the previous example, the resale value of the plane becomes a relevant consideration in the decision to operate the plane. In this instance, the company can sell the plane and recoup part of its investment. If it decides to operate the plane, it is effectively deciding to forgo the opportunities that could have been had with the funds secured from resale. In this situation the relevant cost is the resale price, not the price that was paid for the plane.

Many stores stay open at night even though they have very few customers and fewer sales. If the calculated costs of operating the store include a prorated portion of such expenses as rental payments, depreciation expense, and interest on loans made for equipment, staying open late may appear to be a losing proposition. However, many of the expenses, such as these, which a firm includes in its accounting statements are irrelevant to the decision to stay open at night; they are sunk costs. They are costs the firm will have to pay whether or not the hours are extended, and they are (virtually) unaffected by the nighttime operations. The decision to stay open must be based on only those costs which are actually incurred because of that decision. These costs may include the few additional hours of labor expense, use of electricity, and possible additional costs associated with nighttime shoplifting. Since these expenses can be quite modest, the store may find nighttime operations profitable; they need only a few sales to cover these costs.

During 1971, Congress debated the question of whether or not the SST (Supersonic Transport) project should be continued. At the time they had already spent over $700 million on its development and had committed themselves to additional expenditures. The issue was being reconsidered at the time primarily because of the environmental problems which the planes' critics thought would be created. Many members of Congress argued that the project should be continued on the grounds, among other reasons, of past expenditures. From an economic point of view, should those past expenditures have been considered in the debate? The answer is no. The relevant question at the time was whether or not the additional costs which they could anticipate, including the environmental costs, would be greater than the benefits which were to be expected from completion of the project. The fact that developmental costs had already been incurred should have made the future costs lower than if the developers were starting from the beginning in 1971. However, those past expenditures were sunk costs and irrelevant. Even the interest on the debt incurred because of past expenditures was not a relevant consideration in the decision; the interest would have to be paid whether the project was completed or not.

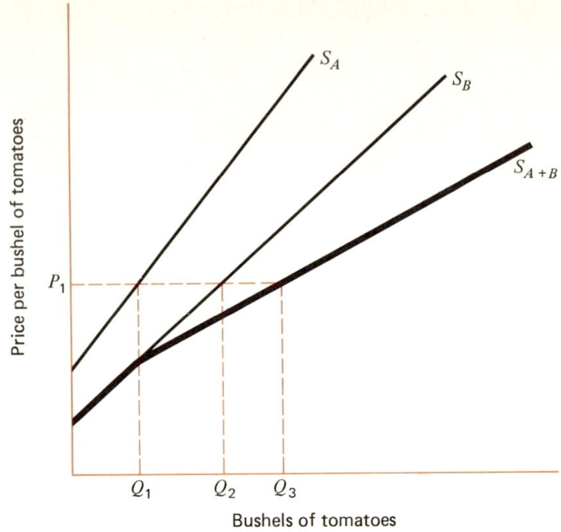

FIG. 4·7 The market supply curve (the heavy curve, S_{A+B}) is obtained by adding together the amounts which A and B are willing to offer at each price. The amounts which A and B are willing to offer at each price are shown by A and B's supply curves, S_A and S_B.

THE MARKET SUPPLY CURVE

One of the purposes in economics is ultimately to talk about people acting in the context of "markets." That means we must turn to the way in which the *market* supply curve is constructed. The market supply of a private good is simply the horizontal summation of individual supply curves. To illustrate, suppose the tomato market consists of two people (or producers or firms) and their individual supply curves are represented by S_A and S_B in Figure 4·7. At a price of P_1, A is willing to offer Q_1 tomatoes and B is willing to offer Q_2. The total market quantity supplied at that price is therefore Q_3. By summing up the quantity of tomatoes which A and B are willing to offer at each and every price in the way just indicated, the *market supply curve*, S_{A+B}, is derived. (The market supply curve is obtained in the same way that the market demand curve is. See Chapter 3.) Along with the market demand curve, the market supply curve will be very useful in our discussion of "competitive" and "monopolistic" markets which begins in Chapter 7.

SUMMARY AND EXTENSIONS

The repeated theme of this chapter has been that cost plays a pivotal role in choice behavior. Cost helps to determine whether or not something will be done or left undone; the way in which cost changes over the range of production will be influential in determining the limit of a person's behavior in any area of activity. The rule for utility maximization is that the individual should produce a good or service or engage in an activity up to the point where marginal cost equals marginal benefit, or, graphically, where the supply and demand curves intersect. This level of behavior generally means more pleasure could have been acquired by having additional units of the good, service, or activity, but the additional costs involved precluded their procurement.

In order for costs to affect behavior, they must be perceived as such by the individual. For this reason the economist, almost by second nature, looks for hidden, implicit costs in all choice situations. These implicit costs will affect the choice ultimately made and, if uncovered, can be helpful in explaining choices which have been made. Much of this book will simply extend, elaborate, and refine the principles made in these four introductory chapters.

QUESTIONS TO PONDER

1 Evaluate the economic content of the adages "Haste makes waste" and "A stitch in time saves nine."

2 If executives' time is so valuable, why can they be found reading the advertisements in the airline magazines while in flight to a business meeting?

3 In terms of demand and marginal cost (or supply) curves, explain the amount of time you have spent reading this chapter.

4 In discussing accident prevention, we assumed increasing marginal costs of preventing accidents. Suppose we had assumed constant marginal costs; would this have affected the essence of the argument?

5 Using the analysis of "optimum friendship," develop an economic analysis of "optimum pollution."

6 People take measures to avoid being the victims of crimes. Why do they not take greater precautions? What does rational behavior on the part of people in attempting to avoid and prevent crimes have to do with the ability of the criminals to commit crimes?

7 What will be the effect of the following changes on the "optimum level of friendship"? Explain in terms of the individual's demand and marginal cost curves.

- **a** A person's circumstances change in such a way that friends can yield greater benefits.
- **b** A person takes a course on "How to Win Friends."
- **c** A person moves to a remote area of a wilderness forest.
- **d** The mobility of the population and the frequency with which people move increase.

8 If the money price of a good goes from $5 to $10, the economist can predict with confidence that less will be purchased. However, he cannot say with the same level of confidence that denying a child a dessert will have a negative effect on the child's misbehavior. Explain.

9 Suppose you are interested in buying a $500 refrigerator and you have a choice of financing the refrigerator at 10 percent for 3 years or including the price of the refrigerator in your 20-year mortgage loan which carries an interest rate of 7 percent. Which would be the least-cost method of financing? How much would you save?

RECOMMENDED READINGS

Fels, Rendigs, and Robert G. Uhler: *Casebook of Economic Problems and Policies: Practice in Thinking* (New York: West Publishing Company, 1975), cases 1, 2, and 7.

Leftwich, Richard H., and Ansel M. Sharp: *Economics of Social Issues* (Dallas: Business Publications, Inc., 1974), chap. 1.

McKenzie, Richard B., and Gordon Tullock: *The New World of Economics: Explorations into the Human Experience* (Homewood, Ill.: Richard D. Irwin, Inc., 1975), chaps. 5, 6, and 10.

APPENDIX

The purpose of this appendix is to explain why an individual's or firm's supply curve is the upward sloping portion of the marginal cost curve. In terms of Figure 4·2, it is that portion of the marginal cost curve which is above point *a*.

The typical marginal cost curve, like the one developed in this chapter, is pictured in the accompanying Figure 4A·1. In developing the basic shape of this curve, we considered an example in which only one cost, labor, varied with production. There are other costs which also vary with tomato production, such as the cost of the plants themselves and of fertilizer, but we ignored them to keep the example as simple as possible. At any rate, these costs, for obvious reasons, are called "variable costs." They vary with the level of production in the short run, that is, a period of time during which costs such as land and some pieces of heavy equipment cannot be changed in amount. During the short run costs of land and heavy equipment cannot be increased or diminished. They are, therefore, referred to as "fixed costs" or "sunk costs." During the time period that their level cannot be changed, fixed or sunk costs are irrelevant in deciding whether or not the resources involved are to be used or left unused.

However, so long as the producer has control over the level of such variable costs as labor, plants, and fertilizer, these costs must be covered

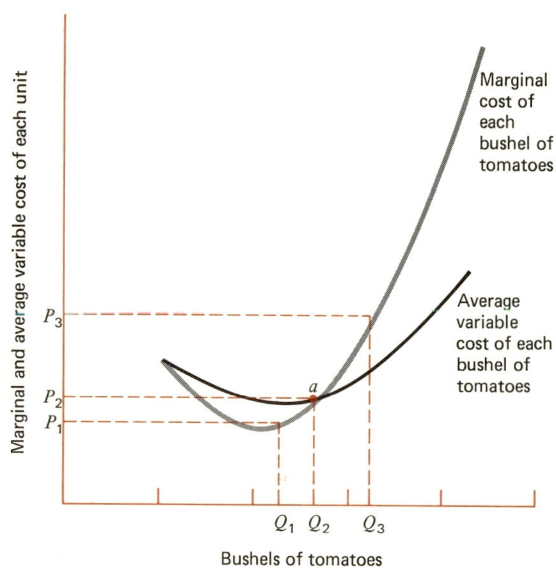

FIG. 4A·1 When the marginal cost falls and is below the average variable cost, the average variable cost must also be falling. On the other hand, when the marginal cost is above average variable cost, the average variable cost must rise. The average variable cost curve must also rise. The rational producer will not produce if the price falls below P_2 because the producer's variable costs of production will then not be covered by the revenues from sales.

through the sale of tomatoes. Otherwise, the producer incurs a loss equal to the fixed costs plus that portion of the variable costs which is not made up by income from sales. For instance, if fixed costs are \$100, variable costs are \$75, and receipts from the sale of the harvest are \$50, the producer loses \$125 (\$175 in total costs minus \$50 in revenues). The producer's losses are increased from \$100 when nothing is produced and only the fixed costs of \$100 are incurred. The point is simple: in order to justify producing anything, the producer must cover the variable costs. This brings us to the further development of Figure 4A·1.

If the marginal cost is decreasing, as it is in the first part of the marginal cost curve in Figure 4A·1, the average "variable" cost of producing additional tomatoes must also be decreasing. If the variable costs of the first bushel of tomatoes are \$10 and those of the second bushel are \$5, the average variable cost drops from \$10 when only one bushel is produced (\$10 of total cost at that point divided by 1) to \$7.50 when 2 bushels are produced (\$15 of variable costs divided by 2). Further, so long as the marginal cost is below the average variable cost, the average variable cost must fall. Once the marginal cost exceeds the average variable cost, the average variable cost must rise. To see the relationship between the average and marginal figures more clearly, consider a basketball player who starts the season with a very high game point average. If the player scores progressively fewer points in each of several following games, his or her average score will start and continue to fall. The average score will continue to fall so long as the score of each successive game is below his or her previous average. If at some point in the season the player's average is 35 points per game and the player scores 25, 26, and 27 points in three consecutive games, his or her average score will continue to fall. The average score will not rise until during some game the player scores more points than the previous average.

Because of this line of reasoning, we know that the "average variable cost curve" in Figure 4A·1 must be falling so long as marginal cost is falling and so long as the marginal cost is below the average variable cost curve. However, once the marginal cost curve peaks above the average variable cost curve, as it does at point a, the average variable cost curve must also rise, as it does in the figure. Point a is, therefore, the low point of the average cost curve.

Why is the marginal cost curve above point a considered to be the producer's supply curve? Again, through production a firm (or individual producer) must cover all variable costs, or else it increases its losses over and above what they would be if nothing were produced. If the price of each bushel is above point a, say P_3, the price for each of Q_3 bushels is above the average variable cost. (This is indicated by the variable cost curve.) The firm is receiving more on average for each bushel than it costs on average in terms of resources like labor. This is also true for every other price above P_3.

At a price like P_2, at which Q_2 bushels will be produced, the price is equal to the average variable cost of each bushel. The firm is just breaking even on each bushel produced and will, accordingly, be indifferent about producing at a price like P_2. However, at prices below P_2, like P_1, the firm will not produce anything. This is simply because the prices on each of Q_1 bushels will then be below the average variable cost. The firm will collect less revenue on each bushel than it incurs, on average, in labor costs. It will be better off producing nothing and incurring the loss, which will then be no more than its fixed or sunk costs.

In summary, the firm or individual producer will not produce at a price below P_2 (or point a); it will produce where its price is equal to marginal cost so long as the price is above P_2. Therefore, as we asserted earlier in the chapter, the relevant portion of the producer's marginal cost curve is that portion of the curve above a point like a; and that is the producer's supply curve.

Part Two
Social Order

Order is not a pressure imposed upon society from without, but an equilibrium which is set up from within.
J. Ortega y Gasset

Individual actions typically occur in the context of a social setting—that is, in the context of *groups*. Indeed, the actions and anticipated reactions of others to our own actions are major constraints on how we behave. The purpose of this section is to apply the principles of individual behavior that we learned in the first four chapters to the question of how we can expect people to behave in groups of other similarly motivated people. We begin in Chapter 5 by exploring the meaning and relevance of property rights in the social interactions of people. In Chapter 6 we develop an economic theory of group behavior which suggests that people in large groups fail to pursue interests which they share in common. These two chapters are important building blocks in our understanding of markets, which are groups of people interested in trading with one another, a topic that we take up at the beginning of Chapter 7.

5

The Emergence of Social Order: Defining Behavioral Limits

The end of law is not to abolish or restrain but to preserve and enlarge freedom; for in all the states of created beings capable of laws, where there is no law, there is no freedom. For liberty is to be free from restraint and violence of others, which cannot be where there is no law; but freedom is not, as we are told: a liberty for every man to do what he lists—for who could be free, when every man's humor might domineer over him?—but a liberty to dispose and order as he lists his . . . actions, possessions, and his whole property, within the allowance of those laws under which he is.

John Locke[1]

PREVIEW OF CHAPTER

Central question

Why do *property rights* exist?

Major objectives

1. To define property rights and to explain their social meaning
2. To demonstrate the productivity of a *social contract* in which the behavioral limits of people are specified and, thereby, to show the purpose of law
3. To show the tenuous nature of any social contract
4. To explain how and under what circumstances trades will emerge once the social contract is agreed upon

[1] John Locke, *The Second Treatise of Government*, ed. by Thomas P. Peardon (New York: The Liberal Arts Press, Inc., 1954), pp. 32–33.

5 To reveal the limitations of *communal property rights* and, thereby, to show the advantages of *private or state property*

Major conclusions

1 Property rights determine the behavioral limits of people's actions; they are, therefore, equivalent to behavioral rules.

2 Without a social contract specifying behavioral limits, resources must be diverted away from production of goods and services to predatory and defensive behavior. When rights are protected, more resources can be devoted to production and the welfare of people can rise. This is the reason for a social contract.

3 Even though one person is more productive than another in the production of all goods, trade between them can still be mutually beneficial.

4 Communal property rights can lead to inefficient (or wasteful) use of resources. Private property rights are a means of "internalizing" the harmful effects which one person's behavior may have on others.

Important terms and concepts

Property rights
Private property rights
Communal property rights
State property rights
Social contract
Social cost

The first four chapters outlined the economist's view of *individual* behavior. We learned that although an individual has choice, his choices will be constrained by physical environmental factors, which affect the costs and benefits of any particular choice situation. In most circumstances the individual's behavior will also be constrained and influenced by the behavior of others. The purpose of this chapter is to initiate a discussion, which will extend through the book, of individual behavior in the context of a *social* setting—that is, a group. Individuals acting rationally within a social group must adjust and readjust their behavior; they must recognize, implicitly or explicitly, the limitations of their own and others' behavior; and they must establish institutions which will attempt to efficiently accomplish individual and collective goals. How these objectives are accomplished forms the basis of this and following chapters.

We begin this chapter by exploring the meaning and importance of *property rights* in society. We do this because, again, our concern is with social behavior of individuals; and as we will see, property rights are instrumental in defining the boundary of social behavior. Indeed, that is their purpose. However, in order to fully understand the importance of property rights, we must understand why they arise; for this reason, we consider social behavior of people in a state of anarchy, in which property rights do not exist. With this background, we are in a position to talk about the emergence of a "social contract" and "exchanges" among people, which we do in the second half of this chapter. In later chapters, we extend our analysis of group behavior in general and market behavior in particular. First, the definition of property rights.[2]

[2] For most of the insights recorded in this chapter, we are indebted to the recent work of Armen Alchian, James Buchanan, and Harold Demsetz. In turn, their contributions are in many ways founded upon the work of other economists who, over the past two decades, have developed an extensive literature in the area of property rights as they pertain to social organization. For appropriate references to the work of these economists, see the "Recommended Readings" section at the end of the chapter.

THE MEANING AND IMPORTANCE OF PROPERTY RIGHTS

Property rights pertain to the permissible use of resources, goods, and services; they define the limits of social behavior and, in that way, determine what can be done by individuals in society.

They also specify whether resources, goods, and services are to be used privately or collectively by the state or any smaller group.

Property rights are a social phenomenon; they arise out of the necessity of individuals to "get along" within a social space in which all wish to move and interact. Where individuals are isolated from one another by natural barriers or are located where goods and resources are abundant, property rights have no meaning. In the world of Robinson Crusoe, shipwrecked alone on an island, property rights were inconsequential. His behavior was restricted by the resources found on the island, the tools he was able to take from the ship, and his own ingenuity. He had a problem of efficiently allocating his time within these constraints—procuring food, building shelter, and plotting his escape; however, the notion of "property" did not restrict his behavior—it was not a barrier to what he could do. He was able to take from the shipwreck, with immunity, stores that he thought would be most useful to his purposes.[3]

After the arrival of Friday, the native whom Robinson Crusoe saved from cannibals, a problem of restricting and ordering interpersonal behavior immediately emerged. The problem was particularly acute for Crusoe since Friday, prior to coming to Tibago, was himself a cannibal. (Each had to clearly establish property rights to his body.) The system which they worked out was a simple one, not markedly different from that between Crusoe and "Dog." Crusoe essentially owned everything. Their relationship was that of master and servant, Crusoe dictating to Friday how the property was to be used.

The notion of property rights is broadly conceived by economists. Property rights are most often applied to discussions of real estate and personal property (bicycles, clothes, etc.); they are also applicable to what people can do with their minds, their ability to speak, how they wear their hair, and if and when they must wear their shoes:

> In common speech, we frequently speak of someone owning this land, that house, or these bonds. This conventional style undoubtedly is economical from the viewpoint of quick communications, but it masks the variety and complexity of the ownership relationship. What is owned are *rights* to *use* resources, including one's body and mind, and these rights are always circumscribed, often by prohibition of certain actions. To "own land" usually means to have the right to till (or not to till) the soil, to mine the soil, to *offer* those rights for sale, etc., but not to have the right to throw soil at a passerby, to use it to change the course of a stream, or to force someone to buy it. What are owned are socially recognized rights of action.[4]

Property rights are not necessarily distributed equally, meaning that people do not always have the same rights to use the same resources. Students may have the right to use their voices (i.e., a resource) to speak with friends in casual conversation in the hallways of classroom buildings, but they do not, generally speaking, have the right to disrupt an English class with a harangue on their political views. The English professor, however, although his behavior is circumscribed, has the right to "allow" his or her political views to filter into the English lectures. And if the President of the United States walked into that same English class and began speaking extemporaneously on *his* political views, it is not likely that anyone would object. A person has the right to go without shoes on a beach, but one does not *always* have the right to enter a restaurant without shoes. On

[3] The absence of human beings affected also his idea of what was useful. Crusoe, in going through the ship, came across a coffer of gold and silver coins: "Thou art not worth to me, no, not taking off the ground; one of these knives is worth all this heap [of gold]." At first, he evaluated the cost of taking the coins in terms of what he could take in their place and decided to leave them. But on second thought, perhaps taking into consideration the probability of being rescued, he took the coins with him! See *Robinson Crusoe* by Daniel Defoe.

[4] Armen A. Alchian and Harold Demsetz, "The Property Rights Paradigm," *Journal of Economic History*, vol. 33, p. 17, March 1973.

the other hand, the restaurant owner's best friend may have that right. By the same token, although students generally pay a minor portion of their educational expenses, they have the right to university facilities such as tennis courts and the university bookstore, but nonstudent taxpayers do not have the same rights to these facilities.

In other words, property rights can be recast in terms of the *behavioral rules* which effectively limit and restrict our behavior. Behavioral rules determine what rights we have with regard to the use of resources, goods, and services. The rights we have may be the product of the legislative process and may be enforced by a third party: usually the third party is the government or, more properly, the agents of government. In this case property rights emerge from laws.

On the other hand, rules which establish rights may not have third-party enforcement. In this case they carry weight in the decisions of individuals simply because individuals recognize and respect behavioral limits for themselves and others. They may do this because of the value they attach to "living up" to their contractual agreements, which may be implied in their associations with others, and because their own rights may be violated if they violate the rights of others. Two neighbors may implicitly agree to certain modes of behavior, such as not mowing their lawns on Sunday mornings or playing their stereo equipment late at night.[5] Their behavior may be founded upon their notion of what it means to be a "good neighbor" and on their recognition of what life can be like if limits to their behavior are not observed. The neighbor who starts his mower early Sunday morning may hear music late at night or may find his rights invaded in other ways. More will be said on this, but for now we mean only to point out that the behavior of each through "offensive and counteroffensive" maneuvers may deteriorate into a state in which both parties are worse off than they would have been if restrictions on their own behavior were commonly observed. From this we see the basis for *behavioral rules* or, what amounts to the same thing, *property rights*.

Property rights are important to any inquiry of social order because it is on the basis of such rights that the terms *individual* and *state* are given social meaning, that actions are delimited, and that a specific social order will emerge. The existing property rights structure is predicated upon specific social and physical conditions. Changes in those conditions can cause a readjustment in the nature of social order.

PROPERTY RIGHTS AND THE MARKET

In the private market economy people are permitted to initiate trades with one another. Indeed, when people trade, they are actually trading "rights" to goods and services or to do certain things. For example, when a person buys a house in the market, he is actually buying the right to live in the house under certain conditions, for example, so long as he does not disturb others. This market economy is predicated upon establishing patterns of *private* property rights; those patterns have legitimacy because of enforcement by government and, perhaps just as important, because of certain precepts regarding the limits of individual behavior which are commonly accepted and observed.[6] Without recognized property rights, there would be nothing to trade—no market.

How dependent are markets on government enforcement for the protection and legitimacy of private property rights? Our answer must of necessity be somewhat speculative. We know that markets existed in the "Old West" when *formally* instituted governments were nonexistent. Further, it is highly improbable that any government can be so pervasive in the affairs of men that it can be the arbiter of all private rights. Cases in which disputes over property rights within college dormitories are settled by student councils are

[5] This is an example used by James M. Buchanan, *The Limits of Liberty* (Chicago: University of Chicago Press, 1975), p. 20.

[6] In addition, there is considerable *private* enforcement of property rights. Almost all people take some measures to secure their own property. They put locks on their doors, leave lights on at night, and alert their neighbors to take their newspapers in when they are out of town.

relatively rare, and the disputes which end up in the dean's office or at police headquarters are rarer still. Most conflicts over property rights are resolved at a local level, between two people, and many potential disputes do not even arise because of generally accepted behavioral limits.

Finally, the concept of property rights helps make clear the relationship between the public and private sectors of the economy—that is, between that section of the economy organized by collective action through government and that section which is organized through the actions of independent individuals. When government regulates aspects of the market, it redefines behavioral limits (in the sense that people can no longer do what they once could) and can be thought of as realigning the property rights between the private and public spheres. When the government imposes price ceilings on goods and services, as it did during the summer of 1971, it is redefining the rights which sellers have with regard to the property they sell. One of the purposes of economics is to analyze the effect which a realignment of property rights has on the efficiency of production.

ANARCHY: A STATE OF DISORDER

Property rights are so much a part of our everyday experience that we are inclined to think of them as being "natural," a part of our birthright. The Declaration of Independence speaks of "certain unalienable rights." Indeed, it is hard to imagine a world in which people interact within a defined social space without the existence of property rights. The purpose of this section is to envision such a state in order that we may gain some insight into the origins of property rights and, therefore, social order.

Thomas Hobbes, a seventeenth-century political scientist philosopher, envisioned a state in which there was a complete absence of property rights, either those rights which have legitimacy because of their social acceptability or those which exist because of legal enforcement. He called this "the state of nature," and his analysis was not very attractive. Because Hobbes gave very little credence to social acceptance as a basis for property rights, his attention was on the role of the state. He believed that "during the time men live without a common Power to keep them in awe," every man will be pitted against another in continual struggle for dominance and protection. Life will be "solitary, poore, nasty, brutish, and short." Where there is no state, he argued, there will be no law and, therefore, "no Property . . . no *Mine* and *Thine* distinct, but only that to be every mans that he can get, and for so long as he can keep it."[7]

One of Hobbes's purposes in writing *Leviathan* was to justify the sovereign state as an absolutely necessary political entity. He tried to convince his contemporaries of the potential for conflict among men without the state; that it is necessary to hand over considerable political power to the state in order that internal conflicts may be minimized. He argued that it is in man's self-interest to swear full allegiance to the state.

In order to make his argument as convincing as possible, it was somewhat natural for Hobbes to describe "the state of nature" in the worst possible terms. One can accept the criticism that Hobbes exaggerated the need for the state without ignoring a cornerstone of his argument: without legally defined property rights, there is considerable potential for conflict among men. The life of man in the state of nature may not invariably be "solitary, poore, nasty, brutish, and short," but it may be markedly less comfortable without property rights than with them.

In an idealized world in which people are fully considerate of each other's feelings and adjust and readjust their behavior to that of others without recourse to anything resembling a dividing line between "mine" and "thine," property rights are no more necessary than they were for Robinson Crusoe alone on Tibago. But in the world as it now exists, there is the potential for conflict. Granted, the potential may not be present in all our interpersonal experiences. People have interests which, for all practical pur-

[7] Thomas Hobbes, *Leviathan*, ed. by C. B. MacPherson [Baltimore, Md.: Penguin Books, Inc., 1968 (first published 1651)], pp. 185–188, with editing by the authors.

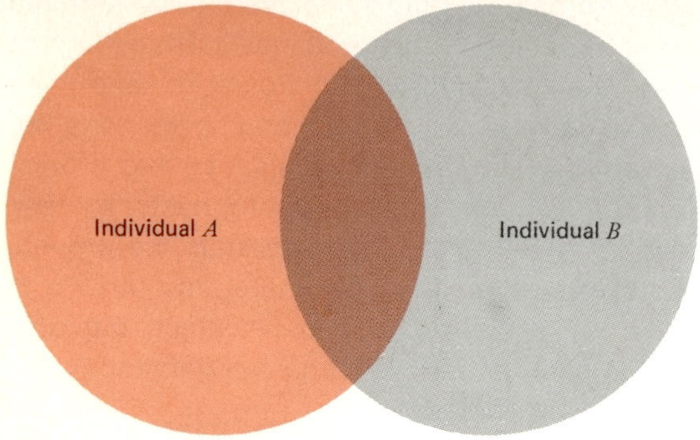

FIG. 5·1 Individuals have spheres of interest which are illustrated by the two circles. The intersection of the two circles represents the area for potential conflict between the two individuals; it is in this area that the property rights (or behavioral limits) of the two must be established.

poses, are independent of one another, and many of our interests are perfectly congruent with the interests of those around us. However, people have spheres of interests (described for two people by the circles in Figure 5·1) which extend outward from themselves and which intersect with the interests of others. A basic axiom of behavior—one developed in Chapter 2—is that most people want more than they have, which means they have an interest in, or can benefit from, that which others have. In other words, they have competing interests—or, in terms of Figure 5·1, areas where their spheres of interests intersect. It is here that the potential for conflict arises, that a dividing line between "mine" and "thine" must be drawn.

Children at play provide us with a reasonably clear illustration of the absence and potential for conflict among people in the larger community. Children can often play together for long periods of time without conflict. They each have interests which do not invade the interests of others (which may be described by the clear portions of the circles in Figure 5·1); for example, one may want to play with a truck, one with a bucket and shovel, and another with toy cowboys. For periods, their behavior may approximate the idealized society mentioned above. On the other hand, when two children want to play with the same toy or play the same role of mother or father in their game of "house" or when one child wants to take over the entire sandbox, conflict is revealed, first with harsh words, possibly in fights, leading to a breakdown of their social interaction—play.

Conflict or the potential for conflict can be alleviated by the development of property rights, held either communally, by the state, or by private individuals. These rights can be established in ways which are similar but which can be conceptually distinguished: (1) *voluntary* acceptance of behavioral norms with no third-party enforcer, such as the police and courts, and (2) the specification of rights in a legally binding "social contract," meaning that a third-party enforcer is established. Most of what we say for the remainder of this chapter applies to both modes of establishing rights. However, for reasons developed in detail in Chapter 6, the establishment of rights through voluntary acceptance of behavioral norms, although important in itself, has distinct limitations, especially in relation to size. More specifically, many behavior norms have a tendency to break down in large-group settings. Because most people hold to the behavioral norm that they should not pollute, and yet at least to some degree they pollute anyway, and because legal codes are filled with specifications of property rights, meaning something has failed, the limitations of behavioral norms may come as no surprise. Be that as it is, holding the discussion of voluntary behavioral rules until the next chapter will permit us to narrow our attention and, perhaps, gain a deeper understanding of the basis of legal property rights. For now, let's step back and consider in more detail the social basis for property rights.

THE EMERGENCE OF PROPERTY RIGHTS

To develop the analysis in the simplest terms possible, consider a model of two people, Fred and Harry, who live alone on an island. They have, at the start, no behavioral rules or anything else which "naturally" divides their spheres of interest. That is, they have nothing that resembles property rights. Further, being rational, they are assumed to want more than they can produce by themselves. Their social order is essentially anarchic. Each has two fundamental options for increasing his welfare: he can use his labor and other resources to produce goods and services or he can steal from his fellow man. With no social or ethical barriers restricting their behavior, they should be expected to allocate their resources between these options in the most productive way. This may mean that each should steal and should continue to steal or attempt to steal from the other so long as more is gained that way than through the production of goods and services.

If Fred and Harry find stealing a reasonable course to take, each will have to divert resources into protecting that which he has produced (*or* stolen). Presumably, their attacks and counterattacks will lead them toward a social equilibrium where each is applying resources to predation and defense and where neither finds any further movement of resources into those lines of activity profitable.[8] This is not an equilibrium in the sense that the state of affairs is a desirable one; in fact, it may be characterized as a "Hobbesean jungle" in which "every man is Enemy to every man."

In an economic sense, the resources diverted into predatory and defensive behavior are wasted; they are taken away from productive processes. If these resources are applied to production, total production can rise, and both Fred and Harry can be better off—both can have more than if they try to steal from each other. It is only through winding up in a state of anarchy or seeing the potential for ending up there that they must question the rationality of continued plundering and unrestricted behavior; and it is because of the prospects of individual improvement that there exists a potential for a "social contract" which spells out legally defined property rights. Through a social contract they may agree to place restrictions on their own behavior, but they will do away with the restraints which, through predation and required defense, each imposes on the other. The fear of being attacked on the streets at night can be far more confining than laws which restrict people from attacking one another. This is what John Locke meant when he wrote, "The end of law is not to abolish or restrain but to preserve and enlarge freedom."[9]

Once the benefits from the social contract are recognized, there *may* still be, as in the case of voluntary behavioral norms, an incentive for Fred or Harry to chisel on the contract. Fred may find that although he is "better off" materially by agreeing to property rights than he is by remaining in a state of anarchy, he may be even "better off" by violating the agreed-upon rights of the other. Through stealing, or in other ways violating Harry's rights, Fred can redistribute the total wealth of the community toward himself.

To illustrate, consider Figure 5·2, which contains a chart or matrix of Fred and Harry's utility levels if either respects or fails to respect the rights established for each as a part of the contract. (The actual utility levels are hypothetical but serve the purpose of illustrating a basic point.) There are four cells in the matrix, representing the four combinations of actions which Fred and Harry can take. They can both respect the agreed-upon rights of the other (cell 1), or they can both violate each other's rights (cell 4). Alternatively, Harry can respect Fred's rights while Fred violates Harry's rights (cell 3), or vice versa (cell 2).

Clearly, by the utility levels indicated in cells 1 and 4, Fred and Harry are both better off by respecting each other's rights than by violating them. However, if Harry respects Fred's rights and Fred fails to reciprocate, Fred has a utility level of 18 utils, which is greater than he will receive in cell 1, that is, by going along with Harry and respecting the other's rights. Harry is similarly better off if he violates Fred's rights while Fred respects Harry's

[8] For a rather difficult discussion of "equilibrium" under anarchy, see Winston C. Bush, "Individual Welfare in Anarchy," in Gordon Tullock (ed.), *Explorations in the Theory of Anarchy* (Blacksburg, Va.: University Publications, Inc., 1972), pp. 5–18.

[9] Locke, *The Second Treatise*, p. 32.

	Harry respects Fred's rights		Harry violates Fred's rights	
	Cell 1		Cell 2	
Fred respects Harry's rights	Fred	Harry	Fred	Harry
	15 utils	10 utils	8 utils	16 utils
	Cell 3		Cell 4	
Fred violates Harry's rights	Fred	Harry	Fred	Harry
	18 utils	5 utils	10 utils	7 utils

FIG. 5 · 2 The payoffs (measured in "util" terms) from Fred and/or Harry either respecting or violating the other's rights are indicated in the four cells of the matrix. Each has an incentive to violate the other's rights. If they do violate each other's rights, they will end up in cell 4, the worst of all possible states for both of them. The productivity of the "social contract" can be measured by the increase in Fred and Harry's utility resulting from their moving from cell 4, the "state of nature," to cell 1, a state in which a social contract is agreed upon.

rights: Harry has a utility level of 16, whereas he will have a utility level of 10 utils if he and Fred respect each other's rights. The lesson to be learned: there is potentially inherent in an agreement over property rights the possibility for each person to gain by violating the rights of the other. If both follow this course, they both will end up in cell 4, that is, back in the state of anarchy.

There are two reasons why this may happen. First, as we stated above, both Fred and Harry may violate each other's rights in order to improve their own positions; the action may be strictly *offensive.* By the same token, each must consider what the other will do. Neither would want to be caught upholding the agreement while the other one violates it. If Fred thinks Harry may violate his rights, Fred may follow suit and violate Harry's rights: he will be better off in cell 4, i.e., anarchy, than in cell 2. Fred and Harry can wind up in anarchy for purely *defensive* reasons. Many wars and battles, both at the street and international levels, have been fought because one party was afraid the other would attack first in order to get the upper hand. The same problem is basically involved in our analysis of the fragile nature of Fred and Harry's social contract.

Fred and Harry's situation is a classic example of what social scientists call a "prisoner's dilemma." The name comes from a standard technique of interrogation employed by police to obtain confessions from two or more suspected partners to a crime. If the method is used, the suspects are taken to different rooms for questioning, and each is offered a lighter sentence if he confesses. But each will also be warned that if the other suspect confesses and he does not, his sentence will be more stringent. The suspect has to try to figure out, without the benefit of communication, how the other will stand up to that kind of pressure and may confess because he cannot trust his partner not to take the easy way out.[10] The problem which the individual suspect has is more complicated the larger the number of partners to the crime who are caught with the individual. There are more people upon whom he must count to hold up under the pressure, which he knows is being brought to bear, and he must also consider the fact that the others may confess because they cannot count on all of them to hold under the pressure.

To prevent violations, both of offensive and of defensive nature, a community may agree to the establishment of a police, court, and penal system to protect the rights specified in the social contract. The system may be costly, but the drain on its total wealth may be smaller than if it reverts back to anarchy, in which case resources will be diverted into predatory and defensive behavior. The costs associated with making the contract and enforcing it will determine just how ex-

[10] There is no wonder that prisoners have such harsh feelings toward those who cave in and "rat on them" or "fink out."

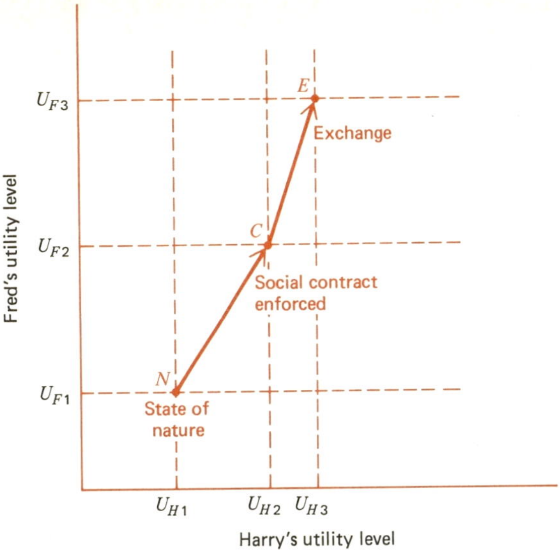

FIG. 5·3 In the "state of nature," in which Fred and Harry each has to use resources to fend off the other, the welfare of Fred and Harry are, respectively, U_{F1} and U_{H1}, or point N. A social contract can move them both to point C. They can further improve their welfare by trading the "rights" to goods and services which they are given in the social contract.

tensive the contract will be, and this matter will be considered later in a separate chapter; but for now, assuming the benefits from the contract exceed the costs of contracting and enforcement, we may summarize the foregoing discussion in terms of Figure 5·3. In the state of nature, Fred and Harry, through allocating their resources among productive, predatory, and defensive uses, will achieve a certain level of welfare. In terms of Figure 5·3, Fred achieves an initial utility level of U_{F1} and Harry, U_{H1}. By developing a social contract, through which they define and enforce property rights, each can move to a higher utility level; Fred to U_{F2} and Harry to U_{H2}. With social contracts, they both can move to higher utility levels because they no longer have to divert their resources to predatory and defensive actions.

THE EMERGENCE OF EXCHANGE

The social contract, which defines property rights, establishes only the limits of permissible behavior; it does not mean that Fred and Harry will be satisfied with the property rights they have been given through the contract. To the degree that some other combination will give them more satisfaction, exchanges can emerge, provided, of course, that the social contract permits them. In terms of Figure 5·3, they can, through exchanges or trades, increase their utility to U_{F3} and U_{H3}.

For example, suppose that the only goods on Fred and Harry's island are coconuts and papayas. The social contract specifies the division of the fruits between them. We need not concern ourselves with the total number of the fruit each has; we need only indicate the relative satisfaction which Fred and Harry receive from the marginal units. Suppose the marginal utilities in the table below represent the satisfaction they received from the last coconut and papaya in their possession:

	Coconut	Papaya
Fred	10 utils	15 utils
Harry	90 utils	30 utils

In the illustration, Fred receives more utility from the last papaya (15 utils) than from the last coconut (10 utils). He would be on a higher level of utility if he could trade a coconut for a papaya. He would lose 10 utils from the coconut but would more than regain that with the additional papaya. On the other hand, Harry receives more utility from the last coconut than from the last papaya. He would gladly give up a papaya for a coconut; he would be 60 utils of satisfaction better off (90 minus 30) than if he did not engage in the exchange. The two should continue to exchange *rights* to the coconuts and papayas until one or both of them can no longer gain via trade.

In this example, we were not concerned with production of coconuts and papayas; we were concerned merely with the benefits from trade resulting from the initial allotments of the fruits. The trades are comparable to those that took place in the prisoner-of-war camps as described by R. A. Radford. (See the first few pages of this text.) If the social contract allocates to Fred and Harry rights to *produce* the fruit, we can also demonstrate that both can be better off through specializing in their production and trading with each other. Consider the information in the following table; it indicates how many coconuts or papayas Fred and Harry can produce with, say, one hour of labor:

	Coconut Production	Papaya Production
Fred	4	8
Harry	6	24

In one hour of labor Fred can produce either 4 coconuts or 8 papayas; Harry can produce either 6 coconuts or 24 papayas. Even though Harry is more productive in both lines of work, we can show that they both can gain by specializing and trading with each other.

If Fred produces 4 coconuts, he cannot use that hour of time to produce the 8 papayas. In other words, the cost of the four coconuts is 8 papayas, or, what amounts to the same thing, the cost of 1 coconut is 2 papayas. Fred would be better off if he could trade 1 coconut for *more than* 2 papayas, because that is what he has to give up in order to produce the coconut. To determine whether or not there is a basis for trade, we must explore the cost of coconuts and papayas to Harry. We note that the cost of 1 coconut to Harry is 4 papayas; this is because he has to give up 24 papayas to produce 6 coconuts. If Harry can give up less than 4 papayas for a coconut, he would be better off. He could produce the 4 papayas; and if he has to give up fewer than that for a coconut, he will have papayas left over to eat, which he would not have had without the opportunity to trade.

To summarize: Fred would be better off if he can get more than 2 papayas for a coconut; Harry would be better off if he could give up fewer than 4 papayas for a coconut. If, for example, they agree to trade at the exchange rate of 1 coconut for 3 papayas, both would be better off. Fred will produce a coconut, giving up 2 papayas, but he can turn around and get 3 papayas for the coconut. Hence, he is better off. Harry can produce 4 papayas, giving up 1 coconut, and trade 3 of the papayas for a coconut. He has the same number of coconuts, but has an additional papaya. Harry is better off.

Although relatively simple, the above example of exchange is one of economists' most important contributions to discussions of social interaction. So many people seem to think that when people trade, one person must gain at the expense of another. If people in the United States trade with people in Japan, someone must be made worse off in the process, or so the argument goes. We will deal with such arguments in more detail in the chapters on international trade; for now we wish to emphasize that we have demonstrated that, through trade, both Harry and Fred are better off, and this was demonstrated even though we postulated that Harry was more efficient than Fred in the production of both fruits!

COMMUNAL PROPERTY RIGHTS

To many, the ideal state of affairs may appear to be one in which everyone has the right to use all resources, goods, and services and in which no one (not even the state) has the right to exclude anyone else from their use. We may designate such rights as "communal rights." Many rights to scarce property have been and still are allocated in this way. Rights to the use of a university's facilities are held communally by the students. No one admitted to the university has the right to keep you off campus paths or lawns or from using the library according to certain rules and regulations. (Such rules and regulations form the boundaries, much as if they were natural, within which the rights are truly communal.) The rights to city parks, sidewalks, and streets are held communally. Before our country was settled, many Indian tribes held communal rights to hunting grounds; that is, at least within the tribe's territory, no one had the right to exclude anyone else from hunting on the land. During most of the first half of the nineteenth century, the rights to graze cattle on the prairies of the western United States were held communally; anyone who wanted to let his cattle loose on the plains could do so. Granted, the United States government held by law the right to exclude people from the plains; but so long as it did not exercise that right, the land rights were communal. The same can be said for all other resources where the "owner" does not exercise his right to exclude.

Communal property rights can be employed with tolerably efficient results so long as one of two conditions holds: (1) there is more of the resource than can be effectively used for all intended purposes (in other words, there is no cost to its use) or (2) people within the community fully account for the effects which their own use of the resources has on others. Without the presence of one of these conditions, the resources will tend to be "overused."

Under communal ownership, if the resource is not presently being used by someone else, no one can be excluded from the use of it. Consequently, once in use, the resource becomes, for that period of time, the private property of the user. The people who drive their cars onto the freeway take up space on the road that is not in use; no one else (hopefully!) can then use that space at the same time. Unless the drivers violate the rules of the road, they cannot be excluded from that space; and if they are rational, they will continue to use the resource until the marginal cost of doing so equals the marginal benefits to them. They may consider most of the costs involved in their use of the road, but one which they may overlook, especially as it applies to themselves personally, is that their space may have had some alternative use: that is, by others.[11] Their presence also increases highway congestion and the discomfort of the other drivers. As a result, they may overextend the use of their resource.

For example, consider Figure 5·4. The individual has a demand for driving on the highway,

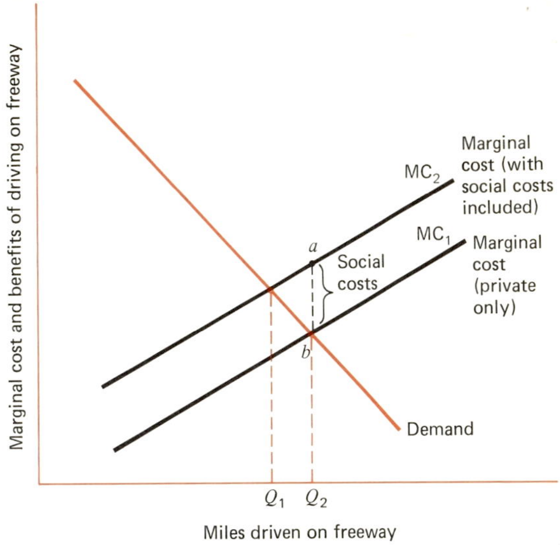

FIG. 5·4 MC_1 reflects the private costs incurred by the individual driver in using the public highways. If all costs, including the *social costs,* of using the roads are considered by the driver, he or she will drive only Q_1 instead of the greater Q_2 miles, which one will drive when only one's private costs are considered. A tax equal to the vertical distance between the two marginal cost curves can induce the driver to drive the optimum quantity, Q_1.

which is represented by the negatively sloping curve. The marginal cost curve MC_1 reflects his private costs, which he considers in his driving decisions. The driver will, given these two schedules, drive Q_2 miles. This is the point at which the marginal benefits of the last mile driven equal the marginal costs. However, there are social costs, mentioned above, to his using the freeway which he may not consider. If these costs are equal to the vertical distance between a and b, and if they are considered by the driver, he will drive less, Q_1 miles. It is in this sense that resources held communally tend to be overused; the driver drives Q_2 miles instead of Q_1. The difference between Q_2 and Q_1 is the "overuse." The state can make the driver consider the social costs in an indirect way by imposing a tax on the driver's use of the road

[11] Environmentalists argue that many roads should not have even been built; the alternative use in this case would be scenery, for example.

equal to the distance between a and b. This is called "internalizing the social cost." Once the state does this—and it is commonly done through gasoline taxes and/or tolls—the rights to the freeway are no longer "communal"; the rights have been effectively taken over by the state.

There are two additional ways that social costs can be internalized. First, people can be considerate of others and account for the social cost in their behavior. Second, the right to the road can be turned into *private property*, meaning that individuals are given the right to exclude others from the use of the resource (i.e., the road). This may seem like a totally undesirable turn of events unless we recognize that private owners can then charge for the use of the road: they can sell "use-rights," in which case the marginal cost of driving will rise, resulting in a movement in the amount of driving toward Q_1 in Figure 5·4.

The prime difference between this private ownership and government taxation is that with private ownership the revenues collected go into the coffers of individuals instead of to the state; this is either "good" or "bad," depending upon your attitude toward government versus private uses of the funds. Furthermore, under private ownership and without viable competitors (and we have an example in which competition *may* not be practical), the owners may attempt to charge an amount which is greater than the social costs in the figure; they may attempt, in the jargon of economists, to acquire *monopoly profits*, and in so doing cause an *underuse* of the road.[12] (A monopoly is a single seller of a good or service which can charge higher prices and reap greater profits than if it had to worry about the actions of other competitors.)

For that matter, the state-imposed taxes may be greater than the social costs. The state may also act like a monopolist. State agencies may not be permitted to make a "profit" as it is normally conceived, but this does not exclude the use of their revenues for improving salaries and the working conditions of state employees. Monopoly profits may be easy to see on the accounting statements of a private firm but may be lost in bureaucratic waste or overexpenditures under state ownership. State ownership does not necessarily lead to waste, but it is a prospect which only the naïve will ignore. More will be said on the subject at various points in the book.

We have now considered the distinction between private and communal property. Several examples will enable us to amplify that distinction and to understand more clearly the limitations of communal property rights and the pervasive use of private property.

Pollution

Pollution can be described as a logical consequence of communal property rights to streams, rivers, air, etc. The state and federal governments, by right of eminent domain, have always held rights to these resources; but until very recently they have inadequately asserted their right to exclude people and firms from their use. As a result, the resources have been subject to communal use and to overuse, in the same sense discussed above.

By dumping waste into the rivers, people, firms, and local governments have been able to acquire ownership to portions of the communal resource—they use it and pollute it. Furthermore, because of the absence of exclusion, those people doing the polluting do not have to pay to draw the resource away from its alternative uses (like pretty scenery) or to reimburse the people harmed by the pollution for the damage done. Under communal ownership, in which government does not exercise its control, the firm with smoke billowing from its stacks does not have to compensate the people who live around the plant for the eye irritation they experience or the extra number of times they have to paint their homes.

[12] To provide for competition and to prevent monopoly profits from emerging, where possible, private rights can be assigned to similar units of the same resource. Although this may not be practical in road construction, it is quite practical in the cattle business, for example. Many different people can own all the resources necessary for cattle production. If one tries to raise his price to achieve monopoly profits, the others can undercut him, forcing him to lower his price. As a general rule, competition requires the dispersion of property rights among different people and groups.

Pollution is often thought to be the product of antisocial behavior, as indeed it often is. Many who pollute simply do not care about what they do to others. However, much pollution results from the behavior of people who do *not* have devious motives. People may view their behavior as having an inconsequential effect on the environment. The person who throws a cigarette butt on the ground may reason that if this cigarette butt is the only one on the ground, it will not materially affect anyone's sensibilities, and in fact it may not. However, if everyone follows the same line of reasoning, the cigarette butts will accumulate and an eyesore will develop. Even then there may be little incentive for people to stop throwing their butts on the ground. Again, a person may reason on the basis of the effects of his own individual action: "If I do not throw my butt on the ground here with all the others, will my behavior materially affect the environmental quality, *given the fact that other butts are already there?*" This type of reasoning can lead to a very powerful argument for conversion of communal rights to private or state rights, with the implied power for someone to exclude some or all of this kind of use.[13]

Fur Trade

According to Harold Demsetz, the hunting grounds of the Indian tribes of the Labrador Peninsula were held in common until emergence of the fur trade there.[14] The Indians could hunt as they wished without being excluded by other members of their tribe. Presumably, given the cost of hunting and the limited demand for meat, there was no inclination to "over-hunt," that is, until there was an adverse effect on the stock of animals in the area.

However, when fur trading commenced and the Indians hunted animals for their skins, the demand and, therefore, the price of animal skins increased. This provided an incentive for the Indians to hunt beyond their demand for meat. Under communal ownership, when a beaver was killed, an Indian hunter did not have to consider the effects which his action had on the ability of the other hunters to trap and hunt. Each hunter, through his own efforts, imposed a cost on the others; when a beaver was killed by one hunter, the task of finding beavers was made more difficult for the other hunters. The cost may be construed as a social cost, much like the congestion a driver can impose upon the other drivers around. Furthermore, under a communal rights structure, there was little incentive for hunters to avoid trapping or incurring the costs of increasing the stock of animals. If a hunter refrains from killing a beaver, perhaps someone else will kill it. In addition, if one person tries to increase the stock of animals, perhaps many others will benefit from his efforts in terms of more animals for them to kill. There was, in other words, no assurance that the Indian who built up the stock of animals would reap the benefits. (For the same reason, we doubt that many buildings would be built if the developers could not reap the benefits of their investment or if what they built would be *communal* property upon completion.) The Indians' solution to the problem of overkill was to assign private property rights to portions of the hunting grounds. Each individual, by virtue of his right to exclude others, had an incentive to control his own take from the land and to take measures, much as ranchers do, to increase the potential stock of furs.

Whales and Seals

Whales have been hunted for centuries, but there has never been a problem with their possible extinction until the last two centuries. Whales have always been more or less communal property; however, because people in bygone centuries did not have the technology we now have to kill and slaughter whales far at sea, the sheer cost of hunting them prevented men from exceeding the whales' reproductive capacity. Theoretically, the

[13] For a similar discussion of why university campuses have dirt paths on the campus lawns, see Richard B. McKenzie and Gordon Tullock, *The New World of Economics* (Homewood, Ill.: Richard D. Irwin, Inc., 1978), chap. 2.

[14] Harold Demsetz, "Toward a Theory of Property Rights," *American Economic Review*, vol. 57, pp. 347–359, May 1964. Demsetz cites Eleanor Leacock, "The Montagnes 'Hunting Territory' and the Fur Trade," vol. 56, no. 5, part 2, Memoir No. 78.

problem could be solved by applying the same solution to the whale overkill as the Indians applied in their hunting grounds: establish private property rights. However, whales present a special problem. The annual migrations of whales can take them through 6000 miles of ocean. Establishing and enforcing private property rights to such an expanse of ocean is an ominous task, even without the complications involved in securing agreement among several governments to respect those rights. These costs have, without doubt, been a major reason why whales remain communal property and are threatened still with extinction.

Communal property rights can also have an effect on the way animals are treated and slaughtered. Armen Alchian and Harold Demsetz have provided us with a vivid description of the seal slaughter in Canada:

> In 1970, the newspapers carried stories of the barbaric and cruel annual slaughter of baby seals on the ice floes off Prince Edward Island in the Gulf of St. Lawrence. The Canadian government permitted no more than 50,000 animals to be taken, so hunters worked with speed to make their kills before the legal maximum was reached. They swarmed over the ice floes and crushed the babies' skulls with heavy clubs. Government offices received many protests that the seals were inhumanly clubbed (by humans) and often skinned alive. The minister of fisheries warned the hunters of the strong pressure he was under to ban the hunt and that he would do so unless the killing methods were humane in 1970.[15]

Alchian and Demsetz point out that the Canadian government had effectively made the first 50,000 baby seals communal property among the hunters; the seals became private property when and only when they were killed. Possession of only the *first* 50,000 baby seals was legal. The rights to the seals were allocated communally on a first-come, first-serve basis, and Alchian and Demsetz stressed that such a rationing system tends to encourage "rapid hunting techniques and to make a condition of their success the degree to which the hunter can be ruthless."[16]

Lawn Mowers, Garden Tools, and Grass Seed

There is a townhouse development in Blacksburg, Virginia. Most of the land within the development is held communally by the owners through the Oak Manor Association. Fearing that owners would shirk their responsibility to make voluntary contributions toward the upkeep of the grounds, the developers stipulated in the purchase contract that all owners would automatically be members of the Oak Manor Association and would pay dues determined by the association. (The dues can, in a manner of speaking, be construed as "taxes" imposed on a local level.) In this way, the potential for the owners to become "free riders" is avoided and the grounds, even though communally owned, are, to this day, reasonably well kept up.

However, not all land in the development is communal property. Each owner has a small parcel of land at the rear of his townhouse, generally fenced, which is the owner's responsibility. In order to facilitate and encourage the owner's upkeep of the "yards," the association began operations by providing the owners with lawn mowers, garden tools, and grass seed. All this was kept in a community shed to which the owners had access; it was communal property and it was treated as such. It was used and abused. After only a year the lawn mowers fell apart because of rough use and the lack of maintenance. The garden tools "mysteriously disappeared" within a few months. Those who bought the grass seed confess that they bought enough seed to cover the entire community several times, implying that much of what they purchased was wasted.

The argument for the community tools and seed was "economies of scale": "It will be more efficient to have one lawn mower for all to use than

[15] Armen A. Alchian and Harold Demsetz, "The Property Rights Paradigm," *Journal of Economic History*, vol. 33, p. 20, March 1973.

[16] Ibid.

for each owner to have a mower which, because of the smallness of the individual plots, will be underused." The system, however, never achieved the perceived economies because of the lack of incentive for the residents to properly use the community property. Furthermore, this happened among a largely homogeneous group of people who, we believe, have an above-average "sense of community." They certainly are not "social reprobates" who go out of their way to damage or destroy public property, or else many of the residents would not live there. Like the whale and seal hunters, they are merely responding to the incentives in communal property.

What we have said in this section does not imply that communal property *always* results in the types of problems we have discussed. The family is an institution in which much property is owned communally with tolerably efficient results. However, this section has served the purpose of describing the problems that communal property can cause and directing our attention to the question of what are the conditions under which such a rights structure will serve the intended purposes.

CONSIDERATION OF OTHERS AS A MEANS OF INTERNALIZING SOCIAL COSTS

If polluters, whale and seal hunters, and townhouse owners would only consider the effects of their own behavior on others, the problem of resources being misallocated or overused and of internalizing the social costs (often called "externalities") would be solved. There would be no need for property rights as we think of them. People would "naturally" consider the costs they impose on others (i.e., social costs); the relevant marginal cost curve would be MC_2 instead of MC_1 in Figure 5 · 4, leading manufacturers to the optimum level of production.[17]

People do account for the external effects of their behavior—at least, most do to some extent. This is primarily true with regard to personal relationships. It is also true that in many often unrecognized ways—such as stepping aside in a hallway to let someone else pass—we consider the effects of our actions on people we do not know. We do at times incur the cost that is necessary to avoid harming others. However, as is evidenced by pollution, in many significant ways, we do not consider the harm that our own individual acts does to others. One reason is that we have real limits to considering others in our decisions; there are limits to our "charity." We cannot always be considerate by stepping aside when we are in others' paths. In a crowded hallway, this could mean excessively slow progress, if not immobility. Furthermore, there is, in a complex, multiperson world, a cost to determining who and by how much people will be affected by our behavior, and there is a rational limit beyond which we are unwilling to incur such costs. It is beyond these limits that communal property rights can have damaging effects on all concerned and that a different structure of rights can be more efficient.

[17] Again, by "internalizing the externalities" we mean that the individual considers the costs that he imposes on others in his own decisions. The costs which one imposes on others are effects which are "external" to him; they are "external costs" or just "externalities." By forcing him to consider them in his own decisions, we are "internalizing the externalities."

SUMMARY AND EXTENSIONS

The purpose of this chapter has been to develop a conceptual basis for the emergence of property rights. We have used Hobbes's description of "the state of nature" as that basis, although we recognize that the Hobbesian "state of nature" need not ever have existed in fact. For the analysis to follow, what is necessary is for people to recognize the *potential* for its existence and for the implied waste of resources. From that description we have been able to argue that total output may be improved by recognized limits on behavior through property rights. Underpinning all we have said is a case for *private-* or *state-*owned property in the sense that the state or private individuals have the right to exclude people from the use of scarce resources. The *assignment* of rights is one means of internalizing the social costs which people's behavior have on others.

From this analysis alone we are unable to say whether private, or state ownership is more efficient in accomplishing people's objectives. Tentative conclusions in this area will have to await a fuller discussion of what can be reasonably expected from state and private ownership arrangements. In the final analysis, our conclusion and your conclusion are likely to be that some mix of state and private property is desirable in any economy. However, most important, this subsequently directs our attention to the problem of drawing the line between public and private ownership. Perhaps further chapters will provide you with a more intelligent basis for drawing that line.

QUESTIONS TO PONDER

1 What do we mean by "property rights?" Why do we have them?

2 If you were going to organize a social order from "scratch," so to speak, would you include private property rights? Why or why not?

3 Using the discussion of problems associated with communal property rights, describe the causes of pollution of some portion of the environment around you.

4 In many respects, communal property rights work very well within a family structure. On what grounds may communal property rights be expected to work more efficiently within a family than within a larger community such as a city?

5 In establishing a "social contract," will the participants necessarily enter into the bargaining process as *equals?* (Before you answer that question you may want to ponder the meaning of "equals.") Would you expect the participants to emerge from the social contract with equal rights? Explain.

6 J. Ortega y Gasset has written, "Order is not a pressure imposed upon society from without, but an equilibrium which is set up from within." After reading this chapter, how do you react to this quotation? In the context of the quotation, what would a condition of "equilibrium" be? What would a state of disorder be?

7 What do enforcement costs have to do with the existence of property rights? What may be the effects of an increase in the productivity of enforcing property rights?

8 Many people argue that communal property ownership breaks down because of "inculcated capitalistic and competitive values." Do you agree? If the argument has any merit, what would be necessary to change the efficiency of communal property rights?

RECOMMENDED READINGS

Alchian, Armen A., and Harold Demsetz: "The Property Rights Paradigm," *Journal of Economic History,* vol. 33, pp. 16–27, March 1973.

Buchanan, James M.: *The Limits of Liberty: Between Anarchy and Leviathan* (Chicago: University of Chicago Press, 1975), chaps. 1 and 2.

Fels, Rendigs, and Robert G. Uhler: *Casebook of Economic Problems and Policies: Practice in Thinking* (New York: West Publishing Company, 1974), case 4.

6

The Logic of Group Behavior

Men journey together with a view to particular advantage and by way of providing some particular thing needed for the purpose of life, and similarly the political association seems to have come together originally . . . for the sake of the general *advantage it brings.*

Aristotle[1]

Unless the number of individuals in a group is quite small, or unless there is coercion, . . . rational, self-interested individuals will not act to achieve their common or group interest. *In other words, even if all . . . would gain if, as a group, they acted to achieve their common interest or objective, they will still not voluntarily act to achieve that common or group interest.*

Mancur Olson[2]

PREVIEW OF CHAPTER

Central question

To what extent can society rely upon voluntary cooperative associations to order people's interpersonal behavior?

Major objectives

1 To develop two competing theories of group behavior
2 To demonstrate the limitations of voluntary cooperative associations or groups as a means of organizing people's social behavior and to show why markets are not only beneficial but necessary

[1] Aristotle, *Ethics*, vol. 8, no. 9, p. 1160a.

[2] Mancur Olson, *The Logic of Collective Action: Public Goods and the Theory of Groups* (Cambridge, Mass.: Harvard University Press, 1971), p. 2.

Major conclusion

A person's actions will have a much more significant effect on his own and other people's welfare in a small group than in a large one. Therefore, a person is much more likely to behave in the interest of all members in a small group than in a large one. In very large groups of people, without coercion applied, members will fail to pursue the common interest of all group members.

Important terms and concepts

Common interest theory of group behavior
Economic theory of group behavior
Public good

In Chapter 5 we established the need for a social contract and property rights. In this chapter our central purpose is to explore how and under what conditions people can organize their behavior in voluntary cooperative associations (groups) in which all work together for the attainment of common objectives. The focus of our attention is on the viability of groups like families, cliques, communes, clubs, unions, and professional associations and societies in which individual participation is voluntary to cohere and pursue the common interest of the members.

We consider two dominant and conflicting theories of group behavior. They are "the common interest theory" and "the economic theory" of group behavior. The former is based on the proposition that a group is an "organic whole" identified by the "common interest" shared by its individual members. Its basic thesis is that all groups, even very large ones, are organized to pursue the common interest of the group members. Taking this theory one step further, it implies that if people share a common interest, they will organize themselves into a group and voluntarily pursue their shared interest.

According to the economic theory of group behavior, the group is a collection of independently motivated individuals who organize voluntarily to pursue their common interest only in small groups, like families or clubs. In large groups the common interest is very often ineffective in motivating group behavior. The logic of this theory seems perverse; but, as we will see in later chapters, it is the basis for almost all economic discussions of markets and explains why governments must be delegated coercive powers to collect taxes and to pursue the "public interest." This is, therefore, one of the pivotal chapters in this book.

However, keep in mind that groups are not the only means by which people's interpersonal or social behavior is organized in society. Economics is basically a study of comparative social systems, an examination of how the different ways of organizing interpersonal behavior can be fitted together in different combinations. We call these means of organizing people's behavior "social organizers" and mention four of them here: markets which involve exchanges of goods and services, government coercion, violence, and voluntary groups. On the surface, violence may not appear to be a bona fide alternative, but we are forced to mention it because of the use made of it throughout the world. The behavior of street-gang members, for example, with respect to people totally unassociated with them, is largely based upon either the existence or the threat of violence. The Cold War was a tenuous truce founded to a sizable degree on the threat of a nuclear holocaust. The persistent violence in the streets of Northern Ireland during the 1960s and 1970s will for many years have a profound influence on what the people of that country can hope to accomplish. Many examples can be cited which illustrate the spread of terroristic activities and the threat they represent to the fabric of social order which has been built on the basis of other social organizers. Aside from what we have already said with regard to anarchy, we will have little to say about violence as a social organizer. This does not lessen the importance which we attribute to violence; it simply reflects the fact that economists have only recently turned their attention to the subject and much remains to be done in the way of theory construction.[3]

The question of how you appraise the roles the various social organizers *should* play in social order appears to be wrapped in one's personal ideology or value system—that is, there appears to be no room for positive analysis. Indeed, what we as individuals want the system to accomplish is surely a factor in how each of us evaluates potential social organizers. Personal values will affect our attitude as to whether or not a given social organizer should be used and, if used, how extensively. The avowed Marxist has very harsh opinions of the market system. But perhaps just as important in our appraisal is what we know about the *relative* effectiveness—the advantages and limitations—of the potential means for ordering behavior. If, for example, we have only a rudimentary understanding of how the market works and fail to appreciate with sufficient clarity the limitations of cooperative efforts, we may naturally place greater reliance on voluntary cooperation than we would otherwise. We, therefore, in this chapter highlight the limitations of voluntary groups as a social organizer in order that we may appreciate why markets, to which we turn in Chapter 7, are not only beneficial but necessary in organizing a society of heterogeneous individuals.

[3] For examples of economists' initial probes into the area of malevolence and violence, see Kenneth E. Boulding, *The Economy of Love and Fear* (Belmont, Calif.: Wadsworth Publishing Company, Inc., 1973), and Gordon Tullock, *The Social Dilemma: The Economics of War and Revolution* (Blacksburg, Va.: University Publications, 1974). These books will be found useful only by those who wish to be challenged.

COMMON INTEREST THEORY OF GROUP BEHAVIOR

There are almost as many theories of group behavior as there are group theorists. However, categorizing theories according to dominant themes or characteristics is sensible in light of our limited space.

All theories of group behavior begin by recognizing the multiplicity of forces which affect group members and, therefore, groups. This is especially true of what we term the *common interest theory*. This point of view, which has been prominent at least since Aristotle, is generally shared by many present-day sociologists, political scientists, and psychologists. The determinants of group behavior most often singled out are the "leadership quality" of specific group members and the need felt among group members for "affiliation," "security," "recognition," "social status," or money. Groups like clubs or unions form so that members can achieve or satisfy a want that they could not satisfy as efficiently through individual action. All these considerations are instrumental in affecting "group cohesion," which, in turn, affects the "strength" of the group and its ability to compete with other groups for the same objectives.

The common interest theory views the "group" as an *organic whole*, much like an individual, as opposed to a collection of individuals whose separate actions appear to be "group action." According to the theory, the group has a life of its own which is to a degree independent of the individuals who comprise it. Herbert Spencer, a nineteenth-century sociologist, often described the group as a "social organism" or as a "superorganic" entity.[4] Karl Marx wrote of the "class struggle" which will bring down "bourgeois capitalism" and of the "proletariat" which will, in its place, erect the communist society. And it was probably the social-organism view of groups that

[4] Spencer was actually somewhat ambivalent on the subject; at times he also wrote of groups as a composite of individuals. This aspect of his writing reflected the influence David Hume and Adam Smith had on his thinking. See Herbert Spencer, *Principles of Sociology* (London: Williams and Norgate, Ltd., 1896).

Aristotle had in mind when he wrote, "Man is by nature a political animal."[5]

Two major reasons are given for viewing groups as a social organism. First, a group consists of a mass of interdependencies which connect the individuals in the group. Without the interdependencies, there would be only isolated individuals, and the term *group* would have no meaning. Individuals are like the nodes of a spider web. The spider web is constructed on these nodes, and the movements in one part of the web can be transmitted to all other parts. Much like the process of *synergism* in biology,[6] the actions of individuals within a group combine to form a force which is greater than the sum of the forces generated by individuals isolated from one another. The group must, so the argument goes, be thought of as more than the sum total of individuals. This argument is often used to arouse support for a labor union. Union leaders argue that the union can get higher wage increases for all workers than all workers can obtain acting independently of one another. The reason is that the efforts of all workers are efficiently coordinated by union leaders. Environmental groups make essentially the same argument: With a few well-placed lobbyists, the environmental group can have a greater political impact than can all the individuals they represent writing independent letters to their representatives at different times.

Second, groups tend to emerge because they satisfy some interest shared by all the group's members. Because all share this "common interest," individuals have an incentive to work with others to pursue that interest, sharing the costs as they work together. Aristotle wrote, "Men journey together with a view to particular advantage,"[7] and Arthur Bentley said, "There is no group without its interest. . . . The group and the interest are not separate. . . . If we try to take the group without the interest, we simply have nothing at all."[8]

[5] Aristotle, *Politics,* Book II.

[6] This is the process whereby two or more substances (gases or pollutants) can come together and combined can have a greater effect than the sum of the effects of each individual taken separately.

[7] Aristotle, *Ethics,* vol. 8, no. 1, p. 1160a.

Having observed that a common interest can be shared by all of a group's members, the adherents of this theory of group behavior argue that a group can, with slight modification, be treated as an individual. The primary modification is the relative tightness or looseness of the ties which bind the group members together. This usually makes group action and reaction less decisive and precise than that of individuals, but the difference between a group and an individual is still a matter of degree, not kind. For instance, the difficulty of passing information about group goals from person to person can make the group's response to new information somewhat sluggish. Nevertheless, a group can be assumed to maximize the attainment of its common objective. Furthermore, the implicit assumption is made that this will be true of large as well as small groups. It is on this deduction that Mancur Olson and many economists take issue with this analysis of group behavior.

THE ECONOMIC THEORY OF GROUP BEHAVIOR

Mancur Olson, on whose work this section rests, agrees that the "common interest" can be influential and is very important in motivating the behavior of members of *small* groups. However, he, like so many other economists, insists that a group must be looked upon as a *composite* of individuals as opposed to an anthropomorphic whole, that the common interest, which can be so effective in motivating members of small groups, can be impotent in motivating members of large groups: "Unless there is coercion in large groups . . ., *rational, self-interested individuals will not act to achieve their common or group interest.*" Furthermore, he contends, "These points hold true when there is unanimous agreement in a group about the common good and the

[8] Bentley, in Peter Odegard (ed.) *Process of Government* (Cambridge: The Belknap Press, Harvard University Press, 1967), pp. 211–213.

methods of achieving it."[9] To understand this theory, we will first examine the propositions upon which it is founded and then analyze some qualifications.

Basic Propositions

Using economic analysis, people are assumed to be as rational in their decision to join a group as they are toward doing anything else; they will join a group if the benefits of doing so are greater than the costs they must bear. As explained in Chapter 2, these costs and benefits, like all others relevant to any other act, must be discounted by the probability that the costs and benefits will be realized.[10] There are several direct, private benefits to belonging to groups, such as companionship, security, recognition, and social status. A person may also belong to a group for no other reason than to receive mail from it and, in that small way, to feel important. A group may serve as an outlet for our altruistic or charitable feelings. If by "common interest" we mean a collection of these types of *private benefits,* it is easy to see how they can motivate "group" behavior. Entrepreneurs can emerge to "sell" these types of private benefits as they do in the case of private golf clubs or Weightwatchers. The group action will be then, essentially, a market phenomenon—that is, a problem in simple exchange.

However, the central concern of this theory is a "common interest" which is separate and detached from these types of *private* benefits. The concern is with public benefits which transcend the entire group, which cannot be provided by the market, and which may be obtained only by some form of collective action. That is, a group of people must band together to change things from what they otherwise would be. Examples include the common interest of consumers in general to obtain better, safer products *than the market would provide without collective action;* the interest of labor unions is to secure higher wages and better fringe benefits than could be obtained by the independent actions of laborers; the interest of students is to have better instruction; the interest of faculties is to educate quality graduates. These are examples of the common interest being a *public good.* (As you will recall, a public good was defined in Chapter 2 as a good—or service—the benefits of which are shared by all members of the relevant group if the good is provided or consumed by anyone.)

Small Groups

Small groups are not without their problems in pursuing the "common interest" of their members. They have a problem of becoming organized, holding together, and ensuring that everyone contributes his part to the group's common interest. This point was illustrated in terms of Fred and Harry's problems of setting up a social contract in Chapter 5, and it can be understood in terms of all those little things which we can do with friends and neighbors but which will go undone because of the problems associated with having two or three people come together for the "common good." For example, it may be in the common interest of three neighbors for all to rid their yards of dandelions. If one person does it, and the other two do not, the person who removes the dandelions may find his yard full of them the next year because of seeds coming from the other two yards. Why do we so often find such a small number of neighbors failing to join together to do something like eradicating dandelions?

We can address this question with the use of the *public goods* demand curve developed in Chapter 3. The common interest is dandelion eradication; and two neighbors, Fred and Harry

[9] Olson, *Logic of Collective Action,* p. 2. A number of economists were moving toward the development of Olson's line of analysis, but the force and clarity of Olson's presentation of this view of group behavior make his book an important reference work.

[10] This type of cost-and-benefit analysis has been explicit, if not implicit, in much of the writing of those in support of the "common interest theory of groups" explained above. There would be little reason for talking about a "common interest" if it did not have something to do with benefits of group participation. See, for example, Dorwin Cartwright, "The Nature of Group Cohesiveness," in Dorwin Cartwright and Alvin Zander, eds., *Group Dynamics: Research and Theory,* 3d ed. (New York: Harper & Row, Publishers, 1968), pp. 91–109.

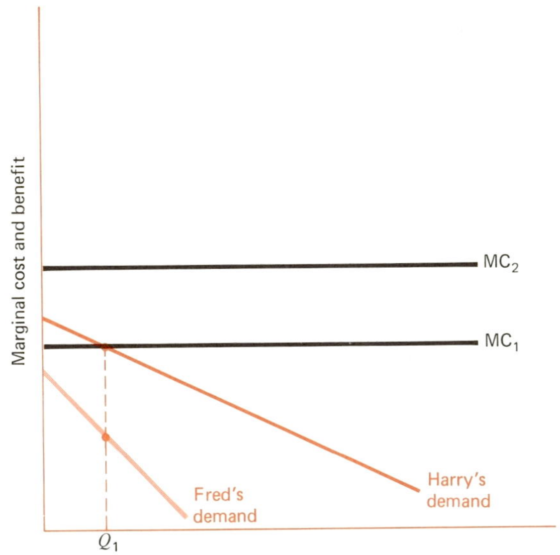

FIG. 6·1 If the marginal cost curve is MC_2, the marginal cost of eliminating even the first dandelion will be too high to take any action at dandelion eradication. However, if the cost were lower, MC_1 instead of MC_2, Harry would be willing to eliminate as many as Q_1 dandelions. Fred would still do nothing.

again, have a demand for this public good.[11] There is no particular reason for us to assume that Fred and Harry have identical demands for this particular public good; consequently, we have drawn Harry's demand for eliminating dandelions in Figure 6·1 greater than Fred's demand.

If we assume, for simplicity only, that the marginal cost of eliminating dandelions is constant, the marginal cost curve will be horizontal. Whether or not either Fred or Harry will individually do anything about his dandelions depends, given their demands, upon the position of the marginal cost curve. If, for example, it is positioned as MC_2 in Figure 6·1, neither Fred nor Harry will be motivated *individually* to do anything about the problem. The marginal cost of eliminating the first dandelion is greater than the benefits that even Harry, who has the greater demand, receives from it. Notice that the marginal cost curve (MC_2) does not intersect either of the demand curves in the graph, meaning that the optimum level of activity for both, *on an individual basis*, is zero. On the other hand, if the marginal cost curve is at MC_1, Fred will still be unwilling to do anything, but Harry will be willing to eliminate, on his own, up to Q_1 dandelions. Fred, however, will benefit from Harry's actions; he will have fewer dandelions in his own yard; he can "free-ride" because of Harry's high demand for dandelion eradication.

Still, the quantity of dandelions eradicated may not be what is socially optimal. Consider Figure 6·2. In that figure we have constructed Fred and Harry's joint, or public good, demand curve. You may remember that this demand curve is obtained by *vertically* summing the demands of the individuals (see Chapter 3). Under individual action, Q_1 dandelions are eradicated by Harry. However, the value which Fred and Harry *collectively* place on the elimination of additional dandelions is greater than the marginal cost. For example, the marginal value of the Q_1th unit to both Fred and Harry combined is MB_1; the marginal cost, MC_1. They can gain by eliminating that dandelion and all others up to Q_3. This is the point where the marginal cost curve and the public good demand curve intersect. By sharing the cost of eliminating the weeds, they can move to Q_3. Harry will not move to that point if he has to pay the full cost for each unit, MC_1, but he will move beyond Q_1 if he can get Fred to take over part of the cost. How they share the cost must, because of the complications involved, be reserved for a later discussion; we need only point out here that there is no reason to believe that an equal sharing of the cost will be the outcome.

Even though Fred and Harry may not ever agree to work out their common problem (or interest) cooperatively, there are several conditions which may lead them to do so. In a small group there is

[11] We realize the imperfections of this example of a public good; much of the benefit of each person's action is private. Only a portion of one neighbor's dandelions may actually affect other people's yards. The example, however, is a reasonably good one for our purposes.

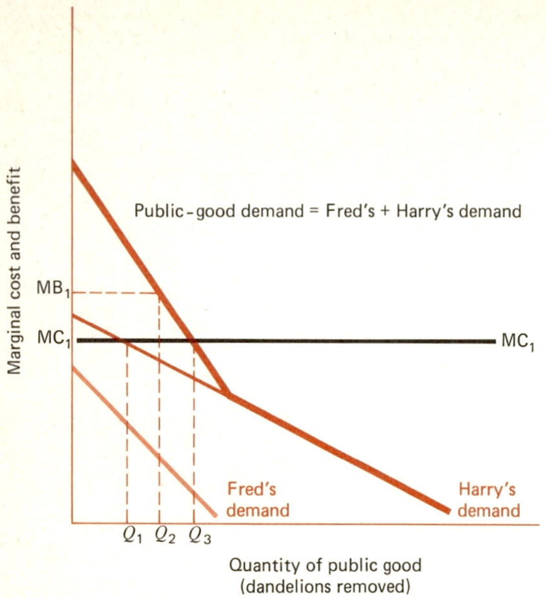

FIG. 6·2 As we studied in Chap. 3, the public good demand curve, which is the darker curve in the figure, is derived by vertically adding the demands of Fred and Harry. Given a marginal cost represented by MC_1, the optimum quantity of dandelions removed is Q_3.

personal contact. Everyone knows everyone else. What benefits or costs there may be from an individual's action are spread over just a few people and, therefore, the effect felt by any one person can be significant. (Fred knows there is a reasonably high probability that what he does to eliminate dandelions from the border of his property affects Harry's welfare.) If the individual providing the public good is concerned about the welfare of those within his group and receives personal satisfaction from knowing that he has in some way helped them, he has an incentive to contribute to the common good; and we *emphasize that before the common good can be realized, individuals must have some motivation for contributing toward it.* Furthermore, "free-riders" are easily detected in a small group. (Harry can tell with relative ease when Fred is not working on, or has not worked on, the dandelions in his yard.) If one person tries to let the others shoulder his share, the absence of his contribution will probably be detected. Others can then bring social pressure to bear to force him to live up to his end of the bargain. The enforcement costs are low because the group is small. There are many ways to let a neighbor know you are displeased with some aspect of his behavior.

Finally, in small groups an individual shirking responsibilities can be excluded from the group if he does not contribute to the common interest and joins the group merely to free-ride on the efforts of others. In larger groups, like nations, exclusion is more difficult and, therefore, more unlikely.

The problem of organizing "group behavior" to serve the common interest has been a problem for almost all groups, even the utopian communities that sprang up during the nineteenth century and in the 1960s. Rosebeth Kanter, in her study of successful nineteenth-century utopian communities concluded:

> The primary issue with which a utopian community must cope in order to have the strength and solidarity to endure is its human organization: how people arrange to do the work that the community needs to survive as a group, and how the group in turn manages to satisfy and involve its members over a long period of time. The idealized version of communal life must be meshed with the reality of the work to be done in the community, involving difficult problems of social organization. In utopia, for instance, who takes out the garbage?[12]

Kanter found that the most successful communities minimized the free-rider problems by restricting entry into the community. They restricted entry by requiring potential members to make commitments to the group, and six "commitment mechanisms" distinguished the successful from the unsuccessful utopias: (1) sacrifice of habits common to the outside world, such as abstinence

[12] Rosebeth M. Kanter, *Commitment and Community: Communes and Utopias in Sociological Perspective* (Cambridge, Mass.: Harvard University Press, 1973), p. 64.

from alcohol and tobacco or, in some cases, celibacy; (2) assignment of all worldly goods to the community; (3) adoption of rules which would minimize the disruptive effects of relationships between members and nonmembers and which would (through, for example, the wearing of uniforms) distinguish members from nonmembers; (4) collective sharing of all property and all communal work; (5) submission to public confession and criticism; and (6) expressed commitment to an identifiable power structure and tradition. Needless to say, the cost implied in these "commitment mechanisms" would tend to discourage many free-riders from joining the society. By identifying the boundaries to societies, these mechanisms made exclusion possible. As Kanter points out, the importance of these commitment mechanisms is illustrated by the fact that their breakdown foreshadowed the end of the community.

Other means of bringing about collective behavior on the part of group members are suggested by the cattlemen's associations formed during the nineteenth century. During the nineteenth century, cattle were allowed to run free over the ranges of the West. The cattlemen had a common interest in ensuring that the ranges were not overstocked and overgrazed and in securing cooperation in rounding up the cattle. To provide for these common interests, cattlemen formed associations which sent out patrols to keep out intruders and which were responsible for the roundups. Any cattleman who failed to contribute his share toward these ends could be excluded from the association, which generally meant that his cattle were excluded from the roundup or were confiscated by the association if they were rounded up.[13]

The family is a small group which by its very nature is designed to promote the common interest of its members. That common interest may be something called "a happy family life," which is, admittedly, difficult to define. The family does not escape difficulties. At present its validity as a viable institution is being challenged by many sources; however, it does have several redeeming features which we think will cause it to endure, imperfect though it may be, as a basic component of social fabric. Because of the smallness of the group, contributions made toward the common interest of the family can be shared and appreciated directly. Parents usually know when their children are failing to take the interest of the family into account, and children can easily ascertain similar behavior in their parents. Family members are able, at least in most cases, to know personally what others in the group like and dislike; they can set up an interpersonal cost-and-benefit structure among themselves which can guide all members toward the common interest. Most collective decisions are also made with relative ease.[14] However, even with all the advantages of close personal contact, the family as a small group often fails to achieve the common interest. Although all family members may be encouraged to "go their own way" up to a point, some individuals may take this too far. They may fail to contribute their share to the common goal and may cause bitterness and, perhaps, the demise of the family. Given the frequent failure of the family as a viable organization with a common interest,[15] the failure of much larger groups to achieve their expressed common objectives is not difficult to understand.

Large Groups

In a large-group setting, the problems of having individual members contribute toward the development of the common interest are potentially much greater. The direct, personal interface

[13] For a very interesting historical investigation of the cattle business during the late nineteenth century, see Rodgers Taylor Dennen, "From Common to Private Property: The Enclosure of the Open Range," Ph.D. dissertation, University of Washington, 1975.

[14] See, for more discussion on the economics of the family, Richard B. McKenzie and Gordon Tullock, "Marriage, Divorce, and the Family," in *The New World of Economics* (Homewood, Ill.: Richard D. Irwin, Inc. 1978), chap. 8.

[15] Approximately one-third of all families based on the institution of marriage end in divorce. Many others fail, in terms of the presence of intense hostility, even though there is no legal recognition of that fact.

which is present in small groups is usually lacking in larger groups; and, by the nature of large groups and the public good they produce, the benefits generated by any one person are generally spread over a large number of people, so much so that individuals may not be able to detect that their actions have a significant effect on anyone, even themselves. As a result, they may perceive neither direct benefits in terms of what their behavior does for themselves, personally, nor indirect benefits in terms of what their behavior contributes to the welfare of others.

On the other hand, an individual may be able to detect benefits from his actions, but he must weigh these benefits against the costs he may have to incur to achieve them. For a large group the costs of providing detectable benefits can be substantial—or they can escalate with the size of the group. This is not only because there are more people to be served by the public good,[16] but also because large groups are normally organized to provide public goods that are rather expensive to begin with. Police protection, national defense, and schools are examples of very costly public goods provided by large groups. If all people contribute to the public good, the cost to any one person can be slight; but the question confronting the individual is how much he will have to contribute to make his actions detectable, *given what all the others do.*

In the context of a *very* large group, suppose there are certain common national objectives to which we can all subscribe, such as a specific charitable program. It is, in other words, in our "common interest" to promote this program. Will people be willing to voluntarily contribute to the federal treasury for the purpose of achieving this goal? Certainly some people will (as Harry does in Figure 6·1 with a marginal cost of MC_2), but many people may not. As they do each April 15 (the deadline for filing tax returns), most will contribute as little income tax as possible. Under a system of voluntary contributions, some people will contribute nothing. A person may reason that although he agrees with the national objective, or common interest, his contribution—that which he can justify—will do little to achieve it. He can also reason that withholding his contribution will have no detectable effect on the scope and effectiveness of the program. (If you or your parents did not pay taxes, would the level of public goods which benefit you be materially affected?) It is for this reason that compulsory taxes are necessary. Olson writes:

> Almost any government is economically beneficial to its citizens, in that the law and order it provides is a prerequisite to all civilized economic activity. But despite the force of patriotism, the appeal of the national ideology, the bond of a common culture, and the indispensability of the system of law and order, no major state in modern history has been able to support itself through voluntary dues or contributions. Philanthropic contributions are not even a significant source of revenues for most countries. Taxes, *compulsory* payments by definition, are needed. Indeed, as the old saying indicates, their necessity is as certain as death itself.[17]

The general tenor of the argument also applies to contributions which go to CARE, a voluntary charitable organization interested mainly in improving the diets of impoverished people around the world. Many of the students reading these pages have been disturbed by scenes of undernourished and malnourished children shown in television commercials for CARE. All those who are disturbed would probably like to see something done for these children. They have had an opportunity to make a contribution, but how many people ever actually contribute so much as a dollar? Needless to say, many do give. They are like Harry in Figure 6·2, who is willing to dig, voluntarily, some of the weeds from his yard. On the

[16] For a pure public good, the costs, by definition, do not rise with a few additional members. However, most groups provide services which are less than a *pure* public good. Education is an example of an impure public good; all education does not benefit all members of society simultaneously and to the same degree. Under these circumstances, the costs can rise, as we have suggested, with the membership, although by a lower percentage.

[17] Olson, *Logic of Collective Action*, p. 13.

other hand, we emphasize the point that a large number of people who have been concerned never make a contribution. (It would be an interesting classroom experiment to see how many students are disturbed by the CARE commercials and how many have ever given to the organization.) There are many reasons for people not giving, and we do not mean to understate the importance of these reasons; we mean only to emphasize that the large-group problem is one significant reason.

True, if all members of a large group make a *small* contribution toward the common interest, whatever it is, there may be sizable benefits to all within the group. But, again, the problem which must be overcome is the potential lack of *individual* incentives from which the collective behavior must emerge. Through appropriate organization of group members, the common interest *may* be achieved, even if the membership is large. This, however, merely shifts our attention to the problem of developing that organization. The organization of a large group can be construed as a public good, and there are likely to be costs to making the organization workable. This is likely for two reasons: first, there are a large number of people to organize, which means that even if there is no resistance on the part of the people to be organized, there will be costs associated with getting them together or having them work at the same time for the same objectives. Second, some individuals may try to "free-ride" on the efforts of others, which means it will cost more to get people to become members of the group. Further, each free-rider implies a greater burden on the active members of the group. If everyone waits for "the other guy to take the initiative," the group may never be organized. It is because of the organization costs that students complain so often about the instructional quality of the faculty or some other aspect of university life without doing anything about it. This is also why most people who are disgruntled with the two major political parties do not form a party with those who share their views. The probability of getting sufficient support is frequently very low, which is another way of saying the expected costs are high.

Because an organization may appear to be an obvious way to promote the public good, individuals who try to organize people for that purpose may go through a learning experience before they conclude that it is too costly a venture for them. Even if the organization is successful, the success may be temporary. Eventually, the free-rider problem emerges and the group may fall apart. During the winter of 1973–74, the United States was in the midst of an "energy crisis." Prices of gasoline and other fuels were being held down in spite of the limited imports of fuel coming into the country from the Mideast. Truckers were having a difficult time obtaining adequate supplies of diesel fuel and of passing their higher operating costs through to the buyers of truck services. Independent truckers sensed that it was in *their common interest* (not the public's, of course) to halt their deliveries of goods and services and, in that way, put pressure on the authorities to increase rates and to allocate more fuel supplies for the use of truckers. The call for cooperation met with some success; some truckers did terminate operations and some caught headlines by blocking traffic on major highways. However, there were many unwilling to go along with the work stoppage—something that was in their *common* interest. Consequently, the supporters of the work stoppage resorted to violence, and it was the threat of violence, and not the common interest, which kept many truckers off the road. If it had not been for the violence and the initial willingness of state police departments to allow truckers to flaunt the law by stopping traffic, including other truckers, it is very doubtful that the truckers would have had as much success as they did.

Qualifications to the Economic Theory

Obviously, there are many cases in which people acting in what may appear to be rather large groups try to accomplish things which are in the common interest of the membership. The League of Women Voters during the mid-1970s pushed hard for passage of the Equal Rights Amendment to the Constitution; labor unions work for wage increases; and the American Medical Association does lobby for legislation which is in the common interest of a large number of doctors. Churches, the Blood Mobile, and other charitable groups are able to work fairly effectively for the "public interest," and several of the possible explanations for this observed behavior force us to step outside the scope of the public goods theory.

Why may people work for the "public interest"? First, as Immanuel Kant, an eighteenth century philosopher, said they should, people can place value on the *act* itself as distinquished from the results or consequences of the act. The *act* of making a charitable contribution, which can be broadly defined to include picking up trash in public areas or holding the door for someone with an armful of packages, may have a value in and of itself. This is true whether the effects of the act are detectable to the individual making the charitable contribution or not. The personal satisfaction (or value) which comes from the act itself is probably the dominant reason why some people do give to CARE. To the extent people behave in this way, the public good theory loses force. Notice, however, that Olson, in formulating his argument, focused on *rational economic man* as opposed to moral man, envisioned by Kant. We expect that as the group becomes larger, greater effort will be made to instill people with the belief that the *act* itself is important.

Second, the contribution which a person has to make in group settings is often so slight that even though the private benefits are small, the contribution to the common interest is also small and can be a rational policy course. This may explain, for example, student membership in groups like the National Association of Student Teachers. All one has to do in many situations like this one is show up at an occasional meeting and make a small dues payment. Further, the private benefits of being with others at the meetings and finding out what the plans are for the association can be sufficient incentive to motivate limited action that is in the common interest.

Third, the benefits received by group members from promotion of the common interest may not be equally shared by all. One or more persons may receive a sizable portion of the total benefits and, accordingly, be willing to provide the public good, at least up to some limit. Many businessmen are willing to participate in local politics or to support advertising campaigns to promote their community as a recreational area. Although a restaurant owner may believe the entire community will benefit economically from an influx of tourists, he is surely aware that a share of these benefits will accrue to himself. Businessmen may also support such community efforts because of implied threats of being socially ostracized.

Fourth, large organizations can be broken down into smaller groups. Because of the personal contact within the smaller units, the common interest of the unit can be realized. In promoting the interest of the small unit to which they belong, people can promote the common interest of the large group. The League of Women Voters is broken down into small community clubs which promote interests common to other League clubs around the country. The Lions Club collectively promotes programs to prevent blindness and to help the blind; they do this through a highly decentralized organizational structure. Political parties are structured in such a way that the local precinct units "get out the votes." The surest way for a presidential contender to lose an election is to fail to have a "grass-roots" (meaning small-group) organization. Churches are organized into congregations, and each congregation is decentralized further into circles and fellowship groups. Most of the work in the Congress is done in committees and subcommittees. Quite often a multiplicity of small groups is actually responsible for what may appear to be the activity of a large group. The decentralization which is so prevalent among voluntary groups tends to support the economic view of groups.[18]

[18] Admittedly, other explanations for decentralization can be made, one of which relates to *diseconomies of scale*. That is, the organization just becomes technically less efficient as its size is expanded. The economic theory of groups rests on the motivational aspect of large organizations, rather than on the technical *capabilities* of the organization.

Fifth, large groups may be viable because the group organizers sell their members a service and use the profits for sales to promote projects that are in the common interest of the group. The Sierra Club, which is in the forefront of the environmental movement, is a rather large group which has members in every part of North America. The group receives voluntary contributions from members and nonmembers alike to research and lobby for environmental issues. However, it also sells a number of publications and offers a variety of environmentally related tours for its members. From these activities, it secures substantial resources to promote the common interest of its membership. The American Economics Association has several thousand members. However, most economists do not belong to the AEA for what they can do for it. They join primarily to receive its journal and to be able to tell others that they belong—both, private benefits. (The AEA also provides economists with information on employment opportunities.)

Sixth, the basic argument for any group is that people can accomplish more through groups than they can through independent action. This means that there are potential benefits to be reaped (or, as some may say, "skimmed off") by anyone who is willing to bear the cost of developing and maintaining the organization. A business firm is fundamentally a *group* of workers and stockholders interested in producing a good (a public good, to them). They have a common interest in seeing a good produced which will sell. The entrepreneur is essentially a person who organizes a group of people into a production unit; he overcomes all the problems associated with trying to get a large number of people to work in their common interest by providing workers with private benefits—that is, pays them for their contribution to the production of the good. The entrepreneur-manager can be viewed as a person who is responsible for reducing any tendency of workers to avoid their responsibilities to the large-group firm. Because it is in their interest to eliminate shirking, the workers may be just as interested as stockholders in having and paying someone to perform this task.[19] An individual worker may be delighted if he is allowed to remain idle while no one else is, but he will want to avoid the risks of all workers shirking. If all shirk, nothing will be sold, the firm will collapse, and workers will lose their wages. We may, therefore, expect that even in communist societies, managers will be paid handsomely (relatively speaking) for the tasks they perform. It is interesting to note that the wage differential between workers and managers is greater in the Soviet Union than it is in the United States.[20]

[19] These points have been made in a much more complete and technical manner by Armen A. Alchian and Harold Demsetz, "Production, Information Costs, and Economic Organization," *American Economic Review*, vol. 62, pp. 777–795, December 1972.

[20] Some managers in the Soviet Union are paid less than industrial workers in the United States; however, the ratio of a manager's salary to a worker's salary is typically greater in the Soviet Union.

SUMMARY AND EXTENSIONS

Economists recognize that such considerations as the "importance of the cause" can significantly affect the willingness of the group members to cohere and pursue the common interest of the membership. However, we have concentrated on "large" and "small" groups to demonstrate that, given other factors, an increase in group size beyond some point can have an adverse effect on the motivation which group members have to pursue their common interest. There is, furthermore, substantial evidence to support this basic conclusion. Several studies have revealed that as far as being able to take action, smaller groups, generally with less than seven or eight members, are more efficient than larger ones.[21] Studies also show that as group size within industry increases, job satisfaction tends to decrease and absentee rates, turnover rates, and the incidence of labor disputes tend to increase.[22]

As Mancur Olson points out, even students of history have noticed a difference in the ability of large and small groups to cohere and survive. Olson provides us with this quote from a book by George Homans:

> At the level of . . . the small group, at the level, that is, of a social unit (no matter by what name we call it) each of whose members can have some first-hand knowledge of each of the others, human society, for many millennia longer than written history, has been able to cohere. . . . They have tended to produce a surplus of the goods that make organization successful.
>
> . . . ancient Egypt and Mesopotamia were civilizations. So were classical India and China; so was Greco-Roman civilization, and so is our own Eastern civilization that grew out of medieval Christendom. . . .
>
> The appalling fact is that, after flourishing for a span of time, every civilization but one has collapsed . . . formal organizations that articulated the whole have fallen to pieces . . . much of the technology has even been forgotten for lack of the large scale cooperation that could put it in effect . . . the civilization has slowly sunk to a Dark Age, a situation, much like the one from which it started on its upward path, in which the mutual hostility of small groups is the condition of internal cohesion of each one. . . . Society can fall thus far, but apparently no farther. . . . One can read the dismal story eloquently told, in the historians of civilization from Spengler to Toynbee. The one civilization that has not entirely gone to pieces is our Western Civilization, and we are desperately anxious about it.
>
> But at the level of the tribe or group society has always found itself able to cohere.[23]

With a reasonable degree of clarity both the theory and the evidence suggest that if society wishes to pursue some interest which is common to people on a very broad scale, some means other than voluntary group cooperation must be found. It is for this reason we begin in Chapter 7 a study of the market and government as social organizers.

[21] See, for example, A. Paul Hare, "A Study of Interaction and Consensus in Different-Sized Groups," *American Sociological Review*, vol. 17, pp. 261–268, June 1952; and John James, "A Preliminary Study of the Size Determinants in Small-Group Interaction," *American Sociological Review*, vol. 16, pp. 444–474, August 1951.

[22] L. W. Porter and E. E. Lawler, "Properties of Organization Structure in Relation to Job Attitudes and Job Behavior," *Psychological Bulletin*, 1965, pp. 23–51.

[23] George C. Homans, *The Human Group* (New York: Harcourt, Brace, Inc., 1950), pp. 454–456, as cited in Olson, *Logic of Collective Action*, p. 56.

QUESTIONS TO PONDER

1 Explain why the "free-rider" problem is likely to be greater in a "large" group than in a "small" group.

2 Discuss the economic value of student government and the faculty senate on your campus. Why do these organizations exist and continue to function? Explain in terms of the analysis of this chapter.

3 The common interest of people who are in a burning theater is to walk out orderly and in other ways avoid a panic. However, why do people so frequently panic in such situations?

4 Relating to Figure 6-2, we wrote that Harry is unwilling to eliminate more than Q_1 dandelions and that Fred must bear a portion of the cost of eradicating dandelions if more than Q_1 dandelions are to be eradicated. Can you explain these statements in terms of the graph?

5 Discuss the costs of making *collective* decisions in large and small groups. What do these costs have to do with the viability of the large and small groups?

6 Intelligent *collective* decisions can be a common interest shared by members of a large group. Does the analysis of this chapter suggest anything about the incentive which individuals have to obtain information or about the intelligence of decisions which a large group will make?

7 In what ways does the market overcome the problems discussed in this chapter relating to large groups?

8 You may have a class in which the professor grades according to a curve, whereby he adjusts his grading scale to fit the test results. This may also be a class in which everyone in it would prefer not to learn as much as they will. If you are in such a situation (or can imagine one like it), the "common interest" of the class members can be for everyone to study less. The same grading distribution can be obtained, and everyone can receive his same relative grade for less effort. Why do class members not collude and restrict the amount of studying they do?

RECOMMENDED READINGS

McKean, Roland N.: "Collective Choice," and James W. McKie, "Changing Views," in James W. McKie, ed., *Social Responsibility and the Business Predicament* (Washington: The Brookings Institution, 1974), pp. 109–134 and 17–40, respectively.

McKenzie, Richard B., and Gordon Tullock: *The New World of Economics* (Homewood, Ill.: Richard D. Irwin, Inc., 1978, chaps. 8, 18, and 21.

Olson, Mancur: *The Logic of Collective Action: Public Goods and the Theory of Groups* (Cambridge, Mass.: Harvard University Press, 1971), chaps. 1–3. This is a most important work in the economic analysis of group behavior.

Part Three
Social Order and the Market for Goods and Services

Economists understand by the term *Market*, not any particular market place in which things are bought and sold, but the whole region in which buyers and sellers are in such free intercourse with one another that the prices of the same goods tend to equality easily and quickly.
Augustin Cournot
(1801–1877)

In this section, the scope of our analysis expands once again to include the *market*. We begin our discussion in Chapter 7 with a review of the historical case for the free competitive market. We then demonstrate how market supply and demand curves can be used to explain price competition among market participants and the efficiency of the competitive market process. In Chapter 8 we reinforce the basic principles developed in the first chapter of this section by applying the supply-and-demand-curve analysis to several real-world problems. Chapter 9 contains an extended discussion of how competition affects our food markets and of how government agriculture policies, while directed at helping farmers, have contributed to inefficiency in our food markets. In Chapter 10 we evaluate the extent to which monopoly power in markets reduces people's welfare.

7

The Competitive Market: Many Buyers and Many Sellers

. . . By directing that industry in such a manner as its produce may be of greatest value, he [the self-interested person] intends only his own gain, and he is in this . . . led by an invisible hand to promote an end which was no part of his intention. Nor is it always the worse for the society that it was no part of it. By pursuing his own interest he frequently promotes that of the society more effectually than when he really intends to promote it.

Adam Smith[1]

PREVIEW OF CHAPTER

Central question

How does the competitive market work?

Major objectives

1 To present the historical case for free competitive markets by reviewing the arguments of Adam Smith
2 To develop the concept of the competitive market as a *process* by which people freely interact to obtain what they want
3 To distinguish between price and nonprice competition and to show how market supply and demand curves can be used to explain how competitive markets work

[1] Adam Smith, *An Inquiry into the Nature and Causes of the Wealth of Nations.*

4 To show how competition coordinates the behavior of buyers and sellers by pushing the market price toward what is called the *equilibrium price*
5 To show how and in what sense price and nonprice competition can be beneficial to people
6 To outline several qualifications to the argument for free competitive markets

Major conclusions

1 The competitive market can best be defined as a process by which buyers and sellers, in an attempt to pursue their own interests, try to outdo, outwit, outdistance, or outmaneuver other people. In the process, market rivals are induced to reveal what, at the limit, they are willing to do, not just what they would like to do under the circumstances.
2 Price competition among producers will push the market price and quantity toward the intersection of the market supply and demand curves, called the *equilibrium.*
3 *Market surpluses* can occur only if the market price is above the equilibrium price, and *market shortages* can occur only if the price is below the equilibrium price.
4 To the extent that the market price and quantity move toward the equilibrium price and quantity, the market is said to be efficient.
5 To the extent that people differ as to the types of goods and services they want, nonprice competition will lead to a greater variety of goods and an increase in the benefits which people receive from the market.

Important terms and concepts

Market	Equilibrium
Competition	Equilibrium price
Market surplus	Equilibrium quantity
Market shortage	Perfect competition

The potential for conflict is all about us. This is because our spheres of interests compete; that is, many of us want the same thing. Voluntary-group associations and the acceptance of behavioral rules are means of moderating the potential for conflict as well as of securing common objectives of group members. However, in the last chapter we listed the limitations of groups as social organizers. This chapter initiates an investigation of the market as a means of extending social order beyond that which can be achieved through voluntary-group associations. The market is not viewed as a substitute for voluntary groups, although the market probably does reduce the need for many group associations. Rather, the market and voluntary groups are viewed as complementary components of a larger social organization, like a country, each component accomplishing what the other cannot accomplish at all or cannot accomplish except at a higher cost. One interest which almost everyone has in common is improvement of their own and the general welfare; the market is seen by its proponents as a system which provides members of a large community with private incentives to pursue this common goal of welfare improvement.

Because the ability of the market to contribute to social welfare is a focal point of many legislative proposals, like price controls and consumer protection measures, we will turn our attention to the efficiency of the market and to the effects of government policy on that efficiency. We do this simply because the effectiveness of an unfettered market in improving welfare must be examined in light of governmental efforts to improve upon the outcome of a free market. As we will see, there are many instances in which government intervention in the market can clearly contribute to an improvement in the welfare of the people; there will be other instances in which government intervention in the market will have distributional effects—some winners and some gainers. In other words, in some instances there will be no clear improvement in social welfare, just a redistribution of it. For now, before we can broach these subjects, we need to lay the groundwork.

THE INVISIBLE HAND OF THE MARKET

Adam Smith wrote in *The Wealth of Nations*, "It is not from the benevolence of the butcher, the brewer, or the baker, that we expect our dinner, but from their regard to their own interest. We address ourselves, not to their humanity but to their self-love, and never talk to them of our own necessities but of their advantages."[2] Taken out of context, as it so often is, this passage may convey a very cynical, harsh, and narrow view of human behavior. However, in context, the statement may sound more reasonable. Smith was trying to make the point that in most advanced societies each individual cannot rely on the benevolence (or altruism) of others for all the things he wants. People are charitable—at least, most people are—but, by the same token, most people have limits to their charity. And, as Smith wrote, the individual "at all times stands in need of the cooperation and assistance of great multitudes [of people], while his whole life is scarce sufficient to gain the friendship of a few persons."[3] Through friendship and altruism, man can enlist the cooperation of a few, but "he will more likely prevail if he can interest their self-love in his favor, and show them that it is for their own advantage to do what he requires of them."[4]

In other words, as early as 1776 Smith made the main point of our discussion of large and small groups. In Chapter 6 we emphasized that voluntary collective action may develop quite effectively within the confines of small groups, where individuals know one another and their contributions to the common goals of the group can be quite significant. However, within very large groups, voluntary collective action will often remain a latent force. Smith saw the market as a means of enlisting the cooperation of those with whom one may otherwise have little contact. "Give me what I want and I will give you what you want" is the type of proposition which Smith saw, and present-day supporters of the market system see, at the bottom of each and every market transaction. The butcher, brewer, and baker were people whom the person fixing the dinner may not have known, yet their cooperation is obtained in the joint task of putting the dinner on the table. By pursuing their own interests, the butcher, brewer, and baker also provided meat, wine, and bread for the benefit of others.

Smith's views stood in opposition to views prevalent during the 250 years prior to the 1776 publication of *The Wealth of Nations*. For this reason alone his work takes on considerable significance. Then, as now, the belief was common that in a market exchange one party must gain at the expense of the other. Smith argued the contrary. If both parties enter into an exchange *voluntarily*, and if each gives up something of value for something else of value, both parties benefit. They may not be as well off as they would like, but their welfare can be improved by the transaction. Furthermore, if people see a potential for exchanges, they can specialize, production can rise, and all can share in the benefits of specialization. Through trade, people can obtain those things they want but do not produce themselves.

Another clearly related view prevalent during

[2] *An Inquiry into the Nature and Causes of the Wealth of Nations* (New York: Random House, Inc., The Modern Library ed., 1937), p. 14.

[3] Ibid.

[4] Ibid.

Smith's time was that only disorder can be expected to arise out of a decentralized, individualistic economy in which private interests are allowed to run headlong after their own ends. The idea that order required detailed guidance from a centralized governmental authority was a focal point of the Mercantilists' position and was responsible for the presence, in the seventeenth and eighteenth centuries, of wage, price, and interest rate controls, controls on foreign trade, regulations concerning the quality of goods and services bought and sold, licensing of labor, and many other controls. The Mercantilists did not see the market as a viable controlling force on producer behavior. They saw centralized control of the economy as a means of ensuring that the ruling class's vision of social justice entered into the determination of what is produced and how it is produced and distributed. They were very skeptical that the "invisible hand of the market" could satisfactorily deal with such complex issues.

To Smith, self-interest is far from being destructive of the "social good." It is a constructive, coordinating force rather than a divisive one. The drive of the individual to seek fulfillment of his own needs means he must appeal to the interests of others; he must offer them something they want. Therefore, people have an incentive to cooperate with others and to coordinate their activities. Profit—that portion of business receipts in excess of costs—represents the incentive the entrepreneur needs to direct his production in accordance with the interests of others. To Smith and those who agree with him, profit is a necessary stimulus. To many opponents of the market system, on the other hand, it is a surplus siphoned off by entrepreneurs, an unnecessary drain on labor earnings.

In Smith's system, competition is the regulating force which keeps profit and any other form of market abuse to a minimum and pushes production toward, but not necessarily to, the lowest possible cost level. If unusually high profits are realized in one industry, self-interest will lead others to enter that industry; production of the good will tend to increase; the price of the good and the profit made on it will tend to fall. Consumers get more of what they want at a lower price. In this way, the drive of self-interest acts like an "invisible hand," guiding social order to an accumulation of improvements in social welfare. Such improvements were, to Smith, in the common interest of all people. The market enabled the participants to achieve this objective, something which could not be accomplished on as large a scale through voluntary collective action. Before closing the discussion of the market, we will deal with the objections to this argument.

In Adam Smith's blueprint for social order, government was necessary, but only for the limited purposes of providing for (1) the national defense, (2) the administration of laws and justice, and (3) certain "public works" such as roads and education, which benefit all within the community, which tend to facilitate the operation of the market, and which cannot be provided profitably by normal market processes.

Smith and those who have followed in his intellectual footsteps tend to object to further intrusions by government in the market for three basic reasons. First, government intervention can mean government coercion; the will of the majority can substitute for the choices of individuals, with no clear improvement in social welfare, or, at best, with only a shift of welfare from one group of people to another. Government coercion also runs counter to the dictates of individualism, which is at the foundation of Smith's system of political economy and which underpins most modern arguments in support of a free market. To Smith and others of his day, *individual choices are important,* in and of themselves; and in order to ensure that people make "good" choices, all must be held responsible for their choices. If individuals are deemed incapable of making reasonably good choices for themselves, much of the argument for the free, unobstructed market loses its force. It is therefore no surprise that we frequently find that the ability of consumers to make reasonably good choices in the marketplace is an issue of legislation designed to protect consumers in such areas as medicine, insurance, and foodstuffs. The question which Smith and his followers may ask is whether or not politicians and government employees can make choices for others which are any more reasonable.

Second, any restriction on the market can disrupt mutually beneficial trades, thus reducing the potential welfare of traders. The imposition of tariffs on imports is a reasonably good example. Such tariffs increase the price of imports and encourage consumers to look for domestic substances which are more costly to produce. Whenever anything is more costly, more resources are used and more in the way of other goods and services must be given up, implying a reduction in welfare.

Third, Smith felt that businessmen would, if given the opportunity, exploit any opportunity which the government is given to manipulate the economy. In short, businessmen would use government powers to further their own private interests. Smith once wrote, "The proposal of any new law or regulations of commerce which comes from this order [of entrepreneurs], ought always to be listened to with great precaution, and ought never to be adopted till after having been long and carefully examined . . . with the most suspicious attention. It comes from an order of men, whose interest is never exactly the same with that of the public, who have generally an interest to deceive and even to oppress the public and who accordingly have, upon occasions, both deceived and oppressed it."[5]

Although he may never have used the word, Adam Smith was well aware of "imperfections" in the market system. He did not see the market as the be-all and end-all to all people. He recognized the potential consequences of monopoly power, which, as he saw it, was primarily fostered by government, and he was opposed to monopoly power of any kind. He is often cited for having observed that businessmen seldom come together except to conspire against the public, meaning that businessmen attempt to restrict trade in ways that suit their personal interests. Competition will not eliminate this tendency; it will only minimize it. Smith recognized the slowness with which the market often adjusts to changes in social conditions and that the market may fail to produce certain goods in adequate quantities without government encouragement.

The case for the market system which Smith constructed did not prove that it is a perfect system or that its flaws are of no consequence. Rather, the case which he attempted to make is that the market system is "better" within very broad boundaries than the alternatives, which, as he saw it, are also flawed. As we pointed out at the start of the book, the efficiency or desirability of any system must be judged in terms of its alternatives, not just against some ideal which may be constructed for purposes of theoretical inquiry.

[5] Smith, *The Wealth of Nations,* p. 250.

THE MEANING OF THE COMPETITIVE MARKET PROCESS

Our discussion of Adam Smith and the market has been quite general. The very briefness of that discussion should reveal that our treatment of the market has not been exhaustive, nor was it meant to be. However, in that opening section we were able to introduce the major arguments which have historically been offered in support of a free competitive market; and, in that way, we have set the stage for a more in-depth study. In this section we add precision to our understanding of the market by first defining what we mean by the *market,* or more properly, the *market process,* and what we mean by *competition.* In later sections we advance the discussion by describing the central tendency of the market process and by indicating in what (limited) sense that process can be considered "efficient." First, the definitions.

The Meaning of the Market

Those unfamiliar with economics think of the market as a geographical location, such as a shopping center, an auction barn, or the business district of their home town. This view of the market is perfectly valid; however, because we wish to direct attention to human behavior in a social context, we prefer to define the market as a process:

The market is a process by which buyers and sellers interact for the purpose of obtaining information about what they are willing to buy and sell and for determining the terms of trade, that is, the prices of goods and the amounts to be bought and sold.

It is a process by which the market participants search for information which is relevant to their own interests. Buyers search for information on the variety of available goods and on the prices which they must pay—they look for information on the seller's supply curves and on the demand curves of other consumers. Sellers, on the other hand, search for information on what types of goods and services buyers want and the prices that buyers are willing to pay for them—they look for information on the buyers' demand curves and on the supply curves of the other sellers. Further, the market is the process by which buyers and sellers deduce courses of actions they should take in buying and selling, and it is the process by which buyers and sellers revise their plans on the basis of whether or not past plans were realized. As Israel Kirzner has written:

> The overambitious plans of one period will be replaced by more realistic ones; market opportunities overlooked in one period will be exploited in the next. In other words, even without changes in the basic data of the market (i.e., in consumer tastes, technological possibilities, and resource availabilities), the decisions made in one period of time generate systematic alterations in corresponding decisions for the succeeding period. Taken over time, this series of systematic changes in the interconnected network of market decisions constitutes the market process.[6]

In a few words, the market is made up of people, consumers and entrepreneurs, who have definite goals to buy and sell on the best terms possible. It is through the groping process of give-and-take that the market participants move from a state of relative ignorance about what other participants want or are willing to do toward some rationally determined level of understanding about how much can be bought and sold and at what prices. In still fewer words, the market is an ongoing informational system and exchange mechanism.

The Meaning of Competition

The concept of competition cannot be fully separated from the concept of the market because, in the economist's way of thinking, they are part and parcel of the same process. By defining competition as we do here, we are merely expanding our understanding of what we mean by the market, or, rather, the *competitive market process.*

Competition is the market process by which participants, in trying to pursue their own interests, attempt to outdo, outdistance, or outmaneuver other participants.

It is also the process by which participants attempt to avoid being outdone, outdistanced, or outmaneuvered by other participants.

Competition does not occur *between* buyers and sellers, but among buyers or among sellers. Buyers compete in the sense that they attempt to outdistance other buyers. Competition requires that buyers become aware of what other buyers are doing and that they offer better terms to the seller, a higher price for the same product, or accept a lower-quality product for the same price. Sellers compete with other sellers by trying to outdistance them. To compete, they must acquire information on what their rivals are doing and make a conscious attempt to do something different or better: to sell at a lower price, to improve the quality of their product, or to enhance the product's appeal to the public. Competition is essentially the fuel which runs the market process as an informational system; it forces participants to reveal what they are willing to do and to accept deals which are less desirable than those that could have been had in the absence of competition. For this reason alone, market rivals have an interest in controlling competitive forces. As an informational system, Friedrich Hayek, a Nobel laureate in economics, has stated the function of competi-

[6] Israel M. Kirzner, *Competition and Entrepreneurship* (Chicago: University of Chicago Press, 1973), p. 10.

tion in a slightly different dimension of the competitive process:

The function of competition is here precisely to teach us *who* will serve us well: which grocer or travel agency, which department store or hotel, which doctor or solicitor, we can expect to provide the most satisfactory solution for whatever particular personal problem we may have to face.[7]

The meaning of competition among buyers is clearly revealed at auctions. Before the sale begins, buyers can be observed looking over the merchandise that will be sold; they can also be observed looking at each other in an attempt to assess the "market demand" for various goods and the price that may have to be paid. During the auction, very specific information is revealed as each buyer calls out the price he will pay and as others try to top it. Typically in department stores, there is very little that buyers can do, by themselves, to affect the price the store charges. Competition is often restricted; however, there are means by which they can compete. Buyers can compete by looking for sellers who are willing to sell at lower prices or by trying to get to the scene of sales before others do.

Competition among sellers has been revealed in the behavior of hand calculator producers over the past decade. We will have more to say on the subject in a few pages; for now, we merely note that hand calculators were first offered in the United States at very high prices and with limited capabilities. As information spread on the prices that were initially charged, the costs and technology of production, and the potential profits to be made, different producers made offers to consumers for lower-priced and higher-quality calculators. In the many ways that are illustrated by the variety of styles and prices of hand calculators presently available, sellers have tried to outdistance and outmaneuver their rivals. We stress, however, that what we observe in the hand calculator business today is not competition; rather, it is the *competitive outcome,* the result of the give-and-take process described above. In short, competition is a process and not a situation.

The competitive process is also evident in areas of social behavior which are normally thought to be outside the study of economics. Children are said to "compete" for the attention of their parents; and men and women are often said to "compete" for the affection of the opposite sex. Considering the nature of competition in these nonbusiness areas of social behavior may add "fullness" to the meaning of the term. An example which is not strictly comparable to competition in the hand calculator business but which may be familiar to students is competition for grades among students. This reveals the nature of the competitive predicament and the problems inherent in attempts to control competitive forces.

Whether you recognize it or not, if you are in a reasonably large class, say larger than 30 students, you are probably in a competitive classroom environment. We say "probably" because you may not be in a competitive environment; you may be in a class in which the professor intends to give all A's, in which case there is no reason for you to "outmaneuver" your classmates (through studying or other means) in order to obtain one of the limited number of high grades. Normally, you are competing for grades and, possibly, recognition, because the number of very high grades is typically limited.

In class you are, in a sense, producing something: understanding (or the appearance of understanding) of the subject matter. Through your performance on a test, you are producing evidence of the level of your understanding in exchange for a given grade and any recognition or further reward that may go with it. How much you learn is, without question, a function of your desire to learn and the standards of the professor; however, to the extent that the standards of the professor are related to the performance of class members, the amount you learn is dependent upon the competitive behavior of class members—how much they are willing to study to "outwit" you on examinations and to avoid your "outwitting" them. Accordingly, you probably spend some

[7] Friedrich A. Hayek, "The Meaning of Competition, "in *Individualism and Economic Order* (Chicago: The University of Chicago Press, 1948), p. 97.

time before and after class trying to figure out how hard your classmates are working.

To establish with some degree of clarity your and other students' position as "classroom competitors," let us focus on student behavior with regard to the final examination for a course for which the professor grades on a curve. If students can assume that, regardless of their overall performance on the exam, the grade distribution will be approximately the same after the final exam as it was before, they can reason that all students should study less. This conclusion is particularly relevant for required courses which students are taking merely for credit hours. Why wouldn't students in such a course readily agree to reduce, by collective action, their studying time? Why should all students work hard if to do so will not change their relative class standing?

However, great difficulties (costs) need to be surmounted before the students can agree to collude. These costs may be extensive or even prohibitive, particularly since some may consider a collective move to restrict studying to be unethical. One has to persuade these students to go along, adding a time cost. Furthermore, each student may fear that some other student or students will chisel on any agreement which is reached. As opposed to reducing their studying time, they may maintain their old studying habits or even increase their study time. If they do, they can benefit by moving up in the grade distribution. Fearing that others may chisel on any agreement which may be reached, you may chisel in order to prevent your relative class standing from falling.[8] With students scattered over several dormitories and apartment complexes, the extensive costs of enforcing the agreement can mean no enforcement; and without assurance of enforcement, it is unlikely that students will be willing to run the risks involved. Note that the costs of developing the agreement and enforcing it can escalate with the size of the class. From this we may deduce that the larger the class, the less likely the students are to reach an agreement, the more likely they will "compete," and the more likely they will wind up studying as if no agreement had ever been considered.

These conclusions will probably hold even if the professor gives his or her students time in class to develop the agreement and sanctions their attempts to collude. One of the authors has tested these hypotheses in class, and, as was expected, students in large classes (those of about 40) took only a few minutes to determine that their efforts would be futile. They reasoned that they would incur more costs trying to reach and enforce the agreement than they would incur by studying for the examination.

Obviously, there are some small classes in which collusion may be effective. A class of two need spend few resources coming to an agreement to collude. If need be, they can enforce the agreement by following each other around between the time of the agreement and the time of the test. For even a slightly larger group, however, enforcement costs may be too great. In another test of the hypothesis, a class of 10 students was given the opportunity to either skip the examination as a group or take the exam. All were completely satisfied with their grades, and all wanted to minimize their studying time. They were told, however, that they could raise their grades by taking the exam. The students began their attempts to collude confident that they would reach an agreement; but after 15 minutes of talking among themselves on the first day, they gave up, unable to trust their fellow students. The next class period, they tried again. This time they all signed a hastily drawn contract. The agreement lasted for several days, but it eventually broke down as students began acting independently of each other—competing. The enforcement costs had become too high.

This type of competitive behavior is endemic in large groups; in fact, an analysis of competitive markets is largely an extension of the theory of group behavior which was developed in Chapter 6. However, although large groups' size may be a *sufficient* condition for competitive behavior, it is not a *necessary* condition. The necessary condition is the presence of prohibitively high agreement and enforcement costs; large numbers imply high costs of this nature. However, freedom

[8] If each student fears that everyone else will chisel, a breakdown of the agreement is assured.

of entry, by which is meant the capacity of people to compete, to try to outdo rivals, also increases enforcement costs. Persons interested in thwarting competitive behavior must gain the cooperation not only of persons in the market but also that of all those potential unknown competitors who will enter the market if profitable opportunities are left unexploited. Freedom of entry, therefore, significantly dictates how willing competitors will be to direct their energies toward outdistancing one another rather than toward trying to thwart competitive behavior.

The Dimensions of Competition

Competition among market rivals occurs in numerous dimensions of product development and marketing: these include price, quality, weight, volume, color, texture, power, durability, smell, and credit terms. Market participants can also outmaneuver their rivals by appealing to the basic human drives of hunger and sex and to people's fears of death, falling, and loud noises. The task of competitors is to search through all these dimensions and to find profitable opportunities to exploit; their task is complicated by the fact that the dimensions of competition change over time with changes in market technologies and preferences of consumers and producers.

Be that as it is, economists categorize the many dimensions of competition into two categories, price and nonprice competition, the latter being a very broad category which includes all dimensions other than price. As can be seen by the contents of this book, economists have historically been much more concerned with price competition than with nonprice competition. The reason is that economists have primarily been interested in explaining how price, as an important information source for market participants, acts as a coordinating force and brings the amount produced into line with the amount consumers are willing to buy. Further, a full understanding of the pricing mechanism will enable us to analyze the effect of any market or government efforts to control price.

In the next section we construct a basic supply and demand curve model of the market. We will use that model to explore the central tendency of price competition; nonprice competition is considered in a later section. The market process takes place in a variety of competitive conditions, called *market structures* by economists. We start the discussion in this chapter by hypothesizing the most competitive market condition (or structure) that we can conceive, referring to it as *perfect competition*. Our purpose is to describe the absolute limit of the competitive market process. We stress that we are talking only about the theoretical *limit*, and not what may actually emerge in the real and imperfect world in which market participants must literally grope their way through a complex maze of information and obstacles. These imperfections in the market will retard the advance of the market toward its limit. However, by establishing what the limit is, we at least have some indication of the directional movement of the market, given market conditions. We also have some indication of how the directional movement will change when changes in market conditions occur. In a later chapter (Chapter 10), we consider the other limit, a market that has been fully "monopolized"—that is, a market in which all competitive behavior has been eliminated. Our purpose is to establish the extreme boundaries within which various degrees of competitive behavior occur. Within these boundaries, we may not be able to predict precisely what the price or market production level will be. However, establishing boundaries improves our ability to assess the *relative* efficiency of the market as a social organizer: "It ain't much, but at least it's something" is the only credible defense we can offer for asking you to read the next few chapters.

SUPPLY, DEMAND, AND PRICE COMPETITION

A fully competitive market must be composed of many buyers and sellers who are either in the market searching out beneficial opportunities or ready and willing to enter the market when beneficial opportunities are observed. In other words, either "actual competitors" (those already in the market) or "potential competitors" (those who stand ready to enter the market) must exist in order for the market to be described as competitive. A fully competitive market offers "freedom of entry," which means that two or more people must be able to enter the market.

To see the limit to which price competition will go in a *given* market for a *given* good, let us assume a market where *perfect competition* exists.

By definition, this requires complete freedom of entry into and exit from the market; anyone can enter the market and duplicate the standardized good produced in search of profitable opportunities to exploit; anyone can try to outdistance or outdo his rivals in search of those opportunities. Furthermore, each competitor produces such a small share of the total industry output that he cannot significantly influence the market price by either expanding or contracting his production level: the individual competitor is, in essence, the proverbial drop in the bucket.

This market setting can be described and analyzed in many different ways; however, economists have found *market supply* (developed in Chapter 4) and *market demand* (developed in Chapter 3) curves very useful in depicting the limit toward which this idealized market will move. Our discussion will be conducted in terms of the market for "widgets," which, according to legend, are gadgets produced during the 1930s. (The firms producing them have ended production, but economists still use them as an example, although no one seems to remember what widgets are.) Once we explore the hypothetical world of perfect competition and have dealt with nonprice competition, we will explore the real-world competition which has been observed in the hand calculator industry. Remember, by dealing with the idealized world of perfect competition, our purpose is to describe the directional tendency of competitive markets. Although the force of competition may not be as great in real-world markets, the directional tendency of the market can still be there.

Demand

By designating widgets as a "good," we assume that individual consumers who enter the widget market have a demand, and downward sloping demand curves at that, for widgets. Their individual demand curves add horizontally to the "market demand curve." That market demand curve, illustrated by D_m in Figure 7 · 1, represents the maximum quantities that consumers are willing to buy at each possible price and the maximum price they are willing to pay for each quantity. The competitive market process is a process by which consumers are induced to reveal their own individual demand curves and, accordingly, the market demand curve: they are induced to reveal what they are willing to pay at the maximum. If consumers do not reveal the maximum price they are willing to pay for the good, someone else will buy it. That is the nature of competition. In a less than perfect world, the curve is not perceived

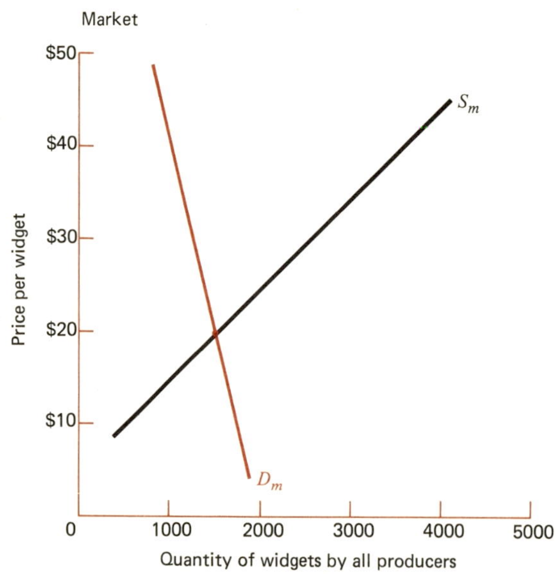

FIG. 7 · 1 D_m is the market demand curve, which is the sum of all consumer demand curves. S_m is the market supply curve, which is the sum of all producer marginal cost curves.

with precision by producers. Still, its position and shape will be more fully known because of the competitive process than if consumers do not have to compete and can do what they want. Indeed, the demand-revealing process is largely what price competition is all about.

The demand curve of Figure 7·1 is the collective consumers' demand for widgets. It is not, however, the demand which consumers have for widgets from *any one* producer-seller. The market demand indicates what consumers will do if the price of widgets from *all* producers rises. When all producers raise their prices, consumers have only the option of moving to other products in other markets. They, therefore, buy fewer widgets but do not reduce their purchases to zero. On the other hand, when one producer raises his price independently of what the others do, consumers have the option of moving *either* to other products or to other widget producers; in a "perfectly competitive" market, by definition, they can make these moves with ease and they can reduce their purchases of widgets from *any one* producer to zero. The potential for substitution is much greater when only one producer raises his price than when all producers raise their prices. If widget producer A raises his price independently of others, his customers can buy from producers $B, C, D, \ldots, Z$. The demand faced by the individual producer is consequently far more elastic than the market demand for the product. (For a review of the determinants of elasticity of demand, see Chapter 3.) Indeed, when talking about a purely competitive market in which entry is open, the demand curve is horizontal at the going market price: it is "perfectly elastic." If producer A, for instance, raises his price by some minute amount above the going market price, consumers in the market, eager to minimize the price they have to pay, can move to other producers already in the market or to producers who will enter the market to take over the sales of producer A. Therefore, at any price above $20 in Figure 7 · 2 producer A sells nothing. On the other hand, if producer A lowers his price by some very small amount below $20, consumers will swamp him with orders as they move from other producers who are now at higher prices. Because the price change necessary to bring about consumer movement in the purely competitive market can be so small—infinitesimal, in fact—the individual competitor is referred to as a "price taker": he essentially accepts the going market price as the price to charge. He is a price taker in the sense that it does not take much of a price change to bring about considerable consumer response.

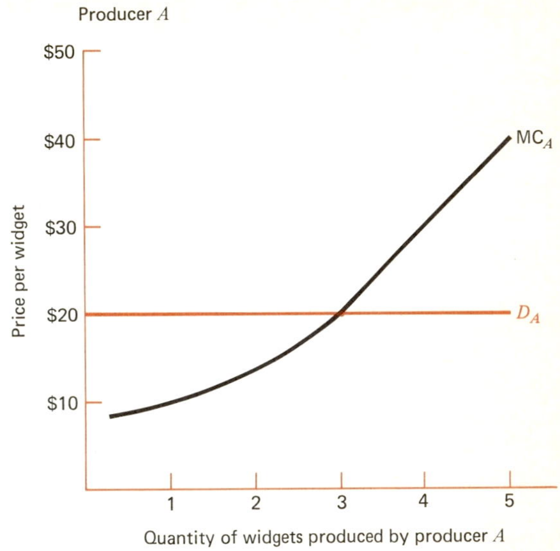

FIG.7·2 The perfect competitor is a price taker. This is illustrated by the horizontal demand curve. At a price of $20 the perfect competitor can sell all that he is willing to sell, which is three widgets. If a competitor raises the price, he will sell nothing, as consumers move to other producers who continue to sell at $20.

Supply

On the supply side of the market, there are a number of actual or potential producers who are willing to produce widgets. How much each is willing to put on the market depends on the conditions of production, such as the cost of resources, the available technology, and many other conditions which need not be listed here.

Given these conditions, producers should be expected to respond to an increase in price by producing more. If production is subject to diminishing returns, the marginal (or additional) cost of producing additional units rises as the volume increases (see Chapter 4). As the price of widgets rises, a producer can justify incurring the higher marginal cost of expanded production and can, accordingly, be expected to expand production in response to a price increase. Assuming all producers have the same shared supply curves that *A* has, the market supply curve, which is the summation of producer supply curves, is also upward sloping. We have drawn producer *A*'s supply or marginal cost curve as MC_A in Figure 7 · 2.

Price Competition and Equilibrium

In order to examine how and why market rivals compete through price and how price directs market behavior, consider the predicament of buyers and sellers at various prices. This can all be done with reference to the supply and demand curves in Figure 7 · 3*a* and *b* and Figure 7 · 4*a* and *b*.

Market surpluses To begin, suppose that the price of widgets is $40 in Figure 7·3*a* and *b*. At that price the market demand curve (Figure 7·3*a*) indicates that consumers are willing and able to buy only a total of 1000 widgets. On the other hand, producers are willing to supply as many as 3500. Producers are willing to supply *at that price* many more widgets than consumers are willing to buy *at that price*. Consumers will buy more if the price is lowered—the law of demand predicts this; the point is, however, that at $40 there is an inconsistency between what consumers and producers are willing to do. There is a *surplus* of 2500 widgets on the market.

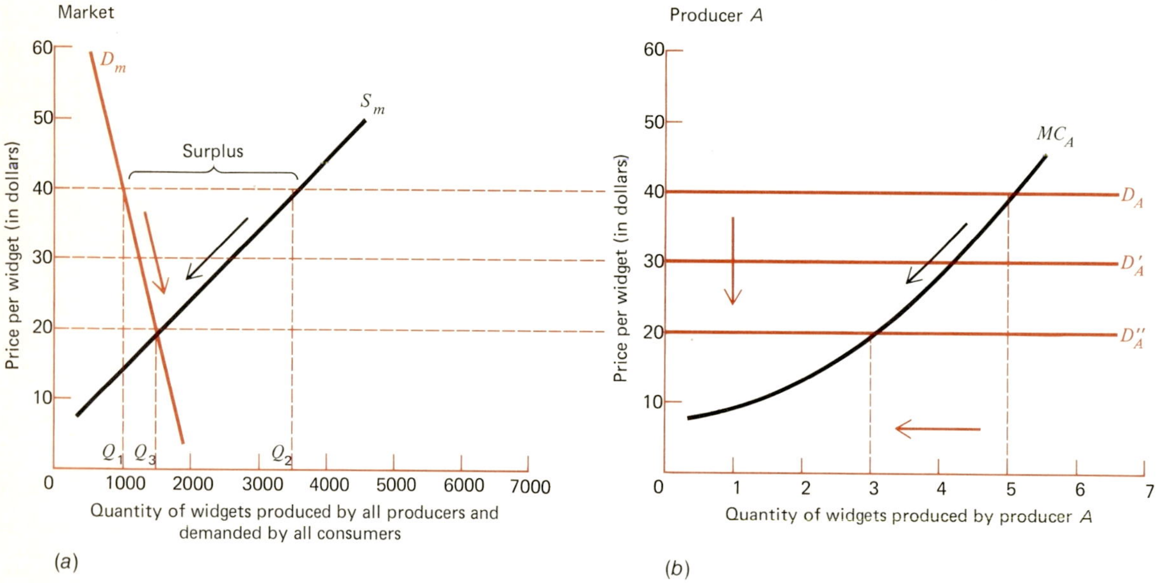

FIG. 7 · 3 At a price of $40, producer *A* will want to sell five widgets. All producers would like to sell as many as 3000 widgets, which exceeds the 1000 widgets which consumers are willing to buy at that price. There is, in other words, a market surplus at a price of $40. Through competition, the price will fall, increasing the number of widgets which consumers are willing to buy and reducing the number producers are willing to sell. The equilibrium price and quantity are $20 and 1500 widgets sold.

Indeed, the definition of a market surplus is the amount by which the quantity supplied by producers exceeds the quantity demanded by consumers.

Individual producer-competitors are in a real dilemma when the price of widgets is $40. There are producers in the market who are either not selling anything or not selling as many units as they would like. Furthermore, the market supply curve in Figure 7·3*a* shows that there are producers who are willing to offer widgets for a lower price than $40. (The supply curve, you may remember, indicates what price producers are willing to accept for each quantity. Therefore, in terms of Figure 7·3*a* producers are willing to offer each of the units up to 3499 at a price below $40. For instance, some producer is willing to offer the one-thousand-first widget for a little more than $15.) In short, there are producers who would like to sell more than they are selling and who are willing to do so at a price less than $40. How would you expect the producers to behave? If individual competitors lower their price slightly below $40 and other producers do not, and in this way they attempt to outdo their rivals, they will attract customers away from the other widget producers and to themselves. Because there are many other producers and because of the consumer response, they can sell as many units as they wish.

To illustrate, consider the predicament of our representative producer, producer A, whose marginal cost curve is pictured in Figure 7·3*b*. Let us suppose that A is one of those producers who is not selling any widgets at $40. His horizontal, perfectly elastic demand curve, D_A, indicates that a *very* small drop in price below $40 will bring about a significant consumer response. Although he may sell nothing *at* $40, he can sell as many as he can produce at a price just below $40—so close to $40, in fact, that it cannot be distinguished from $40 in our graph. At a price just below $40, producer A will sell up to five widgets because producer A's marginal cost of producing each of the first five widgets is less than the price that he can sell it for. He makes a profit on each unit, and we should expect producer A, as a competitor, to seek that profit by doing what is required—by lowering his price by the small amount that is necessary. (Notice that A will not sell a sixth widget because the marginal cost of producing it is greater than he can sell it for.)

Each competitor, like A, must also fear what other producers will do or how they will react to the surplus on the market. Like the student who studies because he cannot trust his classmates to refrain from studying, an individual producer may lower his price because he fears that others will lower their prices and thereby effectively eliminate his chance to sell widgets. Given the number of producers in the market and the number who can move into the market, given freedom of entry, the cost of any one competitor trying to keep other producers from lowering their prices is prohibitively high, so high that the only rational thing for such a competitor to do is to lower his price or stop producing widgets altogether. The dilemma which each faces independently leads all of them to lower their prices.

As the price falls, consumers will demand more widgets, as indicated by their downward sloping market demand curve in Figure 7·3*a*. Some widget producers will get out of the business altogether, since their marginal cost now exceeds the new lower market price; others, like A, will simply adjust their production levels. Some widget producers will divert some or part of their resources to the production of other goods which are now relatively more profitable lines of production. If the price falls to $30, producer A can profitably produce only 4 widgets; the cost of the fifth widget, which approximates $40, is greater than the market price. At a price of $20 per widget, A can profitably produce only 3. Hence, the number offered for sale decreases as the price falls.

The central point of this scenario is that the initial competitive predicament of producers will lead to a reduction in the surplus which results from the gap between what the buyers are willing to buy and sellers are willing to produce. There are forces at work which are pushing the market *toward* the intersection of the supply and demand curves. In a perfectly competitive market with complete freedom of entry and in which buyers and sellers can easily adjust and readjust their market decisions, the price will fall all the way to $20, the intersection of supply and demand. However, in more real-world markets, in which the conditions of the perfectly competitive market are not met, the price will not fall that far. There certainly is, however, no pressure for the price to fall below $20; at $20 producers are willing to produce only as many widgets as consumers are willing to buy.

For a perfectly competitive market, the intersection of the supply and demand curves is called the *market equilibrium*. It is the price and quantity toward which the competitive market will tend to move; it is the "consequence" of the competitive process, distinguishable from the process itself. Because of imperfections, primarily in the form of restrictions on entry, the market may never move exactly to the intersection; but we do know that competition can be a powerful force pushing the market in that direction. Given the positioning of the curves, the intersection is the limit beyond which the market will not move.

One interesting aspect of this particular example is that the widget producers have an interest in keeping the price at $40. At that price they sell, as a group, 1000 units for a total revenue of $40,000 ($40 × 1000); however, competition pushes the market toward a price of $20 and a quantity of 1500. At that price industry revenues are $30,000; the demand is obviously inelastic.[9] At 1500 widgets produced, greater production costs are incurred than at 1000 simply because more are being produced. The revenue is less and the costs are greater at 1500 widgets produced. Therefore, the profits of producers must also be less.

The competitors have a "common interest" to restrict their production, to reduce the tendency of individuals to act independently (competitively), and to push the price up to $40 (or even beyond) and keep it there. At that price level they can share the market and the higher profits. However, the general principle developed in Chapter 6 regarding the behavior of members of a *large* group is applicable to the competitive market: Large groups tend to be unable to pursue goals which may be in the common interest of all members. This holds for competitors even if all see the adverse consequences of independent, individual behavior. The large number of producers makes agreement and enforcement costs too high to expect collusive (or collective) behavior. (The same problem exists for much smaller groups if, for some reason, agreement and enforcement costs are high.)

What if there are only a few competitors in the market and they find that a workable agreement is possible? The agreement will not last if entry is free and open. If the colluding competitors make significant profits, other competitors will be attracted into the market. Competitors newly entering the market can undercut existing competition by charging less, and the price will start to tumble. In short, although existing and potential competition can reduce the collective welfare of the producers, it can benefit the consumers. Consumers receive, because of the competition, a price below $40 and a quantity of widgets above 1000. At the same time, the producers will consider the price decrease to be undesirable (in their particular line of business) and will take whatever reasonable opportunity they have at their disposal, through government or otherwise, to restrict competitive behavior.

Market shortages The supply and demand curves of Figure 7·3*a* and *b* are duplicated in Figure 7·4*a* and *b*. Given these curves, at a price below $20 there will be an inconsistency between the quantity desired by consumers and the quantity producers are willing to offer. At $10 the market demand curve indicates that consumers are willing to buy as many as 1750 widgets; producers are willing to offer less, only 500. The gap between what producers are willing to offer and

[9] The same general conclusions can hold for demands which are elastic; however, the example of an inelastic demand brings the incentive structure into clear focus. (As a matter of review, the demand is inelastic if the total revenues go down when the price falls. The demand is elastic if the total revenues increase when the price falls. See Chap. 3.)

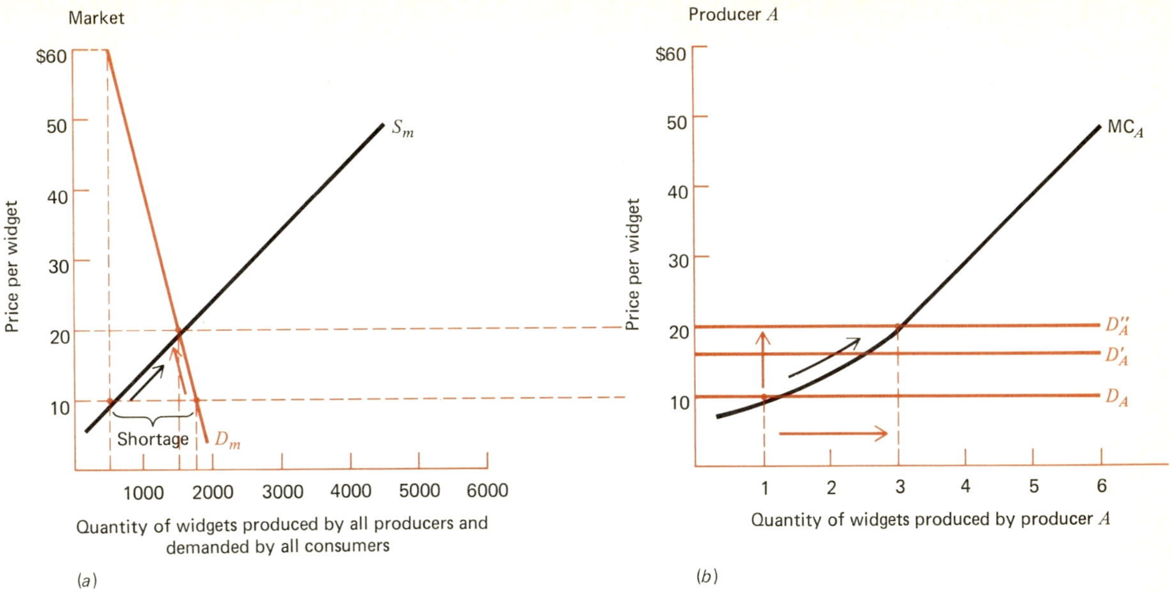

FIG. 7·4 At a price of \$10, producer *A* will want to sell only one widget. All producers would like to sell only 500 widgets, which is less than the 1750 widgets which consumers want to purchase. There is, in other words, a market shortage at a price of \$10. Through competition, the price will rise, causing consumers to cut back on the number of widgets they want to buy and causing producers to expand their production of widgets. As in Figure 7·3, the equilibrium price and quantity are \$20 and 1500 widgets sold.

what buyers are willing to purchase is the *market shortage*.

More precisely, a market shortage is the amount by which the quantity demanded by consumers exceeds the quantity supplied by producers.

This can occur only at prices below the equilibrium price.

In a competitive market the price will not remain at \$10. Consumers place a higher value than \$10 on each widget between 500 and 1500. This is shown by the position of the demand curve, which is above \$10 up to 1500 widgets. Those consumers who are unable to buy as many widgets as they would like at a price of \$10 have an incentive to "compete," to offer, as at an auction, a higher price. Producers, perceiving that consumers will actually pay more than \$10, can offer to sell additional widgets at prices above \$10. Either way, the horizontal demand curves facing each producer shift up as the price increases. Each producer can then profitably produce additional units. Hence, competition leads to price increases, consumers cut back on the quantity they want (remember the law of demand), and producers can profitably expand production. (Can you see why in Figure 7·4*b*?)

At a price of \$20, producers are offering as many as 1500 widgets, which is all that consumers want. There is, therefore, no incentive for the consumers to bid the price up further. If producers try to charge a higher price, a surplus will appear, and the market price will move back down toward \$20. The market is in equilibrium, once again, at a price of \$20 and a quantity of 1500 widgets; no further beneficial opportunities remain to be exploited by either producers or consumers.

Without doubt, consumers would prefer to have

the price remain at $10, but at that price they are on the horns of a dilemma. They would like to get the widgets for as little as possible; they do not want to pay more than $10 (they would pay less if they could get away with it). However, some are willing to pay more, and by paying more they are able to induce producers to incur the necessary production costs. Nevertheless, the price increase will cause consumers to leave the market; others will adjust their purchasing plans downward and move to other goods and services which are now relatively less expensive.

Interim Conclusions

All this discussion of shortages and surpluses leads to several conclusions. First, forces exist in the market which are "stabilizing," that is, which tend to push the market toward one central point, *equilibrium*. To that extent, the tendency of the market, at least on a theoretical level, is predictable. To that extent, the competitive market contributes to social order. A word of caution is necessary, however. We have developed a supply and demand model *as if* the price moves smoothly toward equilibrium. That might be the case in a market in which all participants, buyers and sellers, have perfect knowledge of what everyone else is going to do. However, the market, by definition, is beset with the problem of imperfect knowledge; in fact, we said that the function of the market is to generate the necessary information which people need to interact with one another. We have, therefore, shied away from assuming a market in which people have perfect knowledge because that would be tantamount to assuming away the very process that we wish to explore.[10] In a world of imperfect information, the price may not, and probably will not, move directly toward equilibrium. The market participants will continuously grope for the "best" price as they see it from their individual perspectives. At times, sellers will overshoot equilibrium—that is, produce too much—and, at times, they will undershoot equilibrium—that is, produce too little. Still, the analysis of a competitive market indicates that market rivals will repeatedly revise their decisions in such a way that they will move in the direction of equilibrium. To argue the contrary is to argue that the market is not an informational system and that market participants do not learn from their experiences.

Second, although all resources or raw materials are limited in quantity, a true "market shortage" can exist only if the price is below equilibrium. That shortage can be eliminated with some price increases—how much, we cannot say from theory alone. But we can say that in a competitive market forces will be at work to boost the price upward and to eliminate the shortage. We also know that a surplus of a good exists because its price is above equilibrium. Competition will lead to a reduction in the price and an elimination of the surplus. As we will see in later chapters, if the price is controlled, that is, if it is not permitted to respond to market conditions, surpluses or shortages are to be expected.

Finally, the competitive market is *efficient* in one important sense:

The marginal benefits of the last unit produced equal marginal costs.

At any point below 1500, the equilibrium quantity in Figure 7 · 4*a*, the supply and demand curves show that consumers value an additional widget (marginal benefit) at more than it costs to produce it. The price, which is an indication of relative value, is greater than the marginal cost, which, as explained in Chapter 4, is an indication of the value of those things which are forgone. Take, for example, the five-hundredth widget. Someone is willing to pay as much as $60 (i.e., the marginal benefit) for that unit; the marginal cost of it is $10. The marginal benefit is greater than the marginal cost. By having the resources employed in the production of the five-hundredth widget, the welfare of consumers is raised; consumers receive more pleasure out of the additional widget than they could have received from the other good that could have been produced. Furthermore, the marginal benefit of each unit between 500 and 1500 is greater than the marginal cost, and people

[10] Hayek, "The Meaning of Competition," pp. 92–106.

can experience a net increase in welfare by having each of those units produced. Notice that we have argued all along that competition will tend to push the market toward a production level of 1500; in perfect competition 1500 will in fact be produced. In the sense that market-expressed values are maximized, perfect competition is considered to be *efficient*.

THE NONPRICE DIMENSIONS OF COMPETITION

Markets in which competitors compete solely in terms of price are relatively rare. Table salt is one basic, relatively uniform commodity sold in a market in which price is an important competitive tool; but even in that market, producers of salt compete in terms of real or imagined quality differences and the reputation and recognition of brand names. Kansas wheat farmers, who may be unable to change the nature of their products at harvest time, may then have to compete solely in terms of price. However, in most industries, competition can be expressed in the many dimensions of marketing a product, such as quality or the appearance of quality, design, and durability. When caught in a competitive dilemma, the entrepreneur can use price or any of these other features when trying to outwit competitors. In general, competitors can be expected to choose a competitive strategy that gives them the greatest profit.

Price competition is very often employed by competitors to outwit their rivals; however, price competition is not always the best method of competition. This is so because a price reduction not only means lower average revenues but also can be costly to communicate to the consumers through advertising. Consumers may not take note of price reductions as readily as they do of quality improvements. This may mean that improvement in quality of additional features may be used as a means of countering market pressure to lower price. Furthermore, quality changes are not so easily duplicated by competitors as are price changes, and consumers may prefer a quality improvement or other changes to a lower price. These preferences for quality, as opposed to price reductions, should be reflected in the profitability of making quality improvements. Many consumers, for instance, may prefer a hand calculator with more digits and functions at a constant price than a reduction in the price of a basic model. Producing the more sophisticated model can, depending upon the costs of adding the features, be more profitable than producing the basic model at a lower price and communicating the lower price to consumers.

We have shown that consumers can benefit from price competition among producers who produce the same product. However, we can also demonstrate that consumers can benefit through nonprice competition, through product differences. To do this, we must step out of a perfectly competitive market structure and into a market structure called *monopolistic competition*.

This is a market structure in which product differences are the norm and producers have some measure of control over the price they charge: because producers have their own identifiable products which cannot be readily and perfectly duplicated, entry is more restricted (costly) than is the case in perfect competition.

This is a much more complicated market structure, but it is one which is more realistic. In this section we explore only the nonprice dimensions of competition in this market structure; in Chapter 10, after having developed additional tools of analysis, we will explore price competition in this type of market.

If all consumers had exactly the same preferences for a product in terms of size, color, and so on, producers would be expected to produce that particular product and to compete through price alone. Realistically, however, in the markets for most products, people's preferences differ. To keep the analysis simple and to the point, let us explore nonprice competition in terms of one dimension, product size. For a given product for which size is important, such as television sets, let us view consumers as being distributed along the continuum in Figure 7·5. We have assumed that

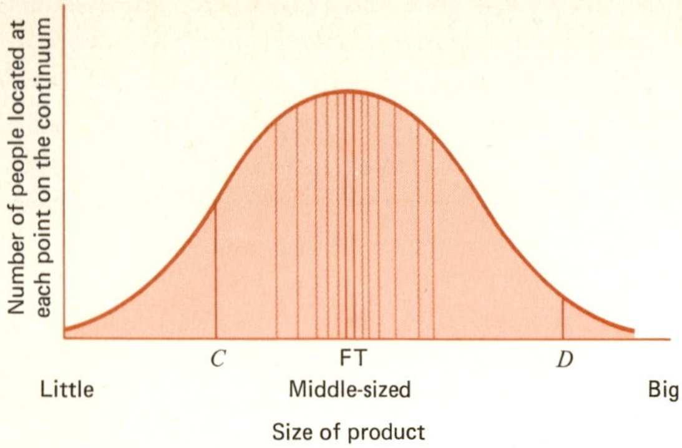

FIG. 7·5 We assume that consumers differ in what they want but that they are distributed along the continuum in such a way that most want a "middle-size" product; fewer consumers want product sizes which are out in the wings of the distribution.

the distribution is bell-shaped. This distribution in Figure 7·5 illustrates that, for the product category under consideration, most consumers are clustered in the middle of the distribution and want a "middle-size" product; fewer consumers want a product of a size in the wings of the distribution.

Everything else being equal, the first producer to enter the market, Terrific TV, will probably offer a product which falls somewhere in the middle of the distribution, for example, at T in Figure 7·5. In this way, Terrific TV offers a product which directly reflects the preferences of the largest number of people; furthermore, as long as there are no other competitors, the firm can expect to pick up customers to the left and right of the center of the distribution. For the consumer who prefers a very large or small television, the product being offered in the center may not come very close to satisfying his wants, but it is the only product available. Terrific TV has a significant incentive to locate in the center because the closer Terrific TV comes to reflecting the preference of the greatest number of consumers, everything else, like consumer income, being equal, the higher the price it can charge and the greater the profit it can make.

The first few competitors who enter the market may also locate close to the center—in fact, several may come close to duplicating what Terrific TV has done. They may conclude that they will enjoy a larger market by sharing the center with several competitors than by moving out into the "wings" of the distribution. In the wings they may be able to charge a higher price for a product that more closely reflects the preferences of those consumers, but there are simply fewer potential customers at either end of the distribution. To illustrate, assume competitor Fabulous Focus locates at F, close to T. By doing this the competitor can appeal to consumers to the left; that is, its product will be preferred to Terrific TV's in the left half of the distribution, since its product more closely reflects those consumers' preferences. Terrific TV, on the other hand, can appeal to consumers in the right half of the distribution. If Fabulous Focus had located at C, it would have appealed to consumers to the left of C and to some of the consumers to the right. However, Terrific TV would have been closer to some of the consumers located between C and T. In short, Fabulous Focus would have a larger potential market at F than at C. For similar reasons, additional entrants into the market may also locate near the center, expecting to outwit competitors and/or expecting a larger market by dividing the large center of the distribution than by taking the wings of the distribution.

At some point, however, as more and more competitors move into the market to exploit available profit opportunities, the center will become crowded, so much so that potential new competitors will find that it is to their advantage to move out from the center and to offer a product located in the wings, at C or D. At C or D the market may not be as large as in the center, but producers may be able to charge higher prices there than in the center, where they would have to compete directly with many other producers. Just how far out on the wings they move depends on tradeoffs they will have to make between the number of customers they can appeal to and the price that can be charged. Like price reductions, these movements of competitors to the wings of the distribution lead to welfare improvements for consumers whose tastes (wants) are different from those of people in the middle of the distribution. These consumers now have a product which comes closer to or directly reflects their own preferences.

Just how many different-sized products are made available is dependent upon the freedom of entry into the market and upon the costs of any one producer expanding the firm's scale of operations to accommodate larger groups of customers. If there are restrictions imposed on entry into the market, for example, through control of a strategic resource by one competitor or through government regulation, the variety of products will not likely be as great as under an open, competitive market. If only two or three competitors are allowed to enter the market and everything else is equal, we would expect them to cluster in the middle of a normal distribution. For example, the number of television stations permitted to operate in a given geographical area is strictly regulated by the Federal Communications Commission. It should be no surprise to those who have studied this section that we find the stations that are operating in a given area carrying programs which predominantly appeal to the "mass audience," that is, to the middle of the distribution of television watchers. The Public Broadcasting System, PBS, was in part organized by the government to provide programs with less than "mass appeal" which the major networks do not offer; even now PBS is constantly being criticized for broadcasting programs which appeal only to the "culturally elite." Magazine and newsstand operators would behave very much like television managers if they could offer only two or three magazines; they would tend to choose those magazines, like *Newsweek,* appealing to the largest number of people willing to pay the highest price. For instance, most motel operators have room for only one small newsstand, and they tend to choose those magazines which appeal to the largest number of their customers.

Even without restrictions on entry into television markets, the variety of programs depends upon the cost of production and the prices which people are willing to pay for the variations. This is true for other products as well. Although they may prefer a product which perfectly reflects their tastes, many people in the distribution may decide to buy a product that is not perfectly suitable if they can buy it at a lower price. Producers can offer such a product at a lower price because of "economies" (cost savings) associated with selling to a large market. Students take classes in large lecture halls instead of under private tutors who may design the course especially for them largely because the mass lecture, though possibly less effective, is substantially cheaper. At any rate, in a market which is open to entry, producers will take advantage of these opportunities.

Further, if one or several producers in one area of the distribution attempt to "exploit" consumers by charging a "high" price, over a period of time other producers can move into that particular portion of the market, competing by way of price and pushing the price down; consumers can move to other, similar products. In these ways, an "optimum" variety of products can eventually emerge in a free, although not perfectly competitive, market. Seen this way, the argument for a *free* market is an argument for this kind of *emerging* process. Without the freedom of entry, we cannot tell whether or not the combination of products produced can be "improved" upon. A free competitive market gives market rivals a chance to see if improvements can be made. The case for the free market becomes even stronger when we recognize that market conditions and, therefore, the optimum mix of products are constantly changing.

COMPETITION IN THE HAND CALCULATOR INDUSTRY

In terms of growth in sales, advancement in technology and design, and the downward movement in prices, the hand calculator industry in the United States during the first half of the 1970s is an almost perfect textbook example of what the forces of price and nonprice competition can accomplish. The first hand calculator was introduced in the United States in 1969; it was Japanese. From that point, sales rose steadily until in 1976 they were over 16 million. Many of the early calculators were simple—some did not even have a divide key. The first basic model was the size of a large paperback book. In 1976 a hand calculator was being advertised which weighed 3½ ounces and measured 9/16 by 2 by 3½ inches.

The first hand calculator which was introduced in 1969 sold for $395. It had an eight-digit display and performed the four basic functions of addition, subtraction, division, and multiplication. In 1970, Texas Instruments, Inc., introduced a model for $400. A year later Canon and Sharpe came out with one which weighed 1½ pounds and had features similar to the first Japanese model but was still in the $350 to $400 range. By December 1971, Bowmar had an eight-digit, four-function model which sold for $240, substantially less than the price charged by existing competitors. All the while, the forces of competition led producers to improve upon existing technology of production.

The year 1972 saw substantial reductions in price and several important features added to calculators. In that year Hewlett-Packard introduced a scientific model which could perform many more than the basic four functions, but the price was still at the $395 level. However, by the end of the year Bowmar, Sears, and other firms had broken the $100 barrier. Some firms introduced memory capabilities, AC adapters, and 1500-hour batteries in an effort to maintain high prices. In spite of these efforts, Casio, a foreign competitor, announced at year's-end a basic model selling for $59.95.

In 1973 prices continued to fall. By the end of the year, National Semi-Conductor was offering a six-digit, four-function model for $29.95. Hewlett-Packard was forced to lower the price of its scientific model by $100; the company also began adding features in order to maintain the price. This effort and that of other firms to differentiate their products were successful to the extent that price reductions were partially resisted.

In 1974, six-digit, four-function models were selling for as little as $16.95. Eight-digit models comparable to models selling three or four years earlier for well over $300 carried price tags of $19.95, and in 1976 consumers could find six-digit models for $6.95. The brief table below of basic eight-digit, four-function models advertised in Sears' catalog indicates the dramatic drop in prices in four years. During the 1971–1974 period, the prices for all goods rose at rates never seen before in modern, peacetime United States, meaning that the relative price of hand calculators actually fell by much more than these rather dramatic decreases in nominal prices indicate.

TABLE 7·1

1971	None was advertised.	
1972	Craig model	$179.95
1973	Sears model	98.95
1974	Sears model	59.95
1975	Sears model	16.95

Notes: In different years, the Sears models do carry different model numbers and there may be slight differences in the models. However, from the advertisements, the models whose prices are given in the above table are highly similar.

The decrease in the price of hand calculators was to be expected. Although the high prices being charged when the calculators were first introduced reflected in part the higher costs of production that were experienced then, the prices also meant high profits, and this was incentive for many firms to move into the industry, to duplicate and advance the existing technology in design and production, and to increase their productivity in an attempt to beat the competition and to avoid being beaten by it. Firms that were unwilling to move with the competition were in fact beaten as their share of the consumer calculator market eroded.

SHORT-RUN AND LONG-RUN EQUILIBRIUM

The development of the hand calculator industry in the last decade can be partially explained using supply and demand curves. We say "partially" because, to use supply and demand curves, we must focus solely on one type of calculator, for instance, the "basic model." The curves also permit us to illustrate the difference between "short-run" and "long-run" market equilibriums.

In 1969, the supply of hand calculators was

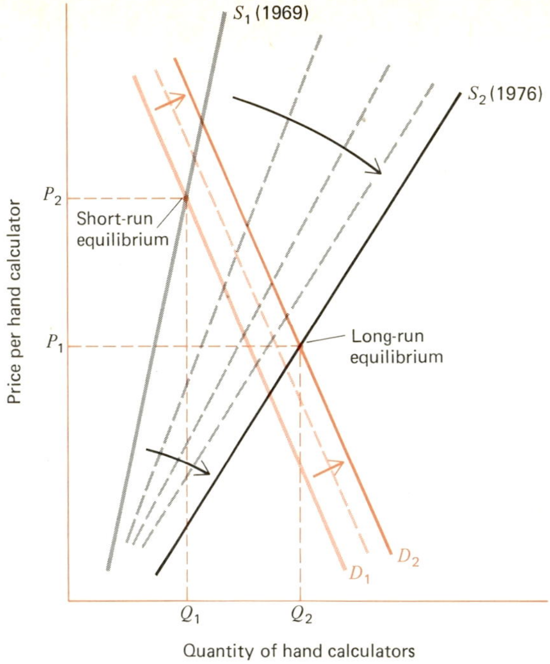

FIG. 7·6 With supply and demand curves for hand calculators at D_1 and S_1, the short-run equilibrium price and quantity are P_2 and Q_1, respectively. However, as firms in the industry are able to expand their scales of production and new firms are able to enter the industry, the supply curve shifts to S_2. An increase in consumer awareness of the availability and advantages of hand calculators shifts the demand to D_2. The long-run equilibrium price and quantity are P_1 and Q_2, respectively.

restricted by the technology of production and the number of firms actually producing basic calculators. The demand was also restricted because the product was new: consumers simply did not know very much about hand calculators at that point, and some were skeptical about buying anything that had not been market-tested for several years. Given these facts, let us assume that the supply and demand curves were initially S_1 and D_1 in Figure 7·6. The initial equilibrium price is described in the figure as P_2. This price and the accompanying quantity, Q_1, represent the equilibrium that existed in the market in 1969. It is called the *short-run equilibrium*. The short-run equilibrium is the price-quantity combination that will exist so long as producers do not have the time to expand their scale of operations.

In years following 1969, the original competitors were able to expand their scale of operations, and new competitors were able to convert plants that were producing other electronic equipment and to build new ones to enter the hand calculator market. Furthermore, technological breakthroughs occurred and the cost of production fell significantly. In fact, several important circuits in the hand calculator were reduced to a very small "chip" and their cost fell from over \$150 to under \$2. Graphically, the supply of the product increased. On the consumer side of the market, because of advertising and word-of-mouth contacts, people became more familiar with the product and the market demand increased.

In terms of Figure 7·6 these events mean that the supply curve gradually increases from S_1 toward S_2, and the demand curve increases from D_1 toward D_2. Because the supply increased by more than the demand, the price in the graph falls from P_1 to P_2; the quantity rises from Q_1 to Q_2. The equilibrium price and quantity, P_2 and Q_2, caused by expanded production capacity and increased consumer demand, are called the *long-run equilibrium* in the market.

The market may not necessarily move smoothly from the short-run to long-run equilibrium. Because competitors do not know exactly what others are doing and because they do not know exactly what is happening to the consumer demand, overproduction, resulting in losses, can occur. Prices in 1976 had fallen to the point where several companies in the hand calculator business were losing money and preparing to get out of the business or significantly reduce their production plans.

The above is an example of long-run market adjustments causing a drop in the market price; this occurred because supply increased by more than demand. The opposite can occur: the demand can increase by more than supply. In this case, as illustrated in Figure 7·7, the price will rise along

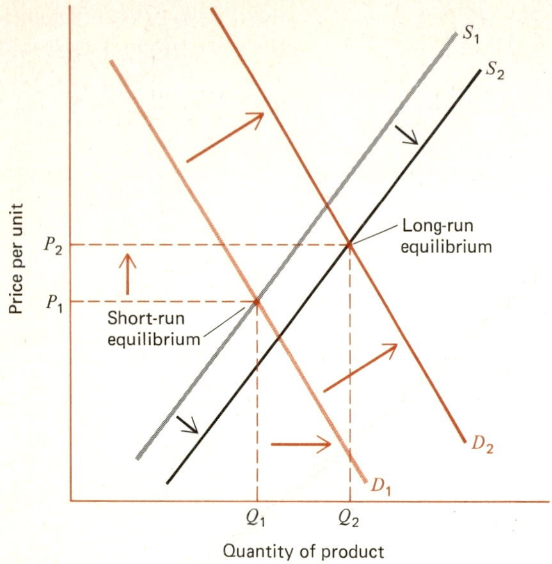

FIG. 7·7 If the demand increases by more than supply, the price and quantity sold will rise.

This was developed in an earlier section. However, consumer demands and, therefore, revealed market benefits are dependent upon ways in which incomes are distributed. If that distribution is changed, demands will change and resources will be allocated differently. For example, if income is taken from the rich and given to the poor, fewer expensive cars may be purchased by the rich and more clothing may be purchased by the poor. The results of competition may be efficient, in a strict economic sense, but they may be considered "socially desirable" by you or others only to the extent that you consider the underlying income distribution to be "just," "fair," or "equitable." As economists, we cannot say what is "just" or "fair"; all we can do is demonstrate, as we do in later chapters, how incomes are distributed in a market system. You must ultimately be the judge of whether or not the distribution which emerges is "just."

with quantity. The price rises from P_1 to P_2, and the quantity produced rises from Q_1 to Q_2. Alternatively, the supply and demand may adjust in such a way that price remains constant while the quantity increases. These changes are described in Figure 7 · 8.

QUALIFICATIONS TO THE ARGUMENT FOR COMPETITIVE MARKETS

The competitive market system has deficiencies, and we must note several qualifications to our argument for the competitive market before we close this chapter. Our discussion will be limited here, however, because further examination of market deficiencies will be more appropriate in various later chapters.

First, the competitive market process can be quite efficient in the sense that production can approach, but not necessarily reach, the level at which the marginal benefit of the last unit produced equals the marginal cost of producing it.

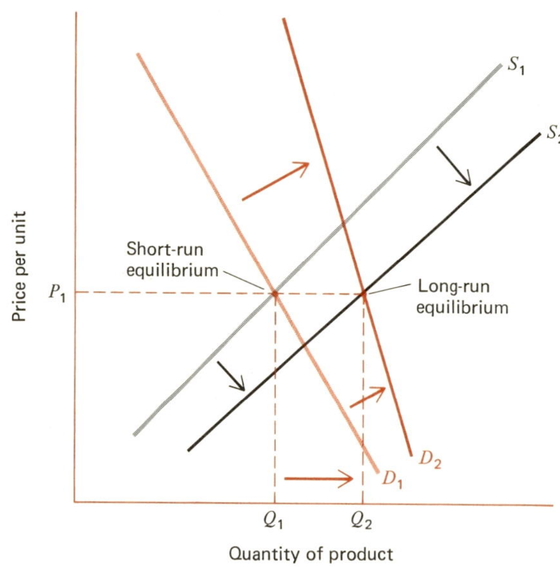

FIG. 7·8 In this example, the supply and demand curves increase in such a way that the price of the goods remains at the same level in short-run and long-run equilibrium. The quantity produced and purchased still goes up, as was the case in Figures 7·6 and 7·7.

Second, to the extent that production costs are imposed on people who are not a party to the "market transaction," as in the case of industrial smoke pollution, the market will not achieve an efficient outcome. The people whose house paint peels because of the smoke bear a portion of the production costs; the price the consumer pays for the product is lower than it would be if all costs, including the pollution, were incurred by the producers. Because of lower prices, consumers will buy more than the "efficient" quantity (1500 widgets in Figure 7·4). In a sense, this is an example of "overproduction." Because all costs of production are not included in the producer's marginal cost curves, price is artificially low.

Third, competition can be undesirable in the production of undesirable products. For instance, if many people consider the consumption of some drug, like cocaine, to be undesirable, a competitive market in cocaine will lead to lower prices for the good and greater quantities consumed. If contract murders are considered to be "bad," competition among hit-men will tend to lower the price of contract murders and increase the quantity demanded. In other words, competition can be "good" in the production of things which people consider beneficial; it can be "bad" in the production of those things which people consider nonbeneficial. It follows that restrictions on the ability of people to compete can, in some instances, be desirable social policy. Obviously, there is danger in overextending this argument to products which small groups of people dislike.

Fourth, opponents of the market system contend that competition (of the monopolistically competitive kind) leads to "produce proliferation" and to waste in the production and advertisement of goods and services. Because there are so many different products available, production of each product takes place on a very small production scale and no plant is fully utilized. This may indeed be the case; but the validity of this objection hinges on whether or not you believe the choice range which product differentiation brings compensates for the production inefficiency that may exist. The relevant question is, Should we collectively force product standardization in order that firms will compete solely in terms of price? What will happen to the welfare of those people who want something that differs from the standardized product? What will happen to social friction and unrest?

Fifth, competition is the process by which one competitor attempts to outdistance his rivals. To outdistance a rival, a competitor may employ "backhanded" techniques, such as releasing false information about other competitors and using "bait-and-switch" promotional gimmicks. In short, competitors can take advantage of customer ignorance. On the other hand, competition can eliminate some of these abuses; competitors will let consumers know when their rivals are misrepresenting their products. Still, fraudulent sellers can move from market to market, staying one step ahead of their reputations.

SUMMARY AND EXTENSIONS

Voluntary cooperative associations of people, such as families and groups of friends, are important means by which people can achieve shared objectives. However, in Chapter 6 we described the limitations of these types of associations. For the purpose of organizing a whole society in pursuit of the common objective of raising all people's welfare, some other social organizer must emerge to complement, to add to, the social order achieved through voluntary associations. In this chapter we have extended Chapter 6's discussion to analyze a social organizer that works in large groups.

The *market* is a system which provides individuals with *private* incentives to produce goods and services for other people. Social benefits emerge as an outgrowth of people's attempts to respond to private incentives. Exchanges can develop among people who seek fulfillment of their own wants, and the exchanges can be mutually beneficial. All people seeking their own interest can mean that they will compete with one another, and it is this competition which drives market participants and controls the behavior of the market participants. A "free market" implies that individuals (sellers and/or buyers) can freely respond to incentives—that they have options and can choose from among these options. It does not mean that behavior is totally unconstrained, that people can do exactly what they want—or that their options are unlimited. What a competitor can do is constrained by what market rivals are willing to do. The pursuit of self-interest and competition *can mean* that people's behavior will be guided in directions which are *efficient*. An *efficient* level of production cannot be strictly equated with a *good* level of output. The goodness of an outcome must be an individual judgment.

The market system is not a perfect system. People have problems in acquiring sufficient information to make reasonably intelligent decisions. It takes time for people to respond to incentives, and producers can make high profits while others gather their resources to respond to the existence of profit. The electronics industry took three to four years to get the price of a basic-model hand calculator down from over $300 to under $40. Some consumers are still not getting exactly the kind of calculator that they want. We must also emphasize that a free market carries with it the very real prospect that monopoly power can be acquired, thus restricting people's ability to respond to profit incentives, to produce more, and to push price and profits down. More will be said about monopoly power in Chapter 10.

QUESTIONS TO PONDER

1 As a matter of review, why does the demand curve have a negative slope and the supply curve have a positive slope?

2 The Mercantilists argued that a country's wealth consisted of its holdings of "gold bullion" (or money). To keep the gold in the country, they proposed restrictions in the form of tariffs and quotas on the importation of goods and services. How do you react to that argument?

3 What is meant by "economic efficiency in production"?

4 In this chapter, we write that competition in the production of "bads" can be "bad." Explain.

5 In order to support a free market is it necessary to accept the philosophical position of "individualism"? Why?

6 List what you consider to be deficiencies of the market system. Is the existence of such deficiencies sufficient grounds for being opposed to a free market? Explain.

7 Why is the intersection of the supply and demand curves the price-quantity combination toward which the competitive market will gravitate? What may keep the market from moving all the way to that intersection?

8 Under what conditions can competition lead to "destabilizing" price movements, that is, movements away from equilibrium?

9 Suppose the demand for blue jeans suddenly increases. Discuss the possible short-run and long-run equilibriums.

RECOMMENDED READINGS

Friedman, Milton: *Capitalism and Freedom* (Chicago: The University of Chicago Press, 1962).

Hayek, Friedrich A.: *The Road to Serfdom* (Chicago: The University of Chicago Press, 1944).

Nozick, Robert: *Anarchy, State, and Utopia* (New York: Basic Books, Inc., 1974), possibly a difficult book for the beginning economics student but still a modern philosophical statement of basic arguments for the market.

Nutter, G. Warren: "Freedom in Revolutionary Economy," in *The American Revolution: Three Views* (New York: American Brands, Inc., 1975), pp. 91–122.

Smith, Adam: *An Inquiry into the Nature and Causes of the Wealth of Nations* (New York: Random House, Inc., The Modern Library ed., 1937), especially the editor's introduction.

8

The Competitive Market: Applications to the World about Us

Without bandying jargon or exhibiting formulae, without being superficial or condescending, the scientist should be able to communicate to the public the nature and variety of consequences that can reasonably be expected to flow from a given action or sequence of actions. In the case of the economist, he can often reveal in an informal way, if not the detailed chain of reasoning by which he reaches his conclusions, at least the broad contours of the argument.

E. J. Mishan[1]

PREVIEW OF CHAPTER

Central question

How can supply and demand curve analysis be used to analyze real-world problems?

Major objective

To demonstrate how supply and demand curves can be used to illuminate the consequences of public policy.

Major conclusions

1. An increase in the price of imported foreign oil can lead to an increase in the price and quantity sold of domestically produced coal and to an increase in the profits of the coal producers.

[1] E. J. Mishan, *Popular Economic Fallacies*, 2d ed. (New York: Praeger Publishers, 1973), p. 11

2 Making the purchase and sale of transplantable kidneys legal can lead to an increase in their price but also to an increase in the quantity of kidneys made available for transplant.
3 The shortages of such university facilities as tennis courts can be eliminated by the introduction of a pricing system.
4 If an excise tax is imposed on a commodity like margarine, the price of margarine will rise and consumers will buy less. In addition, after making allowance for the tax, the effective price received by producers will decrease as a result of the excise tax. Therefore, producers have an incentive to oppose such taxes.
5 Domestic producers of textiles, on the other hand, have an interest in supporting measures to impose tariffs on imported textiles from foreign countries.

In this chapter we consider several problems which will allow us to demonstrate how supply and demand curves can be employed to understand social issues and to predict directional movements in market price and quantity of a good purchased. Supply and demand analysis does not tell us all we may like to understand about the market—for example, *how much* price and quantity change—but it can indicate "general tendencies" and, to that extent, can help clarify issues which may otherwise remain obscure.

WHY COAL PRODUCERS LOVE OPEC

When the 13 countries that make up the Organization of Petroleum Exporting Countries (OPEC) restricted output and forced up the world price of oil back in 1973, coal producers in this country and elsewhere smiled. The action of OPEC enabled them to achieve windfall profits they would not otherwise have had. Reference to simple supply and demand curves can illustrate why this was the case.

Increases in the price of oil cause energy consumers, acting rationally, to seek substitutes for oil. This is a restatement of the law of demand which we studied in Chapter 3 and expanded upon in Chapter 7. Coal is a particularly good substitute because many electric utility plants are equipped to burn either oil or coal, depending on which is the cheaper at the time. Therefore, as a consequence of OPEC's actions, the demand for coal increased. In terms of Figure 8·1, the demand curve shifts from D_1 to D_2 to reflect the increase in demand. At the original market price for coal, P_1, a shortage develops which, as discussed in Chapter 7, embodies the necessary ingredients for an upward movement in market price. The price in this example rises to P_2. As the price rises, production becomes more profitable and producers can justify incurring the higher marginal costs of production.

Because of OPEC's actions, the profit of the coal industry increased. The coal industry's revenues, before oil prices increased, are equal to the then current price of P_1 times the quantity sold, Q_1, which in the figure is equal to the area $0P_1aQ_1$. After the increase in the price of oil, and subsequently in the price of coal, the revenues of the coal industry expand to the higher price, P_2, times the higher quantity Q_2, or the area $0P_2bQ_2$. The increase in revenues is indicated by the L-shaped, shaded area on the graph. The supply curve tells us the marginal cost of each additional unit of coal produced; therefore, the total cost of expanding production from Q_1 to Q_2 is the portion of that shaded area which is under the supply curve and still in the shaded area (Q_1abQ_2). The additional profit, which is the additional revenue minus the additional cost, is that portion of the shaded area which is not underneath the supply curve (P_2baP_1). It is this additional profit which

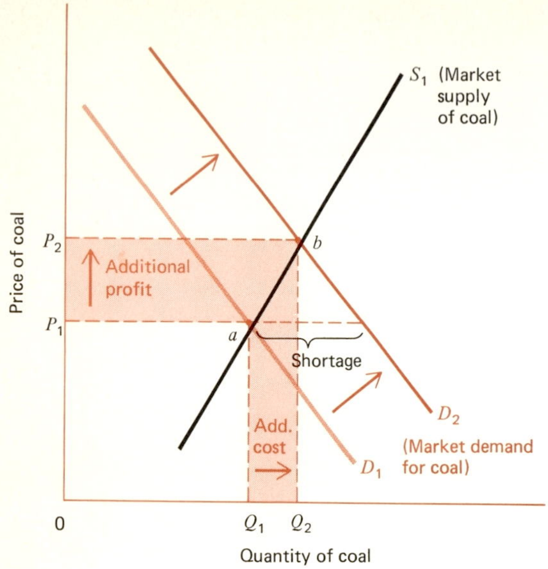

FIG. 8·1 An increase in the price of oil will cause people to shift to its coal substitute. The demand for coal will, for example, shift upward from D_1 to D_2. The price of the coal will rise from P_1 to P_2 and the quantity of coal sold will rise from Q_1 to Q_2. Revenues received by the coal producers increase by the shaded area in the figure. Production costs rise by the area Q_1abQ_2; the profits of producers rise by the area P_1P_2ba.

caused coal producers to smile when OPEC made its announced price increases.

There are several energy substitutes for oil, and the foregoing analysis applies just as readily to these substitutes as it does to coal. OPEC's actions, for example, served the purpose of making wind and solar energy more attractive to energy consumers and, because higher prices can be charged, more profitable to investors. As the price of gasoline rose, reflecting higher oil prices, people began looking for alternative ways of accomplishing the things that could be accomplished with a gasoline engine. There was an explosion in the demand for bicycles; their prices rose and the quantity sold expanded considerably. As producers caught up with the dramatic increase in demand, we also experienced, as expected, a drop in the price of bicycles. In these ways, the increase in OPEC prices sets in motion a whole series of actions which will gradually eat into the energy market over which the Middle East countries may think they have more influence than they actually do.

A MARKET FOR BODILY ORGANS?

An individual has legally recognized property rights to his body and the parts of it. He can therefore do many things with his body and his organs: he can build them up through exercise and diet, or mistreat them through lack of care or drugs. He can give them away or even destroy them. (Suicide is, in general, not illegal, although it used to be. In general, today only attempted suicide is illegal!) But there is one thing state laws do not permit: a person cannot sell his organs to transplant recipients or his body to medical science for use after death in laboratory research or classroom instruction. If laws allowed free commerce in bodily organs, much of the medical profession would resist such sales on ethical grounds. One spokesperson for a kidney transplant center has commented that it "without question would never even consider such a proposal [purchase or sale of a kidney]. Such a thing might open up a whole new concept that is abhorrent."[2] Even the suggestion of a market in bodily organs is shocking to some readers. However, reflection on how a market system may affect the availability of transplantable organs may make the idea somewhat more palatable.

The quantity of any transplantable organ, like a kidney, is presently dependent solely upon the charity of potential donors, and charity in this area is not an insignificant motivational force; without it, many people would die. From 1953 to the middle 1970s, nearly 19,000 kidney transplants were performed with donated kidneys. However, many potential donors are reluctant to

[2] As quoted in Marvin R. Brams, "Property Rights in the Human Body: New Dimensions of Individual Choice and Freedom," paper presented at the Atlantic Economic Society Conference, Washington, D.C., September 1975. This paper inspired this section.

give to medical schools for training purposes or to people in need for reasons which may seem strange to others but which are nonetheless very important to them. Some people object to donating their organs totally on religious grounds; others resist the idea of donating their organs for fear of going to their "eternal reward" with some of their "pieces" missing. (They may not have all their marbles, but they want to have their kidneys and corneas just in case they are needed.) Still others resist giving their bodies or parts of their bodies to medical schools because they recoil at the thought of medical students making jokes about them.

If the legal prohibition against sale of, say, kidneys is lifted, the quantity of transplantable kidneys can be more than the quantity made available out of strictly charitable motives. People may experience some discomfort in having to give up a part of themselves to which they have become attached, but many—not all—can be persuaded at some price to "donate" their kidneys to a worthy cause. One person advertised in a newspaper his willingness to buy a kidney in good order for $3000 and had 100 people calling, willing to sell.[3] As the price rises, more and more people will overcome their hesitancy to give up one of their kidneys (either before or after death) and to offer them for sale. In short, there is likely to be some quantity of kidneys made available when the price is zero; this quantity is depicted by Q_1 in Figure 8 · 2 and reflects people's altruism. From that point in the graph outward, the supply curve rises in a normal positive direction, illustrating that a larger quantity will be made available to "buyers" as the price rises.

The demand for kidneys is a function of several factors. It is related to the size of medical schools and their need for kidneys in research and instruction and to the number of people who experience kidney failure. Since kidney failures can be caused by a person's eating and drinking habits, these habits can also affect the demand for kidneys. Further, the demand for kidneys is related to known techniques of organ transplants.

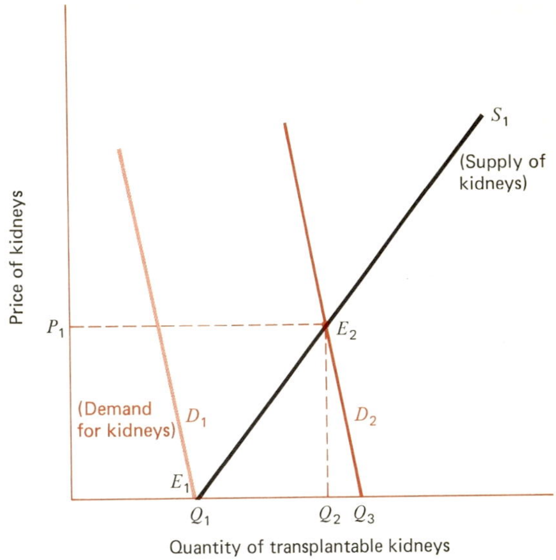

FIG. 8 · 2 If the supply and demand for transplantable kidneys are positioned at S_1 and D_1, there will be no shortage in the market at zero price. However, if the demand is greater, say, D_2, a shortage will exist at zero price. A "free market" in transplantable kidneys will cause the price to rise to P_1, but also the quantity of kidneys available for transplant will rise from Q_1 to Q_2.

As the techniques in this area are perfected, the willingness of doctors to operate may increase, increasing the demand for transplantable kidneys.[4] The demand may be highly inelastic, as is the curve in Figure 8 · 2, but it should still exhibit the normal negative slopes of all other demand curves. As the price of a kidney rises, some people may be willing to stay with the then cheaper dialysis machine; others may be excluded from the market because of insufficient funds to buy at the higher prices.

Under a completely altruistic system, no serious problem arises as long as the demand for kidneys is no greater than D_1. With a supply equal to S_1,

[3] Ibid., p. 14.

[4] New techniques in organ transplants with respect to prevention or rejection can reduce the number of kidneys "wasted" and, to that extent, can reduce the demand for kidneys.

charitable donors are willing to give Q_1 kidneys, and that is all potential demanders want even at a zero price. In this case, equilibrium is at E_1 with a price of zero. In the real world such an outcome is likely to be a rare occurrence, if for no other reason than that the demanders and suppliers are two different groups of people and are in the market for largely different reasons.[5] One might reasonably expect the demand for kidneys to be so great relative to supply that at a zero price there will be a shortage of kidneys. This is the case when the demand in Figure 8·2 is positioned at D_2; the quantity demanded is Q_3, which is greater than the quantity being offered out of altruism, Q_1. Granted, it is possible that with campaigns to enlist new donors, the gap between supply and demand at a zero price can be closed; barring that, which we must point out can be an expensive process, the shortage means that many people will go without kidneys—some will die. Marvin Brams, who has written on the subject, estimated the number of people on dialysis machines in mid-1974 at 18,000 in the United States. Of these, 40 to 50 percent are candidates for transplants.[6] There is also a severe shortage of corneas for corneal transplants.

If a free market in kidneys, or any other organ, were allowed to function, the price of a kidney would rise toward the intersection of supply and demand, or P_1, which in real life can be several, if not tens of, thousands of dollars. At present, the only viable alternative to a transplant for many patients is dialysis through a machine which can cost, in terms of 1973 medical prices, $6000 a year for self-administered care at home and $30,000 a year in a hospital or kidney center. The process can also be time-consuming in terms of time on the machine and time in travel to and from the kidney center.[7] Furthermore, the patient may have to relocate near a dialysis center and may have to endure all the anxiety that goes with waiting until the right donor comes along. Indeed, when the costs are totaled, one can see that many kidney patients may be willing to pay a handsome market price for a kidney *because it is cheaper than its best alternative.*

The prospects of individuals charging for "their God-given organs" is repulsive to many people because it will force some potential buyers out of the market. The people who take this position may simply have a strong ethical position which makes the sale or purchase of an organ "wrong"; they may also see that the quantity of organs demanded falls from Q_3 at zero price to Q_2 at P_1. Perhaps nothing can be said to many people who may be against the sale of kidneys which will cause them to change their minds, but there is one important point evident in the figure which should not be overlooked. At a price of P_1, the quantity of transplantable kidneys is greater than what is available under a completely altruistic system: people offer a total of Q_2 instead of Q_1. *Because of the pricing system more people will have kidneys;* fewer people will be strapped to a dialysis machine for the rest of their lives and fewer will die.

Clearly, the people who are willing to buy the kidneys, even at what may be considered a very high price, are made better off. The price they pay is evidence of the net benefit. The persons selling the kidneys are also better off, or, at least, they expected to be when they sold the organ. If they give up their kidney while they are still alive, they run the risks associated with having only one kidney. Presumably, the price they receive compensates them for suffering those risks. The person who receives payment for a kidney which he gives up upon his death is compensated for the anxiety he

[5] There will be cases in which a father may consent to having a kidney removed in order that it may be given to his son or daughter. In these cases the wants of the parties can, in a sense, be said to be mutually consistent.

[6] Ibid., p. 14

[7] *Newsweek*, July 16, 1973, p. 93. The actual cost is a function of the degree of renal failure. Total failure of a kidney can mean daily dialysis, which requires hospital care. The costs for these patients can soar to virtually unlimited levels. The cost of a kidney transplant was $15,000 to $20,000 in 1973. Furthermore, according to the *Newsweek* article, an estimated 2000 to 5000 people per year died in the early 1970s for lack of care.

may feel from knowing that he will be taken apart upon death.

Furthermore, doctors will have a greater variety of kidneys to choose from; and, as Brams points out, the greater variety can mean that doctors can more closely match the kidney to the recipient, reducing the possibility of rejection. The doctor will tend to receive a larger number of kidneys from live donors. Since experience indicates that the rejection rate is lower with kidneys from live donors than from cadavers, further reductions in the rejection rate can be achieved.

The market system is not without its difficulties in this area. As noted, some people in need of a kidney will be unable to buy one because of their limited financial resources. However, the introduction of a market for kidneys may reduce, but need not preclude, altruistic donations of kidneys. These donated kidneys can go to those people who have financial difficulties. In addition, such persons' financial problems can be solved in the same way that we now solve many other health-related problems of the poor, through charity and governmental aid. The market system has one redeeming feature, and that is the government and charitable groups will have more kidneys which they can buy and give to the poor.

FROM BODILY ORGANS TO TENNIS COURTS

The principles developed in the last section relating to kidney transplants are readily applicable to the way most universities allocate their facilities among students and faculty who want to use them. Consider the way tennis courts are allocated; this example can reveal both the advantages and the limitations of the market system as an allocator of scarce resources.

Typically, universities do not charge a price for the use of such facilities as tennis courts. This usually means that there is a shortage of tennis courts; more people want to use them during certain hours of the day than can use them. The courts are typically rationed on a first-come-first-serve basis. (Some may suggest that this amounts to "allocation by congestion.") Because of this system, many people take the time which is necessary to show up at the courts to see if one is open only to be turned away. Or they may have to waste time waiting until a court becomes available. Many others may like to play the sport, but do not play because they figure that the probability of a court being open when they want it is too low to take the necessary trouble of trying to play. In any event, the cost of such a system to individuals can be extensive.

There are many ways by which the congestion can be reduced and the courts allocated among the competing "buyers," but we will concentrate on two: (1) the pricing system and (2) the sign-up system. When a price is charged, the number of people wanting to use the courts will diminish. Indeed, the price for different hours of the day can be set at a level whereby the number of people wanting to use the courts will equal the number of courts available. The number of courts available may not be affected by the revenues, since the sizes of athletic facilities are normally determined by legislative decisions in state capitals, but the price can serve the very useful function of rationing the courts among potential buyers. It can, thereby, save many people the cost of going to the gymnasium in search of a court and not being able to find one. Still, we cannot overlook the problem that is created in any market for a good: that is, the market system discriminates against those with limited *financial* resources; however, so long as people have competing spheres of interest, discrimination (i.e., rationing) is necessary in one form or another.

Many students and faculty members, even after considering the advantages of using price to ration the courts, may favor the first-come-first-serve system and would vote for it if a referendum were held on the matter; others may favor the pricing system. There are many reasons why opinions differ; however, the one which we would like to highlight is the possible differences in the opportunity cost of students' and faculty's time. Those students and faculty who have a very low opportunity cost for their time—for example, they can earn only $2 an hour or are unemployed—may favor the first-come system. The cost to them in terms of the time wasted can easily be less than the equilibrium price which would be set in the market. On the other hand, a person whose time is very valuable—say one can earn $25 an hour—may gladly pay a rather high price to ensure that he will be able to get a court when wanted and to ensure that no time is wasted on futile trips going to and from the courts.

It is by no means certain that under a pricing system faculty will always outbid students for the tennis courts. First, there are probably a number of students on campus who make more at a part-time job than do faculty members at teaching. Further, even students who do not work while in school may be willing to pay a higher price than faculty members. One reason is that they may enjoy the sport more. Another, possibly unnoticed, reason is that students, while in school, are "capitalists": They are investing in their future earning power, something which economists call "human capital." If they play tennis, they may reduce their future earning stream. In short, the opportunity cost of these students' time can exceed the opportunity cost of faculty members' time; in other cases, the opposite is true. The opportunity cost of one's time is largely a subjective matter; however, the market system permits such considerations to creep into the determination of how resources and goods, like tennis courts, are allocated.

Alternately, the congestion at the tennis courts can be reduced by "sign-up sheets"; players simply sign up for the times they wish to play. Although this system also has an element of first-come-first-serve in it, it does reduce the amount of time a person may have to wait for a court. This system may be used because it is simpler than the pricing system—it does not require that a cashier be present—and it is generally less costly to administer. Indeed, the pricing system may not yield sufficient revenues to cover the cost of administering it. Additionally, the sign-up system may be considered more "equitable" than the pricing system. People can register the intensity of their preferences in a pricing system; but they can also, perhaps with less precision, register the intensity of their preferences under a sign-up system by their willingness to get to the sign-up sheet first. Since price has little to do with the number of tennis courts a university has, it may, therefore, be understandable why the pricing system is rarely used to allocate tennis courts.

THE TAX, THE TAX, WHO PAYS THE TAX?

The general public is convinced that when the government imposes an excise tax on a commodity like margarine, the producers pass the tax, readily and completely, on to consumers in the form of higher prices. On the other hand, every time Congress or a state legislature considers imposing an excise tax or raising one already in existence, producers of the affected commodity will beat a path to the legislators' doors trying to persuade them not to pass the tax. They will spend hundreds of thousands of dollars in their campaigns. If the tax can be completely passed on to consumers, why do they spend so much money attempting to defeat the legislation? The obvious answer is that, as a general rule, producers are adversely affected by taxes imposed on their products; and supply and demand curves can illustrate why.

Suppose that S_1 and D_1 in Figure 8·3 represent the margarine industry's supply and demand curves under free-market conditions. If the market is competitive, the price will tend toward P_2 and the quantity sold, toward Q_3. If the state imposes a $0.25 tax on each pound of margarine sold and the tax is collected from producers, the costs of production, for all practical matters, rise. The producer must now pay a price for the right to use resources, such as equipment and raw materials, *and* a tax to the government for the right to continue production on a legal basis. The supply curve, reflecting the cost increase, shifts up and to the left to, say, S_2. The vertical difference between the two curves represents the additional cost, which in this case is the tax.

The shift in supply causes a shortage to develop in the market, equal to the difference between Q_1 and Q_3 at the initial price P_2. As a consequence,

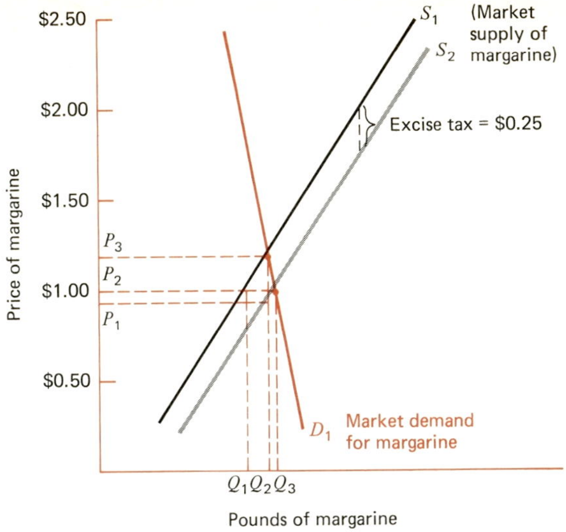

FIG. 8·3 The imposition of an excise tax will cause the supply curve of margarine to decrease. The price paid by consumers will rise from P_2 to P_3, which is less than the tax. The price received by the producers after the tax decreases from P_2 to P_1.

the price charged consumers rises to P_3. However, note that in this example the price increase ($P_3 - P_2$) is not equal to the distance between the two supply curves; it is not equal to the tax which caused the vertical shift in the curve in the first place. Clearly, the *net price* (the market price minus the tax) going to the producer must fall. If he must pay a tax of $0.25, and the price charged consumers rises by $0.20, as it does in the graph, the *net price* received by the producers must fall by $0.05; this price is P_1 in the figure. In other words, the producers, because of the tax and higher price, sell a smaller quantity, but they also sell that quantity at a lower net price to themselves. These changes reduce the profitability of producing margarine. Because of these potential losses, margarine producers can justify spending large sums of money trying to defeat excise tax legislation. The cheapest way of doing this may be to lobby against or simply to "buy off" key politicians.

Butter producers, however, have a clear incentive to see a tax imposed on margarine. The tax on margarine will raise the price of that product, and consumers will then seek substitutes. Butter is clearly a substitute; and as in the case of coal, discussed earlier, the demand for butter rises. Butter producers can charge a higher price, sell a larger quantity, and make higher profits.

There is one condition in the market under which producers' profits go unaffected by an imposed excise tax; it is, however, a rather extreme condition. The demand for the product has to be vertical (or, as economists say, "perfectly inelastic"). That is, no matter what the price is, people will still buy the same quantity. Such a curve is illustrated in Figure 8·4. Again, the vertical distance between the two supply curves represents the tax. Because of the tax, the price in the market rises from P_1 to P_2, which, as can be seen, is equal to the imposed tax. The quantity sold remains at Q_1; the net price of the producers remains at P_1, as

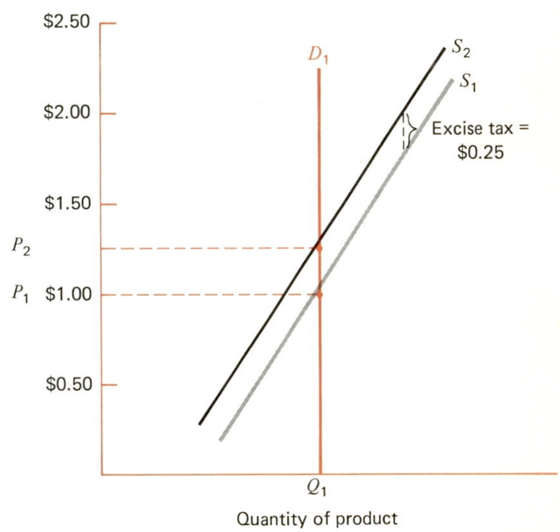

FIG. 8·4 If the demand curve for a product is vertical, a tax imposed on producers will be passed completely to consumers in the form of a price increase equal to the tax.

it was before the tax was imposed.[8] Since economists have a great deal of confidence in the law of demand which states that consumers will buy more at a lower price, this outcome is more of theoretical interest than anything else. The example does, however, serve the purpose of making the general proposition that the more inelastic the demand for the product is, the greater the price increase from an imposed excise tax. The elasticity or inelasticity of demand, as studied earlier, is dependent upon the number of viable substitutes.

A TARIFF ON TEXTILES

A tariff is a special excise tax imposed on goods imported from foreign countries. As in the case of margarine, a tariff on textiles from Hong Kong has the effect of raising the price of imported textiles and reducing the quantity which domestic residents consume of it. This should cause the demand for domestic textiles to rise; domestic producers should be able to raise their prices and sell a larger quantity (refer to Figure 8·1). Like coal producers, domestic textile manufacturers should receive higher profits, and domestic workers in these industries should be able to work more and at higher wages. There is, in other words, ample reason for entrepreneurs and workers in the domestic textile industry to support tariffs on the products of their foreign competitors.

Consumers, on the other hand, have to pay higher prices for their textile products; their *real income* (which is the purchasing power of their money income) falls. One of the reasons why people were buying the imported product before the tariff is that it was cheaper to buy and to make. By encouraging consumers to buy domestic textiles, the government is encouraging them to buy products which are more expensive to make than the products of foreign competitors. In short, because it increases the cost of producing textiles, more resources are needed to produce the domestic textiles; fewer resources are available for doing other things. The tariff, therefore, reduces the production capability of the domestic economy. The textile workers can be better off, but the rest of the country is worse off. (We will discuss tariffs in more detail in Chapter 16.)

[8] If the demand curve were downward sloping and the supply curve were horizontal, an excise tax would cause the horizontal supply curve to shift upward. The market price will increase by the amount of the tax. However, the quantity sold will fall; the producers will lose profits. Accordingly, they should be expected to oppose the tax under these conditions.

HUNGARY'S "TRASH TAX"

Hungary has a tax on "trash." It is not a tax on what we normally think of as trash, but rather on what the authorities wish to consider "trash." The tax is imposed on the sale of selected books which the government in that country wishes to discourage. On the trashy-book list are titles which have been best sellers in this country and other parts of the world; works of Ernest Hemingway have been included. The government does not wish to go so far as to prohibit the sales of these books altogether. However, by imposing a tax, the authorities can raise the books' relative price (that is, the price of books *relative* to other goods); and, as in the case of margarine, people will predictably buy fewer of those titles which are taxed. The government uses the revenues from the "trash tax" to subsidize (reduce) the prices of books which it wishes to encourage; the quantity of subsidized books sold then increases. Because of the tax and subsidy scheme, "trashy books" have been as much as four times as expensive as "classics."

THE ETHIC OF THE COMPETITIVE MARKET

Many people subscribe to the general rule that good motives generate good results; bad motives, bad results. Because the market permits full expression of greed in the social interaction of men and women, the market is viewed accordingly as a corrupting social force. Economists may be able to point to the efficiency of the market, but that is a proposition which may have little impact on reluctant listeners who believe that greed, as a motivational force, must be contained.

As a point in fact, market behavior is in many respects contained by what people consider at the time to be higher social purpose. Even Adam Smith wrote that pursuit of private interest must be tempered by the "virtues of prudence, justice, and beneficence." However, the important point to which supporters of the market must ultimately return to give their argument force is that in the market greed tends to be contained by the nature of the system itself. It is contained within the realm that competition will permit its expression. Indeed, although the *motivation* may conflict with some ethical precepts, the *results* of the competitive process may appear *as if* (but not in fact) people did behave in accordance with what many may see as a reasonable ethical precept: "Do unto others as you would do unto yourself."

To show this, let us consider a short-order cook in two roles, as a producer of hamburgers for himself and as a producer of hamburgers for others in a competitive market. If he produces for himself, it is obviously because he has a downward sloping demand for hamburgers. Assuming that his costs of production, which include his time, meat, mustard, etc., are reflected in an upward sloping supply curve of Figure 8·5, he will produce the quantity of hamburgers shown by the intersection of his supply and demand curves. Up to that quantity, the marginal benefit of another hamburger is greater than the marginal cost (see Chapter 2 for a review). With a demand represented by D_1, he will produce Q_1. With an increase in demand to D_2, because of an increase in preference for them, he will move up along his supply curve and end up with Q_2 hamburgers produced for himself.

Let us turn now to this individual as a producer of hamburgers in a competitive market. Assuming his costs of production do not change because he changes roles, the individual will produce in accordance with the dictates of the price he can receive.[9] If the price which he can receive is P_1, he will find he can profitably produce as many as Q_1 hamburgers. Up to that point, the marginal benefits (measured in terms of the price) exceed the marginal costs of production, indicated by his supply curve. In other words, he will produce as

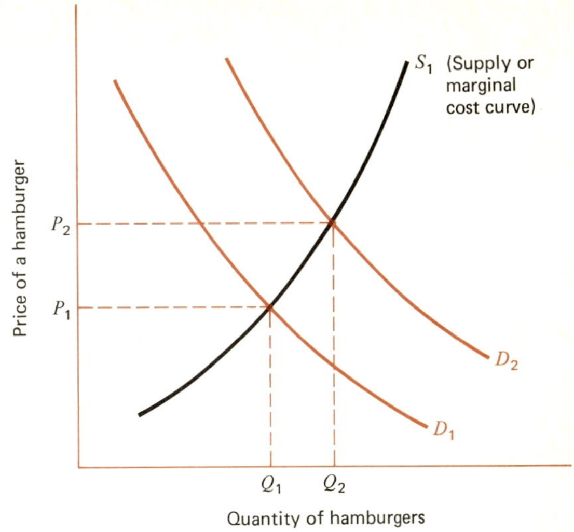

FIG. 8·5 When the short-order cook's demand curve for hamburgers is D_1, he will cook Q_1 hamburgers for himself, which is the same number of hamburgers he will cook and sell to others when their market price is P_1. When the cook's demand is D_2, he will cook Q_2 hamburgers. This is also the number of hamburgers he will cook and sell when the price of hamburgers is P_2.

many hamburgers for the market as he would for himself, given a demand of D_1.

If the market price of hamburgers increases to P_2, the producer will expand production to Q_2, for the same reason discussed earlier. The point which is in need of emphasis is that the producer expands his production along his marginal cost curve. He behaves the same way that he would have behaved if he were producing for himself. It is in this sense that the competitor behaves as if he is following the rule: "Do unto others as you would do unto yourself."

We might prefer that people behave according to the Golden Rule, "Do unto others as you would have them do unto you," but that is a rule to which only a very few among us can adhere on any consistent basis. The "ethical results" of the competitive market may be the best that can be reasonably expected, given human nature.

[9] If costs change, most likely they will fall as *economies of scale* are achieved through catering to a larger number of consumers. This does not materially affect the central point.

SUMMARY AND EXTENSIONS

The market system can perform the very valuable function of rationing scarce resources among all those who want them. It avoids the problems of congestion that will develop when no price is charged for the uses of the resources, goods, and services. Further, the system allows people the opportunity to reveal their relative preferences for a good. A student with very few financial resources may have an intense desire to play tennis; the intensity of his preference can be expressed through his willingness to pay the market price for the good. Because the market price can be an incentive to suppliers, the available quantity of the good can be expanded through the market system.

In this chapter we have shown that when the supply curve is upward sloping and the demand curve is downward sloping, an increase in market demand will cause the price of the good and the quantity sold to rise. A decrease in supply will cause the price to rise and the quantity sold to fall. With additional examples, we can show the opposite: a decrease in demand will cause the price and quantity to fall; an increase in supply will cause the price to fall and the quantity to rise. Even if the supply curve is not upward sloping—for example, if it is horizontal––changes in demand and supply can cause consumers and producers to adjust their plans until the market clears. All this requires a competitive market. In Chapter 10 we consider the phenomenon of monopoly.

QUESTIONS TO PONDER

1 Is a tax on margarine "efficient" in the economic sense of that term?

2 If margarine producers have an excise tax imposed upon them, why will they prefer to have both butter and margarine taxed? Why will a tax on both butter and margarine be more "efficient" than just a tax on margarine?

3 By observing that exporters of oil to the United States prefer not to have a tariff imposed on their oil, we can deduce that they are hurt by such a tariff. With the aid of supply and demand curves, graphically illustrate the harm that a tariff does to oil exporters.

4 Punishment for crimes is a kind of tax on people who engage in illegal activity. What effects would legalizing marijuana have on its supply and demand? What will happen to market price? Quantity sold? Illustrate with supply and demand curves.

5 In the early 1970s the United States government paid Turkish poppy farmers not to grow poppies. What effect should (did) this policy have on the heroin market in other countries in the short-run? Long-run? (Heroin comes from poppies.)

6 In the areas of the United States where beer and liquors cannot be sold on a legal basis, bootleggers are known to be major supporters of community and church efforts to keep the area dry. Explain the logic of this support in terms of supply and demand curves.

7 If tennis courts were allocated by a pricing system, why would you expect different prices for different times of the day? Would this be efficient? Equitable? Would a majority of potential consumers vote for a system of different prices for different times of the day? Explain.

RECOMMENDED READINGS

Fels, Rendigs, and Robert G. Uhler: *Casebook of Economic Problems and Policies: Practice in Thinking*, 1975–76 ed. (New York: West Publishing Co., 1973), cases 4, 5, 6, and 8.

Leftwich, Richard H., and Ansel M. Sharp: *Economics of Social Issues* (Dallas: Business Publications, Inc., 1974), chap. 4

McKenzie, Richard B., and Gordon Tullock: *The New World of Economics* (Homewood, Ill.: Richard D. Irwin, Inc., 1978), chaps. 5, 6, 9, 11, 12, 13, 15, and 19.

North, Douglass C., and Roger Leroy Miller: *The Economics of Public Issues*, 2d ed. (New York: Harper and Row, Publishers, 1973), chaps. 2, 3, 4, 6, 16, 18, and 30.

9

The Government and the Market for Food

Egg prices have always gone in cycles. Once a hen starts her laying cycle of 60 weeks, she keeps on producing. There's no tap short of the soup plant that will shut off the supply. This makes the supply curve very price inelastic in the short run, and economic theory tells that in such a situation any shift in demand produces a very sharp change in prices.

Patrick Howe[1]

PREVIEW OF CHAPTER

Central question

What are the sources of the economic difficulties which farmers have faced over the decades and of the high prices of food which consumers have had to pay?

Major objectives

1. To explain the problems which farmers face in producing food
2. To describe the causes and consequences of governmental programs designed to help farmers
3. To explain the causes and consequences of the Soviet wheat deals

[1] Patrick Howe, "Unscrambling the Egg Market: A Lesson in Economics," *Common Sense Economics*, vol. 2, no. 2, p.42.

Major conclusions

1 The prices of agricultural goods tend to fluctuate widely in the short run because of (*a*) the inelasticity of demand for most agricultural goods, (*b*) the competitive nature of the agriculture industry, and (*c*) the dependency of the industry on the weather.

2 The farm population has dwindled over the decades because of the competitive tendency of many farmers to innovate and increase their productivity and, therefore, to push the prices of farm commodities down, making it unprofitable for many farmers to stay in business.

3 In an attempt to help farmers at the expense of taxpayers and consumers, the government instituted price support programs in the 1930s. The result of the programs was large surplus stocks of agricultural commodities which the government had to buy. The government has tried other programs which reduce the supply and increase the prices of certain other commodities.

4 The Soviet Union's crop failure of 1972 reduced the world supply of certain grains and increased the demand for the grains in the United States markets. The Soviet Union received very attractive prices for the grain it bought in the United States in 1972 because it was able to keep the magnitude of its intended purchases secret. The episode reveals that the Soviets know something about dealing in "capitalist" markets.

"People are starving in Bangladesh." "Consumers are muttering in supermarket aisles." "Longshoremen are refusing to load wheat destined for Russia." "Some cattlemen are killing their calves, and small groups of dairymen are dumping their milk." "The Canadian government is destroying eggs, and newborn biddies are being thrown in the trash." "Consumer prices jump at rates not seen since the Second World War." "Farmers complain about bumper corn harvest." These have been some of the headlines of the 1970s. . . . Could it be that something is amiss?

In evaluating the markets for food, we must start with the observation that men and women are the sole buyers and sellers; and we must end, somehow, with the conclusion that problems are mostly man-made. If only we could claim that all our problems were the consequence of an "act of God"! The intent of this chapter is to explain many of the market problems we detect as we shop for groceries.

AN OVERALL VIEW OF THE FOOD MARKET

Most farm commodities, such as wheat, cotton, and potatoes, are sold in highly competitive markets. There are many buyers and many farmers in almost all lines of produce. Consumers benefit from competition in agriculture because they receive more of the kinds of food they want at lower prices. On the other hand, because of competition, farmers are beset with the problems endemic to similarly competitive markets: in the short run, the prices of agricultural goods respond with reasonable rapidity to the forces of supply and demand. Prices can change substantially during a growing season, that is, between the time the crop is planted and the time it is placed on the market. In addition, over the decades farmers have faced a constantly expanding agricultural technology and have felt the pressure to keep abreast of it or to confront the threat of being forced out of business, as so many have.

Farmers have, however, only rarely been able to conspire *on their own* to control competitive forces. That is, they have not joined together for very long to restrict output, divide the market, raise their prices, and thereby increase their incomes. (They fall into the "large-group" category that is discussed in Chapter 6.) Given their predicament, they have, understandably, turned to a willing government for assistance in accomplishing that which they have been unable to do by themselves. Accordingly, although many different kinds of produce are still free of control by the government, the Department of Agriculture has over the years used tax dollars to encourage farmers to produce more of a number of commodities than can possibly be sold in the market and then, because of these excess supplies the Department has paid farmers to take land out of production.

It should be no surprise that many of these government forays into the agricultural market were initiated in the 1930s when farm families represented 30 percent of the population and, based on a one-person-one-vote rule, had more than their share of federal and state legislative votes, i.e., more than 30 percent. The commodities which have, in one way or another, been supported by government programs were chosen for support, more than anything else, on the basis of the political interests of the representatives serving on key legislative committees. Today, with a smaller farm population, with legislative apportionment more nearly reflecting the distribution of people between rural and urban areas, and with greater consumer awareness of the adverse consequences which government policies have had on the purchasing power of their food dollars, support for past programs has begun to dissipate and there is much talk of returning many areas of agriculture back to free-market status. How much of this talk will be translated into action is unclear at this point. In this chapter, however, we consider the predicament of farmers, both in the short and long run, and the consequences of past government policies.

SHORT-RUN PROBLEMS OF FARMERS

Several characteristics inherent in farming can create problems for farmers in the short run. First, it is documented that short-run demands for most farm commodities tend to be highly inelastic, consumers respond relatively little to price changes. Also farm revenues can fall with a reduction in prices and prices can fall substantially with relatively small increases in supply. Inelasticity of demand reflects consumer unwillingness or inability to make use of substitutes when the prices of foods they eat go up.

Second, modern farming typically requires substantial investment in land and equipment. This means that farmers have significant fixed expenses, such as payments on mortgages and leases on land, which vary little with production in a given year and which must be covered by the revenue from the sale of their crops. Furthermore, by the time farmers must harvest their crops, most of their expenses relating to planting and cultivation have been incurred. Accordingly, at harvest time these "sunk costs" cannot be considered in the decision to harvest or not to harvest and therefore will have little or no influence in determining the supply of any crop on the market at that time (see Chapter 4 for a review of this point).

On what basis, then, does the farmer decide how much to harvest? One must decide whether or not the market prices at harvest are sufficient to cover only the costs of harvesting and transporting the crops to market. Even at very low prices the revenue acquired will probably easily cover the *additional* costs associated with the harvest. On the other hand, the revenue the farmer receives from the sale of the crops may not be sufficient to cover *all* costs, including the costs of planting and of land and equipment use. For example, before harvest a given farmer may have incurred $10,000 in expenses associated with the preparation of land and in planting the corn crop. The cost of harvesting the crop is $1000.

If at harvest time the market price of corn is $2.50 a bushel and the farmer has 3000 bushels to sell, total revenues from the sale will be $7500, which is more than enough to justify spending the $1000 to harvest. However, the total expenses are $11,000, and $4500 is lost on the crop for the year. Although one may lose money in terms of all costs, one is financially better off by selling the crop than by leaving it in the field. If the crop is not taken to market, the total losses will be equal to all the costs incurred before harvest, or $10,000. Most reasonable farmers will sell under these conditions. At times they will leave their crops to rot in the field; this will be the case when expected revenues are less than harvest costs, which in our example would be when the price of corn is less than 33 cents a bushel. (Can you see why?)

There is very little that farmers can do at harvest time to alter the available supplies of their crops. They can store some, but not necessarily all, and storage can be expensive. Farmers also run the risk that prices will not get any better and may get worse. In addition, by delaying their sales, they will not be able to pay off their loans and will add to their interest expenses on outstanding debts. For these reasons, the supplies of most farm commodities, in the short run, tend to be highly inelastic, meaning the quantities available tend to change very little with market price movements.

All of these conditions lead to the conclusion that market prices and farm profits in any one year can be substantially affected by such factors as climate, over which farmers have no control. Interestingly, if good weather prevails for *all* farmers producing the same commodity and a bumper harvest ensues, farmers can find themselves in more financial difficulty than if weather conditions are bad and production is down. The irony is self-evident, and to illustrate why it may be so we have drawn, in Figure 9 · 1, highly inelastic demand and supply curves for corn which represent the conditions existing in most farm markets. For this hypothetical case, we have scaled the price of corn along the vertical axis and the quantity of corn in millions of bushels along the horizontal axis. Given the demand, if the weather is poor and

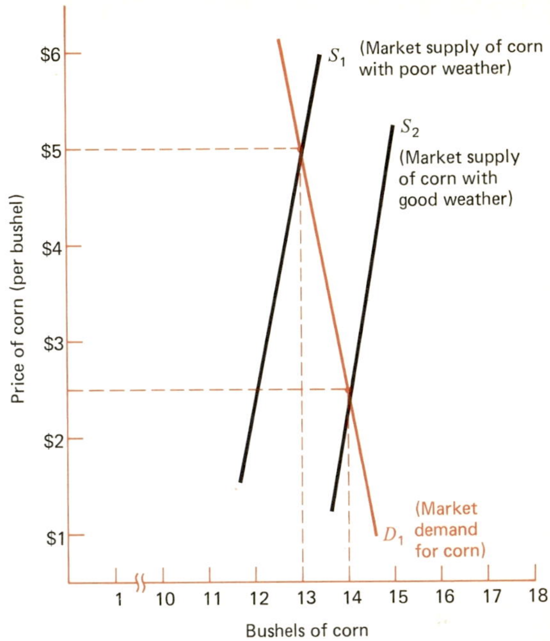

FIG. 9 · 1 Because of the inelasticity of the demand for corn, an increase in the supply of corn in the short run will cause a substantial decrease in the price of corn.

the supply of corn is restricted to S_1, the equilibrium price of corn is $5, and 13 million bushels of corn are sold. The total revenue received by farmers as a group is $65 million ($5 × 13 million bushels).

If, on the other hand, the weather is more favorable, notice from the information in the graph that the financial position of the farmers as a group is worsened. With good weather, the supply of corn will be further out to the right; in the graph we have positioned it at S_2. The equilibrium price is then $2.50 a bushel, with 14 million bushels of corn sold. *The total revenues fall from $65 million to $35 million ($2.50 × 14 million bushels).*

The price falls because of competitive forces, and revenues fall because of inelasticity of demand. With good weather, farmers' total costs of production change very little, causing the difference between revenues and total costs to fall. The farmers may not lose money at $2.50 a bushel, but it is clear that they prefer a market supply curve of S_1 to S_2. (They prefer to sell 14 million as opposed to 13 million bushels of wheat at a price of $5, but given the demand for their corn, that is not an option open to them.)

When interviewed, most farmers appear to hope for good weather and lament over dry, or in other ways poor, growing conditions. Their remarks may appear to contradict our previous conclusion: poor growing conditions *for all farmers* can be preferred to good growing conditions *for all farmers in the short run*. However, an individual farmer, viewing the market from his own geographical location, may prefer good weather for himself for two reasons. First, good weather can mean that he will harvest more; and since *his* total output has very little influence on market price, *given what others do*, his revenues can be greater with a good harvest than with a poor one. For example, if our hypothetical farmer sells 5000 bushels at $2.50, he will have more revenue than if he harvests only 3000 bushels and the price remains approximately the same.

Second, from an individual perspective, as opposed to a "global" perspective of the foregoing discussion, the farmer faces the possibility that any poor weather he experiences may not occur elsewhere. If he has poor weather and farmers in other parts of the country or world have a good growing season, supplies may remain relatively large and prices will not rise materially. Since the farmer with poor weather will have less to sell, his total revenue from sales will fall.

Perhaps it should go without saying that for farmers in a small geographical location, representing a small part of the total market, the most favorable conditions to have, at least *in the short run*, are very favorable growing conditions while conditions are poor elsewhere. Indeed, the welfare of United States farmers has, for short periods of time, been markedly improved by major crop failures in such places as the Soviet Union, a topic to which we will turn in a moment. We emphasized the fact that the financial benefits of even prolonged crop failures elsewhere may be short-lived. This is so because the profit potential in the United States resulting from consistent crop failures elsewhere can mean that more farmers will enter the market and farmers already in the market will expand production. All these movements will increase supply and put downward pressure on market price in the long run.

Our analysis permits several observations which can be generalized to most farm commodity markets. First, small changes in the expected harvest, resulting from any disturbance which affects supply, can lead to significant price fluctuations. Second, as we will see in discussing the Soviet wheat deals, small, unexpected changes in demand can also significantly affect farm revenues because of the inelasticity of the short-term supply of farm products. Third, the potential for price fluctuation may be greater in agriculture than in other markets because consumers and producers are less willing and/or less able to respond readily to price changes in food. Fourth, there is, therefore, an element of uncertainty involved in farming, but we must emphasize that this element is present in all lines of production in which planning and incurring costs are separated by a period of time from the sale of the output. An element of uncertainty has surely been present in the hand calculator business (see Chapter 7) over the past decade. Fifth, where this element of risk is present, producers incur, over the long run, what economists call a "risk cost." This added cost will tend to restrict the long-term supply of farm commodities, and the long-run price of farm commodities should be expected to compensate farmers for accepting the risks involved in their business. These comments are not meant to down-play *short-term* difficulties of farmers but are means to introduce a discussion of the way in which the market can handle the problems of risk in the long run.

LONG-RUN PROBLEMS OF FARMERS

The prices of most farm commodities have risen over the years. This is particularly true of commodity prices during the 1970s. However, the

TABLE 9·1 LONG-RUN DECLINE OF AGRICULTURE EMPLOYMENT*

Year	Civilian Labor Force (CLF) (in thousands)	Agriculture Workers (in thousands)	Percent of CLF in Agriculture
1929	47,630	10,450	21.9
1940	47,520	9,540	20.0
1950	48,920	7,160	12.1
1960	65,778	5,458	8.2
1970	78,627	3,462	4.4
1974	85,936	3,492	4.0

* SOURCE: *Economic Report of the President*, 1975, p. 575.

long-run *relative* prices of farm commodities, which are the ratios of farm prices to nonfarm prices, have tended to fall. This is because the prices of nonfarm goods have risen faster than the prices of farm goods.[2]

Farmers have experienced a substantial long-term rate of growth in agricultural productivity; that is, they have been able to grow more crops with fewer resources. Government agriculture research programs and the competitiveness of the farm sector have stimulated much of this productivity growth. In turn, the productivity growth, which has been much greater in farming than in the nonfarm sector, has been a major reason for the *relative* fall in farm prices. Those farmers who have taken advantage of the new technology, who have made the necessary investment and have taken the associated risks, have been able to cope with the higher costs of such investment and the higher costs for labor and fertilizer. They have had to pay higher prices for their fertilizer and seeds, but they have been able to produce more. In other words, because of their increased productivity, these farmers have been able to accept lower relative prices for their output.

However, the farmers who have not been so aggressive have been confronted with increased costs for fertilizer and labor with no compensating increase in their production. They have faced a price-cost squeeze. Their net income, which is what is left from revenue after costs have been subtracted, has evaporated. Many have been forced to seek employment in the nonfarm sector. The migration away from the farm is clearly revealed in Table 9·1. Because of an inability or unwillingness to make the adjustment from the farm to urban and industrial life, many low-income farmers have stayed on their farms, tending to lower the average incomes of all farmers.

GOVERNMENT AS A MODERN-DAY ROBIN HOOD

According to legend, Robin Hood and his men stole from the rich and gave to the poor; in this way, they redistributed income in an open and direct manner. Through its agriculture policies, government has also contributed to a redistribution—in this case, from consumers and taxpayers to farmers. However, the methods employed have not been nearly as open and direct as those used by the rogues of Sherwood Forest. In fact, many consumers are unaware that their tax dollars have been used to increase the price of bread and other grocery items they want for their families or themselves. Furthermore, the redistribution has not occurred as a clear-cut movement of income from the rich to the poor. Many well-to-do farmers have been the beneficiaries of government agri-

[2] During several years in the early and mid-1970s, the prices of many farm commodities rose faster than those of nonfarm goods. This, however, does not contradict our point which relates to the trend of farm prices over the period from, say, the 1930s to the present.

culture aid, and very poor people have had to pay higher prices for food. To that extent, the poor have contributed their share to improving the welfare of farmers, who have claimed distress in terms of low average incomes. In the process, the government has encouraged farmers to literally waste many very valuable farm resources, such as seed, fertilizer, labor, land, and equipment. Let us explain by turning to the specific example of the wheat market and the government's intervention in it.

Government as a Buyer of Last Resort

Suppose that the long-run supply and demand for wheat are represented by the curves in Figure 9·2; under these conditions the free-market price will be P_1. However, suppose the government, because of political pressure from farmers, determines that this price results in an income for farmers in general which is too low for a decent living or that farmers deserve higher incomes for their efforts. The government can consider passing a law to the effect that anyone wishing to buy wheat must pay no less than P_2, a level considerably above the free-market price.

The problem with selling wheat at the higher price of P_2 becomes clear when you look at the graph. A higher price encourages consumers to buy less wheat, while it encourages producers to expand production. A surplus emerges in the sense that producers are willing to offer more on the market than buyers are willing to take from it. There may be farmers in the market now unable to sell any wheat, in which case they are clearly hurt by a program designed to help them. Other farmers are unable to sell as much as they would like at P_2. All of them have an incentive to sell their wheat illegally, and they can, in all probability, find willing customers if they lower their price below P_2. In other words, in order to hold the price at P_2 by fiat, government must incur all the costs necessary to enforce it. If the price is held to P_2, the government must cope with problems of excess supply and how to give each farmer his "fair share" of the market that is available. (Remember, only Q_2 can be sold at the higher price.)

In order to settle these problems, government can enter the market as a buyer of last resort, willing to pay as much as the support price, in our example P_2, for each and every bushel of wheat. If farmers cannot get P_2 from the market, they can sell their supplies to the government. In this way, government effectively takes the surplus off the market, eliminates any competitive pressures to lower prices, and forces market buyers to pay P_2 for their wheat. Fundamentally, this is the way the Department of Agriculture has supported, since the 1930s, the price of wheat, cotton, feed grains, dairy products, peanuts, rice, and tobacco.[3]

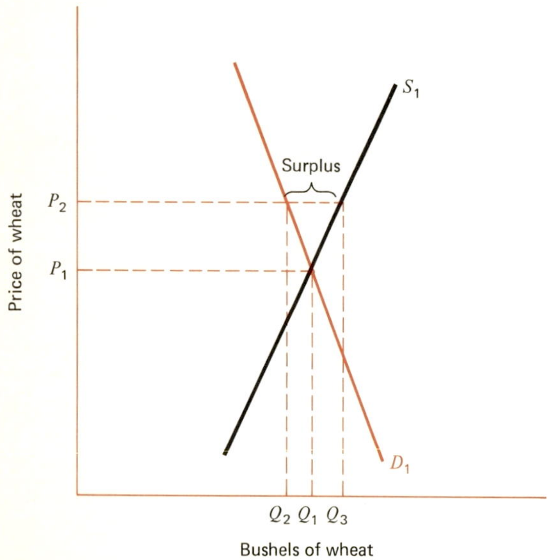

FIG. 9·2 Any price above the equilibrium price which is "supported" by the government will create a market surplus. The government must buy this surplus.

[3] The mechanics of the program are more complex than is indicated here. Prices are actually supported through the Commodity Credit Corporation (CCC). During the growing season, the CCC loans the farmer an amount based on the estimated size of his harvest multiplied by the announced support price. The crop is used for collateral. If at harvest the farmer is unable to sell his crop for at least as much as the support price, he can default on the loan (with no stigma attached) and surrender his crop to the CCC. If he can get more than the support price in the marketplace, the farmer is free to sell the crop in the market and to pay off his loan with the CCC.

Some farmers have benefited from this price support scheme. The prices for their crops have been relatively more stable and their incomes higher. How much and how long they have benefited is a question to which we will return. On the other hand, the price of bread has been higher than it would otherwise have been because the government has artificially kept the cost of wheat above the market price. The higher cost of feed grains has meant that fewer cattle have been raised and meat prices have risen; higher prices for cotton have meant higher clothing costs for consumers. Because more farm land, fertilizer, etc., have been used in crops where prices have been supported, fewer resources have been available for other nonsupported crops. The supply of these other, nonsupported crops has been restricted, and their prices have been higher than they otherwise would have been. Furthermore, the government has had to pay for the crops it has purchased. The funds have come from general tax revenues, meaning that federal taxes, in part, have been used to raise the price of groceries!

What to Do with the Surplus?

Once it buys surplus commodities from the farmer, the government must decide what to do with the surplus. The available options are more restricted than one might think. Government cannot sell in the domestic market what it has purchased at P_2, because the market demand has been satisfied at the support price; indeed, that is the reason for the government purchases in the first place. If the commodities are offered for sale domestically at a price below P_2, buyers will buy from the government instead of the market. Farmers will be unable to dispose of even Q_2 in the market and must sell what they have to the government. Any attempt by the government to sell the crop at anything below the support price, P_2, can mean that the government will end up buying almost the entire crop and selling it at a lower price.

Part of the crop can be given away, and this has been done through domestic and foreign aid programs, but the government must be careful in doing this. If it gives food to people who will not otherwise be in the market, no adverse effect will be recorded; however, if the surpluses are given to those who would otherwise be *prospective buyers*, the market demand will fall, leaving more for the government to absorb.

If the government tries to sell its holdings in world commodity markets, it may run headlong into the objection from other countries that the United States is "dumping" its excess crops on them and is in this way depressing the prices their farmers can otherwise expect to obtain. The United States government may have to heed such objections because other countries can retaliate with similar practices in United States markets. Foreign governments can also retaliate by imposing higher tariffs on United States exports. Reductions in world commodity prices are desirable for consumers in all parts of the world; but if a country's wheat farmers are injured by United States practices and have sufficient political clout to influence their country's diplomatic positions, multilateral price reductions cannot be anticipated. Consumers in the United States may also object to their government's selling wheat or other crops abroad for less than they can buy them for in their own country.

Another way for the government to handle the surplus crops it has purchased is to destroy them. For some crops, destruction may be unavoidable. For example, in 1972 Canadian provincial governments began supporting the price of eggs at levels above their free-market price. The consequence, as expected, was a quick oversupply of eggs, due in part to the fact that United States farmers began shipping eggs to Canada to take advantage of the higher prices there. (The shipments were illegal, but the system was not well policed.) The excess supply had to be purchased by one of the provincial egg boards and later, when it was organized, by the Canadian Egg Marketing Agency. Eggs cannot be stored very long in their natural state. In one instance, 28 million of them rotted at one time and had to be destroyed.[4] When millions are starving throughout the world and newspapers are eager to provide their readership with vivid accounts of waste, politicians and

[4] Howe, "Unscrambling the Egg Market," pp. 42–47.

agricultural officials who support such programs will find destruction of surplus food creates much adverse publicity and is, therefore, a very unattractive option. Programs of destruction may also reveal to the public the extent of the waste of such agricultural policies.

Another option open to the government is to store its purchases of excess market supplies for emergency use in future years. Some crops can be held to soften the consequences of natural disasters.[5] However, if support prices are continually held at levels above market prices, the stored commodities will accumulate, leading to greater and greater storage costs. This is exactly what happened in the United States during the 1950s and early 1960s. The peak holdings of supported crops are indicated in Table 9·2, and the storage costs, at one time, ran well over $1 million a day. Some of the crops stored over the years have rotted, indicating that it would have been better in terms of the tax load on the public if the government had paid farmers to dig those proverbial ditches and cover them over again. Then, at least, the cost of purchasing and storing many crops would have been avoided. One reason why this and other similar agricultural programs have been politically successful is that they are complicated and indirect and, to that extent, removed from public scrutiny.

[5] If natural disasters frequently occur in a particular country, private firms have an incentive to buy crops in good years and store them for sale later. The crops can be purchased at low prices and sold later, during a disaster, at higher prices. During a disaster, the supply of one or more crops will be in short supply; their prices should then reflect their greater relative scarcity, and those who have the goods in storage can make a return sufficient to cover the costs of storage. Because of this, we can assume that any argument suggesting that the government must store the crops is an argument that the market will somehow not adequately handle the problem or that the government should store more crops than is actually reasonable in light of the threat of natural disaster. If the market is free and competitive, the prices charged need not be (although they may at times be) at extortionist levels; existing competition will push the prices in disaster toward those levels which will enable the holders of the crop to cover their expenses. Even the government, when it stores crops for emergency use, must cover its expenses.

Government as a Regulator of Supply

Because the demand for most agricultural commodities is inelastic, the welfare of all farmers can be improved if all work together to restrict their production. Farm commodity prices can be raised and, as a consequence, revenues from the sale of the harvest will be increased.[6] Cartels, although prohibited in most nonfarm, industrial sectors of the economy, are specifically permitted in the farm sector by the Clayton Act of 1914. Farmers, however, as pointed out earlier, face formidable problems in attempting to restrict total farm production through collusion. Farmers tend to spurn any form of collective action. In addition, farmers constitute a significant segment of the population and are spread over a large geographical area, making the cost of all agreeing to restrict output and effectively enforce the agreement very high—so high that long-term workable agreements have been rare in the annals of agriculture history.

Farmers are intelligent businesspeople; they can see the benefits of reducing the market supply of a particular product. But, at the same time, an individual farmer in a large-group setting can reason that if all cut back on production, the price will rise. And, if any one farmer fails to follow suit, the price will not be affected. He can be better off if he and all others cut back on production, but he can be even better off than that if he lets others cut back and he continues to produce as much as he finds profitable at the higher price. Furthermore, the individual farmer may be very hesitant about cutting back because he fears that others will not cut back. Hence, attempts to collude tend to be nipped in the bud.

There are, at times, some frustrated farmers who vent their anger by staging a demonstration at which they dump their milk in a ditch or shoot and discard a few of their calves in full view of

[6] Some improvement in revenue can possibly be realized from a restriction in market supply even if farmers face an elastic *demand* curve. This would be true if the cutback in production causes their costs of production to fall more rapidly than revenues fall. A clear understanding of this proposition will have to await the discussion of monopoly in Chap. 10. For now, we focus solely on the inelastic demand in order to explain a clear case for collective restriction of supply.

TABLE 9·2 PEAK LEVELS OF CCC COMMODITY INVENTORIES

Commodity	Unit	Record Inventory Quantity	Record Inventory Value (millions)	Date of Record Inventory
Beans, Dry Edible	Cwt.	9,802,905	$ 80.3	Aug. 31, 1950
Cotton				
Extra Long Staple	Bale	148,648	38.1	Aug. 31, 1966
Upland	Bale	11,864,188	1,783.4	Aug. 31, 1966
Cottonseed Oil				
Crude	Pound	39,185,302	4.4	Feb. 28, 1959
Refined	Pound	1,024,573,416	173.2	April 30, 1954
Dairy Products				
Butter	Pound	520,847,552	327.0	Sept. 30, 1954
Butter Oil	Pound	110,729,453	87.2	Sept. 30, 1963
Cheese	Pound	463,363,100	174.0	Oct. 31, 1954
Milk, Dried	Pound	744,533,582	109.8	July 31, 1963
Feed Grains				
Barley	Bushel	100,839,675	98.9	July 31, 1959
Corn	Bushel	1,472,845,459	1,878.2	Nov. 30, 1961
Grain Sorghum	Bushel	720,936,582	781.1	April 30, 1962
Oats	Bushel	199,644,553	124.1	Sept. 30, 1971
Rye	Bushel	27,340,241	28.4	Aug. 31, 1971
* Flaxseed	Bushel	27,098,555	72.5	July 31, 1971
Honey	Pound	6,167,922	0.7	June 30, 1953
Linseed Oil	Pound	528,027,934	150.1	Feb. 28, 1951
Peanuts				
Farmers' Stock	Pound	324,805,409	35.8	Jan. 31, 1952
Shelled	Pound	105,773,769	15.0	July 31, 1960
Rice				
Milled	Cwt.	14,337,127	154.0	Sept. 30, 1956
Rough	Cwt.	16,046,379	85.7	May 31, 1957
Soybeans	Bushel	182,407,689	472.7	Oct. 31, 1969
Tung Oil	Pound	42,049,479	10.5	Nov. 30, 1970
Wheat	Bushel	1,276,830,359	2,552.4	May 31, 1961

* Quantity of flaxseed as of 7-31-71 exceeds quantity as of 1-31-49, but value is less as of 7-31-71 because carrying charges not included. Carrying charges were included in 1949 value. Revalued basis of inventory (which excludes carrying charges) started June 1953.

SOURCE: Agriculture Stabilization and Conservation Service, U.S. Department of Agriculture, "Acquisition and Disposal of Farm Commodities by CCC," *ASCS Background Information*, no. 3, July 1974, p. 13.

television audiences. To the extent that such episodes bring pressure to bear on politicians to come to the aid of farmers, the demonstrations can and have been useful. However, barring political interference, the farmers who destroy any part of their crops must settle simply for the satisfaction of having "made a statement."

With the power of enforcement and tax revenues on its side, government can force or entice farmers to behave as a unified collective group (or "monopoly"). It can bring about a reduction in the supply of food and can, therefore, avoid going into the market as a buyer. In so doing, it raises market prices and short-run incomes of farmers. In short, government encourages farmers to act collectively in ways that a free and competitive market would not have allowed.

To illustrate, if in Figure 9·3 the price "desired" by government is P_2 and the free-market supply of wheat is S_1, the desired price can be achieved by reducing the supply to S_2. To do that the government must intervene in the production plans of individual farmers. Since an appeal for voluntary cooperation will have no effect, in the past the government has sought to restrict the supply of several commodities in three basic ways: (1) by assigning acreage allotments, (2) by assigning market quotas, and (3) by paying farmers not to produce as much as they would freely choose without the payment. The effect of all three methods is to divide the available quantity that can be sold at P_2, which is Q_2, among the potential farmers.

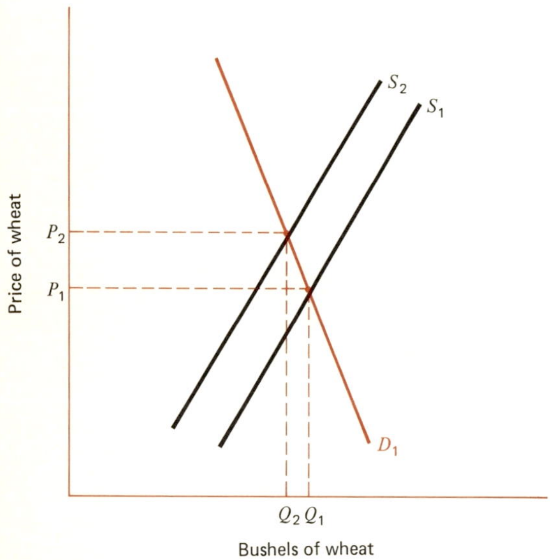

FIG. 9·3 A reduction in the supply of wheat will lead to an increase in the price of wheat and, because of the inelasticity of demand, to an increase in the revenues of farmers. The reduction in supply can be accomplished by any one of the following government policies: (*a*) the assignment of acreage allotments, (*b*) the assignment of marketing quotas, and (*c*) payments to farmers for reducing production.

The *acreage allotment method* restricts output by reducing the number of farm acres that can be used to produce a given crop. The acreage is distributed among the farmers in a predetermined manner. In the case of tobacco, the acreage allotments were initially distributed proportionally, based on the farmers' history of production. Marketing quotas for individual farms are similar to acreage allotments. Instead of being allowed to use only a certain amount of land to produce a given crop, farmers are told how many pounds, bushels, etc., they can take to market. There is, however, one important difference. Under acreage allotments, the behavior of farmers is restricted only in terms of the amount of land that can be used. They are free to cultivate the land as *intensely* as they wish. They can apply more fertilizer and more labor and can increase the land's productivity. In Canada, control of the egg market was organized through control of the number of hens that farmers could have; farmers reacted by introducing a new breed of chicken which is able to lay more eggs; and a new vaccine was used to wipe out a disease which had, in the past, killed 1 to 5 percent of laying hens.

We would expect the cost of producing bushels of wheat, corn, or tobacco to be higher under acreage allotment programs than under free-market conditions. If farmers have an incentive to farm their allotted land more intensely, the tendency must be for them to substitute more expensive resources like fertilizer for the less expensive resource of land. This raises the cost of producing any given quantity. If this is not the general tendency, why were farmers using so much land before the establishment of the acreage allotment schemes? The reason must have been that that was the cheapest way to produce, given the known technology.

Under a *marketing quota system*, the number of pounds or bushels that will be coming onto the market is known with more precision (that number is not dependent on how intensely the land is farmed) and the farmer cannot benefit by attempting to raise his output. His sole objective must be to minimize the costs of producing that which he is allowed to sell. In the final analysis, both systems, acreage allotment and marketing quota, tend to restrict entry into farming and the competitive forces leading toward innovation.

In 1956 President Eisenhower initiated what has since been known as the *soil bank program*. Under this program the Department of Agriculture paid farmers to take a part of their land out of production. (The difference between the soil bank program and acreage allotment is that under acreage allotment no payment is made; coercion is used.) Although the program is now defunct, farmers benefited from the soil bank program by getting direct payment for not producing; because land was taken out of production, the program tended to restrict supply of farm commodities and raise their prices. However, the supply of crops that reached the marketplace did not drop proportionally to the number of acres taken out of production. There was a tendency, to the extent permissible, for farmers to take their worst land out of production. Furthermore, by having less land to farm, farmers were able to farm their remaining land more intensively.

A Change in the Subsidy Program, 1973 Style

Beginning with the Agricultural and Consumer Protection Act passed in 1973, the government has moved away from "support prices" to what is now called "target prices." The act brought about a change in the way in which farmers are subsidized, as well as a change in terminology. For a specified list of commodities, the government no longer supports the market prices by purchasing surpluses. Instead, it announces a "target price" for the various crops and lets the market seek the equilibrium price, given the amount farmers have produced. If the market clearing price is below the target price, the government pays farmers the difference between what they received in the market and the target price. For example, if the target price for a bushel of wheat is $5 and a farmer can sell his wheat in the market for $4.50, the government pays the farmer $0.50 ($5.00 − $4.50) for each bushel sold. Although under this scheme consumers get the benefits of a lower market price than if the government purchased the crops, they still have to foot the bill for the subsidy to farmers. The system also contributes to inefficiency in the agriculture sector; farmers will tend, under the system, to produce beyond that point at which the marginal cost of an additional bushel is equal to the marginal benefit. (Explain why.) At the least, the subsidy is more obvious to taxpayers. In fact, this scheme has been proposed for many years but has been opposed by farm groups, one very plausible reason being the explicit nature of the subsidy.

The Long-Run Benefits of Government Agricultural Programs to Farmers

When federal agricultural programs are initiated, farmers then in operation can receive, possibly for a period of years, windfall gains. However, if the programs remain intact, will all these benefits remain in farming in the long run? As long as government is unwilling to control all aspects of farming, including the rental and sale of farm property, the answer is a qualified no. The benefits of some farm programs will tend to be "capitalized" in (or incorporated into) the market price of the farms, in the market price of the marketable acreage allotment, or in the rental payments paid by tenant farmers.

To explain, if an acreage allotment program makes growing tobacco more profitable in the short run, the demand for the farms with such acreage allotments will rise. Because of the increased demand for such farms, the price of the farms will rise accordingly. Farmers will have to pay a higher price for their farms; they will, therefore, have to make a greater investment than before the allotment program. The person who owns a farm and obtains an allotment at the time the program is established benefits in terms of a higher selling price for his farm. However, the person who buys into the farm after the program is established may receive no greater rate of return on his investment than he would have if the allotment program had never been established.

For example, suppose that a farmer can buy a small tobacco farm for $50,000 before an allotment program is set up; the profit on the farm is $5000. The annual rate of return on investment is, therefore, 10 percent. If the supply of tobacco is restricted through allotments on each farm and the price of tobacco rises, the profit can rise to $10,000. If the price of the farm rises to $100,000, the person who owns the farm experiences a $50,000 increase in wealth. However, anyone who buys the farm receives the same rate of return, 10 percent, as the person receives when the required investment is $50,000. Because of market imperfections, the price of the farm may not adjust in such a way as to reduce the rate of return all the way back to pre-allotment levels; we should, however, expect the price to move in that direction. Anyone who has tried to buy a farm with a 25-acre allotment in eastern North Carolina realizes that this line of analysis has merit.

If landowners have to pay more for their land or if they can sell their land for a higher price because of the allotment, the required rental payment on the land must be raised to compensate them for their out-of-the-pocket investment in the land or the higher opportunity cost of not selling their land at the higher price. (The higher rental payment is the inducement that is needed to keep the land from being sold.) If allotments are detached from the land, as they have been in recent years, and marketed in the same sense as stocks and bonds, the farmer who wants to grow tobacco must now buy land *and* allotment rights, again increasing the necessary investment.

Farm price support programs and soil-bank-type programs can also increase demand for farm lands, increasing the price of farms and the necessary investment and tending to lower the rate of return back toward the competitive level established before government intervention in the market. Given that more land can be opened up for farming, the rate of return a farmer or farm buyer receives on his investment will not fall all the way to the pre-government level. We should expect, however, that after farm support programs have been in effect for a number of years, as they have been at this point in American history, there will be an understandable resistance on the part of farmers to their demise. Like many others, most farmers do not want to lose a good thing. In addition, many farmers in business have now bought their farms at prices which have been inflated because of the government programs. The elimination of the farm programs would mean that the demand for farm property would fall, and many farmers would lose as a result of the expected drop in the value of their property. An adjustment back to free-market status may be strewn with the lost investments of people who assumed that these programs would remain in effect for a long time, if not indefinitely.

SOVIET WHEAT DEALS

The Soviet Union began buying heavily in United States grain markets in the spring and summer of 1972. Its representatives bought 19 million tons of several kinds of grain; about one-fourth of the United States wheat crop for that year was included in the deal. The Soviets received very favorable terms—so favorable, in fact, that before the grain had left America, they indicated a willingness to sell some of what they had purchased back to us—at higher prices, of course. As might be expected, the deal became politicized. Questions concerning why it happened, how the Soviets pulled it off, and the consequences of further trade with the Soviet Union became buried in rhetoric. In 1975, longshoremen refused to load shipments of grain to the Soviet Union unless they could be guaranteed that these sales would not affect domestic food prices and that the grain would be shipped on United States ships. A Pennsylvania congressman proposed legislation that would have required the Secretary of Commerce to issue "domestic food price impact statements" before large deals with foreign countries, primarily the Soviet Union, could be closed. Many other politicians and journalists proposed that sales of grain be tied to purchases of oil and natural gas from the Soviet Union. No one seemed particulary interested in keeping American farmers from selling in the world market, but many were in favor of restricting the ability of the Soviet Union to buy in United States markets. The whole series of Soviet grain purchases represents a good example of how supply-and-demand-curve analysis can clarify the issues and how a large purchaser, keeping the magnitude of his intentions secret, can manipulate a market. First, a brief look at the situation farmers face in the Soviet Union.

The Soviet Union grows most of its grains in the Ukraine and Kazakstan provinces. Kazakstan, which is in the southern part of the Soviet Union and east of the Ural Mountains, making it a part of Siberian Russia, has only recently been opened up to grain production, and it is in this marginal grain-growing area that the Soviet Union has experienced most of its production problems. The Kazakstan region has three important geographic features. First, much of the area is so dry that it approaches desert conditions. On average it receives 15 inches of rain a year, which is marginal for most grain crops. However, the basic problem is that rainfall is highly variable. The region can have more than sufficient rain one year and very little the next. What are marginal growing conditions can rapidly deteriorate to almost impossible conditions. Second, the moisture in the area can be affected significantly by the "Sukhovey Winds." These are very high and extremely dry winds which flow from Siberia down through Kazakstan toward the Middle East. They can suck moisture right off the ground, and when the Sukhovey is up, a crop failure of some magnitude is almost certain. Third, the land is what geographers call "steppe lands," or short-grass lands, meaning that the humus (good farming soil) is very shallow. All the conditions necessary for a significant crop failure are present about once every two years. In contrast, grains in the United States (as well as in the Ukraine) are grown in areas where the average annual rainfalls are greater (15 to 20 inches) and much less variable. Although grain in the United States is also grown in short-grass lands, most of it is grown in areas where the humus is much thicker than in Kazakstan. Crop failures are not expected nearly as frequently in the United States as in Kazakstan.

Be that as it may, the Soviet Union had a series of crop failures beginning in 1972. The crop failure of 1972, which occurred in other parts of the world as well as in the Soviet Union, meant that there was a significant drop in the world supply of grains. The Soviet Union and other nations turned to the United States, which up to that time had been accustomed to large surpluses. The increase in demand for United States grains wiped out the surplus; the equilibrium price was then above the Department of Agriculture's support price. In terms of Figure 9·4, the entry of the Soviet Union and other world buyers into the United States market meant that the demand for wheat shifted from D_1 to D_2. At a perceived equilibrium price of P_1, this meant that there was a shortage, equal to the difference between Q_2 and Q_1. The true equilibrium price was then P_2; this is the price that *could* have been received from the Soviet Union.

However, the Soviets were able to get a price of $1.65 a bushel of wheat, which, in terms of the graph, is close to P_1. They were able to get this very attractive price because of how and when they made their purchases. While their crops were still in the fields, many United States farmers had already contracted to sell them to grain storage companies; the supply price received by farmers was therefore pretty much set. If the farmers had known, which they did not, that the Soviet Union was going to be in the market as heavily as it was, they would have held onto their crops, asking for a higher price. The Soviets, on the other hand, bought from several grain exporting companies, placing large orders with each. The grain exporters and the Department of Agriculture, unable to

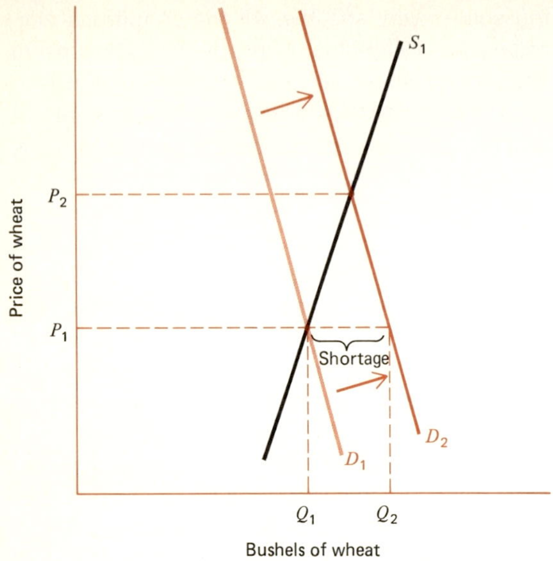

FIG. 9·4 Because of their crop failure in 1972, the Soviet Union turned to United States markets for certain grains they needed. The result was an increase in the market demand for grains like wheat and an increase in their prices in the United States.

compare notes, were not fully aware of the true dimensions of the Soviet grain purchases. The result was that the Soviets were able to purchase a portion of United States supplies at a price that was below the market price. With hindsight, a reasonable market price for wheat in the summer of 1972 has been estimated at \$2.65 to \$3.20 per bushel.[7] Because of the difference between actual purchase price and estimated market price, and given the size of the purchase, Robert Kerton argues that the effective subsidy given the Soviets on their grain purchases in that one year closely approximates \$1 billion.[8] Because of the deal, which depleted United States grain reserves, and because farmers and grain speculators expected further purchases by the Soviet Union and others during the following year, the price of wheat one year later went to \$4.92 a bushel. A year after that, the 1974 price of a bushel was nearly \$6, and bakers were receiving considerable press attention by claiming that the price of bread could rise from a then common price of \$0.50 a loaf to \$1.

Out of the debacle of 1972 the suggestion has emerged that United States grain markets be closed to the Soviet Union. Supposedly, by not selling directly to the Soviet Union, the prices of grains and hence of processed foods would be kept from rising. However, in order to keep the price of food down, the government would have to be willing to keep the United States farmer from selling in the world grain markets in general. If the Soviet Union has a crop failure, it will have to buy its grain from some place—if not the United States, then Canada or Australia. This means that the world price of grain will rise, providing an incentive for United States farmers to sell abroad. They may not, in this instance, sell directly to the Soviet Union; but to the extent that the world price is up, they will continue to sell abroad until the domestic price of grain approximates what they can receive in the world market, and United States consumers will, whether they like it or not, have to pay that price. In other words, regardless of where the Soviets buy their wheat, the price of bread will be forced up by approximately the same amount.

Finally, there seems to be a feeling that United States residents do not benefit from the Soviet wheat purchases unless the purchases are tied explicitly to United States purchases of something like oil. The inaccuracy of this position can be easily uncovered. If the Soviet Union buys wheat from us, they must pay for the wheat in either dollars or rubles (the Soviet currency). If they pay in terms of dollars, the Soviets got the dollars by selling something of value to us. If they pay in terms of rubles, we have rubles which can be used to purchase something from the Soviet Union. In fact, the rubles can be used to buy many (but because of restriction, not all) Soviet goods and services. Oil is, without question, a very valu-

[7] Robert R. Kerton, "The Billion Dollar Blunder," *Common Sense Economics*, vol. 2, no. 2, pp. 48–51.

[8] Ibid.

able resource—something we Americans would like more of; but there may be other things, like chrome ore (or vodka), which we value more than oil. If we take rubles for wheat, we can buy anything conditions at the time dictate we need most. Of course, people who would like to have oil more than the other things may like to see the wheat tied explicitly to oil purchase agreements.

SUMMARY AND EXTENSIONS: EQUITY AND GOVERNMENT POLICY TOWARD FOOD

In enlisting the support of government in their cause, farmers have used the argument that their incomes are low and need to be raised. Although this may sound like a reasonable and laudable request, careful attention must be paid to the consequences of government policy designed to benefit farmers. Through the tax system, many wealthy taxpayers have contributed to the goal of raising the incomes of many poor farmers. However, many low-income taxpayers have also had their taxes used to raise the incomes of many well-to-do farmers. An additional noteworthy consequence of government agricultural policy is that its cost has been channeled, in part, through higher prices on food. Most economists would argue that this is a rather haphazard way of redistributing income. Clearly, it conflicts with the dictates of a progressive tax system, the system which attempts to raise people's tax rates as their incomes rise. Since poor people tend to spend a larger portion of their income on food, higher food prices tend to reduce the real purchasing power of the poor more than the purchasing power of those with higher incomes. Indeed, because of the burden which the poor have felt with respect to their food budgets, the government has initiated the food stamp program. Justification for the food stamp program, and the required taxes to pay for the program, would not be as strong if it had not been for the fact that government policy had been keeping the prices of groceries higher than they would otherwise have been.

Because United States crops have been restricted in supply, world food prices have been kept high. In addition, the amount of food available in the world is inversely related to the world's level of starvation and malnutrition. To this extent, United States policy has contributed to world health problems. Certainly, the United States has given much food away, but the question which must be addressed is whether or not giveaway programs have helped as much as our policies of restricted supplies have hurt.

Furthermore, the price support system and soil-bank-type programs have tended to help wealthier farmers more than less wealthy farmers. If a price support system raises the price of wheat by $0.50 a bushel above the free-market price, the total subsidy effectively going to the farmer producing several hundred thousand bushels of wheat is greater than the total subsidy going to the farmer who produces a few thousand bushels. Also, the larger a farmer's landholdings, the more land the farmer can take out of production, and the more benefits will be received from subsidy payments which are geared to the number of acres taken out of production. Therefore, since the wealth and income of farmers tend to be directly related to farm output and number of acres, the farm programs tend to aid the more affluent farmers more.

What benefits there may be in government agricultural programs in the short run can largely dissipate in the long run as the benefits of the program become capitalized in the value of farm assets. As explained, these benefits are received by the farmers (and their heirs) who own the farms at the time the programs are initiated. Surely, the ethics of any program which tends to have negative effects on the general population and no effect on the long-run welfare of farmers have to be questioned. Suggested alternatives to past farm programs must of necessity be second-best solutions, because the alternatives are also likely to have consequences which are unacceptable or undesirable to some groups in the economy. However, most economists would probably argue that if government is intent on helping low-income farmers, it should do it through direct income grants to those who are deemed needy, and not through the more indirect method of manipulating prices. Income grants may have negative effects on the willingness of people to work, but at least the aid and the possible negative effects are more clearly revealed to those legislators and voters who must ultimately pass on such social issues. The cost of the programs can be distributed through normal legislative processes and not, perhaps, haphazardly through market price increases. With all its deficiencies, the legislative process does provide a well-established means for making social welfare decisions and for checking the expansion of such programs.

Farmers often contend that they should be singled out for special governmental help because of the need to preserve farming as a way of life. Whether or not the argument is valid is a social decision which we cannot presume to make here. We can only ask whether or not farmers have any greater claim to the preservation of their way of life than cobblers or owners of corner grocery stores. Can any collective decision-making process long endure if it is opened up to special-interest demands? Should aid to farmers not be incorporated in more broadly conceived legislation designed to help *all* low-income people?

QUESTIONS TO PONDER

1 In 1972 the Soviet Union purchased several kinds of grains. The prices of the grains rose during the course of that year. If the Soviet Union had purchased only wheat—nothing else—what would have happened to the prices of the other grains not subject to Soviet purchase? Explain in terms of supply and demand curves.

2 If United States farmers had expected the Soviet Union to continue their purchases at the 1972 level for several years, should we have expected the price of grains to rise or fall in future years? Explain.

3 Is an agricultural policy which keeps the price of sugar above its equilibrium price "efficient" in the economic sense of that term?

4 If the price of sugar is supported through purchases by the Department of Agriculture, must the United States restrict the importation of sugar from foreign countries? Why?

5 Discuss the effects over the decades of the tobacco acreage allotment program on the distribution of income within this country.

6 Is the long-run demand and supply of corn likely to be more or less elastic than the short-run demand and supply curves?

7 Suppose that potato farmers throughout the world have a poor crop, as they did in 1975. What will happen to the price of potatoes and the incomes of potato farmers? What may happen to the price of potatoes the following year if the weather remains just as poor?

RECOMMENDED READINGS

Hathaway, Dale E.: *Problems of Progress in the Agricultural Economy* (Chicago: Scott, Foresman and Company, 1965).

Leftwich, Richard H., and Ansel M. Sharp: *Economics of Social Issues* (Dallas: Business Publications, Inc., 1974), chap. 2.

North, Douglas C., and Roger Leroy Miller: *The Economics of Public Issues*, 2d ed. (New York: Harper and Row, Publishers, 1973), chap. 7.

10

Private Control of the Market through Monopoly Power

That competition is a virtue, at least, as far as enterprises are concerned, has been a basic article of faith in the American Tradition, and a vigorous antitrust policy has long been regarded as both beneficial and necessary, not only to extend competition forces into new regions but also to preserve them where they may be flourishing at the moment.

G. Warren Nutter[1]

PREVIEW OF CHAPTER

Central question

What effect does monopoly power have on the efficiency of the market, and why and to what extent does monopoly power give rise to arguments for government control of the market?

Major objectives

1 To define monopoly (or monopoly power) and to contrast the concept with the concept of competition
2 To outline the origins of monopoly power
3 To define the market constraints on monopoly power

[1] G. Warren Nutter and Henry Adler Einhorn, *Enterprise Monopoly in the United States: 1899–1958* (New York: Columbia University Press, 1969), p. 1.

4 To describe the central tendency of monopoly in the market
5 To compare and contrast the market efficiency of pure monopoly with that of pure competition
6 To explain the incentive which competitors have to collude and to "chisel" on any collusive agreement they make

Major conclusions

1 Being the antithesis of competition, monopoly is the absence of the tendency of market rivals to try to outdo and avoid being outdone by others.
2 The primary source of monopoly power is barriers to entry.
3 The monopolist will tend to produce where the marginal cost of the last unit produced is equal to the marginal revenue gained from selling it.
4 The marginal revenue curve is derived from the monopolist's demand curve and is downward sloping like the demand curve.
5 The monopolist will tend to charge a higher price and sell less than competitors will in a competitive market. Because of its goal to maximize profits, the monopolist will fail to produce units of the good for which the marginal benefit to consumers exceeds the marginal cost of production.
6 The inefficiency generated from monopoly power is related to the number and closeness of substitute goods: generally, the greater the number of substitutes, the more efficient is the market.
7 In any cartel of producers designed to reduce industry output and raise the price, each competitor has an incentive to "chisel" on the collusive agreement. The larger the number of competitors involved in a cartel, generally speaking, the greater the incentive which each competitor has to reduce his price and expand his share of the market.
8 Because there are costs involved in any government action against monopoly power, proof of the existence of monopoly power alone is not *sufficient* grounds, from an economic point of view, to justify the government action. One must demonstrate that the benefits of the government action exceed the cost of the government action.

Important terms and concepts

Monopoly (or monopoly power)
Pure monopoly
Monopolistic competition
Oligopoly
Cartel
Efficiency range
Marginal revenue
Marginal revenue curve
Price discrimination

At the bottom of almost all arguments against a free market is a deep-seated concern over the "distorting," "corrupting," "inequitable," and "unethical" influence of monopoly power. A sizable portion of producers is viewed by many people not as being controlled by the forces of competition, but as holding considerable monopoly power, readily exercised, in the absence of government control, for selfish benefits. This concern has been fundamental to the writings of John Kenneth Galbraith, whose works are familiar to economists and lay people. In one of his books he states one of his most familiar themes:

> The initiative in deciding what is produced comes not from the sovereign consumer who, through the market, issues instructions that bend the productive mechanism to his ultimate will. Rather it comes from the great producing organization which reaches forward to control the markets that it is presumed to serve and, beyond, to bend the customers to its needs.[2]

The purpose of this chapter is wide-ranging; it is to develop our understanding of monopoly power in the market for goods and services, to place the limitations of monopoly power into proper perspective, and to more clearly reveal the benefits of competition and of enforcement of antitrust laws. A central question we address is why monopoly power gives force to arguments for government control of the market. The model of monopoly we develop in this chapter can be applied to markets in which firms have various degrees of monopoly power. These markets, which we discuss, are called *monopolistic competition* and *oligopoly*.

THE MEANING AND ORIGINS OF MONOPOLY POWER

In Chapter 7 we defined the competitive market as the process by which market rivals, in pursuit of their own private interests, strive to outdo and avoid being outdone by one another. The competitive market process enables market participants to obtain more information about what other participants are willing to do, greater production levels, lower prices, and a greater variety of goods and services than can be achieved without the force of competition.

Monopoly is the antithesis (i.e., the conceptual contrast) of competition; it is the absence of the competitive tendency of market participants to outdo or avoid being outdone by others. There is, therefore, an absence of the competitive outcome described above.

A monopolist is a market participant who does not have to compete—who does not have to strive to outdo others—because there are no market rivals with whom he must compete either to garner a share of the market or to retain that share.

The Origin of Monopoly

What gives rise to monopoly? To answer that question clearly we must reflect once again on the basis of competition. Competition occurs because market rivals are interested in exploiting profitable opportunities and because they are able to enter markets where such opportunities exist. In the extreme case of perfect competition, a market structure developed in Chapter 7, no barriers to entry exist, as is exemplified by the numerous competitors who are in the market. In a perfect market, entrepreneurs are on the lookout for any beneficial opportunities which entry into the market might secure. Indeed, the individual competitor in that market is incapable of raising his price without facing the possibility that his or her rivals may move in to cut the price and take all his or her customers. If, for example, an individual wheat farmer asks for a price above the market price, potential customers can move to other wheat farmers willing to sell at the lower market price. Although individual farmers can lower their price below the market price, the best price is the market price, and for this reason the competitors are called "price takers." They effectively have no control over (or power to manipulate) the market price.

The necessary condition for competition is *freedom of entry*, which in the case of perfect competition is assumed to be complete. Being antithetical to competition the necessary condition for a monopoly (or monopoly power) is the existence of barriers to those who may want to enter a market to exploit profitable opportunities. The monopolist has what is called "market power" to manipulate

[2] John Kenneth Galbraith, *The New Industrial State* (Boston: Houghton Mifflin Company, 1967), p. 6.

the price because he is protected from being undercut by rivals who find market entry difficult.

Barriers to entry can arise from several sources. First, the monopolist may have sole ownership of a strategic resource used in the production of the monopolized product. Others cannot compete because they do not have the resource that is needed. Second, the monopolist may have a patent or copyright on the product that is produced, making it impossible for other producers to duplicate the product legally. For years, until Eastman Kodak developed a new process for taking instant pictures, Polaroid had a patent monopoly on the instant-picture market. Third, the monopolist may have an exclusive government franchise to sell a given product in a defined geographical area. Consider the exclusive franchises which the telephone company has to provide telephone service in designated areas or which your electric utility has to provide electrical service in your area. Fourth, the monopolist may have a well-known brand name among a very loyal group of customers; in this case, the barrier faced by new competitors is possibly the costly one of trying to get customers to try their product. Fifth, production in the monopolized industry may be conducted on a very large scale, requiring huge plants (land and buildings) and large amounts of equipment. Finally, the need for very large financial resources can preclude many potential competitors from entering a market. All in all, barriers to entry can be reinterpreted as costs which must be borne by potential competitors before they can compete and which, in some cases, may be prohibitively high, making competition impossible.

Pure Monopoly

The extreme, quintessential example of competition is a market structure called *perfect competition;* its direct opposite, the consummate example of monopoly, is called *pure monopoly.*

The pure monopolist is the only producer of a product with no close substitutes. This pure monopolist has the power to raise the price of his product and yet remain confident that the monopolist's customers will not move to other producers of the same product, because there are no other producers in that market. The monopolist is also confident that other producers will not enter the market to offer lower prices or a similar product because of the prohibitively high entry barriers that must be surmounted.

A pure monopolist simply does not have to compete.

Since, by definition, the pure monopolist is the only producer of a particular product, the demand confronted is the demand for that product (as opposed to the demand for a portion of the product's market). The monopolist's demand curve is therefore downward sloping, like the demand for all products; the sole producer has the market power to significantly reduce the quantity that will be sold and to sell that quantity for a higher price. The perfect competitor does not have that power.

MONOPOLISTIC COMPETITION AND OLIGOPOLY

Almost all real-world markets lie somewhere between the polar extremes of perfect competition and pure monopoly. This is because entry into most real-world markets is neither completely free (in the sense that entry is costless) nor completely blocked. All these "realistic market structures" can be described in much the same way that a 12-ounce beer stein with only 6 ounces of beer in it can be described: it is either "half empty" or "half full," depending upon your perspective and, possibly, the point that you wish to make. Similarly, real-world markets can be described, as they frequently are, as either "more or less competitive" or "more or less monopolistic."

Participants in these intermediate markets generally have some incentive to attempt to outdo others or to attempt to avoid being outdone by them; however, they do not, generally speaking, have to be concerned that any very small price increase will result in a total and immediate loss of all customers. On the other hand, because entry is not blocked, they must recognize that there is some price increase which will encourage potential rivals to enter the market and compete. Over time, other producers can surmount the entry barriers that do exist and can produce a similar, if not an identical, product. In all these markets, the power of the producers is checked to one degree or another. The extent of the market power which each producer has, however, is related to the ease (or cost) of entry: the more costly entry is, the lower is the competitive tendency and the greater the power of individual producers. The opposite is also true.

Economists group these real-world market structures into two very broad categories: *monopolistic competition* (a name which suggests the blend of competitive and monopolistic elements) and *oligopoly*.

A monopolistically competitive market is one in which there are a number of competitors selling a similar but differentiated product. Entry, although not free, is relatively easy.

Examples might include makers of hosiery and textbook publishers.

An oligopolistic market is one in which there are few major competitors, generally not more than six and certainly no more than a dozen, who sell similar or differentiated products. Because there are only a few producers, the competitive actions of one producer can significantly affect the market position of each of the other producers. Therefore, each of the producers must be alert to the actions of each of the others. Entry is generally not blocked; however, because of consumers' attachment to the brand names of the oligopolistic producers and because of the large capital requirement for operating in oligopolistic markets, entry is typically very difficult.

Examples of oligopolies are the steel, automobile, cigarette, aluminum, and light bulb industries.

The analysis we will follow in this chapter will be conducted mainly in terms of the pure monopolist's influence on the market. We emphasize this market structure for several reasons. First, pure monopoly is a relatively simple market structure to study, and with this basic model we can convey many essential points about monopoly power in general and about markets in which that power may be less than complete. Second, although the models of monopolistic competition and oligopoly may begin with more realistic assumptions of market behavior, it is easier to understand monopolistic market behavior using a pure monopoly. We can then extend our analysis in a rough way to cover monopolistic competition and oligopoly. Finally, by focusing on the purely competitive and purely monopolistic models, we are able to establish the limits—which we call the *efficiency range*—within which production in real-world markets will normally take place. What output is actually produced within those limits and at what price it is sold depend upon the degree of competitiveness of the markets. This, in turn, depends on the mobility of resources (cost of entry) and, as economist Gary Becker has noted, on the ease with which members of an industry can organize and maintain a *cartel*.[3] (*A cartel is an organization of producers designed to restrict competition.*) Perhaps the best-known international cartel is OPEC (Organization of Petroleum Exporting Countries), which is made up of Middle East countries; its main function is to restrict the production of oil.

THE LIMITS OF MONOPOLY POWER

The monopolistic producer has power in the market that the competitive seller is unable to achieve; it is the power to withhold supplies from the market and to charge a higher price for what is to be sold. However, the monopolist producer's power is not completely unchecked; it is restricted in two major ways. First, without the assistance of government, the monopolistic producer's power to coerce people into buying what he has to offer is never complete. (We use "coercion" to mean the absence of viable choices.) Even if a number of industries in an economy have true monopoly power, an individual consumer typically has the ability to choose from among a number of goods that are produced by both monopolistic and competitive producers.

[3] Gary S. Becker, *Economic Theory* (New York: Alfred A. Knopf, Inc., 1971), p. 100. For an advanced treatment of monopoly power, this is an excellent resource book.

For instance, in many parts of the country, AT&T is the only firm permitted to provide telephone service, but it is possible for most people to communicate in other ways. They can talk directly with one another; they can write letters or send telegrams; they can use their children as personal messengers. In a more general sense, consumers can use their incomes to buy rugs or bicycles instead of private lines, extra phones, or long-distance calls. To the extent that the individual has alternatives, his consumption of any good must, to one degree or another, be construed as voluntary.

Friedrich Hayek, a Nobel laureate in economics, expressed it this way:

> If, for instance, I would very much like to be painted by a famous artist (one who has monopoly power) and if he refuses to paint me for less than a very high price, it would clearly be absurd for me to say that I am coerced. The same is true of any other commodity or service that I can do without. So long as the services of a particular person are not crucial to my existence or the preservation of what I most value, the conditions he exacts for rendering these services cannot be called "coercion."[4]

This is not to say that the effects of monopoly power are all positive. If monopoly power results from one firm's garnering the assets and markets of its competitors, monopoly power can be viewed as a force which reduces a consumer's viable choices. Although the coercive power of the monopolist may not be complete, the "degree of coercion" is in this way enhanced and consumer freedom is restricted. Monopoly power can be opposed on these grounds.

Monopoly power occurs for other reasons, however. A firm may have monopoly power because it "has built a better mousetrap" or developed a good which was previously unavailable. In other words, sometimes a firm is the only producer because it is the first producer and no one has been able to figure out how to duplicate the product. In this instance, monopoly power has emerged in tandem with an expansion of consumer choices; it is productive in a very meaningful sense. Furthermore, in such cases monopoly power may be only temporary because other competitors will maneuver to break the hold which the first producer has on the market.

The second major way in which a monopolist's behavior is constrained results from market conditions, i.e., the costs of production and the downward sloping demand curve for the good which is sold. The monopolistic firm can raise its price, but it must be prepared to sell less. How much less depends upon the closeness and availability of substitutes. The important point is that the monopolistic firm will have a range of prices at which it can sell different quantities as shown by its demand curve. Its task is to *search* through the available price-quantity combinations with the purpose of achieving its objectives, a principal one being, presumably, maximization of profit. Furthermore, the monopolist's behavior is constrained by the costs of expanding production or of trying to preclude competitors from entering the market.

In a free and open market, monopoly power is most subject to dissolution *in the long run.* This is so because, as mentioned before in Chapter 7, there are numerous dimensions within which competition can occur; in the long run it is possible for potential competitors to find unprotected dimensions through which they can invade the market domain of a monopolist and produce a similar but not identical product. The Reynolds International Pen Company had a patent monopoly on the first ball-point pen, which it introduced in 1945. However, the monopoly position of Reynolds quickly eroded during the following two years as other pen companies found ways of circumventing the Reynolds patent and producing their own ball-point pens. Prices on ball-point pens fell from an initial price of $12.50 to the low prices of today.

Many products that you can think of were first sold by producers with short-run monopoly power. The incompleteness of the power, however small, is very important. Like the proverbial hole in the dike, it can cause the ultimate destruction of any monopoly power presently exercised.

[4] F. A. Hayek, *The Constitution of Liberty* (Chicago: The University of Chicago Press, 1960), p. 136.

In the long run excessively high prices, restrictions on supply, and high profits provide other potential competitors with the incentive to find and take advantage of the imperfections in the monopolist's power and to enter the monopolized market.

One of the most effective ways for the monopolistic firm to keep market power in the long run is to enlist the coercive power of the state to protect its boundaries, and to extend those boundaries whenever necessary against encroachment from competitors. This has been done quite effectively for decades in agriculture (see Chapter 9). The insurance industry and the medical profession, which through licensing procedures are protected from competition, are two of many other examples. However, even the power of the state to shield an industry against competitive encroachment can at times be broken down in the very long run. This is so because consumer tastes and the technologies of production and delivery can change dramatically over a period of many years. For example, the franchise monopoly of electric power companies is being weakened by the introduction of home solar power plants. In addition, the railroad industry has been protected by the state for almost a century. Its market has been gradually eroded by the emergence of new competitors (also protected and subsidized by the state) to the point where the railroad industry is now critically ill. In the long run continued protection of any one industry can mean expansion of that control over the competitors who arise to break the monopoly power that the state is attempting to protect.

Without state protection, monopoly may very well dissipate—eventually. Therefore, the relevant public policy questions are, How long will the power persist? And in the meantime, what is the extent of the damage done to economic efficiency and the distribution of income? Since manpower and the machinery of government must be used to do anything about monopoly power, the decision regarding the "appropriateness" of prosecuting antitrust violations will hinge in part on the relationship between the costs and benefits of antitrust action. Many cases of monopoly power will warrant a government response; however, not all cases will, mainly because the benefits to be achieved, in terms of avoiding the damage that would otherwise be done, cannot justify the costs of government action. For example, in 1969 the first seller of hand calculators had a temporary monopoly in the United States market. However, given the rapidity of developments in that industry, few people would now think that antitrust action, involving a long, drawn-out court battle, was warranted.

The relative value of benefits and costs associated with any move to break up a particular monopoly is partially a matter of judgment for those in charge of administering the Antitrust Division of the Justice Department. One may, therefore, not be overly surprised if political considerations, including campaign contributions or even outright bribes, enter into the decision-making process. These are the political considerations in what has come to be known as the "monopoly problem." In the next section we focus strictly on the economic features of the monopoly problem, including the inefficiency in production which can emerge from monopoly power.

THE CENTRAL TENDENCY OF MONOPOLY POWER

In deciding how many times to play tennis during the course of a week, a tennis player will tend to employ a behavioral rule which we previously considered in Chapter 2. The player will weigh the estimated benefits of each game off against the costs that must be incurred. He or she will continue to play tennis until the marginal benefits of an additional game are equal to the marginal costs. At that number of games, the player has maximized his satisfaction from the sport; if one goes beyond that level, the marginal cost will exceed the marginal benefits, lowering one's total utility.

Producers of a good for the market must follow a very similar procedure. The main difference in the type of calculations made is that the benefits of production are measured, not in terms of utility, but in terms of revenue acquired: the producer will produce a unit of a good if the additional (or marginal) revenue acquired from the sale of the unit is greater than the additional cost incurred from production. The difference between the revenue from sales and the cost incurred is called the *profit*. If the marginal revenue from additional units produced is greater than the marginal cost, the profits of the firm will expand.

The firm should, therefore, expand production up to the point where the marginal cost (MC) and the marginal revenues (MR) are equal.

This is a fundamental rule which all firms wishing to maximize profits follow.

To see how this applies to monopolies, consider this example. Suppose you are in the yo yo business. You have a patent monopoly on edible yo yos which come in three flavors, vanilla, chocolate, and strawberry. (We will assume there is a demand for such.) The cost of producing the first yo yo is $0.50, but you can sell it for $0.75. Your profit on the unit is $0.25 ($0.75 − $0.50). If the second unit costs you $0.60 to make (assuming increasing marginal cost)[5] and you can sell it for $0.75, by producing and selling two yo yos your profit will rise to $0.40 ($0.25 profit on the first yo yo plus $0.15 profit on the second). It should go without saying that, if you intend to maximize your profits, you should continue to expand production until there is no longer a gap between marginal revenue and marginal cost; in other words, you should expand production until they are equal (MC = MR, where the abbreviations stand for *marginal cost* and *marginal revenue*, respectively).

This general rule of behavior applies directly to the production decisions of a monopolist. The only change from the above example—and it is a complicating one—is that the marginal revenue from selling additional units does not remain constant for the monopolist; it falls over the relevant range of production. To see why this is the case, consider the schedule in Table 10.1 which reflects the demand of a monopolistic yo yo producer:

TABLE 10·1

Quantity Sold (1)	Price of Yo yo (2)	Total Revenue (1) × (2) (3)	Marginal Revenue △(3) (4)
0	$11	0	0
1	10	$10	$10
2	9	18	8
3	8	24	6
4	7	28	4
5	6	30	2

The price and quantity in the schedule are inversely related, reflecting our assumption that a monopolistic producing firm faces a downward sloping demand curve for product. (Remember, the monopolist is the only producer of a product.) As the price falls from $10 to $6 per yo yo (in column 2), the number sold rises from one to five (in column 1). If all the firm wishes to sell is one yo yo, the producer can charge as much as $10; its total revenue at that level of production is then $10. In order to sell more, say two yo yos, the price for each must fall to $9; the total revenues are now $18, as indicated in column 3. By multiplying column 1 times column 2, the rest of column 3 can be filled in. Notice in the table an interesting phenomenon: as the price is lowered and the quantity sold rises, the total revenue rises from $10 when one unit is sold to $30 when 6 units are sold. However, as the quantity sold rises by increments of one unit, the total revenue does not rise by equal amounts. In fact, total revenue rises by *declining* increments, first by $10, then by increments of $8, $6, $4, and $2. These increments are the *marginal revenue* of each unit, recorded in column 4, which the monopolist must compare with the marginal cost of producing additional yoyos. The firm will extend production to where MC = MR, as discussed previously.

Another notable feature of Table 10 · 1 is that the marginal revenue at an output level of one yo yo is equal to the price, but at every other output level the marginal revenue is below the price that can be charged for that quantity. The reason for this is

[5] This assumption is not completely arbitrary. For an explanation of why we assume increasing marginal cost see Chap. 4.

straightforward. For example, the marginal revenue from the *second* yo yo is $8 while the price at which each of two units can be sold is $9. Because of the downward sloping demand curve, the second yo yo cannot be sold unless the price is reduced from $10 to $9; this means that the revenue acquired on the first yo yo goes down by $1 in order that the second yo yo can be sold. The second yo yo can be sold for $9; however, if we account for the $1 in revenue lost on the first yo yo in order to sell the second, the net revenue from the second is $8 (the selling price of $9 minus the $1 lost on the first yo yo). In order to sell the third yo yo, the price on the first two must fall. The loss in revenue on them is equal to $2. Therefore, the marginal revenue for the third yo yo is the $8 selling price less the $2 loss on the first two units, or MR = $6.

The marginal revenue curve is derived directly from the demand curve. If we graphically illustrate the relationship between the demand curve (columns 1 and 2) and the marginal revenue curve (columns 1 and 4), they will take on the relationship described in Figure 10·1: the marginal revenue curve is below the demand curve and the distance between them becomes greater as the price falls.[6]

In Figure 10·2 we have added the monopolist's marginal cost curve to the demand and marginal revenue curves of Figure 10·1. Our purpose in doing this is to discuss the central tendency of monopoly power, that is, the price and quantity combination which the monopolist will tend to choose. Following the rule that in order for profit to be maximized, production will be extended only to that point where marginal cost is equal to marginal revenue, we can conclude from the graph that our monopolistic yo yo producer will

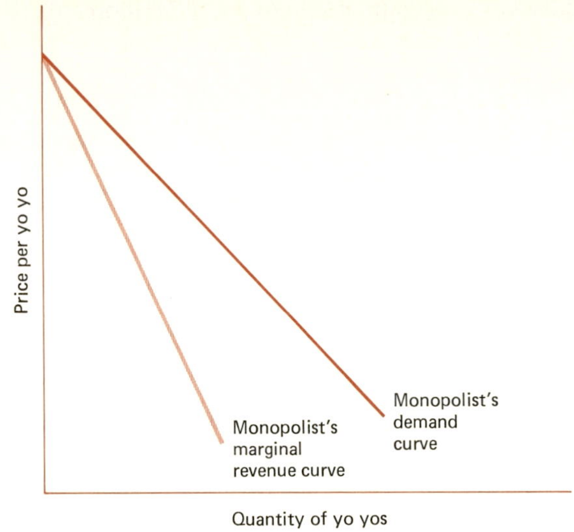

FIG. 10·1 The demand curve faced by a monopolist is downward sloping. The marginal revenue curve is computed from the information contained in the monopolist's demand curve. The marginal revenue curve is derived in Table 10·1.

produce Q_2 units. Note that at that quantity (Q_2) the marginal cost and marginal revenue curves intersect, meaning that the marginal cost and revenue are equal. If the monopolist produces less than Q_2 yo yos, profits will be missed that could have been had by expanding production. For example, suppose the output level is Q_1. By vertically moving up through the graph from Q_1, we can see that the marginal revenue (MR_1) acquired from selling the Q_1 yo yo is greater than the marginal cost (MC_1) of producing it. Further, marginal revenue exceeds marginal cost for all units between Q_1 and Q_2. In other words, by expanding production from Q_1 toward Q_2, the monopolist can add more to total revenues than to total costs. *The firm's profits, therefore, rise up to an output level of* Q_2.

Why does the monopolist firm not produce more than Q_2? If it does the marginal cost will be greater for all additional units than the marginal revenue; profits will fall if more than Q_2 is pro-

[6] Prove this for yourself by simply plotting the information in cols. 1 and 2 and cols. 1 and 4 on a sheet of graph paper. Another simple way of drawing the relationship between the linear demand curve and the marginal revenue curve is to extend the demand curve until it intersects the vertical and horizontal axes. The marginal revenue curve should then be drawn from the point of the demand's intersection with the vertical axis to midway between the origin and the point of the demand's intersection with the horizontal axis. This is essentially how the curves in Fig. 10·1 were positioned.

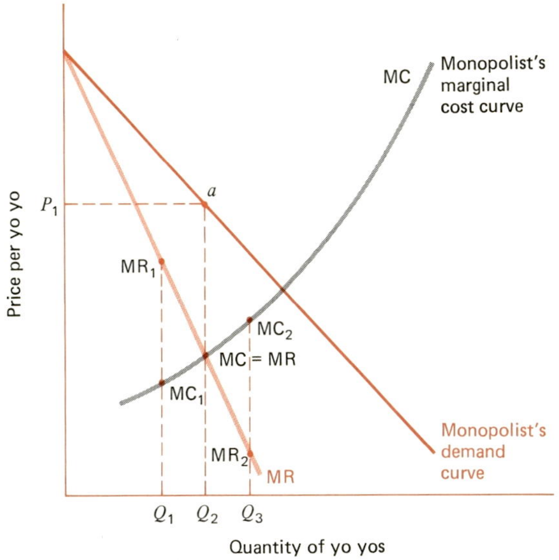

FIG. 10·2 Given the above demand, marginal revenue, and marginal cost curves, the monopolist will move his production level toward Q_2. At production levels below Q_2, the marginal revenue is greater than marginal cost, meaning that the monopolist can increase production and increase its profits. At output levels greater than Q_2, marginal cost is greater than marginal revenue. This means that the monopolist can contract its output, reducing cost by more than revenue and increasing profits.

duced. By producing Q_3 yo yos, the firm may make a profit, but it will not make *maximum* profits. The marginal cost of the Q_3 unit (MC_2) is greater than the marginal revenue received from selling it (MR_2). By producing the Q_3 unit, the monopolistic adds more to cost than to revenues, thereby reducing profits.

Once the monopolistic firm selects the output at which it wishes to produce, the price of the good on the market is simultaneously determined. in this illustration, the price that can be charged for Q_2 yo yos can be found by going up from Q_2 on the horizontal axis to the demand curve in the graph; it is P_1. (Remember, the demand curve indicates the price that can be charged for any quantity, like Q_2.) Therefore, out of all the possible price-quantity combinations open to the monopolist on the demand curve in Figure 10·2, the one that will be chosen is combination *a*.

THE COMPARATIVE EFFICIENCY OF COMPETITIVE AND MONOPOLY MARKETS

In Chapter 7 we concluded that firms in a perfectly competitive market tend to produce at the intersection of the market supply and demand curves. As you may remember, this quantity, represented by Q_c in Figure 10·3, is the *efficient* production level in the sense that the *marginal benefit* to the

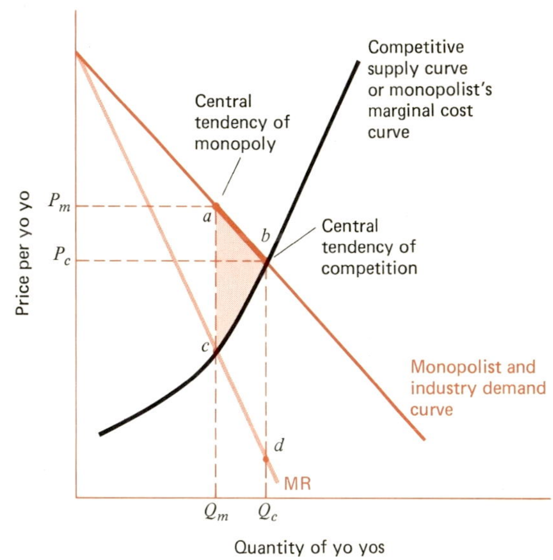

FIG. 10·3 The central tendency of the competitive market is point *b*, and the central tendency of the monopolist is point *a*. Therefore, the price will tend to be lower and the quantity produced will tend to be greater in a competitive market than in a monopolistic market. The inefficiency of the pure monopoly, as compared with the purely competitive market, is represented by the shaded triangular area. This is the total amount by which the benefits of producing $Q_c - Q_m$ units of the good exceed their marginal cost of production.

consumer of the last unit produced is equal to the *marginal cost* to the producer (shown by point b). All units for which the marginal benefits exceed marginal costs are produced, and all possible net benefits to the consumer have been extracted from the production of the good.

When this supply and demand model is converted to represent a monopolist as opposed to a number of competitors, the industry supply curve becomes the monopolist's marginal cost curve and the industry's demand curve becomes the demand facing the sole producer. Whereas individual competitors cannot choose which price-quantity combination they prefer along the demand curve, the monopolist can. Being in sole control of the industry's resources, the monopolist can withhold resources from production and sell the lower quantity produced at a higher price. Barriers to entry preclude competitors from entering and undercutting the monopolist's price. As we have just explained, the monopolist will tend to produce the output level at which the *marginal cost* of production is equal to the *marginal revenue*, not to the output level where marginal cost is equal to the *marginal benefit*.

In short, the monopolist fails to produce the efficient output level: the monopolist produces Q_m which is less than the competitive level of production, Q_c.

The units which are not produced by the monopolist but are provided in a perfectly competitive market are represented by the difference between Q_c and Q_m. For each unit between Q_m and Q_c the marginal benefits, as illustrated by the heavy portion of the industry (or market) demand curve, are greater than the marginal costs of production. These are net benefits which consumers would like to have; but the monopolistic firm, because of its interest in maximizing profits as opposed to maximizing consumer welfare, does not produce an amount which will permit extraction of the net benefits. These lost net benefits are graphically shown by the shaded triangular area. The resources that are not used by the monopolist must then either remain idle or be used in a line of production in which their market value is less. In this sense, economists say that resources are misallocated. Too few resources are used in the monopolistic industry and too many resources are used elsewhere.

Why would consumers prefer that an industry be competitively organized? The answer can be seen in the graph. As revealed by the market demand curve, consumers receive additional benefits for units Q_c minus Q_m equal to the area bounded by Q_mabQ_c. (The demand curve indicates the marginal benefit of each of those units; this area in the graph, Q_mabQ_c, indicates the total benefits for *all* units between Q_m and Q_c.) On the other hand, the marginal revenue curve shows the additional revenue received by producers for each of the $Q_c - Q_m$ yoyos; alternately, the marginal revenue curve represents the *additional* amount consumers will spend for each of those units. Therefore, in order to buy $Q_c - Q_m$, consumers will have to spend an additional amount that is graphically equal to the area Q_mcdQ_c. Notice that the total additional benefits to the consumers (Q_mabQ_c) are greater than the total additional consumer expenditures (Q_mcdQ_c): consumers gain by having Q_c yoyos produced. On the other hand, the graph illustrates clearly why the monopolistic firm is not interested in providing these additional units. It has to incur an additional cost equal to the area Q_mcbQ_c, whereas it can expect to receive only the area Q_mcdQ_c in additional revenues. Those extra yoyos simply cost the monopolistic firm more than it receives in revenues. Again, profits are lower at the competitive output level.

THE TOTAL SOCIAL COST OF MONOPOLY

The total social cost of monopoly power is actually greater than can be illustrated by our supply and demand model used in Figure 10·3. Because firms can benefit from monopoly power, many firms are likely to invest resources in an effort to acquire it—to erect barriers to entry into their markets. These resources are directed away from the production of other goods which could increase benefits to consumers. The total social cost of monopoly should also include the time and effort which the Antitrust Division of the Justice Department must devote to thwarting attempts by firms to gain monopoly power and to breaking the monopoly power when it is acquired. The redistributional effects of monopoly power constitute another social cost. Because of monopoly power, consumers pay prices that are higher than under perfect competition (P_m instead of P_c in Figure 10·3). The real purchasing power of consumer incomes is decreased while the incomes of the owners of monopolies go up. Monopolized industries tend to be owned by those in higher income brackets; to the extent that the monopoly power increases the price of the good and the profits of the producer, the general effect of monopoly is to redistribute income from lower-income consumers to higher-income entrepreneurs. Many consider these redistributional effects to be "socially undesirable" and a part of the total cost of monopoly.

Finally, it is possible for monopolistic firms, through political campaign contributions, paid lobbyists, and outright bribes, to exert undue influence on the level and the distribution of government expenditures. Furthermore, because of their dependency on government contracts, large monopolistic firms have an incentive to use their powers to compete through the manipulation of the political process. According to one school of thought, some firms have an incentive to promote expansion of the highway system beyond the socially optimal point because they can then sell more concrete and bigger cars. Other monopolistic firms may have an incentive to continue and, if possible, to intensify the arms race. According to Galbraith, the modern American economy has seen the emergence of the "new industrial state." The new industrial state is that sector of the economy which is made up of large firms to which he attributes extensive monopolistic power. These firms have an interest in making people believe that economic growth (meaning the production of more and more material goods) and technological development should be central goals of mankind. Galbraith and others see considerable social danger and waste in these goals:

> If we continue to believe that the goals of the industrial system—the expansion of output, the companion increase in consumption, technological advance, the public images that sustain it—are coordinate with life, then all of our lives will be in the service of these goals. What is consistent with these ends we shall have or be allowed; all else will be off limits. Our wants will be managed in accordance with the needs of the industrial system; the policies of the state will be subject to similar influences; education will be adapted to industrial need; the disciplines required by the industrial system will be the conventional morality of the community.[7]

How to calculate the total social cost of monopoly power in the real world is largely a matter of judgment. There is still considerable debate among economists as to what should be included in any estimate of the cost of monopoly power. As we will see in the next section, a firm may have monopoly power, but its power may have little detrimental effect. Consequently, the distortions that occur in the allocation of resources may not be very great.

COMPETITION AMONG PRODUCERS WITH MONOPOLY POWER

To this point in the chapter, we have considered the market position of the pure monopolist: the firm which is the sole producer of a product with no close substitutes and which is protected by prohibitively high barriers to entry. Needless to say, the pure monopoly model is descriptive of very few markets. (Can you name one that fits the description exactly?) Typically, even in the short run, producers in real-world markets compete with several or even many other producers of sim-

[7] John Kenneth Galbraith, *The New Industrial State* (Boston: Houghton Mifflin Company, 1967), p. 398.

ilar products. In short, they compete in the context of markets called *monopolistic competition and oligopoly.* General Motors competes with Ford, Chrysler, American Motors, and a large number of foreign car producers. McDonald's Restaurants compete directly with Burger King, Hardees, and a host of other establishments which specialize in hamburgers. They also compete less directly with Pizza Hut, Kentucky Fried Chicken, and Long John Silver's for fast-food customers. Peoples Drug stores compete with other chain and locally owned drug companies and with department and discount stores for the many other nondrug products which they sell. In the long run, all these firms have to compete with companies that are formed explicitly to surmount the entry barriers and to compete in their markets. As we will see in this section, the limited amount of competition which exists in these real-world markets may move markets away from the equilibrium position of the pure monopolist and toward, but not to, the equilibrium position of perfect competition.

Substitutes, Barriers to Entry, and Market Efficiency

The greater the number and variety of substitutes for any good, the greater the elasticity of demand for that good, that is, the more consumers will respond to a price change. This is a proposition which we studied in Chapter 3. By definition, a firm in a monopolistically competitive market, like the market for fast-food service in many metropolitan areas, faces competition from a number of firms already in the market and from firms that are capable of entering that market. Accordingly, if Burger Bippy independently raises its hamburger prices, consumers can move to any one of the other restaurants which offer similar food and service. Because of consumer ignorance and consumer loyalty to the "Big Bippy," Burger Bippy is very unlikely to lose all its customers by slightly raising its price. It can, therefore, charge more than the ideal competitive price. However, there is a limit to how much Burger Bippy can raise its price without substantially reducing the number of its customers. How much more depends upon the number of other competitors, the facility with which other firms in the market can expand their business, the ease with which new firms can enter the market, and the public's awareness of price differences. Still, given the nature of the market, the demand facing a monopolistic competitor should be relatively elastic. It should also be more elastic than the demand facing an oligopolist. In an oligopolistic market, you may recall, there are fewer competitors to whom customers can turn, and entry is more difficult.

A firm in a monopolistic competitive market may deviate little from the price-quantity combination of perfect competition. Observe, for example, the highly elastic demand curve for hamburgers in Figure 10·4. In this example, the price

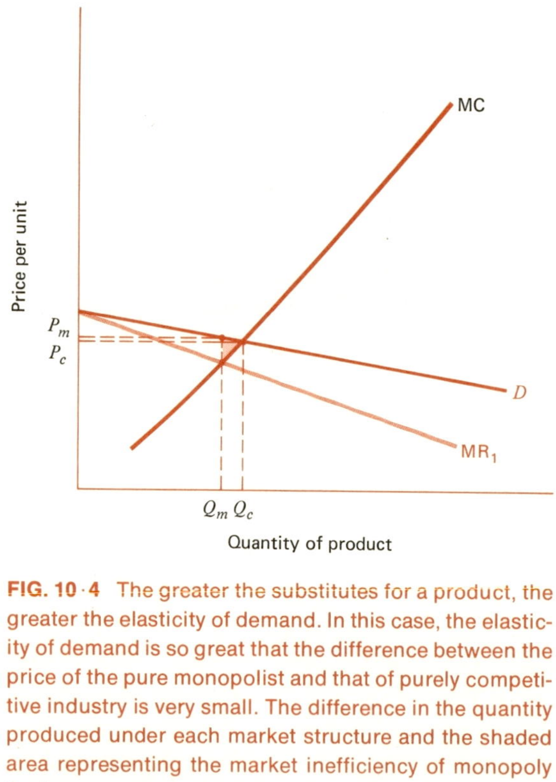

FIG. 10·4 The greater the substitutes for a product, the greater the elasticity of demand. In this case, the elasticity of demand is so great that the difference between the price of the pure monopolist and that of purely competitive industry is very small. The difference in the quantity produced under each market structure and the shaded area representing the market inefficiency of monopoly is also very small.

charged by the monopolistic competitor, P_m, is only slightly higher than that which is achieved under perfect competition, P_c. Also, the quantity sold, Q_m, is only slightly less than the amount sold under perfect competition, Q_c. (Remember, the firm in perfect competition produces goods and services at that point where price is equal to marginal cost, which is at the intersection of the marginal cost and demand curves.) Furthermore, the market inefficiency, indicated by the shaded triangular area, is not very great.

The short-run profits of firms in a monopolistically competitive market may be substantial. If profits are more than enough to cover the costs of entry into the market, in the long run new competitors will enter the market. The market will be divided among a greater number of competitors and the demand facing each competitor will fall, which can cause all competitors to trim the price they charge.

On the other hand, if there are few competitors and if entry is difficult—that is, if the market is an oligopoly—the demand facing any one competitor will be less elastic (or steeper) than the demand curve in Figure 10·4. It will probably look more like the curve in Figure 10·5. If Burger Bippy (now assumed to be an oligopolist) raises its price, consumers have few viable alternatives to which they can turn. Therefore, in the face of a price increase, more consumers will have to stay with Burger Bippy; the consumer response will be lower, the demand curve will be less elastic. In addition, the price-quantity combination will be further removed from the competitive solution. This can be seen in Figure 10·5. The oligopolist's price is significantly above the ideal competitive price, and the quantity produced is significantly below the ideal competitive output level.

Unlike the monopolistically competitive market, in the oligopolistic markets significant barriers to entry deter many new competitors from entering. Therefore, firms in the protected (oligopolistic) industries will be able to retain their short-run positions for a much longer period of time than can firms in a monopolistically competitive market.

Oligopolies are normally associated with the markets for automobiles, cigarettes, and steel, which include some very large corporations. The financial resources required for establishing production units that can be competitive is a formidable entry barrier for many firms; and to this extent, the oligopolies are protected from some competitors. However, one cannot conclude that all competition is precluded. Some very large firms have the financial capacity to move into other fields of production if sufficiently high profit opportunities exist. If, for instance, firms in the electric light bulb market fully exploit their short-run profit opportunities by restricting production and raising their price, firms like General Motors have the capacity to move into the light bulb market and compete directly with the producers already in that market. Indeed, General Motors has moved out of strictly automobile production and into the markets for electrical appliances, television sets, and many others. By

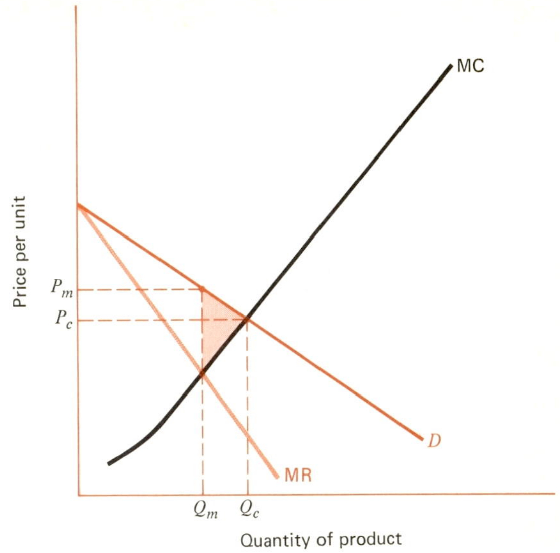

FIG. 10·5 With few competitors, the demand is more steeply sloped than the demand curve in Figure 10·4. Each firm with monopoly power, called an *oligopolist* in this case, can produce significantly less and charge significantly more than it would be able to under purely competitive market conditions.

making this point, we do not mean to suggest that the monopoly power of many large firms should not be a matter for real concern. Rather, we intend only to emphasize that the basis for competition is the *relative* capacity of firms to enter markets where profits can be made, and not the *absolute* size of firms. Seen this way, many markets of 100 years ago which were isolated from one another by a lack of transportation and communication facilities were possibly less subject to competitive pressure than markets of today which contain firms that are, in an absolute sense, substantially larger.

The Cartel: Collusion and the Illusion of Collusion

Several firms in a competitive market may see that their profit positions can be improved if all will collude. By that we mean that they agree to restrict their individual output levels and raise the market price—in other words, they behave *as if* they are a unified monopoly. The analysis in the preceding sections has shown the accuracy of their design; that is, it is accurate as far as it goes. The competitors have a problem. They *are not* one unified monopoly, and it may be impossible for them to behave as if they are. Granted, the profits which are possible under monopoly conditions provide an incentive for competitors to collude. However, once they have colluded and thereby reduced the market supply and raised the market price, they also have an incentive, as individuals, to "chisel" on any collusive agreement made. The individual competitor has an incentive to cut price below the cartel price in order to create the potential for considerable expansion of his or her sales and profits. *If competitors are willing to "chisel" on antitrust laws for the purpose of improving their individual welfare, we must also admit to the possibility that they will be willing to "chisel" on cartel rules for the purpose of enhancing their individual welfare.* What is true for one competitor can be true for all; hence, there is a built-in incentive which can cause the demise of the cartel. If the cartel works for very long, one reason can be that some form of external costs—such as the threat of violence—is imposed on "chiselers."[8] Furthermore, although a small number of competitors makes a workable cartel more likely, all that we have said can be true for industries in which there are very few competitors.

To add some measure of precision to the analysis, consider an oligopoly market with only two producers, called a *duopoly*. To keep things simple, assume that each has the same cost structure and identical demand. Their combined marginal cost curve is indicated by MC_1 in Figure 10·6; the market demand curve for the good is D_1. These two producers can generate monopoly profits if they restrict the quantity that they collectively offer on the market to Q_m, selling that amount for P_m. Dividing the total quantity sold between them, each sells Q_1 at the monopoly price ($2 \times Q_1 = Q_m$). Once in that position, each producer may reason that if he reduces the price he is willing to accept ever so slightly below the cartel price to, say, P_1, disguising what he is doing (through customer rebates or more attractive credit terms), he can sell to the entire market. He alone can then sell as much as Q_2. The marginal revenue, equal in this case to P_1, is clearly greater than the marginal cost of the expanded output. Again, if one producer has an incentive, both have that incentive; and the price can fall as the duopolists "chisel" on the agreement and undercut each other. Such behavior leads the producers back *toward* (but not necessarily to) the competitive equilibrium which is at the intersection of the marginal cost and demand curves. Just how far they move in that direction will depend upon the ability of the cartel to impose a cost on the firm (or firms) that chisel.[9]

[8] As we studied in Chap. 6, the group may provide members with some private benefit which can be denied nonmembers. For example, local medical associations can deny nonmember doctors the right to practice in local hospitals. In these cases, a cost is imposed on chiselers by excluding them from membership in the group.

[9] For a more detailed explanation of the competitive predicament of duopolists, see G. Warren Nutter, "Duopoly, Oligopoly, and Emerging Competition," *Southern Economic Journal*, April 1964, pp. 342–352, reprinted in William Breit and Harold M. Hochman, ed., *Readings in Microeconomics* (New York: Holt, Rinehart and Winston, Inc., 1968), pp. 285–296.

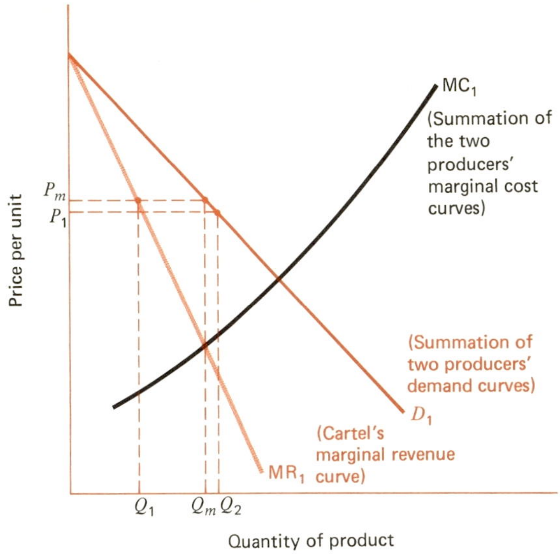

FIG. 10·6 Two firms that make up an industry, called a *duopoly*, have an incentive to collude to restrict their combined output level to Q_m and charge a price of P_m. However, having established that price-quantity combination, they each have an incentive to "chisel" on the collusive agreement. By lowering the price he charges and taking over a larger share of the market, each producer can increase its profits if the other fails to follow suit.

The number of firms in an industry and the freedom with which other firms can enter are important determinants of the strength and viability of any cartel. The larger the number of actual or potential competitors in the market, the greater the cost of agreeing to cartelized operations, of detecting chiselers, and of enforcing the cartel's rules. In addition, if firms differ in their production capabilities, the task of establishing each individual firm's share of the market is made more difficult. If one firm believes that it is receiving a smaller share of the market than it can achieve in a noncartelized market, it has a built-in incentive to chisel on the cartel almost from the start. If the cartel breaks down, it will be no worse off for it. Because of the built-in incentive for cartel members to collude and to chisel, we can anticipate that the history of a cartel will be "cyclical": periods in which output and prices are successfully controlled will be followed by other periods in which chiseling emerges, leading to the destruction of the cartel's price structure.

Government can be a critically important determinant of the success of a cartel. It can encourage or discourage a cartel. Through regulatory government agencies which fix prices, determine market shares, and impose penalties for violations of regulatory rules, government can provide the necessary force to keep competitors or cartel members from doing what comes naturally—chiseling. Insurance companies in most states oppose deregulation of their insurance rates; one reason may be that the state is providing an important service for the competitors. It is forcing all to charge the same minimum price. In seeking regulation, the regulated industry may figure that it is easier for them to control its regulatory agency than to try to control member firms and those who would come into the industry were it not for the regulation. In 1975, President Ford proposed to Congress that the power of the Federal Aviation Commission to set rates and determine airline routes be sharply curtailed. The proposal was met with instant hostility from industry representatives. The *Wall Street Journal* reported,

> The administration bill quickly drew a sharp blast from the Air Transport Association, which was speaking for the airline industry. The proposed legislation "would tear apart a national transportation system recognized as the finest in the world," the trade group said, urging Congress to reject it because it would cause "a major reduction or elimination of scheduled air service to many communities and would lead inevitably to increased costs to consumers."[10]

Why would the airline industry oppose deregulation? Which seems the more reasonable answer, the argument given by the industry or the ex-

[10] "Less Regulation of Airline Sector Is Urged by Ford," *Wall Street Journal*, Oct. 9, 1975, p. 3.

pected 15 to 20 percent reduction in airline passenger rates estimated by the Council of Economic Advisers?[11]

Government can suppress competition in many ways that have nothing to do with price. For example, many people believe that it is socially desirable to prohibit the sale of hard liquors on Sunday. The prohibition can benefit those who share this concern, but it benefits liquor dealers, who, because of competition, might otherwise have to open on Sundays if it were not for the Sunday blue laws. Until 1975 there was a prohibition against Sunday liquor sales in Pinellas County, Florida. One of the local state representatives, thinking he would be doing the liquor dealers in his area a favor, managed to get a law through the Florida legislature that would permit Sunday liquor sales. A liquor dealer, who hardly appreciated the move, stated, "That McDonald [state representative] pulled the boner of the year. We pay those people to do a job up there and all they do is play around."[12] None of those interviewed in the report indicated that they wanted the ban lifted; the ban prevented all store owners from competing by staying open on Sundays. The store owners preferred to give up the extra sales in order to have more leisure time.

On the other hand, through vigorous enforcement of antitrust laws—meaning principally the Sherman Act (1899), the Clayton Act (1914), and the Federal Trade Commission Act (1914)—government can contribute to the instability of cartels. Succinctly, the Sherman Act makes illegal "every contract, combination in the form of a trust or otherwise, or conspiracy, in restraint of trade or commerce among several states, or within foreign nations." In the decade following the enactment of the Sherman Act the courts took a very narrow interpretation of what is meant by "restraint of trade or commerce." As a result, congressmen drew up a detailed list of over 100 practices which the authors of the initial legislation wanted declared illegal. The bill which was finally passed, the Clayton Act, specified only four practices deemed illegal: (1) price discrimination, (2) tying contracts, (3) interlocking directorates, and (4) the acquisition of one corporation's stock by another when the effect is to lessen competition. On the other hand, the Clayton Act made collusive arrangements among laborers and within agriculture legal. The Federal Trade Commission Act established the Federal Trade Commission, which was given power to initiate antitrust action against firms. The Commission was also given the responsibility of preventing unfair methods of competition.

These acts can make agreement among competitors more costly by forcing conspirators to work surreptitiously. It can increase the expected costs of collusion by increasing the probability of conspirators being caught and convicted and by imposing penalties in the form of fines and prison sentences if they are convicted. An increase in the cost of collusion can reduce or eliminate the net benefits conspirators believe they can achieve from collusive efforts.

"THE INCREDIBLE ELECTRICAL CONSPIRACY"

During the 1950s the major manufacturers of electrical equipment in the United States conspired to set prices and divide the market on everything from $2 insulators to turbine generators.[13] Their conspiracy can show us the incentives which competitors have to collude and to chisel on the collusive agreement. The conspiracy involved, among others, General Electric, Westinghouse, Allis-Chalmers, and Southern States Equipment. As a result of the court case, which ended in 1961 and terminated the conspiracy, nearly $2 million in fines were levied against the conspirators and the companies they represented. Six corporate executives were sent to prison and 24 others were fined and given suspended sentences. It was the largest case brought to trial in the history of antitrust laws, and it is a classic example of the benefits and pitfalls of industrial conspiracy.

[11] Ibid.

[12] *St. Petersburg Times*, June 7, 1975, p. 1-B.

[13] For a more detailed account of the case see Richard Austin Smith, "The Incredible Electrical Conspiracy," parts I and II, *Fortune*, April and May 1961, pp. 132 ff. (April) and pp. 161 ff. (May).

During World War II the prices of various types of electrical equipment were regulated by the Office of Price Administration (OPA). The manufacturers, under the umbrella of the National Electrical Manufacturers Association, met on a regular basis during the war years to determine the means by which they could meet the demands being made on them for supplies of electrical equipment. After their regular meeting the members of the conspiracy would regroup and talk about how they could get the OPA to raise their regulated prices.[14] When the war was over, when prices were no longer controlled and the major manufacturers had to face price competition from a growing number of smaller companies, the meetings continued. This time, the talk centered on fixing prices and determining methods of dividing the market. Because buyers had turned increasingly to sealed bids as a means of getting the lowest possible prices on their purchases, the conspirators decided on a plan whereby, in the cases of bids on heavy equipment, they would rotate the privilege of being the one with the lowest bid. All others, after finding out what the "lowest bid" was going to be, agreed to make higher bids. The volume of business each company received was determined on the basis of past sales. In the circuit-breaker business, for example, GE received 45 percent of the business; Westinghouse got 35 percent; Allis-Chalmers, 10 percent; and Federal Pacific, 10 percent.[15] The conspirators used code names and numbers and kept in regular contact with one another by memoranda and telephone. They had working meetings every ten days to two weeks. At the meetings they would review who had gotten what in recent weeks and who could take what bids in the future. The places of their meetings were never revealed on their expense account reports. At times they held their meetings on the golf course.

The conspiracy had its benefits, but as Richard Smith recounts, the firms were no more reluctant to violate the rules of the cartel than they were to violate the Sherman Act:

"Everyone accused the others of not living up to the agreement," Clarence Burke [General Manager of the High Voltage Switchgear Department at General Electric] recalled, "and the ones they complained about tried to shift the blame onto someone else." The most constant source of irritation occurred in the sealed-bid business, where chiseling was difficult to detect. But breaks in book price to the utilities in the open-bid business also generated ill will and vituperation. *Indeed, one of the many ironies of the whole affair is that the conspiracy couldn't entirely suppress the competitive instinct.* Every so often some company would decide that cutthroat competition outside was preferable to the throat-cutting that went on in the cartel; they would break contact and sit out the conspiracy for a couple of years.[16] [Emphasis added.]

In 1953, the cartel began to show signs of wear. Westinghouse, which was under pressure to increase its business, cheated on a turbine deal in 1954. Others began to cheat on the cartel, and price cuts came rapidly. By 1954–55 prices being quoted to switch-gear buyers were as much as 40 percent off book price. By 1957–58, deals were being closed at as much as 60 percent off book, which, for all practical purposes, ended, although temporarily, the cartel. The circuit-breaker cartel started up again in 1959, only after GE, Westinghouse, and Allis-Chalmers had conceded a part of their market share to the demands of Federal Pacific I-T-E. However, the Justice Department broke the case after TVA reported that it had been receiving identical bids from several companies on equipment which it intended to purchase. Several conspirators, put in a classic prisoner's dilemma, began to tell all in order to save their own hides.

MONOPOLY POWER AND PRICE DISCRIMINATION

From time to time a grocery store will advertise one can of beans at $0.30, two cans for $0.55.

[14] Ibid., April, p. 137.

[15] Ibid., April, p. 36.

[16] Ibid., April, p. 171. Clarence Burke once said in 1953, "No one was living up to the agreement and we at G.E. were being made suckers. On every job someone would cut our throat." Ibid., p. 172.

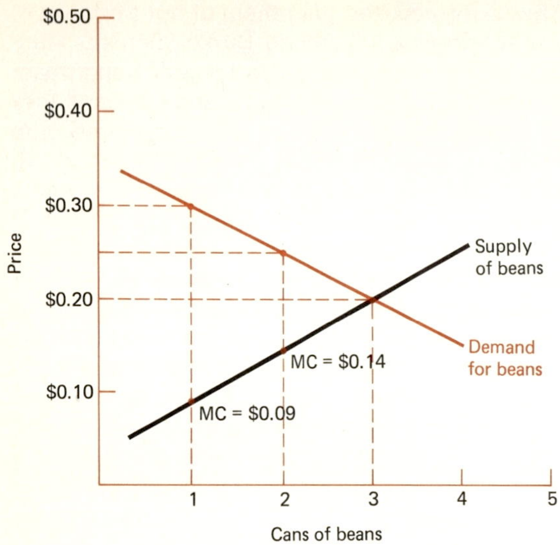

FIG. 10·7 A grocery store with monopoly power, facing the downward sloping demand curve above, can offer customers the following deal: one can of beans for $0.30, two cans for $0.55, and three cans for $0.75. By pricing its beans this way, the store can collect more revenues than if it prices all three cans at $0.20 each. In each case, the consumer with this demand for beans will buy three cans.

Does this pricing technique indicate that the store is trying to give its customers a break and/or that the cost of additional cans of beans decreases as more are sold? More than anything else, the pricing scheme indicates that customers' demand curves for beans are downward sloping and that the company can generate greater profits in this way than by trying to sell cans of beans at one constant price. Consider Figure 10·7. Suppose that the demand curve represents your demand for beans. The supply curve is the store's marginal cost of producing and offering the beans for sale. If the store charges the same price for each can of beans, it will have to mark the cans at $0.25 each in order to induce you to buy two. However, notice from the graph that you are willing to pay more for the first can ($0.30) than for the second ($0.25). If the store sells each can for $0.25, its total revenues are $0.50 (2 × $0.25). However, it can sell the first can for $0.30, which is what you are willing to pay for it. They do this by offering one can for $0.30 and two cans for $0.55. That deal will still entice you to buy two cans, but the company's revenues are $0.55 instead of $0.50, which is what revenues would have been if the company had simply sold each can for $0.25 and had allowed you to buy as many cans as you wished at $0.25.[17]

The deal does not change the marginal cost of providing each can, which, as you can see in the graph, is below the selling price of each. In other words, the company's total revenues are greater; that is, its profits are greater. Indeed, to entice you to buy three cans the company can offer to sell one can for $0.30, two cans for $0.55, and three cans for $0.75. At the same time, the store's profits will rise further. (Notice that if the cans had been priced at $0.25 apiece, you would have purchased only two cans. Can you explain the apparent contradiction?)

A firm can discriminate in this way only so long as its customers are unable to resell the additional cans they buy to other customers who want only one and so long as other firms are unable to move into the market and lower the price of beans. To the extent buyers can benefit from reselling the cans for a higher price than they paid for them, price discrimination will not work for the firm. However, resale is not very practical in the case of canned beans. The person who contemplates buying three cans with the intention of selling the third has very little incentive to seek out a person who is willing to pay $0.25 for only one can. The profit potential in the resale transaction ($0.05) is just not great enough to get people to break the monopoly power. However, imagine a car dealer with two identical automobiles with a book price of $5000 each. If that car dealer were to offer one car for $5000 and two cars for $9000, many people would be willing to buy two cars and take the time to find someone who is willing to pay only $4500 for one car. The $500 gain ($4500 − $4000) can be

[17] Note that if the store had tried to sell all its cans of beans at $0.30, you would have bought only one can. It would have forgone a profit opportunity on the second can. (Why?)

sufficient to cover the time and effort cost incurred in resale. These examples help to explain why we see *this type of price discrimination* much more frequently in grocery stores than in car dealerships. This is not to say that car dealers do not discriminate with regard to price; they do indeed. The salesperson who asks your age, income, place of work, etc., is actually trying to figure out your demand curve with the purpose of getting as high a price as possible.

In short, in preceding sections we have indicated the output level of a monopolist at Q_m in Figure 10·7. However, that level will be the one sought by a monopolist firm *if it is unable to price-discriminate among buyers and among the units bought by a given buyer.* For a monopolist who has the power of price discrimination, the output level can be greater than Q_m. His profits can also be greater than at Q_m. For example, if the monopolistic firm represented in Figure 10·3 can charge a different price for each unit sold between Q_m and Q_c, it will expand production. This is simply because the price it charges for each of the additional units sold will be above the marginal cost of production, indicated by the marginal cost curve. In fact, the monopolistic firm can move very close to, if not to, Q_c; how far depends upon its ability to discriminate.

While the monopolist increases profits through price discrimination, consumers get more of what they want, although not necessarily at the price they want. They are willing to pay the prices necessary to get more than Q_m units. To this extent, price discrimination can increase the efficiency (in an economic sense) of the monopolized industry. Consumers would be better off if they could pay one constant price, P_c, for Q_c, as they would under competition, but that is a choice the monopolist does not allow.

SUMMARY AND EXTENSIONS

The main purpose of this chapter has been to demonstrate the consequences of monopoly in the marketplace. Succinctly, the consequences are higher prices and lower production levels than are forthcoming under market conditions of perfect competition. Also, as we have shown in the chapter, monopoly power can result in inefficiency in production. Consumers prefer that more resources be used in the production of the monopolized good; and for additional units of the good, they are willing to pay a price which exceeds the cost of production. However, because of its interest in maximizing profit, a monopolistic firm will not produce beyond the point at which its marginal cost equals its marginal revenue. Therefore, monopoly power can mean that consumer choice is restricted, and it can be opposed on the grounds that it restricts individual freedom as well as on the grounds that the power that it has results in an inefficient output level.

We have dealt with the extreme case of monopoly power called *pure monopoly;* however, we have also been able to use the model that we have developed to talk about market structures called *monopolistic competition* and *oligopoly.* With regard to these latter market structures, our analysis has been quite general. Accordingly, without considerable empirical work, we are unable to say very much about the relative efficiency of specific markets, for example, the automotive, light bulb, and cosmetic markets. All we can say with reasonable accuracy is that monopolistically competitive and oligopolistic markets will achieve an efficiency level somewhere in between the extremes of perfect competition and pure monopoly—i.e., the *efficiency range.* As we mentioned above, how one evaluates these intermediate markets largely depends upon one's point of view. In the case of the 12-ounce beer stein with 6 ounces of beer in it, pessimists will say that it is "half empty"; optimists will say that it is "half full." In a similar manner, proponents of the market system tend to emphasize the degree to which the existence of any market competition moves the market away from the equilibrium of pure monopoly; opponents of the market system, on the other hand, tend to stress the degree to which the market fails to achieve the equilibrium of perfect competition. Regardless of one's point of view, the analysis of this chapter leads to the conclusions that competition and economic efficiency can be enhanced by the reduction or elimination of arbitrary barriers to entry.

QUESTIONS TO PONDER

1 National news magazines typically offer multi-year subscriptions on a lower per-year rate than they offer one-year subscriptions. Explain the logic of this pricing scheme. Why may this be evidence of "monopoly power" on the part of the magazines?

2 "The larger the number of colluders, the greater the temptation for any individual colluder to chisel on the cartel." Do you agree? Explain your answer with the aid of a graph.

3 Explain why and under what conditions less will tend to be produced under a monopolized industry than under a competitively organized industry.

4 "If a monopoly retains its market power in the long run, there must be barriers to entry into that market." Explain this statement. List possible restrictions on the mobility of resources which may lead to the retention of monopoly power.

5 Provide an economic analysis of why antitrust action may not be taken against all forms of monopoly power.

6 "In an economy in which resources can move among industries with relative ease, a cartel attempting to maximize its short-term profits will sow the seeds of its own destruction." Explain.

RECOMMENDED READINGS

Bain, Joe S.: "Conditions of Entry and the Emergence of Monopoly," *Essays on Price Theory and Industrial Organization* (Boston: Little, Brown and Company, Inc., 1972), pp. 74–94.

Hayek, F. A.: "The Meaning of Competition," in *Individualism and Economic Order* (Chicago: The University of Chicago Press, 1948), pp. 92–106.

Leftwich, Richard H.: *The Price System and Resource Allocation,* 5th ed. (Hinsdale, Ill.: The Dryden Press, 1973), chaps. 11–13.

Smith, Richard Austin: "The Incredible Electrical Conspiracy," parts I and II, *Fortune,* April and May, 1961, pp. 132 ff. (April) and pp. 161 ff. (May).

Part Four
Public Control of the Market

Regulate unto others
As you would have them
Regulate unto you
John Dunlop's "Bronze Rule"
(Dunlop was Secretary of
Labor under President Ford)

In previous chapters we developed economic models of competitive and monopolistic markets, and we showed how these models can be used to illuminate the effects of such market changes as an increase in the price of oil on the market for coal. In the next three chapters we employ these same models to evaluate policy proposals which are designed to control market forces. Specifically, we consider in Chapter 11 the effects of governmental controls on the prices of goods and services which we all buy. Our analysis of government controls is further refined and extended in Chapters 12 and 13, in which we present the pros and cons of policy proposals designed to regulate business production and consumer purchases. The arguments that are presented will help us appreciate the public controversy which continues to surround these issues.

11

Public Control of the Market through Price Ceilings

. . . Wage-price controls are necessary and ultimately inevitable in an economy dominated by an organizational sector where wage and prices are determined by trade unions and corporate policy.

Robert Solo[1]

The common image of price-wage control is entirely wrong. The image is that a little band of dedicated, objective, analytical men in Washington would keep a few heads of powerful corporations and unions from "exploiting us." The fact is that it is "us" who would be and would have to be controlled. And the control would not be managed by Moses, or Buddha, or Galbraith (at least not forever) but by the same kind of people who run and operate all the other agencies in Washington. That is to say, they would be political and bureaucratic.

Paul McCracken[2]

PREVIEW OF CHAPTER

Central question

What is the case for and the case against the control of prices in the economy?

[1] Robert A. Solo, *The Political Authority and the Market System* (Cincinnati: South-Western Publishing Company, 1974) p. 296.

[2] Paul W. McCracken, "Galbraith and Price-Wage Controls," *The Washington Post*, July 28, 1971. At the time the article appeared, Paul McCracken was Chairman of the President's Council of Economic Advisors.

Major objectives

1 To develop the case for and the case against price controls with the use of the tools of analysis developed in earlier chapters
2 To relate the arguments to the real-world experiences of the United States in the control of gasoline prices and interest rates on borrowed money

Major conclusions

1 The proponents of price controls make the following major points:
   a Government control of prices is necessary to ensure justice and equity in the distribution of income.
   b Price increases have little effect on the quantity of goods produced, and, therefore, price controls have little effect on national production.
   c Large corporations control the market, not vice versa. Government control is necessary to check the power of large corporations.
   d Price controls imposed on monopolistic firms can result in an expansion of production.
   e Workers demand higher wages because they *expect* prices of the things they buy to rise, and management concedes to the demands of workers because they expect to be able to raise their prices. Prices must be controlled to change people's expectations about future price increases and break the inflationary spiral.
2 The opponents of price controls make the following major points:
   a Competition is a sufficient controlling force in the market, and government intrusion is unnecessary.
   b Government control is an affront to individual freedom and must be avoided for that reason alone.
   c The task of controlling a large segment of an economy is simply too difficult for a relatively small group of government officials to accomplish successfully.
   d The control of market prices will generally lead to competition among those who are being controlled for special treatment by the controllers.
   e Price controls invariably lead to shortages and "black markets."

Important terms and concepts

Administered prices
Black markets
White markets

In the first year and a half of the 1970s the rate of price increases on goods which people buy and the rate of unemployment were at unusually high levels. President Nixon was being pressed by even his own party to "do something." On the evening of August 15, 1971, Nixon announced what he considered to be "the most comprehensive new economic policy to be undertaken in this nation in four decades."[3] In one fell swoop, he cut loose the dollar from its tie to gold, a bond which had been officially recognized since the 1930s. He imposed a 10 percent "surcharge," meaning an additional

[3] As quoted in *The Wall Street Journal*, Aug. 16, 1975, p. 1.

tariff, on imported goods. He asked Congress to raise the "investment tax credit"[4] from 7 percent to 10 percent and to repeal the 7 percent excise tax on automobiles, and he proposed to cut the federal work force by 5 percent. In addition, and what is particularly relevant to this chapter, he ordered an immediate 90-day freeze on all prices, wages, and rents. In so doing, he reversed his long-held political position against controls, he invalidated numerous contracts negotiated in good faith, and contradicted his chairman of the Council of Economic Advisors who, 17 days before, had articulated the administration's opposition to controls (see the head of this chapter). During the ensuing three years, the country went through four phases of price controls which, as it turned out, were actually phases leading to decontrol.

With the 1972 Presidential election 14 months away, this "comprehensive" policy constituted a brilliant "political package": it had something for everyone. In the area of controls, political considerations won out over what the President and his economic advisors apparently thought was good economic policy. The intent of this chapter is to develop the arguments in favor of price controls (wage controls will be considered in Chapter 15) which are imposed on all or a major segment of the economy and to explain the arguments in opposition to them. Economists support both sides of the issue.

DIOCLETIAN'S EDICT OF 301 A.D.

President Nixon was by no means the first head of government to institute wage and price controls, nor is he likely to be the last. Wage and price controls were in effect in this country during the Second World War and the Korean conflict. Rent controls have been used at various locations in the United States. Prime Minister Trudeau of Canada imposed controls on the economy of his country in the fall of 1975. Going back into history, the first recorded legal code, the Babylonian Code of Hammurabi, developed in the twenty-first century B.C., contained regulations governing the maximum wage, housing prices, and rents on such property as boats, animals, and tools.

In 301 A.D., the Roman Emperor Diocletian issued an edict in which he decreed maximum prices for most everything from poultry to gold and maximum wages for almost everyone from lawyers to the cleaners of the sewer systems. The penalty for violating this edict was death to merchant and customer or to employer and employee, as the case may have been. To those who favor controls, whether in ancient times or in our times, their purpose is to bring about stability and an element of fairness in the prices of labor and goods and services. Prior to the edict, prices had been unstable. The consumers of Rome had begun to turn more and more toward the East for goods which they wanted, and the currency in use had lost much of its purchasing power (i.e., how many goods could be bought).

Some prices, particularly in the area of textiles, were strictly controlled. However, although numerous death penalties were meted out for violations, the control system was a failure and helped bring about the abdication of Diocletian in 305 A.D. Cheating on the system was widespread, and the controls actually had only limited success within a small portion of the empire, mainly the countries of the eastern Mediterranean. This happened even though the state attempted to control production in order to ensure that the supplies of many commodities met the demand at the control prices. Furthermore, the system was plagued with the problem of many goods being sold illegally.

THE CASE FOR PRICE CONTROLS

Fairness, Equity, and Justice

The case for price controls (that is, "price ceilings") is multifaceted. First, on one level, there

[4] With a 10 percent investment tax credit, a firm can deduct 10 percent of the value of that year's expenditure on plant and equipment from its tax liability. For example, a firm that invests $100,000 in a plant can deduct $10,000 (10 percent of $100,000) from what it owes the government in taxes. The credit reduces the cost of the equipment and, therefore, encourages investment by private businesses. This policy proposal was recommended as a means of "stimulating" the economy, by which is meant that production and employment will be increased.

is the simple belief, shared by many people, that the prices of the things should be controlled in order that they may not be made worse off by the eroding effects of inflation. The argument may be heard in many disguised forms from those who believe that they are in a particularly disadvantageous position in an economy in which prices are allowed to fluctuate in response to the forces of supply and demand. The fairness of a price control system may have special legitimacy for those persons, such as the elderly, who are on fixed incomes and have limited means of increasing their money incomes to compensate for the effects of price increases.[5] However, the argument is also frequently heard coming from union headquarters. Too often those who demand controls believe that everything should be controlled except their wages and the prices of goods they sell. Although seemingly perverse, this attitude is understandable from a strict economic point of view, that is, the "selfish" view described by Adam Smith and discussed earlier.

In other words, when prices start to rise, deleterious effects on the distribution of personal income are inevitable. The status quo is disrupted, and people can be expected to question the "fairness," "equity," and "justice" of the changes that are taking place. Many people firmly believe that goods and services *should* be allocated on the basis of something other than prices; some other rationing mechanism must then be employed. What that mechanism should be, however, is not a simple question in a heterogeneous population, and it inevitably leads to controversy. As we will see, with imposed price controls, nonprice rationing schemes can and must be considered.

Unresponsive Producers

Many proponents of controls view the supply curve for a good or goods to be controlled as es-

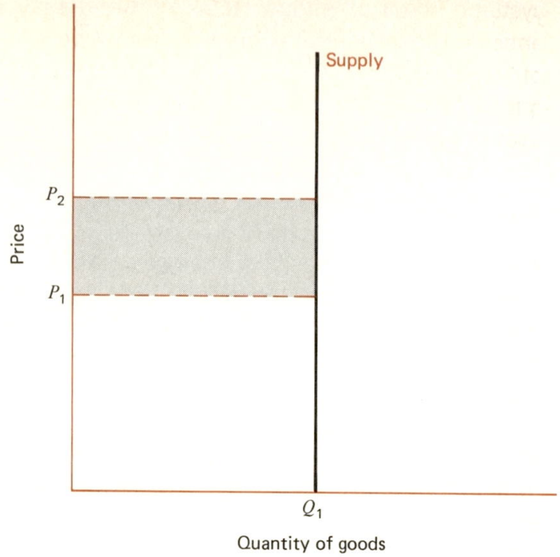

FIG. 11·1 When the supply curve for a product is vertical, an increase in the price of the good has no effect on the quantity which producers sell. It affects only the total revenues of producers and total expenditures of consumers.

sentially vertical. That is to say, if the price is not controlled and rises, the quantity provided on the market is unaffected. Consumers get nothing more in the way of goods; the producers merely reap a windfall profit from being able to raise their prices. The profit is not viewed as an incentive to do anything, but as a "surplus" or a form of "exploitation" by those companies who happen to be fortunate enough to be in the market at the right time. To see the effects of a price rise for a commodity with a vertical supply curve, consider Figure 11 · 1. If the price goes from P_1 to P_2, the quantity offered by producers remains the same, Q_1. The revenues of producers (which equals the expenditures of consumers) rises from P_1Q_1 to P_2Q_1, or by the shaded area.

Furthermore, prices are seen by many as a means of determining incomes and not as a means of rationing the available supplies among competing consumers who, through the pricing

[5] At one time, economists included people on social security in the group of income recipients with relatively fixed incomes. Now, however, social security payments are adjusted periodically for price increases.

system, may register the intensity of their preference for the good. For those who have this point of view, controls do not have adverse consequences, mainly because prices do not serve any useful function—or so the argument goes.

Administered Prices

The third argument is the most technical and the one most often articulated by economists and public officials who favor controls. Many economists argue that a significant segment of the business and industrial community, that is, the larger firms and the firms which control a sizable portion of industry sales, is no longer controlled by the forces of supply and demand. Control by the government must, therefore, fill the vacuum left in the absence of the forces of supply and demand. If it does not, inefficiency in production and inequitable effects on income distribution will result. As John Kenneth Galbraith, a leading advocate of controls, has written, "Controls are made necessary because planning has replaced the market system. That is to say that the firm and the union have assumed the decisive power in setting prices and wages. This means that the decision no longer lies with the market and thus with the public."[6] Robert Solo, in one of the quotations which heads this chapter, echos this basic theme.

Many other economists support this view, which they justify as follows: Firms in the concentrated industries, such as steel, automobiles, nonmetalic minerals, paper, and tobacco, have the power to override the market forces of supply and demand. They can, by manipulating their output, set (or "administer") their prices, and they can manage the demands for their particular products through appropriate expenditures on advertising campaigns. In this way, and not through price, the demand for their products can be brought into equality with the supply which they have decided to produce:

> Most industrial prices are administered prices, not classical market prices. The bulk of such prices are set by the administrative action of the seller. In the steel industry, prices are not set for periods of time, but for such long periods that a price change often becomes front page news. Many prices are set in open-ended contracts negotiated between buyers and sellers for a year or more at a time, with the actual purchase transaction not occurring until the buyer decides how much to buy from time to time at the agreed-upon price. This procedure has also become traditional for wage rates, with the "price" set either by the employer or by an open-ended contract negotiated between management and labor. The actual amount of labor employed is then usually determined by the requirements of the employer.[7]

If one accepts this argument, it follows that

1 Companies in the concentrated industries, of their own will, can push up prices, contributing to what has been called "administered inflation."[8] How long this practice can continue—just how much inflation can be generated in this way—is not always made clear, but the argument is that it is a factor.

2 These companies can also, in the face of a recession or high unemployment, accept higher wage increases for their unionized employees than the market deems acceptable. They, having control of the market, can pass the implied cost increases along to consumers in the form of higher prices. Because of the higher prices, consumers may not initially buy as many goods, and additional unemployment may result. However, these effects only increase the pressure placed on government to stimulate demand for goods and services by buying more goods and hiring more people itself and by lowering income taxes so that consumers will have more to spend. Furthermore, the government has the constitutional power to create money. If it does increase the number of dollars (which is called the "money stock"), which

[6] John Kenneth Galbraith, *Economics and the Public Purpose* (Boston: Houghton Mifflin Company, 1973), p. 315.

[7] Gardiner C. Means, "Simultaneous Inflation and Unemployment. A Challenge to Theory and Policy," *Challenge*, September–October 1975, p. 8.

[8] The phrase comes from the argument that prices are determined or "administered" by large corporations, not competitive forces.

people have to spend and they spend them, more dollars will chase after the available goods and services. In this event, what do you think will happen? Very likely, prices will rise, and businesses can now pay the higher wages they negotiated. Any worker laid off can be hired back. The problem is that, in the process, the country has experienced inflation, which is simply a general increase in prices of goods and services.[9]

Furthermore, administered prices can mean that prices in the concentrated industries are relatively "rigid," that is, they do not respond to policy actions which are designed to reduce the rate of inflation. A government, wanting to reduce the rate of inflation, may restrict the growth in the money stock (or, yet, may even reduce it, although this may be a rather drastic action). By reducing the growth in the money stock, there will be fewer dollars than otherwise chasing after goods and services. As opposed to deflating prices, the firms may keep their prices virtually constant. The effect of the reduced demand for goods and services is thereby felt in the area of employment. In other words, the traditional policies outlined here to bring inflation under control will not work in the concentrated industries. If they will not work, other policy options must be used, one of which is price controls.

Figures 11·2, 11·3, and 11·4 contain the type of empirical information which is offered in support of the "administered price" hypothesis. Figure 11·2 contains the movement of wholesale prices for five groups of industries between 1926 and 1942. The industries are categorized to the extent that prices are either administratively determined or market determined. The chart shows that since the 1920s the wholesale prices of goods produced by industries which are highly concentrated—that is, in which there are few firms—have tended to change less during years of recession or depression than the prices of goods in industries which are not so concentrated and in which firms are forced to respond to market forces. Compare, for example, the movement of prices for group A, which is made up of concentrated industries, with the movement of prices for group E, which is made up of market-oriented industries. The drop between 1929 and 1933 for group A was much less than for group E. During the mid-1930s, the economy began to move out of the bottom of the Great Depression, and, as the chart reveals, the prices of market-oriented industries went up by much more than their counterparts. The opposite is true during the late 1930s, when the economy began to slip back from its upward movement.

The same basic pattern of price movements between concentrated and competitive industries is reflected in Figures 11·3 and 11·4. During the mid-1950s, the economy was bothered with a nagging, high level of unemployment. As indicated in Figure 11·3, the prices in several highly competitive industries, principally agriculture and textiles, actually fell. However, the prices in concentrated industries continued to rise, and at substantially higher rates than in less concentrated industries. The United States experienced another recession during 1967–70. This was brought about by restrictions on the growth of the money stock and a tax increase which were intended to reduce demand and, thereby, reduce the country's rate of inflation. Figure 11·4 illustrates what happened to prices during this period of adjustment in income and employment: the prices in concentrated industries rose much more rapidly than the prices in competitive industries. Again farm prices fell. In those industries in which prices did not fall production and employment did.

The deduction made is that market process does not control the prices of those firms which account for the production and sales of goods in concentrated industries. Control must come from outside—more specifically, from the government, in the form of regulated prices.

Monopoly Power and the Expansion of Production under Price Controls

Our theory of markets does, in fact, suggest that price controls can actually cause firms with

[9] More will be said on the subject of money and inflation in Chaps. 23–26. We are providing only a brief introduction here in order that you may grasp arguments for controls.

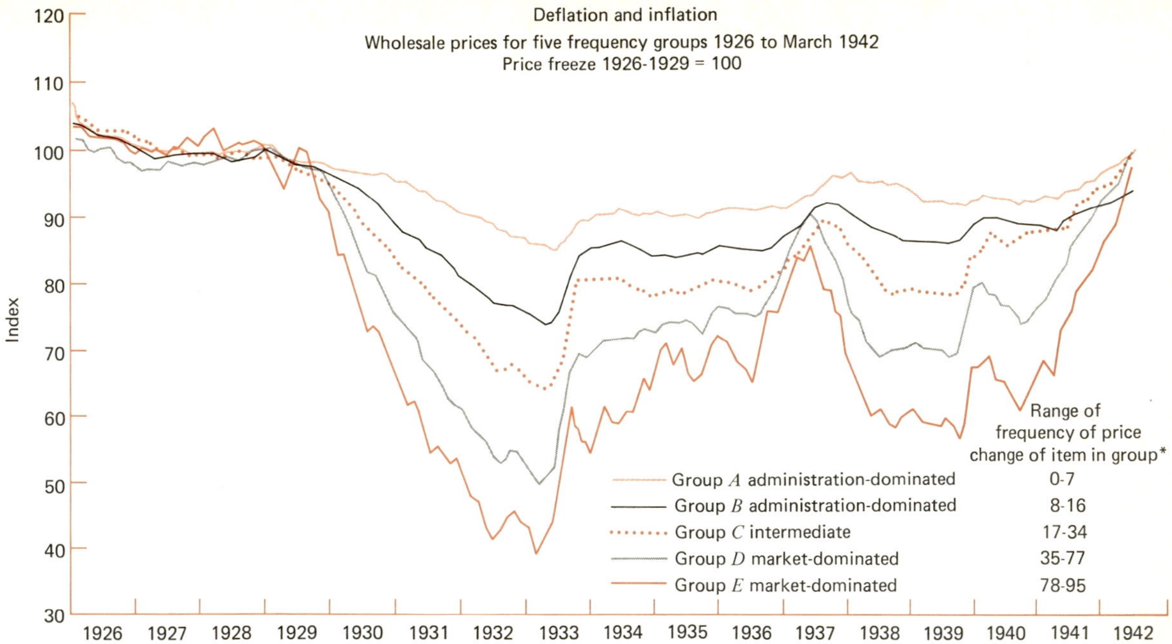

*Price indexes are for 731 items included in the BLS wholesale price index grouped according to frequency of price change in the months of the period 1926 to 1933

FIG. 11 · 2 When industries are grouped according to the frequency of their price changes, as they are in the figure, we can observe that industries which are dominated by a few firms (for example, group A) have experienced modest price changes as compared with industries which have many producers in them and are controlled by competitive forces (for example, group E). (SOURCE: Gardiner C. Means, "Simultaneous Inflation and Unemployment: A Challenge to Theory and Policy," *Challenge*, September–October 1975, p. 10.)

monopoly power to increase their output. This may not always be true; but to the extent that it is true, the argument for price controls is given force. Consider Figure 11 · 5. It is the graph which we used in Chapter 10 to explain the central tendency of monopoly power in the yo yo business. Without government price control, a firm with monopoly power will produce Q_m yo yos and sell that quantity at P_m. If the government deems that price to be too high for purposes of social equity, the government can force the firm to sell at a lower price, for example, P_1. That, then, is the legal maximum price the firm can charge. At that price it can sell as many as Q_1 yo yos. Because it can sell each and every one of these yo yos at P_1, the marginal revenue of each yo yo is also equal to that amount, P_1. Every time the firm sells an additional yo yo, its total revenues will rise by P_1.[10] Therefore, with the price controlled at P_1, the marginal revenue curve for the Q_1 units is P_1a. (Remember, the marginal revenue curve is downward sloping only when the firm can raise its price.)

As we discussed in the last chapter, a firm's ideal production level is that point at which marginal cost is equal to marginal revenue. If full equality cannot be achieved, the firm should strive to come as close to equality as possible.

[10] You may recall from Chap. 10 that the marginal revenue is the additional revenue a firm receives from selling one additional unit of the good.

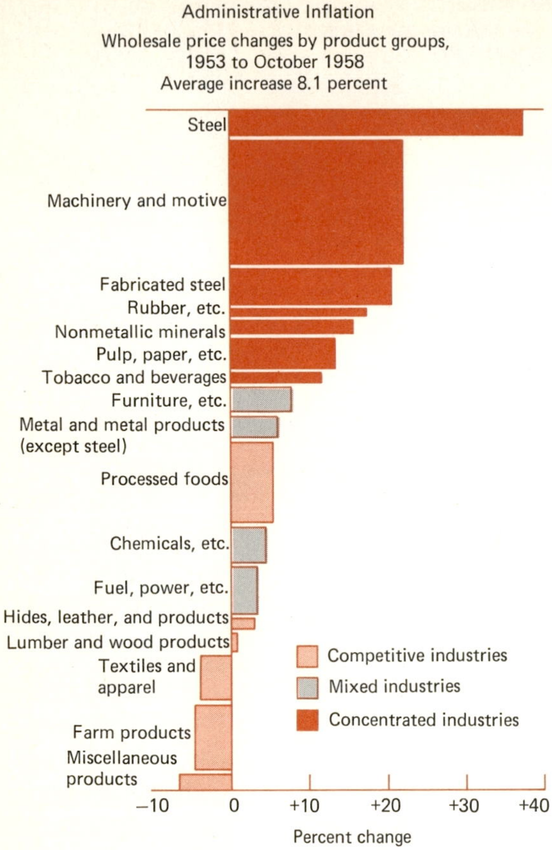

FIG. 11·3 Between 1953 and October 1958, the prices of goods produced in competitive markets, such as those of textiles and farm products, fell. On the other hand, the prices of products in concentrated industries, like steel, rose significantly. SOURCE: BLS. (Secondary source: Gardiner C. Means: "Simultaneous Inflation and Unemployment: A Challenge to Theory and Policy," *Challenge*, September–October 1975, p. 11.)

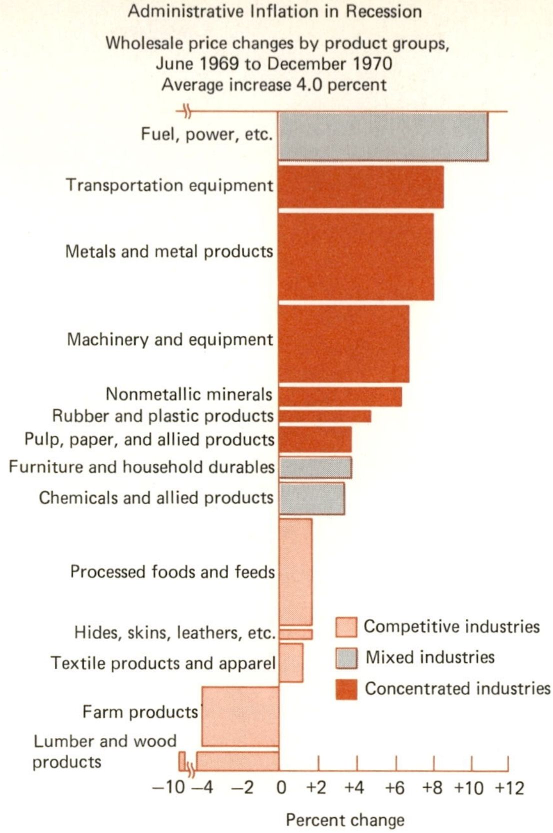

FIG. 11·4 Between June 1969 and December 1970, the prices of farm products and wood and lumber products, which are produced in competitive industries, decreased. The prices of processed foods, which are also produced in competitive markets, rose; however, the prices of more concentrated industries, like metal products, rose by greater percentages.

With the maximum price controlled at P_1, the firm can increase its revenues by selling up to Q_1 units, which is all the demand will permit. Marginal revenue at that point (which is equal to P_1) is not equal to marginal cost; but if the yo yo producer cannot expand production until marginal cost is equal to P_1, he can no longer sell all that has been produced. He should settle for second best, which is to produce only Q_1. Notice, however, that Q_1 is greater than the amount the firm was producing under a free but monopolized market. In short, price controls can cause the firm with market power to expand production. There are some exceptions which will be described later.

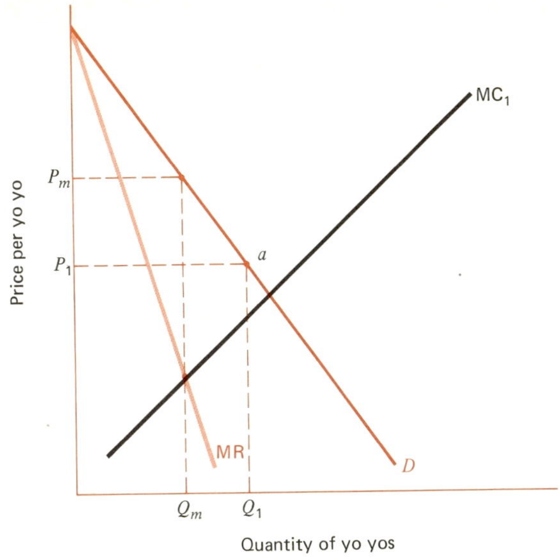

FIG. 11·5 A monopolist whose price is uncontrolled will produce Q_m yoyos and will sell them for P_m. If the firm's price is controlled at P_1, the firm's marginal revenue is equal to P_1: the firm will produce Q_1, which is greater than the amount produced in an uncontrolled market.

Controls as a Jolt to Price Expectations

A final argument in favor of price controls concerns the effect which they may have on people's expectations about future price increases. If people believe that prices will rise in the future by, say, 10 percent, they will include these expectations in their wage demands. Historically, this has been particularly true of union wage negotiations, and managements are often willing to concede to such wage demands because they too assume that prices will continue to rise. They expect, in other words, to be able to cover the added labor costs by charging higher prices. Consequently, the government may have to take action to ensure that prices *can* rise and that businesses *can* pay the wages that have been incorporated in contracts. Otherwise, business may not be able to cover their higher wage bills and unemployment may result. By freezing prices, or by controlling them less severely, the government puts laborers and executives on notice that past expectations of future price increases no longer hold. Labor and management may then be willing to negotiate smaller wage increases and accept lower price increases.

THE CASE AGAINST PRICE CONTROLS

The Controlling Force of Competition

The case *for* price controls is tied very closely to the existence of monopoly power within the market. In fact, as normally developed, advocates of controls feel they should be applied to a limited segment of the total market—that segment in which prices are "administered." In a similar manner, the case *against* controls rests heavily upon the competitive model of market behavior. Economists who do not favor controls feel that through competition the market exerts the necessary control over business and industry behavior, including behavior with regard to price. Indeed, in a highly competitive market, the individual firm has little or no choice over the price it will charge for its products. Prices are not, in this sense, "administered," at least, for a large segment of all firms. Whatever market power there may be in a given market will, in time, tend to dissipate, and if it does not, it can be dealt with effectively and directly with antitrust action. Additional control, in the form of an extension of the arm of government into pricing decisions, is both unnecessary and destructive of the efficient results achieved through competitive processes. One may deduce from this line of argument that price controls are an admission that the government has been unable to control monopoly power through antitrust action. This admission, in turn, raises questions about the ability of the government to carry out the far more complex task of controlling prices.

Individual Freedom

the case against controls inevitably falls back on *individualism* for much of its strength and the bulk of its persuasive content. The ability of the individual to act unencumbered by government fiat is seen as a "good"—an inherent right—to be maximized both for its own sake and because it is a critical ingredient in the ability of a society to adjust and readjust to social and environmental changes.

Pervasive government price controls typically represent an abrupt change in the "package of rights" which a person buys when he acquires property. The individual can sell his property, but he cannot legally sell it for a price that is above the price which is specified by government. To that extent, the range of choices which a person has is narrowed. Because of this, government intrusion can be viewed as a coercive force. It can be seen as a legal form of monopoly power, which, because of the government's ability to tax and police, is a far more complete form than can be achieved by private firms. The case against controls is, in this way, consistent with opposition to monopoly power in any form.

Freedom is the absence of coercion emanating from any source. For economists and social philosophers such as Friedrich Hayek, Milton Friedman, and Robert Nozick, the best way to maximize freedom is to disperse power among so many different decision makers that no one of them will be able to significantly affect the behavior of others. Government control of prices is a marshaling of power. A free-market system, to the extent that it is competitive, disperses power. It tends to maximize freedom. Again, the elements of monopoly power, from this point of view, should be dealt with directly, through antitrust suits. (Of course, how much of this type of action should be taken is a matter of continuing debate among economists.) In the final analysis, individuals who oppose controls stand ready to accept *some* potential for monopoly power that is garnered by business to avoid the monopoly power of government. It is a matter of the less harmful of two evils.

The Limited Abilities of the Controllers

Realistic assessment of the effectiveness of price controls, as the case is developed, must begin with full recognition of the ability of the government to control, that is, the ability of the controllers to handle information that may be relevant to pricing decisions. When price controls are instituted, a central planning board or a regulatory agency—called the Cost of Living Council under the Nixon Administration—is usually established to judge the "appropriateness" of price increases. Prices in general may be frozen, but the board is typically given permission to make exceptions—to allow, for example, firms to pass "legitimate" cost increases through to consumers. When dealing with requests for price increases from even medium-sized firms, controllers must be able to decipher mountains of statistics and accounting data to determine if a price increase is "justified." They must, in other words, determine in a relatively short period of time; whether or not the company asking for a price increase is lying; some deception is to be expected. As we noted in Chapter 10 in discussing the electrical conspiracy of the 1950s, when prices in this industry were controlled during World War II, the company executives conspired to persuade the controllers to raise their ceiling prices. The pricing decisions of control boards may not be very accurate. Because of this and because of the time and trouble industry executives must take to make a convincing case before the control boards and their staffs, and because of the policing costs, the costs of controls can exceed the perceived benefits of controlled prices.

Furthermore, any modern economy is a complex web of input-output relationships. For instance, coal is an input (or resource) into the production of steel, and steel is an input into the production of a wide range of commodities, such as appliances, trucks, and lamps. In turn, trucks are used in construction and transportation of almost all resources and products, including coal, steel, and also other trucks. The circular relationships like this one are numerous. In granting exceptions to wage and price freezes, the Cost of

Living Council must be able to understand the impact of its own decision on other industries. If price increases are allowed in the coal industry, the steel industry may have cause to seek price increases to cover its greater cost. The truck industry may then have a valid case for a price increase, giving the coal industry grounds for an additional price increase. With all these possible price increases, wage earners may then seek allowances for higher wages. In short, the Cost of Living Council's problems may just begin when it seeks to rectify cost-price problems in one sector of the economy. The opponents of wage-price controls argue that the necessary technical expertise that is required to make all these intricate decisions is simply too great to expect a council of even the brightest men and women, with a very large back-up staff, to command. Indeed, the opponents point out that the market is a system which reduces the amount of technical expertise any one person or group of persons must have to generate reasonably efficient production results, and it is a system whereby individuals and firms can adjust and readjust in many small ways to the information they receive on a daily basis. The market allows not only specialization in production, but also specialization in decision making; price controls require centralization of the decision-making process and a dramatic increase in the information which must be absorbed by a limited number of people.

From Price to Political Competition

If prices are to be controlled by government, what do we mean by "government"? Can "government" be equated with a living organism which can consistently reflect *the* "public interest"? Is "government" immune to human failings? The opponents of price controls, such as Paul McCracken, emphasize that the pricing decisions made by control boards will reflect the will of the controllers, who are no better and no worse than most other government bureaucrats. Their preferences as to what constitutes a "just price" and a "just allocation" of goods and services will loom large in their decisions.

Ethics and a sense of fair play may have important roles in the decision-making process. However, political considerations can also play, perhaps, a dominant role in that process. Those persons with talents at political maneuvering and in obtaining special favors from control boards will be in greater demand by special-interest groups under a control system. We should expect their talents to be more fully employed and to be employed at higher prices. Persons with these talents will, therefore, have a private interest in having controls imposed. They may be expected to work for controls.

Competitive behavior, in other words, is not necessarily reduced; its revealed form may simply move from the pricing front to the political front.[11] If price controls are complemented by a government system for allocating the available supplies, as was done with fuel and gasoline in the mid-1970s, pressure in the form of strikes, demonstrations, violence, and/or threat of violence may be used to influence the allocators' decisions. Those wanting special treatment can withdraw these pressures (i.e., costs) in exchange for what they want, which is typically more for themselves and, as a consequence, less for others.

During the 1973–74 energy crisis, the government regulated the allocation of fuel production between gasoline and diesel fuels. Truckers claimed that they "needed" much more fuel than they were getting (this claim, of course, was made by almost everyone). To pressure government allocators into succumbing to their demands, independent truck drivers struck, threatening to paralyze the country unless they got more fuel at lower prices. To ensure "cooperation" among the many independent truckers, those most in favor of the strike blocked roads, vandalized the equipment of those truckers who would not voluntarily cooperate, and actually shot at truckers who ventured out on the road. At least one trucker was killed; others were seriously injured. As far as many truckers were concerned, the action was quite productive, in a perverse sort of way, at least for a

[11] See Armen A. Alchian, *Pricing and Society* (New York: Transatlantic Arts, Inc., 1967).

short period of time. Government allocators did agree to shift more energy production toward diesel fuels and to lower the federal excise tax on it. Later, however, the courts declared the government's moves illegal.

University facilities are generally "sold" to students at below-market prices, sometimes at no price at all. This system has given university administrators and faculty considerable latitude in determining who will use what facilities.[12] Under this type of system, the distribution of the best parking spaces on campus between students and faculty is quite predictable. The system has also, understandably, led to many legitimate demands of students being ignored. The demonstrations and destructive outburst by students on college campuses in the late 1960s and early 1970s reflected student recognition of how the system could be manipulated for legitimate and illegitimate purposes. The methods some students used in their opposition to university policies present a clear example of how violence or the threat of violence can be one means of replacing price, a positive incentive, as an allocator of resources with a negative one.

During the years of the Nixon controls, George Meany, president of the AFL-CIO, was a member of the board charged with regulating prices and wages. He occasionally demanded higher wage increases from the board in return for his continued participation in the proceedings of the board. Although detrimental to the workings of the wage-price control system, his strategy reflected the then relative importance of political pressure.

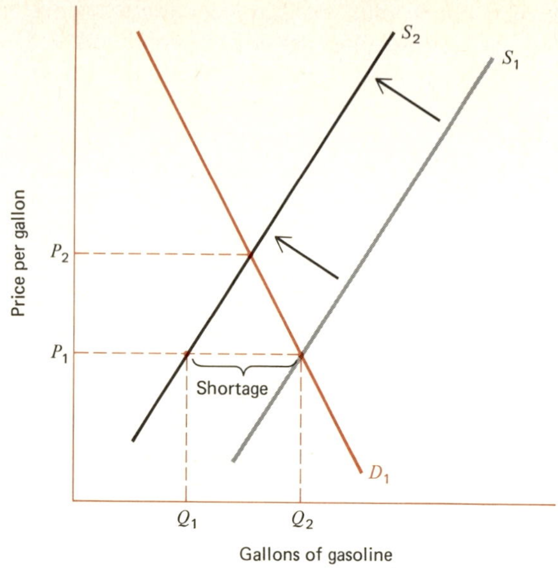

FIG. 11·6 If the supply of gasoline is reduced and the price of gasoline is controlled at P_1, a shortage equal to the difference between Q_1 and Q_2 will emerge.

Price Ceilings and the Inevitability of Shortages in Competitive Markets

In a competitive market, any restriction on upward price movements will lead to shortages. Consider, for example, Figure 11·6, which contains supply and demand curves for gasoline. Suppose that the supply and demand curves are initially S_1 and D_1 and that the equilibrium price, that price toward which a free competitive market will move, is initially P_1. However, suppose that the supply of gasoline falls to S_2, but that the government believes that the new higher equilibrium price, P_2, is "unjust." Consequently, the government "freezes" or "controls" the price of gasoline at P_1.

What will happen in the market? We can clearly see in the graph that at price P_1, which is now below equilibrium, the number of gallons demanded by consumers is Q_2; however, the number of gallons that are supplied is lower, Q_1. The shortage is the gap between Q_1 and Q_2 in the graph. This means that some consumers will not get all the gasoline they want at the ceiling price; very possibly, it means that some customers will be unable to get any gasoline.

The existence of the shortage means an inconvenience to consumers; it means that consumers will have to stand in line to get whatever amount

[12] Richard B. McKenzie and Gordon Tullock, "University Setting," in *The New World of Economics* (Homewood, Ill.: Richard D. Irwin, Inc., 1978), chap. 19.

of gasoline they do get. In order to avoid long lines, they may try to reach the service station early, but others may do the same. The line may be shorter, but in the end obtaining a prime position in line can mean sitting at the pumps before the service station opens. The moral of the story: although the pump price of gasoline may be held constant at, say, P_2, the actual price paid by most consumers rises. The actual price is the sum of the pump price per gallon plus the time cost of waiting in line or maneuvering in other ways to avoid waiting in line. Waiting in line in winter for many means wasting gas to keep warm.

The Arab oil embargo During the winter of 1973–74, OPEC (Organization of Petroleum Exporting Countries) restricted the amount of oil which they would allow to be exported to the United States by 25 percent. To keep the price of gas from rising, a price ceiling was imposed at about \$0.50 per gallon. The available gallons of gas were rationed, not by price, not by coupons, but by "congestion" at service stations. Many service stations took it upon themselves to allow each customer, regardless of car size, 10 gallons of gasoline. Often, people had to stand in line for 2 hours in order to get 10 gallons. A person earning \$3.50 per hour (or who valued his time at that amount), paid \$5 (10 × \$0.50) to the service station attendant and incurred a time cost of \$7 (2 × \$3.50). The total cost of the gasoline was \$12, or about \$1.20 a gallon! In other words, the price ceiling on the pump did not keep the actual or effective price of a gallon of gasoline from rising. Note that the effective price was even higher for people whose wage rate was much higher than \$3.50 per hour. It was lower for those with lower opportunity cost for their time. Seen this way, it is understandable why many people with very high wage rates were paying other people to sit in filling station lines and have their cars filled up. Granted, many people earnestly believe that the rich should bear a disproportionate share of the cost of controlling prices; however, even if we accept that position, we run headlong into the question of whether or not price controls are the most efficient or, in some other sense, the "best" means of bringing about equity through redistribution of incomes. Should we not consider using personal income and wealth taxes instead?

Shortages and monopoly power In developing the case for price controls, we showed that in a monopolized market controls can result in great production. At that control price (P_1 in Figure 11·5), the quantity supplied was equal to the quantity demanded—no shortage. However, control of even monopolists' prices, if the control is severe enough, can create shortages. For instance, suppose that the control price is P_1 in Figure 11·7. The quantity that the monopolist will be willing to offer at that price is Q_2 (why?); the quantity demanded, however, is greater, Q_3. As in the competitive market, a shortage develops in this market, and all the problems associated with shortages in competitive markets can be revealed in this type of market.

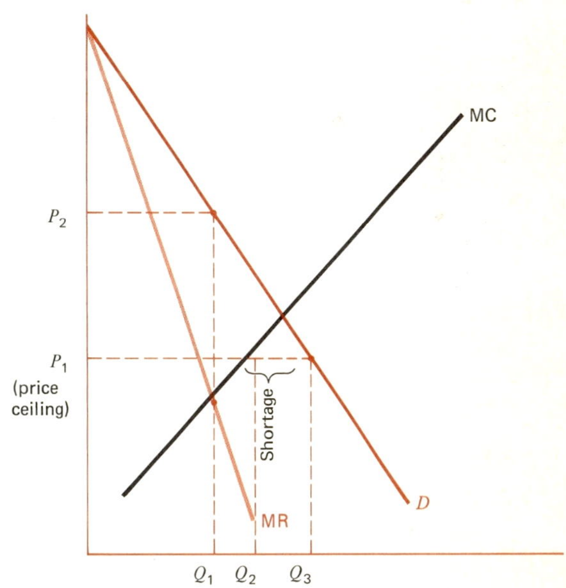

FIG. 11·7 If the price of a monopolist is controlled at P_1, a shortage equal to the distance between Q_2 and Q_3 will result.

The Many Dimensions of "Price Increases"

Control of the pump price is control of only one dimension in which competitive behavior can be expressed in the market. Price control can mean that competitive behavior which would otherwise have been reflected in a price increase will be reflected in other areas of doing business. For example, if a service station owner has a long line of customers waiting to get gas, and he knows that he cannot service all of them in the way that he once did (and, for that matter, he does not have to), he can change the "quality" of his service. He can neglect to clean windshields and check oil levels and, in general, be more abrupt with his customers. All these things happened during the energy crisis of 1973–74. As a result, the effective price of gasoline rose, even though the pump price remained constant. Some service station owners went several steps further; they started closing on weekends and at nights, making the purchase of gasoline less convenient. Still others required customers to negotiate long-term purchase contracts for gasoline and pay in advance. To the extent that an interest cost was involved, the price of gasoline actually rose further than what officially recorded statistics indicated. Others refused to serve anyone other than their regular customers.

Price controls on meals offered in university restaurants can have interesting effects, all of which mean that effective prices actually rise. At one college, during the summer of 1971, the student center offered a breakfast special which included two eggs, bacon, toast, and milk and sold as a unit for $0.65. It was quite a bargain. All the items could be bought separately, but then the total price was $0.95. The college planned to raise the price of the unit breakfast in the fall of 1971. However, President Nixon's announcement of the price freeze in August abruptly terminated those plans. The college resolved its dilemma by eliminating the unit breakfast from its menu. The same breakfast could still be bought in its component parts, but, as we indicated, that cost $0.95. In other words, price controls were successfully circumvented.

At another university, one of the restaurants sold a double-decker hamburger with two patties of meat. When cafeteria officials were held back from raising the price of the sandwich, they eliminated one of the two meat patties. In other words, there are many ways by which the "effective price" of most goods can be raised; increasing the price tag is just one of them. In order to *fully* control price, all dimensions of competitive behavior must be controlled. Even with a sizable police force, this is a task of Herculean proportions, especially in the long run when producers are given time to develop ways of disguising their effective price changes.

Black Markets

Many business maneuvers to evade price controls may be legal, such as the elimination of the bargain breakfast, given the guidelines developed by the control board; others may not. For example, it is illegal for gasoline stations to fill their premium tanks with regular gasoline and to sell the gas at premium prices; but this was frequently done during the winter of 1973–74. A greater shortage of heating oil developed during that winter than was expected. One of the reasons was that truckers, able to get only a portion of their diesel fuel needs at the control price, found that home heating oil could be used in their trucks. Although illegal, they paid home heating oil dealers a higher price for fuel oil than the price at which the dealers could legally sell it to homeowners, thus reducing the available supplies. In short, there is the ever-present prospect of some sellers ignoring price controls and dealing in the "black market" for their goods. The benefits of controlling prices must exceed the cost of enforcing the controls. The further the ceiling price is removed from the market equilibrium price, the greater the benefits from selling the controlled commodity illegally, and the greater the task of controlling the price. Furthermore, to the extent that supplies of a good enter the black market, the shortages on the legitimate market are increased.

COUPON RATIONING

If prices are not used as a rationing mechanism and shortages of goods occur on the market, some other means of rationing must be employed. If nothing else is done, supplies will be rationed on a first-come-first-served basis or, as we have said, by congestion.

The Typical System

One of the most frequently mentioned nonmarket methods of rationing is through the distribution of coupons which entitle people to buy so much of the rationed commodity. The consumer must, under this system, still have the money to buy the goods under control, but he must have the appropriate number of coupons before he can legally use his money for that purpose. By limiting the number of coupons, the (revealed) demand for gasoline can be reduced from D_1 to D_2 in Figure 11·8 and, as is done in the graph, the number of gallons demanded by consumers can be brought into line with the estimated number of gallons available. Thereby, the shortage and the problems of a first-come-first-served market can be alleviated.

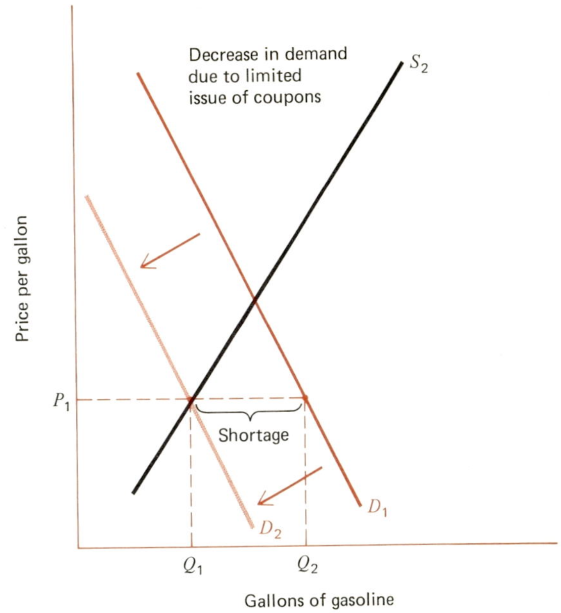

FIG. 11·8 A price control can create a shortage. However, by issuing coupons which must be used in the purchase of gasoline and by restricting the number of coupons issued, the government can reduce the demand for gasoline from D_1 to D_2 and eliminate the shortage.

At this level of consideration—and it is a level beyond which politicians who favor rationing rarely go—the coupon system appears deceptively fair and simple. However, the question which is too infrequently faced is how the coupons are to be distributed. Certainly, the government would not want to auction them off. How, then, do we distribute them? Do we distribute the coupons equally among all registered drivers? Not everyone lives the same distance from their place of work or from school. Some people—for instance, salespeople—have to travel much more than others. Commuting college students have to drive further to school than students who live on campus. One of the reasons why many students choose to live on campus, although they may prefer to live elsewhere, is that they can save money that would otherwise be used for gas in going to and from school, for entertainment purposes, or for going home on the weekends. Do we give the commuting students and salespeople more gasoline than others? If we do, how much more? Some salespeople have to travel more than other salespeople; some students live much further from campus than others. Do we discriminate in the amount of coupons that we give to different salespeople and different college students? If we allow for such differences, will this encourage people to lie about their situation? These are formidable questions that must be answered if the system is going to be "equitable" in any meaningful sense. One redeeming advantage of the pricing system is that it allows the *intensity* of people's needs and preferences to be reflected in just how much of the commodity will be purchased.

"White Market" for Coupons

However the coupons are distributed, should the recipients be allowed to sell them to others? Should "white markets" (that is, legal markets) for coupons be allowed to spring up? If coupons are to be used, most economists are in favor of white markets in coupons for a very simple reason. If the deals made in the white market are voluntary, both parties to the exchange benefit. The person who pays someone else for coupons is better off by having more coupons and, therefore, more gasoline which he, at that time, values more than his money. The person who sells his coupons will not be able to drive as much because of the sale but will have more money to buy other things. In agreeing to make the exchange, he must figure that these other things more than compensate him for his lost trips.

The coupons have a market value because if the price of gasoline is controlled, a shortage will occur; and the further the control price falls below the market clearing price, the greater the value of the coupons. This brings to light another question of some importance regarding the reasonableness of price controls. If there is a price attached to coupons, has the price of a gallon of gasoline been held constant? The answer is no! If the price of an extra coupon for one gallon of gasoline is $0.50 and the pump price of a gallon is $0.70, the total price to the consumer is $1.20 ($0.50 + $0.70). The consumer who uses the coupons distributed by the government to purchase gas incurs an opportunity cost of $0.50 for each coupon used. The total price is, therefore, as we indicated, $1.20. The total cost of a gallon is quite clear for the person who goes into the white market to buy extra coupons in order to buy extra gallons of gasoline.

In plainer terms, the existence of a white market means that, although there may be a redistribution of income, the *price* of gasoline rises. *The main difference is that the price to the consumer will be greater under that type of system than if the price of gasoline at the pump were allowed to rise!* Why, you ask? The benefits of the price increase are received not by the oil companies, refineries, and service stations, but by the people who were fortunate enough to be registered drivers (if that is the criterion used for coupon distribution) when the coupons were distributed. They typically have nothing to do with the production of gasoline. Therefore, the price increase does not provide anyone with an incentive to supply more gasoline to the market. If the price increase were received by producers, they might make greater profits, but they would also have a greater incentive to search for new sources of oil and to step up their production plans. However, under a price control system, this is not a likely consequence. The lower supplies, therefore, mean higher prices! Since less is produced, less income is earned by people in total, but the resulting redistribution of income can be seen as a desirable outcome by those who favor controls.

RENT CONTROLS: NEW YORK'S LONG-RUN PROGRAM TO DESTROY HOUSING

Following World War II, most major cities in the United States did away with controls on rent; New York City, however, retained them. As late as 1971 approximately two-thirds of that city's private rental units were under control. The rental units which were not controlled were mainly luxury apartments for the affluent. Presumably, the rich could afford to be "taken" by landlords.[13]

During the postwar years until about 1970 construction costs for rental units rose an average 6 percent a year; maintenance costs went up an average of 3 percent a year; and city real estate taxes rose 4 to 6 percent a year. While costs were going up at these rates, the city rent control board allowed rents on the controlled units to rise an average of 2 percent a year.[14]

[13] Actually, there were many well-to-do people who had rent-controlled apartments and therefore benefited from the program. Those who were hurt the most by the program were those who newly entered the housing market.

[14] RAND Corporation, "The Effects of Rent Control on Housing in New York City," *Rental Housing in New York City: Confronting the Crisis*, RM-6190-NYC, February 1970, condensed and reprinted in Robert W. Crandall and Richard S. Eckaus, eds., *Contemporary Issues in Economics: Selected Readings* (Boston: Little, Brown and Company, 1972), pp. 251–252.

In the short run, rent controls can be expected to have very little effect on a city's inventory of rental units; there are just a few things that landlords can do in the short run to affect the supply of housing. However, given time and a growing cost squeeze, economic theory predicts that, if the market is competitive, a shortage of *controlled* rental units will emerge. If rents cannot be raised in the face of rising costs and the shortage, landlords can be expected to seek other means of effectively raising the rental payments. One of the more obvious ways is to change the "quality" of the rental unit by allowing it to deteriorate over time.

New York's rent controls had all these effects and a couple more that may seem a little surprising. During the 1960s, when controls began to have a serious binding effect, a study by the RAND Corporation revealed a decline in construction of those kinds of rental units which would have come under rent control. Between 1960 and 1967, the stock of "dilapidated" housing units grew by 44 percent; the stock of "deteriorating" units grew by 37 percent. An estimated 114,000 units were withdrawn from the housing market between 1965 and 1967, an effect much of which can be attributed directly to rent controls.[15] Some landlords found that they could escape rent controls by substantially upgrading the quality or in other ways changing the classification of their rental units. This had the effect of providing more housing for the well-to-do, but it also had the perverse effect of reducing the available housing supply for lower-income people, whom, supposedly, the control system was designed to help. Furthermore, the city's rent controls had the effect of encouraging urban sprawl. Because rental property was not profitable, construction companies began to build more heavily than they otherwise would have in suburban areas where rents were not controlled; and because of the housing shortage in New York, many people were forced to look to the suburbs for places to live.

RAND also reports, "To retain the benefit of controlled rents, many families have held onto large controlled apartments despite departure of some family members from household; thus 74 percent of all persons living alone in rent-controlled apartments occupy three or more rooms, as contrasted with 52 percent in uncontrolled apartments. . . ."[16] Succintly, the controls had the effect of inefficiently allocating the available supply of housing.

Finally, not all tenants in controlled apartments actually benefited from the control system. Tenants who had leases with controlled rents found that they could sell those leases to others who were willing to pay more than the controlled rental payment for an apartment. For example, *Newsweek* reported in 1971 that "Rent-controlled digs are so sought after that a tenant giving one up—say a three-room apartment for $60 a month—can 'sell' a lease for as much as $5,000 in "key money.'"[17] As in the case of the gasoline coupons discussed earlier, the problem is that this money, $5,000, does not go to those who need an incentive to provide more housing. Understandably, for the past several years New York has been gradually moving toward the decontrol of rent.

USURY LAWS: HOW TO REDUCE THE AVAILABILITY OF CREDIT TO THE POOR

Throughout history there have been laws designed to restrict interest rates charged on loaned money. Diocletian prohibited money being loaned at more than 12 percent interest. A later emperor lowered the ceiling interest rate to 8 percent for commercial loans and 6 percent for individual loans.

The arguments put forth in favor of usury laws, that is, laws to control interest rates, are all very familiar. (1) Low-income people cannot afford to pay high interest rates for credit. Furthermore, they do not have the sophistication to understand the meaning of interest rates and can be taken advantage of unless the state comes to their aid in

[15] Ibid., p. 251.

[16] Ibid., p. 254.

[17] *Newsweek*, June 7, 1971, p. 117.

the form of controls on interest rates. (2) Banks and lending institutions have monopoly power and, without government intervention, can charge exorbitant interest rates. (3) Money lending is unproductive and, therefore, any return on the lending of money is a form of exploitation. If the exploitation cannot be eliminated, it should be controlled by the state. Finally, (4) low interest rates encourage borrowing and consumer purchases and business investment.[18]

An interest rate on credit is the price that one must pay to buy credit. The main difference between this price and most other prices is that the interest price is stated as a percentage of the money loaned. However, like all other prices, an interest rate serves the important function of rationing the available supplies of credit among the potential borrowers. If the rate is controlled and not allowed to move up toward the equilibrium rate, just as in the case of rent controls, a shortage of credit will develop. There will be more people wanting to borrow money at the ceiling rate than there are funds to go around. This means that some nonprice means of rationing the available credit must be used; and, very likely, the system employed does not work for the benefit of low-income people.

Banks and lending institutions tend to favor those persons who have the highest credit ratings. In this way banks and other lending institutions minimize the "risk costs" which they have to accept in doing business. Needless to say, poor people tend to have, by virtue of their low and, possibly, unstable, incomes, very low credit ratings. As a result, when usury laws are in effect, the poor are the ones most likely to be rationed out of the market. In fact, in order to obtain credit, poor people—or, for that matter, anyone with a low credit rating—have to pay high interest rates, not so much because the extra charges enable credit institutions to fill their tills with profits, but because credit institutions are covering the risk costs they have to incur in making loans to people with low credit ratings. On the accounting statements of banks, the risk costs are reflected in high rates of default and high collection costs.

This is not to suggest that banks, for example, are not profitable businesses. For the most part, they are. However, any unusually high rates of return made by banks reflect, more than anything else, federal and state government control, that is, restriction on entry of new banks into the banking field. In that way, governments restrict the competitiveness of the banking industry and contribute to unrestricted interest rates being higher than they otherwise would be. For now, we bring this topic up to make the point that *given the existing control of entry into the credit industry,* an additional control in the form of usury laws can be harmful to those people the laws are designed to help.[19]

[18] For a brief historical account of arguments for and against usury laws, see Norman N. Bowsher, "Usury Laws: Harmful When Effective," *Federal Reserve Bank of St. Louis Review,* vol. 56, pp. 16–23, August 1974.

[19] But, then again, perhaps, the upper middle- and higher-income groups, who generally have political clout on matters like interest rate ceilings, may see that by restricting the interest rates lower-income people will be rationed out of the market and they themselves will actually be the beneficiaries of the usury laws. At least, this is a point of view to think about.

SUMMARY AND EXTENSIONS

Price controls are seen by many as a relatively straightforward and simple means of controlling a spiraling rate of inflation across commodities or of controlling intense pressure for a price increase in a particular market. The appearance is, as this chapter has tried to show, deceptive. *If* a relatively small number of firms with monopolistic power can be identified, *if* control can be restricted to them for a relatively short period of time, *if* the controllers are immune to political pressure, *if* they are objective, and *if* nonprice means of raising the "effective price" can be controlled, price controls might work and, indeed, might result in an increase in output of the controlled industries. (See the discussion relating to Figure 11·4.) However, there are many very important *ifs* on which this conclusion hinges.

As we have argued, price controls can create monumental problems of allocation and enforcement of the controls. The costs of overcoming these problems can be greater than the benefits expected to be achieved. One would, therefore, think that they would be used as a policy course of last resort in dire emergencies, not as a normal policy option. The resulting allocation of goods and services may be no more equitable than that which will be achieved under a free-pricing system.

Furthermore, monopolistic power cannot be the cause of a continuing long-run rise in the price level. Given consumer purchasing power, there is a limit to the ability of even monopolistic industries to influence consumer demand for their products. Given that demand, as we studied in Chapter 10, there is a limit to the price which they will charge and there is a limit to how far they can raise their prices.

QUESTIONS TO PONDER

1 If the price in a competitive market is controlled below the market equilibrium price, is the resulting output level an efficient output level? Explain.

2 In the chapter we suggested that price controllers can lower the price of a monopolistic producer and cause the output level to increase. Can the price be lowered so much that a monopolistic producer will actually reduce production?

3 Why do students tend to be assigned more remote parking places on university campuses than faculty? Explain in terms of the pricing system used to admit students to the university.

4 In the chapter we presented data which showed that during recessions the prices of firms in so-called "concentrated industries" fell less than the prices of firms in "competitive industries." The production and employment levels fell more in the concentrated industries. Explain why this may be the case.

5 What effect do price controls have on the incentive of firms to innovate? Explain.

6 "If the prices in only one competitive industry are controlled, the shortage will be greater in that industry than if the prices of all industries are controlled." Do you agree? Explain.

7 "Price controls can be more effective in the short run than in the long run." Explain.

8 Consider government housing subsidies to the poor as an alternative to rent controls. What are the effects of subsidy schemes on housing prices, the availability of housing, and the distribution of income? How do these effects compare with the effects of rent controls?

9 Assume there is a legal interest ceiling on home mortgage loans. What effect will the ceiling have on home building during a period of high rates of inflation?

RECOMMENDED READINGS

Alchian, Armen A.: *Pricing and Society* (New York: Transatlantic Art, Inc.), 1967.

Bowsher, Norman N.: "Usury Laws: Harmful When Effective," *Federal Reserve Bank of St. Louis Review*, vol. 56, pp. 16–23, August 1974.

Campbell, Colin D., ed.: *Wage-Price Controls in World War II, United States and Germany* (Washington, D.C.: American Enterprise Institute for Public Policy Research, 1971).

Friedman, Milton: *Capitalism and Freedom* (Chicago: The University of Chicago Press, 1962.

———: *An Economist's Protest: Columns in Political Economy* (Glen Ridge, N.J.: Thomas Horton, Inc., 1972), chaps. 2 and 8.

Galbraith, John Kenneth: *Economics and the Public Purpose* (Boston: Houghton Mifflin Company, 1973).

Hayek, Friedrich, A.: *The Road to Serfdom*, rev. ed. (Chicago: The University of Chicago Press, 1971).

McKenzie, Richard B., and Gordon Tullock: *The New World of Economics* (Homewood, Ill.: Richard D. Irwin, Inc., 1978), chap. 19.

Means, Gardiner C.: "Simultaneous Inflation and Unemployment: A Challenge to Theory and Policy," *Challenge*, September–October 1975, pp. 6–20.

RAND Corporation: "Rental Housing in New York City: Confronting the Crisis," in Robert W. Crandall and Richard S. Eckaus, eds., *Contemporary Issues in Economics: Selected Readings* (Boston: Little, Brown and Company, 1972), pp. 249–255.

12

The Regulation Jungle

The state—the machinery and power of the state—is a potential resource or threat to every industry in the society. With its power to prohibit or compel, to take or give money, the state can and does selectively help or hurt a vast number of industries.
George Stigler[1]

PREVIEW OF CHAPTER

Central Question

How can we explain the emergence of agencies which regulate various industries?

Major objectives

1. To briefly describe several of the more important regulatory agencies
2. To develop three major theories of why regulatory agencies have arisen. These three theories are discussed under the following headings:
   a. The Public Interest Theory of Regulation
   b. An Economic Theory of Regulation
   c. Regulation as Taxation

Major conclusions

1. The public interest theory of regulation is founded primarily upon the contention that externalities are associated with many products and that

[1] George J. Stigler, "The Theory of Economic Regulation," *The Bell Journal of Economics and Management Science*, vol. 2, p. 3, Spring 1971.

substantial economies of scale in some industries will mean that only one producer can survive any competitive process.

2 Many empirical studies raise serious questions as to whether or not several regulatory agencies were actually organized to serve the public interest.

3 The economic theory of regulation is based on the proposition that firms in some industries, who do not wish to compete, have a demand for protective regulations from government. This theory views the government as the supplier of such regulatory services as the protection of firms in the industry against price reduction by existing or new competitors.

4 Regulation can also be seen as a method of taxation. Some consumers of certain products are forced to pay higher than free-market prices for the products or services they buy in order that the prices can be lowered for other people. In other words, regulation is a means of redistributing income.

Important terms and concepts

Various regulatory agencies (see chapter for descriptions)
Natural monopoly
Economies of scale
Average cost
Declining marginal cost curve
Declining average cost curve

Name an industry which does not, in some way, come under the authority of a government regulatory agency. Give up? At the start of the century that would have been a relatively simple task. Today, however, with the arm of government extending in all directions in the marketplace, the task is not so simple. The list of government regulatory agencies almost spans the alphabet: ABC, CAB, FAA, FDA, FEA, FPC, FRS, FTC, ICC, NTHSA, OSHA, SEC. This list is hardly complete, and it does not include all the various state utilities commissions, licensing boards, health departments, consumer protection agencies, and so forth.

The list of regulated occupations and industries is equally impressive for its inclusiveness: air transport, telephone, trucking, natural gas, electricity, stockbrokerage houses, health care, taxicabs, massage parlors, drugs, postal service, television and radio broadcasting, toys, beauticians, ocean shipping, lawyers, slaughterhouses, doctors, embalmers and funeral services, optometrists, oyster fishing, banking, and insurance. The list could be extended much further. With the passage each year of numerous laws which constrain the behavior of businesses, regulation itself has become one of our country's fastest-growing industries.

This chapter continues the discussion of price ceilings of Chapter 11. Regulation of an industry often entails government control of the upward movement of prices. However, regulatory agencies affect industry in more ways than that. An industry is frequently required to set minimum prices as well as maximum prices. A government agency may impose control on the entire rate structure and also entry into that industry. And an agency can stipulate detailed rules as to what types of services and goods will be provided, at what levels, and to whom. In short, regulation can pervade all dimensions of production and distribution and sell off many of the goods and services we buy in the marketplace.

Although we see a good deal of regulation around us, explaining it, as Richard Posner has observed, is a major challenge to social theory.[2] There are several theories of regulation prominent in economic literature; in many respects they are quite insightful. Unfortunately, economists' understanding of the regulatory process—why it happens[3] and how it happens—is incomplete at this point in the development of economic theory. Statistical tests of current theories have been spotty, and the data used in many of these tests have, of necessity, been very crude. There are also many instances of regulation and changes in regulatory policy which are left unexplained by current theories. Nonetheless, our study of regulation must begin with a review of what we know about regulation and what current research indicates may be the final verdict about the efficacy of regulation.

In this chapter we begin by briefly describing several of the major federal regulatory agencies. We then proceed to a review of current theories of regulation, paying particular attention to their defects. The regulatory agencies are coming in for some hard knocks from many diverse sources, from free-market economists and businessmen, consumers, the regulated industries themselves, and even such consumer advocates as Ralph Nader and his "raiders." A major purpose of this chapter is to explain this controversy surrounding United States regulatory policies.

THE ALPHABET OF REGULATORS

Before dealing with the thorny issues of why regulation occurs and what its consequences are, we provide skeleton descriptions of the origins and functions of several federal regulatory agencies. With this descriptive background we will be better able to understand the regulatory process.

[2] Richard A. Posner, "Theories of Regulation," *Bell Journal of Economics and Management Science*, vol. 5, p. 335, Autumn 1974.

[3] As we will see, not all industry regulations have been proposed to further the "public interest."

ICC

The Interstate Commerce Commission (ICC) was established in 1887 to deal with problems which were emerging in the railroad industry. Specifically, several railroad companies had formed a cartel to divide the market and set prices. The cartel was being weakened through rebates to customers and price discrimination. The ICC was charged with the responsibility of prohibiting these practices. Understandably the railroad companies, along with those being discriminated against, supported the formation of the ICC. In years since, the regulatory authority of the ICC has been expanded to cover all motor carriers (except air) engaged in interstate commerce—mainly trucks and water carriers. It has also been given the authority to set minimum and maximum rates for all the different modes of transportation and the responsibility of ensuring what it deems to be adequate service to different parts of the country.

The Interstate Commerce Commission is composed of seven members. The Commissioners are nominated by the President and approved by the Senate for terms of 7 years. No more than a simple majority of the commissioners may be from one political party, and any commissioner may be removed for "just cause." Just cause may, of course, include conflict of interest.[4]

In recent years, the ICC has come under attack from economists and consumer advocates alike for practices favoring those who are regulated at the expense of consumers. Ralph Nader, the consumer advocate, has recommended that the ICC be abolished in its present form.[5] President Ford in 1975 asked Congress to sharply reduce the ICC's ability to set rates, restrict entry into the transportation market, and establish routes. This proposal was nothing new. Economists have advocated these changes for years, and President

[4] One commissioner resigned in 1970 after admitting that he accepted travel expenses from one of the companies the ICC regulates.

[5] *The Interstate Commerce Commission*, The Ralph Nader Study Group Report on the Interstate Commerce Commission and Transportation; Robert C. Fellmeth, project director (New York: Grossman Publisher, 1970), p. 324.

Kennedy made a similar proposal during his administration.

FTC

The Federal Trade Commission (FTC) was set up by an act of Congress in 1914. The original purpose of the five-member commission was to investigate any tendency toward greater industrial concentration and to advise the President and Congress on matters relating to antitrust law. To carry out these duties, it was given the power to probe through corporate records and to require corporate executives to appear at hearings relating to antitrust practices, unfair business practices, deceptive or false advertising, and discriminatory pricing practices. The commission has the power to hold public hearings, to issue formal complaints, and to order the company to cease its illegal acts. The respondents have recourse to the courts. Again, the commissioners are appointed for 7-year terms.

CAB

The Civil Aeronautics Board (CAB) was established in 1938. It has the power to license United States airline companies, to set their rates, and to establish their routes. No United States airline company can engage in either interstate or international operations without a CAB license. Although a large number of local carriers, all-freight carriers, and helicopter carriers have been licensed, it may be of some interest to note that no new major trunk airline company, like United or Eastern, has been granted a license since the CAB was organized. The members of the board are appointed for 6-year terms by the President and can be removed only by him. As in the case of the ICC, President Ford, followed by President Carter, proposed legislation which would reduce the ability of the CAB to control the rates (or ticket prices) of airline service. The proposal was opposed by most of the airline companies because it would introduce more competition into the determination of their rates.

FCC

The Federal Communications Commission (FCC) was established by way of the Communication Act of 1934. It holds regulatory authority over communications by wire, that is, telephone and telegraph, and over the broadcast media, television and radio. It has the power to set rates for interstate telephone and telegraph services. States retain regulatory authority over *intra*state service. In the area of commercial and noncommercial broadcasting, the FCC's powers come primarily from its authority to issue licenses for radio and television stations. The FCC determines, in other words, who and how many can engage in broadcasting and prescribes the nature of the services to be rendered by the stations, the location of stations, and the area to be served by them. Licenses are issued for periods of 3 years, after which the programming of the station is reviewed before the license is renewed. In order to ensure renewal of a license, a station must engage in some public service broadcasting and follow program guidelines laid down by the FCC. The seven FCC commissioners are appointed for terms of 7 years.

To the extent that not all frequencies are presently in use for radio and television transmission, the FCC has restricted entry into the broadcast business. It has also held up the introduction of pay-TV service through cable companies. Cable service vastly increases the potential sources of programming for television.

FPC

The Federal Power Act of 1930 set up the Federal Power Commission (FPC). Its authority was first limited to regulation of water power. However, in 1935, the FPC was given the authority to regulate rates, service, corporate practices, and security issues of interstate electric utilities. Beginning in 1938, its authority was further expanded to cover the fixing of rates for interstate natural gas service. The commission has five members who serve 5-year terms.

In the late 1960s and early 1970s, the FPC came under attack by many economists for its tight control on the price of natural gas shipped across state lines. In 1975, 1976, and 1977, a number of states had serious shortages of natural gas because the FPC was restricting the interstate price to one-fourth of what the gas could be sold for in Texas and elsewhere.

SEC

As a response to the large number of cases of stock fraud and the precipitous drop in stock prices which occurred during the previous 5 years, the Securities and Exchange Commission (SEC) was established in 1934. The SEC has the authority to license stock exchanges and to police their activities. It also has the authority to regulate the fees charged by brokers carrying out transactions for customers. Beginning in 1975, the SEC allowed stockbrokers' fees to be determined competitively. Those fees fell almost immediately by 30 percent or more. The SEC also has the authority to supervise corporations when they issue new securities and to determine rules for disclosure of relevant information relating to those issuances and to reports to stockholders. The SEC is made up of five members appointed by the President for terms of 5 years.

FDA

Various foods and drugs have been regulated to one degree or another since the turn of the century. However, it was not until 1931 that the Food and Drug Administration (FDA) came into existence under the Department of Health, Education, and Welfare. The FDA is charged with the responsibility of regulating the purity, safety, and accurate labeling of certain foods and drugs. Specifically, the drug must be deemed safe and effective by the FDA before it can be sold on the market. The agency is also responsible for enforcing a wide variety of consumer protection laws pertaining to such items as labeling, packaging, and advertising of food and drug products.

THE PUBLIC INTEREST THEORY OF REGULATION

Regulation exists in many industries; and in their search for an explanation for its pervasive existence, many people, economists included, have accepted the argument that regulation serves the public interest. Generally, this means that regulation is intended to increase the efficiency of the market. As the argument is most frequently developed, two sources of inefficiency are seen in a free market: (1) externalities and (2) monopoly power. Therefore, the existence of externalities and monopoly power are the two prime arguments for regulation.

The Externality Problem

We have discussed the problems which "externalities" cause in a free market before, and we can assure you that these same problems will surface in the context of other topics before this book is closed. However, a brief review of the externality problem will be useful at this point to clarify the public interest theory of regulation.

Safety is a good which people want but which can create problems in a market. If a degree of safety is provided in a given product line, say automobiles, people who buy the safety equipment can be the sole beneficiaries of the purchase. The driver, for example, is the sole beneficiary of shock-absorbing steering columns, and the market can handle the sale of this type of good with reasonable efficiency. However, with regard to other safety devices which can benefit persons other than those who make the purchase, the market may fail to provide an "efficient" quantity of those types of equipment. For example, shock-absorbing bumpers can benefit the person who buys a car, but people who do not buy the bumpers also benefit. (They receive an "external benefit" from those who buy bumpers.) If a person who does not buy bumpers happens to run head on into a car with shock-absorbing bumpers *at low speeds*, the damage to both cars will tend to be less.[6] However, the person who does not buy protective bumpers does not have, in a completely free market, to pay for these benefits and can take a free ride on the purchases of others. Needless to say, the quantity of bumpers purchased will, in an unregulated market, be less than what is economically optimal. Therefore, according to the public interest theory, there is a need for regulation, a need to make automobile producers sell their cars with shock-absorbing bumpers, as well as headlights, brakes, etc., of given qualities.

In addition, all producers can be harmed by the actions of a few producers. If people in general believe that a given product line is "safe," there is the ever-present possibility that some competitors will take advantage of people's faith in that product. A competitor can reduce the safety of his or her product and thereby reduce the production costs and cheat customers of what they thought they were buying. The disagreeable experiences which consumers sometimes have with some producers can make them skeptical of all firms, reducing the price consumers are willing to pay for the good. (Consumers have to "pay" more in determining which products are safe; that is, they may require information or use trial and error to get the good that is satisfactory. Therefore, they are unwilling or unable to pay as much for the product.) These reasons have been very important in the debate over the regulation of the food and drug industries and of toys, and over many other consumer protection laws; we will return to this argument and discuss the pros and cons of it in greater detail in Chapter 13. For now, we simply wish to make the point that whenever the problem of an industry's reputation arises, the externality–public interest argument is usually found undergirding the movement for regulation of that industry. To the extent that the FDA, the CAB, and the SEC contribute to the drug, airline, and securities industries' reputation for safety, fairness, and honesty, the regulators can be seen as producers of *public goods* in quantities not otherwise achieved in the market.

[6] A person who slams into the side of another car at 100 miles per hour is likely to be killed with or without the protective bumpers.

The Monopoly Problem

Regulatory agencies are thought to be organized to deal with the problem of monopoly power. An industry, such as the railway industry, may be so concentrated in the hands of a few large corporations that these companies are capable of forming a workable cartel; that is, they are able to behave as if they were a monopoly. They can divide the market, restrict output, and raise prices to consumers; they can also engage in price discrimination. During the 1970s, charges of monopoly power have been very prominent in proposals to regulate the United States oil industry, the automobile industry, and a host of others.

Figure 12·1 is a replica of a graph used to discuss monopoly power in Chapter 10. The carte-

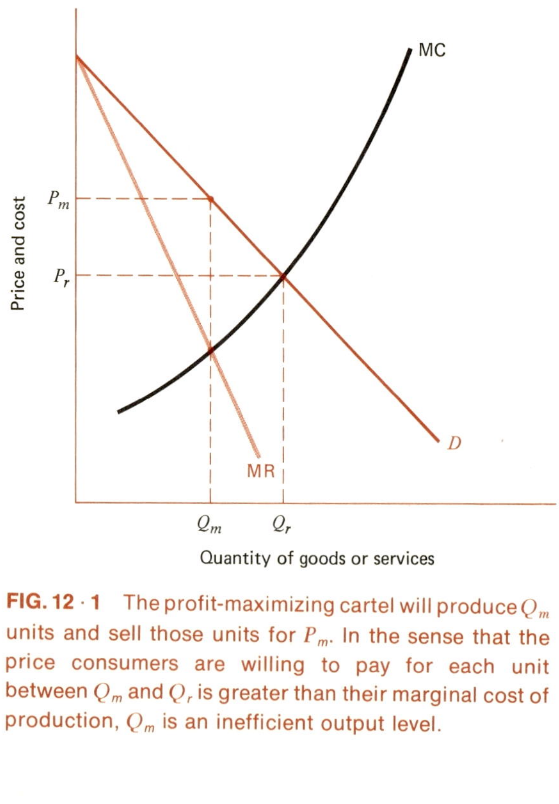

FIG. 12 · 1 The profit-maximizing cartel will produce Q_m units and sell those units for P_m. In the sense that the price consumers are willing to pay for each unit between Q_m and Q_r is greater than their marginal cost of production, Q_m is an inefficient output level.

lized industry tends to produce at an output level of Q_m and sell at a price of P_m. That output level is inefficient in two respects. It is less than can be produced within the constraints of the cost of production (MC curve) and the demand for the good (D), and the marginal benefit of the last unit (equal to the price) is greater than the marginal cost of producing that unit. Consumers are willing to pay more than it costs to produce additional units; but, because of the monopoly power, they do not get the chance to buy those units. Furthermore, that price-quantity combination can mean "excessive profits" for the owners of the firms involved and an "inequitable" or "unjust" distribution of income.

Regulation can mean that the firms which operate in the regulated industry are forced to sell at lower prices and to produce and sell larger quantities. Ideally, firms can be forced to produce Q_r units of the good or service and sell that quantity at P_r, which is, incidentally, the same price-quantity combination to be achieved under highly competitive conditions. It is also an *efficient* output level in the sense that the marginal benefit of the last unit is equal to the marginal cost. (You may want to review what economists mean by efficient output levels if this discussion seems a little hazy. See Chapter 7.)

Ideal results are never really expected from the regulatory process. That is to say, the regulators may not be able to make the firms they regulate produce at Q_r, the efficient output level, and sell at P_r. This may be because of the difficulty (i.e., cost) that regulators encounter in determining what the "ideal" price-quantity combination is. However, to the extent that the regulators are able to force the prices charged by the cartel producers below that which they would otherwise charge and to coerce or encourage these firms to expand production, increases in market efficiency result. To this extent, regulators serve, in a way, the public interest.

As suggested above, the regulatory process can be very costly. If the regulation is to serve the "public interest" in the sense that the efficiency of the entire social system is increased, the rise in market efficiency (i.e., benefits) must exceed the costs of regulation. Too often the cost of regulation is overlooked; therefore, regulation can be perceived as a more attractive "social organizer" than perhaps it should be.

The Tendency toward "Natural Monopoly"

Our discussion of monopoly power to this point has been based on an asumption of a rising marginal cost curve for firms within the industry. (See the marginal cost curve in Figure 12·1.) One very significant argument for regulation of industries like electric utilities is based on a contrary assumption, that the marginal cost of producing additional units of electricity decreases, at least in the long run. As opposed to being upward sloping, the marginal cost curve is, within the relevant range, downward sloping. In such event, the argument made is that there is a "natural tendency" for the industry to become dominated by one firm, which, once established, will have monopoly power to make monopoly profits. Let us explain; but in order to do the argument justice, we need to introduce the concept of *average cost*. (Average cost is simply total cost divided by quantity produced.)

Let us assume that the marginal cost of additional units of electricity decreases. This is a technological assumption, resulting from *economies of scale*. By producing on a larger scale, a firm can take advantage of the known technology embodied in very large plants and pieces of equipment. One can imagine that a large turbine, say the size of a house, can be more efficient in generating electricity than can several much smaller ones. By moving from smaller turbines to larger ones, the greater efficiency is translated into a lower cost of producing additional megawatts of electricity. How long one can increase the size of the generating plant and lower the cost of production is a matter which is open to some debate, as we will see later. Suffice it to say that proponents of this line of argument believe that economies of scale are considerable—so extensive that in order to produce power at the lowest possible cost, only *one* very large electric company can operate in a

TABLE 12·1 THE MARGINAL AND AVERAGE COST OF PRODUCING MEGAWATTS OF ELECTRICITY

Megawatts (1)	Marginal Cost (2)	Total Cost (3)	Average Cost [(3) ÷ (1)] (4)
1	$50	$ 50	$50
2	40	90	45
3	30	120	40
4	20	140	35
5	10	150	30

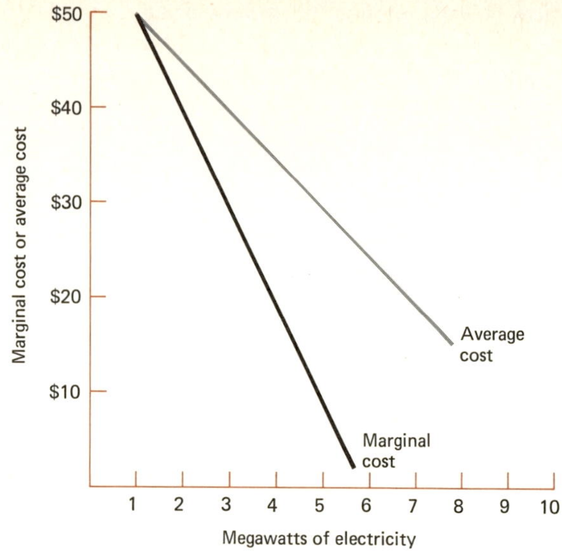

FIG. 12·2 When the marginal cost curve is downward sloping, the average cost curve must also be downward sloping and must be above the marginal cost curve. See Table 12-1 for an example of how the average cost figures are computed.

large geographical area, sometimes the size of a state.

If the *marginal cost* of producing additional megawatts of electricity diminishes, the *average cost* of each unit also decreases, but at a slower rate. Consider Table 12·1. The marginal cost of producing each additional megawatt of electricity is indicated in column 2; it decreases from $50 for the first megawatt to $10 for the fifth. Notice however, that the average cost and marginal cost for the first unit are equal, $50; but from that point on average cost decreases by less than marginal cost.[7]

With this type of information, we can plot a corresponding marginal cost curve and average cost curve on a graph. They will tend to take on the shapes illustrated on Figure 12·2. The marginal cost curve will be below the average cost curve. (If you have some difficulty understanding how the curves in the graph are obtained, we suggest that you plot the information in columns 1 and 2 to obtain the *marginal cost* curve and plot the information in columns 1 and 4 to obtain the *average cost* curve. The curves should take on the general shape of the curves in Figure 12·2.)

In Figure 12·3 we have included the average and marginal cost curves of Figure 12·2 and have superimposed the market demand curve and the marginal revenue curve on it. The traditional argument suggests that a firm with decreasing cost curves like the one in this figure will tend to expand production, lower the cost of production as output is expanded, and arrive at a size at which it can influence price by its production decisions. The firm, thus achieving monopoly power, will produce where all monopolists produce, at that point where marginal cost is equal to marginal revenue. In terms of Figure 12·3, the monopolistic firm will sell Q_m megawatts of electricity for an average price of P_m. In the process it will, so the argument goes, generate monopoly profits.[8] There is, in other words, a "natural tendency" for firms in decreasing-cost industries to become

[7] Again, *average cost* is simply the total cost of the units produced divided by the number of units produced. The total cost of two megawatts is $90 ($50 for the first megawatt plus $40 for the second); the average cost for each megawatt is $45 (90 divided by 2 units). The average cost of three units is $120 ($50 + $40 + $30) divided by 3 units produced, or $40. The table is completed in this way.

[8] Can you indicate in terms of the graph the area which describes the profits?

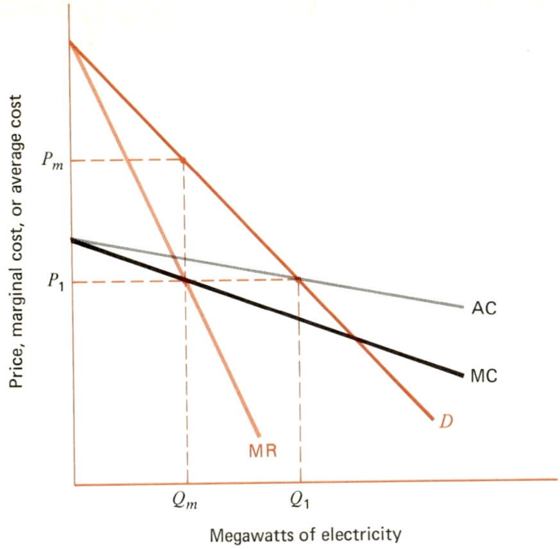

FIG. 12·3 Even with declining marginal cost, the firm with monopoly power will produce where marginal cost is equal to marginal revenue. This equality occurs at Q_m. However, unless there are barriers to entry, other firms can enter the market, causing the price to fall toward P_1 and the quantity produced to rise toward Q_1. At that price-quantity combination, only one firm can survive.

monopolies; accordingly, they are called *natural monopolies.* These industries are seen as prime candidates for regulation. The regulation is needed to keep the industries from exerting their market power; regulation is a *countervailing force.*

Although it is true that a firm with decreasing cost can expand until it is a major, if not the only, producer in the industry, we see very little merit in the conclusion that these firms will necessarily be able to exercise significant power over price. It is therefore, not necessarily true that such industries must be regulated. To explain, let us suppose that a natural monopoly flexes its market muscle and charges P_m by restricting its production to Q_m. The problem which this firm confronts is that, in the free-market system, another firm can enter and expand its production to a greater level, charge a lower price, and attract the customers to itself. To protect its interest, the firm which behaves like a monopolist will have to cut its price and expand production to acquire the benefits of the *lower average* cost.

Predictions as to how far the price will fall and the output rise must be tenuous, but it does seem reasonable to conclude that only one firm will survive. One firm can offer to sell to the entire market at a price which cannot be undercut by competitors. That price approximates P_1 in Figure 12·3. The total revenue of the firm would be that price times Q_1 (or $P_1 \times Q_1$). Notice that the average cost of producing Q_1 megawatts of electricity is also equal to P_1. (To see this, go up in the graph from Q_1 to the *average* cost curve.) Therefore, the total cost of production (which is equal to the average cost times the quantity sold) is equal to the firm's revenue. The firm is just covering its costs of production; the owners of the firm are receiving something for their investment, but it is only enough to cover such implicit cost as the risk cost associated with their investment. (Risk cost must be included in any calculation of average cost and, therefore, total cost.) Being alone in the market, the firm may then think it can restrict output, raise price, and reap economic profit. However, again, it must face the ever-present threat of some other firm coming into the market and selling at a lower price.

From a purely theoretical perspective, the natural monopoly argument is not by itself a sufficient argument for justifying regulation. Something else must be added, and generally those seeking the regulation supply the further justifications. An argument frequently heard is that some industries, the electrical power utilities, for instance, require such huge amounts of capital investment that no competitor can reasonably be expected to enter the market if the existing firm acts like a monopolist. In brief, potential producers are barred from competing by their inability to raise the needed capital. This may be possible, but it is a presumption which reflects the general impression that electric power production must take place on as large a scale as it presently does. This is not necessarily the case, and the capital requirements may be raised by any number of large corporations. This is particularly true if a firm intends to compete only in a segment of the market dominated by the one firm.

Second, another argument put forward to promote government regulation of electric utilities is that a firm must have a set of transmission lines. Competition may mean that several sets of power lines will run down city streets, creating what most people would see as an environmental mess. This may be an argument for a governmentally protected and regulated firm that is responsible for *transmission* of electricity, but it does not appear to have anything to do with the question of whether or not regulation is required in the *generation* (as opposed to *transmission*) of electricity. To see the argument in proper perspective, consider the interstate pipelines for carrying gasoline products. The pipelines are regulated. However, there is competition (and the potential for competition) on the production end of those lines; a number of firms is refining gasoline. Even if there were only one firm refining gasoline, that one firm would have to determine its production and pricing decisions based on what it thinks other potential firms would do if it tried to extract monopoly profits. The electric power generation industry can be organized in a similar way.[9]

A third argument for regulation is that production in natural-monopoly industries generally requires large quantities of fixed capital assets. Once purchased, the cost of these assets becomes a *sunk cost*, to be ignored, like all sunk costs, in short-run production and pricing decisions. Industries which are characterized by decreasing cost functions, so the argument goes, are vulnerable to destructive price wars. In a price war, firms ignore fixed costs and determine price on the basis of the short-term costs associated with using the equipment they have already purchased. If this happens, firms will destroy themselves.

Although appealing and frequently heard, this argument seems to assume that entrepreneurs will actually enter an industry in which self-destruction is a likely outcome. The argument cannot be dismissed out of hand, but it must be questioned. We do see many industries—oil production and automobile production, to name two—in which capital needs are quite extensive and in which at least a modest amount of competition exists. Producers of neither oil nor automobiles seem likely to destroy themselves any time soon.

Fourth, even if an unregulated industry produces Q_1 units and prices that output at P_2, the efficient output level is not being achieved. As we have studied in previous chapters, the *efficient* production level is the level at which marginal cost is equal to marginal benefits, or the point at which the marginal cost curve intersects the demand curve. The production level of Figure 12·3 falls short of the efficient output level. By referring to Figure 12·4, we can see why the efficient level of output is not achieved.

In Figure 12·4, the efficient output level is Q_2. Given the market demand curve, the firm can sell that output level for only P_1. Total revenues are, therefore, P_1 times Q_2. Note, however, that the average cost of producing that output level is greater; we have indicated average cost at that point at AC_1 in the graph. Total costs ($AC_1 \times Q_2$) are therefore greater than total revenues. The actual loss to the firm, trying to produce what economists consider to be the efficient output level, is indicated by the shaded area of the graph. In order for the efficient output level to be achieved, the company must be given subsidies equal to the shaded area, or it must be allowed to price-discriminate among units sold and customers, something it supposedly cannot do without government protection. By charging prices higher than P_1 for the first few units sold, the firm can offset losses in moving from Q_1 to Q_2 of Figure 12·4.

Again, we question whether this argument alone justifies government protection of an in-

[9] For an insightful discussion of the potential for competition in electric power generation, see Robert M. Spann, "Restructuring the Electric Utility Industry: A Framework for Evaluating Public Policy Options in Electric Utilities," in William H. Shaker and Wilbert Steffy, eds., *Electric Power Reform: The Alternative for Michigan* (Ann Arbor, Mich.: Institute of Science and Technology, University of Michigan, 1976).

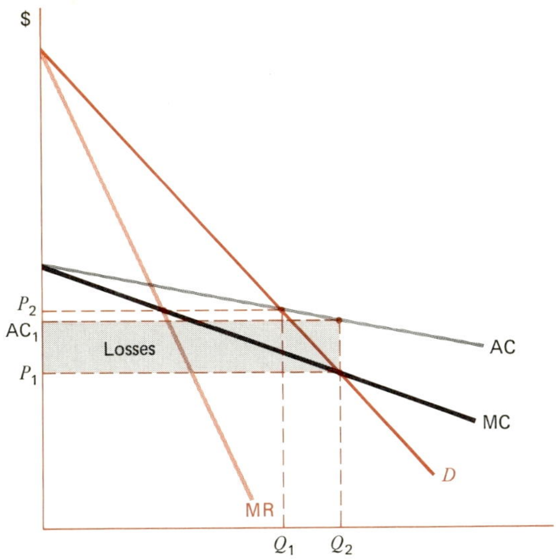

FIG. 12·4 The natural monopolist who cannot price-discriminate will at most produce Q_1 megawatts of electricity. However, Q_2 is the efficient output level. The one firm producing Q_1 megawatts of electricity and selling them for P_2 will not be producing at the efficient output level, Q_2. If the firm produces Q_2, it will have losses equal to the shaded area.

dustry. The unregulated firm can charge a price equal to P_2 for megawatts up to Q_1. It is thereby able to cover all its costs on those units. If the good cannot be easily resold, the free-market firm can then undertake a little price discrimination of its own. It can charge a slightly lower price for a few additional units beyond Q_1 and a slightly lower price for units beyond that. It can lower the *marginal price* on additional units until Q_2 is reached. So long as the marginal prices it charges are on the demand curve and above the marginal cost of additional units, the firm not only moves toward the efficient output level, it covers all its costs. It can do all this without providing any other firm an incentive to move in and compete; however, its product must meet the condition for price discrimination. Otherwise, people will buy at the lower marginal prices and sell to those who are paying P_2.

An Evaluation of the Public Interest Theory

Up to this point our criticisms of the public interest theory of regulation have been related mainly to its theoretical flaws, which, we admit, are at least subject to debate. In recent decades economists have begun to go further: they have questioned not only whether regulation serves the public interest but whether regulation in many instances is actually *intended* to serve the public interest.

The evidence accumulated from economic research on the subject provides ample support for the skepticism of some economists. Richard Posner, in his review of a sizable portion of economic literature on regulation, has written, "Some fifteen years of theoretical and empirical research, conducted mainly by economists, have demonstrated that regulation is not positively correlated with the presence of external economies or diseconomies or with monopolistic market structures."[10] Posner goes on to suggest that few respected economists will argue that the prices charged by and entry into industries such as trucking, taxicab service, stockbrokerage, and ocean shipping can be justified on efficiency grounds: "Even the danger of 'market failure' in such traditionally unquestioned areas of regulation as health care, the legal profession, and the safety of drugs and other products is increasingly discounted [as a basis for regulation]."[11]

Does regulation make a difference in the behavior of an industry? Contrary to what the public interest theory suggests, economists are hard pressed to find evidence that indicates regulation actually harms industries that are regulated. Instead, they have often found that regulation is beneficial to regulated industries. Using data from 1912 to 1937 on the electric utility industry, George Stigler and Claire Friedland con-

[10] Posner, "Theories of Regulation," p. 336.

[11] Ibid.

cluded that the introduction of regulation in that period had virtually no effect on the level of rates and rate structure of that industry. They found that regulation had a slight, statistically insignificant effect on the wealth of stockholders. The effect was thought to be so small as to be unimportant.[12]

Raymond Jackson undertook a similar study of the electric power industry for the years 1940, 1950, and 1960. For 1950 and 1960, Jackson's findings are essentially the same as those of Stigler and Friedland. If regulation had any effect, it tended to be in favor of industrial and commercial users and not residential users. In 1960, however, he found some evidence that regulation had begun to depress the price of electricity to consumers.[13] Thomas Moore found that between 1952 and 1962 the depressing effect of regulation on prices was no more than 5 percent.[14] William Jordan, who has reviewed these as well as many other studies, commented, "Taken together, these three studies indicate that regulation has had a limited effect on lowering electric utility rates, and that most of its benefits have been enjoyed by commercial and industrial consumers rather than the more numerous residential consumers."[15]

More recently Robert Spann has found evidence which reveals that the rates of return for electric utilities were being depressed by the regulatory process in the late 1960s and early 1970s. He points out, however, that the regulatory process has always introduced a lag between the time when a utility's costs rise and the time when the utility can raise its rates to adjust for cost increases. The late 1960s and early 1970s was a period of unusually high rates of inflation; the costs of electric power production tended to rise even faster. Spann concludes that the reductions in the utilities' profitability can be attributed more to the "lag effect" than to a change in regulatory policy. He goes on to question whether electric power production is in fact a decreasing-cost industry. His findings, which support the findings of others, indicate that significant economies of scale can be achieved in electric power production. However, within the range of market demand the long-run cost curve of the firm is not downward sloping. This suggests that more than one producer of electricity is possible in a given region; at least some modest amount of competition in electric power *production* (as opposed to *transmission*) is possible. The conclusion being drawn by some economists is that regulation is not a necessity, as has been conventionally thought.[16]

Economists have questioned the usefulness of regulation in other industries. For example, Richard Caves comments on regulation in the airline industry: "Paradoxically the Board's [CAB's] policies, on the whole, have probably had little effect on the rate of profit earned by the industry; but, without the Civil Aeronautic Act and the Board, these profits would have resulted from quite a different sort of operation."[17] Ronald Coarse has noted the effective way by which the FCC has restricted entry into the broadcasting industry

[12] George J. Stigler and Claire Friedland, "What Can Regulators Regulate? The Case of Electricity," *Journal of Law and Economics*, vol. 5, p. 16, October 1962, reprinted in Paul W. MacAvoy, ed., *The Crisis of the Regulatory Commissions: An Introduction to a Current Issue of Public Policy* (New York: W. W. Norton and Company, Inc., 1970), pp. 39–52. The authors use data from the years 1912 to 1937 because during that period of time there were some utility companies which were regulated and some which were not, and they therefore had a basis for comparison.

[13] Raymond Jackson, "Regulation and Electric Utility Rate Levels," *Land Economics*, August 1969.

[14] Thomas Gale Moore, "The Effectiveness of Regulation of Electric Utility Prices," *Southern Economics Journal*, April 1970.

[15] William A. Jordan, "Producer Protection, Prior Market Structure, and the Effects of Government Regulation," *Journal of Law and Economics*, 1972, p. 156.

[16] Robert M. Spann, "Federal Regulation of Electric Utilities via Taxation and Litigation: An Analysis of Changes and Alternatives in Electric Utility Regulation," and "Restructuring the Electric Utility Industry: A Framework for Evaluating Public Policy Options in Electric Utilities" (Blacksburg, Va.: Center for the Study of Public Choice, Virginia Polytechnic Institute and State University, 1975).

[17] Richard W. Caves, "Performance, Structure, and the Goals of Civil Aeronautics Board Regulation," *The Crisis of the Regulatory Commissions*, p. 134.

and has enabled firms in that industry to make substantial profits.[18]

More than any other agency the ICC has come under heavy attack for having restricted entry into the trucking industry and for having raised the rates which truckers are permitted to charge for hauling cargo. Each year the ICC turns down hundreds of applications by firms who want to get into the trucking business or who want to extend their service area and compete with other firms. Figure 12·5 provides a vivid illustration of the growth in applications for truck licenses and the number of licensed carriers in the United States. Although applications have risen, the number of licensed carriers has generally decreased since trucks began to be regulated by the ICC in the late 1930s. Because of rules and regulations which are designed to ensure a "stable trucking industry," trucks frequently have to follow routes which take them miles out of their way, adding to the cost of hauling cargo. Furthermore, after hauling cargo to one destination, the rules of the ICC forbid them to pick up cargo for the return trip. Mark Frazier provides us with these descriptions of inefficiencies generated by ICC regulation of the trucking industry:

> A truckful of furniture, en route from Dallas to San Diego, detours 800 miles out of its way—adding 12 hours to the trip and squandering 160 gallons of fuel. . . .
>
> In Atlanta, Ga., a trucking company announces plans to lower rates on truckloads of tire treads bound for Ohio to save its customers $400 a trip. But it is prevented from making the cut. . . .[19]

One can cite many cases in which regulatory agencies have denied firms rate increases and have required railroads and airline companies, for example, to maintain routes that they would not otherwise choose to maintain.[20] However, the weight of the evidence strongly suggests that regulatory agencies, in many instances and perhaps as a rule, have not been pursuing in any systematic way the "public interest." In the one important area in which regulation seems to have had a significant effect on market price—natural gas—most economists agree that the effect of regulation has been to stimulate greater con-

[18] Coarse wrote in his 1967 article, "We know from recent figures that the profits of television stations in the first fifty TV markets represented, on an average, 36 percent of gross revenues and that the rate of return on capital for some stations was 200 or 300 percent per annum (after taxes)." Ronald H. Coarse, "The Economics of Broadcasting and Public Policy," *The Crisis of the Regulatory Commissions*, p. 95.

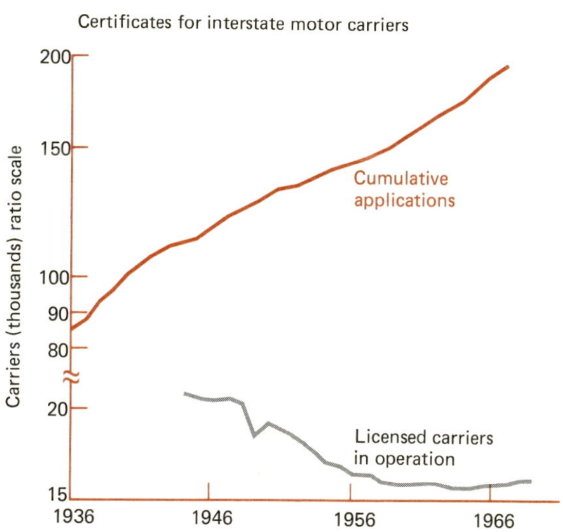

FIG. 12·5 During the period from 1936 to the late 1960s, the cumulative applications for licenses from truck companies gradually rose. However, the number of licensed companies in operation declined. (Reproduced from George J. Stigler, "The Theory of Economic Regulation," *Bell Journal of Economics and Management Science*, vol. 2, p. 6, Spring 1971.)

[19] Mark Frazier, "Highway Robbery—Via the ICC," *Reader's Digest*, January 1975, p. 72.

[20] Jordan reports on one study in which the majority of the rate decreases for Consolidated Gas Electric Light and Power Company of Baltimore between 1910 and 1953 were initiated by the company and not by the regulatory commission. In fact, 39 of the 65 rate decreases during the period were initiated by the company. One could argue, on the other hand, that the Consolidated Gas and other companies may have initiated rate decreases because they expected action by the regulatory commission. Jordan, "Producer Protection," pp. 157–160.

sumption of that resource, an unwarranted depletion of reserves, and market shortages. In other words, the regulation of natural gas has also led to inefficiencies in production and consumption.[21] With this type of evidence mounting, it is no wonder that economists have looked to theories other than the public interest theory to explain the regulatory process.

AN ECONOMIC THEORY OF REGULATION

Generally, economists who have studied the effects of regulation have found that regulation has tended to have little, if any, effect on the profitability of industries (e.g., utilities) which may have otherwise been monopolistic and has tended to increase profitability in industries which would otherwise have been workably competitive.[22] These findings can be explained in several ways.

First, it may be argued that regulators have been inept at carrying out their assigned tasks or that regulation is too difficult a task for any competent group of men and women to handle properly. The problem is especially difficult since regulated firms have an incentive to deceive the regulators. Through juggling their books, regulated firms can make their costs appear greater than they actually are and can justify rate increases that could not be justified if the true cost of operations were known with sufficient accuracy to the regulators.

Second, if regulators concentrate on price regulation and restriction of entry into an industry, firms will be able to maintain profits by reducing the quality and therefore the cost of their service.

Third, the intent of regulation has been circumvented in one other important respect. Regulators of electric utilities, for instance, have tended to determine prices to consumers on the basis of what the regulators think is a "fair rate of return or profitability" on investment. This has given utilities an incentive to substitute capital assets (plant and equipment) for other resource inputs, such as labor, in order to maintain or boost profits. For example, suppose that a utility commission considers 7 percent a fair rate of return on capital investment. (This means that the firm will be allowed to make profits equal to 7 percent of the value of its plant and equipment.) Further, suppose that the same *additional* amount of electricity can be generated by spending $1 million on plant and equipment *or* $1 million on labor. If the firm invests in the plant and equipment, it can argue before the utility commission that its rates should be adjusted upward to allow for an additional $70,000 in profit (7 percent of $1 million of new capital). If labor is used, there will be no increase in investment and no basis, given the rate-making rule, for a price increase to consumers. By making production capital intensive, electric utilities are able to circumvent the intent of the regulation.

Fourth, although regulation is begun with the good intentions of those who promote and pass the laws, somewhere along the line regulators may become pawns of the regulated firms. According to this line of argument, regulatory agencies have become stacked with men and women whose professional careers have been bound to the industries which they regulate; and regulated firms have had an undue influence on regulatory policies. The consumer's voice has not been adequately represented.

The Supply of Regulation

Many economists, following the lead of George Stigler,[23] have begun to shed the public interest theory of regulation and to look for a more powerful explanatory theory. As opposed to viewing regulation as being *thrust* upon the firms, these economists have begun to view regulation as being *procured* by the regulated firms. Govern-

[21] Robert B. Helms, *Natural Gas Regulation: An Evaluation of FPC Price Controls* (Washington: American Enterprise Institute for Public Policy Research, 1974).

[22] Jordan, "Producer Protection," especially his concluding section, pp. 174–176.

[23] Stigler, "The Theory of Economic Regulation." See also George J. Stigler, *The Citizen and the State* (Chicago: University of Chicago Press, 1975).

ment (meaning politicians and bureaucrats) is viewed as a *supplier* of "regulatory services" to firms in an industry. These services can include (1) price fixing, (2) restriction on entry, (3) subsidies, and (4) suppression of substitute goods and promotion of complementary goods.[24] These services are offered to industries which are willing to pay the "price" for them. In the political world, this price can be paid in the form of campaign contributions, supplements to government pay, and legal work for back-home law firms of politicians who support regulation. It can also be paid in the form of time which company employees spend on political campaigns and in the form of the number of votes which the firms, in other ways, can marshal for supporters of regulation.

The Demand for Regulation

If all firms within an industry decide to form a workable cartel, monopoly profits can be achieved. However, if a cartel is formed in a free market, it may not hold together for long for two very important reasons. First, there is the ever-present threat of new firms entering the market and forcing the price back down to the competitive level. Second, as we studied in Chapter 10, there is the distinct possibility that firms will chisel on any cartel agreement. The cost of reaching a collusive agreement and ensuring that the agreement is obeyed can be extensive. Government regulation can be a less costly means for firms to gain control over the market and to form a workable cartel. Consequently, firms have a demand for regulation.

From this theoretical point of view, regulation is seen as emerging from the interaction of the suppliers of regulation (governments at all levels) and the demanders of it. Regulation will be provided to those who are willing and able to pay the price for the regulation. From even the most casual review of the history of regulation, this view seems to have some merit. As Richard Posner has observed,

> The railroads supported the enactment of the first Interstate Commerce Act, which was designed to prevent railroads from price discrimination, because discrimination was undermining the railroad's cartels. American Telephone and Telegraph pressed for state regulation of telephone service because it wanted to end competition among telephone companies. Truckers and airlines supported extension of common carrier regulation to their industries because they considered unregulated competition excessive.[25]

To this list we can add that barbers, beauticians, and lawyers, as well as a number of specialists in other professions, have sought government licensing, which is a form of regulation. Farmers have been behind political moves to regulate the supplies of their commodities. Furthermore, whenever deregulation is proposed, the affected industry will almost always oppose the proposal.

Small Groups and Large Groups

To the extent that regulation provides benefits to *all* regulated firms, the regulation, itself, is a public good. All firms within the regulated industry can benefit to one extent or another, even firms which have not contributed anything to procuring the regulation. As in the provision and production of any public good, some firms within the industry will try to "free-ride" on the efforts of those who secure the regulation. If all firms within the industry free-ride, that is, do nothing, obviously the regulation and collective benefits will not be procured.

As explained in Chapter 6, the free-rider problem is particularly acute in very large goups. In a large-group setting, the cost of organizing the group for the purpose of collective action can be

[24] As examples of the latter form of regulatory service, milk producers in Wisconsin have been able in past years to suppress the sale of margarine in that state. Commercial television stations have, through the FCC, been able to suppress the introduction of pay-TV through cable companies. On the other hand, airlines have encouraged the government to subsidize airports and to build bigger and better ones to accommodate larger and faster planes.

[25] Posner, "Theories of Regulation," p. 337.

substantial simply because of the number of people involved. Group organization must be initiated by someone: someone must bear at least the initial cost of organization. Because the benefits of the collective action will be spread more or less evenly over the entire group, the cost of initiating it can be greater than the benefits which each individual receives. The collective action needed to secure regulation may not be taken; each individual member of the group rationally decides to free-ride on the efforts of others, which may not be forthcoming. The free-rider problem may explain why some large groups (such as secretaries) have not yet secured government protection; everyone in the group is waiting for everyone else to take the necessary action and incur the necessary costs to organize and obtain the protection. As a consequence, the group retains its competitive status.

Small groups, on the other hand, may have much more success because the organizational costs are proportionally smaller and each individual receives a larger share of the group benefits. The fact that there were few railroad companies in the 1880s may explain why railroads were able to effectively lobby for the formation of the ICC, while other groups did not succeed or did not try.

An Evaluation of the Economic Theory

This economic theory of regulation is not without flaws. Several reasonably large groups, like the truckers and farmers, have been able to secure a high degree of government protection through market regulation, and many highly concentrated industries, such as electrical appliances, have been unable to secure the degree of protection from domestic competitive forces that the truckers have. There are several possible avenues of explanation for these observations. First, in highly concentrated industries the development of private cartels is less costly than procurement of government regulation. (Remember that, according to this theory, government suppliers charge a price, and that price may be substantial.) Industries which are not so concentrated and which are less able to collude may have a greater demand for regulation. Furthermore, in industries which consist of a large number of firms, the cost of securing the regulation can be spread over all of them. Any one firm within a large group of firms may have very little incentive to join in the group's action; at the same time, its share of the cost can be quite small. If the cost of securing regulation is $10,000 and there are 1000 firms in the industry, the cost per firm is $10. For a market in which there is a smaller number of firms, the incentive to cooperate in collective action may be greater, but the cost to each firm is also greater. Of course, the opposite can be true, making regulation more likely among the smaller group of firms.

Second, a large group of firms can control a sizable voting block. A candidate for public office may assume the role of a "politician entrepreneur" and offer to "produce" regulation for an industry if the owners and employees in that industry will pay him with their votes. In this event, creating an organized lobby to seek regulation is unnecessary.

Third, there are ways to get around the free-rider problem. Mancur Olson suggests that a trade association can be formed for the express purpose of pushing for protective legislation. To enlist the support of the people within the industry, the association sells trade magazines and other informative services and uses its publication profits for the production of public goods, such as the procurement of regulation.[26,27] Furthermore, the benefits of regulation do not have to be distributed equally among the firms within the industry. The benefits can be distributed to only those firms which in fact make a contribution to the procurement of the regulation. For example, truck and airline routes can be assigned to those firms which belong to the associations that

[26] Mancur Olson, *The Logic of Collective Action* (Cambridge, Mass.: Harvard University Press, 1971).

[27] For this to work very effectively, there must be barriers to entry into the trade association business. If one trade association actually makes enough profits to provide public goods to the industry, some other association may become established and sell the same types of publications at a lower price. This is because the new association does not have to work for the provision of the public good.

lobby for the establishment of the regulatory agency. The individual firms, therefore, have a private incentive to participate in a collective action.[28]

All in all, the economic theory of regulation can explain a great deal of what we observe in the area of government policy, and that is a part of the problem with the theory. It can explain so much that, at this point in its development, predictions about the emergence of regulation are difficult to make. We cannot now predict precisely which industries are likely to achieve regulation.

REGULATORY ANARCHY

The economic theory of regulation highlights a simple point often overlooked: firms within a regulated industry can benefit from the regulation. While arguing that regulation is in the "public interest," an industry may be pursuing its private interests. Why else are such large sums spent in lobbying efforts?

If one industry secures *protective* regulation, other industries may have an incentive to pursue the same course. To the extent that all industries pursue that course, the country's standard of living is reduced. If, for example, the output of all industries is reduced through restrictive practices, there must be fewer goods and services to go around. With less production, there are fewer goods to buy and less earned income to spend.

In other words, if the political process permits the type of protective regulation we have discussed, the ensuing competition for regulation can lead to the worst of all possible worlds, "regulatory anarchy." Once that state is achieved, people may be willing to take constitutional steps to preclude protective regulation. However, taking those steps may be very difficult because each special-interest group has an incentive to fight to keep its protection from market forces.

To see the problem more clearly, consider the case of a simple two-industry (*A* and *B*) economy. In Figure 12·6 we have drawn the relative real incomes (which is the purchasing power of money

	Industry *A* does not seek protective regulation		Industry *A* seeks and obtains protective regulation	
	Cell 1		Cell 2	
Industry *B* does not seek protective regulation	*A*'s real income	*B*'s real income	*A*'s real income	*B*'s real income
	$10	$15	$16	$8
	Cell 3		Cell 4	
Industry *B* seeks and obtains protective regulation	*A*'s real income	*B*'s real income	*A*'s real income	*B*'s real income
	$5	$19	$7	$10

FIG. 12·6 The real incomes of industries *A* and *B* are highest in cell 1, in which neither industry seeks protective regulation. However, each has an incentive to seek protective regulation. If they both obtain the protective regulation, they will both end up in cell 4, in which their separate and collective real incomes are less than they are in cell 1.

incomes) of people in those two industries under different states of regulation. If neither *A* nor *B* seeks regulation, they both end up in cell 1, with $10 of real income going to the owners and employees in *A* and $15 going to the owners and employees in *B*. If, however, *A* seeks and obtains regulation and *B* does not, the relative income of *A* goes up from $10 to $16. The income of *B* goes down from $15 to $8. (They both move from cell 1 to cell 2.) By the same token, industry *B* can raise its relative real income by seeking regulation if *A* does not. *B* can raise its income from $15 (in cell 1) to $19 (in cell 3). In other words, they both have an incentive to seek protective regulation. However, if they both seek and obtain regulation, they will wind up in cell 4, which, as shown in the figure, is a worse solution than would have been achieved if neither had sought regulation. (To *A* and *B*, cell

[28] Collective action in this case is very much like the kind of collective action we find exhibited in the marketplace.

1 should be preferred to cell 4. Cell 4 reflects the anarchistic solution.)

In a two-industry model, like the one we are using here, the participants can easily see what they have done by their independent actions and can agree on a constitutional arrangement whereby protective regulation is ruled out. On the other hand, in an economy in which there are many industries, the costs of seeing clearly what is happening and agreeing on an appropriate regulatory policy are compounded by sheer numbers. Still, the damage from protective regulation may, at some point, be so great that it is recognized that some form of across-the-board *de*regulation is pursued. The rash of proposals for deregulation and reform of the regulatory process in recent years may reflect a growing, popular recognition of the present failures of our regulatory agencies.

REGULATION AS TAXATION

Richard Posner suggests a third theory: that much of the regulation we observe can be explained as an indirect form of taxation.[29] As he sees it, the essential feature of taxation is that it is a means whereby the government extracts money from one group in order that certain goods and services can be provided and that the incomes of other groups can be subsidized. Many cases of regulation seem to be quite consistent with this view of taxation. For example, airlines were permitted until 1975 to charge fares for long-haul flights which were above their operations costs. The extra revenues were used, in part, to defray the below-cost pricing of short-haul flights. Airlines have been required to provide service to airports that are not profitable for them to serve; on the other hand, the fares charged at other airports more than compensated them, at least in good years, for the losses at low-volume airports. In effect, some airline passengers were being taxed to subsidize the ticket prices of other airline passengers.

The postal service is a closely regulated industry. For years postage collected on first-class letters has been used to offset losses on the system's handling of magazines and other bulk-mail items. Again, the regulation has been a means by which one group of customers is taxed for the benefit of another. This policy appears to be a rather clumsy way of administering national tax policy; it raises serious issues of equity in the distribution of the tax burden.

[29] Richard A. Posner, "Taxation by Regulation," *Bell Journal of Economics and Management Science*, vol. 2, pp. 22–50, Spring 1971.

REGULATORS AS UTILITY MAXIMIZERS

In this chapter we have so far discussed three theories of regulation. This review of regulatory theory is not exhaustive; there are other theories. For example, there is one theory which views regulators as utility maximizers who have an interest in raising their monetary income and nonmonetary income (such as the free time they have at work). One way they may be able to raise their nonmonetary income is to follow courses of action which minimize the flak they receive from the firms they regulate and from consumers. Changes in regulatory policies can then be seen as a natural consequence of changes in the abilities of the different groups—the regulated firms and consumers—to apply pressure on the regulators.[30]

[30] For an extended discussion of this point of view see Gordon Tullock, "Regulating the Regulators," in Svetozar Pejovich, ed., *Government Controls and the Free Market: The U.S. Economy in the 1970's* (College Station, Tex.: Texas A & M University Press, 1976), pp. 141–159.

SUMMARY AND EXTENSIONS

By treating the different theories of regulation separately, as we have done in this chapter, we may give the impression that regulation in any given area can be explained by one, and perhaps only one, of the theories. In the real world the problem of explaining regulation is not so simple. Regulation of the airline industry, for instance, has probably come about as a consequence of a combination of forces. Some people have wanted to use regulation as a means of pursuing the "public interest" as they see it; other people, especially those connected with airline firms, have supported regulation because they see it as an opportunity to protect their markets. The precise nature of any particular regulation probably reflects the strengths of these separate forces and the extent to which our political institutions allow them to be expressed.

This leads us to an important final point. The public interest argument, especially as it relates to improving market efficiency, is a valid basis for industrial regulation; however, it can be easily exploited. Although pretending to be pursuing the public interest, promoters of regulation can pursue their own interests instead of what may be claimed to be in the public interest. The statistical studies which have been cited in this chapter indicate that this is not a trivial problem. How can we, through government, allow for some public interest regulation without opening up the floodgates to protective regulation, without allowing the whole process to degenerate into a state of regulatory anarchy? How are we going to regulate the regulators and do it efficiently? These are the central questions which must be addressed in any movement for regulatory reform.

QUESTIONS TO PONDER

1 The economic theory of regulation developed in this chapter suggests that entrepreneurs have an economic incentive to support protective regulation. Do the workers in those industries have a similar incentive? Under what conditions would they support protective regulation? Under what conditions would they not support the regulation?

2 Producers of aircraft have tended to support CAB restrictions on prices which airline companies can charge their customers. Explain their support.

3 Can you develop a public interest case for the regulation of barbers and beauticians?

4 If electric utility commissions determine prices by way of a rule which specifies a "fair rate of return on investment," what effect will this have on the efficient use of fuels used in the production of electricity? Should fuel oil producers be in favor of the fair-rate-of-return method for regulating utilities?

5 In the 1970s electric utility commissions allowed electric companies to pass increases in the cost of their fuels on to their customers through "fuel adjustment clauses." Most economists agree that such a pricing scheme reduces the incentive which electric companies have to reduce the use of their fuel consumption and to seek out the cheapest fuels. Does this mean that the fuel adjustment clauses are, in the total context of regulation, an efficient device for adjusting rates? If there is a cost to making rate adjustment through normal regulatory processes, does this fact affect your reasoning?

6 Which theory of regulation seems to be most persuasive to you? Why?

7 Again, assume that the rates which electric utilities can charge are based on the "fair return" method. Economists argue that if electric utilities charge higher prices for the use of electricity during periods of peak demand, less electricity will be used during those hours. Many people will change their behavior in such a way that they will tend to use electricity at other times when the price is lower. By shifting the demand through what is called "peak-load pricing," the needed electric generating capacity is lowered. Should we expect electric utility companies to be in favor of peak-load pricing in view of the "fair return" method for determining profits? Why?

8 Given the data in the following table, plot the marginal cost, average cost, and demand curves on a graph. Label the efficient output level. Will the firm produce that level? Why or why not?

Quantity	Marginal Cost	Price Consumers Will Pay
1	$21	$45
2	18	36
3	15	27
4	12	18
5	9	9
6	6	0

RECOMMENDED READINGS

Helms, Robert B.: *Natural Gas Regulation: An Evaluation of FPC Price Control* (Washington: American Enterprise Institute for Public Policy Research, 1974).

Jordan, William A.: "Producer Protection, Prior Market Structure, and the Effects of Government Regulation," *Journal of Law and Economics*, Winter 1972, pp. 151–176.

MacAvoy, Paul W., ed.: *The Crisis of the Regulatory Commissions: Introduction to a Current Issue of Public Policy* (New York: W. W. Norton & Company, Inc., 1970).

Phillips, Almarin, ed.: *Promoting Competition in Regulated Markets* (Washington: The Brookings Institution, 1975).

Posner, Richard A.: "Theories of Economic Regulation," *Bell Journal of Economics and Management Science*, vol. 5, pp. 335–358, Autumn 1974.

Stigler, George J.: *The Citizen and the State* (Chicago: University of Chicago Press, 1975).

13

Consumer Protection: A Question of Who Should Be Responsible

As many of you know, there is a move afoot in Washington to reexamine a great deal of what has long been presumed to be socially useful regulation. What is being questioned is our tendency to turn to government to solve all our problems . . . . It has been suggested that we reconsider these regulations, weigh their costs and benefits, and decide whether we are paying more than we are getting in return.

Lewis Engman[1]

PREVIEW OF CHAPTER

Central question

What is the case for and against laws designed to protect consumers from unsafe and shoddy merchandise?

Major objectives

1 To present in some detail the most frequently heard arguments for and against laws designed to protect consumers

2 To stress that consumer protection always comes at a cost and to point out that a central question in the consumer protection controversy is how much cost will be incurred, who will pay that cost, and how will it be paid

[1] Lewis A. Engman, "The Fairness Doctrine: Competition and the First Amendment," speech to UCLA Communications Law Program, Oct. 29, 1975. Mr. Engman was at the time chairman of the Federal Trade Commission.

Major conclusions

1 The case for consumer protection legislation involves the following major points:
   a Consumers need to be protected when external benefits and costs are involved in the production and/or consumption of goods and services.
   b Consumers need to be protected against the abusive use by businesses of their monopoly power.
   c Consumers need to be protected because they are incapable of understanding the many complexities involved in the production and consumption of goods and services.
   d Consumer complaints to businesses are in many significant ways public goods. Government protection is a means by which consumers can make their complaints heard collectively. It is a way of producing a public good that is not (and cannot be) produced in sufficient quantities in the private market.

2 The case against consumer protection laws involves the following major points:
   a Although imperfect, competition provides consumers with a rationally determined level of protection.
   b People differ in their willingness to accept risk, that is, to use products which are not perfectly safe. Consumer protection laws invariably reduce the capacity of people to buy products of lower quality at lower prices, which many prefer.
   c Consumer protection laws impose a particularly heavy burden on the poor, who, because of their low incomes, tend to buy cheaper but lower-quality products. They are forced to pay higher prices for the goods they buy.

3 If products are made safer by way of government standards, many people will respond by being less careful in the use of the products they buy. Consumer protection laws will, therefore, not aid in reducing injuries as much as might be expected.

Important terms and concepts

Caveat emptor
Caveat venditor

Many people firmly believe that responsibility for product safety, quality, and effectiveness ought to rest squarely in the lap of the producer/seller. They believe that government can best accomplish this by setting product standards and using the power of the state to protect the consumer from abuses of the marketplace. However, before conclusions are drawn, the consequences of such changes in product liability must be considered. This is precisely what this chapter is about.

FROM CAVEAT EMPTOR TO CAVEAT VENDITOR

Less than 100 years ago the general rule of the marketplace was *caveat emptor*—"Let the consumer beware." In the purchase of goods and services, the consumer was usually held fully responsible for the safety, quality, and effectiveness of what he purchased. In short, the consumer had to look out for himself. Liability for the safety and effectiveness of goods and services could be assumed by the seller, but this had to be demonstrated through a contract endorsed by both seller and buyer. Even if the buyer had a contract, the rule of *caveat emptor* held that he had to beware of what he was signing. Sellers could be sued for breach of contract or fraud, but the consumer could not look to a government agency to initiate a suit or to protect him in other ways from the "devious maneuvers" of businessmen.

During the twentieth century, through a number of significant court cases and changes in the law, product liability was gradually shifted to the producer and/or seller. One important change in product liability law came in the 1916 court case of *MacPherson v. Buick Motor Company.* The court held the producer liable for damages suffered in an automobile accident because of evidence demonstrating that there had been "negligence" in the manufacture of the car. According to Roland McKean, on whose work this short review of legal history is based, this decision was applied to a wide range of cases involving such goods as food, beverages, firearms, and explosives, and to other varied items such as a defective bar stool.[2] In more recent years producers have been held responsible not only for explicit warranties, but also for any implied warranty made in the promotion of the product. For example, Ford Motor Company was held responsible for a windshield which shattered when hit by a stone because the company had advertised the windshield as shatterproof. In a 1960 case, *Henningsen v. Bloomfield Motors, Inc.*, the court held Chrysler responsible for an automobile accident in which no evidence had been offered to demonstrate that Chrysler had been negligent in the manufacture of the car. The court ruled: "An implied warranty that it [the product] is reasonably suitable for use as such accompanies it into the hands of the ultimate purchaser,"[3] meaning that the seller can be held responsible, within limits, for *how* the product is used. McKean writes,

[2] Roland N. McKean, "Product Liability: Implications of Some Changing Property Rights," *Quarterly Journal of Economics*, November 1970, pp. 611–626.

[3] Ibid., p. 615.

"Within a few years the Henningsen precedent was applied to a wide variety of products, including a glass door, shotgun, dental chair, and hula skirt. Liability to bystanders, and other extensions of manufacturer liability, have been established more recently."[4]

Although the shift from the rule of *caveat emptor* toward the rule of *caveat venditor*—"Let the seller beware"—has been clear, courts have made some effort to avoid holding the seller responsible for minor hazards or for misrepresentations which imposed minor cost on consumers. In 1970 the Transportation Department's National Traffic Safety Administration ordered General Motors to notify owners of 1959 and 1960 Cadillacs of a defective Pitman arm which could cause steering problems and loss of control. In 1975 the court ruled that GM did not have to notify the owners and make the necessary repairs because the one accident caused by failure of the Pitman arm "didn't prove that it [failure] would happen sufficiently often to create an unreasonable risk to safety."[5]

THE CASE FOR CONSUMER PROTECTION

The case for consumer protection through product standards and the assignment of product liability to the seller is in many respects similar to the case for regulation of industries that we studied in the last chapter. The case relies heavily upon the problems created by externalities and monopoly power in the marketplace. However, there are significant differences in the arguments, in emphasis if not in kind, and for this reason alone the subject of consumer protection must be treated separately.

External Benefits

In Chapter 12 we developed an example concerning shock-absorbing bumpers for automobiles. People who do not buy them can benefit from the purchases of those persons who do.

[4] Ibid., p. 616.

[5] *Wall Street Journal*, Apr. 30, 1975, p. 2.

When two cars, one with and one without shock-absorbing bumpers, collide at low speeds, both cars will be damaged less and both drivers will be injured less because at least one had protective bumpers. To the extent that the car buyer does not consider the benefits which others receive from his purchase, the quantity of shock-absorbing bumpers purchased will be less than may be considered socially desirable or economically efficient.

Suppose that the supply curve in Figure 13 · 1 is the industry's marginal cost curve for producing protective bumpers. The demand curve, D_1, represents the market demand of consumers, based on *private* benefits, for bumpers. Under competitive conditions, the quantity produced and sold in the market is Q_1. If people fully account for the benefits which their purchases have to others—and we suggest that to some extent they do—there is nothing wrong with Q_1 bumpers being purchased. However, many people either ignore or do not fully consider the impact which their purchases have on others; these *external* benefits are, to this extent, not reflected in their market demands. Many people are not able to justify purchasing the bumpers; others may purchase fewer bumpers for their cars than they would if they considered the benefits received by others.[6]

These *external* benefits of each bumper are indicated by the vertical distance between the two demand curves in the graph, D_1 and D_2. D_2, in other words, is where the market demand curve would be *if all* benefits, private and external, were reflected in consumers' demands. The quantity purchased would be Q_2. However, in a completely free market Q_2 will not be purchased even though one can demonstrate through the graph that there are sufficient benefits generated to cover the costs of the additional units between Q_1 and Q_2.[7] For this reason, economists will agree with consumer advocates who contend that the market will result in a lower level of safety than is socially desirable. Through government intervention in the form of product standards—i.e., requiring bumpers of shock-absorbing capability—a greater level of safety can be achieved and the amount of damage done in low-speed automobile accidents can be reduced. The same general line of argument can be extended to a wide range of goods and serv-

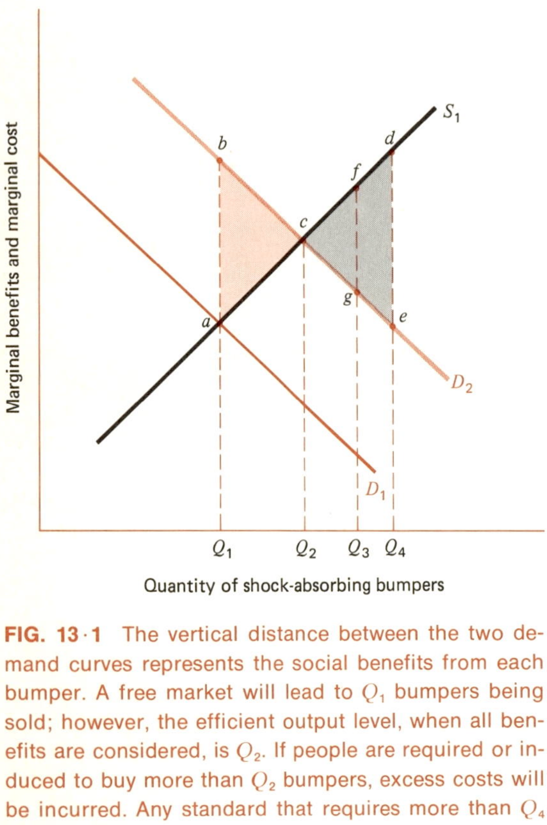

FIG. 13·1 The vertical distance between the two demand curves represents the social benefits from each bumper. A free market will lead to Q_1 bumpers being sold; however, the efficient output level, when all benefits are considered, is Q_2. If people are required or induced to buy more than Q_2 bumpers, excess costs will be incurred. Any standard that requires more than Q_4 bumpers be purchased will, in the net, make people "worse off."

[6] For example, the cost of a protective bumper may be \$100 more than an ordinary bumper, but the additional *private* benefits to the consumer may be estimated at \$75. In this case, the bumper will not be purchased even though \$50 worth of benefits are being received by others in terms of reduced expected damages in the event of an accident. However, with the external benefits added to the private benefits, purchase of the bumper can be justified. (Total benefits equal \$125.) We can also imagine a person justifying, on the basis of private benefits alone, the purchase of a protective bumper for the family car which is used for most trips around town, but, because of diminishing marginal benefits, not for a second car which may be rarely used.

[7] Notice that the marginal benefit, as shown by demand curve D_2, for each unit between Q_1 and Q_2 is greater than the marginal cost of producing those units.

ices, from brakes to safety caps for drugs to protective devices for explosives, where *significant* external benefits are present.[8]

Although valid as stated, this line of argument has limits beyond which it cannot be pushed. On *a priori* grounds alone, we cannot conclude, for example, that *all* automobiles must have shock-absorbing bumpers.[9] A requirement that all cars have protective bumpers may mean a quantity of bumpers purchased far in excess of Q_2, which is the socially desirable (or efficient) quantity.

If the government intervenes in the market and forces people to expand their purchases of bumpers from Q_1 to Q_2, social benefits are achieved. These additional benefits are represented by the orange-shaded area *abc*.[10] If the government forces consumers to buy more than Q_2 bumpers, the marginal cost of each unit beyond Q_2 is greater than the marginal benefits. There is an excess burden (or net social cost) when the number of bumpers the public is required to purchase is extended beyond Q_2. There is, therefore, some quantity of required protective bumpers which will not be socially desirable.

To explain, if the required number of protective bumpers is Q_4, this excess burden is the gray-shaded area *cde*. (For each unit between Q_2 and Q_4, the marginal cost is greater than the marginal benefit. The gray-shaded area, *cde*, is the total of this excess cost which can be measured by the goods that could have been produced but are not.) As we have drawn the illustration, the two triangular areas, *abc* and *cde*, are equal. The additional social benefits of expanding the number of protective bumpers from Q_1 to Q_2, *abc*, is equal to the social cost of extending their purchase beyond Q_2 to Q_4, *cde*. Consequently, there is no real *net* social benefit to moving to Q_4. If the required number of bumpers is greater than Q_2 but less than Q_4, there is some net social benefit. At Q_3 the social cost is equal to *cfg*, which, as can be observed in the graph, is less than *abc*. It goes without saying that if the number of bumpers consumers are required to purchase is greater than Q_4, people are in the net worse off than they would have been without this "consumer protection." They lose more than they gain.

All this may seem rather abstract and unrealistic, but the lesson is quite simple. Consumer protection up to a point can be socially beneficial. However, there can be too much of a good thing, and what consitutes "too much" depends upon people's supply and demand curves for the good. In more concrete terms, it is possible to make the world so safe that few resources are available for doing anything else.

Why do governments tend to settle on standards like required bumpers on *all* cars or safety caps on all prescription-drug bottles? Those in favor of such consumer protection argue that determining with precision the optimum point for protective bumpers, Q_2, is difficult and costly—so much so that the blanket rule is the more desirable, less costly policy. However, the argument may also be turned around by opponents to consumer protection. That is, the blanket rule may be or is too costly (it causes the number of bumpers purchased to go beyond Q_4); it is less costly than trying to determine Q_2. Consequently, people can, in terms of economic efficiency, be better off by not having this form of legislation. But then again, and we emphasize this point, the blanket rule may move us toward a point like Q_2 or even Q_3, in which case it would be socially desirable legislation. The matter, of course, ultimately reduces to an empirical question, that is, what the actual costs and benefits are and exactly what the rule is.

[8] We have italicized "significant" because ultimately the benefits from government intervention must justify the cost of government intervention.

[9] If that judgment is made, it must be based on analysis of factors not introduced to this point. From the analysis to this point we can legitimately draw only the conclusion that the number of protective bumpers installed should be greater than will be installed in a completely free market.

[10] The shaded area *abc* is the total amount by which the additional benefits of $Q_2 - Q_1$ bumpers are greater than the additional costs of producing them. To explain further, the demand curve D_2 represents the total (private and social) marginal benefits of consuming each additional unit. The total additional benefits of consuming $Q_2 - Q_1$ additional units is therefore equal to the area under the curve in that part of the graph (Q_1bcQ_2). The total cost of producing $Q_2 - Q_1$ is equal to the summation of marginal costs of each additional unit, which is, again, equal to the area under the marginal cost curve (Q_1acQ_2). Net social benefit is equal to the difference between the total additional benefit and the total additional cost, or *abc*.

External Costs

The external cost argument for consumer protection is symmetrical to the external benefit argument just developed. Succinctly, the consumer-user of a certain product does not bear all the costs associated with its use. As a consequence, he or she will tend to consume more of this good than is socially desirable or efficient, imposing a cost on others in the process. Product safety and effectiveness are forms of "social pollution," much like industrial smoke.

Consider, for example, spray deodorants. A person buys a spray can and incurs a private cost equal to the price of the can. However, during the mid-1970s several scientists came to the conclusion (which has been questioned in some scientific quarters) that the release of certain chemicals from these aerosol cans is having a detrimental effect on the ozone layer in the upper atmosphere. Because the destruction of the ozone layer, can mean that more of the sun's rays will get through to earth, resulting in harmful effects on the earth's inhabitants and environment, those who use spray deodorants and many other products dispensed through aerosol cans impose a *cost* on people who do not use them. At the very least, the public incurs a risk cost.

In terms of Figure 13·2, D_1 depicts the consumers' market demand for spray deodorant. S_1 shows the marginal cost of producing the good, exclusive of the ozone effect. In a free, competitive market the quantity purchased is Q_2. However, if the producers have to account for the social or external cost imposed on others through the use of their product, the producers' supply curve will be S_2, with the vertical distance between S_1 and S_2 representing the external (or ozone) cost of each spray can sold. The quantity purchased will then be Q_1. In a free market, more cans of spray deodorant are purchased, Q_2, than is socially desirable, Q_1. By moving consumption back to Q_1, social welfare can be raised by an amount equal to the shaded area *abc* in Figure 13·2. (Why?)

Again, as in the case of external benefits, this line of argument does not necessarily imply that all spray cans should be banned. Whether or not

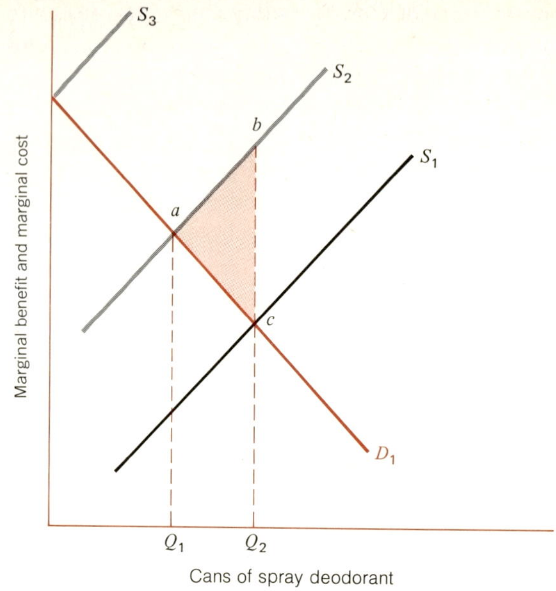

FIG. 13·2 The vertical distance between S_1 and S_2 is the social cost of producing each can of spray deodorant. A free market will lead to Q_2 cans being produced, which is greater than the efficient output level, Q_1. The difference between Q_1 and Q_2 is the "overproduction" which results when social or external costs are involved in production.

we should accept a complete ban depends upon the extent of the external costs. If the use of spray cans will ultimately cause the destruction of life on earth during the next 50 years, the external costs are obviously quite high and a complete ban on the use of such cans can be reasonable.[11] However, the costs can be far less than that, and some less stringent policy may be the appropriate course of action. But then, on the other hand, many consumer advocates argue that the potential harm in this area, as well as many others, cannot be measured. By allowing the spray cans to be sold, we are, in other words, playing a very dangerous game. That may be true in certain

[11] For that matter, if the supply curve, which includes all social costs, is equal to or above S_3 in Fig. 13 · 2, a complete ban is appropriate policy: zero production is the efficient output level.

areas, such as with the problem of spray cans and the ozone layer, but we must be careful in how we apply the argument to other products.

In certain areas the size of the external costs can be measured with reasonable accuracy. For instance, if a spray can explodes while a person is carrying it out of the store and bystanders are injured, the external costs can be measured by the injuries suffered by and loss of income to the bystanders. By making the producers liable for the safety of the product, the external costs are internalized. That is, the producers must consider the payments they make to injured third parties as a component of their total cost. However, this will mean a decrease in production and an increase in social welfare only if consumers also are initially not responsible for third-party injuries. If consumers are responsible beforehand—that is, before the liability for product safety is imposed on the producer—the consumers have to pay for all injuries to bystanders. They therefore have to consider these (expected) costs in their purchases and to adjust their purchases to take account of these costs. The consumers are then already considering the social costs of their actions, and the efficient output level is already achieved. In short, the *assignment* of liability to producers *or* consumers can reduce the quantity bought and sold to the point where it is equal to the socially desirable quantity. However, a *shift* in produce liability from consumer to producer need not change the quantity bought and sold.

Monopoly Power

Many consumer advocates believe that there are firms in the United States and elsewhere which use their market power to restrict the variety of products available and to reduce the quality, safety, and effectiveness of the products which they do offer. The monopolist, in other words, can choose not only what quantity of a given product will be offered (as we discussed in Chapter 12) but also the nature (quality, safety, etc.) of that product. If left unconstrained by government, the monopolist will tend to maximize profits by finding that one combination of price, nature of product, and quantity which will make the difference between total cost and total revenue greatest.

Consumer advocates feel that most consumers want products of higher quality than they can presently obtain. Consumers want safer products, more effective products, and they are willing to pay the necessary cost, under competitive market conditions, to get what they want, or so the argument is developed. Consumer advocates contend, however, that consumers are not given that choice in a monopolistic or oligopolistic market. Furthermore, they are not willing to pay the "extortionist" prices charged by firms with monopoly power. According to many consumer advocates, these firms, therefore, need to be told what to do by the only viable countervailing force—government.

We see two possible rebuttals to this line of argument: (1) the advocates of consumer protection overrate the power of even very large firms in the market; and (2) if a sufficient number of consumers wants a safer or more effective product, a firm can be set up to provide that product on a profitable basis. On the other hand, consumer advocates see the concentration of major industries in the hands of a very few firms as evidence of market power and they see significant financial and other barriers to new firms who may want to enter the market. We cannot hope to settle this dispute here. We can point out, however, that the latter argument may indicate only that not enough consumers are willing to *pay* for the safer product; there is, therefore, insufficient incentive for firms, in the short run, to overcome the barriers to entry. Advocates of government protection may then argue that profit should not be the sole criterion for determining whether or not and in what quality such things as drugs and baby cribs are sold.

Complex Modern Technology and Information

Modern technology makes for an extremely complex world. Proponents of consumer protection argue that it is impossible for the average consumer to know and comprehend the ins and outs of a clock radio, much less a color television set or many prescription drugs. Furthermore, the production process is so far removed from the consumer that he has little or no idea of the conditions under which his cereal and meat are produced; chemicals which are added cannot be detected by ordinary sense perception. Without adequate information and the ability to comprehend whatever information is available, the consumer cannot be expected to make rational choices: he does not know the *true* costs and benefits of his purchases. The consumer must, therefore, be protected by those who do "know" the costs and benefits—politicians and government bureaucrats.

Consumers may have the incentive to acquire some information about what they buy; they may read the labels or listen to television commercials. But, given the costs of going further, they may acquire less information than is socially desirable. In one respect, this line of argument will bother most economists. The argument may come from people who view themselves as a part of the consuming intelligentsia and who may wish to impose their preferences on others, and it fails to recognize that information is an economic good.

Information can be very useful, but there is also a cost of acquiring it. The individual must judge whether or not the information acquired is worth the expected costs.[12] As in the purchase of any good, the consumer will tend to purchase information up to that point at which the marginal benefits of an additional unit equal the marginal costs. This may mean that the consumer remains largely ignorant of the fine points of what is bought. However, in remaining ignorant—or maintaining some degree of ignorance—the consumer is implicitly or explicitly trading off information on the safety, quality, and effectiveness of given goods for greater quantities of other goods. For instance, you can increase your knowledge of the safety and effectiveness of most things, from automobiles to lawn mowers to cake mixers. You can do this by subscribing to a periodical like *Consumer Reports* (or by writing for a wide variety of government publications). However, there is a cost to reading and subscribing to *Consumer Reports*, and many people rationally decide to take their chances with their purchases rather than pay to receive publications. They, and possibly you, prefer to use the money on beer or even for a contribution to UNICEF. Information can be beneficial but less beneficial than these other goods. Government can produce the information; but, again, there is no such thing as free information. The cost will be borne by taxpayers.

The information argument is, however, very attractive in another sense. Like the shock-absorbing bumper, information can possibly benefit far more people than those who actually pay for it—that is, there are external benefits associated with its provision. To the extent that this is true, the market demand for information, like the market demand for protective bumpers, will not fully reflect the societal benefits. The quantity of information produced and purchased will fall short of the efficient level (as bumpers do in Figure 13·1). The government can intervene in the market to supplement the information flow and increase social welfare.

The Public Good of Consumer Complaints

Whenever possible, airlines book more people for flights than they have seats on their planes. This is done because more people generally reserve seats than show up to claim them. Even with overbooking, planes frequently take off with empty seats. One reason is the fact that the individual customer does not bear the full cost of his failure to show for a flight. The cost of the empty seat is spread over all customers through higher ticket prices.

Every now and then, however, people show up at the ticket counter and are unable to get seats. Ralph Nader was once one of these unfortunate people. He sued the airline company which caused him this inconvenience; and by drawing

[12] Recall that we considered the trade-off between study of economics and conversations in Chap. 2. To gain economic information, the cost is the forgoing of hours in some other activities like conversations.

attention to this practice, he imposed a heavy public relations cost on the airlines. Nader believes that if everyone would take the time to challenge business practices detrimental to consumers, such practices would change.

Hotels also follow the practice of overbooking, and at one economics convention a particular economist found that, although he had confirmation for his room reservation, the hotel desk clerk did not have a room for him. He told the clerk, therefore, that if he did not get a room soon, he would proceed to undress in the lobby, change into his pajamas, and use one of the couches in the lobby for a bed. He convinced the clerk that he meant what he said, and as a result the hotel was "able" to find him a room within a very few minutes.[13]

We all often find ourselves in similar situations: we do not get what we bargain for. Unlike Nader and the economist, however, we may do little more than grumble to ourselves. Most people passively accept the shoddy merchandise or the unfortunate circumstances which befall them in dealing for goods and services. Their behavior can be quite rational. Consumers can make a fuss; they can take their case all the way from the salesclerk to the president of the company. The merchandise may eventually be replaced or they may receive redress for the wrong that has been done to them. The process, on the other hand,can be quite costly in implicit time, emotional and energy costs and explicit money costs—so much so that the consumers do not bother to do anything except look for another airline or hotel.

Like shock-absorbing bumpers and information, consumer complaints can also be *public goods*. If an individual consumer's complaint is effective and forces the company to alter its business practices, people other than the complainant benefit. These external benefits may not be considered by a large segment of the consuming public to whom wrongs have been done. Although *total* benefits from complaints may be greater than the costs, many complaints will go unmade because the *private* costs to the individual consumer are greater than his private benefits. This is simply another example of how people, acting in a large-group setting, may decide to free-ride on the actions of consumer activists. (See Chapter 6.) By setting up a government agency, like the FTC, to investigate consumer complaints and seek redress, a public good is produced at public expense.

[13] This example is taken from Leland Yeager's presidential address to the Southern Economics Association, Nov. 14, 1975.

THE CASE AGAINST CONSUMER PROTECTION

Arguments against consumer protection have been embedded in the foregoing discussion. In this section we seek to reemphasize those arguments, to uncover their flaws, and to bring to light points not previously mentioned. On balance, these two sections of the chapter reveal the complexity of the consumer protection issue and the delicate problem of finding a solution for a major social problem.

Competition as a Form of Consumer Protection

The protection which a person can reasonably expect to have against the whims and exploitive efforts of businesses is never complete. Complete protection means incurring prohibitive costs. The benefits of being protected against some forms of business abuse are simply too small to justify the costs of the protection.

The market system does not produce complete protection; abuses are prevalent. However, the case against consumer protection via government does not have to be founded upon the argument that the market, if left alone, will yield perfect results—that is, complete protection or no abuses. All that needs to be shown is that the market system in some ways protects the consumer and that it does this with greater completeness or efficiency than alternative systems.

The individual consumers in a free market may have little power to coerce producers into providing them with safer or more effective goods and services. On the other hand, consumers have two very important tools of persuasion. First, they can offer to pay for a safer product, and there is some price which profit-maximizing entrepreneurs will accept to provide it. Second, consumers can turn to other producers to obtain what they want or to avoid the abuses of individual producers. If producers do not offer consumers what they want, if they repeatedly sell shoddy merchandise or fail to live up to their end of the bargain, more and more consumers can move to other producers of the same good or to producers of substitute goods. The fear of losing customers helps to keep producers in line and puts pressure on them to offer the type of good their customers want. If Coca Cola, for example, persisted in selling drinks that had lost their carbonation, consumers could move to Pepsi or 7-Up and many new drinks which would come onto the market.

Granted, when buying a Coke, the consumer cannot be completely assured that the quality of the product that has been purchased will be good; it is quite possible that if one drinks enough Cokes, one will buy one which is "dead." The market does not yield complete protection. It would be impossible for Coca Cola to guarantee the effectiveness of their drinks 100 percent of the time. Furthermore, reducing the risk of their product having faults can mean greater production costs and higher prices. The consumer may prefer to accept some risks at lower prices than to pay the higher prices to avoid those risks altogether. Life would very likely be a rather dull experience if consumers tried to reduce their consumption risks to the absolute minimum.

In the market, consumer protection emerges as a consequence of the consumer's ability to patronize sellers of alternative goods and services. Monopoly power, by definition, means that consumer choice is, for one reason or another, restricted. The consumer's protection against the whims and abuses of the monopolist is correspondingly reduced: if the monopolist attempts to exert his market power by offering shoddy merchandise, the consumer does not have sellers of close substitutes to which to turn. Therefore, the economists' argument for competitive markets is, in a manner of speaking, an argument for a form of consumer protection. It is a form, however, which broadens consumer choice and, as we have discussed in Chapter 7, a form of protection which leads to the efficient allocation of resources. Through setting standards for product quality and safety, government intervention can mean a restriction of consumer choice and an increase in monopoly power for those firms which can meet the production standards. Medical doctors, for instance, have been able to increase their market position—their monopoly power—by erecting legal barriers against less qualified persons practicing medicine.

The case for consumer protection through a competitive market is not a recommendation for the complete absence of government in the marketplace. The government has a role; it is to set and monitor (through police, courts, etc.) the legal framework within which exchanges can be made. To the extent that exchanges rely on their legal enforceability, the government's role is a very important one. Still, the system is not without its flaws. A contract may be legally enforceable, but the consumer may have to pay the costs of having it enforced (through taxes and/or legal fees) and may be unwilling to do this. In such case, the only protection the consumer may have is the drive for competitive survival among firms. Furthermore, the problems of lack of accurate information and of safety as a public good, discussed in the previous section, are flaws in the case against consumer protection which cannot be overlooked. Proponents of the market system argue, however, that government intervention to remedy these problems can be supported only if the expected benefits exceed the costs of the government's efforts.

Differences in Risk Aversion

People differ in their willingness to assume the risk that the goods and services that they buy may be defective, ineffective, or unsafe. These differences should be reflected in their individual demands to avoid risks, and the differences can be explained in several ways. First, people differ as to their preferences toward "risk aversion." Some people simply place a higher personal evaluation on avoiding risks than do others. Some people are willing to assume the risks associated with hang gliding; others would not dare. Many people are willing to accept the risks of buying a used car or a used electric toaster, while others have a strong aversion to buying secondhand merchandise. If we are to believe the surveys, most drivers are willing to accept the risks associated with driving around in their cars with their seat belts unfastened; a few will not go around the block without them on. The central point is that, if everything else is equal, people who have a strong aversion to risk have greater demands for safer products than other people whose preferences are less intense.

Second, the differences in people's willingness to assume risk may reflect the differences in their economic circumstances. Given their risk aversion, income can affect people's demand for safer products. One very reasonable hypothesis is that income and demands for safer products are positively related. Many people with low incomes buy their lunches in "greasy spoons." Their incomes may place an absolute restriction on their ability to eat in restaurants with Grade A ratings. On the other hand, they may reason that they are *better off* by eating where they do at lower prices than going elsewhere and reducing their risk of food poisoning but paying higher prices.

People also differ in their ability to cope with risk from a technical standpoint. Some parents have developed habits which force them to keep drugs and house-cleaning fluids out of the reach of children; others do not have children and generally do not concern themselves with open bottles of drugs left on the kitchen counter. Some people are inclined to read instructions more carefully and are more patient in making sure they use the products they buy correctly than are others. In summary, people with a comparative efficiency in coping with risk can afford to buy less safe products. Although they may have to incur a risk cost, the total cost—the price they pay for the product plus the risk cost—is less than the cost of a safer product purchased on the market.

If all consumers were willing to accept the same degree of risk, the answer to the problem of protecting the consumer, through establishing product standards, would be a relatively straightforward one. Government regulators would simply have to determine that *one* level of risk acceptable to any one person, and therefore acceptable to all, and set their standards accordingly. However, the problem is not easily solved. Invariably, consumer choices will be restricted, meaning that some less safe or ineffective products can no longer be offered for sale.[14] Those consumers who are comparatively efficient in coping with risk or who have no real aversion to risk will be forced to buy safer products; assuming that safety is not a free good, the cost of what these consumers buy will increase. In economic terms, this amounts to a misallocation of resources—a social waste. For example, people without children must still pay for child-proof drug bottles.

There are social benefits to people who believe that they should be protected for any of the reasons that we have given; on the other hand, consumer protection, according to the opponents, imposes a social cost on many people. These costs are clearly revealed by the many sets of automobile seat belts which are never used. The cost is less clearly revealed in other areas. Producers are now required to make children's sleepwear fire resistant. However, in order for the products to retain their fire-resistant quality, parents must give the sleepwear special treatment in wash cycles; they must use soap as opposed to detergent. For parents who never take the necessary care with what they have purchased, the fire-resistant quality is shortly lost after purchase—they have been forced to purchase something that they have never fully used.

If, as opposed to the setting of product standards, the liability for the safety or effectiveness of a product is shifted in full to the producer, meaning that the consumer can no longer *choose* to assume the risk himself, the same types of problems can develop, except that they may be

[14] If government regulation did not reduce the range of consumer choice, there would be no point to the regulation.

less severe. The producer has to assume the risk and may avoid those risks by discontinuing those product lines in which the risk is significant. In order to continue to offer the good on the market, he must either incur the cost of lawsuits and/or damage claims or buy insurance to cover the newly acquired risk cost. Prices can be expected to rise in line with the increased cost to the producer. Through the producer, consumers are effectively forced to buy an insurance policy against the product being unsafe or defective. They no longer have the choice of self-insurance at, perhaps, a lower price.

The Distributional Effects

Many people support consumer protection measures because of their sincere concern for the poor. The poor are viewed as being unable to buy the necessary consumer protection information in order to make reasoned choices. The poor are also the ones who are least capable of understanding the technical information and who are least able to endure the hardship of the once-in-a-while defective goods and services. However, opponents of consumer protection measures point out that the poor often buy low-quality goods and services because, as noted above, they are better off by paying less and having more of other things. If less-safe products are removed from the shelves, the burden of consumer protection is disproportionally felt by the poor. People in higher-income groups are often already buying the safer goods and services, and their relevant choice range is hardly affected, or so the opponents of consumer protection may argue.

The Behavioral Response of Consumers

The level of safety achieved through the purchase and use of a product is dependent upon the inherent characteristics of the product *and* the way in which the consumer uses the product. If consumers are forced to buy a safer product, paying a higher cost for it, and are led to believe that they are being protected by a government agency, they may change the way they use the good: in short, they may be inclined to be more careless in the reading of labels and instructions and in the use of the product. In the net, the level of people's safety may be increased but, perhaps, not as much as one may think by considering only what the government does. The behavioral response of the consumer, in other words, increases the cost-benefit ratio.

Seat belts are an example of a safety measure which may have a slight but perverse effect on the level of *public* safety.[15] Seat belts reduce injuries to persons driving cars; they therefore reduce the cost of automobile accidents to drivers and the cost of reckless or high-speed driving. Assuming a downward sloping demand for reckless and high-speed driving, the required seat belts should increase the amount of reckless and high-speed driving. This can make highways less safe for people in other cars; the seat belt requirement imposes a social cost on others around them.

[15] See Richard B. McKenzie and Gordon Tullock, *The New World of Economics: Explorations into the Human Experience* (Homewood, Ill.: Richard D. Irwin, Inc., 1978), chap. 2.

SUMMARY AND EXTENSIONS

With the growing number of legislative proposals for increased government protection of consumers, the debate over *caveat emptor* has been joined. Product safety has become more controversial and important. Unfortunately still, the public debate very infrequently moves beyond the emotional, normative level. The real issues and implied trade-offs are only superficially considered.

The purpose of this chapter has been to clarify some of the major themes on both sides of the debate, their extremes as well as their areas of possible reconciliation. The public policy course which will probably be taken will be some compromise between the extreme calls for full consumer protection by government and those for a complete reign of the market system. Just how much consumer protection government provides will reflect the voters' and politicians' recognition of its costs and benefits and their willingness to trade off freedom of choice and individual initiative for whatever benefits government protection may bring.

It is very difficult for even the most ardent free-market economists to be against legislative proposals for greater accuracy and completeness in product labeling. The information received can, for those who will bear the costs to understand it, only improve consumer choices. The costs are very slight. On the other hand, if the government increases the required proof of the effectiveness and safety of drugs, as it did through the 1962 Kefauver-Harris amendment to the Food, Drug and Cosmetic Act of 1938, critical questions of benefits and costs are raised. That act of Congress increased the costs of drug development and the time lag between the date on which the drug is developed and the date on which it can be offered for sale.

By increasing testing requirements, some potentially unsafe drugs may be kept off the market; several deaths and human deformities due to drug use may be avoided. On the other hand, many new drugs may never be conceived because of the expected costs of their development; many drugs which are effective in reducing deaths may be held off the market for a period of years. The act may have reduced the number of deaths from unsafe drugs, but it may have also increased the number of deaths because safe, effective drugs have been withheld from the market for 2 to 8 years. Before we can make rational choices on social policy we must know what the trade-off in this area is. Sam Peltzman, in a study of the 1962 amendment, has concluded that the greater testing requirements have generated fewer benefits than costs.[16] The importance of this issue is particularly acute if the legislation causes drugs which can cure cancer or reduce heart attacks to be withheld from the market. Clearly, the legislation itself is a form of social experimentation.

There is no way of ensuring that the more sophisticated drugs being developed today are perfectly safe. Over a series of tests, because of the inability of doctors and scientists to completely control their experimentation, we can expect mixed results. Any determination of the effectiveness or safety of a drug will be founded upon judgment as to what the "weight" of the evidence shows. In addition, there are frequently trade-offs between the toxicity of drugs and their effectiveness or between the risk of causing cancer and effectiveness in curing another disease. Just how much cost are we willing to bear? What kinds of trade-offs are we willing to make? Since people's preferences are different on these issues, whose

[16] Sam Peltzman, *Regulation of Pharmaceutical Innovation: The 1962 Amendment* (Washington, D.C.: American Enterprise Institute for Public Policy Research, 1974). William M. Wardell and Louis Lasagna have drawn similar conclusions and have found that the more stringent United States regulations have resulted in net social costs for the United States as compared with the British experience; see *Regulation and Drug Development* (Washington, D.C.: American Enterprise Institute for Public Policy Research, 1975).

preferences will be reflected in the force of law? These are the basic questions to which the issue of consumer protection ultimately reduces.

QUESTIONS TO PONDER

1 Explain why over the decades there has been a growing public demand for consumer protection through government intervention in the market. Does the growth in this demand have anything to do with the general rise in personal income and changes in the relative prices of product safety and material comfort?

2 Explain how education can influence the demand for and supply of consumer protection. Hint: Think of education as a factor of production within the family unit.

3 On what grounds can a requirement that all new cars must come equipped with seat belts be deemed a socially desirable policy? A socially undesirable policy?

4 Many people who argue against product standards as a means of protecting consumers will argue, instead, for more consumer education. Which policy do you prefer? Do the relative costs of each means of correcting consumer choices have any bearing on your views? What are the costs associated with greater consumer education? With higher standards for products? Why, in view of your analysis, would you expect some producers and politicians to be in favor of product standards? Which producers would be in favor of the product standards?

5 With the aid of supply and demand curves, develop an argument for the optimum level of safety.

6 Assuming that consumers are normally distributed along a continuum indicating their willingness to assume risk, and assuming that a democratic government is considering imposing *one* standard of acceptable risk, what level will that standard be in the distribution? If an ardent consumer advocate were allowed to make that decision, what would you suspect would be his choice? Which choice will minimize "social friction"?

RECOMMENDED READINGS

Buchanan, James M.: "In Defense of Caveat Emptor," *University of Chicago Law Review*, vol. 38, pp. 64–73, Fall 1970.

Campbell, Rita Ricardo: *Food Safety Regulation: A Study of the Use and Limitations of Cost-Benefit Analysis* (Washington, D.C.: American Enterprise Institute for Public Policy Research and Hoover Institution on War, Revolution, and Peace, Stanford University, 1974).

McKean, Roland N.: "Product Liability: Implications of Some Changing Property Rights," *Quarterly Journal of Economics*, Fall 1970, pp. 611–626.

Nader, Ralph, and Donald Ross: *Action for a Change: A Student's Manual for Public Policy Research* (New York: Grossman Publishers, 1971).

Peltzman, Sam: *Regulation of Pharmaceutical Innovation: The 1962 Amendment* (Washington, D.C.: American Enterprise Institute for Public Policy Research, 1974).

Posner, Richard A.: *Regulation of Advertising by the FTC* (Washington, D.C.: American Enterprise Institute for Public Policy Research, 1973).

Wardell, William M., and Louis Lasagna: *Regulation and Drug Development* (Washington, D.C.: American Enterprise Institute for Public Policy Research, 1975).

Part Five
Social Order and the Market for Labor

Governments, long hostile to other monopolies, suddenly sponsored and promoted widespread labor monopolies, which democracy cannot endure, cannot control without destroying, and perhaps cannot destroy without destroying itself.
Henry C. Simmons

In previous chapters, our central purpose has been to explain how markets for goods and services, like bicycles and entertainment, work. In the next two chapters, our attention turns to the market for labor which is used to produce the goods and services we buy. We explain not only how people's wage rates are determined and why they differ, but also how government policy can influence the employment opportunities which people have. In Chapter 14 we focus on competitive labor markets; our attention then turns in Chapter 15 to employer and employee groups which have market power to significantly affect the wage rates and employment opportunities of workers. In all our discussions, we will see that many of the principles studied in earlier chapters are applicable, with only minor modification, to labor markets.

14

The Absence of Power in the Labor Market

Labour, like all other things which are purchased and sold, and which may be increased or diminished in quantity, has its natural price and its market price.

David Ricardo[1]

PREVIEW OF CHAPTER

Central question

How are wage rates determined, and why do they differ among different groups of workers?

Major objectives

1 To explain how wage rates are determined and why they differ in competitive labor markets

2 To explain how nonmoney benefits from employment affect the wage rates of workers

3 To show the effects of laws which specify minimum wage rates which workers must be paid and to explain the political support of minimum wage laws

4 To explain how housing standards for migrant workers can affect the employment opportunities of migrant workers

[1] David Ricardo, *The Principles of Political Economy and Taxation* (London: J. M. Dent and Sons, Ltd.), p. 52.

Major conclusions

1. The *demand for labor* is dependent upon the *marginal product* of workers and the price of the product they produce.
2. The demand for labor is downward sloping like the demand for all other goods and services.
3. The wage rate and number of people hired in a given competitive labor market are determined by the interaction of supply of and demand for labor.
4. Nonmoney benefits from employment tend to increase the supply of labor in that market, reduce the money-wage rate, and increase the number of people hired.
5. Minimum wage laws tend to increase the income of some workers but reduce the employment opportunities and income of other workers.
6. Imposed housing standards for migrant workers tend to reduce the demand for migrant workers, reduce the money wage received, and reduce the employment opportunities for some migrant workers. However, the economic position of some (or most) migrant workers can be improved.

Important terms and concepts

Demand for labor
Marginal product of labor
Supply of labor
Equilibrium wage rate
Human capital
Nonmoney benefits from employment

Professional football players earn more than ministers or nurses. Social workers with college degrees usually earn less than truck drivers who may not have completed high school. Generally speaking, given equivalent educational background and teaching experience, professors of accounting earn more than professors of history. Indeed, you may believe that a particular professor of history is an outstanding teacher—he or she is able to communicate effectively and is concerned about his or her students; nonetheless, he or she probably earns less than a mediocre teacher of comparable rank and experience in the accounting department. Does this make for social justice? We cannot pretend to answer in full that very difficult question; however, we can broach the subject of social justice by addressing the more manageable questions of why people earn what they do and why earnings differ among occupations.

In previous chapters we have dealt with the market for final goods and services like hand calculators, automobiles, and dry cleaning. In this chapter we deal specifically with the market for labor, an important resource in most production processes. Admittedly, labor is only one of many resources that firms use in production. However, the general principles developed with regard to the labor market are applicable to markets for other resources: principally, land and capital (i.e., plant and equipment). Further, you should realize that there are many forces which determine who is employed and at what wage; they include such factors as the employee's background and social status, appearance, sex, race, and range of acquaintances, all of which may be considered to be noneconomic determinants of employment. By concentrating on the economic determinants of employment—those which relate most directly to production and promotion of a product—we do not mean to suggest that other factors are unimportant. Indeed, they are very important, as is indicated by the laws which are required to reduce sexual and racial discrimination in employment. Our purpose in this and the next chapters is simply to show how economic forces work to influence the wage that is paid, the working conditions of employment, and the numbers of employees that are hired. Although constructed primarily for the purpose of showing how labor markets work, the model we develop can be used to explore the effects of minimum wage laws and housing standards for migrant workers.

This chapter deals solely with competitive labor markets. Chapter 15 is concerned with market power in labor markets in the form of unions and what are called "monopsonistic employers."

THE DEMAND FOR AND SUPPLY OF MOUSETRAPS AND MOUSETRAP MAKERS

Labor, in its many forms, is a special kind of commodity; it is a commodity in which most people have a personal stake. The *wage rate* is the price at which the employer buys this commodity; alternately, it is the price which the individual laborer receives in exchange for his efforts. In a competitive market that "price," like the price of most everything else, is determined by the interaction of the supply of and demand for labor. To understand why a person earns what he does, we must consider the determinants of the supply and demand for labor. First, the demand.

The Demand for Labor

If there were no demand for mousetraps, there would be no need—no demand—for mousetrap makers. This is a general principle which is applicable to all other kinds of labor in a free and open market. You are able to sell your services, whether you are a plumber, a textile worker, or a writer, because there is a demand for the product or the service you can offer; the greater the demand for that product, the greater the market price for it and the greater the demand for your labor. As we will see in a few pages, the greater the demand for a given kind of labor, if everything else is equal, the higher the wage rate.

The productivity of labor—that is, how much a worker can produce per unit of time—is also a critically important determinant of the demand for labor. Labor productivity determines how much laborers can produce, and the price of the final product gives a market evaluation to laborers' output. These two factors—labor productivity and market price of what is produced—work together to determine the market value of labor to employers and, therefore, employers' demand for labor. In addition, we can predict that the demand for labor should rise and fall with increases and decreases in labor productivity and market price for the product.

For example, suppose that mousetraps are sold in a competitive market; that is, as we studied in Chapter 7, the price of mousetraps is set at the intersection of their supply and demand curves. Further, assume that mousetraps are produced under conditions of *diminishing marginal returns:* as more units of labor are added to a fixed quantity of plant and equipment, output expands, but by diminishing increments.[2]

The employer's basic problem once he enters the range of diminishing returns is to determine how many laborers he will employ. Consider Table 14·1. The assumption of diminishing returns is illustrated in column 2. The first unit of labor added to a fixed quantity of plant and equipment can produce six mousetraps per hour: therefore, the *marginal product* (that which the first employee alone contributes to production) is six. From that point on, however, the marginal product of each additional laborer diminishes; first the marginal product diminishes to five mousetraps for the second laborer employed, then to four mousetraps for the third laborer, and so on.[3]

[2] For a review of the "law of diminishing returns," see Chap. 4.

[3] The reason why the marginal product of each additional laborer diminishes is not that laborers are inherently different. We have assumed that all units of labor are more or less alike in their capabilities. It is a technological fact that the fifth unit of labor added to production is not able to add as much to total output as the fourth unit because others are already working with the plant and equipment; nor is the fourth able to add as much to total output as the third laborer.

TABLE 14·1 COMPUTATION OF THE VALUE OF THE MARGINAL PRODUCT OF LABOR

Units of Labor (1)	Marginal Product of Each Laborer (per hour) (2)	Price of Mousetraps in Product Market (3)	Value of Each Laborer to Employer (Called "Value of Marginal Product") [(2) × (3)] (4)
1st laborer	6	$2	$12
2nd laborer	5	2	10
3rd laborer	4	2	8
4th laborer	3	2	6
5th laborer	2	2	4
6th laborer	1	2	2

Column 3 lists the market price for each mousetrap. To keep the market analysis simple and representative of highly competitive markets, we assume that each firm can sell its mousetraps at a constant price.[4] By multiplying the dollar price of the mousetraps in column 3 times the marginal product of each laborer in column 2, we can determine the value of each laborer (or, more properly, the "value of the marginal product") to the employer. The value of each laborer is indicated in column 4. This is the amount that the employer will, at the limit, pay each laborer. If less than each laborer's "value of marginal product" has to be paid, the employer earns a profit.

If the wage rate for each laborer is slightly below $12, we can see from the table that the employer will hire only one worker. He cannot justify the second worker if he has to pay him $12 for an hour's work and receives only $10 (which is second laborer's market value) in return. On the other hand, if the wage rate is lowered to slightly below $10, the employer can justify hiring two laborers. Then the return to the employer from each laborer is greater than the wages paid to them. If the wage rate is dropped even further, to slightly below $4, the employer can hire as many as five workers. As we can see from the table, the value of the marginal product for five workers is then greater than or equal to $4.

Because of the line of reasoning presented above, economists argue that the *demand curve* for labor, like the demand curves for other goods, is downward sloping: that is, the lower the wage rate, if everything else is the same, the greater the quantity of labor an employer will hire. Theoretically, if this is true of one employer, it is true of all: the *market* demand curve for a given type of labor, suitable for a given use, is also downward sloping. We have, accordingly, drawn the market demand curve for mousetrap workers downward sloping in Figure 14·1.[5] This is a deduction which is more or less obvious once stated; however, as we will see, this inverse relationship between the wage rate and employment opportunities often

[4] From our study of competitive markets in Chap. 7, we concluded that competitors tend to be "price takers," meaning they must accept the going market price as a given. See Chap. 7 for a review of why this is true.

[5] The reader may get the impression that the market demand curve for labor is derived by horizontally summing the labor demands of individual firms, which in turn are derived directly from tables like Table 14·1 for each firm. Strictly speaking, this is not the case. However, to be perfectly correct in deriving the market demand curve for labor, the analysis would have to be further complicated, which is unnecessary for our introduction to the workings of labor markets. In addition, the conclusions we have developed regarding the general shape of the demand curve still hold in more sophisticated treatments. For further study, consult Richard H. Leftwich, *The Price System and Resource Allocation*, 5th ed. (Hinsdale, Ill.: The Dryden Press, 1976), Chap. 14.

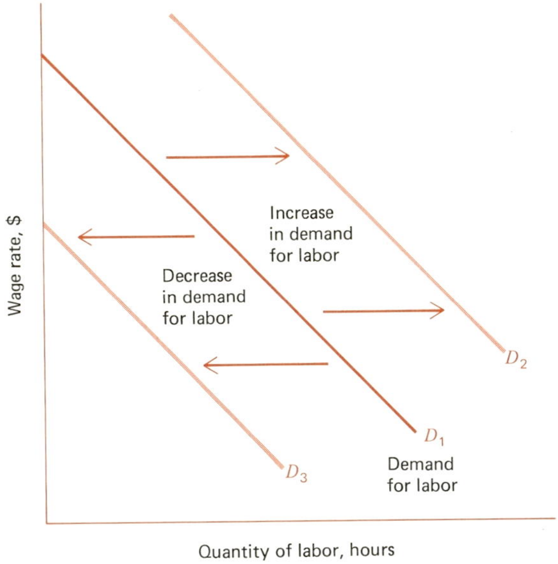

FIG. 14·1 The demand curve for labor, like all other demand curves, is downward sloping. A rightward shift in the demand curve from D_1 to D_2 represents an *increase* in the demand for labor; a leftward shift in the demand curve from D_1 to D_2 represents a decrease in the demand for labor.

becomes overlooked in public policy discussions on minimum wage legislation and on other laws relating to employment conditions of workers. The important point to remember is that profit-maximizing employers, except in cases of faulty judgment and for short periods of time, will not employ people if they have to pay them in wages and fringe benefits more than they are worth. How much they are worth is dictated by their productivity and what can be gotten in the market for what they produce.

If the price of the product, mousetraps in this example, increases, the employers' demand for mousetrap makers will rise, say, from D_1 to D_2 in Figure 14·1. Because the market value of the laborers' marginal produce will rise, producers will want to sell more mousetraps and will hire more workers to produce them.

Refer back to Table 14·1. Suppose the price of a mousetrap rises from \$2 to \$4. At a wage rate of \$10, the employer can then hire as many as four workers because the value of their marginal product is then above \$10. (The value of the marginal product of the fifth laborer would be only \$8 [2 mousetraps produced times \$4].) In a like manner, if the price of the final product falls below \$2, the demand for workers will also fall below D_1.

If worker productivity rises as the result of technological change, this can result (but not necessarily) in an increase in the demand for workers. If workers produce more, the value of their marginal product may rise and the employer can then afford to hire more of them. We must hedge our conclusion, however. An increase in worker productivity *can* result in a decrease in the demand for labor in that market. For instance, suppose worker productivity increases *across the industry*, not just in one or two firms. Increased productivity can mean more mousetraps are offered on the market and the price of mousetraps, because of the downward sloping demand for that product, will fall. The drop can be so great that it more than offsets the favorable effect of the productivity increase. In other words, the net effect on the value of the marginal product schedule *can be* negative—the demand will fall. In such event, an increase in productivity can be beneficial for consumers, who will pay less, but it can be harmful to employees in the mousetrap industry, who now have fewer employment opportunities and lower wages. Again, we emphasize that this seemingly perverse result is only a possibility and not a certainty. The opposite can result; the demand for labor can rise.

The Supply of Labor

The supply curve of labor generally slopes upward: in other words, more workers will be willing to work and they will be willing to work more hours at higher wage rates than at lower wage rates. For this reason, we have drawn the supply curve as S_1 in Figure 14·2. This rule can be demonstrated by asking class members how many are willing to work and how many hours they are willing to work at a given job for \$3, \$5, and \$7 per

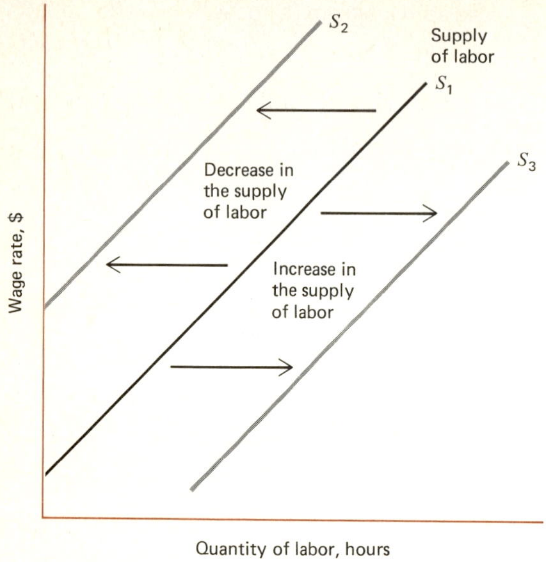

FIG. 14 · 2 The supply curve for labor is upward sloping. A rightward shift in the supply curve from S_1 to S_3 represents an increase in the supply of labor; a leftward shift in the supply curve from S_1 to S_2 represents a decrease in the supply of labor.

hour. We suspect that more students will be willing to work more hours at $7 per hour than at $4, illustrating that the supply curve is upward sloping.

There is a more complex explanation for the assumed upward sloping supply curve. Workers have many different things which they can do with their time. They can use their time to work at the construction of mousetraps, to work at any number of other jobs, to go fishing, etc. As we explained earlier in Chapter 2, the worker will rationally allocate his time in such a way that the marginal benefits of an hour spent doing any one thing are equal to the marginal benefits of the time that can be used elsewhere. Because some kinds of work are unpleasant, a wage must be paid to induce the worker to allocate some of his or her time away from, say, fishing into the production of, say, mousetraps. Rational workers will give up doing those alternative things that are of least value to them. The wage rate must be further raised to entice them to allocate even more time to the job, away from alternatives which are relatively more valuable.

Let us look at the problem of the employers who want to hire a greater number of workers instead of paying more money to get more production time from the same workers. If the wage rate is $4 per hour, employers will hire people who value their time spent elsewhere at less than $4 per hour. There are people who value spending their time elsewhere at more than $4 per hour; and if employers of mousetrap makers raise wages to $5 per hour, they can attract some of these people into making mousetraps. In both illustrations, the basic point is clear. The supply curve of labor is upward sloping: more labor is supplied at higher wages.

The supply curve of labor can change, and it will change, if the value of employees' alternatives changes. For example, if the wage which mousetrap makers can earn in toy production goes up, the value of their time has increased. The supply of labor to the mousetrap industry should then decrease from S_1 to S_2 in Figure 14·2. This type of shift in the supply curve of labor means that, at a given rate, a lower quantity of labor will be forthcoming into a particular market; and in order for the employer to be able to hire the same quantity of labor, a higher wage rate must be offered to the workers simply to keep them from taking their improved alternative.

The same general effect will occur if the value which workers place on some leisure-time activity increases. Because most people value staying at home with their families on holidays like Thanksgiving or July 4th, employers who want to keep their shops open or continue production generally have to pay substantially higher wages to those who will work. Needless to say, if for any reason the value of workers' alternatives decreases, the supply curve of labor will increase: if wages in the toy industry fall, more workers will want to move into the mousetrap business.

Equilibrium in the Labor Market

A competitive market is one in which neither individual employers nor individual employees have

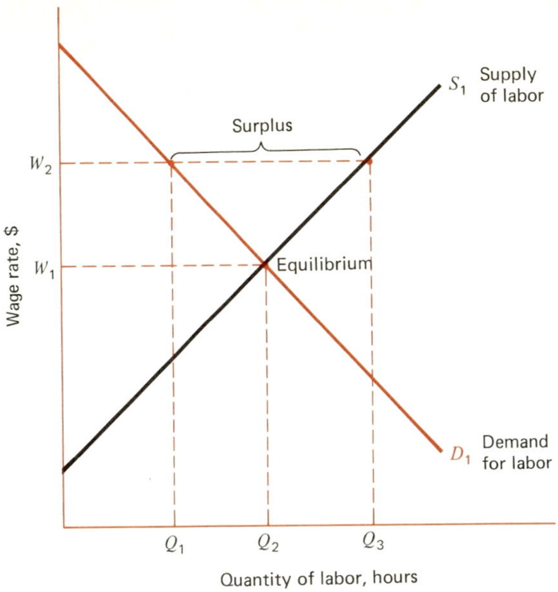

FIG. 14·3 Given the supply and demand for labor, S_1 and D_1, the equilibrium wage is W_1 and the equilibrium quantity of labor hired is Q_2. If the wage rate rises above W_1, a surplus of labor will emerge. At a wage rate of W_2, the surplus is the difference between Q_3 and Q_1.

the power to influence the wage rate. This is illustrated by the market demand and supply curves for labor in Figure 14·3. The wage rate will tend to settle at W_1. The quantity of labor employed will be Q_1. Note that at that combination, i.e., the intersection of the supply and demand curves, the laborers who are willing to work for W_1 can find jobs.

The equilibrium wage rate is determined in the competitive market in a manner which is very similar to the way the prices of goods and services are determined. At a wage rate of W_2, for example, the quantity of labor that employers are willing to hire is Q_1, whereas the quantity of workers willing to work is Q_3. Clearly, at that high wage rate there is a surplus of labor on the market. Notice that some of this labor, indicated by the supply curve, is willing to work for a wage that is less than W_2; the opportunity cost of their time is simply less than W_2. The workers who cannot find jobs in this labor surplus market can be expected to accept a lower wage; in doing so they will begin, over time, to replace those workers who have jobs. The workers who have lost their jobs must then compete by the only effective means they have at their disposal, that is, by lowering the wage they are willing to accept. In this manner, the wage rate falls toward W_1, and the quantity of labor that employers can afford to hire expands toward Q_2. The surplus of labor will be further reduced because some workers will withdraw from the market, reducing the quantity of labor supplied from Q_3 toward Q_2. As the rate falls, some workers will find that they have an opportunity, such as going fishing or getting another job, that is more highly valued than the opportunity to produce mousetraps. The surplus is eliminated at a wage rate of W_1. (Actually the *money* wage rate—i.e., how many dollars earned per hour—may not fall. What may happen instead is that the money wage rate may stay constant while the prices of what workers buy increase. In this event, the *real* wage rate—i.e., what the money wage rate will buy—falls, leading to the same general effects. Therefore, when we talk about wage increases or decreases, we are really talking about changes in *real* wage rates.)

We have not illustrated this in a graph; but if the wage rate were below W_1, we could show that the quantity of labor demanded by employers would be greater than the quantity of labor supplied. As a result of the shortage of labor, the employers, eager to hire more workers, would compete for the available supply of labor by offering higher wages. The higher wages would cause some employers to cut back on their hiring plans; this, in turn, would cause an increase in labor *supplied* on the market. In short, the wage rate would rise toward W_1 in a competitive market. There are, therefore, forces in a competitive market pushing the wage rate toward the equilibrium level, W_1.

NONWAGE DETERMINANTS OF EMPLOYMENT

We have conducted the discussion to this point *as if* the wage rate is the key determinant of employment, perhaps giving the impression that such considerations as job satisfaction and the way employers treat their employees are of little or no importance. Needless to say, this impression must be corrected, if for no other reason than that the authors consider the nonmonetary aspects of their employment conditions to be very important. Many people live in the Appalachian Mountains or the Rockies; in order to do this they may have forgone monetary income to acquire the benefits of the beauty of the surrounding area. Professors work in academe mainly because it affords them the opportunity to teach and write and to set their own work schedules: these are significant nonmonetary benefits. The congeniality of one's colleagues is another important determinant of where and how much people work. Others are attracted to their jobs because of the power that goes with the jobs or the public attention they receive, such as in TV news reporting.

These types of nonmonetary considerations affect many people. Ultimately this means that there are trade-offs between monetary and nonmonetary returns to work. The greater the number of people who desire the nonmonetary aspects offered by a given type of employment, the greater the number of people who will be willing to work at that type of employment. The supply will be greater—for example, S_2 as opposed to S_1 in Figure 14 · 4. The money wage rate will be correspondingly lower, W_1 as opposed to W_2. The workers naturally prefer W_2 to W_1. However, even though the money wage rate is lower, because of the nonmonetary dimensions of that employment, the workers, according to their own values, are better off. The nonmonetary benefits are equal to the vertical distance between S_1 and S_2. The *full* wage rate of employees is equal to this vertical distance plus the money wage they earn, W_1. Notice that the summation of these two components of the wage structure add up to *more* than W_1.

Two interesting observations should be made. Often when workers in different occupations compare money wages and find they are being paid different amounts, the issue of social justice is raised. This is frequently because the *full* wages (money plus nonmoney wages) are not being compared. One worker may be earning less in terms of money but receiving more in terms of nonmoney benefits (which are nontaxable, we might add). Worker A may be working less intensely and may suffer fewer pressures (and is therefore in a different labor market). If these factors are considered, the one earning the higher money wage rate may actually be earning less on a full-income basis. Certainly, many (but not all) executives who earn very high salaries have to give up much in the way of a home life and independence of thought. If they knew how to coach, many faculty members would probably require much higher salaries before they would take the job of their college's football coach, with all the risks of being fired that go with it.

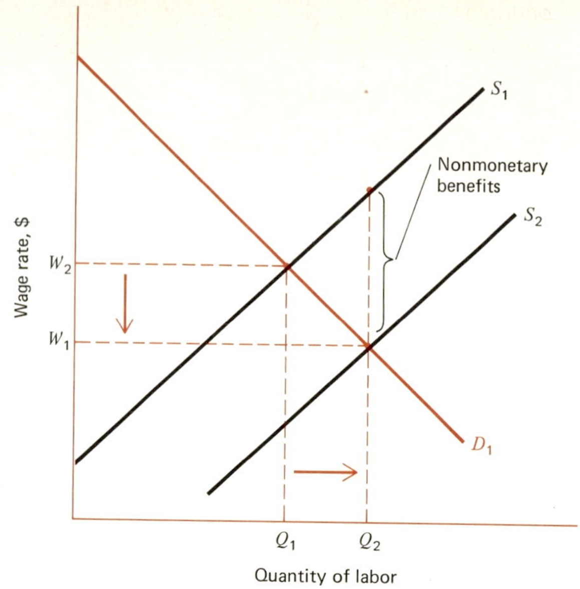

FIG. 14 · 4 The supply of labor will be greater for jobs which have nonmonetary benefits. This means that the money wage rate of workers who receive nonmoney benefits from their jobs will be lower. Given the demand for labor, the wage rate will be W_1 for workers who receive nonmoney benefits, illustrated by S_2. The wage rate will be higher, W_2, for workers who do not receive the nonmoney benefits, illustrated by S_1.

Employers can also benefit from providing their

employees with a favorable working climate: they can attract more workers and pay them less. At the same time, the workers' welfare may be enhanced over what it would have been if wages were higher and nonmonetary benefits lower. The benefits frequently are costly to employers, but they should still be used if they lower their wage bills by more than they raise their costs of production in other ways. In other words, employers have some economic incentive to be nice to their employees, to provide air conditioning, and to lower the noise level for them while they work. These things can raise worker productivity and lower the money-wage bills. Needless to say, there is a limit to how much the employer will do in these areas because there are trade-offs which must be considered. The employer may, for example, have to forgo building a company swimming pool in order to air-condition the working area. Again, the employer will not pay in terms of the *full* wage rate more than the worker is worth, and he will tend in a competitive labor market to pay all employees a wage rate equal to the marginal value of the last employee hired.

WHY WAGE RATES DIFFER

We are now in a position to address another question raised at the start of the chapter: Why do people receive different wages? An obvious response to that question is that the supply and demand conditions are different in different labor markets. As can be seen in Figure 14 · 5, given the available supply of labor, S_1, the greater the demand for labor, the greater the wage rate. With demand equal to D_1, the wage rate is W_1; the wage rate is higher, W_2, for the greater demand D_2. The wage rate is, given the demand for labor, lower for a greater supply of labor. With the supply equal to S_1 in Figure 14 · 5*b*, the wage rate is W_2; however,

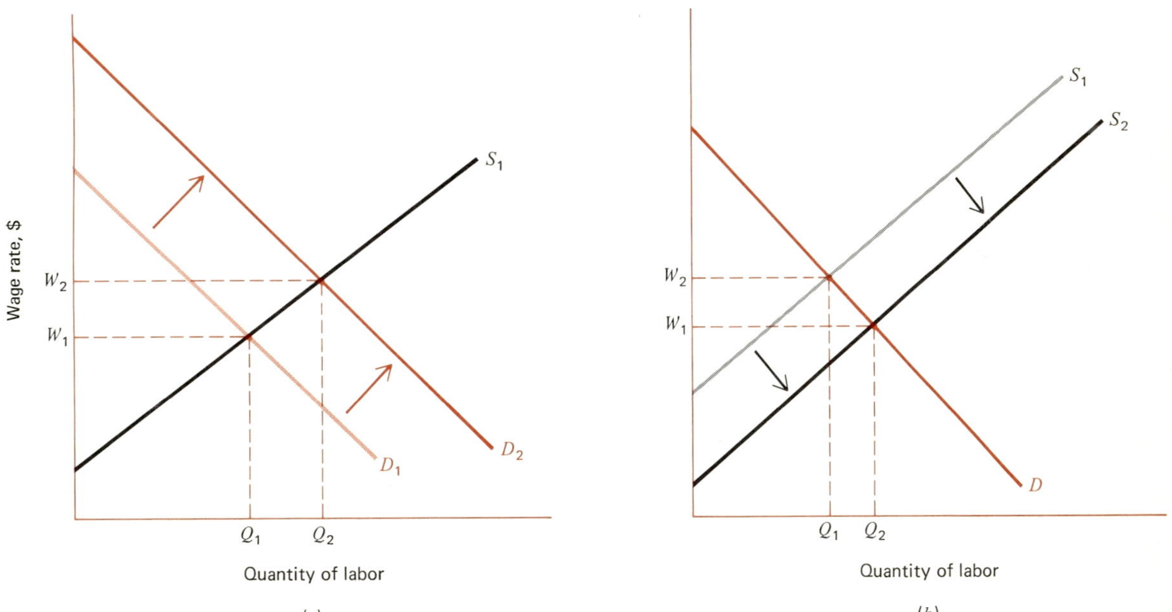

FIG. 14·5 As illustrated in part *a*, an increase in the demand for labor in a competitive labor market will result in an increase in the wage rate and the number of workers hired, and vice versa. As illustrated in part *b*, an increase in the supply of labor will result in a decrease in the wage rate and an increase in the number of workers hired, and vice versa.

the wage rate is lower, W_1, with the greater supply S_2.

In addressing the question of why wage rates differ, a more satisfactory answer can be developed. First, let us consider people in the same line of work. They may earn different wages because some are more productive than others. It follows, therefore, that they are in different labor submarkets with respect to the demand for labor. If one group of workers is more productive than another, employers may not only *have* to pay higher wages to more productive workers, but employers *can* pay them more. Employers will *have to* pay them more because their services are competitively sought. Employers *can* pay them more because their marginal product is greater to the firm.

Catfish Hunter has been, for a number of years, a highly paid baseball player. The New York Yankees have been able to justify his high salary because of his attraction to their fans. When he pitches, more people show up at the ball park. Furthermore, he has been a successful pitcher. Since a winning team generally attracts more supporters for all games than a losing one, Catfish's presence on the team has an additional, indirect effect on the team's earnings. He is, in other words, in a submarket for baseball players described by D_2 in Figure 14 · 5*a*, whereas other players are in a market which may be described by D_1.

Second, people in different lines of work earn different wages because consumers value differently the products that are produced. Automobile workers may earn more than textile workers because people place more value on (that is, they are willing to pay more for) automobiles than for clothing. This situation contributes to differences in the value of the marginal product of workers and to differences in the demand for labor. This explanation, *by itself,* however, cannot explain why wages in the automobile and textile industries are different over the *long run.* If wages are different in the two industrial areas, and there are no other compensating differences in employment, workers in the textile industry will, attracted by the higher wages in the automobile industry look for work there. The supply of labor in that industry will rise and the wage rate will be depressed. In the long run, the wage differential will tend to disappear.

The persistence of wage differential can be attributed to several factors. Because of their attachment to life in North and South Carolina, textile workers may be resistant to moving to Michigan, where automobiles are made. There may be nonmonetary benefits associated with textile work, as compared with automobile production, which actually make the full wage of each group more nearly equal. In addition, if textile workers do not have the skills necessary to do the work of automobile workers, the cost of their acquiring the needed skills can be a barrier to their entering the market for automobile workers. Finally, as we will explain in more detail in Chapter 15, unionization of automobile workers and the fact that many textile workers are employed by *monopsonistic employers*[6] may explain why wages are held up above their free-market rate in the automobile industry and are held below the competitive level in the textile industry.

Third, although wages may appear to be paid solely for the purpose of compensating the worker's effort, most wages are payment both for effort and for use of what economists call *human capital. Capital* is generally thought of as plant and equipment, for instance, the factory building and the machines it contains. The use of the term *human capital* may appear to be a strange twist of words. However, a capital is a man-made means of production—it is something which is produced or developed for the purpose of being used in the production of something else. Education enables a person to acquire (produce or develop) skills which can be used in the production of other things. The skills or knowledge a person acquires

[6] A *monopsony* is a single *buyer* of something, a single employer of a resource. (Remember that a *monopolist* is a single *seller*.) A firm with *monopsonistic power* is one which is such a large purchaser of the available labor supply relative to the size of the market that its employment decisions have a significant effect on the wage rate earned by workers. A firm in a highly competitive labor market is one whose employment decisions do not cause the wage rate to rise or fall.

are a form of capital—human capital. Wage differences reflect differences in effort which different workers are willing to expend at work *and* differences in the amount of human capital which different workers bring to the job. The educated worker, whether a top-notch mechanic or a registered nurse, is, in a manner of speaking, a capitalist; this person holds within himself capital assets and earns a rate of return on his investment. In acquiring that capital the individual, much like the business entrepreneur, takes a risk that these human capital assets will be outmoded before the person has a chance to fully utilize or exploit them. In the 1970s students majoring in history and social studies, expecting to teach, found this particular investment in human capital unprofitable; many have been unable to get positions which will make use of their skills.

Fourth, wage differences can be a consequence of social discrimination—sexual, racial, religious, ethnic, and political. Social discrimination is the process by which potential employees are grouped according to some easily identifiable characteristic, such as sex or skin color, and by which employment decisions are made, not on the basis of *individual* merit, but mainly on the basis of the *group* to which the individual belongs. For instance, a woman may be excluded from consideration for an executive job because, although she may be individually qualified, women as a group have been excluded. To the extent that employers believe, although incorrectly, that certain groups like women and blacks are less productive, or to the extent that employers have a distinct preference for working with certain groups like men, the labor market will be segmented. In a segmented labor market, employee groups in different submarkets face different demand curves and are unable to move easily from one market to another where different wages will be paid.

Without legal interference, discriminatory practices may remain in markets. However, competition among producers in the final goods market can *weaken* (but not eliminate) the forces and extent of discriminatory practices. Suppose that employers have a deep-seated prejudice against women; they believe that, on the average, women are less productive than men. Consequently, the market demand and wage rates for women are less than they are for men. If, on the average, women are in fact as productive as men, a producer, trying to outdo his market rivals, can hire women, pay them less, sell a product for less, and take away part of the rivals' markets. Caught in this type of competitive bind, market rivals will also have to hire women to keep their market shares. The result is that the demand for women rises while the demand for men falls, causing a general increase in the wages of women and a general decrease in the wages of men. The wage differential between men and women may not be eliminated by competition, but it can be less than what it otherwise would be: if everything else is equal, we should expect wage differences to be less in markets which are essentially competitive than in markets in which employers have significant market power. Put in other terms, the persistence of market power among employers can mean the persistence of social discrimination and, possibly, differences in productivity due to inculturated attitudes and skills.[7]

A fuller explanation of why wages differ may entail an inquiry into why the ability to work and attitude toward work differ among different labor groups. However, that is a task which would take us too far afield. We will leave it for advanced courses in sociology, psychology, and business administration. For now, we will employ the competitive labor market model to investigate the consequences of minimum wage laws and housing standards for migrant workers.

MINIMUM WAGE LEGISLATION

Congress enacted the first federal minimum wage law in 1938. At that time, the minimum wage was set at $0.25 an hour, and it carried the full support of unions. In 1977, the minimum wage was $2.30 an hour, and expectations are that it will rise fur-

[7] For more on sexual discrimination, see Richard B. McKenzie and Gordon Tullock, "Equal Pay for Equal Work," in *The New World of Economics* (Homewood, Ill.: Richard D. Irwin, Inc., 1978).

ther. Minimum wage laws have considerable support within the public; indeed, in some quarters opposition to them is met with the same resistance as opposition to motherhood. Nonetheless, most economists see significant deficiencies in this form of welfare legislation. The explanation emerges directly from the model of the labor market which we have developed.

The Employment Effects of Minimum Wage Laws

Consider Figure 14·3 again. If the market is competitive and left free of government intervention, the wage rate will settle at W_1. Suppose, however, that politicians consider this market wage too low to provide a "decent living" for the workers in this particular market. Therefore, they pass a law which requires employers to pay no less than W_2 (W_2 stands for the minimum wage, $2.30 in 1977). The predicted effect of the law is to reduce the employment opportunities of those workers who happen to be in the market: employers cannot afford to hire as many people, and the quantity of labor demanded falls from Q_2 to Q_1. Those persons who retain their jobs and receive the minimum wage are obviously better off; their take-home pay increases. However, these benefits may be small comfort to those workers who, because of the minimum wage, are no longer able to find a job in this market. These workers are in this market, presumably, because it is the best, if not the only, employment opportunity that they have. The minimum wage law forces them out of employment in their best alternative and into a market which they deem less desirable. Their *full* wage rate, that is, money plus nonmoney benefits, is reduced. The wage rate of some workers is reduced from a level which is deemed "unacceptable" by politicians and the public to the level of zero; that is, some workers will become unemployed.

Furthermore, we may note by reference to Figure 14·3 that the number of laborers willing to work increases with the introduction of the minimum wage. This means that the workers who would have otherwise had a job at W_1 have fewer employment opportunities at W_2 and have to compete with a larger number of workers for the available jobs.

It is easy to doubt these predictions of the effects of minimum wage laws. Admittedly, there is some theoretical support for the skepticism (which will be considered in Chapter 15). However, almost all empirical studies which have been done on the subject over the last three decades support the prediction. John Peterson and Charles Stewart have reviewed these studies and have concluded:

> The impression created in most government studies that federal minimum wage policy has produced no adverse effects is erroneous. . . . The general model of economic theory [that is, the competitive model] most clearly corresponds to the observed results of statutory minimums [that is, minimum wages], whereas the alternative models used to be nonpredictive in theory and in fact . . . .
>
> Minimum wage rates produce gains for some groups of workers at the expense of those that are the least favorably situated in terms of marketable skills or location.[8]

In a more recent study, Marvin Kosters and Finis Welch found that minimum wage laws tend to increase the instability of employment for people who are covered by the law, particularly nonwhites and the young.[9] When the demand for goods and services has fallen, indicating a need for a drop in market wages, wages cannot fall below the statutory minimums; and, consequently, employers have had to adjust to the changing market conditions by reducing employment. They cannot lower wages and, therefore, they cannot lower prices in order to boost sales.

[8] John M. Peterson and Charles T. Stewart, *Employment Effects of Minimum Wage Rates* (Washington: American Enterprise Institute for Public Policy Research, 1969), pp. 151–155.

[9] Marvin Kosters and Finis Welch, "The Effects of Minimum Wages on the Distribution of Changes in Aggregate Employment," *American Economic Review*, vol. 62, pp. 323–331, June 1972.

The most recent study of the employment effects of the minimum wage rate by James F. Ragan corroborates the earlier work. As expected, he found that the wage legislation was particularly detrimental to teenagers, especially nonwhite males. Using unpublished data collected by the Bureau of Labor Statistics, Ragan found that the boosts in the minimim wage from $1.25 in 1966 to $1.60 in 1972 increased the unemployment rate among teenagers by 3.8 percentage points. He goes on to suggest that the increases in the minimum wage rate between 1972 and 1977 have probably increased that figure to 4 percentage points. To the extent that Ragan's findings are correct, the minimum wage law explains why the unemployment rate among the young is so much higher that it is among other age groups.[10]

The Social Effects of Minimum Wage Laws

Strictly from an economic point of view, we may hypothesize three social consequences of minimum wage laws in competitive labor markets. First, to the extent that people are unable to find work, minimum wage laws can increase the number of people on welfare and unemployment. Second, minimum wage laws can have a positive effect on the level of criminal activity. One alternative to employment in legitimate labor markets is employment in the "crime industry." Some, but by no means all, of the workers displaced by minimum wage requirements may seek to earn a living by what is perhaps then the only means available to them, criminal activity. This hypothesis has not been tested; however, when a test is made, we would expect the effect to be particularly strong among teenagers, who are most likely to work in low-paying jobs and to be affected by the minimum wage laws.

Third, since at the minimum wage more people want a job than can find one, the employer, if he wishes, can discriminate on the basis of sex, race, religion, or any other grounds; just what basis he chooses to use depends upon his preference or prejudices. In short, although the effect may be small, minimum wage laws probably inadvertently encourage racial and sexual discrimination.

[10] James F. Ragan, "Minimum Wages and the Youth Labor Market," *The Review of Economics and Statistics*, 59, pp. 129–136, (May 1977.)

Other Nonmonetary Effects

To the extent that minimum wage laws keep *full* wage rates above their market equilibrium levels, employment opportunities will be reduced. However, the full wage rate will not rise by as much as the minimum money wage which must be paid. As we have explained, employers usually pay their employees partly in terms of money wages and partly in the provision of pleasant working conditions and other nontaxable fringe benefits. Assuming that employers are paying their employees as much in monetary and nonmonetary wages as their productivity will allow, an increase in the minimum money wage will cause employers to reduce their payments in nonmoney forms. Employers, for example, can reduce the "quality" of working conditions; they can turn down the air conditioning or raise productivity quotas. They can do this because the minimum wage law causes a surplus of labor on the market. The workers who retain their jobs may experience an increase in money wages, but they should also receive less in nonmoney forms.

The Political Support for Minimum Wage Laws

In view of these rather formidable arguments, why do minimum wage laws attract so much political support? Part of the answer is that the voting public is largely unaware of the effects of minimum wage legislation. Clearly, adverse employment effects are obscured by the myriad forces operating in the labor market. Furthermore, those who perceive the demand for labor as being vertical, or perfectly inelastic, will understandably be in favor of minimum wages; increasing the wage rate, from their perspective, does not affect employment opportunities. Another reason, just as important, is that a large segment of the population benefits from the minimum wage laws. Those who retain their jobs in spite of the legislation benefit directly in terms of a higher paycheck and have an incentive to support the legislation. Many college students favor minimum wage because they, being more productive and, perhaps, more knowledgeable than those who have not finished high school, are among those people who are least likely to be adversely affected by the laws.

Labor unions have a definite incentive to support minimum wage laws. To the extent that the government raises wages in the nonunion sectors of the economy, unions will be in a better bargaining position. The unions run less of a risk that their wage demands will cause their employers to move to nonunion sectors of the economy. A primary reason for union support of the first minimum wage legislation in the late 1930s is that many companies were moving out of the unionized North to the nonunionized South. The union expected, correctly, that minimum wage laws would retard this movement: the laws reduced the net benefits to firms moving south. Finally, minimum wage laws tend to impose a disproportionately heavy burden on young, unproductive workers who do not have the vote and who are least likely to understand those factors contributing to their employment problems.

THE HOUSING PROBLEM OF MIGRANT WORKERS

Beginning in the 1960s, a number of television news documentaries vividly portrayed the substandard, even squalid housing conditions of migrant workers. Most migrant workers typically lived in houses without bathrooms and running water. They often had to sleep on dirty mattresses thrown on the floor. To many people the obvious solution to this problem was to impose higher and stricter housing standards on employers who hire migrants for work in the fields. The consequence of the legislation has been reduced employment opportunities for migrants.[11] Many have benefitted from the standards; others, whose employment opportunities evaporated with the imposed standards, were made worse off.

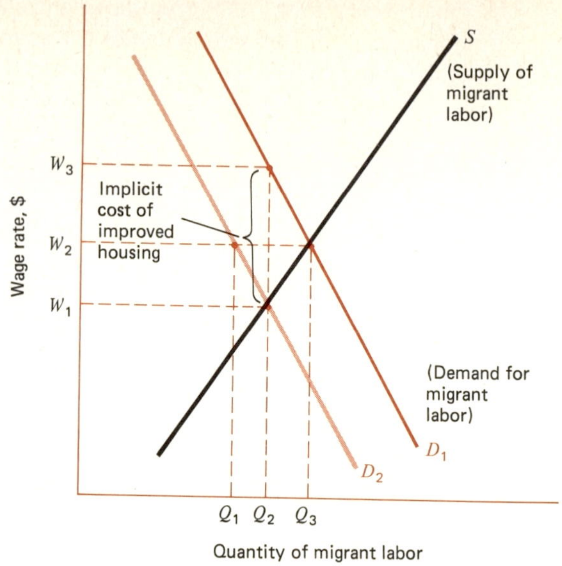

FIG. 14·6 Imposed higher housing standards for migrant workers reduce employers' demand for migrant workers. The reduced demand for migrant workers will lead to a lower money wage rate, W_1 instead of W_2, and fewer employment opportunities for some migrant workers.

To see why, consider Figure 14·6. We have depicted the supply and demand for migrant labor in that graph. Given the housing employers are willing to provide, D_1, the figure shows the *money wage rates* they are willing to pay migrants for their labor in a completely free market. If employers are forced to pay workers more in terms of higher housing standards, they will pay them less in money terms. Higher housing standards should cause the demand for migrant workers to fall vertically by the implicit cost of the improved housing. The new equilibrium money wage rate falls to

[11] Milton Friedman, "Migrant Workers," *Newsweek*, July 27, 1970, p. 60, and "Housing Dispute Spurs Migrant Farmers to Switch to Machines from Migrant Help," *Wall Street Journal*, June 29, 1970, p. 18.

W_1 and the employment opportunities fall to Q_2. Again, as in the case of imposed minimum wages, migrant housing standards can benefit those migrant workers who are able to find jobs; their *full* wage rises from W_2 to W_3 (W_1 in money wages plus W_3 minus W_1 in nonmoney housing form). However, for those workers who are then a part of the unemployed, the housing standards can reduce their real income below its already very low level; they may not agree that housing standards are a desirable public policy.

The employers of migrant workers may be viewed as unfeeling capitalists; and many of them, no doubt, have little concern for migrant workers. However, there may be many who are concerned but are caught in a competitive bind. Consumers want to buy their food at the lowest possible price. Producers must be able to sell their produce at a competitive price; this means that they must minimize their costs of production, including the *full* wage rate which they pay their employees. If they are forced to pay for better housing for their laborers, they must seek ways of keeping costs to the minimum. One way of doing this is to substitute other more productive forms of labor for relatively unproductive, unskilled migrant workers; another way is to substitute machinery for the hands of migrants. The increase in the cost of housing the migrants makes these alternatives relatively more attractive. This is precisely what has happened in many farm areas after stricter housing standards were imposed. It is for this reason that the employment opportunities of migrants may be predicted to fall.

The government may then try to correct the social problem that it has created with an imposed minimum wage. As we have explained earlier, this can only aggravate the employment problem of migrants. If the minimum money wage rate is set at W_1 in Figure 14 · 6, the employment opportunities will fall further to Q_3. Conceivably the government can enter the market and force employers to continue to hire as many workers as they once did, but this policy course makes for a political trade-off between individual freedom and welfare improvements for one group.

SUMMARY AND EXTENSIONS

In competitive labor markets, wage rates are determined by the interaction of willing suppliers of labor (employees) and demanders of labor (employers). The supply of labor is significantly influenced by nonmonetary benefits of employment and by the value which workers place on their alternative opportunities; the demand, on the other hand, is influenced by the price of the laborer's product and the laborer's productivity. Given the supply and demand model of labor which we have developed, two points are stressed: first, differences in money wage rates may not mirror true differences in the *full* money and nonmoney incomes of employees. Without complete recognition of the nonmoney component of incomes, faulty policy conclusions can be drawn. Second, in a competitive market any attempt to change workers' incomes through minimum wage laws and standards for working conditions can benefit some workers at the expense of others.

Conservative economist Milton Friedman has written, "The old saying is that Quakers went to the New World to do good and ended up doing well. Today, well-meaning reformers go to Washington to do good and end up doing harm."[12] Minimum wage rates do benefit some, if not most, of the people that

[12] Milton Friedman, "Migrant Workers," *Newsweek*, July 27, 1970, p. 60.

they were intended to benefit. However, the benefit comes at the expense of others whom the laws harm. Can the implied redistribution of income be construed as a clear-cut welfare improvement? Economic analysis cannot answer that highly subjective question; but economic analysis of the kind presented in this chapter will reveal the detrimental effects of such laws and will cause us to seek ways by which we can increase the employment opportunities of those whom we seek to help rather than reduce them.

QUESTIONS TO PONDER

1 In what ways are market-determined wages "just" or "unjust"? Explain.

2 The government requires that employers pay their employees time and a half for hours worked beyond 40 hours per week. What effect has this law had on the quantity of labor demanded? Why?

3 Does union support of laws preventing children from working have anything to do with the private interests of union members? Should society protect its members from some kinds of employment, regardless of the pecuniary elements? Why?

4 What effects have the minimum wage rate and migrant housing standards had on the prices of consumer goods? Explain those effects, using supply and demand curves.

5 Suppose that the government requires employers to pay a minimum wage rate of $10 per hour for workers over 22 years of age. What effect should such a law have on the employment opportunities of those persons over 22? What effect should such a law have on the employment opportunities and wage rates of persons less than 22 years of age?

RECOMMENDED READINGS

Fels, Rendigs, and Robert G. Uhler: *Casebook of Economic Problems and Policies: Practice in Thinking,* 2d ed. (St. Paul, Minn.: West Publishing Co., 1975), case 26.

Friedman, Milton: *An Economist's Protest: Columns in Political Economy* (Glen Ridge, N.J.: Thomas Norton and Company, 1972), chap. 8.

McKenzie, Richard B., and Gordon Tullock: *The New World of Economics: Explorations into the Human Experience* (Homewood, Ill.: Richard D. Irwin, Inc., 1978), chap. 7.

15

The Presence of Power in the Labor Market

Labor associations can do nothing to raise wages but by force; it may be force applied passively or force applied actively, or force held in reserve, but it must be force . . . . Those who tell you of labor unions bent on raising wages by moral suasion alone are like those who tell you of tigers who live on oranges.

Henry George[1]

PREVIEW OF CHAPTER

Central question

How do employer cartels and unions affect the wage rate that is paid and the employment opportunities of workers?

Major objectives

1 To explain how and to what extent firms with *monopsony* (*or market*) *power* in the labor market can affect wage rates and employment opportunities

2 To explain how and to what extent unions can affect wage rates and employment opportunities

3 To describe the inefficiency resulting from market power in labor markets and the benefits of competition

[1] Henry George, *The Condition of Labor: An Open Letter to Pope Leo XIII* (New York: United States Book Company, 1891), p. 86.

Major conclusions

1 The *marginal cost of labor curve* is derived from and lies above the supply curve.
2 Compared with a competitive labor market, a *monopsony* or an *employer cartel,* like the National Football League, will hire fewer players and pay lower wages.
3 Unions can raise the wage rates of their members by
   a Restricting the supply of labor in a given market
   b Negotiating for a higher wage rate through strikes or the threat of strikes
   c Increasing the demand for the product that union members produce
4 In most cases unions tend to reduce employment opportunities by artificially raising wages above the competitive level. They thereby tend to reduce the quantity of goods and services produced and the real incomes of consumers.

Important terms and concepts

Monopsony
Monopsony power
Marginal cost of labor
Marginal cost of labor curve
Unions

Competition is "bad" for those who have to compete. We emphasized this point in our discussion of competitive markets for hand calculators and farm commodities. However, the rule is just as applicable to employers who would prefer to control the competitive forces for labor as opposed to being controlled by them. The individual employer would prefer to have the option of paying employees less than the market wage; but competition, to the extent it exists, does not give an employer that choice.

In a like manner, the worker finds that competition for available jobs results in a reduction in the wage he might otherwise receive. Medical doctors, truck drivers, and barbers all have a definite interest in restricting the competition which exists in their own particular markets and, if necessary, in moving to labor markets where the force of competition is less intense. To the extent that they can band together and act as a group, workers can acquire a measure of control (i.e., "power") over their available employment opportunities and the wages they receive. As we will see, this power is difficult to maintain without the back-up support of the law or the threat of violence, whether real or imagined; and it comes at the expense of the consumer, who will have fewer goods and services available and will have to pay higher prices for what is bought. Simply stated, this chapter examines the existence of power in the labor market, the conditions that allow power to persist, its influence on the allocation of resources, and how it affects the real incomes of workers, consumers, and entrepreneurs.

A significant number of people in modern society is engaged in the acquisition of market and political power. A central theme of this chapter is that the exercise of power by one group in society can lead to market inefficiencies and to attempts by other groups to counter the power exercised by any one group. The end result can be a reduction in the general welfare of the community. This is a sweeping statement which we will explore in the next several pages. As seen from the perspective of this chapter, the economist's argument for competitive markets is an argument for the dispersion of power—not the garnering of it—in such a way that each individual (or firm) is unable to affect the general movement of the market and is free of the potentially destructive effects of power exercised by others.

THE POWER OF THE EMPLOYER

Power is never complete. It is always circumscribed by the imperfect nature of knowledge and the forces of law, custom, and the market. To understand the impact of power in the labor market we must begin by recognizing the limits to which any individual or group can accumulate and use market power. Within limits, employers can hire and they can fire; they can decide what products they will produce and, accordingly, what type of labor they will employ. However, there are presently many laws which restrict the conditions of employment as well as the employer's ability to discriminate among employees as to sex, race, age, and religious affiliation. Such legal restrictions impose costs on employers for going outside the legal boundaries and reduce the benefits from and the inclination toward discrimination.

Rules of common decency restrain an employer from "dressing-down" one of his workers for accidents or ineptness in front of others; such rules of common decency have also at times reinforced legal restrictions against racial and sexual discrimination. A competitive market imposes additional constraints on the behavior of employers. By definition, the employer in a highly competitive market is in a large-group setting. There is either a large number of employers in the same basic labor market or, given the freedom of others to enter, many other employers who stand ready to enter in the event that profit opportunities emerge. Competition for labor among the many employers pushes the wage up to a given level, forcing some employers to retreat from the market but permitting the ones who remain to hire the number of workers deemed desirable at that wage rate.[2]

There is no *economic* reason why the individual employer should pay (in money and nonmoney terms) more than this market wage. By the same token, if the employer tries to offer the workers less than the market wage, the employees can look for other jobs to any one of the other employers in the group, or to the employers who enter the market to take advantage of profit opportunities.

The individual employer in the highly competitive labor market (i.e., in the large-group setting) cannot restrict materially the employment opportunities of workers; in this limited sense alone, the competitor is said to lack significant market power.

He cannot control the employees' alternatives and, therefore, cannot control their wages. For the individual employer, the freedom of the competitive market is a highly constrained freedom.

Restrictive Employment Rules in Professional Sports and Universities

Owners of professional sports teams have developed complex sets of rules to govern the employment of athletes by teams within a given league. Teams of the National Football League (NFL), for example, acquire rights to negotiate with promising college players through the "annual draft," and these rights are assigned in an inverse relationship to a team's win-loss record during the previous season. That is, the team with the poorest record is given first choice in each round of the draft; the team with the best record, the last

[2] The competitors for the services of labor who actually do not hire employees but who would if the wage were sufficiently low are just as important to the determination of the wage rate as are people at an auction who bid on items but who never buy because the price always goes above the price they are willing to pay. They keep the price from falling. The market power of the Southern textile firm to lower wages is constrained by many other employers who will move into town if the wage there falls. The wage in this sector of the economy still is quite low.

draft choice.[3] Once the player has been drafted by one team, no other team in the league can negotiate with him. Teams can buy and sell draft rights and rights to players once drafted, but the rules explicitly prohibit league teams from competing with one another for the services of any player.[4] Violations of the rules carry stiff penalties or, ultimately, revocation of the team's franchise. Why do you suppose this is true?

The National Collegiate Athletic Association (NCAA for short) also has rules which govern the recruitment and retention of college and university athletes and which, as far as intent is concerned, are similar to those which characterize professional sports. The NCAA restricts the number of athletic scholarships schools can give for different sports and the stipends and fringe benefits athletes can receive. Furthermore, once enrolled in a four-year college or university, a player cannot change schools without losing a year of eligibility. Why?

The University of North Carolina system, which is composed of 16 campuses scattered throughout the state, is a major employer of faculty within its geographical region. Like most other state university systems, North Carolina has a very interesting rule governing employment. One university, such as East Carolina University, cannot consider hiring an art professor from, say, the University of North Carolina at Chapel Hill unless the artist first applies for the position and unless the Chancellor at East Carolina has permission from the Chancellor at Chapel Hill to consider the artist for employment. In fact, no one at East Carolina is even supposed to talk with the artist about employment until permission is obtained to do so.[5] Rules of this kind are typically called "antipirating" agreements and have been developed, usually in less overt terms, among other employer groups. Why do they exist?

The argument used in support of the type of employment rules found in professional sports and university systems is that the rules protect the "weak" from the "strong." The NFL contends, for instance, that without the draft system and the reserve clause, which after employment contractually ties a player to a club, the financially strong teams would be able to raid financially weaker teams for their good players, making for a noncompetitive sport. This may be true. However, these rules can cause other results as well. We will analyze this situation in the next section using our supply and demand model. For example, we show that these rules can be a means by which the intensity of competition for athletes and faculty members is reduced and by which salaries of workers in these specialized areas are held down. The rules, in short, are a means by which employers, through collusive action, have tried to acquire a degree of *market power* or, what amounts to the same thing, *monopsony power* over the workers they hire.[6] As we will show, where the rights to players can be sold to other employers, as is true in professional sports, the rules cannot protect the weak from the strong and do not hold down the cost of business; they merely redistribute income from workers and consumers to employers.

[3] One qualification needs to be added: the winner of the Super Bowl is given the last draw, regardless of its regular-season win-loss record. Furthermore, at this writing the draft system is being challenged in the courts, and it is uncertain whether or not it will be permitted to continue. Our discussion of professional football employment rules is meant to explain why the system was organized in the first place and why players may challenge it in the courts.

[4] Teams in different leagues, however, can compete for the same players. Teams in the Canadian Football League, for example, compete with the NFL for players.

[5] Administrative Memorandum No. 6 from President William Friday, University of North Carolina system, Nov. 1, 1972. Actually, the policy stipulated here applies to all university personnel, including clerical workers, and the rule has been unanimously endorsed by the chancellors of the 16 member institutions.

[6] A *monopsonist* is defined as the sole *buyer* of any good, service, or resource, and the term stands in contrast to *monopoly*, which is a single *seller* of a good or service. An example of a monopsony is, perhaps, a large coal-mining company in a small town with no other industry. However, the term is most frequently used, as it is here, to indicate a sole or dominant employer of labor in a given market. Strictly speaking, a firm which is not the sole employer but is a dominant employer of a given type of labor is said to have *monopsony power*. A firm has monopsony power if in order to expand its use of labor it must increase the wage rate, i.e., if it faces an upward sloping labor supply curve. To say the same thing in another way, a firm with monopsony power can influence the market wage rate by changing its demand for labor.

The Employer Cartel in Professional Football

To illustrate the benefits to employers in cartels like those found in sports and university systems, consider a model of the football players' market which, admittedly, is not fully descriptive. The model can be made more descriptive and more complicated once basic points have been made. Assume that all football players in a given submarket are alike in most important football skills. Furthermore, assume that the downward sloping demand curve D_1 in Figure 15·1 reflects the *market* demand for these players by the teams in the professional league and that the upward sloping supply curve S_1 represents the number of players who are willing to play at different wage rates.

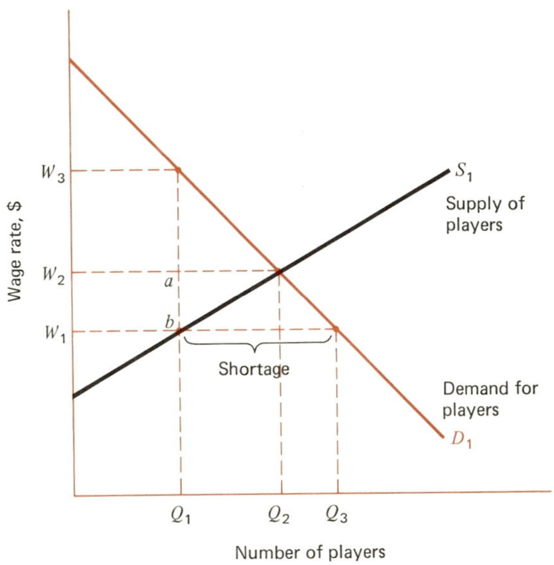

FIG. 15·1 In a competitive market, the wage rate will be W_2. However, in pushing up the wage rate to that level, employers impose costs on one another. For instance, if the wage rate were W_1, there would be a shortage of labor, employers would compete for the available labor by offering a higher wage, and all workers would have to be paid the higher wage rates that are bid.

If all teams act independently of one another—that is, if they act competitively—the market wage rate will rise toward W_2; the number of players signed will move toward Q_2. These movements occur because at any other wage rate there are gaps (shortages or surpluses) between the number of players demanded by teams and the number of players willing to play ball. At a wage of W_1, below equilibrium, the number of players demanded is Q_3, which, as can be seen in the graph, is greater than the number of players willing to sign, Q_1. There is, in other words, a shortage of players in this market equal to the distance between Q_3 and Q_1. As indicated by their demand for players, teams are willing and able to pay more than the low wage of W_1; indeed, one or more of the teams are willing to pay the Q_1 players as much as W_3. Given what teams are willing to do and the existing shortage, the market wage will rise as team owners bid for players.

An increase in the wage rate encourages more players to offer their services to the teams. However, what is most important for you to understand is that as long as there is a shortage, the competitive bidding which occurs in the market imposes costs on the teams. The team that bids for a player at a wage higher than W_1 imposes a (external) cost on the other teams. The other teams must then bid a comparable wage in order to retain the players whom they have, or, if they want to acquire additional players, they may have to bid an even higher wage for them. Then other teams must counter with a higher wage. In this manner, the competitive process (as in an auction) results in all teams imposing reciprocal costs on one another as they bid, a situation which is beneficial to players but detrimental to owners. Wherever possible, owners should be expected to seek, through collusion, ways of reducing the reciprocally imposed cost. The goal of reducing the intensity of competition is in the "common interest" of team owners; and as we studied in Chapter 6, where the group is sufficiently small, the common interest can serve as a motivational force for group action. The "common interest" is paticularly easy for professional sports teams to pursue since teams can be excluded from the

TABLE 15·1

Number of Players Willing to Sign (1)	Annual Wage of Each Player (2)	Total Wage Bill [(1) × (2)] (3)	Marginal Cost of Additional Player [Δ(3)] (4)
1	$20,000	$20,000	$20,000
2	22,000	44,000	24,000
3	24,000	72,000	28,000
4	26,000	104,000	32,000
5	28,000	140,000	36,000
6	30,000	180,000	40,000

Note: The annual wage rates are hypothetical, stated only to make a general point.

league if they fail to abide by the contractually agreed upon rules.

In a competitive labor market, the cost of each additional player to the league (as opposed to any given team) is actually greater than that which is indicated by the wage paid to him. This is because, in a competitive market, any increase in wages paid to one player must be extended to all players who are more or less equal, even if some of them were originally willing to work for less than the going market wage: the cost of each *additional* player is the wage paid to him in order to retain his services plus the extra salary that must be paid to all previously hired players.[7] To see this more clearly, consider the hypothetical data in Table 15 · 1. (The number of workers in this table has intentionally been kept small to simplify, as much as possible, the required computations. Besides, the general points made are the same as those derived with an example involving much larger numbers.)

The first two columns of the table describe the assumption underlying normal labor supply curves: as the wage rate rises, a greater number of players is willing to play ball. (Because we want only to make a general point, these figures are hypothetical.) If only one player is demanded by all teams, the annual salary required to hire him is what is indicated in column 2, $20,000. The *total* cost of this player to the league is also equal to this amount (shown in column 3). If, on the other hand, two players are demanded, and if the second player will not sign until the going salary is raised to $22,000, in order to have two players in the league the salary of both players must be raised to $22,000. If the first player's salary is not raised, he can quit, leaving the league with only one player. The first player can, therefore, demand and receive a $22,000 salary when the second player is hired. The cost of the second player coming into the league is, therefore, $24,000, as indicated in column 4 of the table: $22,000 for his services plus the $2,000 raise given to the first player.

The cost of each additional player, which is recorded in the remaining portion of column 4, can be derived in a similar manner. Assume the third player will not work for less than $24,000; then the cost of the third player to the league is greater than this. It is equal to the $24,000 salary paid to him plus the $2,000 raise which must now be given to each of the first two players: $24,000 plus $4,000 equals the cost of the third player, $28,000. Skipping down the column, the cost of the sixth

[7] Because the wage rises from W_1 to W_2, the total wage bill for the first Q_3 players rises by the wage increase $W_2 - W_1$ times Q_1 players, or by the area W_2bW_1 in Fig. 5 · 1.

player is the $30,000 salary paid to him plus the $2,000 raise that is given to each of the first five players for a total league cost of $40,000. The extra salaries that must be paid in each case are the reciprocal costs mentioned above.

Except for the first player, the marginal cost of each additional player is greater than the wage that is paid to any one player at each level of employment. Furthermore, the gap between the marginal cost of labor and the wage paid expands as the number of players hired increases. When only two players are hired, the gap is $2,000 ($24,000 − $22,000); the gap is much greater when six players are employed, $10,000 ($40,000 − $30,000). The *marginal cost of labor curve* is simply a plotting of points contained in columns 1 and 4. Therefore, if we graphically illustrate the relationship between the marginal cost of labor curve and the supply curve, they will take on the general appearance of the two curves in Figure 15·2, with the marginal cost of labor curve lying above the supply curve.

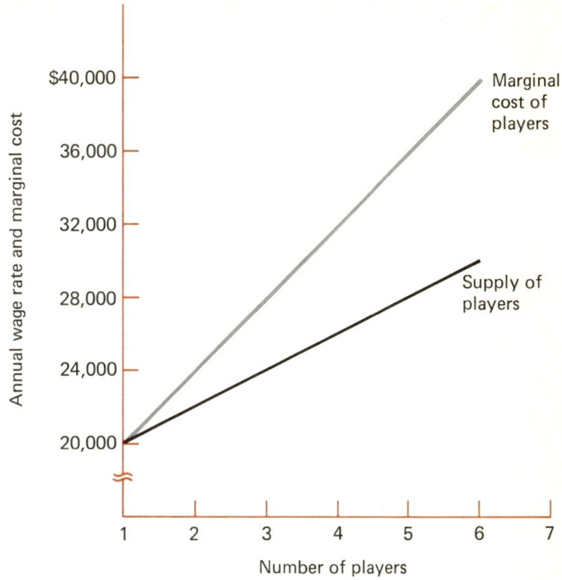

FIG. 15·2 An upward sloping supply curve means that a higher wage rate must be offered to attract more workers. This means that the marginal cost of workers, as for football players, is greater than the wage that is paid. Therefore, the marginal cost of labor curve lies above and diverges from the supply curve of labor. (See Table 15·1 for the information underlying the curves.)

A football league breaks down the competition for players by devising rules for employment and through forming a kind of "employer cartel."[8] In trying to maximize league profits and, therefore, individual team profits, the employer cartel will devise rules in such a way that the marginal cost of the last player (MC_L) hired by the league is equal to the marginal value of the last player (MV_L) hired by the league. The league's market demand curve for players reveals the marginal value of each player to the league. To graphically illustrate the optimum employment level of the cartel, combine the marginal cost and supply curves of Figure 15·2 with the market demand curve of Figure 15·1. This is done in Figure 15·3. Following the rule for optimum employment ($MC_L = MV_L$), the profit-maximizing cartel will tend to hire only Q_2 players.

Why does the employer cartel hire only Q_2 players? Why not some other number? The answer is revealed in the graph. Suppose the cartel employed only Q_1 players. By vertically moving up through the graph we can see that the marginal *value* of the Q_1st player (in terms of additional revenues gained by the league) equals MV_1; the marginal *cost* of that player, on the other hand, is much less, MC_1. The league can increase its profits by hiring that player plus every other player between Q_1 and Q_2: the marginal value of each player between Q_1 and Q_2 is greater than the marginal cost to the league; the employment of each of these players, therefore, raises the league's profits. Beyond Q_2, the reverse is true: the marginal cost of each player to the league is actually greater than his marginal value to the team. Therefore, the league's profits are reduced by hiring more than Q_2 players.

[8] Under competitive market conditions, the number of players employed is the point at which the labor supply and demand curves intersect, or Q_3 players. This number, as can be seen, is greater than what we would expect to be hired when the market is cartelized, as is the case in the football league.

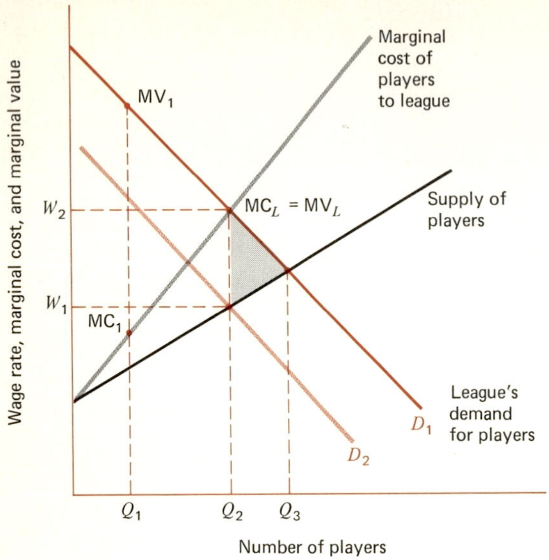

FIG. 15·3 Employers will hire labor up to the point where the marginal value of the last worker equals his or her marginal cost. For a monopsonistic employer of football players, the optimum number of players hired is Q_2. The inefficiency in this employment level is illustrated by the shaded area in the figure.

Having decided on Q_2 players, the league can develop employment rules that will reduce the market demand for labor to D_2, which means that the market wage will be W_1. Notice that W_1 is all the teams have to pay to ensure that Q_2 players are hired. Of course, if the teams were forced by circumstances to pay more, they would be willing to do so; in fact, they would be willing to pay as much as W_2 for Q_2 players. The cartel, however, is organized to prevent teams from competing with one another and paying players their market value.

Wage Discrimination in Professional Football

To this point we have explicitly assumed that all players in the football submarket are more or less alike in their abilities and salary levels. However, most players differ significantly in their abilities and have different opportunity costs for their services. Some players are able to run and block better than others, and some have nonfootball opportunities which are more lucrative than those of other players. Through the draft system, team owners are given exclusive rights to negotiate with each player they draft; and, as we can show, this usually means that owners can discriminate among players as to the wages they pay.

In a fully cartelized labor market, all a player can do in negotiating with the team that has drafted him is either play or withhold his services from that team; he does not have the option of turning down one team's offer in favor of another. If he withholds his services, the best salary he can receive is equal to his best nonfootball opportunity. Therefore, of two players, the one with the higher opportunity cost will be able to bargain for a higher salary, if everything else is equal. His higher nonfootball salary has put him in a better bargaining position vis-à-vis the team; he has a greater incentive to hold out for a higher salary. Indeed, we should not be at all surprised to find cases in which players of more or less equal football abilities but different opportunity costs are paid differently. In fact, a player's higher opportunity cost can, in the bargaining process, be more influential in determining his salary than his football abilities. This is so simply because employment rules reduce the degree to which teams have to compete for players on the basis of their athletic abilities.

Our discussion of wage discrimination is not meant to suggest that players are never able to negotiate salaries which are greater than their opportunity cost—many of them obviously do. However, cartel rules significantly reduce the strength of players' bargaining positions and, to that extent, the wages they are able to receive. If this were not the case, we would be hard pressed to explain the employment rules of the National Football League.

Nevertheless, there are several reasons why players may be paid more than their opportunity cost. First, there is some competition between the National Football League and the Canadian Football League. Second, some players are more adept at bargaining over salaries than others; they are able to bluff their way into salaries which exceed their best nonfootball opportunity. In addition, certain players have unique talents and personalities which are virtually impossible to duplicate. There is only one O. J. Simpson, and he has considerable *monopoly* power over the sale of his skills. When a *monopsonist* (like a football league) faces a *monopolist* (like O. J. Simpson), the final negotiated wage depends largely upon the relative market strengths and bargaining skills of the parties involved.

Third, a player's ability to perform on the field depends heavily on his mental state. A player who is seriously disgruntled because he considers his salary "unfair" may not play up to his ability. Furthermore, if a player whose skills are better than those of other players is not paid commensurately with his skills, he may reduce the effort he makes to the point where his "output" is equal to that of others. So long as he is doing as well as his teammates for the same pay, the team will have no incentive to replace him. Consequently, a team is usually willing to pay its better players more than their opportunity wage to ensure that it will be able to demand more from them. Fourth, a team actually runs a risk when it allows a superstar to hold out for even a part of a season. With the player absent from the lineup, attendance can fall off, causing a significant drop in the team's gate receipts. To avoid this risk, a team has an incentive to concede to the player's demands.[9]

The Sale of Player Rights

Professional football teams can, given league rules, sell or trade their "rights" (contracts) to players once players have been drafted and signed. A team interested in maximizing its profits always stands ready to sell, at some price, the rights to its players. Furthermore, to the extent that players are signed for less than their true market value, other teams will want to buy the rights to those players; that is, there will be a market demand for player rights. Through the interaction of supply and demand and the implied competitive forces among the owners, market prices will be placed on these rights which are roughly equivalent to the difference between the true market value of the player and the contracted salary. For instance, if the present value[10] of the salary paid to a player over the course of his expected sports career is $100,000 and the present value of the benefits a team can expect to receive from having the player playing with them is $200,000, the rights to this player should sell for roughly $100,000. It follows that the greater the market value of a player and/or the lower the negotiated salary, the higher the market price for the player's rights.

Recognition of market price for player rights brings to light two very important points. First, to the extent that the rules of the employer cartel permit teams to negotiate salaries with players who are paid less than their true market price, the price of the player's rights is raised by the employment rules. The rules tend to benefit the owners of the teams, who can sell those rights at the expense of the players. The teams, therefore, incur costs of employing players which approximate the players' true market wage. If a team buys rights to players from other teams and uses the players, it incurs a cost equal to the salary of the player plus the interest income lost on the money paid out for the player's rights.[11] If the team continues to employ a player the rights to whom can

[9] For further discussion of factors determining player salaries in professional sports, see Simon Rottenberg, "The Baseball Players' Market," *Journal of Political Economy*, June 1956, pp. 242–258, reprinted in Harry G. Johnson and Burton A. Weisbrod, eds., *The Daily Economist*, (Englewood Cliffs, N.J.: Prentice-Hall, Inc., 1973), pp. 57–76.

[10] You may recall from Chap. 2 that the present value of any future expenditure is less than any equal expenditure made currently. By suggesting that the present value of the player's salary is $100,000, we are saying that the team would just as soon make a $100,000 payment to the player now as meet his regularly scheduled annual salary payments in future years which add to more than $100,000.

[11] Remember, if a team pays $100,000 for the rights to a player, they do not have the $100,000 to place in a savings account or to invest in bonds. Therefore, when a team spends $100,000 on a player, it loses the interest income from the savings account or bonds.

be sold to another team, the team incurs the cost of the player's salary, plus the payments it could have received from the player's rights, plus the interest income that could have been had if the rights had been sold and the acquired funds invested. Again, the full explicit and implicit cost of the player will approximate the player's market value.

Second, as noted earlier, the NFL contends that the draft system and the reserve clause in players' contracts are needed to protect financially weak teams from being raided of their good players by financially strong teams. If rights to players can be sold, this argument clearly loses much of its force. If the financially strong teams cannot hire a player by bidding directly for him in the labor market, they can hire him by buying the rights to him from the team that acquired the rights in the draft. If the weak team is unwilling to pay the full market wage for the player, it will be unwilling to pass up an offer from another team for the player's rights which is equal to the difference between the player's salary and what the player would receive in a competitive labor market.

Furthermore, as economist Simon Rottenberg has noted, there is no reason to believe that a financially strong team will actually raid other teams of *all* their good players.[12] If game attendance is dependent, at least in part, on close, exciting games, a team that raids other teams of their best players and, accordingly, consistently demolishes its opponents on the field may find that its attendance and its gate receipts fall. Therefore, there is some point at which hiring an additional highly skilled football player hurts the financially strong team more than it helps. In other words, there is some optimum number of good players that even the best team will seek in order to develop a team which wins often enough to keep the game interesting. The experience of the New York Yankees illustrates the principle developed here. The Yankees found that during the 1950s and early 1960s, when they were winning baseball pennants almost by habit, the attendance at their games began to fall off. There are many reasons for the drop in attendance; however, this section suggests one possible reason which may be overlooked. At any rate, when the Yankees began to lose in the mid-1960s, attendance picked up again.

The Efficiency of the Employer Cartel

To the degree that an employer cartel, like that in football, restricts the employment level, as to Q_2 in Figure 15·3, the labor of workers is inefficiently allocated among the employees' alternative employments. A little reflection on the meaning of the curves in Figure 15·3 will tell us why. The supply curve reveals the minimum wage football players are willing to accept to play ball; this minimum wage, in turn, can be thought of as the value of the players' time in their best nonfootball employment opportunity. The league's demand for players, on the other hand, reveals the value which team owners place on their players' efforts in football.

Notice in Figure 15·3 that between Q_2 and Q_3 the marginal value of each player, shown by the demand curve, is greater than the wage.[13] In short, the time of these players is valued more highly in football than it is in their best nonfootball alternative; players can create more market value for consumers by playing football than they can by doing anything else. However, to the degree that the employer cartel is unable to discriminate among players in wages paid, the number of players hired will fall short of Q_3 (the competitive level) and will approximate Q_2 (the cartel level). In this sense, resources are allocated inefficiently. The extra consumer value which is lost is equal to the shaded area in Figure 15·3; this is the amount by which the marginal value of each player in football exceeds the players' opportunity cost. In short, the fans as well as the players lose from the employers' cartel.

Those people who believe there is too much emphasis on football in our country and too little emphasis on the production of other goods and

[12] Ibid.

[13] Beyond Q_3 the marginal value of each additional player is less than what the player can earn elsewhere.

services may see hidden benefits in the employer cartel. Because of the cartel, some potential football players ($Q_3 - Q_2$) will not be hired. However, these players can then seek employment elsewhere and eventually, perhaps, will increase the production of some other good. This argument suggests that the restrictions in professional football can be "socially beneficial," as defined by those who dislike football, to the extent that nonfootball goods and services are produced; all we can do is note that there is in the argument a criterion for judging how resources should be allocated which is distinctly different from the market criterion used by economists. Admittedly, the economist's efficiency criterion is defective in establishing what is "socially good or just." However, it is a criterion which is manageable and takes account of the preferences of consumers as they are revealed in the marketplace.

Some General Comments

The model which we have developed for the employer cartel in football is applicable to a wide range of employment rules which restrict competition, and it illustrates why employers like to set up such rules. Our model suggests that the National Collegiate Athletic Association, for instance, has formulated very rigid rules for recruitment of college athletes because, among other reasons, it reduces what universities have to pay their players. University athletic administrations and the student body benefit. Essentially, the system imposes a tax on players, the benefits of which are received, through the restricted market, by others who own and manage the teams.

There are other employment rules which have the same effect. A salary schedule is laid down by the Civil Service Administration for federal workers that admittedly reduces the cost of deciding how much federal workers must be paid; but it also reduces the competition among departments for government workers and, thereby, may reduce the salaries they are paid. Furthermore, many large companies which represent a significant force in their own particular labor markets set restrictions on the salaries which different departments can pay for various categories of workers. To the extent that the rules are obeyed, the firms gain the benefits of their monopsonistic market position.

As an example of restrictive employment rules within a large firm, consider the situation of one of the authors. His secretary is paid out of nonuniversity funds—mainly grants from federal and private sources. At the time of this writing, the author would like to pay his secretary more than the limit authorized by the university's salary schedule for secretaries. However, although the money which constitutes this secretary's salary does not come out of university funds, the university will not allow her to be given a raise. Officials insist that her salary must parallel the salaries of other secretaries paid by the university. This is simply because the university fears, correctly, that if it decrees otherwise, a precedent will be set that will lead to intradepartment competition for the services of the university's secretaries. To prevent this and keep the best secretaries from going to those professors who can pay more through grant monies, the university will have to raise the salaries of secretaries who are paid directly from university sources. The employment rules restrict competition and reduce the total wage bill of the university. The rules, however, contribute to inefficiency in the allocation of labor and raise questions concerning the legitimacy of the resulting income distribution.

Although employer cartels are easy to set up in some labor markets, collusion among employers can be very difficult to develop and maintain. If a large number of employers each hires only a very small fraction of the total labor force, collusion is particularly difficult. For instance, it is very difficult for owners of hot dog and hamburger stands in large metropolitan areas to effectively collude on their individual demands for the types of workers they hire. If all employers manage to collude and decide collectively to reduce their demand for labor, the wage can fall. However, once the wage has fallen, there is an incentive for each firm to take advantage of the lower wage by expanding the number of workers employed. If the individual firm is small, an increase in employment will not alone materially affect the market wage rate. Furthermore, in a free market, new firms will enter the labor market to take advantage of the artificially low wage. In other words, each employer—each owner of hamburger stands—has an incentive to chisel on any collusive agreement in the labor market. If many employers chisel, competition will return, leading to increases in the market wage rate. Given the incentive to chisel, the cost of forming a workable cartel can be so great that no one will attempt to form one. This is typical of most labor markets; it is certainly characteristic of employers of workers for hamburger stands. Only in labor markets dominated by a small number of employers are we likely to find workable cartels. The employer cartels in professional sports work in part because the number of teams is relatively small and, more important, because the league can impose costs on teams for violating the cartel rules by revoking franchises.[14] The government's employment rules work because of the controls which the federal government has on the budgets of departments; positions are simply not funded for more than the salary limits.

THE POWER OF THE EMPLOYEE

In a highly competitive labor market, an individual worker *in that market* is, by definition, powerless to do anything about the wage he earns or the conditions of his employment. This powerlessness is largely due to the behavior of his fellow workers, not to his employers, although the market position of employers is involved. The individual worker must accept the going market wage; by demanding a higher wage, the worker may be turned down in favor of other workers in the same market who are willing to accept the market wage. The ordinary textile worker is in this type of competitive bind. When applying for a job, he must accept the offer made by the personnel officer who interviews him—little or no bargaining is involved. Similarly, the textile worker is unable to object to his annual wage increment, because it generally reflects conditions in the textile labor market.

In short, competition means that the welfare of the individual worker in a labor market is controlled by what others, acting independently of one another, are willing to accept as terms of employment. The willingness of one worker to accept the market wage imposes a cost on those workers who would like to see the wage pushed up to some higher level. Nevertheless, individual workers can surmount these forces in two fundamental ways: (1) skill differentiation and (2) union organization.

Differentiation of Labor Skills

By making use of one's natural mental and physical talents or by developing new ones through acquisition of human capital (e.g., education), the individual worker can "differentiate" his labor from that of others. One may move into a totally new and different labor market, a market which one has all to oneself or in which there are few competitors who are not inclined to accept low wages and/or poor working conditions. In either case, what the individual worker must accept as the terms of employment is less dependent upon what other workers are willing to do and more dependent upon what consumers are willing to pay for his services, isolated from the services of all other workers.

Although we hear considerable discussion of the ability of unions to marshal market power for workers, over the decades skill differentiation has probably been the single most important means by which workers have acquired some control over their own employment. High school students accept jobs as menial workers in order that at some later date the work experience gained will make them relatively more attractive to employers in a different labor market. Students go to college for the social life and, at times, for the joy of learning; but many go also to improve their skills

[14] Even in professional sports, teams have found legitimate ways to circumvent employment rules and chisel on the cartel. To eliminate these loopholes, the cartel's employment rules have over the years become increasingly complex.

and to make themselves more employable.[15] College graduates go to graduate school to differentiate their skills from the mass of people receiving college degrees. Musical groups work to develop a "style of their own" which will separate them from the other groups competing for stardom. Beauticians try to be the first to learn new styles; authors try to improve their writing skills; basketball players spend long hours on the court after school; law secretaries train to become legal assistants. All of these efforts and many more are attempts to override the forces of competition.

Granted, to the extent that all workers follow the course of skill differentiation, its benefits are reduced: wages will be depressed. However, gains can be made by those who reach a different market first; and although the benefits may be temporary, they can be sufficient to cover the cost a person must incur in differentiating his skills.[16] Furthermore, consumers benefit to the extent that worker efforts enable the consumers to get more of what they demand in the way of final products. Differentiation means variety and choice.

Union Organization

In a large and competitive labor market, an individual worker has no power to influence the wage he receives. This is so because his efforts represent such a miniscule part of the total labor supply and because he can be replaced at the *competitively* determined wage rate. The worker who withdraws himself completely from that market imposes no cost on employers—employers lose nothing of significance in the way of production; they hire someone else. Accordingly, only the laws of morality and common courtesy may apply with sufficient strength to induce employers to concede to the demands of the individual. On the other hand, if a group of workers is large enough and acts collectively, it can impose substantial costs on employers. If a group of employees can reduce the available supply of workers by a significant amount, their action may cause employers to have to cut back production and take a loss on sales. Employers, then, have an incentive to heed the demands of a group of workers acting collectively (i.e., as unions), whereas they may have little incentive to even listen to the demands of the individual.

Through strikes and picketing, unions can reduce the available supply of labor to employers. With this power they can bargain for higher wages and/or better working conditions. In a competitive market, the net effect of this kind of union action is a reduction of the employment opportunities in the unionized market. Consider Figure 15·4, which represents the competitive labor market for textile workers. Without union interference in this market, the supply of labor is S_1. The market wage rate is W_1 and the number of workers hired, Q_2. By

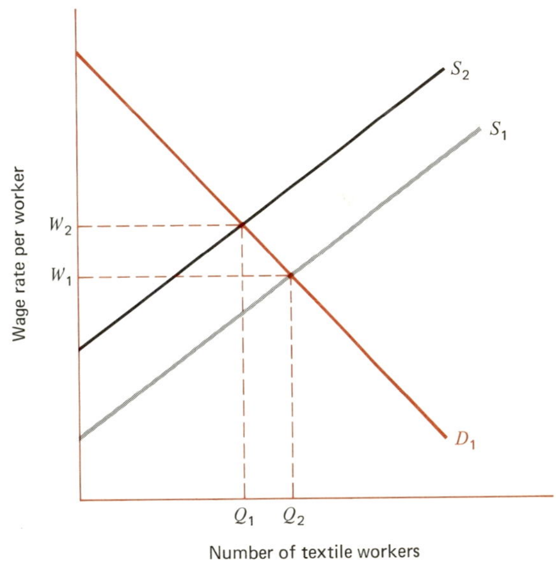

FIG. 15·4 Unions can increase the wage rate by reducing the supply of laborers from S_1 to S_2. Alternately, the union can negotiate a wage rate of W_2. In either case, the number of workers hired will be Q_1, which is less than will be hired in a competitive market.

[15] Many students also attend college to ensure that they will not be pushed, by those who do attend college, into labor markets which require few skills and are highly competitive.

[16] On the other hand, the person who trains to become a neurosurgeon "has it made" simply because few people are willing or able to make the same investment in human capital.

organizing the textile labor market and excluding some potential workers from membership, a union can restrict the supply of labor in this market to S_2. Because of the shortage of labor which will then exist in the market at a wage of W_1, the going wage rate will rise to W_2. The number of workers hired at that wage rate falls to Q_1. Employers will hire only Q_1 workers because now beyond Q_1 each additional worker costs more at the unionized wage rate than he is worth to the employer.

On the other hand, if the market is controlled by a single employer or a cartel of employers, like the one that exists in professional sports, a union can raise the wage up to some limit without affecting the number of workers hired. To see this, consider Figure 15·5, which is a duplication of Figure 15·3 used earlier. The monopsonistic employer will tend to hire Q_1 workers and tend to pay them a wage of W_1. Employers are willing to pay their workers a wage equal to as much as W_3. Through strikes, threats of strikes, and bargaining strategy, unions can raise the wage of their members up to W_3. If the wage goes above W_3, the number of workers hired will fall; however, the point we wish to emphasize is that so long as the wage stays within the range of W_1 to W_3, at least the same number of workers will be hired.

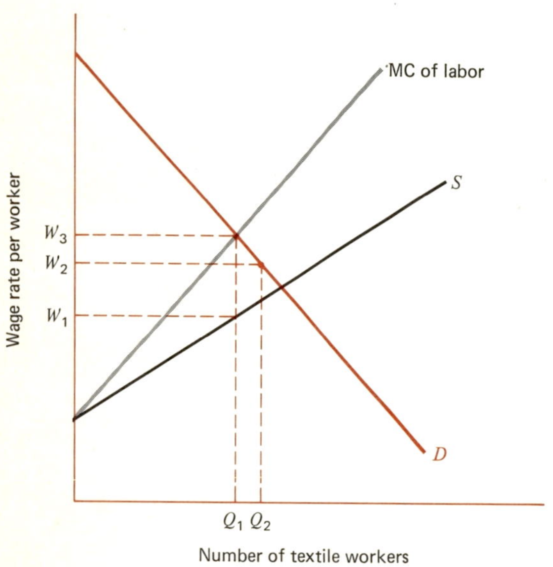

FIG. 15·5 In a monopsonistic labor market, a union can raise the wage rate from W_1 to, say, W_2 and increase the number of workers hired from Q_1 to Q_2.

However, if the wage rate is raised to some level below W_3, say to only W_2, the number of workers hired will increase from Q_1 to Q_2. The union wage rate which is paid to each worker then becomes the marginal cost of labor. The marginal cost of labor curve is no longer upward sloping; rather, it is horizontal at a wage rate of W_2. As in our previous discussion, the monopsonist will hire labor up to the point where the marginal cost of labor, which is now constant at W_2, equals the marginal value of labor. This occurs at the higher employment level of Q_2. (If the union wage rate were set at the intersection of the supply and demand curves, the competitive employment level would be achieved. Can you explain why in terms of the graph?) The same can be said of minimum wage laws which are imposed on monopsonistic labor markets: so long as the minimum is below W_3 in Figure 15·5, employment will expand. Once this new employment equilibrium of W_2 and Q_2 is reached, however, further increase in either the minimum wage or union wage rate, without an accompanying increase in labor demand, will reduce the level of employment. For instance, if the union wage rate were set at W_2 in Figure 15·5, employment would be Q_2. If then the wage rate were raised from W_2 to W_3, employment would fall from Q_2 back to Q_1.

In these cases, unions and government can be seen as countervailing forces against the power of the employer; at the same time, employment opportunities in the industry are increased. The economic argument for unions and minimum wage laws is, consequently, most powerful when employers also have significant market power. Furthermore, we should expect to find the most successful unions in monopsonistic labor markets rather than in competitive ones. In competitive labor markets, union wage demands are more restricted by the adverse effects that the wage demands have on total employment and union membership; as the union wage is raised, the number of jobs falls along with the number of dues-paying members. Minimum wage laws are applied to markets whether or not they are monopsonistic. As we demonstrated in the preceding chapter, such laws have a negative effect on employment in competitive markets. Here we have shown that they can have a positive impact on employment, depending upon the level at which the minimum wage is set. (That is, the wage must be between W_1 and W_3 on the graph). The net effect of such laws depends upon the extent of the competitive and monopsonistic elements in labor markets. Studies conducted over the past 30 years, such as the ones cited in Chapter 14, have supported the view that the net effects of minimum wage laws across all markets is negative—that is, they have reduced employment opportunities.

Unions can have a positive effect on the employment opportunities of their members in another way: they can increase the demand for the product or service which the union members produce. The greater demand for the final product will mean a higher price for the product and, as we explained earlier, a greater demand for the union worker. As illustrated in Figure 15·6, an increase in the demand for labor from D_1 to D_2 causes the wage rate to rise from W_1 to W_2 and the number of workers hired to rise from Q_1 to Q_2. With union dues, the union can increase the demand for the product that the members produce by advertising the product or by lobbying for governmental appropriations which will increase the demand for the product. For example, unions representing automobile workers typically lobby for increases in government expenditures on highways. Similarly, unions representing aircraft workers lobby for increases in the military budget and against proposals designed to reduce military expenditures. It does not follow, however, that such union efforts necessarily increase the employment of *all* workers. An increase in government expenditures on military aircraft, for instance, can mean that the government has less to spend on other programs which would have led to employment opportunities for other workers. Alternately, an increase in military aircraft purchases can lead to a tax increase and to a reduction in the amount consumers have to spend on such goods as furniture and houses. Fewer consumer expenditures on furniture and housing will mean fewer employment opportunities in those industries. In other words, while it is true that overall employment may rise, union efforts to increase the employment opportunities probably lead to distortions in government expenditures and employment opportunities.

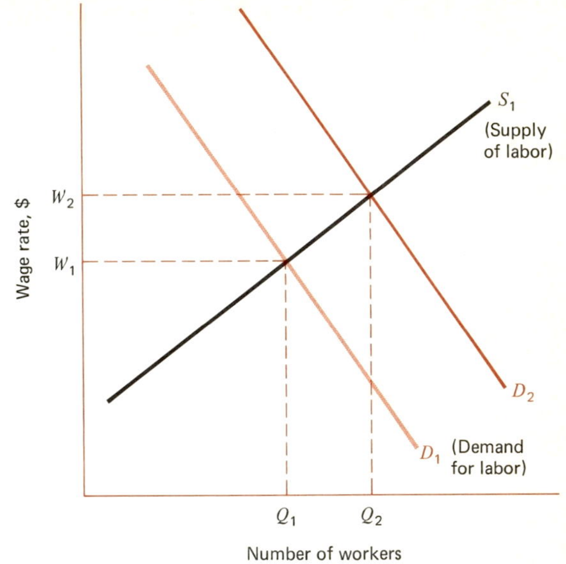

FIG. 15·6 A union can increase the demand for the final product, increase the price of the final product, and, thereby, increase the demand for the employment of union members. With the increase in the demand for labor from D_1 to D_2, the wage rate paid will rise from W_1 to W_2 and the number of workers hired will rise from Q_1 to Q_2.

Small Groups, Large Groups, and Public Good of Unions

The preceding analysis of the economic effects of unions was based upon the assumption that workers can act collectively in a group that is large enough to materially affect the market supply of labor. The effectiveness of a union is, therefore, dependent upon how well the union is organized, and in a free and open market securing the needed collective action may be difficult. This is particularly true when the number of workers needed for the collective movement is large and the use or threat of violence is prohibited by law. The explanation for these statements flows directly from our analysis of large- and small-group behavior in Chapter 6.

Any effort that a union makes to restrict the labor supply and raise wages in a particular labor market is a public good to the workers in that labor market. If the wage is increased through labor supply restrictions, some workers must bear the cost of bringing about those restrictions; some group of workers must refuse to work (strike) and must be willing to bargain. However, if the group of striking workes retains their jobs and receives higher wages, all workes in the market benefit from the group's actions. As explained in Chapter 6, collective action is much more likely to be achieved within a small group than in a large one. In a small union, each worker, by definition, represents a significant part of the total labor supply; his behavior can make a significant contribution to his own welfare and to the welfare of other group members. The individual can detect the benefits, in terms of higher wages, of his own actions, which in this case may be participation in a strike. The worker should, consequently, be willing to bear some cost (lost pay) to receive those benefits. Further, a small group, in which there may be ties of friendship, provides many opportunities for imposing social sanctions on those persons who do not participate in collective action, such as union movements. It is, therefore, understandable why unions first emerged, contrary to popular belief, in small-group settings, in situations in which employers and employees worked closely together, and not in large industrial settings in which the relations between employers and employees were strained and made impersonal by the sheer size of the labor force.[17] Large-scale union organizations developed much later, after smaller unions were organized into federations and these larger organizations found that they could increase their membership by selling them private goods and services, such as insurance policies, recreational facilities, and seniority rights.

A worker in a large group, on the other hand, represents a very small fraction of the total labor supply. His or her individual actions, for all intents and purposes, are insignificant in the context of the labor market. As noted earlier, the individual worker can withdraw completely from this market with no detectable effect on the market supply of labor or the going wage rate. Similarly, the worker should not be able to detect his or her individual contribution to the effectiveness of any large union movement. If no one else will strike, striking alone will have no effect. Conversely, the wage rate may rise because of labor supply restrictions, but the individual worker can reason that his participation in the strike made no detectable contribution to the goal of increasing the wage rate. The market wage will be the same with or without the person's participation in the large union movement. Therefore, although all workers in a labor market may sense the benefits of unionization, they may fail to participate in any movement toward that end. They have insufficient private incentive to incur the implied costs (lost income, etc.) of participation in the large union movement; their incentive is perverse—to take a "free ride" on the activities of other workers.

Without the existence of laws which support organized unions or without the use of force (violence) or the threat of force, many large union movements would fail because of the tendency of people to try to get a "free ride." However, those most interested in seeing a union formed can overcome the free-rider problem by force or, in

[17] Mancur Olson, "The Labor Union and Economic Freedom," in *The Logic of Collective Action: Public Goods and the Theory of Groups* (Cambridge, Mass.: Harvard University Press, 1971), pp. 66–97.

the case of small union movements, social ostracism. Faced with the threat of violence if he crosses the picket line, an individual worker incurs a private cost (in terms of bodily injury or property damage) for his actions. He must then weigh that cost off against the cost which he must incur by participating in the union movement. If the police look the other way or are unable to deal with the scope of the lawlessness, the violence cost imposed on those who are otherwise free-riders can become so great that participation in union activities becomes a rational act for most workers.

Laws have been written which are supportive of union movements. That is, the government can impose a cost on workers who do not wish to participate in union activities. In this way government aids the union in reducing the free-rider problem and, therefore, the cost of union organization. Presently, a plant or firm can be organized as a union shop. In a union shop all workers, once employed, must belong to the union if a simple majority of the workers votes for unionization. If 51 percent of the workers have voted for a union and a worker refuses to join the union, he or she is simply denied employment in that firm; this is a rather substantial cost for nonparticipation.

Before plants could be organized through democratic election procedures, union organizers had to generate much more support among workers than is implied by a simple majority vote. Without elections, a few workers could undermine union efforts to organize a plant. A few workers would cross the picket lines, causing others to follow suit; or the strike breakers could be workers who moved into the labor market to lay claim to the jobs of the strikers. It is no wonder that strike breakers have been met with so much hostility and violence throughout the history of the labor movement and have been referred to as "scabs." Democratic elections have been a way of reducing the potential for violence; at the same time, they have been a boon for unions. They have reduced the cost of organization to those sympathetic with the union cause.

Union Effects on Nonmoney Competition

Unions are usually seen as countervailing forces to the market power exercised by large and powerful employers and employer cartels. It is true that by imposing significant costs on employers through strikes and work slowdowns, unions are able to exert some control over the supply of labor. This includes not only organizing a large portion of the potential work force, but also maintaining some control over the input, in terms of both quantity and quality of union members who may try to compete by working harder and improving job-related skills.

Union members have an interest in keeping each other from accepting a lower market wage because the end result of the ensuing competition can mean lower wages for all. Similarly, members have an interest in keeping each other from trying to improve their market position and wages through harder work and skill improvement. If some workers compete in this way, all members may have to follow suit and all will end up working harder for the same wage rate. For this reason, unions that are really interested in reducing nonmoney competition among workers should be expected to seek, wherever possible, wage schedules and wage increases which are not based on such job performance considerations as "merit," "hard work," and "aggressiveness." Interestingly, evaluation of job performances on these criteria is often considered impractical by unions. In most union movements wage rates are generally based on years of seniority, and wage increases are usually distributed in equal portions across the board to the membership. Hard work and skill improvements often do not pay; and to this extent unions contribute to the perpetuation of production inefficiencies.

SUMMARY AND EXTENSIONS: A QUESTION OF HOW MUCH POWER

As we have demonstrated, the power of the employer to control the demand for labor and the power of the employee to control the supply of labor can lead to inefficiencies in the allocation of resources. However, in a free market, one in which resources can move with reasonable facility to take advantage of profit opportunities, the market power of employer and employee groups cannot be complete. Even employer cartels must compete with employers outside of their particular cartel for the available supply of labor. Other employers can move into labor markets in which the wage is being artificially held down by employer collusion, and employees can move to other labor markets and to other employers. If various labor markets are cartelized, the power of any one cartel is constrained by the inevitable competition for labor that will exist among the cartels. The wage may be held down below perfectly competitive levels; but because of the limited competition that does exist, the distortion may not be very great. As illustrated by the competition for players that existed during the early 1970s between the National Football League and the now defunct World Football League (two employer cartels), competition can be quite intense even among a limited number of alternative employers.

If workers organize and cause wage rates to rise, employers after a period of time may move to nonunionized locations in the economy, reducing the ability of employees to gain from their union efforts. Obviously, employers and employees have good reason for wanting to extend their control. However, these types of extensions invariably meet with the difficulties that most large groups face when their members try to form an agreement to pursue a common purpose. As the group expands, the significance of any one person or firm decreases and the free-rider problem becomes more pronounced. Furthermore, the continued expansion of the collective labor movement will eventually run into the open resistance of those who do not wish to see their job opportunities constricted by a cartel or a union vote.

To the extent, however, that laws facilitate expansion of large-group movements, that is, reduce the costs of organization, those laws should lead to greater concentration of market power in the hands of employers and/or employee groups. Because of the benefits involved, we should expect groups to take advantage of whatever power their positions will allow them to develop, the end result being reduced efficiency in production. More resources will be devoted to power-group organization (employer cartels and unions) and more will be used in the exercise of that power. These changes mean that fewer resources are available for production and/or that resources are inefficiently allocated among their alternative uses. With reduced outputs, consumers will have less to buy and will, accordingly, have lower real incomes. Some economists are opposed to concentration of power by employers and employees for just this reason; they favor competition because it minimizes these types of waste. Even those economists who do not believe that the best outcome for society is the elimination of all power groups nonetheless argue that government should do nothing that will encourage power groups.

QUESTIONS TO PONDER

1 If unions are able to raise wages in the unionized sector of the economy, explain what will happen to the supply of labor in the nonunionized sector of the economy.

2 In what sense is the individual laborer in a competitive labor market in a "prisoner's dilemma"? (See Chapter 2 for a discussion of the meaning of "prisoner's dilemma".)

3 We have suggested that violence or threat of violence can be a means by which union members enlist the support of nonunion members in union strikes. Why? Without the support of the law, why are unions unstable? Can violence be used by employers to prevent the unionization of their firms? Explain in economic terms.

4 Why might the industrious workers in a labor market be opposed to unionization?

5 Unions often prefer to unionize an entire labor market for a given type of worker. Explain.

6 Under what conditions will an employer cartel fail to hold together and accomplish its intended objectives?

7 If team owners can sell the rights to their football players to other teams, players will be paid more than if the rights cannot be sold. Do you agree? Explain.

8 If the "draft system" of the NFL is declared illegal by the courts (as may already have happened by the time you read this), what changes would you expect in player salaries, ticket prices, and number of players signed?

9 If employers have to pay union workers more than their competitive market rates, firms will move to geographical areas where they can hire nonunion workers. What effects do such shifts have on wage rates in union and nonunion sectors of the economy? On the unemployment in these areas? On the efficiency in the allocation of resources?

RECOMMENDED READINGS

Neale, Walter C.: "The Peculiar Economics of Professional Sports," in Harry G. Johnson and Burton A. Weisbrod, eds., *The Daily Economist* (Englewood Cliffs, N.J.: Prentice-Hall, Inc., 1973), pp. 46–56.

North, Douglas C., and Roger Leroy Miller: *The Economics of Public Issues*, 2d ed. (New York: Harper and Row, Publishers, Inc., 1973), chaps. 11, 12, 23, and 29.

Rees, Albert: *The Economics of Trade Unions* (Chicago: University of Chicago Press, 1962), chaps. 1–4.

Rottenberg, Simon: "The Baseball Players' Labor Market," in *The Daily Economist*, see above.

Part Six
The Extended World Market

"Why should a thing made in Brussels, for example, cost more when it reaches Paris?"

Now, it did not take me long to perceive that the rise in price results from the existence of *obstacles* of several kinds between Paris and Brussels. First of all, there is the *distance*. . . .

Now, among these *obstacles* between Brussels and Paris there is one that we ourselves have set up, and at great cost. There are men lying in wait along the whole length of the frontier, armed to the teeth and charged with the task of putting difficulties in the way of transporting goods from one country to the other. They are called *customs officials*. They act in exactly the same way as the mud and the ruts. They delay and impede commerce; they contribute to the difference that we have noted between the price paid by the consumer and the price received by the producer, a difference that it is our problem to reduce as much as possible. . . .

Really, I wonder how we could have ever thought of doing anything so fantastic as to pay many millions of francs for the purpose of removing the *natural obstacles* that stand between France and other countries, and at the same time pay many other millions for the purpose of substituting *artificial obstacles* that have exactly the same effect; so that the obstacles created and the obstacles removed neutralize each other and leave things quite as they were before, the only difference being the double expense of the whole operation.

Frederic Bastiat

Frederic Bastiat, *Economic Sophisms* [Irvington-on-Hudson, N.Y.: The Foundation for Economic Education, Inc., 1964 (originally published 1845)], pp. 64–65.

In previous chapters, we have developed a number of principles of economic analysis. We have shown how these principles can be applied to markets within a country like the United States. In the next two chapters, we demonstrate how many of these same principles are applicable to trade of goods and services among different nations.

16

International Trade and the Extended World Market

It can be of no consequence to America, whether the commodities she obtains in return for her own, cost Europeans much, or little labor; all she is interested in, is that they shall cost her less labor by purchasing than by manufacturing them herself.

David Ricardo[1]

PREVIEW OF CHAPTER

Central question

How and to what extent can countries benefit from international trade?

Major objectives

1 To explain the gains to countries from international trade and thereby to develop the case for free international trade
2 To describe the distributional income effects from international trade, that is, to describe who gains and who loses from trade between countries
3 To explain why domestic firms which have to compete with foreign producers have an interest in imposing tariffs on imported goods
4 To evaluate commonly articulated arguments for tariff protection against imports
5 To consider the "politics of protection," that is, the uneven political support for tariffs

[1] David Ricardo, *Notes on Malthus' Principles of Political Economy*, as quoted in Jacob Viner, *Studies in the Theory of International Trade* [New York: Augustus M. Kelley, Publishers, 1965 (originally published 1937)], p. 441.

Major Conclusions

1 When trade occurs between two parties in two different countries, both parties gain from the transaction.

2 Even though one country can produce all goods and services more efficiently than can another country, trade between the countries can be mutually beneficial.

3 Although there are net gains from international trade to the countries as a whole, there are distributional effects which must be considered. Those firms which have to compete with foreign producers can lose income because of free trade in their product area. On the other hand, consumers who buy products which are exported have to pay higher prices for those products than they would have in the absence of international trade.

4 Domestic producers who have to compete with foreign producers in the domestic market can benefit substantially from and have a concentrated private interest in asking Congress for tariff or quota protection from the imports. Even though tariffs or quotas on imports cause consumers to pay higher prices for the products they buy, consumers generally have little incentive to oppose legislation designed to restrict imports. The reason is that the cost of opposing the tariff legislation is generally greater to the individual consumer than the benefits that can be achieved through lower consumer prices.

5 Tariffs and quotas on imports reduce international trade and, therefore, the aggregate incomes of countries that engage in international commerce. Most arguments presented in favor of tariff legislation are seriously flawed.

Important terms and concepts

Comparative advantage
Tariff
Quota

Nations never really trade—people who happen to live in different countries actually do the trading. This simple point is important. It helps us see clearly how most of the concepts and principles developed thus far in this book apply to discussions of international trade. These concepts and principles that we have developed so far affected people who buy and sell in the marketplace; the geographic scope of our market was not delineated. In this chapter, our marketplace will be the world.

There are, of course, differences between international and domestic trade, and these differences make international economics an important subdiscipline within the economics profession.

There are the obvious differences, like the many different national currencies that are involved in international trade. One of the most intangible yet significant differences is between people's attitudes toward domestic and international policies. As Abraham Lincoln is reported to have said, "Domestic trade is among us; international trade is between us and them." However true this may be, people in different parts of the world trade with each other, at a fundamental level, for the same reason that people in different regions of a country do: they are, by and large, trading to *gain*, and they want to deal with those persons who will help them most in accomplishing their individual objectives.

Understanding that people (not nations) trade is important for another reason. If the focus of attention is solely on the gains from international commerce to nations, as opposed to individuals, the distributional effects—the gains and losses to different people—from that trade can be overlooked. As we will show, international trade can result in an increase in a nation's *total* income while, in the process, some people's incomes may be reduced. With these income losses hidden, the political efforts of some groups who want government protection from competition in the extended world market may be evaluated incorrectly. We emphasize the distributional income effects of trade in order that the political objectives to free, unimpeded trade among nations can be seen in proper perspective.

A major theme of this book has been that each individual competitor has a vested interest in being protected from the forces of competition. Accordingly, firms which produce domestically and must compete with foreign importers have an interest in being protected from their foreign competition via tariffs (i.e., a tax) on imported goods. However, as we will show, protection increases the price consumers have to pay for goods, and if all sectors of the economy are protected because of the narrow interests of each sector, the income of everyone can be reduced. It is this latter prospect which makes the case for *free* international trade. These points will be illuminated in the following pages. First, consider the advantages of international trade from the perspective of the nation.

THE GAINS FROM TRADE

The gains from international trade are clearest when there is no domestic substitute for an imported good. The United States does not have any known reserves of such basic resources as chrome, manganese, and tin. For these resources, which are widely used in industry, we must rely on foreign suppliers, and we must trade away goods which we value less for these resources. The gains from trade also are clear when we can produce the same type of goods as are imported only under unfavorable conditions. For example, cocoa and coffee can be domestically raised but only under the difficult and expensive conditions of greenhouse farming. Obviously, it is less costly for the United States to import the coffee in exchange for some good, such as wheat, for which our climate is well suited.

There are, however, benefits from international trade which are more difficult to understand. Foreign producers who market their goods in this country increase the scope and intensity of competitive forces in the United States. They reduce the market power of domestic firms, and to that extent they tend to reduce product prices and to expand the domestic output levels. Further, foreign suppliers increase the variety of goods which are available domestically. Without the 20 or more foreign automobile producers which sell in the United States market, the Big Four auto makers in this country would each sell to a much larger percentage of the market and would need to be less concerned that instigating a price increase will cause consumers to move to other manufacturers. Collusion among the Big Four would be much easier and more probable without the presence of foreign competitors in the market.

Some of the benefits of specialization through international trade are clear. By concentrating on producing a smaller number of goods than would be necessary under autarky (national self-sufficiency) and by selling to the world market, the people of a country may become more proficient at what they do and reap the technological benefits of economies of scale, that is, the cost savings that come with large-scale production. However, there are resource savings which are not so apparent; indeed, under the conditions in the example about to be discussed, some readers may doubt that the trade among the parties can be mutually beneficial. A little reflection will indicate otherwise.

To illustrate the inevitable benefits from trade in

TABLE 16·1 AN EXAMPLE OF COMPARATIVE COST ADVANTAGE

	Maximum Units of Textiles with Zero Beef	Maximum Units of Beef with Zero Textiles	Domestic Cost Ratios in Each Country	Mutually Beneficial Trade Ratio to Both Countries
United States	30	90	1 textile costs 3 beef	1 textile trades for 2 beef
Japan	25	25	1 textile costs 1 beef	

the simplest but yet most dramatic terms, let us visualize a world in which there are only two goods, textiles and beef, and two countries, the United States and Japan. Further, assume that the United States is more efficient in the production of both textiles and beef; that is, with the same resources the United States can produce more beef and more textiles than can Japan.[2]

The relevant data for our illustration are provided in Table 16·1. With the same labor, capital, and so on, as Japan, the United States can produce 30 units of textiles whereas Japan can produce only 25 units. Alternatively, if all these resources are used in the production of beef in both countries, the United States can still outproduce Japan in the ratio of 90 units of beef to 25. From these data one might think that the United States will not benefit in any way from trading with Japan; however, traders in the United States are not likely to see the matter that way. The principal concern of traders is not with just how efficient in absolute terms the United States is in comparison with Japan. Their principal concern is whether or not they, in the United States, can make a better deal with traders in Japan than they can make with themselves.

In a sense, the United States does trade with itself every time it produces either beef or textiles. If the United States produces beef, it gives up some of the textiles that could have been produced, and vice versa. In our example, every time it produces 1 unit of textiles, the United States, on average, gives up 3 units of beef. (The United States gives up 30 units of textiles in order to produce 90 of beef, or an average of 3 units of beef for each textile.) The United States will trade beef for textiles if it can give up fewer than 3 units of beef for each unit of textiles supplied by Japan. Interestingly, Japan domestically gives up, on average, 1 unit of beef for each unit of textiles it produces. Therefore, if Japan can get more than 1 unit of beef for each unit of textiles that it trades, Japan gains by the trade. Japan, in other words, is willing to accept fewer than 3 units of beef for 1 unit of textiles which it produces; it is *not* willing to accept fewer than 1 unit of beef for each of the textiles. It can give up 1 textile and produce 1 beef domestically; why should it then accept less than 1 beef for its textiles?

In short, if the trade ratio between beef and textiles is greater than 1 unit of beef for 1 unit of textiles but less than 3 units of beef for 1 unit of textiles, both Japan and the United States gain by the trade. For example (and this is only one of several possible examples), suppose the exchange ratio is 2 units of beef for 1 unit of textiles. The United States will gain in trade because it now has to give up fewer units of beef (2 as opposed to 3) than it will have to give up if it tries to produce the textile

[2] Strictly speaking, if know-how is considered to be one of the resources used in the production processes, the two countries cannot have equal resources and different production abilities. To circumvent this objective, we admit to some inequality in the know-how which is available to each country.

itself. By producing the textile itself, the United States has to give up 3 units of beef; by trading with Japan it has to give up only 2 units of beef. The United States can, accordingly, produce 3 units of beef, giving up a textile in the process, and then trade 2 units of beef for the textile in international trade: the United States has its textile and 1 extra beef. Alternatively, the United States can trade all 3 units of beef for 1½ textiles.

Similarly, Japan can gain from trade if the trade ratio is 1 unit of textiles for 2 units of beef. Domestically, Japan can give up 1 unit of beef in order to produce 1 unit of textiles; it can then turn around and trade that 1 unit of textiles for 2 units of beef. In order to have 2 units of beef under conditions of self-imposed autarky, Japan would have to give up 2 units of textiles.

Therefore, both countries can gain from international trade, and they gain because they specialize in the production of that good for which they have a comparative cost advantage. Granted, by the design of this example the United States is in absolute terms more efficient than Japan in both goods. (It has what economists call an *absolute advantage* in both products.) However, Japan does have a comparative cost advantage (or *comparative advantage*) in the production of textiles. One unit of textiles costs Japan 1 unit of beef; on the other hand, 1 unit of textiles costs the United States 3 units of beef. Similarly, the United States has a comparative cost advantage (or *comparative advantage*) in the production of beef: 1 unit of beef costs the United States ⅓ unit of textiles. One unit of beef costs Japan more, 1 unit of textiles. By the two countries specializing in domestic production in that commodity for which they have a comparative cost advantage, resources are saved on an international scale and these resources can then be translated into greater production internationally. Table 16 · 2 contains the hypothetical production levels of the two countries in beef and textiles. Before trade, the United Sates produces 15 units of textiles and 45 of beef; Japan produces 3 units of textiles and 22 of beef. Total production of the two countries is seen in the last column of the table, 18 units of textiles and 67 units of beef.

Under the conditions of international trade,

TABLE 16 · 2 THE GAINS FROM INTERNATIONAL TRADE

	United States	Japan	Total of U.S. and Japan
(1) Production and consumption levels before international trade	15 textiles 45 beef	3 textiles 22 beef	18 textiles 67 beef
(2) Production levels in anticipation of international trade (Complete specialization is assumed.)	0 textiles 90 beef	25 textiles 0 beef	25 textiles 90 beef
At an exchange ratio of 2 beef for 1 textile, U.S. and Japan agree to trade 40 beef for 20 textiles, resulting in the following consumption levels after trade:			
(3) Consumption levels after international trade	20 textiles 50 beef	5 textiles 40 beef	25 textiles 90 beef
(4) Increased consumption (after subtracting before-trade consumption levels)	5 textiles 5 beef	2 textiles 18 beef	7 textiles 23 beef

these two countries will specialize in the production of that good for which each has a comparative cost advantage: with complete specialization, the United States will produce 90 units of beef and Japan will produce 25 units of textiles. At an international trade ratio of 1 unit of textiles for 2 of beef, let us suppose that the United States and Japan agree to trade 40 units of United States beef for its equivalent, 20 units of Japanese textiles (for each unit of textiles, the United Sates has to give up 2 units of beef). The United States will end up after trade with more beef (50 units as opposed to 45) and more textiles (20 units as opposed to 15). As can be seen in row 3 of the table, Japan also ends up with more of both commodities. Total "world" production rises to 25 units of textiles (from 18) and to 90 units of beef (from 67). As can be seen in rows 3 and 4, both countries can enjoy greater consumption levels of textiles and beef. In these very real senses, the aggregate incomes of both nations increase. The benefits of trade are, therefore, demonstrated despite the intuitive idea that the United States would not be better off.

United States Trade Figures

The benefits to the United States from international commerce are revealed in the international *balance of trade statistics,* that is, statistics about what we export to other countries and what we import from them. In 1975 the United States exported goods and services valued at $148 billion. This figure represented approximately 10 percent of the country's total domestic production, up from approximately 6 percent in 1960. On the other hand, in 1975 we imported from other countries $131 billion of goods and services, or an amount equal to almost 9 percent of the country's total production. The difference between exports and imports is partially, but not totally, explained by $4 billion in gifts which the United States government, charitable organizations, and individuals made to people in foreign countries. The monetary gifts Americans make to foreigners represent claims against United States production and usually end up as exports of goods. Also, a part of the income received from the sale of United States goods abroad went into the purchase of foreign stocks and bonds and into overseas investments by United States firms. Although these investments are not in themselves exports or imports, and therefore are not included in the above figures, they do not generate interest and dividend incomes for Americans which are a part of the export figure. In fact, in 1975 Americans received approximately $18 billion in interest and dividend incomes from previous investments made in foreign countries. Foreigners received about $12 billion in interest and dividend payments from their investment in prior years in American businesses and government bonds.

Many of the imports bought by Americans were finished products, such as automobiles and television sets, and were sold in stores with the familiar "Made in Japan" or "Made in Germany" labels. Other imports were raw materials, like crude oil and tin, and product parts, such as transistors, which were then used in the production of so many of the goods you buy on a daily basis. Some of the raw materials were used in products which were ultimately exported to other countries.

THE DISTRIBUTIONAL EFFECTS

With the numerical example in Table 16·2, we were able to demonstrate a very important economic principle: even a country that is more efficient in the production of *everything* than any other country can still benefit from trade. Admittedly, no country is the most efficient producer of everything, but that is the importance of the illustration. We can demonstrate the case for freedom of international commerce in the most unlikely of conditions. Further, if voluntary trade takes place, we must assume that both parties gain from that trade; why else would the parties voluntarily agree to trade with each other? The increase in real income for both countries is revealed in highly concrete terms: goods are obtained from abroad that cannot be obtained from domestic sources and/or more of those goods are obtained than can be produced domestically.

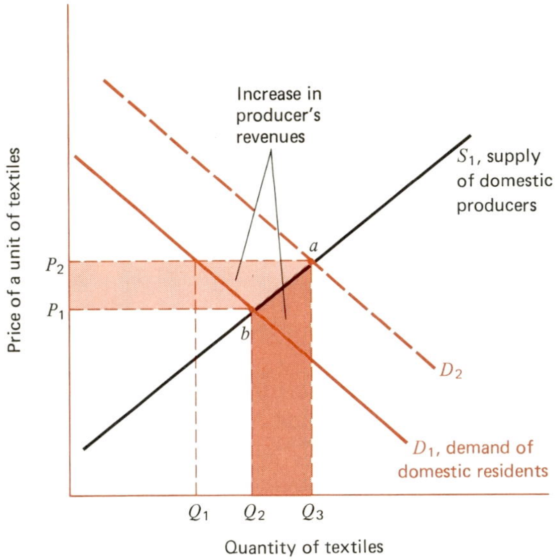

FIG. 16·1 The opening up of foreign markets to United States producers increases the demand for products which can be exported. Domestic producers of exported products can increase the price they charge and sell a larger quantity. Their revenues and profits go up.

The Gains for Exporters

Many people experience income increases from free international commerce. Those who export domestic goods to foreign countries gain because they now have more markets for their goods in which a larger quantity of goods can be sold. If exporters can sell a larger quantity, they may be able to sell that quantity at a higher price. Consider Figure 16·1. In that graph we have drawn as S_1 the domestic textile producers' supply, which can be sold either in the domestic market or in markets of other countries. Without international trade, the demand faced by domestic textile firms is simply the demand of domestic residents, which is illustrated in the graph by D_1. Under conditions of autarky, the competitive price that can be charged by producers is P_1; the quantity that can be sold, Q_2. If, however, foreign buyers can make purchases in the domestic textile market, the overall demand will rise to, say, D_2. Domestic producers can then sell more, Q_3, at a higher price, P_2; the domestic textile producers, including their workers and suppliers, obviously have an interest in expanding their international market as much as possible. They gain in terms of more employment opportunities, higher prices, and greater incomes.[3] Consumers, on the other hand, in the narrow context of the textile market, are hurt by the trade, because they have to compete now with foreign buyers, they pay higher prices, and, because of that, reduce their consumption of textiles (to Q_1 in the figure).

For reasons which are apparent from this demonstration, farmers supported the sale of wheat to the Soviet Union that began in the early 1970s and complained loudly when the United States government, for a time, held up the sales for political reasons. On the other hand, many consumers and members of Congress objected to the sales on the grounds that the Soviet wheat deal would increase the price of wheat and, therefore, of bread.

In a narrow context, consumers of a particular exported product have an interest in restricting its exportation. However, in the broad, multicommodity context of international trade, restrictions can work against many people's private interests, even the private interests of consumers of bread. Trade is ultimately a two-way street. In order to import goods and services which can be produced more cheaply abroad than domestically, a country must export something to some other country. No country will continually export a part of what it produces without getting something in return. Therefore, to the extent that exports are restricted to suit the private interests of some

[3] Producers' revenues rise from a low of P_1Q_2 (point b) to P_2Q_3 (point a), the increase being equal to the L-shaped shaded area, $P_2aQ_3Q_2bP_1$. The cost of producing these additional units is equal to that portion of the L-shaped area under the supply curve (the darker-shaded area). Why? The increased profits to the domestic textile producers are equal to the area bounded by P_2abP_1 (the lighter-shaded area). Producers benefit because they receive greater profits; workers and suppliers of raw materials benefit because their services are in greater demand and because they receive greater payments for their services. The benefits to workers and suppliers are revealed by the area Q_2baQ_3.

group, imports of other commodities also are restricted. Restrictions on the exportation of wheat, for example, may prevent a rise in the price of bread. However, because there will be fewer imports, these restrictions can also lead to increases in the price of many imported goods, such as radios and television sets, which we can produce domestically but only at higher costs. Restrictions on a group's exports effectively reduce imports and raise the prices of many goods the group buys.

Losses to Firms Competing with Imports

Foreign producers can gain a foothold in the domestic market in three ways: (1) by providing a product that is better than anything available from domestic sources, (2) by selling a product similar to domestic substitutes at a lower price, and (3) by providing a product previously unavailable in the domestic market. Few people object to the importation of any product that has previously been unavailable; indeed, most people welcome it. However, those who face competition from foreign producers have a private incentive to object to the importation of those products with which they have to compete. To the extent that a good is imported, the total domestic supply of the good increases; the domestic competitors sell less and may have to sell at a lower price. In short, domestic producers experience a fall in employment opportunities and real income.

These predictions are illustrated in Figure 16·2. Without the importation of foreign textiles, the domestic demand and supply curves are assumed to be D_1 and S_1. In a competitive domestic market, producers will sell Q_2 units of textiles and will sell that quantity for a price of P_2. Total receipts are P_2 times Q_2 (or P_2Q_2). However, the importation of textiles means that the total supply available in the domestic market expands; we have illustrated this new and greater supply as S_2. The supply curve, S_2, is the summation of the domestic and foreign supplies of textiles, and the difference between the two supply curves is the amount of imported textiles at each price. The greater supply will cause the domestic price of textiles to fall

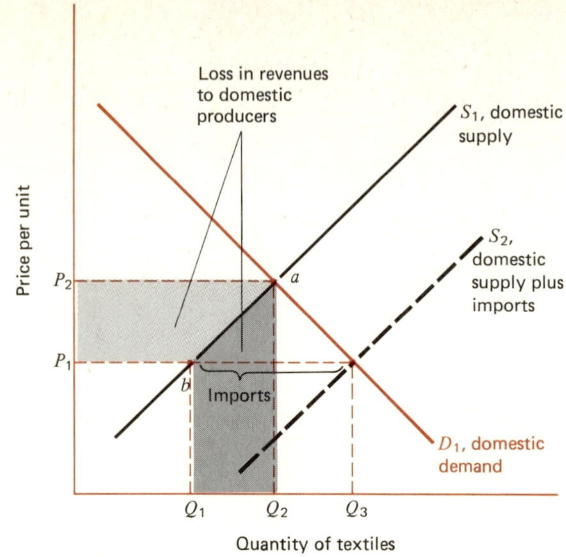

FIG. 16·2 The opening up of the domestic market to foreign trade increases the domestic supply of textiles. As a consequence, the price of textiles falls in the domestic market. Domestic producers not only receive a lower price but sell a lower quantity. Consumers benefit from the imports to the extent they are able to pay the lower price and to increase the quantity of textiles they buy.

from P_2 to P_1. Because prices are lower, consumers increase their consumption from Q_2 to Q_3. Consumers obviously benefit; they get more for their money. On the other hand, the losses experienced by domestic firms, their workers, and their suppliers of raw materials are evidenced by the reduction in domestic production and the reduced revenues resulting from lower textile prices and lower domestic output levels.

Because prices are lower, domestic producers must move down their supply curve (S_1), and at the lower price they sell a lower quantity, Q_1 instead of Q_2. The total revenues of the domestic producers fall from P_2Q_2 to P_1Q_1; this is shown by the L-shaped shaded area bounded by $P_2aQ_2Q_1bP_1$. Of this total loss in revenues, owners lose by the lighter area bounded by P_2abP_1; the loss in incomes of workers and suppliers of raw materials is shown by the darker area Q_2abQ_1. This latter area is the cost the domestic firms would incur in producing a quantity from Q_1 to Q_2. These costs are payments made to workers and suppliers which are no longer made after the introduction of foreign textiles. Looked at another way, workers (and other resources) are employed in the domestic textile industry presumably because, in the broadest possible sense, the industry provides them with their best, most appealing employment opportunity. The introduction of foreign substitutes, however, reduces a country's demand for its domestic labor in textiles. The market wage drops below what it would otherwise be, and some workers are induced to move to what were previously their second-best employment opportunities.

Tariffs and Quotas

Because of these consequences of foreign competition, domestic producers have a private incentive to seek government restrictions on textile imports. Two forms of protection are commonly used, *tariffs* and *quotas*.

A tariff is a special tax on imported goods.

If tariffs are imposed on foreign textiles (or any other good) coming into this country, the price of foreign textiles will rise and the foreign supply of textiles will decrease (say from S_2 toward S_1 in Figure 16 · 2). This will cause a price increase for all textiles and an increase in domestic production. If the supply shifts all the way back to S_1, all foreign textiles have been excluded from sale in the domestic market. However, a much smaller tariff can have a more modest effect on the total supply; the supply curve may shift only a portion of the way back toward S_1, in which case the domestic price of textiles will still rise and domestic producers will expand their production levels. However, with the total supply curve located to the right of S_1, imports will come into the country.

Quotas are quantitative restrictions on the amount of a good which can be imported from abroad.

A quota may specify the amount of oil that can be imported into this country on a daily basis or the amount of sugar that can be imported on an annual basis. Regardless, a quota has the same general effect as a tariff. It reduces the total supply available in the domestic market, raises the market price, and encourages domestic production. There are two main differences between quotas and tariffs: first, quotas firmly restrict the amount of a product that can be imported, regardless of market conditions. Tariffs, on the other hand, permit the importation of a product so long as people are willing to pay the price of the product plus the tariff. If the demand for the product increases, more can be imported under a system of tariffs. Under the quota system, however, the quantity which can be imported does not increase without administrative action, whether demand increases or not. Second, any one foreign producer can sell as much as he can under a system of tariffs. Under a quota system, the quota is typically rationed among a specified group of foreign producers. Otherwise, all foreign producers would rush to sell their goods before the quota is filled. To the extent that the quota is rationed, quotas require more detailed government intervention in international markets.

The Politics of Protection

Because of the private benefits to be had, we should expect tariff and quota restrictions to be sought by an industry so long as the implied market benefits exceed the political costs of securing them. As we explained in Chapter 12, politicians are likely to "charge" for providing market protection. They often expect the voting support of those with a vested interest in the protected industry and contributions to their political campaigns in return for the congressional services they render in securing passage of appropriate tariff legislation. The industry's firms can make the necessary contributions out of the increased revenues they expect to receive as a result of the elimination of foreign competition. The difference between the increase in industry profits due to import restrictions and the amount paid out as political contributions can be construed as profits derived from diverting industry from market to political activity.

Consumers, on the other hand, have reason to oppose tariffs or quotas on imported products because such legislation will cause the price of what they buy to rise. However, the effects of tariffs cannot be seen in the prices of goods purchased in stores. Stores do not tack on the import charge (the cost of the tariff which is passed on to the consumers) at the cash register as they do a sales tax. Further, many consumers, never formally exposed to economics, are not able to reason through the complex effects which a tariff has on consumer prices. In fact, most consumers accept the proposition that what is good for the textile industry or the automobile industry or the electrical appliance industry is good for the country and for themselves, especially because of "Buy America" slogans and advertisements describing the loss of United States jobs.

As we will explain in greater detail in Chapter 21 of this book, consumers as a group have less private incentive to oppose tariff legislation than any specific industry has to support it. (For that matter, consumers have little incentive to push for restrictions on exports.) The benefits of a tariff accrue principally to a relatively small group of firms which may already have its lobbying organization well entrenched in Washington. These firms have a definite personal incentive to listen very closely to what politicians from their districts have to say with regard to tariffs; they have an incentive to be fully informed on the issue. They also have an incentive to make a significant contribution to the campaigns of politicians willing to support their private interests. On the other hand, the harmful effects of a tariff are diffused over a very large group of consumers. The financial burden borne by any one consumer may be very slight, particularly if the tariff itself is small. Indeed, most tariffs represent a small percentage of the selling price of the final product. As a result, the individual consumer may have very little incentive to become informed about a politician's position on any particular tariff when the issue is up for legislative consideration. The consumer has little incentive to make any kind of political contribution. All consumers, taken together, may have a collective interest in opposing tariffs; but collective, political actions must be initiated by individuals who must receive sufficient private benefits before they will be willing to incur the necessary costs of organizing any collective, political action.

This is not meant to suggest that consumers will not, at some point, oppose tariff legislation; they will have the necessary incentive at some level of tariff legislation. It is for this reason that Congress has rarely passed tariffs on imported goods which are high enough to make American importation of a good totally unprofitable for the foreign firm. At the same time, we emphasize the unequal political influence of consumers and industry representatives when they consider modest tariffs or, for that matter, any other legislation designed to benefit a special-interest group.

Regardless, tariffs are beneficial to that sector of the economy which is protected by them. They have the effect of reducing total real income while, at the same time, redistributing income toward the protected sector. To paraphrase a common expression, the size of the pie is reduced but the protected sector of the economy gets a bigger slice of a smaller pie. People who are more interested in the size of their share than in the size of the pie will find tariffs or quotas an attractive policy option.

THE CASE FOR FREE TRADE

In the first section of this chapter we demonstrated that international trade can result in an increase in the total incomes (meaning the summation of all individual incomes) of countries engaged in that trade. Accordingly, anything which reduces the scope of trade results in a reduction in the total real incomes to the countries involved. Tariffs are one means by which imports coming into a country can be reduced. To the extent that trade is a two-way street—that is, to the extent that exports trade for imports, at least in the long run—a reduction in imports leads to a reduction in exports, and, therefore, mutually beneficial trade to the countries involved is reduced. The reasoning is straightforward. A country which wishes to buy goods and services from us is dependent upon being able to sell to us: it is dependent upon our imports. From our imports the Japanese get the dollars they need to buy American products (exports). Therefore, if we reduce our imports, they will sell less to us and have fewer funds with which to buy from us. Tariffs reduce the two-way trade and the real incomes of both countries.

On the other hand, what is true for one sector of the economy is not necessarily true for all sectors. Tariffs reduce the quantity of goods available in the domestic market; and, therefore, they reduce a country's *total* real income. If all sectors are protected by tariffs, all sectors can (but do not necessarily) experience a drop in real income from the level that could have been achieved under conditions of free, unprotected trade. When everyone's income is reduced by protection, the case for free trade is strongest, clearest, and most likely to receive political support. Consider an example of a two-industry economy of automobiles and textiles, both of which have to compete with imports.[4] The relevant hypothetical data are presented in the matrix in Figure 16·3, which, as you may recall, is very similar to the matrixes used in Chapters 5 and 12. If neither industry seeks protection, both operate in cell I at a combined real income of $50, with $20 going to the textile industry and $30 going to the automobile industry. If the automobile industry does not seek protection but the textile industry does, the economy moves to cell II, in which case the economy's real income falls to $48. However, notice that the income of the textile industry rises from $20 to $23 as a result of the protection. The real income of the automotive sector, of course, falls from $30 (in cell I) to $25 (in cell II). The people in the automobile sector, because of the tariff on imported textiles, have fewer textiles available and have to pay higher prices for what they buy. The people in the textile sector also pay higher prices for textiles, but they get the benefits of the higher prices paid by people in the automobile industry. Therefore, the textile industry has an incentive to seek protection.

	Textile industry does not seek tariff protection		Textile industry seeks and obtains tariff protection	
	Cell I		Cell II	
Automobile industry does not seek tariff protection	Real income of textile: $20	Real income of auto: $30	Real income of textile: $23	Real income of auto: $25
	Cell III		Cell IV	
Automobile industry seeks and obtains tariff protection	Real income of textile: $15	Real income of auto: $34	Real income of textile: $17	Real income of auto: $26

FIG. 16·3 If both the textile and automobile industries do not obtain tariff protection, they can be in cell I with the highest possible industry and collective incomes. However, each industry has an incentive to obtain tariff protection. If they both obtain the protection, they both will end up in cell IV, a state in which each industry has less income than it could have had.

Similarly, the automobile industry has an incentive to seek protection. If the textile industry does not seek protection while the automobile industry does, the economy moves from cell I to cell III. The real income of the country falls from $50 to $49, but the automobile industry is better off. Its income rises from $30 (in cell I) to $34 (in cell III). It, too, has an incentive to seek protection. Indeed, either industry has an incentive to seek protection even if the other sector is already protected. For instance, if the textile industry has protection and the automobile industry does not (that is, the economy is in cell II), the automobile industry can seek protection and move to cell IV, in which

[4] The example is deficient to the extent that we do not consider an export sector; however, by ignoring this added complexity we lose nothing in the way of basic points we seek to make.

event its real income rises from \$25 (in cell II) to \$26 (in cell IV). If the automobile industry has protection and the textile industry does not, by acquiring protection the textile industry can move from cell III to cell IV; the real income of the textile industry rises from \$15 to \$17.

As a consequence, without some constitutional constraint preventing the two sectors from receiving protection in the form of tariffs on imports, each sector has a vested interest in seeking protection, *regardless of what the other sector does.* If both sectors seek it and laws are passed to oblige both, the economy will wind up in cell IV, in which the total real income is less (\$43) than it would have been with no protection for either sector (\$50 in cell I).

	Textile industry does not seek tariff protection		Textile industry seeks and obtains tariff protection	
	Cell I		Cell II	
Automobile industry does not seek tariff protection	Real income of textile	Real income of auto	Real income of textile	Real income of auto
	\$20	\$30	\$23	\$25
	Cell III		Cell IV	
Automobile industry seeks and obtains tariff protection	Real income of textile	Real income of auto	Real income of textile	Real income of auto
	\$15	\$34	\$17	\$31

FIG. 16·4 If tariff protection is not obtained, the textile and automobile industries will have incomes of \$20 and \$30, respectively. If both receive tariff protection, the income of the textile industry falls to \$17; however, the income of the automobile industry rises to \$31. In this case, the automobile industry has no incentive to agree to elimination of *all* tariffs.

The conditions in this example are quite favorable for the emergence of a prohibition against all forms of protective tariffs. There are only two sectors that need to reach an agreement, and the costs involved in reaching such an agreement are relatively small. However, in the economics of the real world, there are many economic sectors, and the costs of reaching a decision on tariff prohibition are much greater for two basic reasons. First, more sectors must be considered in the decision-making process. Second, any one sector of the economy may resist the elimination of the tariff on its foreign competitors because it reasons, perhaps correctly, that the detrimental effect of the tariff, taken by itself, is very slight; on the other hand, the benefits for its owners and workers are quite significant. The resistance of each sector to the elimination of tariffs in its sector adds to the decision costs.

Without a constitutional restraint against tariff protection, both industries in Figure 16·3 end up in cell IV with lower real incomes. However, in reality the effects of tariffs will be different for different sectors. Although the *total* real income of *all* sectors is lower, the real incomes of several (or many) sectors may be higher with protection throughout all sectors than without protection in any industry. Consider the information in Figure 16·4. The *total* real income of the two sectors is less in cell IV (\$49) than in cell I (\$50). On the other hand, the real income of the automobile sector is greater in cell IV (\$31) than in cell I (\$30). It is the textile sector which bears the brunt of the tariff protection in both sectors. The automobile sector in this example (and all other sectors like it in real-world economies) has a private interest in exerting political pressure to retain protective tariffs. Those sectors of the economy which, for one reason or another, have a "comparative advantage" in the manipulation of the political process will be the sectors least willing to see the political arena closed to competition for tariff protection.

The case for free trade is a subtle one. It is a case made in full recognition of what can happen if the political process is opened to legislation designed to benefit special-interest groups such as entrepreneurs, labor organizations, and consumer groups. These interest groups can be expected to compete in the political arena for favors and benefits in the same way they compete in the domestic market. The political favors obtained by one sector come at the expense of other sectors, and if all sectors receive the same treatment, all sectors can be worse off. If all are to be treated alike under the law, we must choose between free trade and protection for all—between cell I and cell IV. Economists generally choose cell I, free trade, because of the obvious total income benefits it provides for most members of a country. This, however, is a general position taken by economists. There are, as we will see, qualifications to this argument. These qualifications inevitably result in the political process being used to pursue legitimate national goals, such as the production of public goods through foreign trade policies. Yet even trade restrictions necessary for the "public good" are abused by those who would exploit them as a means of securing protection for private purposes.

THE CASE FOR RESTRICTED TRADE

Tariffs are never publicly proposed on the grounds that they will have the effect of serving the private interests of the protected industry, raise consumer prices, and reduce the domestic availability of the protected good. Such a proposal would most assuredly meet resounding political defeat. Instead, tariffs are usually put forth as the most efficient means of accomplishing some national objective. Any private benefits which accrue to the protected industry are portrayed as mere side benefits which emerge from achieving the overriding objective of serving the public interest.

Most pro-tariff arguments camouflage the underlying issues; however, there is one important and partially valid argument for tariff protection. It has to do with the maintenance of a strong national defense industry. If imports are allowed to flow into a country unabated, certain industries which are needed in time of war and other national emergencies can be undersold and will be run out of business by foreign producers. In time of war or national emergency, the United States will then be dependent upon foreign suppliers for needed defense equipment or material, and these suppliers may be either hostile or politically restrained from supporting the United States position.

Although the United States may be able to convert existing industries to the production of war-related goods, the length and complexity of the conversion process will impede our military response. Tariffs, then, protect defense industries from foreign competition. They may create inefficiencies in the allocation of world resources, but, so the argument goes, that is one of the costs we must bear to maintain a strong national defense posture.

Given the unsteady popularity of United States foreign policies and the uncertain support of our allies, the argument has merit. Israel has found over the past decades that it cannot count on the support of many of its Western allies in time of war. At one time it had purchased planes from France; but because France disagreed with Israel's policies with relation to its Middle East neighbors, France failed to provide Israel with needed spare parts. Israel was, accordingly, forced to expand its own defense industries. The United States could, conceivably, find itself in a similar position if it has to rely on foreign exporters for such goods as planes, firearms, and oil.

Like so many arguments whose boundaries are only vaguely defined, this tariff protection argument is easily abused by groups interested in seeking the private benefits of tariff protection. The argument has been used by the textile industry in the Carolinas and by candle manufacturers who, in their petition to Congress for increased tariff protection, have argued that candles are "a product required in the national defense to such an extent as to utilize the full capacity of the industry."[5]

In years past, United States oil producers have contended that a healthy domestic oil industry is vital to the national defense and that the health of the industry can be maintained only via protection

[5] "Petition of the Candlemakers—1951," in Paul Samuelson, ed., *Readings in Economics* (New York: McGraw-Hill Book Company, 1973), 7th ed., p. 237.

from the importation of cheaper oil.[6] The primary problem with this argument is that the tariff increases consumption of domestic oil by making foreign oil more expensive. The tariff permits domestic producers to raise their prices, encourages consumption of domestic oil, increases the depletion rate, and can make us more dependent on foreign energy sources in the future.

In formulating his energy policy, former President Ford took the national-interest argument one step further. In 1973 the OPEC oil cartel imposed an embargo on the exportation of oil to the United States. It used United States dependence on its oil reserves as a bargaining tool in its efforts to reduce United States political and economic support of Israel. President Ford contended in 1974 that a tariff should be imposed on imported oil in order to stimulate domestic exploration for new energy reserves, to make the United States energy independent by the 1980s, and, thereby, to reduce the threat of political blackmail from the Middle East.

There are many other arguments in support of tariffs, most of which are very weak from a practical as well as a theoretical perspective. We will deal briefly with five of them:

1 *Labor is paid less in foreign countries than in the United States. Therefore, United States industries cannot hope to compete on an equal footing with foreign imports. Tariffs are needed as a means of equalizing the cost of production and of making competition fair.*

Because this argument assumes, for the most part correctly, that wages are lower elsewhere than in the United States, it has an appealing ring. However, the direction of trade is not directly linked to the absolute wages in the United States or in foreign countries. What counts is the relative cost of production. Wages in the United States may be quite high in absolute or relative terms; however, so long as United States workers are much more productive than workers abroad, the costs of producing a good *can be* lower in the United States than elsewhere. Therefore, it is possible that, even with higher wages, United States firms can successfully compete with foreign firms for domestic customers.

Still, not all United States firms which are more efficient than their domestic counterparts and pay higher wages will be able to fend off foreign competition. Let us go back to the textile-beef example used earlier. The United States was more efficient in the production of beef and textiles than Japan, meaning that, generally speaking, fewer resources were being used to produce those two goods in the United States. Very possibly, the incomes of United States workers in both industries were on the average higher than in Japan. However, we noted that Japanese firms had a *comparative cost advantage* in textiles and, as a result, were able to undersell textile firms in the United States. However, if we impose tariffs (or quotas) on textiles because Japan has a comparative advantage in that product, we destroy the basis for trade. We destroy the basis by which we are able to export goods to Japan; and we destroy the mutual benefits of international trade.

2 *Abe Lincoln is reported to have once said something to this effect: "I don't know much about the tariff, but this I do know: if we trade with other countries, we get the goods and they get the money. However, if we trade with ourselves, we get the goods and the money." The statement seems to suggest that we are somehow better off by trading domestically than internationally and that tariffs are a means of encouraging domestic trade.*

Lincoln was clearly right when he said, "I don't know much about the tariff," because the rest of the statement demonstrates that he did not. He failed to recognize the real-income benefits from international trade. Tariffs reduce those benefits. Further, he seems to have confused a country's welfare with its monetary holdings. If we buy goods from abroad, we *do* get the goods and they

[6] During the energy crisis of the early 1970s, imported oil became more expensive than domestic oil. Import restrictions for oil were accordingly reduced or eventually eliminated.

do get the money.[7] But what is the other country going to do with the money it receives? If it sits on the money and never uses it, who is better off? In this case, we are. We have gotten some foreign goods in exchange for some paper bills, which, by the way, are relatively cheap to print. Foreign exporters and their countries will not long continue to export goods in exchange for paper money; at some point they will want to get something in return for their labor and materials. Then they can use the dollars they have to buy goods from us. Again, we see that trade is a give-and-take process by which benefits flow to both countries.

3 *Foreign countries impose tariffs on the United States goods they import. Unless we restrict, through tariffs or quantitative controls (i.e., quotas), the importation of their goods into our country, foreign producers have the benefits of selling in both our markets and their own. In order for United States firms to survive, foreign competitors must be restricted from coming into United States markets. Besides, if we cannot compete with foreign firms in their own markets, fairness dictates that they should not be allowed to compete with United States firms in the United States.*

This argument has a significant flaw: by restricting imports, countries like Japan reduce the ability of the United States and other countries to buy from them. In order to buy Japanese goods, Americans need yen; we get yen by selling to Japan. If Japan reduces its imports from the United States, Americans will have fewer yen to buy Japanese goods. The Japanese, thereby, restrict their own exports via tariffs. Their actions reduce international trade and, to that extent, the total (or aggregate) real income of the world. The Japanese harm both us and themselves. If we respond to their actions by imposing tariff restrictions on goods coming into this country, we reduce trade further. The harm done is compounded, not negated.

On the other hand, if we increase our tariffs in response to tariff increases in other countries, we may improve our bargaining position in international trade conferences designed to reduce tariffs on a multilateral basis. To the extent that all tariffs are in the end reduced by this strategy, world trade is stimulated.

4 *In times of recession, many people in the United States are out of work. If the government imposes tariffs on a wide range of imported goods, the demand for domestically produced goods will rise, more workers will have jobs, and these workers will have higher incomes which they can use to spend on other goods and services produced by other American workers.*

In the short run, more workers are likely to be hired because of tariffs. However, in the long run, as we have repeatedly emphasized, reduced imports will be offset by reduced exports, reducing the markets for United States goods and increasing the number of people without jobs in the export industries. The short-run increase in employment in industries that previously competed with imports will be offset by reduced employment in the export sector of the economy in the long run.

Furthermore, if we reduce our demand for foreign goods to increase the present employment opportunities in the United States, our domestic recession will be transmitted to other countries. Since we will buy fewer foreign-made goods, fewer workers will be needed in foreign industries. This, in turn, gives foreign governments a reason to retaliate by imposing tariffs of their own on the goods we export to them. They can reason that the tariffs will temporarily improve their domestic employment levels and that their tariffs can be used as a bargaining tool in getting us to reduce our tariffs against their products. The end result will be a reduction in total worldwide production and real income.

5 *Because they have only recently begun operations, certain industries must produce on a*

[7] Actually, the transaction may not involve the transfer of paper money. What is more likely to happen, as we will explain in the next chapter, is that payment will be made by transferring funds on the accounts of banks. The importer will experience a drop in his bank balance; the exporter will experience an increase in his bank balance. The essence of the transaction is the same as a transfer of paper money.

very small and noncompetitive scale. They are unable initially to successfully compete with much larger firms which have lower production costs. If protected by tariffs, these industries can establish themselves in the market, expand their scale of production, and eventually compete with foreign producers.

There are three main counterarguments to this position, known as the *infant industry* argument for protection. First, it is very difficult for a government to determine which domestic industries may eventually be able to compete with their foreign rivals once they establish themselves. The problem is particularly acute when we are talking about a long period of time during which market conditions, including the technology of production, will change significantly. Also, if given political acceptance, the argument is easily abused by industries interested in simply expanding their share of the world market. It may be easy for a firm to demonstrate that it can achieve economies of scale if it is allowed to expand via tariff protection. However, in order for the infant industry argument to be valid, the firm must actually be able to demonstrate that the country has a *comparative advantage* (not just economies of scale) in the production of the young industry's products.

Second, the prospect that a firm may eventually compete with its foreign rivals is not wholly sufficient grounds for protection. Once firms become established, consumers may receive benefits in terms of lower prices for the goods they buy. However, tariff protection imposes in the interim a cost on consumers in terms of higher-priced domestic goods. Before protection can be followed as a reasonable policy course, the proponents of protection must be able to show that the future benefits that will be received once the firm is established are (in present value[8] terms) greater than the costs that are incurred in the interim time period between the time the tariff is imposed and the time that the future benefits are received.

Third, if a firm can expand, can cover all costs of production, and can eventually compete with its foreign rivals by expanding its scale of operation, profitable opportunities exist for private entrepreneurs. Through the private capital markets (i.e., the bond and stock markets), firms with profitable growth potential will be able to secure the funds needed for expansion. If a firm is unable to secure the necessary expansion funds from private sources, it is either because there are defects in the capital markets or because the claims of potential benefits from expansion are not accepted by private investors. The returns are insufficient to get investors to accept the risks of investment.

The proponents of protection contend that government is obligated to accept production risks which the private market will not accept. The soundness of this claim is largely a question of one's values and one's perspective on what government should and should not do.

[8] See the discussion of the concept of present value in Chap. 2.

SUMMARY AND EXTENSIONS

The schedule of tariffs applied to various goods coming into the United States is now larger than the Los Angeles telephone directory; the print that is used is just as small. It is difficult to believe that all these tariffs have been imposed simply as a means of pursuing some national interest, such as the maintenance of a strong defense establishment. On the contrary, most tariffs now in effect reflect the political influence of special-interest groups.

The case against special-interest tariff legislation is strong and has perhaps been made stronger, with satire and wit, by Frederic Bastiat, a French economist of the nineteenth century. Pretending to represent the candle manufacturers of his day, he wrote the French Chamber of Deputies in 1845:

> Gentlemen:
>
> . . . We are subjected to the intolerable competition of a foreign rival, who enjoys, it would seem, such superior facilities for the production of light, that he is enabled to *inundate* our *national market* at so exceedingly reduced price, that, the moment he makes his appearance, he draws off all customs for us; and thus an important branch of French industry . . . is suddenly reduced to a state of complete stagnation. This rival is no other than the sun.
>
> Our petition is, that it would please your honorable body to pass a law whereby shall be directed the shutting up of all windows, dormers, skylights, shutters, curtains, in a word, all openings, holes, chinks, and fissures through which light of the sun . . . penetrates into our dwellings. . . .
>
> You may have no longer any right to cite the interest of the consumer. For whenever this has been found to compete with that of the producer, you have invariably sacrificed the first. You have done this to encourage labor, to increase the demand for labor. . . .
>
> Take care—you carry the death blow to your own policy. Remember that hitherto you have always repulsed foreign produce *because* it was an approach to a gratuitous gift, and *the more in the proportion* as this approach was more close. . . .
>
> Choose, but be consistent. And does it not argue the greatest inconsistency to check as you do the importation of coal, iron, cheese, and goods of foreign manufacture, merely because and even in proportion as their price approaches *zero*, while at the same time you freely admit, and without limitation, the light of the sun, whose price is during the whole day at *zero?*[9]

Indeed tariffs force consumers to buy more expensive domestic goods; to that extent they reduce aggregate real income. However, special-interest groups benefit from them and, unfortunately, our political process is easily exploited to that end.

[9] Frederic Bastiat, "A Petition," *Economic Sophisms* [Irvington-on-Hudson, New York: The Foundation for Economic Education, 1964 (originally published 1845)], pp. 56–60.

QUESTIONS TO PONDER

1 Using supply and demand curves, show the effects of a United States tariff on the price and quantity of the good in the foreign country in which it is produced.

2 Import quotas are quantitative restrictions on the importation of specific goods. For instance, the United States may place a quantitative limit on the amount of sugar (by weight) or oil (by volume) that is permitted to be imported into this country. That limit is the import quota. What effect will an import quota have on the domestic price of sugar received by domestic sugar producers? On the price received by the exporting firms?

3 If a tariff is imposed on imported automobiles and the domestic demand for automobiles rises, what will happen to the number of automobiles imported into this country? If a quota is imposed on the number of automobiles imported into this country, and the demand for automobiles increases, what will happen to the number of automobiles imported? Given the increase in demand, will the domestic price of automobiles go higher under a system of tariffs or under quotas?

4 Given the following information about the production capabilities of France and Italy, which country will export wine to the other? Give an example of a mutually beneficial exchange rate between wine and bread.

	Wine		Bread
France	40 units	or	60 units
Italy	10 units	or	5 units

5 Evaluate the following argument: "Tariffs on imported textiles increase the employment opportunities and incomes of textile workers. They, therefore, increase aggregate employment and income."

RECOMMENDED READINGS

Fels, Rendigs, and Robert G. Uhler: *Casebook of Economic Problems and Policies*, 1975–76 ed. (St. Paul, Minn.: West Publishing Co., Inc., 1975), cases 18 and 19.

Johnson, Harry G.: "Economics of the Brain Drain: An 'Internationalist' Model," in Harry G. Johnson and Burton A. Weisbrod, eds., *The Daily Economist* (Englewood Cliffs, N.J.: Prentice-Hall, Inc., 1973), pp. 232–249.

Yeager, Leland B.: *International Monetary Relations: Theory, History, and Policy* (New York: Harper and Row, Publishers, Inc., 1966), chap. 1.

17

International Finance: The Lubricant of Trade

The goal of every science is a conceptual model which shows how the pieces of its universe are related. Economists seek to become the Copernicuses of the international financial system, but their task is complicated since this system has changed substantially in the last one hundred years and continues to change.

Robert Aliber[1]

PREVIEW OF CHAPTER

Central question

How are two people in different countries which have two different currencies able to engage in international trade?

Major objectives

1 To describe the function and importance of *international exchange rates*
2 To demonstrate how international transactions which involve different currencies take place with the aid of commercial banks
3 To explain how international exchange rates are determined in a market uncontrolled by government
4 To explain the consequences of governmental attempts to control the international exchange rate

[1] Robert Z. Aliber, *The International Money Game* (New York; Basic Books, Inc., 1973), p. 12.

Major conclusions

1. The international exchange rate effects the relative prices of domestic and foreign products in the domestic markets.
2. Changes in the exchange rate will change the relative prices of foreign and domestic products and will affect a country's level of imports and exports. More specifically, a *depreciation* of the dollar will result in fewer United States imports and greater United States exports. An *appreciation* of the dollar will have the opposite effects.
3. In an international money market, the international exchange rate is determined by the interaction of the forces of supply and demand.
4. If the government fixes the exchange rate, the consequences will at times be a *balance of payments deficit* and at times a *balance of payments surplus*. For a United States balance of payments deficit which persists for a long period of time, the only solution may be to depreciate the dollar.

Important terms and concepts

International exchange rate
Depreciation of the dollar
Appreciation of the dollar
Balance of payments deficit
Balance of payments surplus
Floating exchange rate system
Fixed exchange rate system
Gold and currency reserves
International Monetary Fund
Currency swaps
Special drawing rights

People rarely use the barter system in trading—that is, exchanging one toy for two pens or three pots for the rear end of a steer. The reason is quite simple. Barter complicates trade because the seller must also be a buyer. In barter, not only must the seller find someone who wants what he has to offer, but the buyer must also have something that he wants in exchange. The seller of pots who wants beef, for instance, must find someone who is both willing to trade beef in exchange for pots and willing to make the exchange at approximately the same rate. The costs which buyers and sellers must incur in finding one another, even in the domestic market, can be extensive. When people are miles apart and separated by national boundaries and different cultures, as they are in international trade, barter is all the more complicated and unlikely. For this reason alone, we rarely observe individual exporters also acting as importers of goods and services with specific exports being exchanged for specific imports.

In the domestic economy, money, in the form of bills, coins, and checking account deposits, "lubricates" trade in the sense that it reduces the cost of consummating exchanges. The seller of pots needs only to find a buyer willing to pay with money; he does not have to accept goods which may be difficult to store, use, and trade. In the international economy, money lubricates trade in the same sense. However, there is one important complicating factor: those involved in trade are in different countries, each with different monetary units and monetary systems. The French have the franc; the Japanese, the yen; the Americans, the dollar. Indeed, there are well over 100 national currencies in the world. A system of international monetary exchange has emerged in order that the importer of goods may pay for the goods bought in the domestic currency of the importing country, whereas the exporter of those goods is paid in the currency of the exporting country. How this system works and the problems inherent in it are the subjects of international finance and this chapter.

THE PROCESS OF INTERNATIONAL MONETARY EXCHANGE

In order to grasp the complexities of international monetary exchange in concrete terms, imagine that you own a small store which carries wine. You may buy stocks of wine either domestically, that is, from New York and California wineries, or from wineries in France. If you buy from a New York firm, the problems of negotiating the deal and making payment are easily solved. Since the price of wine is quoted in dollars and the domestic firm expects payment in dollars, you can pay in the same way that you handle your personal affairs; you can write a check on your bank account. Subsequent to closing the deal, your bank balance falls while the balance of the New York winery rises—only one national currency is involved.

The purchase of wine from a French winery is a little more complex for two reasons. First, the price of wine will be quoted in terms of francs. Second, you want to be able to pay in dollars but the French winery must receive payment in francs; therefore, at some point you must be able to exchange the dollars you have for francs. (Alternatively, the French winery must be able to convert the dollars you give it for francs which it wants. Either way, dollars must be exchanged for francs.) Let us consider each problem separately.

International Exchange Rates

In order to compare the prices of French wine with the prices of domestic competitors in the United States, you need to convert the franc price of wine into the dollar equivalent. For this you need to know the *international exchange rate* between the dollar and the franc.

The international exchange rate is simply the price of one national currency (like the franc) in terms of another national currency (like the United States dollar).

In our example, the *international exchange rate* is the dollar price you must pay for each franc you buy. Table 17·1 gives the prices of several foreign currencies in terms of dollars and cents. As revealed in Table 17·1, the dollar price of a French franc in December 1976 was just over 20 cents. On the same date, the dollar price of a British pound was a little over $1.67.

TABLE 17·1 INTERNATIONAL EXCHANGE RATES BETWEEN THE DOLLAR AND SELECTED FOREIGN CURRENCIES (THE DOLLAR PRICE OF THE FOREIGN CURRENCY), DECEMBER 1976

	Dollar Price of Foreign Currency
British pound	$1.6784
Canadian dollar	0.9820
French franc	0.2005
Japanese yen	0.0034
Spanish peseta	0.0146
Swedish krona	0.2405
West German mark	0.4196

If you are interested in buying wine from France, you will need to convert the franc price of wine into dollar terms. With a knowledge of the international exchange at the time, conversion of the franc price to dollars is not very difficult. Assume that you want to buy F5000 (read "5000 francs") worth of wine and that the international exchange rate between dollars and francs is $0.20 = F1. This means simply that 1 franc sells on the international money market for $0.20 or that 1 dollar sells for F5. Now you can compute the dollar price of the wine as equal to $1000. (Each franc purchased on the international money market costs $0.20. The F5000, therefore, will cost you $1000: $0.20 × 5000.)

Obviously, the international exchange rate between dollars and francs is important: it determines the dollar price of the foreign goods you want to buy. If the exchange rate had been different, the dollar price of French wine would have been either less than or more than the $1000 computed above. For instance, suppose that the exchange rate were raised from $0.20 = F1 to $0.30 = F1. In the jargon of international finance, the change represents a *depreciation* (sometimes called a *devaluation*) of the dollar, since the dollar is now cheaper in terms of francs: it takes fewer francs (F3.33) to buy a dollar than previously (F5). In this case, the change represents an *appreciation* of the franc, since each franc will now buy more of a dollar, \$0.30 as opposed to \$0.20. The important point to note is that at the higher exchange rate, the dollar price of the purchase is \$1500 (\$0.30 × 5000). If the exchange rate is lowered (i.e., the dollar is *appreciated*) from \$0.20 = F1 to \$0.15 = F1, the price of the French wine to you will fall to \$750.

Accordingly, the franc price of wine and the exchange rate go a long way toward determining your willingness to buy French wine. If the franc price of wine increases or decreases, your dollar price also increases or decreases. Changes in the dollar price of francs have similar effects. If the dollar *depreciates* (that is, the dollar price of a franc rises), the dollar price of French wine rises also, and, very likely, you will be inclined to import less, since at a higher cost your customers will tend to buy less French wine. If the dollar *appreciates* (that is, the price of a franc falls), the dollar price falls; and, very likely, you will import more, since you can lower your prices to your customers and they, given their downward sloping demand curve, will tend to buy more wine.

Hence, a depreciation of the dollar tends to discourage imports, whereas an appreciation of the dollar on the international money market tends to encourage imports.

These results of changes in the international rate of exchange and, therefore, the value of the dollar are summarized in Table 17 · 2.

TABLE 17 · 2 THE EFFECTS OF A DEPRECIATION AND APPRECIATION OF THE DOLLAR ON UNITED STATES EXPORTS AND IMPORTS

	Depreciation of Dollar	Appreciation of Dollar
Price of exports	Decrease	Increase
Dollar value of exports	Increase	Decrease
Prices of imports	Increase	Decrease
Dollar value of imports	Decrease	Increase

The Exchange of National Currencies

The second complicating factor of buying the wine from France has to do with the fact that two national currencies are involved in the purchase of French wine. Since your American customers pay for what they buy from you in terms of dollars, not francs, you must ultimately pay for the wine in dollars. That is all you have to make the payment. On the other hand, workers in the vineyards and wineries of France expect to be paid in francs, since that is the currency they need to carry out their personal transactions. As indicated before, the French wine exporter, therefore, must ultimately be paid in francs in order to be able to meet these obligations.

How can you make payment in dollars while the French exporter is paid in francs? The answer to this question is not mysterious. Many large banks, both in this country and abroad, deal in national currencies for the same reason that other businesses trade in other commodities: the banks buy dollars (or any other national currency), paying for them in francs or yen or whatever, with the idea of selling them for a better price to someone else at a later date. An automobile dealer buys cars at a low price with the hope of selling them at a higher price. Banks attempt to do the same thing, except that their "commodities" are national currencies.

Let us illustrate how banks are involved in your purchase of the French wine. If you agree to pay for French wine in terms of dollars, you may write a check made out for the correct dollar amount on your account and, as in the case of the purchase of the New York wine described previously, send the check to the French firm.[2] The French wine-

[2] Instruments of exchange, other than checks, are often used in international transactions. However, the process is the same as that which we describe here; we use checks as an exchange here because we are interested in describing the essentials of the exchange process.

maker will accept the check knowing that the dollars can be traded (that is, sold) to a French bank in exchange for francs at the current exchange rate. If the exchange rate is \$0.20 = F1, and you have sent the winemaker a check for \$1000, the exporter will receive F5000 from the French bank for your check. The balance in your bank account will then fall; and since the French bank now has the dollar check, its dollar account in the United States bank in which it holds its account increases. Remember, banks, even foreign ones, have accounts with other banks just as individuals do. Any time a French importer wants to buy goods from a United States firm, the French bank will sell (or trade) the dollars that it now has on account in a United States bank in exchange for francs.

In the process of buying and selling dollars, the bank may make a profit. For example, suppose the French bank buys dollars from the French winery at a rate of \$0.20 = F1 (or \$1 = F5), paying F5000 for \$1000. The bank can then sell to a French importer the dollars acquired at a higher franc price, say \$0.19 = F1 (or \$1 = F5.26), receiving F5263 for the \$1000 sold. The gain to the bank on these two transactions is F263.

Our discussion of your imagined purchase of French wine leads us to an important observation: Any United States import, be it wine or watches, will lead to an increase in the dollar holdings of foreign banks. Similarly, expenditures of Americans on tours abroad or on the stocks and bonds of foreign corporations will have the same effect—an increase in the dollar holdings of foreign banks. Americans must have francs to buy a meal at a French restaurant or to buy a French corporate bond; therefore, someone must accept American dollars in exchange for francs. In most instances, the foreign banks end up holding the dollars that are sold by Americans.

On the other hand, United States exports to foreign countries reduce foreign holdings of United States dollars because exports are typically paid for out of the dollar accounts of foreign banks. (That is, the dollars are sold to foreign importers of United States goods, who then pay the United States exporters.) Expenditures by foreigners on trips to the United States and on the stocks and bonds of United States corporations have the same effect that United States exports do. They will increase the holdings of foreign currencies by United States banks. Consequently, if American expenditures abroad, in any of the forms mentioned above, exceed foreign expenditures here, the dollar holdings of foreign banks will tend to rise, and vice versa.[3]

If American expenditures abroad exceed for a period of time foreign expenditures here, foreign banks will at some point accumulate all the dollars that they can reasonably expect to use—that is, sell back to their citizens who want to buy American goods. At such a point, the banks have several options open to them. They may first sell their dollar holdings to other foreign commercial banks in exchange for francs, marks, or krona. They may sell the dollars to their government—more properly, the central bank of their country, such as the Bank of France. However, the market may be saturated with dollars; no one, including the central bank, may want to buy them at the going price (\$0.20 = F1 in our illustration). In this event, the banks can induce people to buy the dollars by altering the exchange rate; they can depreciate the dollar. For instance, they can change the exchange rate from \$0.20 = F1 to \$0.30 = F1. In this way, they simply increase the price of francs and decrease (depreciate) the price of dollars.

This change in the exchange rate has several effects which will tend to reduce the excess number of dollars coming into the international money market. As explained earlier, the change will make French wine, as well as every other French good, more expensive for Americans to buy. This will tend to reduce United States imports and, accordingly, the number of dollars that need to be exchanged for foreign currencies. In addition, the depreciation of the dollar will tend to reduce the price of American goods to foreigners. For instance, at an exchange rate of \$0.20 = F1, the

[3] The discussion could be developed in terms of United States bank holdings of francs or any other foreign currency. In this event, the effects of American expenditures on the foreign currency holdings of United States banks are the exact opposite of those described here.

franc price of a $1 million American computer is F5 million; at an exchange rate of $0.30 = F1, the franc price of that same computer is F3.33 million, a substantial reduction. To buy American goods at their new lower franc price, the French will increase their demand for dollars. Thus, because of lower American imports, the quantity of dollars being offered on the market falls. At the same time, because of greater American exports, the quantity of dollars demanded by the French expands, soaking up many of the dollars floating around the market. The gap—or the growth—in foreign holdings of dollars is reduced!

THE DETERMINATION OF THE EXCHANGE RATE

National currencies have a market value (i.e., price) because individuals, firms, and governments use them to buy foreign goods, services, and securities. There is, therefore, a market demand for a national currency like the franc. Furthermore, the demand for the franc (or any other currency) is downward sloping like D_1 in Figure 17·1. To see why, look at the market for francs from the point of view of a United States resident. As the dollar price of the franc falls, Americans want to buy more French goods and will require a larger quantity of francs to complete their transactions. As was explained earlier, this is so because of the effect which the lower dollar price of the franc has on the prices of French goods to Americans. To review, we noted that at an exchange rate of $0.20 = F1, F5000 worth of French wine will cost you $1000; however, at $0.15 = F1, the same quantity of French wine will cost you $750. Americans will import more French goods at the lower dollar price; they will demand a larger quantity of francs to make their purchases. Hence, the demand curve for francs is downward sloping.

The supply of francs coming into this market is a reflection of the French people's demand for American goods, services, and securities. To get American goods, the French need dollars. They must pay for these dollars with francs; in doing so they supply francs to the international money market. Although there is some theoretical argument to the contrary, concerning which we need not elaborate on here, economists generally view the supply curve of a foreign currency as being upward sloping to the right, as is the supply curve of francs, S_1, in Figure 17 · 1. The logic which underpins the slope of the curve should be, by now, familiar. As the dollar price of the franc rises, the price of American goods to the French falls. (Can you illustrate why with an example of your own?) To buy a larger quantity of American goods at a lower franc price, the French need more dollars and offer more francs to get them. Therefore, as the exchange rate rises, the quantity of francs supplied also rises.

The buyers and sellers of francs make up what is loosely called the "international money market" in francs. As we indicated earlier, banks are involved heavily in this market and others like it.

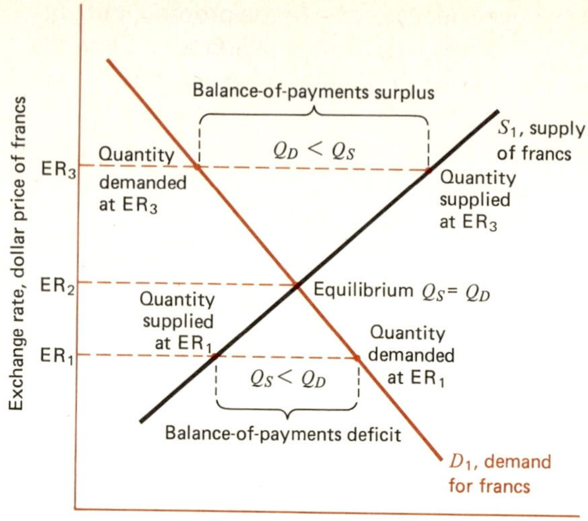

FIG. 17·1 The international exchange rate between the dollar and the franc is determined by the forces of supply and demand. If the exchange rate is below the equilibrium rate, say at ER$_1$, the quantity of francs demanded will exceed the quantity supplied, and the exchange rate will adjust upward as the result of competitive forces. On the other hand, if the exchange rate is above the equilibrium rate, the exchange rate will adjust downward. The price of a foreign currency is thus determined in much the same way that the price of any other commodity is determined.

They act as a middleman in the process: they buy francs from the sellers (suppliers) and sell to the buyers (demanders). As in other markets, the interactions of the suppliers and demanders will determine the price of the currency. Let us explain further. Given the supply and demand curves in Figure 17·1 and a competitive market for national currencies, the dollar price of the franc—that is, the exchange rate—will move toward the intersection of the supply and demand curves. The equilibrium price or exchange rate is ER_2. At that rate the quantity of francs supplied on the market is exactly equal to the quantity of francs demanded. There is no buildup of dollars or francs in the accounts of foreign banks. There is no reason for French or United States banks to change the exchange rate in order to either encourage or discourage the purchase or sale of francs or dollars. There is, in other words, an equilibrium in the net balance of payments coming into and going out of the country—that is, the country's *balance of payments.*

If the exchange rate is below the equilibrium level, the quantity of francs demanded will exceed the quantity supplied. There will be imbalance in the balance of payments. In the jargon of international finance, there is a *balance of payments deficit* for the United States. The excess quantity of a foreign currency demanded over the quantity of that foreign currency supplied on the market is the definition of a balance of payments deficit at the conceptual level. When it comes to the very practical problem of defining the balance of payments deficit in such a way that it is measurable in terms of data collected by the Department of Commerce, economists are at considerable disagreement.[4]

[4] Generally speaking, when a figure for the deficit is given in newspapers and magazines, the figure refers to the drain on United States government holdings of gold (called *gold reserves*) and other foreign currencies (called *foreign exchange reserves*) and the increase in foreign bank holdings of United States dollars. A decrease in reserve holdings is included because the reserves have been used by the United States government, in effect, to buy the necessary foreign currency (francs in our illustration) to help fill the gap between demand and supply. An increase in dollar holdings of foreign banks is included in the measurement of the deficit because (when the country is on a *fixed exchange rate system,* which will be discussed later) the dollar holdings of foreign banks can be, at the will of the banks, exchanged for a portion of the United States reserve.

In terms of the discussion of the preceding section, the excess demand for francs results in an accumulation of dollar balances in French banks beyond that which they can sell; as viewed from the other side of the problem, the banks will not have as many francs as they need. As in any other market, competitive pressures will push the exchange rate up toward ER_2. Those persons wishing to buy francs but who cannot at, say, ER_1, will offer the higher price that banks will then charge for the francs. As the price of the franc rises, French goods will become less attractive to Americans and, accordingly, the quantity of francs demanded will contract. American goods, however, will become more attractive to the French as the exchange rate moves up; the quantity of francs supplied will then rise.

Similarly, if the exchange rate is above ER_2, say at ER_3, the quantity of francs supplied will exceed the quantity demanded—the conceptual definition of a *balance of payments surplus*—and the exchange rate will fall toward ER_2, causing an increase in the quantity of francs demanded and a decrease in the quantity of francs supplied. (Can you explain why these changes occur as the exchange rate falls?)

In short, in a free foreign currency market, the price of a foreign currency on that market is determined in the same way that the price of any other commodity in its market is determined. The same basic forces are at work in the international money market as there are in the cattle market.

CHANGES IN MONEY MARKET CONDITIONS

The price of a national currency on the international market moves in response to changes in market conditions. Any gap between payments going out to foreign countries and payments coming in from abroad can be resolved by appropriate movements in the exchange rate. In a free international money market, government action is not needed to remedy a *persistent* deficit in a country's balance of payments. There is no need to be concerned about a persistent surplus in a country's balance of payments. Any imbalances are corrected by changes in the exchange rate.

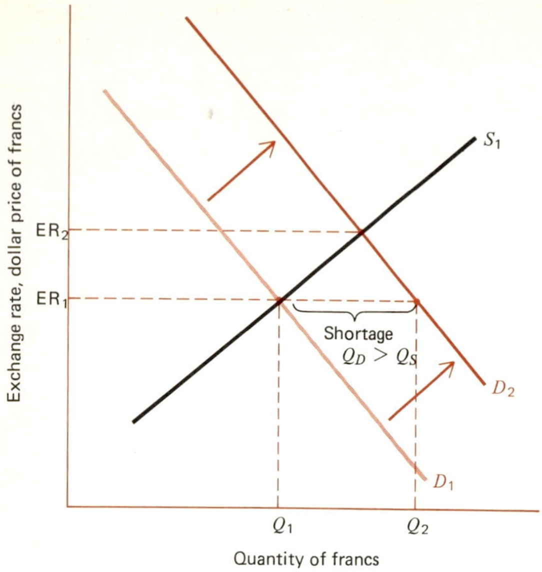

FIG. 17·2 An increase in the demand for francs will result in a shortage of the currency at the initial exchange rate. Competition among the potential buyers of the currency will push the exchange rate upward to a new equilibrium.

A Change in Consumer Tastes

To illustrate how changes in the exchange rate can rectify changes in the demand and the supply of francs, suppose that the preferences of Americans for French goods, for some unspecified reason, increase. The American demand for francs will increase because Americans will need a greater quantity of francs to buy the additional French goods they have come to desire. If, as in Figure 17·2, the United States demand for the franc rises from D_1 to D_2, at an exchange rate of ER_1 (the initial equilibrium rate) the quantity of francs demanded will exceed the quantity of francs supplied. As in our previous discussion, those who want to buy a greater quantity of francs but who cannot (because of the shortage) at ER_1 will offer to pay a higher price for them. Again, the exchange rate will rise toward the new equilibrium level of ER_2. (By definition, the dollar depreciates in value on this market.) At this level the initial imbalance in the money market is expunged. Those people willing to pay the price for the francs get them and can purchase French goods.

A Change in Real Incomes

The international money market can handle other changes in market conditions. For example, suppose that the real incomes of Americans rise. Assuming that consumption goes up with real income, consumers in the United States will be likely to buy more foreign imports. This is because Americans may not make their purchases on the basis of where the goods are produced and also because Americans will buy more domestically produced goods which quite possibly will incorporate materials imported from abroad. Either way, an increase in Americans' real incomes will lead to an increase in the demand for foreign currencies. The demand for francs, for instance, will rise, as in Figure 17·2. The exchange rate will rise to bring about an equilibrium between the supply and demand for francs and other currencies.

A Discrepancy in National Inflation Rates

Inflation is the general rise in the prices of goods and services in a country.[5] During periods when the inflation rates in the United States and in other countries are approximately the same, the exchange rate between the dollar and other currencies will remain stable. This is so because the *relative* prices of goods in the different countries remain the same, and there is no incentive for people to switch from domestic to imported goods, or vice versa.

However, when the inflation rate in the United States exceeds the inflation rate in foreign countries, foreign goods become *relatively* less expensive to Americans, and American goods become *relatively* more expensive to foreigners. There is, therefore, an incentive for Americans to buy some

[5] The problems of inflation will be considered in detail in Chaps. 23–26.

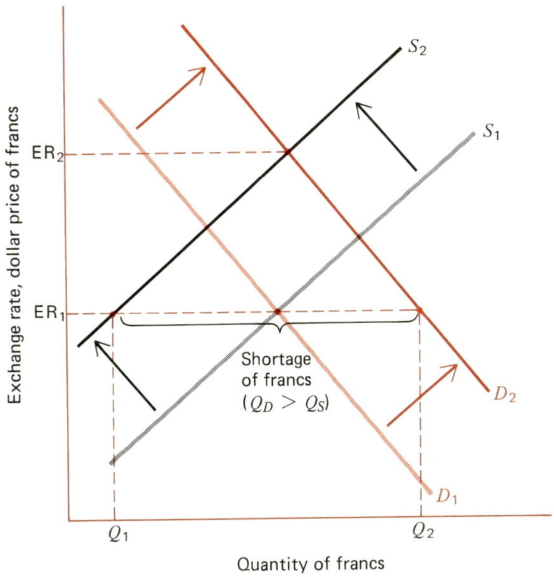

FIG. 17·3 A higher rate of inflation in the United States than in France will cause the demand for francs to rise and the supply of francs to contract. The result is an increase in the exchange rate between the dollar and the franc.

foreign goods to take the place of purchases previously made in the domestic market. Foreigners, on the other hand, have an incentive to buy more of the goods they want from their own country and from those countries whose prices are not rising as fast as prices in the United States. In summary, a higher United States inflation rate should lead to an increase in the United States demand for foreign currencies and a decrease in the supply of foreign currencies.

In terms of the market for the franc, which we have been using to illustrate what may happen in all currency markets, the demand can shift outward, from D_1 to D_2 in Figure 17 · 3, and the supply of francs can shift up and to the left, from S_1 to S_2. Again, at the initial equilibrium exchange rate of ER_1, a gap emerges between the quantity demanded and the quantity supplied. Given this shortage, an exchange rate which is free to move with market conditions will rise, in this case, to ER_2. At that higher rate a balance is reestablished in the money market. The higher rate, on the other hand, means that the dollar price of foreign goods is higher to Americans because of the exchange rate adjustment. In short, the rise in the exchange rate compensates for the differences in domestic inflation rates between the United States and some other country such as France.

CONTROL OF THE EXCHANGE RATE: THE FIXED EXCHANGE RATE SYSTEM

To this point, our analysis of the international money market has implicitly dealt with the *floating exchange rate system.* In this system, the exchange rate is determined by the forces of supply and demand. However, until 1971 international exchange rates were controlled by governments; the rates were not permitted to move in response to changes in supply and demand. Although this system has many names, it is generally referred to as a *fixed exchange rate system* simply because the rates were indeed fixed for long periods of time by government decree. The fixed exchange rate system is no longer in use among major trading countries; but because of its historical importance, we now turn to a detailed discussion of how the fixed exchange rate system worked.

For all its virtues, a free or floating exchange rate system has one disadvantage which causes many of the world's politicians to favor fixed exchange rates at specified levels for long periods of time. A free-moving exchange rate system can increase the risks involved in carrying out international business; this is because a small change in the exchange rate can cause significant losses to people who have closed business deals.

For example, suppose that you negotiate a purchase of wine on the basis of an exchange rate of \$0.20 = F1 and that you agree to pay the exporter \$1000. The French winery will expect to receive F5000. If, however, at the time you send the check, the exchange rate has moved to \$0.21 = F1, the exporter will receive only F4672 (\$1000 ÷ 0.21). The exporter loses F238.

Granted, the exchange rate may move in the opposite direction, in which case the exporter will gain by the change. In addition, short-term adverse changes can be hedged through the future market. However, the point that is emphasized by advocates of fixed exchange rates is that in long-term deals the exporter (or importer, depending upon how the contract reads) runs the risk of losing money because of movements in exchange rates. A risk cost is incurred; that cost will be translated into higher prices for the wine the exporter sells. Under a fixed exchange rate system, exchange rates move only periodically; the risk cost is reduced, and the prices of foreign goods can be lower to domestic consumers. Hence the attractiveness of fixed or controlled exchange rates.

As we discussed in Chapter 11, the control of the price of any good creates problems in that particular market. The foreign exchange rate is another kind of pricing system, and so control of the exchange rate is another form of price control. If the exchange rate is fixed at ER_1 in Figure 17·2 and the supply and demand curves remain stable, there is no problem with the fixed rate. Furthermore, there is no need, in that event, for governments to fix the rate; the rate will, in a completely free market, remain at the level (ER_1) as long as the supply and demand curves for currency stay put. However, if the exchange rate is fixed when market conditions change, problems can emerge. If the demand for francs increases from D_1 to D_2 as in Figure 17·2, a shortage of francs develops in the international money market. There is a balance of payments deficit for Americans. Those who want francs at that price will be unable to get all that they want from normal market sources. The government may have to ration the available supply and police the market against black marketeering. If black markets are not controlled, the price of the currency will rise. The price rises illegally, but it rises nonetheless. In the end the exchange rate has not really been controlled.

FILLING THE GAP

The United States government can keep the exchange rate fixed (that is, at ER_1) by filling the gap between the quantity of francs demanded and the quantity supplied. Under the fixed exchange system, the government holds reserves of francs (as well as other currencies); and it can fill the gap between the quantity of francs demanded and supplied by selling its francs at the officially established price. If buyers can secure francs from the government at a price of ER_1, as in Figure 17·2, there is no reason for them to offer to pay higher prices; consequently, to the extent that the government fills the gap, there is no upward pressure on the exchange rate. In order to do this, however, the United States government must have reserves of francs which it can offer for sale. It can collect these reserves at times when the quantity of francs supplied on the market exceeds the quantity demanded by Americans; during these periods the United States government can buy the excess francs from the French with dollars it has the power to create (i.e., print). The United States government can then sell them—that is, supply them—on the money market when a shortage of francs exists (when the quantity of francs demanded exceeds the supply).

However, if the latter shortage persists, there is what is called a *fundamental imbalance in the United States balance of payments* as opposed to a temporary imbalance to be corrected by future seasonal swings in the market conditions. It is in times of fundamental imbalance that a real problem emerges, one of maintaining sufficient reserves of the currencies in question to continue filling the gap. The problem of not having sufficient international reserves to fill a persistent gap is referred to as a *liquidity problem*. This problem can be remedied, although temporarily, in several ways.

Gold Reserves

Down through the centuries governments have used gold as international monetary reserves, each country defining its national currency in terms of gold. If the United States government establishes the price of gold at $35 an ounce and the French government prices gold at F175 an ounce and a shortage of francs develops on the money market, the United States government can sell some of its gold to France and receive F175 for each ounce. The francs can then be sold on the money market, filling the gap at the official exchange rate.[6] Conversely, if there is a shortage of dollars, the French government can keep the price of the dollar from rising above the official level by selling some of its gold to the United States in exchange for dollars and then selling the dollars received for francs.

Currency Reserves

Since the 1930s, when exchange rates have been fixed, countries have used a combination of gold and other currencies as international reserves. Many countries have used the United States dollar as one form of international reserves. Indeed, the dollar has been used as a form of international money to close deals between two countries neither of which is the United States. For example, an exporter in Brazil may agree to accept dollars in exchange for goods shipped to an importer in Germany. The Brazilian exporter accepts the dollars because of confidence that the dollars can be converted into the currency of Brazil.

Foreign banks have been willing to hold a large balance of dollars because so many transactions are carried out in terms of dollars, because banks need to have dollars available for their customers, because there is a large variety of goods available from the United States and they know that foreigners will always want the dollars, and because before 1971 banks were confident that they could trade their dollar holdings in for gold at any time. Knowing that they could get gold for dollars and that gold is more expensive to store than dollars, choosing to hold dollars was rational for many foreign banks as well as foreign firms, individuals, and governments. These foreign institutions, however, got those dollars by selling goods and services to us. To the extent that they continue to hold onto those dollars for the purpose of carrying out other international transactions, people in the United States have struck a tremendous deal: they have traded money, which is relatively cheap to produce, for textiles, automobiles, and appliances, which are much more expensive.

Foreign banks and governments have accumulated dollar balances from the late 1940s to the present. During the mid- to the late 1960s, the French government was against our policy with regard to Vietnam. French officials realized that by accepting dollars in exchange for goods and services they and other governments were helping to finance a war which they opposed. General DeGaulle, then President of France, proposed that the international monetary system go back to a pure gold standard, one in which gold alone, and not dollars, would serve as a country's reserve asset. DeGaulle knew that this proposed change in the international money system would reduce the ability of the United States to buy the goods and services it needed to continue its war policy. Because of the dominance of the dollar in international transactions, the proposal, although a rational one, given the national objectives of France, failed. It failed partly because it would have constricted international monetary reserves and reduced the ability of countries to control the exchange rates.

The International Monetary Fund

At the close of World War II the International Monetary Fund (IMF) was created to further increase the availability of international reserves which countries could use to fill gaps in their balance of payments. By depositing a portion of its gold reserves and a specified amount of its currency in the IMF, a country receives the right to borrow

[6] The process may not in practice work exactly like this. What may really happen is that, given the shortage of francs, foreign banks will continue to exchange francs for dollars that are presented to them. The banks can then sell the dollars that they collect to the Bank of France, which exchanges the dollars for gold. In the final analysis, the outcome is the same: gold is traded for francs. The shortage of francs is eliminated through the use of gold as an international reserve.

other foreign currencies from the IMF at a modest interest rate. These currencies can then be used to help fill any gap between outgoing and incoming foreign payments. Each country's borrowing rights are restricted, however, to 125 percent of its deposit with the IMF.

To illustrate, suppose that the deposit quota of the United States is $1 billion, 25 percent of which is covered by gold and the remaining part by dollars. Given the established exchange rates, the United States can borrow as much as $1.25 billion worth of francs, pounds, yen, and other currencies. When the imbalance is corrected, the United States can pay back the currencies that it has borrowed. Over the years, member countries' deposit quotas have been increased, which has had the effect of increasing the quantity of foreign currencies that each country can borrow.

Currency Swaps

During the 1960s, countries also increased one another's international reserves of foreign currencies by simply trading their currencies, that is, by engaging in *currency swaps*. The United States might agree to *swap* some of its dollars for marks from West Germany. Each country would then have more of the other's currency available to cover its balance of payments deficit.[7]

The reserves acquired through currency swaps in the 1960s were meant to be used to correct temporary imbalances in a country's international accounts and to get it over rough times in the international finance market. A country was expected to rebuild its depleted reserves during times when its incoming payments exceeded its outgoing payments. However, the system failed to work as expected. Some countries, particularly the United States and Great Britain, failed to take measures to correct their balance of payment deficits which were persistent during this period. Once they got the additional reserves, they used them up. For all intents and purposes, the United States and Britain, through currency swaps, traded some of their currency (which was, at most, paper) for the goods and services of other countries. Through currency swaps, the United States, for example, traded some of its dollars for marks, then through allowing a continued balance of payments imbalance, used the marks to buy goods and services from Germany.

Special Drawing Rights

Gold has been used for centuries as an international reserve. However, gold is expensive both to mine and to store. To use it as a reserve asset, we must not only dig a hole and bring it out of the ground, but we must also go to the trouble and expense of digging another hole in another part of the country (Fort Knox, Kentucky) to store it. Furthermore, we must make annual expenditures on defense systems to prevent the stored gold from being stolen. Gold has served an important role in international finance, but the benefits generated have come at considerable expense to all nations that so use it.

Gold reserves have another disadvantage: they grow only as new gold is mined and distributed to world governments. Growth in world trade can mean increases in the temporary gap between a country's outgoing and incoming payments. These larger gaps must be filled, if the exchange rate is to be held at the same level, with a larger quantity of reserves. However, the growth in world trade and resultant gaps in countries' balances of payments can be greater than the growth in gold reserves and, for that matter, growth in reserves from the other sources discussed above. In the 1960s, because of the expense of increasing world gold reserves and fears that world trade would be impeded, members of the IMF developed plans for a new monetary reserve system called *Special Drawing Rights* (or SDRs). Unlike other reserves, SDRs are mere bookkeeping entries on the accounts of the IMF. Once a country

[7] In addition, during periods of international monetary crisis in which buyers and sellers of a given foreign currency no longer feel that the exchange rate can be held at the officially established level, countries can, as they did in the 1960s, negotiate loans from groups of other countries. These other countries provide the country in trouble with a loan made in their currencies. The country in trouble can then use these borrowed funds to fill the gap in its balance of payments, thereby keeping the exchange rate from rising.

has an SDR account, it can use SDRs to settle imbalances in its international payments or to fill the gap between the quantity of, say, francs demanded and the quantity supplied on the free market. As with gold, a country can sell some of its allocated SDRs to France for francs, using the francs to fill in the balance of payments gap. In 1970 the IMF distributed $3.5 billion worth of SDRs (with 1 SDR equal to $1) to its members in proportion to their accounts. Additional distributions of SDRs were scheduled for later years. Because they can be used much as gold is used, SDRs have been referred to as *paper gold.*

Has a new international money been created? The answer is simple: The members of the IMF have agreed to accept SDRs in settlement of their accounts, just as in the past they have agreed to accept gold. They have agreed that SDRs, even though only bookkeeping entries, are a form of international money. It is the general acceptability of the United States dollar which gives the bills in your wallet value in domestic transactions and makes them money; the same principle applies to gold and to SDRs. More simply stated, money is what people generally accept in trade.

CORRECTING A PERSISTENT BALANCE OF PAYMENTS DEFICIT

International reserves of gold, foreign currencies, and SDRs are a means of solving *temporary* balance of payments deficit problems. If an excess of outgoing payments over incoming payments persists, a nation's reserves will eventually run out; the country will then not be able to keep the exchange rate from seeking its equilibrium level without resorting to elaborate rationing systems. When an imbalance persists, a country must seek other corrective measures; and frankly, there are very few options which can serve as long-run solutions at its disposal. Most are neither economically efficient nor politically acceptable.

Through changes in taxes and its expenditures and through changes in the supply of money people hold, a government can possibly reduce the country's total real income and inflation for short periods of time. (We will study how the government can do this in Parts Nine and Ten of the book.) A lower rate of domestic inflation will make domestically produced goods relatively more attractive to domestic residents and foreigners. A lower aggregate real income will mean that people will have less to spend, leading to less domestic consumption and fewer imports. The reduced demand for foreign goods will be translated into a reduced demand for foreign currencies and a subsequent reduction in the gap between the supply of and demand for any particular foreign currency at the official exchange rate. There will, therefore, be a reduction in the short-run balance of payments deficit. Many economists believe that this was precisely the sort of policy President Eisenhower followed during his term of office. The political and economic objections to these means of correcting the balance of payments deficit are that they add to the nation's unemployment rolls and that they lower the nation's real income and domestic production. Fewer people are needed in production. Further, a reduction of domestic inflation may seem like an attractive policy, but economists have not figured out a policy course which will reduce domestic inflation without creating a short-term unemployment problem.

Another way of correcting a persistent balance of payments deficit is for the government to impose tariffs on imported goods and/or restrict the flow of funds into foreign investments. Both options will tend to reduce the immediate demand for foreign currencies and the balance of payments deficit. These policies have been used by almost all governments. We need only remind you of the objections to restrictions on international trade raised in the preceding chapter.

Finally, after all else has been tried, a country may have to face the inevitable depreciation of its currency in terms of other world currencies. For instance, given a fixed exchange rate of $0.20 = F1, the United States can correct a balance of payments deficit by depreciating the dollar (or revising the exchange rate upward) to $0.30 = F1. The rules of the IMF provide for such a change. The change will make United States exports more attractive to foreigners; it will make foreign imports less attractive to Americans. Consequently, a depreciation of the dollar will reduce the quantity of francs demanded and increase the quantity of francs supplied on the international money market. This solution is reflected in Figure 17·2. With the demand for francs at D_2 and the exchange rate at ER_1, the balance of payments deficit is equal to the difference between the quantity of francs demanded, Q_2, and the quantity of francs supplied, Q_1. This is so because the exchange rate is below the equilibrium rate. A depreciation of the dollar moves the exchange rate toward the equilibrium rate of ER_2; that movement reduces the gap.

THE DEMISE OF THE FIXED EXCHANGE RATE SYSTEM IN 1971

In August 1971, President Nixon withdrew the United States' commitment to maintain fixed exchange rates between the dollar and other world currencies. In so doing, he allowed the overvalued dollar to seek a new equilibrium level and to move with future changes in money market conditions. The system which emerged is often referred to as a *floating exchange rate system.*

Demise of the fixed exchange rate system —sometimes called the *adjustable peg system,* since countries could periodically adjust the rates—was inevitable. The United States had run a balance of payments deficit in almost every year since 1950. Gold reserves, valued at $35 an ounce, had dwindled during this period from a high of $23 billion in 1950 to $12 billion in 1971. At the same time, foreigners had accumulated something in the neighborhood of $80 billion in their bank accounts. Although many of these dollars were necessary to carry on world trade, it was becoming clear to almost everyone that the market was saturated with dollars, that the dollar was overvalued, and that its depreciation was necessary.

People's fear of a depreciation of the dollar can have a disrupting effect on the international money market for two reasons. First, if a depreciation occurs, foreign dollar holdings lose value in terms of other world currencies. For example, at an exchange rate of $0.20 = F1, a $100 bank account is worth F500. However, at $0.30 = F1, that same $100 is worth only F333. In order to avoid an anticipated loss at times when a depreciation of the dollar is expected soon, people will try to sell the dollars they have and buy other currencies. In other words, in times of international monetary crisis, the demand for foreign currencies like francs will increase; this greater demand will increase the gap between the quantity of francs demanded and the quantity supplied. Thus, the United States will experience greater difficulty in filling the gap with its own reserves.

Second, there are speculators in the market who, as opposed to trying to avoid a loss, will try to make a profit on any expected depreciation of the dollar. If a person holding dollars buys francs at $0.20 apiece and sells them back at $0.30 apiece, the purchaser will make a profit of $0.10 on each franc. The expected depreciation, however, increases the demand for francs, again widening the gap between the quantity of francs demanded and the quantity supplied. During the 1950s and 1960s, the British were also having substantial balance of payments deficits, and the same types of problems were emerging in the pound market as in the dollar market.

Beginning in the mid-1960s, people began to suspect that depreciations of the dollar and the pound were about to occur. Every year or so there would be a *run* on the dollar or the pound, meaning that people would try to get out of dollars or pounds and into some other currency, such as German marks. These crises became progressively more frequent in the late 1960s and early 1970s. By August 1971, the runs on the dollar and the pound were so destabilizing to the fixed exchange rate system that abandonment of the system was certain; the timing of the change to a floating exchange rate system was the only question left. President Nixon chose to include the abandonment of fixed rates in his "package program" to lower taxes, stimulate the economy, and control prices in general. It is ironic to note that prices of international currencies were decontrolled at the time that the prices of domestic goods and services were frozen.

At present, finance ministers from the major industrial countries are meeting periodically to hammer out a new international monetary system. The system will probably remain one in which exchange rates will be allowed to move in response to the forces of supply and demand. However, wide and abrupt swings in the exchange rate will be prevented by governmental intervention in the money markets. In other words, the system will be what international finance officials call a *dirty float*, that is, neither completely free nor rigidly controlled. Developed countries will probably make plans to collectively come to the aid of any country which finds its currency rapidly depreciating.

To understand how countries may collectively help one another, consider the predicament of Britain in the spring of 1976. The British economy was experiencing the twin problems of inflation and unemployment, and its balance of payments was in deficit. Because Britain was importing more than it was exporting, its total demand for foreign currencies was greater than the quantity being brought to the international money market. Accordingly, the pound was depreciating. In terms of the dollar and many other currencies, one pound was buying progressively less. The depreciation of the pound is evidenced by the fact that one British pound bought $2.05 in January 1976; as indicated in Table 17 · 1, by December of that year it had fallen to $1.68. Because people feared that the pound would depreciate even further, they tried to get rid of the pounds they had. This increased the supply of pounds and caused the pound to depreciate further. The United States, France, West Germany, and several other countries agreed in early June to loan Britain the equivalent of over $5 billion. By having these currencies available, the British could buy up the pounds that were being offered for sale. They could stave off further depreciation of their own currency. (If the British government is willing to buy each pound offered for $1.75, will anyone sell pounds for less than $1.75?)

One of the major problems facing finance ministers as they strive to develop a new international monetary system is how to prevent a country from going into the international monetary market with the intent of depreciating its currency. By depreciating its currency, a country can increase the demand for its exported goods and lessen the demand for its imported goods. By manipulating the exchange rates, a country can improve, albeit temporarily, its own unemployment problem and worsen the unemployment problems of other countries. As in the case of tariffs, other countries may have to retaliate by trying to depreciate their currencies. Competitive devaluations can make the international monetary system unstable.

SUMMARY AND EXTENSIONS

If international trade is to operate smoothly, a stable set of international exchange rates is a necessary prerequisite. Changes in exchange rates can change the prices of exports and imports. Continual and significant variations in exchange rates can introduce an element of risk into international commerce and can, thereby, reduce the volume of trade. The proposal that exchange rates should be controlled or fixed at constant levels is intuitively appealing. However, as we have tried to emphasize, such a system has serious defects.

Under a floating exchange rate system, exchange rates will vary in response to changes in consumer tastes and the technology of production. We must accept such changes as not only useful but also necessary. However, exchange rates will also vary as a result of changes in domestic and foreign inflation rates and national income levels. In short, the stability or instability of the international monetary system will mirror the stability or instability of world economies. If the economies of the world are unstable because of inappropriate domestic policies, the international monetary system will be inherently unstable.

A primary challenge to those financial ministers who are interested in developing a stable international economic order will be to determine ways by which their efforts will lead to greater stability in the individual economies of the world. Beginning with the next section and chapter, we begin a study of inflation, unemployment, and production at the national level. With the aid of the theory that is developed, we will try to explain the policies which economists and government officials have recommended to stabilize prices and production levels of national economies. We are also partially able to explain the causes of the high rates of inflation and unemployment which we observe in the United States and throughout the world.

QUESTIONS TO PONDER

1 If a country appreciates its currency in relation to other national currencies, what effect will that have on the exports and imports of other countries? What effect will the appreciation have on the propensity of domestic investors to invest abroad?

2 Do you agree that a tax on imports and a subsidy on exports will have the same effect as a depreciation in a nation's currency on the international money market?

3 Suppose that the United States and Great Britain have a fixed exchange rate between their two currencies and that both countries double the price of gold in terms of their own national currencies. What effect will the doubling of the price of gold have on trade between the two countries? Assuming that other countries keep the price of gold constant in terms of their own currencies, what effect will the change in the dollar and pound price of gold have on international trade between the United States and Britain and the rest of the world?

4 Develop a case for and against the fixed exchange rate system.

5 Do you agree that if a country runs a persistent balance of payments surplus, that is, if its outgoing international payments are less than its incoming payments, it is trading goods and services for the currencies of other countries? Why would a country be unwilling to incur a balance of payments surplus for any long period of time?

RECOMMENDED READINGS

Bernstein, Peter L.: "The Dollar Glut," and Sam Shulsky: "The Lure of Gold: I" and "The Lure of Gold: II," are reprinted in *Economics: A Synergetic Approach*, written and edited by Bernard J. McCarney and Virginia Lee Owen (Hinsdale, Ill.: The Dryden Press, Inc., 1972).

Fels, Rendigs, and Robert G. Uhler: *Casebook of Economic Problems and Policies*, 1975–76 edition (St. Paul, Minn.: West Publishing Co., Inc., 1975), case 18.

Part Seven
The Public Sector

. . . Individuals entering into society must give up a share of liberty to preserve the rest. The magnitude of the sacrifice must depend as well on situation and circumstances, as on the object to be obtained. It is at all times difficult to draw with precision the line between those rights which may be surrendered, and those which must be reserved; . . . .

George Washington

Charles Callan Transill, ed., *The Making of the American Republic: The Great Documents, 1774–1789* (New Rochelle, N.Y.: Arlington House, n.d.), p. 1003. The quote is from the letter which Washington, then President of the Constitutional Convention, sent to the Continental Congress as he transmitted the text of the Constitution.

In this section of the book, we turn our attention to the public sector—i.e., government. Specifically, in Chapter 18 we describe the importance of government in the economy and provide explanations for the considerable growth in government which has occurred over the past 40 years. In Chapter 19 we develop the economic justifications for government activity in the economy, and in Chapter 20 we consider the special problems inherent in governmental attempts to redistribute the nation's income from the rich to the poor.

18

The Importance and Scope of Government

. . . That during the time men live without a common Power to keep them in awe, they are in that condition which is called Warre; and such a warre, as is of every man, against every man. . . . In such condition, there is no place for Industry; because the fruit thereof is uncertain; and consequently no Culture of the Earth, no Navigation, nor use of the commodities that may be imported by the Sea; no commodious Building; no Instruments of moving, and removing such things as required much force; no Knowledge of the face of the Earth; no account of Time; no Arts, no Letters; no Society; and which is worst of all, continuall feare, and danger of violent death; And the life of man, solitary, poore, nasty, brutish, and short.

Thomas Hobbes[1]

PREVIEW OF CHAPTER

Central question

How important is government in the economy?

Major objectives

1 To describe the size and scope of government activities in the economy in terms of government employment, expenditures, and tax collections
2 To describe the relative importance of state and local government on the one hand and the federal government on the other
3 To explain the considerable growth in government that has occurred over the past four decades

[1] Thomas Hobbes, *Leviathan*.

Major conclusions

1 Government at all levels—federal, state, and local—is by all measures a very important factor in the economic activity of the country. Government employs over 16 percent of all workers in the country and accounts for a little more than one-third of all purchases in the country. Furthermore, a sizable segment of the population depends on government in one way or another for a part or all of their livelihood.

2 Government has grown substantially at all levels in the past 40 years; however, the growth has been most pronounced at the state and local levels in the past decade. In addition, government expenditures at all levels have grown most dramatically in the area of meeting human needs, like education and medical care.

3 The substantial growth in government that has occurred in recent decades can be partly explained by (*a*) increases in the preferences of people for more goods and services traditionally produced by government, (*b*) increases in the prices of almost all goods and services, (*c*) changes in population growth and distribution, (*d*) changes in social and political philosophy, (*e*) new roles which have been assumed by government, and (*f*) defects in the political system.

Painting is the art of brushing and blending colors on a canvas. The skillful artist usually has not only some generalized notion of what he wants to paint, but also an understanding of the advantages and limitations of the materials and colors that the artist intends to use. In many respects social philosophy is an art form. It is the art of explaining the "composition" of the social order which we observe around us and of hypothetically reconstructing it in such a way that "improvements" may be seen. Instead of water and oils, the mediums of social philosophy are conceptual arguments regarding the motivation of human behavior, the constraints imposed by the social and physical environment on the behavior of individuals and groups, and the results that may be expected of any given societal organization. Like the artist, the skillful social philosopher understands the "mediums" of his trade; the philosopher understands the advantages and limitations of the component parts of social order.

Fundamentally, the study of economics is the pursuit of an answer to the question of how society *should* be organized. How *should* its component parts be blended into a form which is intellectually appealing? How can an "improvement" be made over present circumstances? These are normative questions for which there are no pat answers, and they eventually force the economist to step outside the strict regimen of the economics discipline and into the more artistic realm of social philosophy. In pursuit of the "how should" questions, economics alone cannot yield final answers, but it can be of considerable assistance. It can provide us with a basis for defining the component parts of social order and for illuminating the advantages and limitations of those component parts. In this way the study contributes needed "skills" which permit the development of provisional answers to the question, "How should society be organized?"

In this text we have recognized four component parts of social order, called "social organizers." They are (1) voluntary groups, (2) violence or the threat of violence, (3) markets, and (4) government. Up until now our purpose has been to reveal, as fully as possible, the advantages and drawbacks of both voluntary groups and markets as means of organizing the way people interact in pursuing their own private and collective interests. As we have repeatedly stressed, the viability and acceptability of any social organizer, such as markets, must be judged in full recognition of the marginal advantages and disadvantages of its alternatives. Accordingly, in this chapter we begin an analysis of government as an alternative means of organizing human behavior and for improving upon the accomplishments and failures of voluntary groups and markets.

To begin, we'll briefly review the failings of the market as a social organizer, because it is in those failings that the basis for much government action can be found. In the chapters which follow, we devote considerable attention to those areas of social order in which governmental-collective action is not only beneficial but necessary. We examine policy courses (represented by laws and programs) which government can follow to *improve* environmental quality and to alleviate the persistent social problems of unemployment, inflation, and poverty. There will always be a role for the markets and government; the major problem we face is how to define the permissible boundaries of markets and governments. The boundaries will never be defined with precision; and when the boundaries are tentatively drawn, inevitably reasonable people will disagree. Their disagreement reflects in part the artistic nature of the task facing social philosophy. The techniques of economic analysis help us to draw the boundaries with greater precision and, to that extent, reduce the potential for disagreement.

A demonstration of market failures is not, in and of itself, a clear and convincing case for governmental action. The failures of markets may mirror the imperfect nature of human behavior, upon which government, with the best of intentions and design, cannot improve. Further, government acts in a political and bureaucratic setting, and the imperfections of that setting will, in varying degrees, reduce the efficiency and acceptability of government as a substitute for the imperfect market. In other instances, the failings of the market will be so extensive that even an imperfect government will yield improvements of the sort that we seek. Again, one can determine the degree to which markets, government, and voluntary groups each contribute to our general well-being only when one understands the advantages and limitations of each of these social organizers. Therefore, in Chapters 21 and 22 we draw attention to the deficiencies of democratic processes and their bureaucratic delivery system. In this chapter, before going into more analytical issues, we describe the current and growing scope of government activity at the federal, state, and local levels in the United States. In the next chapter we discuss the basis for the emergence and expansion of government action. Chapter 20 considers governmental efforts to redistribute income. Future chapters deal in more detail with specific governmental policy areas such as inflation, unemployment, and national economic planning.

THE IMPACT OF GOVERNMENT ON THE ECONOMY: THE RECENT RECORD

Before the 1930s, government at all levels in the United States played a relatively modest role in the economy. In 1929 the federal government spent slightly over $3 billion, which represented approximately 3 percent of the total value of the country's production of goods and services. State and local government expenditures were equally modest. In the 1970s, the scope and importance of government in the economy can be seen in the statistics concerning government employment, tax revenues, the amount and distribution of government expenditures, and the number of people in the United States who are beneficiaries of government programs. As data in the following sections will show, growth in government has in recent years been mainly at the state and local levels, leading, in a relative sense, to a form of decentralization of government activity.

Government Employment

Statistics relating to government employment at the federal, state, and local levels are provided in Table 18·1. In 1975, 15 million people worked for

TABLE 18·1 UNITED STATES POPULATION AND CIVILIAN AND GOVERNMENT EMPLOYMENT: 1950 TO 1975

Year	Population (*millions*)	Civilian Labor Force[a] (*millions*)	Government Employees (*millions*)					Total Government Employees as Percent of Population (*percent*)	Total Government Employees as Percent of Civilian Labor Force (*percent*)
					States and Local				
			Total	Federal	Total	State	Local		
1950	151.3	62.2	6.4	2.1	4.3	1.1	3.2	4.2	10.3
1960	179.3	69.6	8.8	2.4	6.4	1.5	4.9	4.9	12.6
1970	203.2	82.7	13.0	2.9	10.1	2.8	7.4	6.4	15.7
1975	221.7	92.6	15.0	2.9	12.1	3.3	8.8	7.1	16.2

[a] The Civilian Labor Force, generally, includes all persons 16 years of age and older who work or are looking for work. A more detailed definition of this statistic is given in Chap. 23.

SOURCE: U.S. Bureau of the Census, *Statistical Abstract of the United States: 1975* (Washington, D.C.: U.S. Government Printing Office).

government at one level or another. This figure represents a little more than 7 percent of the total estimated population for that year and more than 16 percent of what is referred to as the *Civilian Labor Force* or CLF.[2] Generally speaking, the Civilian Labor Force includes all persons 16 years or older who work for a living or who want to work but for some reason cannot find a job. (Persons who are not employed and do not wish to be employed, like many high school and college students and some homemakers, are not included in the calculation of the Civilian Labor Force. For a more detailed description of the CLF, see Chapter 23.) Of the total number of government employees, most (8.8 million) worked at the local level; and more persons worked for the states than for the federal government.

These data also reveal that government employment has been growing over the years both in absolute numbers and as a percentage of the population and the Civilian Labor Force. In 1950 only 10.3 percent of all workers were employed by the government. By 1960 that percentage had risen to 12.6 percent; by 1970 the percentage had moved up to 15.7. Table 18·1 also reveals that the growth in government employment between 1970 and 1975 has been at the state and local levels; the number of federal workers has remained stable.

[2] There are proportionally fewer part-time jobs in the public sector than in the private sector. Accordingly, if we measure employment in terms of "full-time equivalent units" (where 2 half-time workers = 1 full-time worker), the percentage of the labor force in government goes up to 19.4 percent in 1973.

Government Finances

In 1974 government at all levels spent $480 billion on goods and services ranging from agricultural research to war materials, to schools and school lunches, to legal services for the poor, to roads and hospitals. (See Table 18·2.) This expenditure level for 1974 represented 34 percent of *Gross National Product* (GNP), which is the market value of all goods and services produced in the economy. (See Chapter 23 for a more detailed discussion of GNP.) As can be seen in Table 18·2, total government expenditures for 1974 were up from $70 billion and 24.6 percent of GNP in 1950. They are up from $333 billion but still 34 percent of GNP in 1970. In 1977 outlays of the federal government alone will be in the neighborhood of $394 billion. The actual federal government budget for 1978 is expected to exceed $440 billion.

Table 18·2 also shows the changing relative importance of federal expenditures on the one hand and state and local expenditures on the other. In

TABLE 18·2 GROSS NATIONAL PRODUCT AND EXPENDITURES BY ALL GOVERNMENTAL UNITS: 1950 TO 1974

Year	Gross National Product (*billions of dollars*)	Total Expenditures of All Governments (*billions of dollars*)	Federal (*billions of dollars*)	State and Local (*billions of dollars*)			All Government as Percent of Gross National Product (*percent*)
				Total	State	Local	
1950	285	70	42	28	11	17	24.6
1960	504	151	90	61	22	39	30.0
1970	977	333	185	148	56	92	34.0
1974	1,413	480	254	226	86	139	34.0

SOURCE: U.S. Bureau of the Census, *Statistical Abstract of the United States: 1976* (Washington, D.C.: U.S. Government Printing Office), pp. 256–393.

1950 federal expenditures ($42 billion) were 50 percent greater than the combined total of state and local governments ($28 billion). By 1974 state and local expenditures ($226 billion) were much closer to the expenditure level of the national government ($254 billion).

A more complete picture of the role of government in the economy can be developed by considering separately the different levels of governments. Federal tax revenues and outlays for selected years between 1960 and 1978 are presented in Table 18·3 and in Figures 18·1 and 18·2. Table 18·3 shows that individual income taxes, social security taxes, and corporate income taxes, in that order, are by far the most important sources of tax income for the federal government. Indeed, 45 percent of the total federal $265 billion taxes in 1974 came from personal income taxes such as those which are deducted from one's paycheck. Social security taxes accounted for another 25 percent, and corporate income taxes (which are charged on the profits of corporations) accounted for 15 percent. Excise taxes, like those on gasoline, liquor, cigarettes, and certain luxury items; estate and gift taxes; customs, which are taxes on imported goods; and miscellaneous receipts, like the sale of government property, were responsible for the remaining 15 percent of total federal revenues. Figure 18·2 discloses the sources of tax collections for the period 1970 to 1975.

Table 18·3 also reveals the growth in government receipts from the various forms of taxation from 1960 through 1974. Aside from corporate income and excise tax receipts, tax collections grew by more than 150 percent between 1960 and 1974. The most dramatic percentage increase in federal receipts is in the area of social security tax collections; tax receipts in this area grew by 348 percent in the 14-year period, more than twice the percentage growth in individual income taxes. Social security taxes are paid by employees and employers as a percentage of people's earned incomes up to specified income levels. The growth in social security taxes can be explained, in part, by the increase in the overall level of people's incomes; much of the growth, however, can be explained by the increase in the *rate* of taxation and the raising of the income level which is subject to the social security tax. In 1960 the combined employee and employer tax rate was 6 percent of the first $4800 earned by each worker; by 1973 the combined tax rate was 11.7 percent on the first $10,800 earned by each worker. In 1976 the tax rate was still 11.7 percent, but the maximum salary taxed rose to $15,300.

Federal expenditures Federal outlays have risen

TABLE 18·3 FEDERAL GOVERNMENT RECEIPTS, BY SOURCE, AND OUTLAYS, BY FUNCTION: 1960 TO 1978 *(billions of dollars)*

	1960	1970	1974	1978 (*estimate*)	Percentage Increase from 1960 to 1974
Total receipts, by source	92.5	193.7	264.9	393.0	186
Individual income taxes	40.7	90.4	119.0	171.2	192
Corporate income taxes	21.5	32.8	38.6	58.9	79
Social insurance taxes	14.7	45.3	65.9	126.1	348
Excise taxes	11.6	15.8	16.8	18.5	45
Estate & gift taxes	1.6	3.6	5.0	5.8	212
Customs	1.1	2.4	3.3	5.2	200
Miscellaneous receipts	1.2	3.4	5.4	7.2	350
Total outlays, by function	92.2	196.6	268.4	440.0	191
National defense	45.2	79.3	78.6	112.3	74
International affairs	2.9	3.6	3.6	7.3	24
Gen. sci., space, & technology	0.7	4.6	4.0	4.7	471
Agriculture	2.6	5.2	2.2	2.3	−16[a]
Natural res., environ., & energy	1.7	3.6	6.6	19.7	288
Commerce & transportation	5.8	9.1	13.1	19.3	126
Community & regional development	0.4	3.5	4.9	7.9	1125
Educ., manpower, & soc. services	1.0	7.9	11.6	19.4	1060
Health	0.8	13.1	22.1	43.2	2662
Income security	18.3	43.1	84.4	143.9	361
Veterans' benefits & services	5.5	8.7	13.4	18.3	144
Law enforcement & justice	0.4	1.0	2.5	3.8	525
General government	1.1	1.9	3.3	3.9	200
Revenue sharing & gen.-purpose fiscal assistance	0.2	0.5	6.7	8.1	3250
Interest	8.3	18.3	28.1	39.7	238
Allowances				2.6	—
Undistributed offsetting receipts	−2.5	−6.6	−10.1	−16.4	304
Budget surplus (+) or deficit (−)[b]	+0.3	−2.9	−3.5	−46.9	—

[a] The drop in government agriculture expenditures and the increase in natural resources expenditures between 1970 and 1974 reflect, in part, a rearrangement of the expenditures by function.
[b] A budget surplus is the amount by which total receipts exceed total outlays; a budget deficit is the amount by which total outlays exceed total receipts.

SOURCE: 1960 to 1973 budget data from U.S. Bureau of the Census, *Statistical Abstract of the United States: 1976* (Washington, D.C.: U.S. Government Printing Office), pp. 230–231.
1978 budget data from Office of Management and Budget, *The Budget of the United States Government: Fiscal Year 1978* (Washington, D.C.: U.S. Government Printing Office), p. 372.

even faster than receipts, as is also shown in Table 18·3 and Figure 18·2. Between 1960 and 1974 total federal expenditures grew by 191 percent, from $92 billion to $268 billion. The prices of the goods and services which the federal government buys also increased significantly during this period, by approximately 66 percent. Therefore, after allowing for the price increases, federal pur-

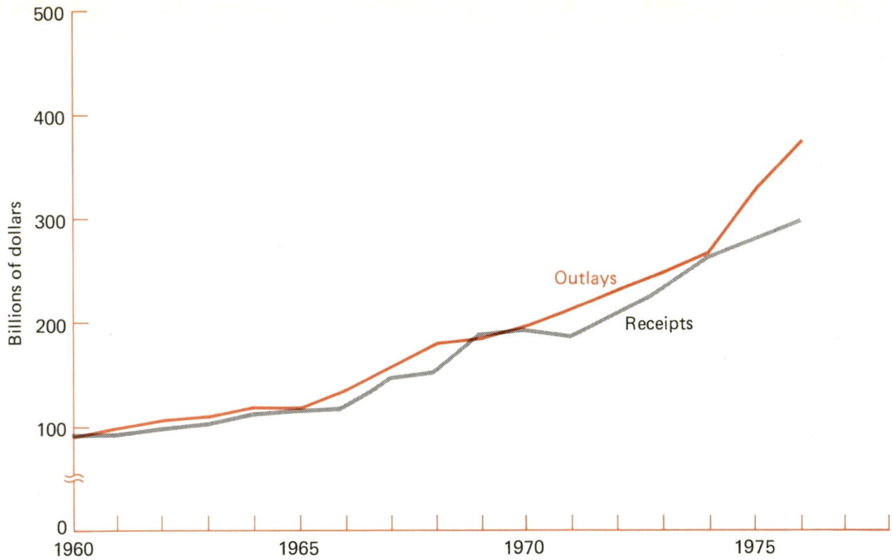

FIG. 18·1 FEDERAL BUDGET RECEIPTS AND OUTLAYS: 1960 TO 1975. Federal government outlays (expenditures) and receipts (tax collections) have increased significantly since 1960. Generally, outlays have exceeded receipts, meaning that the federal government has run a budgetary deficit during most of the years covered by the figure. [SOURCE: U.S. Bureau of the Census, *Statistical Abstract of the United States: 1976* (Washington, D.C.: U.S. Government Printing Office).]

chases of goods and services rose by more than 100 percent. However, as a percent of GNP, federal outlays remained stable at around 20 percent.

The most dramatic percentage increases in the 1960 to 1974 period were in the areas of community and regional development (1125 percent); education, manpower, and social services (1060 percent); health (2662 percent); and revenue sharing and general-purpose fiscal assistance to state and local governments (3250 percent). These substantial increases reflect the government's acceptance of new roles in the economy and a change in budgetary priorities at the national level. During the 1960-74 period, medical assistance for the elderly and disabled through Medicare and Medicaid were finally accepted as social responsibilities of the federal government. Although the federal government had for some time been aiding states and local governments through specific-purpose grants to expand and improve such facilities as hospitals, police protection, and sewage systems, beginning in 1971 it also initiated what has been called its *revenue sharing program.* Under this program, federal grants are not tied to specific purposes at the state and local levels.

Expenditures on national defense have been rising over the years; but in spite of the United States involvement in the Vietnam war, total expenditures on defense between 1960 and 1974 rose at a rate only 8 percentage points faster than the general rate of price increases. Overall, although more resources went into national defense in 1974 than in 1960, the relative importance of defense expenditures fell substantially in the federal government budget. The reason is that expenditures in most other areas increased at much faster paces. In 1960 defense expenditures

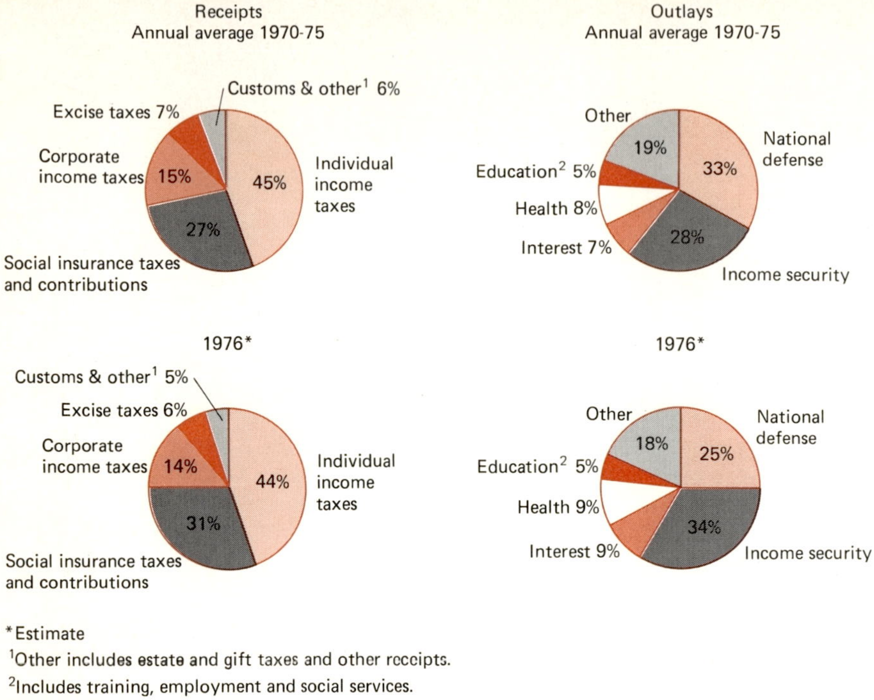

FIG. 18·2 ANNUAL FEDERAL BUDGET: 1970 TO 1975 (AVERAGE ANNUAL PERCENT DISTRIBUTION BY FUNCTION). The figure shows that the individual income tax is the biggest source of government revenue, accounting for 45 percent of federal revenues in the 1970-75 period and 44 percent in 1976. The social security tax collections were the next most important revenue source. In the 1970-75 period defense expenditures were the largest single expenditure category; income security payments, primarily in the form of social security payments, was the next most prominent outlay category of the federal government. The relative importance of these two categories was reversed in the 1976 budget. [SOURCE: U.S. Bureau of the Census, *Statistical Abstract of the United States: 1976* (Washington D.C.; U.S. Government Printing Office).]

accounted for 49 percent of federal outlays; in the 1970-75 period, they represented only 33 percent (see Figure 18·2). The percentage decline continues; in 1978 defense outlays will be approximately 25 percent of expected total outlays.

State and local government revenues State and local governments receive a significant portion of their revenues from the federal government in the form of specific grants for specific purposes and from the more general revenue sharing program. In fact, state and local governments received 41.8 billion or about 18 percent of their revenue from federal sources in 1974. (See Table 18·4 and Figure 18·3.) Table 18·4 and Figure 18·3 show that property, sales, and individual income taxes, in that order, are the most prominent sources of nonfederal tax revenues. For most local governments, property taxes are the single most important revenue source; and sales taxes are the most important tax revenue source of states. As indicated by

TABLE 18·4 STATE AND LOCAL GOVERNMENT REVENUE AND EXPENDITURES: 1950 TO 1974 *(in billions of dollars)*

	1960	1970	1974	Percentage Increase, 1960–1974
Total revenue	60.3	150.1	237.9	294
From federal government	7.0	21.9	41.8	497
From state & local sources	53.3	128.2	196.1	268
General, net of intergovernmental	43.5	108.9	165.9	281
Taxes	36.1	86.8	130.7	262
Property	16.4	34.1	47.7	190
Sales	11.8	30.3	46.1	291
Individual income	2.5	10.8	19.5	680
Corporate income	1.2	3.7	6.0	400
Other	4.2	7.9	11.4	171
Charges & miscellaneous	7.4	22.1	35.2	377
Utility & liquor stores revenue	4.9	8.6	11.7	138
Insurance trust revenue	4.9	10.7	18.4	276
Direct expenditures	61.0	148.1	225.7	270
Direct general expenditures	51.9	131.3	198.6	283
Education	18.7	52.7	75.8	305
Highways	9.4	16.4	19.9	111
Public welfare	4.4	14.7	24.7	461
Health	0.5	1.8	3.4	580
Hospitals	3.2	7.9	12.5	290
Police protection	1.9	4.5	7.3	284
Local fire protection	1.0	2.0	3.0	200
Natural resources	1.2	2.7	3.7	208
Sanitation & sewage	1.7	3.4	6.0	253
Housing & urban renewal	0.8	2.1	3.5	337
Local parks & recreation	0.7	1.9	3.0	329
Financial administration & general control	2.1	4.7	7.5	257
Interest on general debt	1.7	4.4	7.7	353
Utility & liquor stores expenditures	5.1	9.4	14.4	182
Insurance trust expenditures	4.0	7.3	12.7	218

SOURCE: U.S. Bureau of the Census, *Statistical Abstract of the United States: 1976* (Washington, D.C.: U.S. Government Printing Office), p. 264.

the percentage growth, individual income taxes are becoming a more important tax source for both state and local governments. Corporate income tax receipts play a relatively unimportant role in most state and local governments' finances.

Figure 18·4 illustrates the relative positions of federal taxes and state and local taxes per person (or per capita). Over the period 1950-70, the per capita tax bite of the federal government has been consistently higher than the per capita take of state and local governments combined. However,

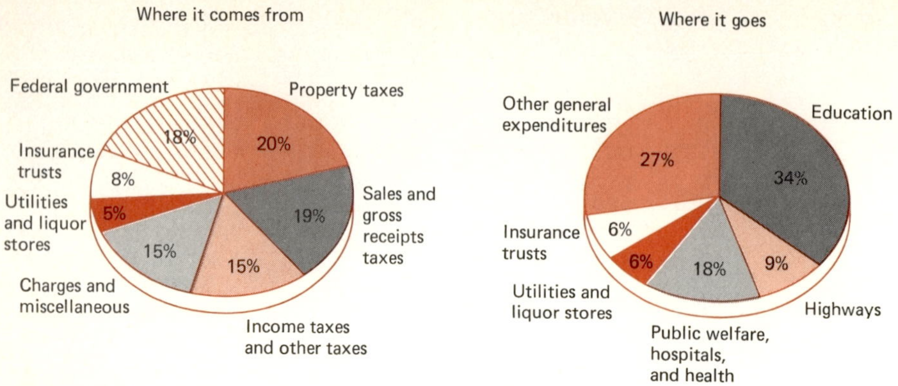

FIG. 18·3 THE STATE AND LOCAL GOVERNMENT DOLLAR: 1974. The main sources of revenue for state and local government were property taxes, sales taxes, and grants from the federal government, accounting for 20, 19, and 18 percent of state and local government revenues, respectively. The largest expenditure category of state and local government was education. [SOURCE: U.S. Bureau of the Census, *Statistical Abstract of the United States: 1976* (Washington D.C.: U.S. Government Printing Office).]

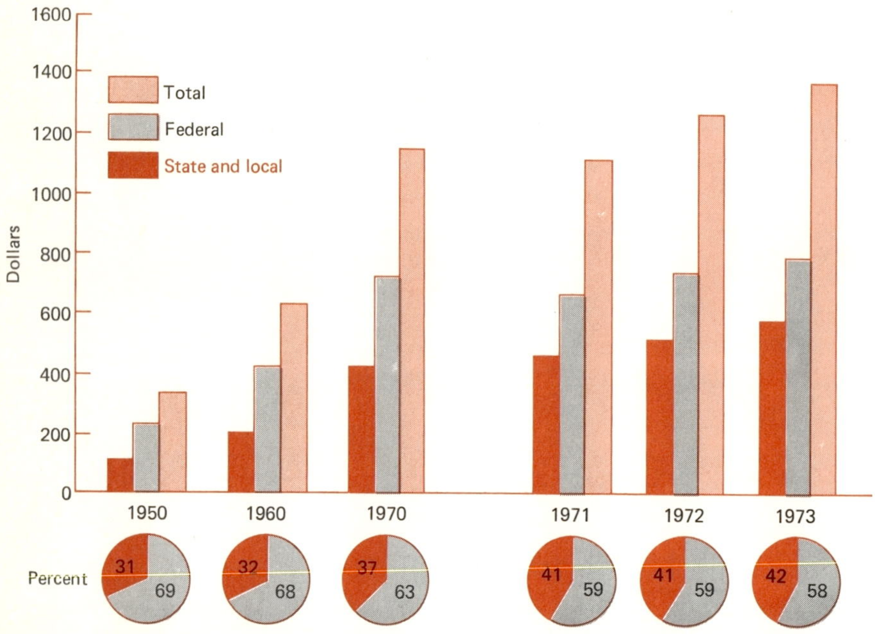

FIG. 18·4 PER CAPITA TAX REVENUE, BY LEVEL OF GOVERNMENT: 1950 TO 1973. Government expenditures per capita (or person) have grown at all levels of government. However, the increase has been most prominent at the state and local government levels. [SOURCE: U.S. Bureau of the Census, *Statistical Abstract of the United States: 1975* (Washington, D.C.: U.S. Government Printing Office).]

as we have indicated, a portion of the tax revenues of the federal government are channeled back to the states.

State and local government expenditures Table 18·4 reveals the substantial increase in state and local expenditures we mentioned before. This table shows that the most dramatic areas of expenditure increases in the 1960-74 period have been public welfare assistance (461 percent), health (580 percent), housing and urban renewal (337 percent), and interest on state and local debt (353 percent). The last statistic, interest payments, has increased because state and local governments have had to pay higher interest rates on the bonds they have issued to finance public works and because deficit spending (going into debt) has been used more frequently as a means of financing programs. Interest rates on many municipal and state bonds have risen by more than the rates paid by other borrowers such as corporations. Because the financial condition of many states and cities, such as New York City, has worsened, investors are demanding higher interest rates to compensate them for the growing risk of default.

Education is the single most prominent function of state and local governments. Still, the relative importance of education in state and local budgets is giving way to a growing emphasis on other social welfare programs. In 1977, states and localities (especially New York City) were pushing the federal government to take over that part of their social welfare programs involving direct assistance to the poor and unemployed. These proposals are being considered sympathetically by the Carter administration. A reasonable prediction is that the federal government will, within the next few years, assume a growing portion of the welfare burdens of state and local governments.

Beneficiaries of Government Programs

The purpose of government is to benefit people. By providing national defense, police protection, and the administration of the legal system, government activities benefit almost all citizens more or less indirectly. However, the benefits of government are not always spread evenly over the entire population. Those who are on government payrolls and who receive retirement income or other welfare assistance benefit directly. It is difficult to calculate accurately the total number of people who receive a portion or all of their incomes directly from government sources. There is a danger of counting those people who receive benefits from more than one source twice or three or more times. However, in Table 18·5, we have listed six categories of people who receive at least a portion of their incomes from government. In this table we include the 15 million government workers at all levels (from Table 18·1). We have also added 32.1 million social security recipients, primarily persons who are either retired or disabled and are entitled to social security benefits. In 1975 there were an additional 25.5 million unemployed workers who, at one time or another during the year, received unemployment compensation payments. Veterans' benefits were paid to a total of 3.2 million, and 19 million people had income supplements in the form of food stamps. The total of these six groups of beneficiaries is nearly 94.8 million persons, a figure which is equal to approximately 45 percent of the nation's population during that year. Without doubt, some people are included in more than one of these categories; to the extent that this is true, the figures are inflated. On the other hand, there are many other government programs, for instance, subsidies to farmers and homeowners and aid to mothers of dependent children. These programs benefit millions of people, many of whom may not be included in the previous calculations. In addition, many industries, including those in what has been called the "military-industrial complex," depend almost totally on government contracts for their continued existence. The incomes of the employees in these industries are indirectly supported by government action. Regardless of the exact numbers involved, it is quite clear that the number of people directly or indirectly dependent upon government represents a substantial portion of the United States population. Most of these people are also voters, and so we may conclude

TABLE 18 · 5 PERSONS RECEIVING SOME PORTION OF THEIR INCOMES DIRECTLY FROM GOVERNMENT SOURCES: 1975 *(millions of persons)*

Federal, state, & local employees		15.0
Federal	2.9	
State	3.3	
Local	8.8	
Social security recipients		32.1
Retired workers	16.6	
Others (disabled workers, widows & widowers, children, etc.)	15.5	
Unemployed workers		25.5
Veterans		3.2
Food stamp recipients		19.0
Total		94.8

Total recipients (94.8 million) as a percent of the U.S. population in 1975 (212.7 million) } 44.6 Percent

SOURCE: U.S. Bureau of the Census, *Statistical Abstract of the United States: 1976* (Washington, U.S. Government Printing Office).

that a sizable number of voters have a special, private interest in the continuation and expansion of various government programs.

Government as a Regulator

The statistics we have presented on government employment, taxes, and expenditures indirectly describe the overall influence of government in the economy. The influence of government is suggested more directly, however, by the controls which federal regulatory agencies have on almost all United States industries and institutions. Federal, state, and local governments dictate the minimum wages that can be paid in various occupations, the permissible level of hazard in working areas, the design and construction of goods from toys to fixed-foundation and mobile homes, the drugs that can be issued, the amount of information which companies must provide on corporate securities and on consumer products, the amount and quality of utility service, the racial mix of educational systems, the permissible routes and rates for trucks, airlines, and trains, and prices of all goods when "price freezes" are in effect.

The full force of government as a regulator of economic activity can be seen in the books containing rules and standards issued annually by various agencies and by the massive paperwork which these agencies impose on private businesses to ensure that the regulations are being obeyed. As an example of government influence in one area of the economy, consider the activity of OSHA (Occupational Safety and Health Administration), which was created in 1971. In the first four years of its operations, OSHA wrote close to 4400 standards relating to the safety conditions of employment. This list covers 800 pages in the Code of Federal Regulations and includes, among other things, about 140 standards pertaining to portable wood ladders used on construction sites.[3] The production of such standards, most of which have been deemed necessary by Congress, has truly become a growth phenomenon in the United States. (For more on the case for and against government regulation, see Chapter 12.)

[3] Robert Stewardt Smith, *The Occupational Safety and Health Act: Its Goals and Its Achievements* (Washington, D.C.: American Enterprise Institute for Public Policy Research, 1976), p. 11.

GROWTH IN GOVERNMENT: SOME EXPLANATIONS

Although a large and pervasive government is relatively new to the United States, such governments are by no means new or unique in history. Indeed, two of the earliest civilized areas, Mesopotamia and Egypt, depended on elaborate government irrigation works for almost all their countries' production of goods and services. Both countries were located in largely arid regions, and the irrigation canals, built and maintained by the governments, were indispensable for raising crops. Further, these early countries had a great deal of direct government management of other aspects of their economy. Price controls, direct government operations in the market, and government control of a large part of foreign trade were characteristic. European governments (including monarchies) during the Renaissance and the early modern period were also highly "interventionist." Although generalizations are always difficult to make, the type of economy in which the government holds a major share has been historically more common than the type of economy in which government is a relatively small and inconsequential part of the economy, such as that of the United States and England in the nineteenth century. In fact, one of the most daring dimensions of the "American experiment" in constitutional government has been the rather limited role assigned to government in the economy.

Growth in the relative importance of government in the United States has been dramatic. Some would say this growth has been too dramatic; others argue that the pace of governmental growth has been too slow to keep up with the growth in the "collective" needs of people. As opposed to entering the debate on how extensive government influence and power *should* be, in this section we seek explanations for the growth in government activity that has been observed in modern times. Of necessity, several arguments cited must be looked upon as tentative hypotheses which may be considered reasonable only after further analysis of the government sector in chapters which follow.

Changes in Preferences and Incomes

An argument frequently offered to explain the growth of government is simply that people's "tastes" for the kinds of public goods and services produced by government have dramatically increased over the past three or four decades. People now want more and better educational facilities, parks, roads, airports, medical services, sewage systems, and care for the elderly and disabled. In other words, government growth mirrors society's collective shift in demand from the private to the public sector.

Going a step further, economists point out that what appears to be a pure change in preferences may reflect, more than anything else, the rising level of people's incomes: the increase in their incomes has given people the capacity to "buy," through the political processes, more of the public goods that they have always wanted but could not afford in the past. Many publicly provided goods, like police protection and elementary education, may be construed as "necessities." However, there are probably many public goods, like space flights and certain kinds of high-quality medical service, which are "luxury goods." The demand for both these types of goods—necessities and luxury goods—in the private as well as the public sector, tends to rise at a faster rate than people's incomes. All purchases taken together can, in the long run, rise no faster than income because people have only their incomes to spend. Therefore, if government purchases rise at a faster rate than income, the purchases of all goods in the private sector must rise at a slower rate than income. On this assumption, as income rises, government grows in an absolute and relative sense.

Increases in Prices

As mentioned before, the price of almost everything has risen substantially over the last decade. Consequently, a part of the increase in government budgets can be explained by the simple need for government in times of inflation to spend more dollars to buy the same real quantity of goods and services. In order to keep abreast of inflation between 1960 and the end of 1976, government budgets at all levels would have had to double.

Inflation also increases the amount of money paid to government in the form of taxes, particularly at the federal level, where income taxes are such an important source of revenue. During inflationary times, people's money income (that is, the number of dollars they earn) increases; and because people are obligated to pay a percentage of their money income to the government, the tax revenue of government also rises. Sales taxes rise as prices rise, and property taxes rise (with, perhaps, some lag) as the market value (prices) of real estate and personal property rises.

In addition, the federal government and, to a lesser extent, many states have what is called a *progressive income tax rate system.* Under this system, people pay progressively higher tax *rates* as their *money* income rises.[4] For example, on the first $15,000 of income a person may be required to pay taxes at a rate of 15 percent; on the *next* $5000 of additional income one may be required to pay tax at a rate of 20 percent. Therefore, in times of inflation, people's tax payments rise not only because of their higher money incomes but also because of the higher *rates* of taxation. Although the purchasing power of people's income may not have risen during inflationary times, the proportion of their income paid to the government goes up. Individuals have less to spend; federal and state governments have more. For the reasons outlined here, economists look upon inflation as a hidden form of taxation.

To see the effects of inflation on tax payments and the real income more clearly, consider the following example. Suppose that in 1976 the Jones family had an income of $18,000. Taking into consideration only federal income taxes, suppose also that in filing their tax returns they were able to claim three personal exemptions and to use the standard deduction, which was, at the time, a maximum of $2800.[5] As can be seen in Table 18 · 6, the Joneses' taxable income in 1976 was $12,950: $18,000 of money income less personal exemptions of $2250 ($750 for each of three exemptions) and less the maximum standard deduction of $2800. On this taxable income, the Joneses' taxes are $2497, as calculated by the progressive rates indicated in the table (15.5 percent on the first $4000 of taxable income, 19 percent on the next $4000, and so forth).

Now, suppose that during the next year prices rise by 10 percent and the Joneses' income also rises by 10 percent: the next year the Joneses earn $19,800; however, given the equivalent price increase, this higher salary provides the same purchasing power as their salary the year before. Notice that the tax system is set up in such a way that the allowable deductions remain at a total of $5050 ($2250 for dependents and $2800 for the standard deduction). The Joneses' taxable income rises to $14,750 from the $12,950 figure of the year before, an increase of nearly 14 percent. Furthermore, given the progressive rates, the Joneses' tax obligation rises to $2947, an 18 percent increase in dollar terms over the year before. *The Joneses were not able to buy any more with their higher salary, but they had to pay more taxes. Indeed, the Joneses'* real *after-tax income, measured in 1975 prices, fell by more than 1 percent.* They are worse off, while the government is better off in the sense that its outlays can be increased. Because of government's propensity to spend what it receives, many economists argue that inflation has been a significant cause of government growth.

[4] A progressive tax rate system is held to be in contrast to *regressive tax rate systems* and *proportional tax rate systems.* Under a regressive tax rate system, the tax rates fall as income rises. Sales taxes tend to be regressive because they are not generally applied to the savings of people. Since the wealthy tend to spend a smaller fraction of their income and save a larger fraction than the poor, the wealthy tend to pay a smaller proportion of their income in the form of sales taxes. The tax rate, as a percentage of income, tends to fall as income rises. A proportional tax rate system is one under which the tax rate, as a percentage of income, remains constant over all income levels.

[5] The *standard deduction* is a deduction from gross income which is allowed those people who do not itemize their deductible items, such as interest on loans and medical expenses. Because it is the simplest method of computing taxes, we use it here. In 1976 the standard deduction was 16 percent of gross income up to a maximum of $2800. Since 16 percent of $18,000 is $2880, the Joneses could take only the maximum of $2800.

TABLE 18 · 6 THE "INFLATION TAX" ON ONE FAMILY

	1976		1977	
Money income of Joneses		$18,000		$19,800
Less: Three personal exemptions at $750 each	$2,250		$2,250	
Standard deduction (maximum allowable)	2,800		2,800	
Total deductions		5,050		5,050
Equals taxable income		$12,950		$14,750
Tax on taxable income				
15.5% on first $4,000 of taxable income	$ 620		$ 620	
19% on $4,000–$8,000	760		760	
22% on $8,000–$12,000	880		880	
25% on $12,000–$16,000	237		687	
Total tax		$ 2,497		$ 2,947
Money income of Joneses		$18,000		$19,800
Less total tax		2,497		2,947
Equals after-tax money income		$15,503		$16,853
Purchasing power of after-tax money income (in 1975 prices)		$15,503		$15,320

Notes on table:
Assumptions: 10% increase in prices
10% increase in Joneses' money income
Results: 18% increase in money taxes
7% increase in the purchasing power of money taxes collected from the Joneses
1% decrease in purchasing power of Joneses' after-tax income
Conclusions: With constant deductions and a tax rate schedule, inflation increases the purchasing power of government.

SOURCE: Adapted from *First National City Bank Monthly Economic Letter*, January 1975, p. 10.

Population Growth and Population Distribution

Between 1950 and the mid-1970s, the population of the United States increased by more than 40 percent. Therefore, one reason government at all levels has grown is that it has had to serve more people. The growth in the population has had an especially heavy effect on state and local governments; they have had to provide more schools, police, and streets and have had to extend their water, garbage, and sewage services to more people and to wider geographical areas.

Between 1950 and 1974, the number of people 65 years and older grew by approximately 75 percent; this age group increased its numbers at a much higher rate than did the general population. As a consequence, the number of social security recipients has become a larger portion of the general population and government bills in this area have gone up. Although the percent of the labor force that was unemployed in 1950 and 1974 was practically the same (5.3 and 5.6 percent, respectively), the *number* of persons unemployed in 1974 was 54 percent greater than in 1950. The number of people with incomes below the poverty line has increased with the population; and, as indicated by the growing crime rate, the number of people who work in what economists often refer to as the *crime industry* has grown disproportionately to the general population. Further, a larger percentage of the population now lives in cities and their sprawling suburbs. Such shifts in the distribution of the population have resulted in the government having to assume greater responsibilities. At one time, families were expected to take care of their elderly and disabled members; the government now takes care of a growing number of those who are unable to care for themselves. Whereas people living in small communities once had their own wells and septic tanks, governments now use tax funds to provide water and sewage services.

The growth and increasing density of the population have had the additional and complicating effect of raising the level of "social congestion." Social congestion is manifest in larger and more frequent traffic jams and greater concentrations of noise and unpleasant sights. Generally speaking, as people become more crowded, their activities have a greater impact on the surrounding physical environment. In other words, if the frequency and degree to which our individual actions affect others is increased, government's traditional responsibility to limit the effects which our actions have on others will expand.

Productivity Growth in the Public and Private Sectors

Economist William Baumol argues that a portion of the growth in government can be explained by the fact that the pace of productivity increase is faster in the private than in the public sector.[6] In the private sector the productivity of workers has been increasing at a reasonably steady rate as new and better machinery has been developed. This means that workers in the private sector have, over the years, been increasing the amount they can produce, and thereby they have reduced the cost of what they produce.

On the other hand, Baumol contends that productivity increases are much more difficult to achieve and have been far smaller in the public sector. This is because the "human services" which governments provide require a relatively fixed relationship between the number of government employees and the number of people served, for example, by schools, welfare programs, and police, and because the *quality* of governmental services is judged in part by the labor input. Given this relationship, there has been an increase in the cost of goods and services provided by government relative to goods and services produced in the private sector. Baumol goes on to argue that if we can reasonably assume that the demand for most government services is *inelastic*,[7] people will spend more on public goods and services. An alternative and, perhaps, complementary hypothesis is that government employees, recognizing the inelasticity of the demand for their services, have had a private interest to resist measures to increase efficiency and, consequently, raise productivity.

Changes in Social and Political Philosophy

Adam Smith, who wrote *The Wealth of Nations*, held a strong belief that people are, to a significant extent, masters of their own fate, that they can make *conscious* decisions about the work that they will undertake and the goods and services they will buy. There was almost a moral imperative that people, having made these types of decisions for themselves, should be held responsible for their decisions. In addition, the technology of the day was not as sophisticated as in recent times, and the ability to understand and make use of it did not have much effect on the distribution of income. The most important determinant of the distribution of income was seen to be the willingness of people to work and to trade leisure for other goods and services. The individual was, therefore, the centerpiece of Adam Smith's writings and of

[6] William J. Baumol, "Macroeconomics of Unbalanced Growth: The Anatomy of Urban Crisis," *American Economic Review*, vol. 57, pp. 415–426, June 1967.

[7] As explained in detail in Chap. 3, an inelastic demand means that consumers respond relatively little to a price change. Therefore, if the price of the product goes up, the total expenditures of consumers and the total revenues of producers go up.

most social theory down through the nineteenth century.

In the past half-century the prominence of the individual in social theory has been on the wane. Instead, sociologists and psychologists have developed theories which are based on the assumption that people's behavior is *determined,* not merely influenced, by genetic, environmental, and social forces. In the most extreme version of this philosophical position, people are not conscious actors but are the victims of the society of which they are a part. The remedy for social problems is, therefore, a change in these environmental and social forces which determine behavior—that is, a change in society which is beyond the capacity of any individual to bring about. According to the proponents of these theories, necessary changes must come through collective action, which, in short, means through government action. In this sense, growth in government can be partially explained by the emergence and acceptance of a new and truly "social" theory of human behavior.

George Lodge, a member of the faculty of the Harvard School of Business and author of *The New American Ideology,*[8] looks at underlying social trends from another perspective. He argues that America has been going through an ideological transformation during the twentieth century, he believes that the old values and beliefs which undergirded nineteenth-century capitalism have lost their "legitimacy" and have been giving and are continuing to give way to new values which are more consistent with present-day conditions. He believes that *communitarianism* is augmenting and replacing the centerpiece of nineteenth-century capitalism, *individualism:* "For most people today, fulfillment occurs through their participation in an organic social process. The community as we conceive it is indeed more than the sum of individuals . . . . Fulfillment for most depends on their place in the community, their identity with a complete social process."[9]

[8] George C. Lodge, *The New American Ideology* (New York: Alfred A. Knopf, Inc., 1975).

[9] Ibid., p. 17.

Second, Lodge contends that the concept of private property has lost its importance as corporations have come to dominate the industrial system and as ownership in them has become so diffused that no one effectively "owns" the corporation, in the sense that the "owners" exert significant control. According to Lodge, the rights of private property are being replaced with the "rights of membership." People now look to the state to control the uses of property which were once controlled by the forces of competition; and since the rights of property have been taken from individuals, "community needs" are now being introduced into decisions as to how property should be used.

Third, whereas at one time people accepted the view that complex tasks could be most effectively accomplished through specialization of effort among many people, no one of whom was necessarily concerned about the entire task, Lodge writes that "there has been a growing acceptance of *holism,* or the theory that nature tends to group units of whatever kinds into wholes, and into a single, great integrated whole."[10] In the wake of the recent ecological movement, people have, according to Lodge, developed a "new consciousness" regarding the interdependence between nature and societies' activities and are demanding that tasks be centrally directed and coordinated to ensure harmony among component parts.

One may reasonably debate the arguments which Lodge offers in support of his claim that an ideological transformation is justified. However, to the extent that the transformation has occurred, Lodge offers one cogent explanation for the growth of government.

Developing Theories of Government Control

Before the 1930s economists generally argued that if problems of unemployment emerged, forces within the market system would come into play to push the economy back toward full employment. In the 1930s a new theory of unemploy-

[10] Ibid., p. 20.

ment developed. A major conclusion of this new line of analysis was that the presumed corrective forces either did not exist or did not work fast enough to alleviate significant short-run problems of unemployment. This theory, developed by British economist John Maynard Keynes, also led to the conclusion that the government could, through its budgetary policies, introduce the needed corrective force. We will develop this theory in detail in Chapters 28 through 30; for now, we mention that one of the ways government can increase employment is to increase its expenditures. An increase in government expenditures means more jobs, more production, and more income for people; these people, in turn, will spend their newly acquired income, creating more employment. Although still prominent in government policies, these theories are now viewed with more skepticism among economists than they were a decade and a half ago. However, to the extent that the theories have been accepted as a basis for policy, the federal government has assumed new responsibilities which it once did not have.

Defects in the Political Process

One view of government is that politicians vote for those things which are in the "public interest" and that government employees attempt to carry out their assigned tasks in the most efficient manner possible. Needless to say, this view of government does not exactly reflect the workaday world of politicians and government bureaucrats. One of our purposes in this part of the book is to explore the deficiencies of the political and bureaucratic arenas (see Chapters 21 and 22). For now, we merely point out that Congress frequently passes laws and makes appropriations which serve the private interests of small segments of the voting population at the expense of the general population and that a portion of the growth in government may be explained by a growth in the inclination of representative bodies (Congress and state legislatures) to serve private interests and by a growth in the facility of private-interest groups to exploit this inclination.

As we point out in Chapter 22, government bureaucracies, once established, have a tendency to develop, mature, and overextend their boundaries—to grow larger than is economically efficient. While several reasons will be given later, two possible ones can be offered at this point for the growth of bureaucracies. First, government workers and their families constitute a significant portion of the voting population; when the rest of the population is split on the continuation or expansion of a government program, government employees themselves may hold the deciding votes. They are, in a limited sense, their own employers. Second, members of Congress have little time to supervise the operations of the many bureaucracies in Washington and to investigate whether or not budget increases are economically justified or even beneficial. Control of bureaucracies is very limited.

APPROACHES TO THE STUDY OF GOVERNMENT

Three approaches have been used by economists in their study of government. The first approach is descriptive. Our analysis in this chapter has utilized this approach as we have traced the forms and amounts of governmental activities. This approach can also involve a description of the institutions of government.

Second, many researchers have traditionally assumed that the fundamental purpose of democratic government is to improve the lot of the people who are governed. Accordingly, another approach to the analysis of government has been to define the deficiencies of voluntary groups and markets, to develop theories which explain the need for government intervention in the economy, and to make policy recommendations on "appropriate" governmental action. We have engaged in this type of analysis in previous chapters. For example, we have discussed the adverse consequences of minimum wage laws and the benefits of multinational tariff reductions. In chapters which follow, we develop theories which suggest how the government can change the money supply (that is, the number of dollars in people's pockets and bank accounts) and can manipulate the federal budget in order to relieve persistent problems of unemployment and inflation.

In the past two decades, economists have begun to take a third approach to the study of government which involves asking the question "Why?" Why is it that when government sets inner cities out on a policy course, such as trying to rebuild intercities, a lot of money is spent but even the guarded expectations of policy makers are infrequently met? To answer this question, economists have had to define with more precision the rationale for government in the first place and have had to investigate in detail the political and bureaucratic processes through which government action is taken. This approach has led to new theories of politics and bureaucracies which utilize the traditional tools of economic analysis. It has also led to some bothersome hypotheses regarding the inherent deficiencies of democratic forms of government. For instance, as we will explain in detail in Chapter 20, there are few incentives in democracies for individual citizens to become and remain politically active. This failure on the part of the general citizenry means that their ultimate control of government is less strong than may have been presumed. Additionally, this failure has tended to open the political process to exploitation by special-interest groups who may, through bribes, personal contacts, and campaign contributions, manipulate politicians to their own advantage. Government may have grown in part because politicians may have been "selling" new and expanded programs to special-interest groups for the "price" of political support in elections.

This last approach to the study of government has also led to the conclusion that growth in government may be partly explained by the considerable monopolistic power which government employees have in the provision of governmental services. Having private interests of their own, government employees have pursued those interests through expansion of their bureaucracies to the point where many are beyond the "optimum size," causing waste in the use of valuable public resources. The logic behind these conclusions will be developed in Chapter 22,

SUMMARY AND EXTENSIONS

In the past four decades the role of the American government in the economy has grown from one of relative insignificance to one of substantial importance. To a considerable extent, the welfare of people is now influenced by the taxing and expenditure decisions which are taken at the federal, state and local governmental levels. Other conclusions derived are:

1 The expenditure of federal, state, and local governments now equal a little more than one-third of the country's total production of goods and services.

2 All levels of government have grown in past decades; however, government at the state and local levels has grown more rapidly than the federal government, thus leading to a form of decentralization of governmental influence.

3 In summary, the major reasons for growth in government are (*a*) increases in the prices of goods and services which the government purchases, (*b*) growth in and change in the distribution of the country's population, (*c*) increases in the cost of government relative to the cost of goods produced in the private sector, (*d*) changes in taste for public goods, (*e*) increases in people's incomes, (*f*) changes in the American ideology, and (*g*) deficiencies in the political and bureaucratic processes. There are, without doubt, other explanations.

The remaining chapters of this book will be a study of governmental behavior in various policy areas, such as the management of national production, employment, price levels, and environmental and energy needs. Our intent is to develop theories which may guide us in making sound policy recommendations for the alleviation of various social ills. We will approach these tasks, however, by first studying the economic justification for government and by considering characteristics of the political and bureaucratic processes which have a bearing on the efficiency with which government can be expected to pursue its assigned tasks. We will then be in a better position to evaluate the relative effectiveness of government and markets as alternative means of organizing society.

By legend, there was a Roman emperor who was asked to judge a contest between two singers. He awarded the medal to the second singer after having heard only the first. In a similar way, many people who see the deficiencies of the market conclude that the government should be called upon to take over tasks previously assigned to the market. They draw this conclusion without critically examining the effectiveness of government in its assigned role. By reintroducing politics into the study of economics, we are suggesting that both singers be heard before the medal is awarded: government and markets must be judged on a relative basis in the imperfect setting of the real world. In this setting, economics is the study of *political economy*, a study of the economics of politics and the politics of economics.

QUESTIONS TO PONDER

1 The list of reasons for government growth given in the chapter is not an exhaustive one. Can you cite additional reasons?

2 Government expenditures on "human services" (education, health, welfare, etc.) have grown over the past decade faster than defense expenditures. Other than changes in people's tastes for these different types of governmentally produced goods, can you explain the relative growth rates of these two expenditure categories?

3 George Lodge (referred to in the chapter) has argued that people's growing understanding of ecology—that is, the interrelatedness of all things in nature—has caused them to take a more "holistic" view of human organization. Do you agree? How may such a change in one's philosophical viewpoint affect his or her perceived role of government?

4 Expanding on Lodge's thoughts (question 3 above), is there a centralized authority which dictates and maintains the delicate ecological balance in nature? In what respects are market systems and ecological systems similar? Dissimilar?

5 We have suggested in the chapter that population growth and shifts in the distribution of population from small towns to urban settings can partially explain the growth in government over the last several decades. In terms of such economic variables as prices, human capital formation (i.e., education) and wage rates, explain the growth and shifts in population (and, thereby, the growth in government).

6 Do you expect government to grow as rapidly in the future as it has grown in the past? Explain your answer.

RECOMMENDED READINGS

Buchanan, James M., and Marilyn R. Flowers: *The Public Finances: An Introductory Textbook*, 4th ed. (Homewood, Ill.: Richard D. Irwin, Inc., 1975), chaps. 3, 6, 16, 20, and 31.

Lodge, George C.: *The New American Ideology* (New York: Alfred A. Knopf, Inc., 1975), chaps. 1, 6, 7, and 9.

19

The Bases of Governmental Action

In its broadest definitional sense, collective action is the enactment and enforcement of law. The justification for all collective action, for government, *lies in its ability to make men better off. This is where any discussion of the bases for collective action must begin.* [*Emphasis added.*]

James Buchanan[1]

PREVIEW OF CHAPTER

Central question

What are the economic justifications for government actions?

Major objectives

1. To develop the case for governmental provision of *public goods*
2. To explain the effects which *external costs* and *benefits* have on the efficiency of production in private markets and to explain how government can correct for the inefficiencies that are generated because of the external costs and benefits
3. To stress the limits to which the arguments for government action can be taken
4. To evaluate the alternative ways the government can carry out its assigned economic functions

[1] James M. Buchanan, *The Bases for Collective Action* (Morristown, N.J.: General Learning Corporation, 1971), p. 2.

Major conclusions

1 Reviewing material covered in Part One of the book, we again explain why certain *public goods* cannot be provided by private markets alone. If public goods are produced at all, people will benefit regardless of whether or not they pay for them. Therefore, beneficiaries have no incentive to make payment and producers have no incentive to provide the good in conventional market settings.

2 External costs lead to *overproduction* in private markets. External benefits lead to *underproduction* in these markets. Government action can narrow the gap between the free-market output level and the "efficient" output level.

3 Not all market inefficiencies should be alleviated by government action. Government action means that costs must be incurred, and the costs of government action may be greater than the benefits to be achieved (that is, greater than the inefficiencies to be eliminated).

4 Government can deal with external costs and benefits in several ways: through (*a*) persuasion, (*b*) assignment of property rights, (*c*) government production, (*d*) regulations designed to force private producers to conform to established standards, and (*e*) user charges and subsidies.

Important terms and concepts

Private good
Public good
External costs
External benefits

What and how much should government do, and what should be left to the market? These two questions define one of the most important issues of our time—the division of social responsibilities between the public and private sectors of our economy. As a general response, economists suggest that government should do those things at which it is, relative to the market, more efficient. Similarly, the market should retain those responsibilities at which it is relatively more efficient.

Economics provides a method for evaluating the efficiency characteristics of markets and government. It enables us to identify those categories of goods and services which the market will fail to produce altogether and to identify others which the market will fail to produce efficiently. At various points in the textbook (specifically, Chapters 5, 10, 12, and 13), we have discussed market inefficiencies—what economists call *market failures*. The purpose of this chapter is to review and to consolidate those failures and, in that way, to provide an economic rationale for the existence and scope of government as an institution for collective as opposed to individual action. Briefly, market failures occur (1) *in the production of public goods*, (2) if *external costs* and *external benefits* arise from goods and services produced by the market, (3) if *monopoly power* exists in the market, and (4) in the distribution of income. Because the question of monopoly power and government intervention was developed so extensively in Chapters 10 through 13, that area of market failure will not be considered again in this chapter. The distribution of income is the subject of the next chapters. The failures of government and the means by which markets alleviate those failures will be considered in later chapters. In this chapter we explain why government must produce "public goods" and why and to what extent government must intervene in markets in which external benefits and costs are generated. We also evaluate the alternative ways government can deal with market failures.

PUBLIC GOODS AND THE MINIMUM STATE

There is a wide range of *private goods*, like bread, which, for one very practical reason, can be produced with tolerably efficient results through the market. Even though bread is available on grocery store shelves, it cannot be obtained unless payment is made. If bakers can withhold their bread from consumers until consumers pay for it and can sell what they produce at a profit, they will have a private incentive to provide their product. Consumers will have a private incentive to pay for what they want; if they fail to pay, they can be denied the satisfaction of eating toast with their breakfasts or sandwiches for their lunches. Mutually beneficial trades to baker and consumer are possible; and we see that, in this case, the private interests of both buyers and sellers will ensure that such trades are sought and consummated.

There is another category of goods, called *public goods*, which in its pure form will not be produced and traded in the market. Clean air, public parks, and police protection are all examples of public goods. The "failure" of the market to provide public goods is *not* a consequence of the inability of buyers and sellers to benefit from these goods; indeed, they do benefit. Rather, the failure on the part of the market is a consequence of the inherent nature of the public goods. As we explained much earlier (Chapter 3), a pure public good is one whose benefits are shared equally and simultaneously by all persons. Furthermore, if the good is provided, no one can be excluded from sharing in the benefits, because the benefits are pervasive and are received automatically. Unlike bread, the production of public goods and receipt of their benefits are part and parcel of the same process.

Therefore, there is a fundamental difference between private and public goods. In the case of the private good (bread), the benefits received are predicated upon payment; without payment the bread stays on the shelf. However, in the case of the public good, benefits are predicated upon production, not on payment in a market sense. The seller of bread has an incentive to produce because he can collect from all who benefit from that good; the producer of a public good, however, cannot collect for the benefits given. This is so because in producing the public goods, benefits are received by consumers before payment is made. The public good producer can be expected to have the same luck in collecting from beneficiaries as a baker would if he flew over a city, tossing out loaves of bread, and *then* went from door to door to ask for payment from all those who picked up the loaves he dropped.

Therefore, if a public good is provided, it must be provided through collective, governmental action. The cost of the public good is covered through forced taxation. People may not like the taxes any more than they like to pay for the bread that they buy. However, forced taxation is the only way that they can get the benefits of public goods which they want. At the head of this chapter, James Buchanan writes, "The justification for all collective action, for government, lies in its ability to make men better off."[2] In the case of the pure public good, government makes people better off by providing goods and services that will be absent in a market economy. Examples of publicly produced goods, which closely approximate the pure form discussed here, are national defense, police protection, and the legal system.

National Defense

National defense for a country like the United States is *the* classic example of a public good which, if it is provided at all, must be provided by the government. Given the enormity of defense expenditures in the United States, no one is capable, much less willing, to pay even a significant portion of the entire cost. Therefore, unlike the

[2] Ibid.

market in which bread is sold, "exchanges to obtain defense" cannot involve one buyer and one seller. To bring the cost per person down to within a tolerable range, an entrepreneur who was considering going into the defense business would have to contract at the same time with a very large number of people, possibly tens of millions. The bargaining that would inevitably go on between the entrepreneur and all these people would, without question, make the "transaction costs" so high that no one would even consider the production of national defense as a reasonable business venture.

Furthermore, even if all agree that some minimum level of national defense is desirable, and even if they are willing to collectively cover its cost, national defense will not likely be provided on a voluntary basis. Each person in this *large-group* setting may reason as follows: "If I pay and no one else pays, no real defense is provided. On the other hand, if everyone else pays and I do not, the security of the country will essentially be unaffected by what I fail to do." Considering the matter individually (that is, not as a collective body), the tendency of each person will be to contribute nothing, hoping others will provide defense protection. This tendency, which we have called the "free-rider problem" increases the transaction costs of developing collective action through markets or voluntary groups.

So, if people see a need for defense, they must agree to produce it collectively; at the same time they must establish a central authority—government—which has the power to force them all to make whatever payments are necessary to cover the cost of the public good. In short, the production of public goods requires that people make collective decisions simultaneously on how much to spend on any given public good and how much to pay in taxes.

Laws as Public Goods

Laws are a product of government. They determine the limits of individual behavior, the type and scope of government programs, and the meaning and rights of state and individual "ownership." In general, the cumulative effect of the stream of laws which legislatures pass over time will determine the type of society we will have. To the extent that laws affect us all, more or less equally and simultaneously—to the extent that we all must be subject to the same legal framework—laws are public goods. Like national defense and for the same reasons, laws cannot emerge from the market processes. In fact, markets depend on laws to establish the property rights which can be bought and sold. Furthermore, just as people must be forced to pay taxes to provide a public good like national defense, government must enforce its laws; law enforcement is another public good. Adherence to law for most can be a matter of duty, of moral obligation. Indeed, it is doubtful that any system of laws can long survive without the support and respect of a large segment of the people whose behavior they are intended to govern. However, in any society there very likely will be many people who, as in the case of defense, will fail to make their contribution voluntarily, as inconsequential as it may be, to social stability or whatever other public benefits the legal system is designed to achieve; in short, they may violate the laws where it is in their private interest to do so. Government can thwart the violators and can "produce" the desired social stability by penalizing those who insist upon going outside the legal system and doing those things which are privately beneficial but destructive of the collective welfare. It follows that government "production" of police, judicial, and penal systems is justified.

Mosquito Abatement Programs

At the local government level, mosquito control is an example of a public good. Acting independently, one person is not likely to have much success ridding a yard of mosquitoes. It will quickly be reinfested as mosquitoes move in from neighboring yards and other sections of town. On the other hand, if a citywide, government-financed mosquito abatement program is instituted, the mosquito population in all sections of town can be significantly reduced; all residents within the community can benefit more or less equally. The level of government which actually deals with a problem like mosquitoes depends upon how widespread the problem is. If mosquitoes cover more than the boundaries of a city, a city's program may meet with little success. Mosquitoes can move into the city from other sections of the country or region. In this event, the mosquito abatement programs will have to be the responsibility of a state or regional governmental agency.

The list of public goods which we have provided here is not exhaustive. In addition, governments offer many other goods and services which are significantly removed from the "pure form" of public goods that we have used as the basis of our discussion. However, most of these goods and services supported by government tend to be private goods with elements of "publicness" about them. For instance, a city bus service, a publicly financed transportation system, can exclude people from receiving its principal benefit unless they pay the stipulated fare. (Passengers who are unwilling to pay can be tossed off the bus!) However, to the extent that city buses reduce the congestion on streets caused by cars, they benefit large segments of the population. In the next section we deal specifically with these types of *mixed* or *quasi-public goods*—goods that involve *external costs* or *external benefits*.

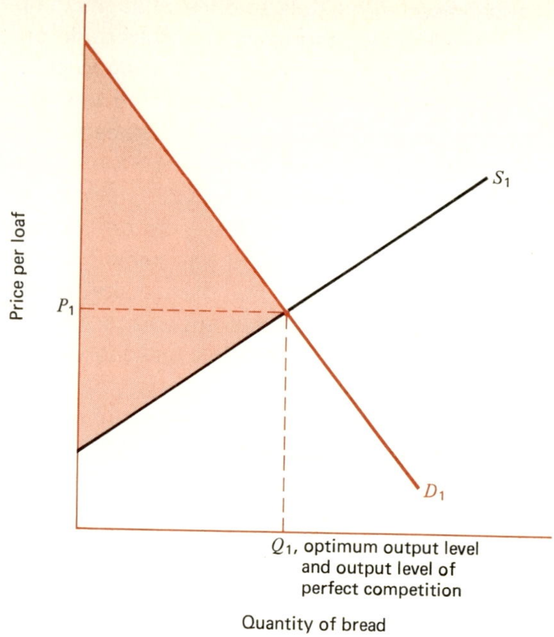

FIG. 19·1 The demand curve reflects the marginal benefits of each loaf of bread, and the supply curve reflects the marginal cost of producing each loaf of bread. For each loaf of bread up to Q_1, the graph shows that the marginal benefits of each loaf are greater than the marginal cost. Therefore, the shaded area is the maximum welfare gain from the production of bread.

EXTERNAL COSTS AND EXTERNAL BENEFITS

In competitive markets producers are induced to minimize their production costs, to lower their prices, to increase their production levels, and to improve the quality of their products. As consumers compete, they demonstrate just what they are willing to pay for a given product and in what amount they are willing to buy it. As we studied in Chapter 7, production in a competitive market for bread will move toward Q_1, the intersection of the market supply and demand curves. (See Figure 19·1.) At this point the marginal cost of the last loaf of bread is equal to the marginal benefit of the last loaf to consumers. To the extent that the market moves toward that position, it is "efficient" in a special sense.

People are presumed to be "better off" so long as the marginal benefit of what they do is greater than the marginal cost; this is a basic proposition that has been with us since the book's start. Notice that for each loaf of bread up to Q_1, the marginal benefit of consumption is greater than the marginal cost of production. People get more value out of each loaf than they can get out of some other alternative good. (Recall that the marginal cost of a loaf of bread is the value of the most attractive alternative forgone to buy the bread.) By producing exactly Q_1 loaves, no more and no less, the market has extracted all possible "surplus" or "excess" benefits, indicated by the shaded area in the graph. It is only in this sense that production and the distribution of resources in the economy are "efficient."

To achieve these optimum results, however, we had to assume not only that competition in the market is quite intense (perfect), but also that all the product's benefits are received by buyers and that all costs of production are incurred by producers. It should go without saying that to the extent that the optimum or efficient output level is not achieved, the market "fails": part of the excess benefits described by the shaded area in the figure will not be received by the purchaser.

When exchanges between buyers and sellers affect people who are not directly involved in the trading, the exchanges are said to have *external effects* or, more commonly, to generate *externalities:*

Externalities are the positive or negative effects which exchanges have on people not participating in the market; they are third-party effects.

When such exchanges give pleasurable effects to third parties, the effects are called *external benefits*. On the other hand, when the external effects are unpleasant or result in a cost being borne by people other than buyers and sellers, the effects are called *external costs*. The consequential effects of external costs and benefits on production and market efficiency can be reviewed with the aid of supply and demand curves.

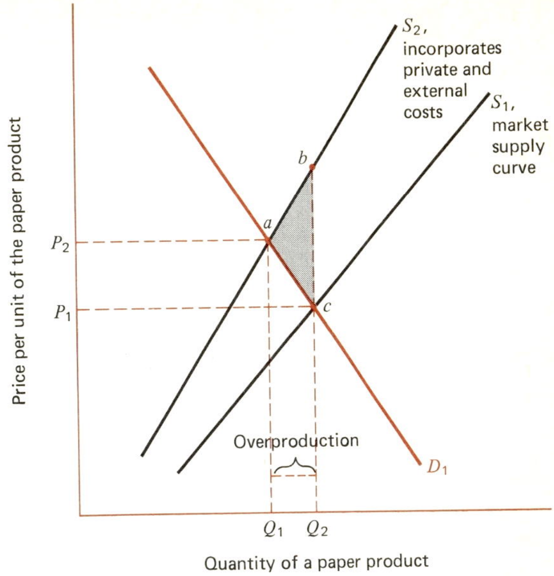

FIG. 19·2 Ignoring the external costs associated with the production of paper products, private producers will base their production and pricing decisions on supply curve S_1. If they include the external costs in their production decisions, they will operate on the basis of supply curve S_2 and will produce less, Q_1 instead of Q_2. The shaded area is the total amount by which the total costs (including private and external costs) of production exceed the marginal benefits derived from the units of paper products between Q_1 and Q_2; it represents the inefficiency of the private market.

External Costs

Consider a market for a paper product, illustrated by the supply and demand curves in Figure 19 · 2. The market demand curve, D_1, summarizes all the benefits which market participants receive from the paper product they buy. In producing paper, the producers have to assume directly the cost of labor, chemicals, and pulpwood. These are the costs on which the paper manufacturers must base their production decisions, and they are the types of costs that go into the construction of the industry's supply curve of paper, S_1. In a perfectly competitive market, with these market supply and demand curves, the quantity of paper product bought and sold will be Q_1 and the price paid by consumers will be P_1.

In the production of paper, however, some costs may not be incurred by its producers. The production of paper can result in considerable amounts of solid waste being dumped into rivers and streams, in gases being emitted into the atmosphere, and in a "stench" which pervades the surrounding community. Because of the solid waste, gases, and stench, towns located downstream will have to incur a greater expense to clean the water they use, the people in the surrounding area may have to paint their houses more frequently and seek medical attention for eye irritation, and homeowners and other businesses may have to accept lower prices for their property. These costs are "external" to producers; but, nonetheless, they are a part of the *total societal* cost of producing paper products. In a perfectly competitive market, in which all participants act independently of one another, these external costs are the types of costs which producers *must* impose on others. An individual producer who voluntarily installs pollution abatement equipment while others do not will incur costs that are higher than those of other producers. The other producers can then underprice the first producer, take over that producer's market, and, perhaps, run the producer out of business. Some producers may be "social reprobates" who do not care if they cause harm to others by polluting the environment; our point is that competition can lead even those producers who are concerned about the environment to pollute and thereby impose costs upon others. These producers in a perfectly competitive market may welcome enforced, government control of pollution of all producers.

Regardless, the supply curve which reflects all private and external production costs, S_2, is up and to the left of the market supply curve, S_1, on which producers of the paper product base their market decisions. If producers have to bear all costs, including the external costs, the price of the product will be higher (P_2 rather than P_1) and consumers will, because of their downward sloping demand curve, buy a smaller quantity of paper products. They will buy Q_1 units instead of the greater Q_2 units that they do buy. Furthermore, the higher supply curve, S_2 indicates that the true marginal cost of each unit of paper between Q_1 and Q_2 is greater than the marginal benefit received by consumers. This means that consumers value other goods that can be produced with the labor, chemicals, and wood more highly than they value the $Q_2 - Q_1$ units of paper product. The paper producers are, in this sense, overproducing, and the social waste of the overproduction is equal to the shaded triangular area bounded by the letters *abc*.

There are other examples of "external costs" which will lead to overproduction. Highway congestion is created by the production of larger and greater numbers of cars, and noise is created by airplanes in and around airports. People who have children increase the public school enrollment and, thereby, the tax burden on taxpayers; they effectively impose a part of the cost of educating their children on people unrelated to their decision to bear children. Granted, people do not make their child-bearing decisions on economic grounds alone; moral considerations as well as "accidents" enter into the process. However, if the costs and benefits are evaluated in the decision to have children, and if parents consider whether or not "they can afford" additional children, public provision of education increases the number of births. (It reduces the private cost of having children and moves people down their demand curves.) In the same sense that pollution costs that are externally imposed can result in the overproduction of paper, the external costs of public expenditures on education contribute to overpopulation, a significant social concern of many people.

Accordingly, the argument that production of goods which involve external costs results in overproduction has been used to justify government intervention in the market in the form of controls on virtually all forms of pollution (water, air, noise, etc.). Government intervention in child-bearing decisions has become more widespread in countries with serious overpopulation problems. In the United States, sex education and planned parenthood programs are publicly supported. India now requires fathers with three children to be sterilized. However, the argument has been extended to many other areas of human interaction:

1 *Controls on speeding and reckless driving.* Those who speed and drive recklessly impose a cost on other drivers; they increase the probability that others will suffer physical, financial, and emotional damage as a result of having an accident. Speeding and other forms of reckless driving are "goods" which many people apparently value. People will produce this kind of driving to the extent that the government does not act to penalize it.

2 *Control on porno districts.* Adult bookstores, X-rated movie houses, and an assortment of bars and massage parlors that go with them tend to impose costs on other businesses in the same location. Because of their gaudy exteriors and because of the prostitutes that tend to congregate around them, they, according to the argument, give the business districts that they are in a "trashy" appearance and tend to scare away many customers not interested in pornography. To combat these problems, many cities have passed zoning codes which force all these "less desirable" types of businesses into limited areas of the town, into what have come to be known as porno districts.

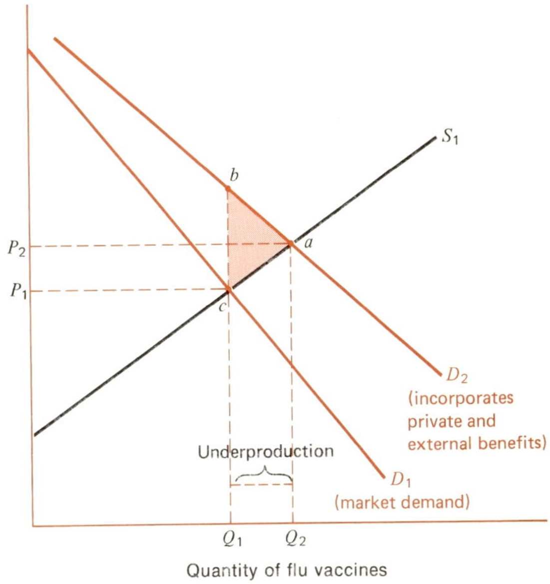

FIG. 19·3 Ignoring the external benefits of getting flu vaccines, consumers will base their purchases on demand curve D_1 instead of D_2, which includes the external benefits. There will, therefore, be fewer vaccines purchased than can be economically justified, Q_1 instead of Q_2. The shaded area is the total amount by which the marginal benefit of each vaccine between Q_1 and Q_2 exceeds its marginal cost of production; it represents the inefficiency of the private market.

External Benefits

To illustrate the effects of external benefits on the allocation of resources, consider the market for flu vaccine. The production costs of the vaccine include labor, research and production of equipment, eggs, and transportation. Assuming that all of these costs are internal to the vaccine producers, the market supply curve is S_1 in Figure 19 · 3. (There is only one supply curve in the figure because of the assumed absence of external costs.) People, without question, can receive important private benefits from being inoculated against flu; the fact that many millions of people pay for flu shots each year illustrates the fact that there is a market demand for the vaccine. Their private demand for flu shots is illustrated by D_1 in the figure However, in the process of getting shots for themselves, people provide benefits for others around them. By not catching the flu themselves, they reduce the probability of others coming down with the illness. Other people can avoid the explicit medical expense associated with flu and the implicit cost of lost work time. Therefore, people who get shots will be more likely to generate *external benefits* for others. These external benefits, however, are not captured in the *market* demand curve. Private and external benefits are captured only in the higher, *societal* demand curve, labeled D_2. On the graph the vertical distance between the market and the societal demand curves illustrates the external benefits of each flu shot.

Left alone, a perfectly competitive market will produce at the intersection of the *market* supply (S_1) and demand curve (D_1), or point *c*. At that point the equilibrium price will be P_1 and the quantity produced will be Q_1. However, notice that when the external benefits are added to the private benefits, the total marginal benefits of additional vaccines beyond Q_1 is greater than the marginal cost of their production. In other words, when all benefits are considered, people place a higher value on having more vaccines than they place on alternative goods and services. (The value of these alternatives is equal to the marginal cost of their production.) Indeed, if all benefits, both private and external, could be expressed in market decisions, a greater quantity of vaccines, Q_2, would be produced and purchased. People's welfare would rise by the triangular shaded area, *abc*, of Figure 19·3; this is the total amount by which the benefits of the additional vaccines, $Q_2 - Q_1$, exceed the additional cost of their production. Furthermore, when all benefits are considered, at Q_2 the marginal cost of the last vaccine is equal to the marginal benefit. In this sense, Q_2 is the efficient vaccine level.

However, a free market will fail to achieve this optimum state; flu vaccines will be underproduced. Since people acting independently of one another cannot capture the external benefits, they are not privately willing to pay the necessary higher price, P_2, to generate a greater quantity of vaccines. Therefore, collective, governmental action to supplement what has been achieved in the market can be supported and (possibly) justified. (The qualification will be explained in the next section.) It is on such grounds that governments assumed the responsibility for inoculating the population against swine flu (which was undertaken on a massive scale in the United States in 1976) and smallpox.

The external benefit argument is employed to support governmental research into preventative medicine and for stopping the spread of communicable diseases in general. The same line of analysis has been advanced to promote governmental activity in the following areas:

1 *City bus service.* As we mentioned earlier, a city bus service provides benefits to its passengers but also to motorists and pedestrians who may then face less congested streets.

2 *Education.* Education, in many ways, provides private benefits to most people. Educated people tend to earn higher incomes, to achieve higher social status, and to be interested in reading and learning about many diverse subjects. However, there are external benefits also from mass education which spread from the educated people to most of the population. To the extent that a nation's people share the ability to read and write in a common language, they can communicate and interact efficiently. Therefore, with the development of general literacy, resources that would otherwise be devoted to trying to communicate can be directly employed in the production of goods and services. The prices of goods and services fall and people's real income rises in line with the resource savings in communication. Because of the external benefits and without government support, it is argued that education would tend to be underproduced.

The ratio of public and private benefits from education at different levels is different; differences in public support may, therefore, be argued. Elementary school education is primarily concerned with the development of the basic communication skills mentioned above; the private benefits to the pupils may be looked upon as unavoidable but fortunate side effects. At the collegiate level, however, the private benefits to students may dominate the public benefits. This line of argument partially explains why elementary education is almost totally supported from public sources while students in colleges and universities are asked to pay a third or a half of their direct educational expenses. (When the opportunity cost of students' time is considered, college students may personally incur 75 percent of the total cost of their education.)

3 *Beautification programs and public parks.* People who plant trees and develop parks benefit privately from the beauty they have provided; however, many others benefit who are not a party to the development projects. Because of these external benefits, the optimum level of beautification and park development will not be provided by the market. Government action, again, is necessary to supplement the efforts of private individuals and firms.

ON DEALING WITH EXTERNALITIES

Probably more often than not, exchanges between buyers and sellers affect others who are not directly involved. Individuals buy clothes partly to remain warm in the winter, dry in the rain, and so forth. However, for many people, much of the time, the appearance of their clothing is at least as important as its comfort. We choose clothing because we want the people who look at it to be pleased or impressed or, at times, irritated by it. The same can be said in varying degrees about cars that we purchase, where we go to eat, the records we buy, the deodorants that we use, and even the colleges that we attend. Indeed, the external effects of our individual actions are purposefully as well as accidentally imposed on others.

Should government always intervene when externalities are involved in our social interactions? For people who value personal freedom, the answer is no. However, economic analyses can be introduced to explain many limitations placed on government intervention. First, the externalities and economic distortions in the market are frequently quite small, if not inconsequential. In developing the concepts of external costs and benefits, we used graphical examples which involved significant market distortions. However, consider Figure 19·4. In that figure, the supply curve (S_2) which incorporates all *private costs* (those incurred by producers directly) and *external costs* (those which are imposed on third parties) is only slightly removed from the market supply curve (S_1) (that supply curve which incorporates only the private costs). The difference between the market output level, Q_2, and the optimum output level, Q_1, is small. Furthermore, the shaded area of the graph which illustrates the lost efficiency, *abc*, is also very small. Therefore, the benefits to be gained by government intervention are very few.

On the other hand, when the government intervenes in any area of social behavior, agencies will be set up, employees hired, papers shuffled, and reports filed. Almost invariably, suits will be brought by the government against firms and individuals who violate government rules and by firms and individuals against the government when it oversteps its authority; this taxes the capacity of the judicial system. In short, significant costs can be incurred.

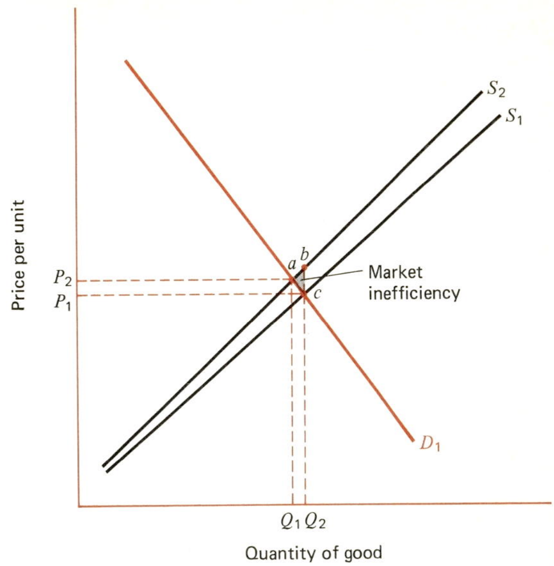

FIG. 19·4 In the market illustrated by the supply and demand curves there are external costs, and the market produces more than the efficient output level. However, the inefficiency in the market, represented by the shaded triangular area *abc*, is quite small—so small that government intervention may not be justified on economic grounds.

Markets may be inefficient in the sense that less or more than the optimum quantities of goods will be produced. However, if the cost of government intervention exceeds the cost of the market's inefficiencies, government action will worsen, not improve, overall efficiency. There are many cases, as we have indicated in the preceding section, in which government intervention is warranted. However, without considering the efficiency or inefficiency with which government bureaucracies work and the cost of government, the degree of government intervention which is economically justified can be exaggerated. For this reason, our goal in this chapter and Part Eight is to examine how the government operates.

The second economic argument for limiting the role of government is to limit the external costs that government actions generate themselves. In a democracy, if government is permitted to dictate the types, styles, colors, and textures of clothing that can be worn, and if it does this on the grounds that external costs and benefits are associated with people's appearance, those people who have the votes to set those standards can impose a cost, one that is external to them, on other people who are in the minority. (Many college students would probably suffer if governments were unconstrained in this area.) Those who have the votes to dictate hair codes can impose a cost on others who disagree. Those who like certain types and styles of cars can impose a cost on those who like other types and styles. In certain cases we might agree with the majority and we may, therefore, benefit from not having to put up with what we consider to be sloppy dress habits. At other times we may be the victim of the whims and fancies of the majority; in these cases, we would suffer. In short, most of us may agree to restrict the domain of government because, even though we may benefit from government action at times, on balance, over a number of policy decisions, we are likely to be worse off. A constitution which restricts the legislative domain of government is a means of forcing governments to consider the positive and negative effects of a whole series of governmental actions and to judge their *net* effect over time.

Granted, the government is not totally constrained in dictating dress, hair, and automobile standards. Governments, through their educational arm in particular, have at times dictated standards in these areas. For instance, until the late 1960s the University of Virginia had dress codes which required that coats and ties be worn by male students. When men started wearing their hair long in the mid-1960s, many parents had to bring suit against public school boards to force the boards to allow their sons to wear their hair long. Police departments have, according to a recent decision of the Supreme Court, the right to set hair length standards for their officers. Costs are imposed on those who must obey these rules. However, to the extent that dress and hair codes are established with greater and greater detail, the external cost of public decisions escalates. Furthermore, the more centralized the governmental decision, the greater the external cost, because people will have fewer opportunities to move to other areas of the country where dress habits are more in line with their own preferences. (It should be noted that the market system is one which involves an extreme degree of decentralized decision making.) Regardless, where it is impossible or very expensive to ensure that government is constrained, tolerance on the part of people for the individuality of others can be a socially desirable trait—one which may reduce the external costs of governmental action. However, tolerance is a social trait which over the course of time may prove to be difficult to maintain.

Third and finally, in certain markets where external costs are present, government action may not be necessary. Some of the *external costs* and *benefits* which are presently causing market distortions may eventually be "internalized"—that is, considered as *private costs* and *benefits*—by private entrepreneurs who are interested in making profits. For example, suppose that the development of a park-type area in the midst of a shopping district generates external benefits to all the surrounding businesses in the sense that more customers are attracted to the shopping district and more sales are made. A firm can internalize these types of benefits by buying a large tract of land and building on it a large shopping mall with a park in the middle. In addition, the firm can add air conditioning and music. Because more customers will be attracted to the mall than to other shopping areas without the park, the air conditioning, and the music, the firm which owns the mall can benefit by raising the rents it charges over and above what are charged elsewhere. Simply stated, shopping centers have risen to "internalize the externalities"; to the extent that they have done this, economic efficiency has been enhanced without government intervention.

When Walt Disney built Disneyland in California, he could hope but did not know that his amusement park would be as successful as it has been. The visitors whom he attracted benefited merchants in the surrounding area. Since Disney failed to buy up the surrounding property, other businesses moved in to take advantage of the benefits that were "spilling over" from the amusement park. The area has become congested; property values have skyrocketed. When Disney set out to build Disney World in Florida, he was determined to buy enough land so that most benefits that spilled out of the amusement park, per se, would still be within the Disney domain. Accordingly, he bought up something in excess of 6000 acres of land near Orlando, Florida. Within that area, virtually everything is available in a very pleasant environment. In addition, Disney World constitutes a quasi-city whose transportation, sewage, and garbage collection services work with reasonable efficiency. Businesses have set up on the perimeters of Disney World; however, the sheer distance between them and the center of Disney World reduces the benefits which they can receive from the Disney operations.

GOVERNMENTAL MEANS OF DEALING WITH EXTERNALITIES

Without question, government participation in the economy can guarantee that certain goods and services are produced more efficiently: the benefits to be achieved by altering people's behavior may be substantial in comparison with the costs of government intervention. Further, a general consensus in favor of government intervention may develop; such a consensus developed in the United States with regard to the environment in the late 1960s. Having made these points, however, we have not determined the *form* of the government intervention. In this section, without going into much detail, we outline the possible forms which government intervention can take. Briefly, they are (1) persuasion, (2) assignment of communal property rights to individuals, (3) government production of goods and services, (4) government regulation of private production to conform to established standards, and (5) changes in the prices of the affected products through government taxes or fines and subsidies. Generally, economists argue that if the government is going to intervene, it should choose that means, given the task at hand, which is most efficient.

Government Persuasion

External costs partially result from our lack of concern over the welfare of others. If we were fully concerned about the adverse effects which our actions have on others, there would be no concept of an external cost. The costs imposed on others would be a private concern—therefore, a private cost. In such a social setting of full concern for others, our individual production schedules would be based, as much as possible, on the total societal costs of the production.

Realizing this basic point and the possibility that people's concern for others can be changed, government can alleviate market distortions by trying to persuade others to be aware of their effects on others. For this reason, government engages in advertising campaigns to make people conscious of their possible contribution to the litter problem and forest fire problems. They also encourage people to drive safely and to cultivate their land in such a way that erosion problems will be minimized. In times of droughts and "energy crises," the government encourages people to conserve water and to not be "fuelish." Although such campaigns may have limited effects, they may be more effective than other means of dealing with the same problem—at least, given the political constraints at the time.

Assignment of Property Rights

As we pointed out in Chapter 5, when rights to property are unassigned or are held communally, anyone can use the property without paying for its use so long as no one else is already using it. Under these conditions, people do not bear the full cost of what they do or what they produce.

They will, therefore, tend to overuse the property in the same sense that we have discussed in this chapter. Accordingly, an external cost is imposed upon others. In Chapter 5 we pointed out that when grazing land is unclaimed, or unassigned as private property, as much of the West was 150 years ago, ranchers may allow their herds to overgraze the land. This occurs because they do not have to pay for the use of the land. The grass that is eaten by one person's cattle cannot be eaten by other rancher's herds. In this way, each imposes costs on the other.

If rights to the land are assigned to the ranchers, they bear responsibility for what their cattle do to the land. If the land is stripped of its grass, the rancher will suffer the cost of not being able to raise his cattle on that land in ensuing months or years. The rancher will also suffer in terms of the selling price of the land or in terms of the rent that could have been charged others for its use.

Therefore, the assignment of property rights, or a clearer statement of the property rights that already exist, by government can alleviate some externalities problems. However, there are resources, such as air and water, the boundaries of which are difficult to identify and divide. In these cases, the property rights solution will not work very well or, possibly, not at all. In such cases, government may consider other methods of control.

Government Production

Government nationalization and production of such goods as steel, automobiles, and paper products may appear to be straightforward solutions to the problems of externalities, and they are advocated by many people. Because the government is assumed to be concerned with the societal effects of production, external costs of individual firms or industries are made internal to government production arrangements. The argument is that government will consider the total cost to society of producing, say, paper and, through public ownership, guide production to the optimum level. It is on the basis of such arguments as these that governments operate such facilities as schools and public health services, national and state parks, transportation systems, harbors, electric power plants (like TVA), and many others.

Government production can be, however, a mixed blessing. Like almost everything else, it is an alternative with advantages and disadvantages. Government production in some areas can mean that there is one more producer in the market and therefore more competition. Many people in the mid-1970s advocated that government should go into the production of oil as a means of stimulating competition in that United States industry. In other cases, however, government production can mean the elimination of competition. Consider, for example, the U.S. Postal Service, which has exclusive rights to deliver first-class mail. A government agency, like the Post Office, charged with producing and selling a good or service (like first-class mail delivery), is not permitted to make profits and distribute those profits to itself. However, because of its monopolistic position, it may possibly allow its costs to go up through wages that are higher and work standards that are lower than would exist under competitive market conditions.

Government direct production of such public goods as national defense may be unavoidable. On the other hand, direct government ownership and production may not be necessary in other cases. As opposed to producing the good with which externalities are associated, government may simply contract with private firms which compete for the business. This is precisely how most states handle their road construction projects. This is also how a few city governments handle their "production" of ambulance, police, and fire protection services.

Government Regulation to Conform to Established Standards

We have dealt with government regulation of private businesses at length in Chapters 11, 12, and 13. Therefore, our discussion here will be relatively brief, and it addresses only one point—the

TABLE 19·1 COST OF REDUCING "UNITS" OF SOLID WASTE DISPOSAL

	Producer A	Producer B	Producer C
Cost of eliminating first unit	$100	$ 50	$1000
Cost of eliminating second unit	200	100	1500
Cost of eliminating third unit	300	200	2000
Cost of eliminating fourth unit	400	400	2500
	Standard		
Cost of eliminating fifth unit	$500	$ 800	$3000
Cost of eliminating sixth unit	600	1600	3500

Cost of Reducing Solid Waste Disposal by Set Standards		Cost of Reducing Solid Waste Disposal by Price	
Cost to A of eliminating 4 units	$1000	Cost to A of eliminating 6 units	$2100
Cost to B of eliminating 4 units	750	Cost to B of eliminating 5 units	1550
Cost to C of eliminating 4 units	7000	Cost to C of eliminating 1 unit	1000
Total cost of reducing solid waste emission to a total of 6 units	$8750	Total cost of reducing solid waste emission to a total of 6 units	$4650

effects of standards on the efficiency of relieving the problems of external costs and external benefits.

If external costs are associated with the production of a product like paper and if there is overproduction, the government can take steps to reduce the production level, an action which, in turn, can lead to fewer external costs. The government can accomplish this goal by either forcing all producers to reduce their individual production levels or forcing each producer to cut back on, say, the amount of solid waste that it dumps into the streams. Consider only the latter alternative, which involves the setting of maximum amounts of solid waste that may be dumped into the streams.[3] Further, suppose that the government takes the extreme stand of requiring the producers to meet the standards or terminate production.

The problem with this solution is that it may not be the most efficient or least costly means of achieving the societal goal of reducing the external cost. This results because firms differ in the efficiency with which they are able to meet the standard. To see why, consider the situation of three firms, A, B, and C, whose costs of reducing the emission of solid waste differ according to the schedules in Table 19·1. We assume that each of these firms is emitting 6 "units" of solid waste into a given stream and that the government agency deems it appropriate to cut back the total units of solid waste from 18 units (3 × 6 units of each producer) to a total of 6; the rule issued is that each producer cannot dump more than 2 units. Therefore, each firm will have to reduce its

[3] You may remember from a much earlier discussion that the optimum level of pollution will not likely be zero pollution. This is because the cost of going that far in improving the environment will in all probability exceed the benefits. The task of government regulators in this area is to establish what the "optimum level of pollution" is and impose standards which achieve that level.

TABLE 19·2 COMPARISON OF TOTAL COST TO PRODUCERS OF STANDARDS AND USER CHARGE METHODS OF ELIMINATING POLLUTANTS

	Producer A	Producer B	Producer C
Cost incurred from eliminating pollutants under standards method (from bottom of Table 19·1)	$1000	$ 750	$7000
Cost incurred from eliminating pollutants under user charge method (from bottom of Table 19·1)	$2100	$1550	$1000
User charge of $1100 for each pollutant emitted	0 (no units emitted)	1100 (1 unit emitted)	5500 (5 units emitted)
Total cost of user charge method to producer	$2100	$2650	$6500
Voting outcome if referendum were held	Vote for standards method	Vote for standards method	Vote for user charge method

emission by 4 units; and, as indicated in the table, the total cost of achieving the standard is $8750: $1000 incurred by A in eliminating the 4 units of solid waste emission, $750 by B, and $7000 by C. Notice that the cost of achieving the goal of only 6 units of solid waste pollutants can be reduced to $5250 by simply requiring A and B to eliminate all their solid waste pollutants and allowing C to continue production as usual. (The $5250 figure is obtained by adding all amounts in the first two columns of Table 19·1.)

Given these cost savings, applying different standards to different firms may seem like the obvious way to lower the cost of pollution reduction from the straight, across-the-board standard for all. However, if the required reduction in their pollution is dependent upon how costly it is for them to clean up, the firms are given an incentive to overstate the actual cost of cleanup. Further, for large numbers of industries, the expense of the government determining the cost of cleanup to the firms can be prohibitively high. In summary, across-the-board standards can work, but they can be expensive.

Changes in Prices of Products through User Charges and Subsidies

If overproduction results because of the existence of external costs, the government can reduce production and the external costs by imposing a tax on the product. The market supply curve can, in this manner, be decreased to conform with the higher supply curve (S_2) in Figure 19·2, which incorporates all private and external costs. Consumers must pay a higher price and will buy less. The market inefficiency is thus eliminated.

Alternatively, the government can apply a "user charge" (a price) on firms for the amount of pollutants, or solid waste, that they emit. Firms will continue to pollute so long as the cost of eliminating the pollutants is greater than the user charge; operating on the same rational basis, they will eliminate those units of pollutants for which the cost of elimination is less than the user charge. The government can achieve whatever level of pollution it desires by simply raising the user charge: the higher the charge, the lower the pollution. This is just another application of the law of demand. Furthermore, by use of this pricing technique, the desired level of pollution will be achieved by the least costly means possible. Consider Table 19·1 again. To eliminate 12 units of solid waste, the user charge must be slightly higher than $1000 per unit of solid waste dumped into the stream. If the user charge is $1100 per unit of solid waste emitted, producer A will find that the elimination of all 6 of its units of solid waste will be less expensive than paying the user charge of $1100. If, for example, A eliminates only 5 units, it will have to pay the government $1100 for the sixth unit of solid waste that it dumps into the stream. It can get by with less expense by paying the $600 for the equipment to eliminate that unit.

Producer B will find that the elimination of 5 units of solid waste will be a more attractive alternative than payment of the user charge. On the other hand, B will pay $1100 for the right to emit its sixth unit because the elimination of that unit would impose a cost of $1600 on the firm. Producer C would eliminate only one unit of solid waste. *However, with the user charge at $1100, producers A, B, and C together will eliminate 12 units and emit only 6, the desired social goal.* Notice that the cost of eliminating those 12 units of solid waste is only $4650 (as compared with the total cost incurred of $8750 via the standards method discussed above). It is because of analyses like this that economists conclude that the user charge is a more efficient (less costly) means of relieving pollution problems than across-the-board standards.

There are, however, two deficiencies in the user charge method. First, the people who are affected by the external cost, the pollution, may not be the ones who receive the benefits of the revenue collected by the government. These people have reason to favor the standards method. Second, to many people the user charge method for dealing with pollution is a means by which businesses can pay for the "right to pollute." Many people fail to see that the user charge will increase the price of the product, cause consumers to buy less, and reduce the amount of pollution. Nonetheless, politicians understandably find it difficult to support "user charges." Instead, they are inclined to support standards which producers must meet to avoid "fines" or "penalties." In the eyes of many constituencies, this method amounts to penalizing people who violate the law. To economists, the fines are simply disguised user charges; they have the same effect.

Problems of external benefits and underproduction can be relieved by the government giving subsidies to firms who produce the affected good. Because of the subsidy, firms will lower their prices and people will buy more, which is the desired goal of the subsidy. North Carolina is one of several states which uses subsidies as a means of increasing the number of people going to private colleges and, thereby, the total number of people who attend college. The state pays private colleges a fixed amount ($400 a year in 1976) for each North Carolina student that they enroll.

User Charges versus Standards in Democracy

Using the information in Table 19·1, we demonstrated that user charges are a more efficient way of reducing pollution than standards. However, does it follow that user charges will be selected as the policy course in a democracy? The answer is clearly no in this particular case if voting is restricted to the three producers. As shown in Table 19·2, the total cost incurred by producers A and B under the user charge method is greater than the total cost they will incur under the standards method; on the other hand, producer C incurs a lower total cost under the user charge method than under the standards method. It follows, therefore, that if a referendum were held on the issue, A and B have an economic incentive to vote for the standards method; and their votes, in this case, will represent a majority of the three voting producers.

In short, even though it is a less efficient (i.e., more costly) means of dealing with pollution, the standards method will be selected. Granted, the producers who are affected are not likely to be the only people voting on the issue. However, the benefits of dealing with pollution efficiently are spread over a large number of consumers through slightly lower prices. The benefits that each consumer receives from ensuring that pollution is dealt with efficiently are probably so small that he or she may have little incentive to learn which method is actually the more efficient. Consumers, as a group, therefore, may be disinterested in what they may consider to be a complicated technical issue. Furthermore, they may side with producers on the issue because the user charge method may be equated with selling "rights to pollute" to producers.[4]

[4] For a more rigorous and complicated argument, see James M. Buchanan and Gordon Tullock, "Pollution's Profits and Political Response: Direct Controls versus Taxes," *American Economic Review*, vol. 65, pp. 139–147, March 1975. Although it is somewhat difficult to do, cost configurations for a table like Table 19·1 can be devised in such a way that the user charge method will receive a majority of the producers' votes in a referendum. The purpose of this section, however, has been only to show how the cost of the standards and user charge methods to producers can explain the observed widespread opposition among producers to the user charge method.

SUMMARY AND EXTENSIONS

Several important conclusions can be drawn from this chapter. First, a market economy will fail to produce altogether *pure public goods*. Second, it will "overproduce" goods and services with which *external costs* are associated. Third, a market economy will "underproduce" goods and services with which *external benefits* are associated. Because of these market failures, government intervention in the economy *possibly* can be justified. To make the case for government intervention, however, the cost of the intervention, realized in terms of larger government bureaucracies, must be less than the benefits to be achieved.

A major purpose of this chapter was to point out that, as might be expected, there are areas of economic activity into which government intervention is clearly warranted. There are other areas, however, where the market can be left alone. In between these two extremes there are many areas of the economy into which government intervention may or may not be warranted. To determine whether or not government intervention is economically justified, the full costs and benefits of each proposed area of government activity must be considered, and much of economists' time is devoted to making such studies.

In Chapter 20 we turn to a study of government's role in affecting the distribution of the nation's income. Our analysis of this chapter will be helpful in explaining the economic basis for this growing role of government. However, we will have to introduce moral and political considerations to fully explain the government's efforts to redistribute the nation's income.

QUESTIONS TO PONDER

1 The U.S. Postal Service is a government agency. On what *economic* grounds can government provision of mail service be justified?

2 One of the main conclusions of this chapter is that the existence of external costs is not a conclusive economic argument for government intervention in, let us say, the production of steel. Why is it not a sufficient condition? What is missing in the argument for government intervention?

3 Government is now involved in the regulation of occupational safety. What economic arguments can be developed for government intervention in this area? From economic considerations alone, what is a more efficient way of handling the task of reducing job-related injuries and deaths: (*a*) the imposition of safety standards, or (*b*) penalties on firms which experience job-related injuries and deaths? Explain.

4 List five goods or services provided by the federal government that are not discussed in the chapter or used in the above questions. Give an economic explanation for their provision through government.

5 This chapter has been concerned primarily with economic arguments for government intervention in the economy. What "moral" arguments can be used to support various government activities?

6 Population growth will lead to more government controls of people's behavior. Do you agree or disagree? Explain.

RECOMMENDED READINGS

Boulding, Kenneth E.: *Beyond Economics: Essays on Society, Religion and Ethics* (Ann Arbor, Mich.: The University of Michigan Press, 1970), pp. 258–288.

Buchanan, James M.: *The Bases for Collective Action* (Morristown, N.J.: General Learning Corporation, 1971).

Leftwich, Richard H., and Ansel M. Sharp: *Economics of Social Issues* (Dallas: Business Publications, Inc., 1976), chaps. 3, 7, and 8.

20

Government and the Distribution of Income

The primary goal of taxation is to transfer control of resources from one group in the society to another and to do so in ways that do not jeopardize, and may even facilitate, the attainment of other economic goals.

George Break
Joseph Pechman[1]

PREVIEW OF CHAPTER

Central question

How can the government affect the distribution of the nation's income?

1 To describe the distribution of the nation's income
2 To evaluate alternative explanations of the causes of poverty
3 To provide economic justifications for governmental relief programs
4 To evaluate alternative methods of redistributing the nation's income
5 To consider the actual effect which governmental relief programs have had on the distribution of the nation's income

Major conclusions

1 Although there are still many poor people, the percentage of the population officially classified as "poor" has dropped substantially since 1965.

[1] George F. Break and Joseph A. Pechman, *Federal Tax Reform: The Impossible Dream?* (Washington, D.C.: The Brookings Institution, 1975), p. 4.

2 There are a number of explanations for poverty. Several of the more prominent explanations are: (*a*) low productivity, which can be due to a number of factors; (*b*) racial and sexual discrimination; (*c*) changes in the overall level of economic activity, especially as that activity relates to the employment opportunities of people with few skills and little education; and (*d*) poverty by choice. This list is not all-inclusive.

3 Governmental attempts to redistribute income and, thereby, to relieve some of the hardships of the low-income groups can be justified on the following grounds: (*a*) Poverty relief is a public good which requires collective action in order to achieve the optimum amount of poverty relief. (*b*) Redistribution of income is a moral imperative; it is the type of governmental program to which people will agree if their income position in society is unsure. (*c*) Governmental programs for poverty relief can be construed as a form of social insurance; that is, people may be uncertain about their future income positions and agree to governmental programs to relieve poverty because they feel they may need an income supplement in the future.

4 There are three basic ways by which government can help the poor: (*a*) *in-kind transfers* in the form of food, housing, medical care, and education; (*b*) *cash transfers*, such as what the *negative income tax* would provide; and (*c*) *direct governmental intervention* in the labor market in the form of, for example, minimum wage laws. Almost all forms of in-kind transfers and cash transfers adversely affect the incentive of people—both the high-income groups who pay the taxes and the low-income groups who receive the benefits of government programs—to produce efficiently.

Important terms and concepts

Median family income
In-kind transfers
Cash transfers
Negative income tax
Implicit marginal tax rate

Why government? Up to this point our answer has been that government is organized to provide certain *public goods* and to minimize the distorting influence of *external costs and benefits* on the production of goods and services. This analysis explains government participation in many areas of the economy. However, the public and political debate in this country over what if anything the government should do is, to a significant extent, concerned with how the country's income can be most "equitably" or "fairly" distributed among different groups of people. In other words, the central question of this continuing discussion is, What can and *should* the government do to promote "economic justice"?

Why is there great political interest in the effect of government policy on the distribution of income? First, government is an organized body through which people can express their values relating to justice, fairness, and equity. These values may emerge from an ethical system which is largely independent of the market system; and people's notions of what constitutes fairness in the distribution of income may be in sharp conflict with the income distribution which emerges from the market process. The political system is a means of settling differences between ethical points of view. Elections and referendums determine which points of view will dominate government actions. Second, if the "public interest" is to be served by the establishment of, for example, a strong national defense or a sound educational system, resources must be bought and profits will be made. People will compete politically for these profits. In seeking their own private interest, politicians frequently shroud their private interests in the oratory of ethics and the public interest. In the real world of practical politics it is not always easy to distinguish between legislation designed to correct for a real ethical concern and legislation which is a disguised means of promoting private interests.[2]

The purpose of this chapter is to complete our survey of the public sector by describing first the distribution of the nation's income and then the means by which income has been transferred from the relatively well-off to the poor. We will discuss both the arguments which have been used to justify government intervention in this area and the inevitable conflict between the achievement of economic efficiency and the attainment of people's concept of justice and equity.

THE DISTRIBUTION OF INCOME

Basic data on the distribution of income among families in the United States are contained in Table 20·1. This table reveals that in 1975 1.8 percent of all United States families had incomes of less than $2000; 10.2 percent had incomes of less than $5000. At the other end of the distribution, 15.1 percent had incomes in excess of $25,000. The large majority of Americans had incomes in between these two categories. In fact, the *median family income*—that income which is at the midpoint of the income distribution—was $14,268 in 1975.

TABLE 20·1 PERCENT DISTRIBUTION OF FAMILIES BY INCOME LEVEL: 1965 AND 1974

Income	1965	1975
	(percent)	*(percent)*
Under $2,000	8.9	1.8
$2,000–$2,999	7.2	1.9
$3,000–$3,999	7.7	2.9
$4,000–$4,999	7.9	3.6
$5,000–$5,999	9.3	3.9
$6,000–$6,999	9.5	4.0
$7,000–$9,999	24.2	12.6
$10,000–$14,000	17.7	22.7
$15,000–$24,999	6.2	31.7
$25,000 and over	1.4	15.1
Median income	$6,957	$14,268

SOURCE: U.S. Bureau of the Census, *Statistical Abstract of the United States: 1976* (Washington, D.C.: U.S. Government Printing Office), p. 404.

As indicated in the table, people's income levels moved upward substantially between 1965 and 1975. In percentage terms, more than twice as many families earned less than $2000 in 1965 as in 1975; and nearly twice as many families earned less than $5000 in 1965 as did in 1975. At the other end of the spectrum, many more people earned incomes in excess of $15,000 in 1975 than in 1965. A portion of these upward movements can be explained by increases in production due to better technology and corresponding increases in most people's earnings between 1965 and 1975. However, a major share of the shifts can be explained by the high rates of inflation experienced during this period. People's money incomes (which is simply the number of dollars they earn) were rising, but so were the prices of goods and ser-

[2] For example, congressional debates on the defense budget are often more centered on where defense bases will be, which companies will receive contracts to produce armaments, and which bureau in the Department of Defense will have control of some portion of the budget than they are concerned with military matters per se. "Eighty members of Congress from nine Northeastern states urged the Army to put more active-duty divisions and Army construction money in their areas." (*Washington Post*, Aug. 17, 1975, p. A3.) Indeed, defense is not unusual in this respect. Debate on flood control legislation often gives the appearance that members of Congress are not interested in preventing floods but are greatly interested in having such construction projects in their districts.

vices. Therefore, the improvement in people's standard of living or real income (which is the purchasing power of their money income) was not as dramatic as the figures in the table indicate. Indeed, in order to keep up with the rising costs associated with inflation, the median income would have had to have risen from the $6957 level of 1965 to $11,867 in 1974. Because the tax burden grew during the period (see Chapter 18), and because many people's money incomes did not keep up with price increases, many families were actually economically worse off in 1975 than they were a decade earlier despite the fact that their salary increases pushed them into higher income brackets.

Table 20·2 provides additional information on those who were classified as having "low incomes" or as being "poor" by the Social Security Administration in 1959 and 1974. The calculation of the "poverty income level" is based primarily on the cost of what the Department of Agriculture considers to be a nutritionally adequate but economically thrifty food plan plus an allowance for clothing and shelter. When the poverty level is calculated, it is adjusted for the family size, the sex of the family head, the number of children under the age of 18, and the difference in the cost of living of farm and nonfarm families. As the cost of living goes up, the poverty income level is adjusted upward also. As indicated in Table 20·2, there were 24.3 million people (or about 11 percent of the population) who were living below the poverty income level in 1974. This figure is significantly lower than the 39.5 million Americans who were considered poor in 1959.

As indicated in the body of Table 20·2, in 1974 most of the poor were members of families. Only about 20 percent were classified as "unrelated individuals." Further, approximately 10 million of the 19.4 million people in poor families were under the age of 18. The table also indicates that most of the poor in the United States are white. However, the table fails to reveal that minorities —primarily blacks, Indians, and Spanish-Americans—constitute about one-third of the total poor in the country whereas they account for slightly more than one-tenth of the population. The number of people who were over 65 in 1974 accounted for about 10 percent of the population and for about 14 percent of the poor.

The statistics in these two tables and in others like them can be criticized on two scores. First, poverty is largely a relative concept. The standard of living at the United States poverty income level in this country would be considered a very high standard of living in many other places in the world. On the other hand, this poverty income level is considered too low by many others both in our country and in some other advanced, industrial nations. In addition, people's definition of poverty changes over the long run; the poverty income level that was decided upon in 1964, when the statistics were first compiled, would not have been the poverty income level decided upon at the turn of the century, when, for example, most people did not have indoor plumbing, radios, electric stoves, and other conveniences which are now commonplace. The poverty income level has not been adjusted upward in the last decade to reflect the change (if any) in people's ideas of

TABLE 20·2 PERSONS BELOW POVERTY LEVEL BY FAMILY STATUS, RACE, SEX OF HEAD, AND AGE: 1959 AND 1974
(in millions of persons)

	1959	1974
All persons	39.5	24.3
Family status		
In families	34.6	19.4
Unrelated individuals	4.9	4.8
Race		
White	28.5	16.3
Nonwhite and minorities	11.0	8.0
Sex of head of household		
In families with male head	29.1	12.5
In families with female head	10.4	11.8
Age		
Persons 65 and older	5.5	3.3
Persons under 65	34.0	21.0

SOURCE: U.S. Bureau of the Census, *Statistical Abstract of the United States: 1975* (Washington, D.C.: U.S. Government Printing Office), pp. 401 and 403.

what constitutes a "poverty income level."[3] Second, the statistics which reflect the number of the nation's poor are based largely on people's money incomes. Many people receive significant income in nonmoney forms. For instance, some of the elderly who are counted as being among the poor own their homes. Therefore, because they do not have to make house payments, the demands on their money incomes may not be as great as the demands on younger people whose annual earnings are greater than the so-called poverty level.

THE CAUSES OF POVERTY

The explanations for poverty being advanced today are almost as varied as the large and growing number of researchers of the subject. However, four economic explanations dominate. First, some people are poor because of their low productivity. They are unable to produce very much during the time they spend on the job and, therefore, are paid very little. Low productivity is often attributed to, among other factors, the inability to meet the basic literacy levels required by modern industry in order to be considered for higher-paying jobs. Indeed, 60 percent of all poor families are headed by a person with only a grade school education. Further, according to many researchers, the poor are largely trapped in a "circle of poverty." Because they are poor, they are unable to afford to stay in school or to move to better school districts. They are also unable to have books and toys which provide learning experiences in the home, and they do not have diets which will permit them to remain attentive while in school. Another argument is that young people lack sufficient motivation to learn because of the low esteem into which formal education has fallen in many low-income neighborhoods and because of a lack of educational aspirations on the part of their parents. Finally, because teachers expect children from disadvantaged backgrounds to learn very little, teachers demand very little and put up less resistance to the poor child dropping out of school than they do to the child from a higher-income family dropping out. All these factors can by the eighth grade result in the poor child's being two grades behind those classmates who are in families with higher incomes.[4]

The second explanation for the existence of poverty focuses on racial and sexual discrimination. Many people are poor because they are members of a minority or because they are female; race, minority status, or sex is used as a basis for assuming the level of their productivity and, therefore, for determining the jobs to be opened to them. As indicated in Table 20 · 2, nearly 50 percent of poor people are at present in households that are headed by women, and approximately one-third of all poor people are members of a minority group. In addition, nearly one-half of the nonwhite population in the country lived in poverty in 1974.

Gary Becker and Lester Thurow have developed two prominent economic theories of discrimination.[5] Becker argues that discrimination against blacks, for example, occurs because whites have a "taste" for not having to work and associate with blacks. Whites, therefore, demand higher wages from employers who hire both blacks and whites than from employers who hire only whites. To reduce the wages they pay white workers, employers, according to Becker, reduce their demand for black workers. Both blacks and whites suffer in terms of money incomes; however, in Becker's theory the whites are compensated for their lost money income by the satisfaction of not having to work with blacks. Many blacks, on the other hand, are relegated into very low-paying jobs or into the unemployment and welfare roles.

[3] For example, recipients of the Aid for Dependent Children program in the late 1940s could not own a TV (which was new, anyway) or have a telephone and still be eligible for public assistance. Today, welfare recipients often have TVs, phones, cars, etc.

[4] Howard P. Tuckman, *The Economics of the Rich* (New York: Random House, Inc., 1973), p. 175.

[5] Gary S. Becker, *The Economics of Discrimination* (Chicago: University of Chicago Press, 1957). Lester C. Thurow, *Poverty and Discrimination* (Washington, D.C.: The Brookings Institution, 1969).

Thurow questions Becker's central conclusion, which is that "when actual discrimination occurs, he [the person doing the discriminating] must, in fact, either pay or forfeit incomes for the privilege."[6] Thurow writes, "If this deduction is correct, empirical impressions are amazingly false. Do the whites of South Africa or the United States really have lower standards of living as a result of their discrimination? If they do, increases in those standards can be used as an inducement to persuade them to give up their prejudices against Negroes."[7]

Thurow concedes that some forms of discrimination may be explained by Becker's analysis; however, he adds that other forms are the consequence of some white employers acting as *monopsonists*.[8] When employers compete, for example, for black employees, they push the wage rate up, increasing the cost of labor to all employers. According to Thurow, through physical, social and economic pressures, dominant white employers are forced to restrain their competitive behavior and their demand for black employees. Although Thurow does not explain the process by which this pressure is applied or why employers do not behave the same way toward white workers, he argues that the net effect is that blacks are, because of the employers' control over the labor market, paid less than their competitive wage rate and fewer blacks are hired in the market.

Unable to get jobs in markets controlled by prejudice, blacks become crowded into occupations, such as house cleaning and janitorial services, in which there exists a necessary "social distance" between the employees—blacks—and the employers—whites. So many blacks are pushed into these job markets that the overall wage rate received by blacks is depressed. If labor markets were freed of the pressures on white employers to avoid hiring blacks, the wages of blacks would rise along with the number of blacks hired. These gains of the black workers would come at the expense of white employers, who would have to pay the higher wages, and of white employees, who would then have to compete with blacks for the available jobs. The same general line of analysis can be applied to sexual discrimination.

The third explanation for poverty is that the number of a nation's impoverished is significantly affected by the overall level of economic activity in the country. If consumers, governments, and businesses reduce their demand for goods and services, fewer jobs will be available. Many people who have jobs will lose them, and many more will have to accept part-time employment or wages which push their incomes below the poverty line. The number of poor people went up significantly during the 1930s because there were many fewer jobs and little income for many people to earn. Researchers, investigating this line of analysis, have found that slumps in economic activity tend to affect blacks and women more than they affect white males. This observed relationship is explained in part by the actual or presumed low productivity of blacks and women, by discrimination against blacks and women, and by employment rules which require that the people last hired (who tend to be blacks and women) be the first fired.

Fourth, many people who are included as a part of the poverty statistics have *chosen* to work very little or to work at jobs which are low-paying but are personally rewarding in nonmonetary ways. For instance, many farmers *choose* to stay on their farms in spite of the higher wages in industrial jobs. In effect, these farmers and others who put job satisfaction ahead of monetary reward are paying a money price for the opportunity to organize their time as they see fit, to stay away from crowded urban settings, and to stay "close to the land," a phrase which means different things to different people. Over the past decade many young people have *chosen* to organize communal-type living and working arrangements in the full knowledge that their material wealth will be less than it might otherwise be. They do this in order

[6] Becker, *The Economics of Discrimination*, p. 6.

[7] Thurow, *Poverty and Discrimination*, p. 113.

[8] As you may remember from Chap. 15, a monopsonist is a single buyer. When the term is applied to the labor market, it means a single employer of labor or a group of employers acting as a single employer. The term *monopsonist* should not be confused with *monopolist*, which is a single seller of a product or resource.

to pursue what they consider to be a more meaningful way of life. Many others, such as gold prospectors, beginning actors and actresses, and some of those who spend their time on highly speculative business ventures follow career courses which offer substantial income if they are successful but continuing poverty so long as they remain unsuccessful. Many succeed, but many fail. All at some times in their lives are likely to be counted as a part of the poverty statistics.

THE BASIS FOR GOVERNMENT RELIEF PROGRAMS

Fifty years ago, governmental efforts to relieve the social problems caused by poverty and to provide the poor with supplemental income, food, and housing were meager at best. Aid to the poor was left largely to charitable individuals and organizations. Today, however, as indicated by the number of dollars spent and the number of people affected, governmental relief efforts are, by historical standards, extensive. On what grounds can collectivization of charity through government be justified? Are there economic arguments which may explain why the government has stepped in to aid the poor? Of course, not all governmental efforts in this area can be explained by economic logic alone. A full explanation, as we have said at the start of the chapter, requires that we step outside the boundaries of strict economic analysis and into a discussion of our ethical precepts of justice and fairness and if and how these precepts conflict with market-determined values. However, for the time being we concentrate on the economic arguments for collective, government action on behalf of the poor. The analysis of public goods, external costs, and external benefits developed in the last chapter will be useful in explaining *some* or our government's efforts to redistribute income from the well-to-do and middle-income groups to people in the lower-income brackets.

Poverty Relief as a Public Good

Dilapidated housing, seriously ill-fed children, sickness, and early death are the familiar sights and signs of poverty. The very presence of a very low-income group of people within a community can be a depressing reality to almost everyone. The *relatively* well-to-do or rich may have a demand for giving aid to the poor because of their simple and deep-felt concern for the poor; the well-to-do may be interested in improving the lot of others, and they may dislike seeing or knowing that others around them are suffering while they are living in relative splendor.

The rich may have a demand for helping the poor for other, less benevolent reasons. The poor, because of their presence, can impose heavy external costs on other people within the community. The property values of the rich can be adversely affected by the unpleasant sights of poverty, and the rich may have to protect their property from the criminal assaults of the poor. To avoid the unpleasant sights and the high crime rates of impoverished areas, the rich may have to incur the cost of moving away from the poor and of erecting social and physical barriers to the poor moving close to them. Housing developments with strict regulations on the minimum size and types of housing that can be built are means by which the rich are able to protect themselves from the poor; however, the cost of the protection is translated into inflated monthly mortgage payments which the poor cannot hope to meet. Governmental aid to the poor can reduce, but not necessarily eliminate, the costs which the rich may have to incur to avoid knowing or associating with people who do not live as they do.

Aid to the poor in the form of money, food, and housing can benefit all within a community in much the same way that national defense and police protection do. Almost everyone can receive some satisfaction from knowing that people around them have something to eat and a place to sleep. Because the aid enables the poor to buy better housing and clothing, it can improve the general appearance of the community and can increase the property values of the well-to-do. As Milton Friedman, who is a staunch supporter of the free-market system, has written,

> . . . I am distressed by the sight of poverty; I am benefited by its alleviation; but I am benefited

equally whether I or someone else pays for its alleviation; the benefits of other people's charity therefore partly accrue to me. To put it differently, we might all of us be willing to contribute to the relief of poverty, *provided* everyone else did. We might not be willing to contribute the same amount without such assurance.[9]

To the extent that all within a community benefit, poverty relief is another example of a public good, a concept which we explored in detail in Chapter 19; and, like all public goods, people, acting individually and independently of one another, may not provide the optimum quantity of the public good: they may give either too little or too much to the poor. They may in total give too little because each, knowing what others are giving, may try to free-ride on the charitable contributions of others. In addition, each may reason that his or her small contribution will have very little effect on relieving the community's total poverty problem. On the other hand, in other, perhaps far fewer cases, people may give in total too much—only in the sense that each of the donors is unaware of the contributions of the other donors and that the total contribution is actually greater than all donors, if they knew what all others were doing, would like to see given to the poor. In these instances the poor may still not be living comfortably. Collectivization of charitable contributions can, therefore, be a means of either expanding or contracting the total amount given to the poor.

In cases in which aid to the poor is expanded by government intervention, everyone is better off. The poor receive more income and the relatively well-to-do have the satisfaction of knowing that they are helping others; there is a clear welfare improvement. However, when government intervention leads to less aid to the poor, the well-to-do may be better off, but the welfare of the poor is reduced. In this instance there is no clear-cut welfare improvement.

To demonstrate the above conclusions with greater clarity, consider a simple, three-person society composed of individuals A, B, and C. C is the poor person whom A and B would like to help. Both A and B have a demand for giving to C; that is, they are willing to pay a certain amount of money for gifts of, say, bread to be given to C. Further, to make the analysis somewhat descriptive of the real world, suppose that A and B differ as to how much they are willing to give. Consequently, their demand curves for giving bread to C are illustrated by D_a and D_b in Figure 20 · 1. Finally, suppose that the marginal cost of loaves of bread to A and B is constant over the number of loaves that they are willing to purchase and that the marginal cost is equal to P_2.

The graph reveals that, if left to himself, B will give as many as Q_b loaves of bread to C. This is because the private marginal benefit of each loaf

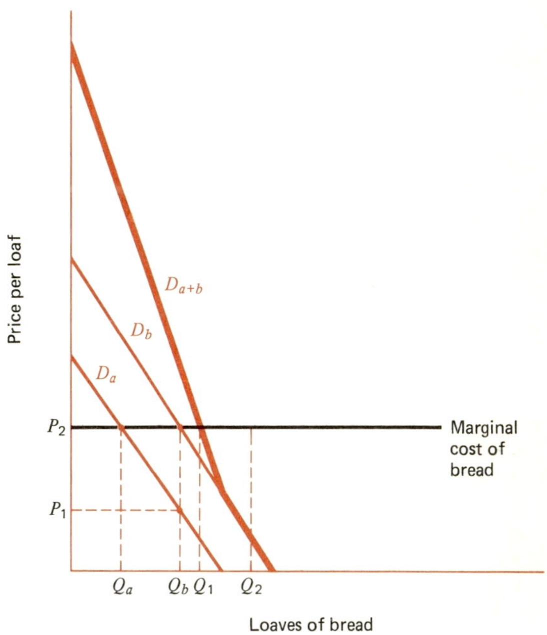

FIG. 20 · 1 The public goods demand curve D_{a+b} is obtained by vertically adding together D_a and D_b. The optimum loaves of bread to be given is Q_1. However, if A and B give independently of one another, more or less than that amount of bread will be given. Governmental attempts to collectivize charity can be construed as an attempt to optimize charitable contributions.

[9] Milton Friedman, *Capitalism and Freedom* (Chicago: University of Chicago Press, 1962), p. 191.

given up to the Q_b loaf is greater than the marginal cost of its purchase; B is better off by giving each of these loaves than by using his money to buy something else. Similarly, if left entirely to himself, A will give Q_a loaves. However, assuming that A and B know of each other's existence, they will take into account each other's gifts. For example, suppose that B has given Q_b loaves of bread to C. A will not be motivated to make any gifts at all. B is giving more than Q_a, so A feels that his contribution is "covered." For A to donate more than Q_a loaves, he must pay a price equal to P_2, which is more than he is willing to pay. However, if A could pay less than P_1, he would be willing to extend the total amount of giving beyond Q_b. On the other hand, if B knows that A has given Q_a loaves, B will give only the amount between Q_a and Q_b when the price per loaf to him is P_2. (Can you see why?)

This amount of bread, Q_b, is not the social optimum quantity of gifts from the standpoint of A and B taken together. If we add their demand curves vertically, and thereby add the amounts which A and B are each willing to pay for each loaf, we produce the public goods demand curve labeled D_{a+b}. (Remember, this darker demand curve is not the same as a market demand for a private good. The market demand for a private good is obtained by adding individual demand curves *horizontally;* a public goods demand curve is obtained by adding individual demand curves *vertically*. See Chapter 3 for further details on the construction of the demand curves in Figure 20·1.) This darker curve in Figure 20·1 shows how much the giving of a loaf of bread is *jointly* worth to the two of them. As we studied back in Chapter 5, the socially optimum amount of bread is where the collective marginal benefit of each loaf is equal to the marginal cost. In terms of Figure 20 · 1, this optimum amount is Q_1. By getting together and sharing the cost of each loaf of bread through some form of government, A and B can bring down the cost of each loaf for both; they will then each want to give more to C. In this case, C, who is poor, will be better off, since he will get more bread. In addition, A and B will be better off by the collective arrangement. The price that they each pay is reduced, and they are, therefore, able to do more of what they want, which is to give bread (or housing or money) to C.

This, then, is the basic argument for government aid to the poor. Through government, people can agree to make charitable contributions, and they can share the cost of the gifts to the poor through the tax system. Because the government has the authority to compel people to pay their taxes, which are then used to pay the poor, the free-rider problem is averted. Since everyone is forced to pay a portion of the poverty relief programs, the quantity of gifts can be increased. Even through government the optimum quantity of gifts may not be given; however, government relief efforts can move the total quantity of gifts toward the socially optimum amount.

Although it may rarely occur, it is possible that governmental relief programs are at times organized to reduce the amount of aid actually given to the poor. In the above analysis, we assumed that A and B knew of each other's gifts of bread to C. This is a condition which may not always hold simply because A and B may not know each other and because they make their gifts at different times and in different places. Further, knowing that A may reduce his gifts if A knows of B's gifts, and vice versa, C, the recipient of the gifts, has an interest in hiding knowledge of the gift of A from B and of the gift of B from A. Clearly, many beggars on city streets at times try to give the appearance of being more impoverished than they really are. Each beggar knows that he must put a few coins in his cup to suggest that others have given to him; however, he also knows that he must periodically remove any "excess" coins from his cup. A beggar who has a pot full of coins may receive very few additional coins. The analogy of the beggar is not easily extended to all poverty problem areas; however, many well-to-do people may have an interest in collectivizing charity through government. If charity is not collectivized by the government, the well-to-do may be confronted with requests for contributions from many different sources, and they may have little idea as to how much has been given by other donors. Therefore, more than the optimum amount of gifts may be made.

To see this point, consider Figure 20·1 again; however, this time assume that A and B are each not aware of how much the other is giving to C. Therefore, A gives Q_a and B gives Q_b. The socially optimum amount is still Q_1; however, notice that the combined total of A's and B's gifts made independently of each other equals Q_2, which is more than Q_1. If A and B knew what the other was giving, they would give less. Government intervention in cases like this can reveal to all how much help the poor are receiving and can result in less in total being given to the poor. At the very least, recognizing the extent of government charity, some people may very well reduce their charitable contributions made directly to the poor and indirectly to the poor through charitable organizations like the Salvation Army and the churches.

Redistribution of Income as a Moral Imperative

The line of analysis in the above section suggests that governmental efforts to redistribute the nation's income can lead to greater efficiency in the allocation of purchasing power (income) and therefore, of resources. However, advocates of governmental programs to redistribute income are frequently unconcerned with the efficiency arguments we have discussed. Indeed, many may view the concept of efficiency as being altogether irrelevant to the question of poverty relief. Rather, many people argue that as a matter of moral imperative, the government should take more money from the wealthy and give to the poor than the wealthy will choose to give. Reflecting the necessary imprecision with which their ethical systems may be defined, advocates of extended governmental income transfers to the poor are frequently unable to justify, except by assertion of what is the right thing to do, their implied moral judgments. At other times, advocates point to specific teachings of the Bible or Koran as the basis for their moral concern; these teachings are viewed as revealed truth and, according to their adherents, should be followed as such in the formation of government policy.

Through the centuries philosophers have grappled with the question, Is there a logical basis for the ethical values which people hold? A primary concern of their struggle has been with developing principles which will enable people to decide whether or not a community's distribution of basic rights (such as the rights of speech and the vote), wealth, and income are socially *just* or *unjust;* in other words, philosophers—economists included—have been in search of the broad theoretical outlines of the *just society.* In recent years John Rawls, a Harvard philosophy professor, has organized what he calls "a theory of justice," in a well-known book by that title, which he believes incorporates the guiding principles people seek.[10] Rawls's theory is founded upon several intuitively plausible postulates. First, people are better off behaving cooperatively in some form of human society than they are alone. Second, there are a number of ways of organizing human interaction. Third, people must have some means or set of principles for judging and choosing from among the various potential social arrangements that arrangement which is "best." "These principles," according to Rawls, "are the principles of social justice: they provide a way of assigning rights and duties in the basic institution of society and they define the appropriate distribution of the benefits and burdens of social cooperation."[11] Examples of basic social institutions to which Rawls refers are the legal protections of freedom of thought and liberty of conscience, competitive markets, private ownership in the means of production, and the monogamous family. Fourth, people are *moral* in the sense that they understand the need for and are prepared to affirm a conception of *justice* by which all societal institutions can be judged.

In developing his theory of justice, Rawls is not interested in seeking and defining principles of justice which flow solely from the dictates of reason or science or which are externally derived

[10] John Rawls, *A Theory of Justice* (Cambridge, Mass.: Belknap Press of Harvard University Press, 1971). For an excellent summary of this book, see John Rawls, "A Kantian Conception of Equality," *Cambridge Review*, February 1975, pp. 94–99.

[11] Rawls, *Justice*, p. 4.

from the teaching of, for example, some form of religion, although religious views may be a part of the process by which the guiding principles are derived. Rather, Rawls is interested in developing those principles which "free and rational persons concerned to further their own interests would accept in an initial position of equality as defining the fundamental terms of their association."[12] It is the *acceptance* of the principles of social justice by *all* people, who may be differently motivated, which is the essential element of the Rawlsian theory. In taking this position Rawls recognizes, as James Buchanan has suggested, that "Unless we are to be rescued by a 'savior' or 'saviors' who will enslave us all, modern men and women must reform their own institutions. Rules can be changed while the game continues to be played, but few players are willing to delegate decisions on such changes to the self-anointed witch doctors."[13] With respect to changes in the distribution of income, the subject of this chapter, Rawls seeks guiding principles that are not imposed upon but that emerge from a social setting of people who recognize the need for general agreement: "The scheme of social cooperation must be stable: it must be more or less regularly complied with and its basic rules willingly acted upon; and when infractions occur, stabilizing forces should exist that prevent further violations and tend to restore the arrangement."[14] In short, without general agreement on basic rules, society may perpetually exist in a "Hobbesian jungle" of the kind we discussed in Chapter 5, a state of noncooperation in which all are worse off.

What are the basic principles of social justice to which people in general can agree? Rawls argues that they are principles which will emerge from a setting in which people choose jointly a social contract that incorporates the principles of justice. In order for the principles to be "fair," the social contract setting, according to Rawls, must be "fair" in the sense that no participant has an advantage in determining what those generally agreed-to principles of justice will be. If anyone has an advantage in determining the principles, the principles will be devised to correspond to the private interests of that individual and will lack the necessary general agreement that is so important in the Rawlsian theory for social stability. A "fair" contract setting is one into which all those who engage in social cooperation enter as equals. Further, they are all behind what Rawls calls a "veil of ignorance." Behind this veil "no one knows his place in society, his class position or social status, nor does any one know his fortune in the distribution of natural assets and abilities, his intelligence, strength, and the like, . . . [his] conception of the good or . . . [his] psychological propensities."[15] Without any knowledge of what their position in society will be, the participants are asked to devise rules for distributing basic rights in society and for distributing the society's benefits—the distribution of income. Rawls argues that two fundamental principles will emerge.

First: each person is to have an equal right to the most extensive basic liberty compatible with a similar liberty for others.

Second: social and economic inequalities are to be arranged so that they are both (*a*) reasonably expected to be to everyone's advantage, and (*b*) attached to positions and offices open to all.[16]

In the Rawlsian system of justice, inequalities in the distribution of wealth and income are *just* only when they are advantageous to everyone, especially the lower-income groups in society. Inequalities in the distribution are *unjust* when they are to the disadvantage of anyone, particularly to someone in the lower-income group. Rawls concludes that justice—a concept developed when people are in the initial contract state behind the veil of ignorance—requires that the income of the

[12] Ibid., p. 11.

[13] James M. Buchanan, "Notes on Justice in Contract" (Blacksburg, Va.: Center for the Study of Public Choice, Virginia Polytechnic Institute and State University), Working Paper CE 76-6-4, 1976, p. 25

[14] Rawls, *Justice*, p. 6.

[15] Ibid., p. 12.

[16] Ibid., p. 60.

lower-income people in society be maximized. This is called the *difference principle.*

Many people who have read Rawls have concluded that the difference principle justifies a massive transfer of income from the rich to the poor of society, because that is a redistribution scheme which even the rich would have accepted in the initial social contract setting behind the veil of ignorance. The difference principle, therefore, justifies present governmental poverty programs and expansions of them. On the surface, a redistribution from the rich to the poor does appear to be consistent with the difference principle; the income of the poor is apparently raised by the design of the program. However, the transfers can be inconsistent with the goal of maximizing the incomes of the poor. Massive governmental programs to redistribute income can reduce the incentive of the relatively rich to work and invest in productive assets. To the extent that the productive efforts of the rich are beneficial to the poor—to the extent that the poor work with capital equipment—a transfer of income from the rich to the poor can conceivably make the poor worse off, at least over a period of time as the poor gradually have fewer capital assets to aid them in production. The poor of today may be better off because they receive supplements to their income which are transferred by the government from the rich. However, the poor of the future may be worse off because the aggregate income of the society then will tend to be less because of depleted capital stocks. In this event, the poor of the future will tend to earn less income (they are less productive because they have less capital to work with), and the government will have less income to transfer from the rich to the poor. Indeed, Robert Nozick, another Harvard philosophy professor, has written a book which contains a major attempt to counter Rawls's basic arguments.[17] A basic thesis of Nozick's work is that the rich, who may be rich because of greater natural or acquired talents and who are more productive, benefit the poor by providing them with mutually beneficial opportunities for trade at lower prices than would otherwise exist.[18] Certainly, it is doubtful that the poor would be better off if the rich did not possess their greater productive skills.

Richard Wagner goes even further and contends that adoption of Rawls's framework for establishing justice in the distribution of income may result in *less* income transfers from the rich to the poor than we now have.[19] Behind the veil of ignorance, people do not know their relative income position; and in that state they will vote for income redistribution schemes which reflect their ignorance of their relative position and the fact that they have an equal chance of being in a high or low income bracket. When the veil of ignorance is lowered, however, they immediately become aware of their station in life—their present and expected future income. Wagner argues that in a world in which people are aware of their relative income standing, people with above-average income will vote for less equalization than formerly; those with below average income will vote for more governmental transfers and greater equalization in the income distribution.

Given the country's distribution of income, there are many more people who have incomes below the average income level than people who have incomes above the average. This is so because the relatively few people who have extremely high incomes pull the average income level upward to the point where more than 50 percent of the people have less than the average income. In the real world of practical politics, in which the veil of ignorance has been dropped and people know their relative position in the income distribution, Wagner argues that people will vote for more income transfer programs than they would adopt behind the veil of ignorance where there is at least some possibility that they each will have an above-average income. Rawls's theory of justice is based on the presupposition

[17] Robert Nozick, *Anarchy, State, and Utopia* (New York: Basic Books, Inc., Publishers, 1974).

[18] A full discussion of the Nozick position involves a treatment of the law of comparative advantage, which we discussed in some detail in Chaps. 5 and 16.

[19] Richard E. Wagner, "Politics, Bureaucracy, and Budgetary Choice: The Brookings Budget for 1974," *Journal of Money, Credit and Banking*, vol. 6, pp. 367–383, August 1974.

that once the principles of justice are accepted, people will adhere to them; they will not change the rules of the game once the veil of ignorance is dropped. However, again in the real world of practical politics this condition may rarely hold, or it may hold only to a very limited extent and for a relatively short period of time. Wagner's suggestion is that by using Rawls's veil of ignorance as a frame of reference in establishing justice in the distribution of income, the present distribution of income, which includes significant governmental transfers, may be unjust in the sense that there is *too much* rather than *too little* in the way of income transfers from the rich to the poor.

Overall, Rawls's theory of justice provides a basis for thinking through the complex issues of justice in the distribution of income from a noneconomic point of reference. However, it adds little to our understanding of how much governmental aid *should* be given to the poor. The argument can, with appropriate blinders to counterarguments, be used to "justify" more or fewer income transfers.

Redistribution of Income as Social Insurance and as an Outcome of Practical Politics

The Rawlsian approach to explaining governmental attempts to redistribute income requires that we hypothesize an initial social setting which is filled with moral people who are interested in working out the guiding principles of justice. However, the basis for real-world governmental programs for the poor may be only incidentally linked to that idealized setting. Instead, present poverty relief programs may be construed as a form of "social insurance" which people elect to buy through government. Because people may be uncertain as to what their future incomes will be, they vote for programs which will provide them with relief if they confront significant hardships. According to this explanation, people can be totally unconcerned with the justice or injustice, taken in a fundamental sense, of proposed poverty programs; they are merely concerned with averting economic disaster for themselves.

In a democratic system, individual votes can represent small claims which people have against the total income earned by all people in the country. The poverty relief programs which we observe may simply be the consequence of people "cashing in" their votes for greater income shares. Also, relief programs can in part represent political services which politicians are able to provide their constituencies. The scope of those services will mirror the size of the constituency that benefits from the programs, the relative productivity of politicians in pushing poverty relief legislation through Congress, and defects in the political process which allow one income group to, in some sense, exploit other groups. For some, income redistribution may be a moral imperative; for others, it is simply a consequence of pragmatic politics—that which emerges from within (and, at times, outside) the constitutional framework of government.

METHODS OF REDISTRIBUTION AND INCENTIVES

From the long list of federal programs, it is clear that there are many different ways of giving aid to the poor, and space restrictions do not allow us to consider all possible forms of aid.[20] However, our intent in this section is to examine the incentive effects of three broad categories of aid: (1) *in-kind transfers* in the form of food, housing, Medicare, and education; (2) *cash transfers* which the poor can spend as they wish; and (3) *direct government intervention* in the market, mainly in the form of minimum wage laws and rent controls.

Regardless of their purpose, redistribution programs tend to affect people's incentive to work, to invest, and to buy certain goods and services which are subsidized. Generally, aid given to the poor by almost any means has two distinguishable effects, an *income effect* and a *relative*

[20] According to a government study, there were 168 different federal programs to aid the poor in 1972. These programs are administered by 12 or more government agencies. (U.S. Congress, Senate, Committee on Finance, *Hearings on Establishing Priorities among Programs Aiding the Poor,* 92d Cong., 2d Sess., February 1972.)

price effect. When the poor are given more income, their set of opportunities changes and they can choose to buy more or less of various goods and services, including leisure. Because aid typically changes the relative prices of goods and services, including leisure, the poor are induced to buy more of those goods whose relative prices have decreased and to buy less of those goods whose relative prices have gone up. In this section, we highlight the different incentive effects of the three categories of aid listed above. In terms of the economist's notion of efficiency, the analysis enables us to see the advantages and disadvantages of the possible ways of helping the poor.[21]

In-kind Transfers

Instead of giving the poor money grants with which they can do as they wish, aid is given in such forms as food, housing, and education at zero or subsidized prices. The aid is tied to specific commodities and, therefore, is referred to as *in-kind transfers.* Because of the special characteristics of the different aid programs, we consider them separately here.

Food Although there are several governmental programs which are intended to supplement the food budgets of the poor, the food stamp program is by far the largest in terms of tax dollars spent and number of people affected. Under this program the poor can buy from the government stamps or coupons which can be used to buy food. Certain categories of grocery store items, such as soft drinks, candy, and wines, are specifically excluded.

The price paid for the stamps is less than their value at the checkout counter of grocery stores, and the difference between the price of the food stamps and their store value is the effective food subsidy or transfer. However, the price which the poor pay is inversely related to family size and directly related to the family's *adjusted income.* The adjusted family income is obtained by subtracting certain expenses, such as for housing and utilities, that are over a stipulated percentage of the family's gross income. The program is set up in such a way that the effective food subsidy goes up with family size and down with increases in adjusted family income. As a family's adjusted income rises, the effective subsidy gradually falls until it is zero at some stipulated income level.

Table 20·3 indicates the subsidy at various income levels for a family of four in 1974. It shows that at a zero adjusted income level (which, given the adjustment, means the family can still be earning something), a family is given (or "sold" at zero price) stamps worth $1800 in the supermarket; the subsidy falls from that point to where it is $288 at an adjusted income level of $6000; the total (adjusted) family income is raised because of

TABLE 20·3 FOOD STAMP BENEFITS FOR A FAMILY OF FOUR (JULY 1974)

Earned or Presubsidy Adjusted Income (1)	Effective Subsidy[a] (2)	Total Adjusted Income [(1) + (2)] (3)
$ 0	$1800	$1800
1000	1572	2572
2000	1308	3308
3000	948	3948
4000	660	4660
5000	444	5444
6000	288	6288

[a] Difference between the price of stamps and their value in the store.

SOURCE: Edgar K. Browning, *Redistribution and the Welfare System* (Washington, D.C.: American Enterprise Institute for Public Policy Research, 1975), p. 41.

[21] In developing this section, we are indebted to Edgar K. Browning, who has written a small but excellent book, *Redistribution and the Welfare System* (Washington, D.C.: American Enterprise Institute for Public Policy Research, 1975). The reader should consult this book for an extended discussion of the points briefly made in this section. Browning's coverage of alternative redistribution programs is also more complete than we can offer here.

the food stamp program [see column (3)].[22] However, the table also reveals that a family with $6000 of presubsidy income [column (1)] actually has only $844 more in total adjusted income [column (3)] than the family with $5000 of adjusted income. In other words, a $1000 difference in presubsidy income results in an $844 difference in total income. In this way, the food stamp program raises and tends to equalize the incomes among people *within* the low-income group. The taxes that are levied on higher-income groups to pay for the program tend to equalize incomes *among* income groups.

The food stamp program has a number of economic effects which should be kept in mind when evaluating the program relative to alternative means of helping the poor. By design, food stamps lower the price of food to the people in lower-income groups who qualify for them; and, given their downward sloping demand curve for food, the lower relative price of food will result in the poor buying a greater amount of food. This is the prime purpose of the program. However, the program also increases the effective income of the poor [see column (3) of Table 20·3]. Further, if the poor, like most other groups, have an inelastic demand for food, the lower relative price of food will result in the poor spending less of their own earned income on food.[23] In this way, the food stamp program enables the recipients to buy more of other goods. A concern of many people who favor the food stamp program as a means of helping the poor over, say, unrestricted grants is the fear that the poor will use any cash grants they receive to buy such things as cigarettes and "booze." Although their ability to buy such products is more restricted under a food stamp program than it would be under a cash grant program, the analysis of this section suggests that food stamp recipients can increase their consumption of "booze" or any other good if they want.

Regardless, food stamps will lead to greater food consumption than will exist under a cash grant program. Under both cash grant and food stamp programs, the real, effective income of the poor is raised. However, under the food stamp program the relative price of food is lowered, causing the poor to buy more food than they would if their incomes were raised while the relative prices of all goods remained the same. Although food stamps may be favored by the taxpaying public, unrestricted cash grants will be preferred by the poor. With the additional money income and knowing their own preferences, the poor can buy more food if they want or they can buy more of other goods if those are preferred. In short, a $1 of food subsidy to the poor is worth less than a $1 cash grant. Put in other terms, the tax cost of a cash grant program will be less than a food stamp program giving *equal* benefits to the poor. Kenneth Clarkson estimates that in order to achieve the same benefits to the poor, 25 percent more tax dollars will have to be spent on a food stamp program than on a cash grant program.[24] For this reason and because cash subsidies are very likely administratively less complicated, most economists favor unrestricted cash subsidies over most in-kind transfer programs.

The poor may not pay income taxes in the sense that they actually write the government a check on the income they earn; however, the food stamp program, as well as other in-kind programs, tends to impose an *implicit income tax* on the poor in the sense that their disposable income does not rise by the amount of their increased earnings. Consider Table 20·3 again. It indicates that if the presubsidy earnings of a family of four rise from $5000 to $6000, or by $1000, the family's effective, usable income rises from $5444 to $6288, or by $844. In effect, $156, or 15.6 percent of their additional income, is taken (or taxed) away by government. The implicit marginal tax rate (which is the

[22] When the deductions are considered, the family's gross income is actually greater than what is indicated in col. (3).

[23] An inelastic demand means that at lower prices people will spend less on food (see Chap. 3). Empirical studies indicate that, in general, people's demand for food is inelastic; we assume here that this is true for food stamp recipients as a group.

[24] Kenneth W. Clarkson, *Food Stamps and Nutrition* (Washington, D.C.: American Enterprise Institute for Public Policy Research, 1975), p. 42.

rate applied to increments of income) varies over different income ranges, as is indicated in Table 20·3; however, Edgar Browning suggests that the implicit marginal tax rate is generally between 25 and 30 percent, a higher marginal tax rate, we might add, than is applied to the incomes of families with much higher incomes.[25] To the extent that the food stamp system is set up in the way that Table 20·3 indicates, it reduces the return and incentive which people have to work and to invest in skills which will raise their incomes. When the gain in disposable income is reduced from $1000 to $844, people effectively earn less for additional work and, therefore, receive fewer compensating benefits for working. This does not mean that food stamp recipients will not work, but it does mean that we can expect a *marginal* adjustment downward in the amount and intensity of work which people do. It should also follow that people should be less inclined to accept those jobs which are higher-paying but are, for some reason, unattractive in terms of the physical or emotional strain that they put on the poor. These predictions are supported by empirical studies.[26]

To avoid the disincentive to work, the government might consider leaving the subsidy unchanged over all income ranges. However, this means that everyone would be eligible for food stamps, and the costs would, without doubt, go far above tolerable limits. Taxes would go up, causing the marginal tax rates on higher-income groups to rise and creating a disincentive for them to work and generate income. Invariably, any welfare program like food stamps forces people to trade off efficiency in the distribution and use of resources for the benefits of greater social justice which are perceived for the program.

Housing Public housing projects, in which the government organizes the construction and manages the housing units, typically have most of the economic effects that food stamp-type programs have. Housing projects reduce the relative price of housing to the poor and cause them to demand more housing than they otherwise would; they also increase the total effective income of the poor who are in the projects. Further, because the aid, again, is in the form of a specific good or service, the value of the aid to the poor is not as great as a cash grant of equal dollar value. The poor must take the aid primarily in terms of the types and sizes of housing that are governmentally provided, instead of in terms of the things that they want most.

However, there is one important and distinctive difference between food stamps and public housing programs. In the case of the food stamp program, the poor can buy as much food as they wish from the market. In the case of public housing programs, on the other hand, the number of housing units and the sizes of the units are determined through governmental processes and are dependent upon specific governmental appropriations for the construction of additional housing. Generally, the subsidized price of public housing and the administratively determined supply have meant that far more people have wanted to get into public housing projects than there have been units available. Indeed, only about 7 percent of the eligible poor lived in public housing in 1960.[27] Although less acute today, the shortage is clearly revealed by the long waiting lists in many areas of the country. The program, therefore, provides a rather significant benefit to a relatively small portion of the people who are considered in need of better housing. Further, law restricts project managers from raising their rents and from allowing those who are eligible to express the intensity of their preferences for better housing through their willingness to pay higher rents. Although seemingly contrary to the intent of the program, rent increases can permit better maintenance and, if the funds can be used for the purpose, additional housing units for those eligible persons on the waiting lists.

[25] Browning, *Redistribution*, p. 42.

[26] Joseph A. Pechman and P. Michael Timpene, eds., *Work Incentives and Income Guarantees: The New Jersey Negative Income Tax* (Washington, D.C.: The Brookings Institution, 1975).

[27] Browning, *Redistribution*, p. 45.

Education Most countries in the world provide free elementary education for all children. In a number of countries there are specialized, high-quality private schools where parents who can afford to do so purchase better-quality education for their children; but this is a minor phenomenon. Most children go to government-provided schools, and more go because of the subsidized price.

In government-provided schools there are a certain number of special programs for the very bright and the very slow students; but, basically, everyone gets much the same education in terms of curriculum and amount of time in school. The amount that is learned in school is proportional to what the student brings with him in terms of innate abilities and home experiences as well as to the formal education he or she receives. Recent studies suggest that children from high-income homes do much better than those from low-income homes. It is not clear whether this reflects superior native intelligence inherited from the parents or the home environment; but in any event it is clear that the school experience is much more valuable for those students who bring a good deal with them to school than it is to those who bring little from their homes.[28]

Thus, the child from a high-income family will typically have a higher predicted lifetime income than the poor student if neither goes to school. It is likely that the school experience will possibly increase this difference. The gains received from schooling by the child are not equal and are likely to be greater for the child from a well-to-do home than for the child from a poor home. Thus, it is by no means obvious that the public educational system should be regarded as redistributing wealth from the well-off to the poor. Everyone may receive greater wealth in the form of human capital and greater future incomes because of public education, but the rich may receive more than lower-income groups.

[28] Howard P. Tuckman, *The Economics of the Rich* (New York: Random House, Inc., 1973), chaps. 9 and 10. Tuckman suggests that public education is a tool which the wealthy use to maintain and expand their share of the country's wealth.

Higher education, another example of direct expenditures of government funds which is frequently regarded as a welfare activity, is fairly definitely a redistribution of funds from the poor to the well-off.[29] Not only are those students who are highly motivated and intelligent more able to gain from a given investment of resources by the state in their education, but the resources invested by the state tend to be rationed so that bright and highly motivated students get much more of them than do the dull and unmotivated. Since, once again, the bright and highly motivated students are the ones who tend to have the highest incomes even if no one got any public education, this is redistribution to the upper-income group.

In general, a relatively high portion of the poorest students (those who have the lowest expected lifetime income) are not eligible for higher education because they cannot meet the entrance requirements. If they do become eligible for higher education, they normally go to schools where the state is investing relatively little. But the brighter and more hard-working students have been selected for receipt of larger subsidies, so that, in addition to their natural talents and ability to learn more from class, they are actually being given a better education.

Cash Grant Transfers

There are many ways by which cash grants can be made to the poor. However, in this section we will draw the broad outlines of one method which is now receiving considerable attention in policy discussion; that method is the *negative income tax* (or NIT). Most income earners pay a portion of their income to the government; their tax payments also rise with their income. In this way, their income is subject to an *income tax* or, more precisely, a *positive income tax*. As the name may

[29] For opposing views on this subject, see W. Lee Hanser and Burton A. Weisbrod, "The Distribution of Costs and Benefits of Public Higher Education: The Case of California," *Journal of Human Resources*, vol. 4, pp. 176–191, Spring 1969; and Joseph A. Pechman, "The Distributional Effects of Public Higher Education in California," *Journal of Human Resources*, vol. 5, pp. 361–370, Summer 1970.

TABLE 20·4 A HYPOTHETICAL NEGATIVE INCOME TAX SCHEDULE

Pretransfer Income (1)	Cash Grant or Transfer (2)	Total Disposable Income [(1) + (2)] (3)
$ 0	$2500	$2500
1000	2000	3000
2000	1500	3500
3000	1000	4000
4000	500	4500
5000	0	5000

suggest, the negative income tax is a cash payment system by which the government pays people with low incomes some amount of money to supplement their incomes; the supplement also rises as the incomes of poor people fall further below the stipulated income level.

Table 20·4 contains one of many possible negative income tax schedules. Under this particular plan, every poor family will receive a minimum governmental transfer of $2500, even if no work is done; this minimum transfer level is often referred to as the *guaranteed income level*. As the family's income rises by increments of $1000, the amount of government cash transfer goes down by $500. At an income level of $5000, the *breakeven income level*, no cash transfer is made. Above the breakeven level, the typical plans call for the family to pay a portion of their *additional* income to the government. Notice that, as in the case of the food stamp program, an *implicit marginal income tax rate* is applied to the income of the poor who benefit from the NIT. When the family's income rises by $1000, the government effectively "taxes" away 50 percent of the increase by reducing the cash transfer which it pays. Further, this *implicit* marginal tax rate is much higher than the *explicit* marginal tax rate paid by people with these and, possibly, four times the breakeven income of $5000; and the implicit marginal tax rate on the poor can be lowered by (1) lowering the guaranteed income level and/or (2) raising the breakeven income level. However, each of these policy courses has inherent problems. A reduction in the minimum income level will provide less protection for those who do not or cannot work. On the other hand, an increase in the breakeven income level will mean that more people will benefit from the negative income tax system and the cost of the program will rise. For example, in order to reduce the marginal tax rate to 20 percent while keeping the guaranteed income level at $2500, the breakeven income level would have to be raised to $12,500, which is not far removed from the medium family income in 1976. In short, a substantial percentage of the population will then be recipients of this form of welfare.

To keep the cost down and the benefits concentrated on the truly poor of the country, it follows that any negative income tax system which is likely to be politically acceptable will incorporate a rather high implicit marginal tax rate. The system will, therefore, have a heavy built-in *dis*incentive to work: much of the benefits of extra work will be implicitly taxed away through reduced subsidy payments. However, economists tend to favor the negative income tax system over other possible welfare programs for several reasons. First, they propose that the NIT replace present welfare programs, many of which are notorious for having an implicit marginal tax rate of 100 percent. In other words, $1 earned leads to a $1 reduction in subsidy, which has an even greater adverse effect on work incentives than their proposed NIT system. Second, since the NIT can be run through the Internal Revenue Service as the *positive* tax system is, the NIT is potentially less costly than the conglomeration of welfare programs now in force. These welfare programs require large bureaucracies to apply and enforce their many detailed regulations to provide the in-kind services. Third, instead of aid in the form of food or housing, the poor are given money which they can spend according to their own calculated needs; fewer tax dollars need to be spent to achieve the same benefits for the poor. However, aside from the work incentive effect, Browning notes that the NIT fails to treat the causes of poverty and to take into account the special needs of people, like heavy medical expenses.[30]

Generally, any aid which is based on income, family size, and family structure, as the food stamp-type programs and negative income tax proposals typically are, tends to have other, potentially significant incentive effects. If the income criterion is based on money earnings, people can be expected to reduce the amount of time they spend earning money and to increase the time they spend, for instance, growing their own food. If the subsidy is adjusted upward for each additional child, the cost of having children is reduced, and this has the effect of increasing the size of many subsidized families.[31] If the aid that is given is based on family structure, the way the aid system is structured can cause the dissolution of families. To illustrate, suppose that the schedule below indicates the cash grants which are given to poor people in three family arrangements.

Family Structure	Cash Grant
1 adult	$3000
1 adult, 2 children	4000
2 adults, 2 children	5000

A family of four—two adults and two children—will, if they stay together, receive $5000. However, note that if the parents separate, or give the appearance that they have separated, and if one parent takes both children, the aid that all receive will rise from the $5000 received when they are together as a family unit to $7000 ($3000 for the single adult plus $4000 for the one adult and two children). This welfare arrangement provides families, many of which may already be unstable, an additional reason to break up. Other schemes can be devised which will lack the above incentive structure; however, the point of this section is that policy makers must be careful in how they design their programs. The Aid for Dependent Children program provided female heads of household with supplemental income; the aid was denied poor families with a male adult in the home. The program was notorious for the number of husbands who deserted (or gave the appearance of deserting) their wives so that they could receive additional welfare benefits. In general, when aid is given on the basis of special characteristics of people and families, people can be expected to adjust *marginally* to meet the qualifications. Still, the equity benefits of poverty relief programs can more than compensate for the adverse incentive consequences; however, the implied trade-off must be recognized by policy makers.

Direct Government Intervention in Markets

Minimum wage laws and controls on the rents of low-income housing have also been means by which the government has attempted to help the poor. However, as we explained in Chapter 14, minimum wage laws tend to boost the wage rate for people in many labor markets above the equilibrium wage. The result is a reduction in the number of people whom employers want to hire and an increase in the number of unemployed people. Minimum wage laws, to the extent they have an effect on wages that are paid, tend to raise the wage rates of those who retain their jobs; however, they lower the wage rates of others from what is considered a very low wage to an even lower wage, possibly zero. Since the poor tend to be some of the least productive workers in labor markets because they lack the needed training and skills, they represent a disproportionate percentage of those who are unemployed when minimum wage rates are raised. (See Chapter 15 for a more extensive discussion of the effects of minimum wage rates.)

When rents for the housing of the poor are controlled, the consequence is a market shortage of housing: more people want to rent the controlled housing than there are housing units available. In this event, landlords can be selective regarding to whom they will rent, and they will tend to choose

[30] Browning, *Redistribution*, p. 38.

[31] Of course, not every aid recipient will have an additional child because of the aid program. For many, the amount of aid may be too small to cover the cost of additional children. However, there are many potential welfare parents who are practically indifferent to having another child; the additional welfare benefits for each additional child will, for many of these people, be the necessary incentive to make an additional child a rational choice.

TABLE 20·5 RELATIVE INCOME DISTRIBUTION *(Expressed as Percentage of Total Money Income Received by Families, by Quintile)*

Year	Lowest Fifth	Second Fifth	Middle Fifth	Fourth Fifth	Highest Fifth
1952	4.9	12.2	17.1	23.5	42.0
1962	5.0	12.1	17.6	24.0	41.3
1972	5.4	11.9	17.5	23.9	41.4
1975	5.4	11.8	17.6	24.1	41.1

SOURCE: 1952, 1962, and 1972 data from U.S. Bureau of the Census, "Money Income in 1972 of Families and Persons in the United States," *Current Population Reports*, series p-60, No. 90 (1973), table 16, as reported in Edgar K. Browning, "How Much More Equality Can We Afford?" *Public Interest*, No. 43, p. 93, Spring 1976. Data for 1974 from U.S. Bureau of the Census, *Statistical Abstract of the United States: 1976* (Washington, D.C.: U.S. Government Printing Office), p. 406.

those renters who are most likely to meet their rental payments consistently. Given the financial difficulties which the poor have, the landlords will tend to choose people with higher incomes rather than the poor. Alternately, because the rent is below the market clearing price and there is a shortage of housing, landlords can reduce the amount they spend on the upkeep of their housing units. Many poor people who are able to keep their housing in the face of rent controls will witness to the deterioration of their apartment buildings. Other landlords may simply close up their rental units and move to other areas where they can charge higher rents. Finally, rent controls will discourage the construction of new housing units. (For a discussion of rent controls in general and New York City's experience with rent controls in particular, see Chapter 11.)

THE EFFECTS OF GOVERNMENT REDISTRIBUTION PROGRAMS

Have governmental poverty relief programs had a significant effect on the incomes of the poor? Many researchers, including people who have been advocates of greater governmental transfers, have concluded that the effect has been small. In support of their position, they point to the very small changes which have occurred in the nation's income distribution over the last two or more decades. Consider the statistics in Table 20·5. In 1952, the 20 percent of all families with the lowest incomes in the country earned 4.9 percent of the nation's total income, whereas the 20 percent of all families with the highest incomes earned 42 percent of all income. As can be seen in the table, in the following two decades those figures changed, but not by very much. In 1972, the 20 percent of all families with the lowest incomes earned 5.4 percent of the nation's income. However, Edgar Browning contends that these figures are misleading. They are based on *gross money incomes earned* and are not adjusted for the governmental cash and in-kind transfers that are indicated by amounts in Table 20·6, for the fact that government collects more taxes from higher-income groups than it does from lower-income groups, and for the fact that there are fewer children in lower-income families (because many poor are elderly).[32] After making adjustments for these considerations, Browning comes out with the *effective* income distribution in Table 20·7. In that distribution, the lowest fifth of all families *received* (as opposed to just *earned*) 11 percent of the value of all income in 1972; this figure represents a 44 percent increase over the relative income share of the poorest group in 1952.

[32] Edgar K. Browning, "How Much More Equality Can We Afford?" *Public Interest*, No. 43, pp. 90–110, Spring 1976.

TABLE 20·6 FEDERAL OUTLAYS BENEFITING LOW-INCOME PERSONS: 1964 TO 1974

	1964	1970	1974	Percentage Increase between 1964 and 1974
Federal outlays (in billions)				
Cash payments	$ 6.4	$ 8.7	$ 12.0	87.5
Food and housing transfers	0.3	1.0	3.2	966.6
Education	0.1	1.4	1.8	900.0
Health	0.7	4.0	6.2	785.7
Manpower	0.2	1.5	2.0	900.0
Other	0.2	1.1	2.0	900.0
Total	$ 7.9	$ 17.8	$ 27.0	241.7
Total federal cash transfers (in billions)	6.4	8.7	12.0	87.5
Total federal in-kind transfers (in billions)	1.5	9.1	15.0	900.0
Federal transfers per low-income person	$219	$700	$1111	407.3
Federal cash transfer per low-income person	177	342	494	179.1
Federal in-kind transfer per low-income person	42	358	617	1369.0

SOURCE: U.S. Bureau of the Census, *Statistical Abstract of the United States: 1975* (Washington, D.C.: U.S. Government Printing Office, 1975), p. 405.

Although there is reason to believe that the increase in the income share of the poor is exaggerated by these figures, Browning does show that the effect of government policy is much greater than the distribution of earned income suggests. A study undertaken for 1975–76 by the Congressional Budget Office draws similar conclusions.[33]

33 "Study Finds 50% Fewer Poor People," *The Washington Post*, Jan. 16, 1977, p. A1.

TABLE 20·7 ADJUSTED RELATIVE INCOME DISTRIBUTION *(Expressed as Percentage Share of Income Received by Quintile)*

Year	Lowest Fifth	Second Fifth	Middle Fifth	Fourth Fifth	Highest Fifth
1952	8.1	14.2	17.8	23.2	36.7
1962	8.8	14.4	18.2	23.1	35.4
1972	11.7	15.0	18.2	22.3	32.8

SOURCE: Edgar K. Browning, "How Much More Equality Can We Afford?" *Public Interest*, No. 43, pp. 90–110, Spring, 1976.

SUMMARY AND EXTENSIONS

This chapter has covered a great deal of ground. We have discussed the way in which income in the United States is distributed, and we have provided several theoretical explanations for the distribution which we observe. We have also developed theoretical arguments for governmental programs to relieve problems of poverty and have briefly indicated the incentive effects of a very limited number of means of relieving poverty. The coverage of this chapter is not exhaustive; we have tried only to suggest the ways in which economics can be used to think through the very important social problem of helping the poor.

There is much that we have not had space to discuss. For example, the money transferred to the poor must be taken from someone; we have only touched on the effects which the required taxes have on the incentive of the well-to-do to work, to invest, and to buy different goods and services. One may think that an obvious solution to the incentive problems of taxation would be to levy the taxes on the profits of businesses. However, such taxes invariably fall on someone; therefore, they also have effects on people's consuming and saving decisions. They have an impact on the relative prices of goods and services and on the real incomes of different groups of people. A study of the true *incidence* of taxes (that is, of who pays the taxes that are levied) could take a whole course in itself.

Finally, we must recognize that the government engages in much redistributional activity that is really not intended to help the poor. Its purpose is simply to redistribute the income among people within the middle- and upper-income groups. Indeed, many governmental programs have many supporters in government bureaucracies because they will increase the incomes of the people who will administer the programs. How and to what extent governmental relief programs will benefit people other than those whom they are supposedly intended to benefit will be more fully explained in Chapter 22.

QUESTIONS TO PONDER

1 In the chapter we gave several explanations for governmental aid to the poor. Can you think of additional explanations?

2 John Rawls argues that behind the veil of ignorance people will agree to fundamental principles of social justice that include the rule that the income of the lowest-income group should be maximized. That is, an income inequality is justified only to the extent that it is to the advantage of the lowest-income group. Why does this rule—called the *difference principle*—not *require* the government to transfer incomes from the rich to the poor?

3 Since the economy can be expected to grow over time in terms of greater productivity and greater incomes of people, there exists an inequality in income between the present generation and future generations. What does the Rawlsian theory of justice suggest should be done about this intergenerational inequality?

4 What do food stamps do to the ability of the poor to purchase education or training in skills which will increase their productivity and earned incomes? We stated in the chapter that the food stamp program contains an implicit tax on the effective incomes of the poor. What does this implicit tax do to the rate of return on investment in training?

5 In the chapter we suggested that public education probably leads to greater inequality in the income of people who receive the education. Does this necessarily mean that poor people are worse off because of publicly provided education? What does public education do to the inequality of income of the parents of students who receive the education?

6 List the advantages and disadvantages of in-kind transfers and cash grants as means of aiding the poor. Given this listing, which method do you prefer? Explain.

7 Consider this argument: "Because the poor have very little education, they are the ones who can benefit most from education; the rate of return on education is to them greater than it is to the rich. The poor have a greater incentive than the rich to acquire skills through education and to pay for the education they receive. Therefore, public support of education for the purpose of helping the poor is unnecessary." What objections can you raise to this line of argument?

8 Early in the chapter, we suggested that governmental aid to the poor is a means by which the rich can reduce the external costs which the poor, through the overt manifestations of poverty, impose on the rich. Using this argument as a basis for governmental action in poverty relief, should government use in-kind transfers or cash grants to provide aid to the poor? What factors must be considered?

9 In the chapter, we argued that under the conditions that well-off people did not know how much each other is giving, they might give "too much." Is it *possible* that, even when this condition exists, the well-off will give too little? Illustrate with a graph.

10 Predict the effects of the food stamp program on

- **a** The real income of the poor who qualify
- **b** The prices of food
- **c** The quantity of food bought by the nonpoor public
- **d** The quantity of food produced
- **e** The real income of nonpoor consumers and farmers
- **f** The real income of nonpoor taxpayers
- **g** The aggregate real income of future generations

RECOMMENDED READINGS

Boulding, Kenneth E.: *Beyond Economics: Essays on Society, Religion and Ethics* (Ann Arbor, Mich.: Ann Arbor Paperbacks of the University of Michigan Press, 1970), pp. 227–238.

Browning, Edgar K.: "How Much More Equality Can We Afford?" *Public Interest*, No. 43, pp. 90–111, Spring 1976.

———: *Redistribution and the Welfare System* (Washington, D.C.: American Enterprise Institute for Public Policy Research, 1975).

Clarkson, Kenneth W.: *Food Stamps and Nutrition* (Washington, D.C.: American Enterprise Institute for Public Policy Research, 1975).

Herzog, Elizabeth: "Facts and Fiction about the Poor," *Perspectives on Poverty and Income Distribution* (Lexington, Mass.: D.C. Heath and Company, 1971), pp. 100–117.

Okun, Arthur: *Equality and Efficiency: The Big Tradeoff* (Washington, D.C.: The Brookings Institution, 1975).

Pechman, Joseph A., and P. Michael Timpane, eds.: *Work Incentives and Income Guarantees: The New Jersey Negative Income Tax* (Washington, D.C.: The Brookings Institution, 1975), pp. 1–15 and 115–156.

Rawls, John: *A Theory of Justice* (Cambridge, Mass.: Belknap Press of Harvard University Press, 1971), chap. 1.

Thurow, Lester C.: *Poverty and Discrimination* (Washington, D.C.: The Brookings Institution, 1969), chaps. 1 and 3.

Tucker, James F.: *Current Economic Issues and Problems* (Chicago: Rand McNally College Publishing Company, 1976), chaps. 7 and 11.

Tuckman, Howard P.: *The Economics of the Rich* (New York: Random House, Inc., 1973), chaps. 1, 2, 9, and 10.

Part Eight
The Political Economy

But what is government, but the greatest of all reflections on human nature? If men were angels, no government would be necessary. If angels were to govern men, neither external nor internal controls on government would be necessary. In framing a government, which is to be administered by men, the great difficulty lies in this: You must first enable the government to control the governed; and in the next place, oblige it to control itself.

James Madison
"The Social Foundations of Political Freedom," *The Federalist Papers*, No. 51. A modern edition is available in paperback: New York: Washington Square Press, 1964 (first published in 1787–88), pp. 122–123.

In the last two chapters we developed economic arguments for government intervention in the market. In the following two chapters the focus of our attention is on how government goods and services are produced in public bureaucracies. Using basic economic principles, we address the question of "government failure" (we considered the problem of "market failure" in Chapter 19) and evaluate the efficiency of democracy as a political organization and of bureaucracy as a governmental delivery system.

21

The Economics of the Democratic Process

I have no fear, but that the result of our experiment will be, that men may be trusted to govern themselves without a master. Could the contrary be proved, I should conclude, either that there is no God, or that he is a malevolent being.

Thomas Jefferson[1]

PREVIEW OF CHAPTER

Central question

Why is government policy what it is?

Major objectives

1 To explain how and to what extent democracy and the United States Constitution are designed to control the scope and size of government

2 To demonstrate why candidates in a two-party election tend to take political positions which are in the "middle of the road"

3 To show how the voting rule (like simple majority) can affect the cost of making collective decisions and, therefore, the efficiency of collective or governmental action

4 To explore the deficiencies of democracy as a method of making collective decisions

[1] Saul K. Padover, ed., *Thomas Jefferson on Democracy* (New York: Appleton-Century Co., Inc., 1939), p. 19.

Major conclusions

1. The three branches of government, the First Amendment to the Constitution, and the decentralization of government into states, counties, and cities are means of achieving certain governmental ends, but they are also means of limiting the role of government in society.
2. In a two-party democracy, the candidates will tend to represent the views of the *median voter group*.
3. The simple-majority voting rule can be a means of minimizing the combined cost associated with reaching a collective agreement. However, the simple-majority voting rule is not the only possible voting rule, nor is it the way to minimize the costs of making *all* collective agreements. Some issues are too important to be decided upon by a simple majority of the voting population; others are too inconsequential to require that a simple majority of voters agree before a decision can be made.
4. The principal deficiencies of democracy can be summarized as follows: (*a*) Individuals must adjust their behavior to the quantity of the public good provided by government; they cannot adjust the quantity of the public good they consume to their individual preferences. (*b*) Under a simple-majority voting rule (as well as other voting rules), government programs can pass even though the total cost of the programs exceeds their collective benefits; government programs can fail to pass even though their collective benefits exceed the total cost. (*c*) Voters have little incentive to become informed about the political positions of candidates or about the consequences of government programs. (*d*) For reasons which are explained in the chapter, compared with the general population, special-interest groups have a disproportionate amount of political influence.
5. Decentralizing governments is a means of introducing competition into the determination of taxes which people pay and into the determination of the kinds of public goods and services which are provided.

Important terms and concepts

Median voter group
Logrolling (discussed in detail in Appendix 21B)

This book is called *Modern Political Economy*. The title itself implies that our interests extend far beyond the workings of the market system, which was the focal point of the first seventeen chapters. In those chapters we discussed the effects which various government policies have on the operation of markets. For example, we considered the economic impact of price controls and consumer protection laws on the market for final goods and services. Throughout the analysis we assumed that government policies were given to us and that our task was simply to evaluate their effects. The central question undergirding much of the discussion was, "Given the objective of economic efficiency, what are the optimum government policies?" We said little about how government policy is derived or why governments follow the policy courses that they do. In this and following chapters, we make a major shift in our analytical interest. Our main concern is with analyzing the functioning of government itself—that is, the process by which government decisions are made and carried out. Instead of suggesting what the government *should* do, our interest is in commenting on the central tendency of the two-party democratic system, in recognizing the limitations of government as a process for satisfying human wants, and in explaining the political outcome that we observe. In short, we address the question of why the government operates the way it does. Clearly, with government accounting for a substantial portion of the nation's production of goods and services, this is an important question and one which economists can hardly ignore.

We refer to the analysis of this chapter as "The Economics of the Democratic Process" because of the approach we employ. We do not assume from the start that people who vote, who seek to be elected, or who work in government are necessarily motivated to achieve or to do those things which are in the "public interest." Rather, we assume that voters and individuals in government are *rational,* in an economic sense, meaning that they aim to raise their own utility under the special institutional constraints of the democratic system. We then inquire what forms governmental policies will tend to take under the circumstances.

Our reasons for taking this approach are quite simple. First, our primary purpose is to understand how the government works, and this requires that we examine participants in the political process as they are, not as we think they should be. People will vote to obtain what they want and not, necessarily, to obtain those things which we think they should want. Indeed, the secret ballot affirms and protects that right, and we do not wish to propose that that right be changed. Further, although we may like them to behave differently, politicians will espouse programs and platforms which reflect their own private interests, one of which presumably is being elected and reelected. Second, voters and consumers are the same people. John Doe makes purchases and he votes; he is the same man in the supermarket as he is in the voting booth. In both capacities, he can express his public and charitable concerns; however, in both capacities he also has his own private interests and will behave on the basis of those interests. To the extent that people make cost-benefit calculations of the kind we have discussed in all areas of behavior, the economic model of individual behavior in the marketplace is transferable to discussions of the political process. We will see in this chapter that economic analysis can yield very valuable insights into the workings and limitations of the democratic system as a means of allocating scarce resources. In the next chapter, our attention will turn to an investigation of the efficiency characteristics of government bureaucracies.

DEMOCRACY AND SOCIAL CONTROL

The framers of the American Constitution fully recognized the need for government and for restrictions that government imposes on individual freedoms. John Jay in *The Federalist Papers* wrote,

> Nothing is more certain than the indispensible necessity of government; and it is equally undeniable, that whenever and however it is instituted, the people must cede to it some of their natural rights, in order to vest it with requisite powers [to carry out its assigned responsibilities].[2]

The reason for government, which we developed in some detail in Chapter 5, is implied in James Madison's often repeated statement,

> But what is government, but the greatest of all reflections on human nature? If men were angels, no government would be necessary.[3]

Having recognized the need for government, the founding fathers were equally (if not more) concerned with controlling government; Madison continues,

[2] John Jay, "The Dangers of Foreign Force and Influence Threatening the United States," *The Federalist Papers,* No. 2. A modern edition is available in paperback: New York: Washington Square Press, 1964 (originally published 1787–88), pp. 5–6.

[3] James Madison, "The Social Foundations of Political Freedom," *The Federalist Papers,* No. 51 (New York: Washington Square Press, 1964), p. 122.

If angels were to govern men, neither external nor internal controls on government would be necessary. In framing a government, which is to be administered by men, the great difficulty lies in this: You must first enable the government to control the governed; and in the next place, oblige it to control itself.[4]

The framers of the Constitution defined a role for government; however, at the same time they defined, by way of the First Amendment, certain basic rights which would not be subject to infringement by conventional political processes and simple-majority vote: "Congress shall make no law respecting an establishment of religion, or prohibiting the free exercise thereof; or abridging the freedom of speech, or of the press; or the right of the people peaceably to assemble, and to petition the Government for a redress of grievances." They felt that these basic rights were too important to allow them to become the subject of normal political maneuvering; in other words, the potential cost of political infringement on these rights was too great. The First Amendment represents a set of rights for individuals; along with other provisions of the Constitution, it also represents a means of control on government.

Observers of the political process often look upon the political decision-making process incorporated in the Constitution as a means of facilitating the operation and extension of government. However, having recognized the need for government in a limited number of areas, the framers of the Constitution were intent upon establishing a "political obstacle course" which would restrict the scope of government. This is the reason for the division of power between the states and federal government, for the two houses of Congress, and for the veto power of the president. Further, by extending to people the right of the vote, their interest was in dispersing the decision-making power among a great many people and increasing the difficulty by which a majority of people can unite and impose their will on the minority through government. Madison, again, wrote in *The Federalist Papers:*

It is of great importance in a republic, not only to guard the society against the oppression of its rulers; but to guard one part of the society against the injustices of the other part. . . . [By way of the federal republic] the society itself will be broken into so many parts, interests, and classes of citizens, that the rights of individuals, or of the minority, will be in little danger from interested combinations of the majority. In a free government, the security of civil rights must be the same as that for religious rights. It consists in the one case in the multiplicity of interests, and in the other, in the multiplicity of sects.[5]

Clearly, the democratic system that was established was intended to be a mechanism for the social control of government; its purpose was to permit maximum attainment of individual freedom. Further, so long as the government remained relatively small, the democratic system would be a reasonably effective control on government. The framers were concerned, as we will discuss in more detail later, that growth in government would lead to a breakdown in the controlling power of democratic processes. Instead of reflecting the interests of their constituency, the framers of the Constitution were concerned that a large government would mean that representatives would begin to pursue their own interests, and not those of their constituencies, and that bureaucracies would become large, unwieldy, and detached from the controlling influence of the Congress and the voting public.

Still, within the bounds of the constitutional framework, the democratic system which was devised is a means by which politicians, in their competitive efforts to be elected, will seek to represent the interest of their constituencies on issues which are within the purview of government. How a two-party system does this and how economics can be used to answer that question is the subject of the next section.

[4] Ibid., pp. 122–123.

[5] Ibid., p. 125.

THE PRACTICAL POLITICS OF A TWO-PARTY SYSTEM

Elections are held for the purpose of determining the winners of political campaigns; and winning candidates (or issues, when they are up for public consideration) in a two-party democratic system, such as the one which dominates United States politics, are typically "middle-of-the-roaders." They tend to represent the views of the very large group of voters who are neither staunch "liberals" nor staunch "conservatives"; winning candidates usually have moderate views or political positions. Further, there is generally little difference between the candidates of the Republican and Democratic parties. Indeed, a major slogan of George Wallace, who ran for president as a candidate of the American party in 1968 and 1972, was that "There is not a dime's worth of difference between the two of them," meaning his Republican and Democratic opponents. To see the reason why this tends to be the case, consider Figure 21 · 1, which shows all possible political positions on a liberal-conservative continuum. Given that the continuum is all-inclusive, there is some position on the horizontal axis which represents the favored political position of each potential voter. The bell-shaped curve indicates the distribution of voters along the political spectrum. There are a few voters out on the wings of the distribution; however, most voters are assumed to be clustered in the center. Actually, the distribution of voters can vary from the one that is indicated. On the other hand, the distribution that we show seems reasonable, and a change in the shape of the distribution will not affect our analysis.

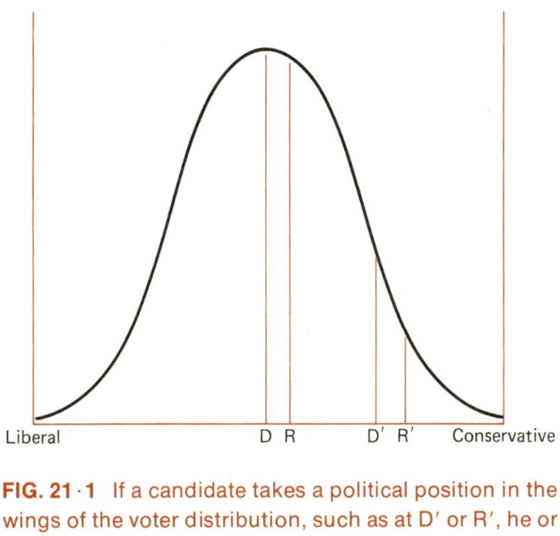

FIG. 21 · 1 If a candidate takes a political position in the wings of the voter distribution, such as at D′ or R′, he or she can be beaten at the polls by a candidate who moves into the middle of the distribution. To avoid losing the election, both candidates in a two-party election are induced to take middle-of-the-road political positions, such as D and R.

Assuming that the candidates of the two parties are intent on winning the election, and assuming that voters will vote for that person who most closely approximates their own preferred political position, politicians will not choose political positions out in the wings of the distribution. To see why, suppose that the Republican candidate chooses a platform which establishes his political position at R′. The Democratic candidate can easily win the election by setting his political position slightly to the left of the Republican's position, for example, at D′. The Republican will take all the votes to his right, which, as indicated by the curve, are very few, and may take roughly half the votes between R′ and D′. However, the Democrat will take all the votes to his left, since he comes closer to their preferred political position than does the Republican; he will also take roughly half the votes between D′ and R′. Clearly the Democrat will have an overwhelming majority.

The smart politician will choose a position near the middle of the distribution in order to avoid being outmaneuvered by his opposition, as above, and ending up losing the election. The opposing candidate must also go to the middle. Otherwise, he or she will lose the election. For instance, suppose that the Republican develops a political platform which puts him at R and the Democrat remains at D′. The Republican will then take all the votes in the left-hand side of the distribution and roughly half the votes between R and D′. He will have more than the necessary simple majority needed to beat his Democratic opponent. In short, in order to contemplate victory or to avoid being beaten, both parties will tend to choose political positions which are close to one another and in the middle of the distribution. Their positions must be sufficiently distinct that they can claim that they are in fact a different party to many voters; but still they must be sufficiently close that they will minimize the number of voters which are in between them.

Many people often criticize politicians for taking similar stands on issues. Their criticism is understandable, since there are many people to the left and the right of the political positions of the major candidates; they would no doubt like to see candidates who more closely represented their own views. However, the analysis of this section suggests that the competition between candidates for votes will lead them to take positions which are in the middle of the distribution and which are similar. The candidates are in a classic "prisoner's dilemma." If the two candidates are ideologically far apart, each can increase the number of votes received (or the probability of winning) by moving closer to the other candidate. Each must also consider the prospects of the other candidate moving closer and making his or her defeat more likely.

Like everyone else, politicians can make mistakes and can misinterpret the political positions of voters. This is so simply because the distribution of voters represented in Figure 21·1 is not known with perfection before an election; politicians must do what they can to determine where the distribution of voters is and to develop their campaigns on that basis. At times, politicians will misread the public's political sentiment and will be defeated because of their mistake. For example, when the political campaign starts, the Democrat may believe, but not know, that the distribution of voters is skewed to the left, as is the orange curve labeled *A* in Figure 21 · 2. Consequently, he or she will take a political position at D′, thinking that it is in the middle of the distribution.

On the other hand, the Republican candidate may believe that the distribution is skewed to the right, as is the orange curve labeled *B*, and therefore may establish a political position at R′.

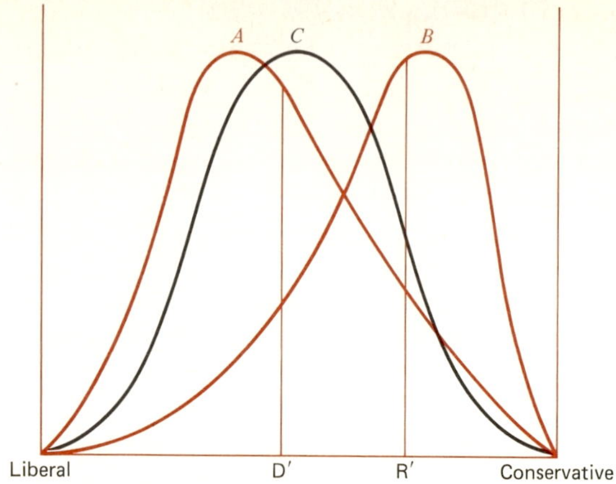

FIG. 21·2 Candidates do not know with perfection how voters are distributed along any political continuum. If the Democrat incorrectly perceives the distribution to be like the one labeled *A* and the Republican perceives the distribution to be like the one labeled *B*, they will each initially establish their political positions at D′ and R′, respectively. Because the Democrat has chosen a position which is closer to the middle of the true distribution, labeled *C*, the Democrats will win the election.

However, the true distribution may be the symmetrical bell-shaped curve labeled *C* in the graph. Since the Democrat is closer to the center of the "true" distribution, the Democrat wins. Over the course of several elections and with the aid of opinion polls, politicians will learn from their mistakes and will "discover," in an imperfect way, what the actual distribution is. They will then move toward the center of the distribution and represent the views of the people in that middle—the so-called *median voter group*. Those in the median voter group will, in a two-party system, tend to have a government which is very much in accord with their preferences. However, other people, particularly those who are in the extreme wings of the distribution, will be continually frustrated by the gap they observe between what they think government should do and what the government actually does.

This median voter model of the political process can be greatly complicated, and we do provide extensions in Appendix A to this chapter. However, the basic conclusions we've drawn here show that public decisions will tend to reflect the views of the median voter group and have considerable predictive power. A number of presidential elections in the post-World War II years, such as the elections of 1948, 1960, and 1968, have been very close; and when the elections have not been close, the losing political party has in succeeding years taken steps to move its political position closer to the position of the other party. When Barry Goldwater lost by a very wide margin in 1964 to Lyndon Johnson, the party made a deliberate effort to pick a more moderate candidate in the 1968 election. The result was that the contest between Richard Nixon and Hubert Humphrey in 1968 was practically a dead heat. After George McGovern went down to a resounding defeat to Richard Nixon in 1972, primarily because McGovern was viewed by the people as much too liberal and Nixon virtually refused to campaign and run the risk of making mistakes, the Democrats realized the need to select a more moderate candidate; their choice in 1976 was Jimmy Carter. In addition, the above median voter model of political behavior described in Figure 21 · 1 has been found to be very useful in sophisticated statistical studies in predicting government policies toward such public concerns as the absolute size of school budgets and conservation programs.[6] Many people are often upset because government tends to favor the preferences of the average person; but, fortunately or unfortunately, that is what a two-party democratic system tends to do: rational politicians, pushed by political competition, will move toward the center of the road in order to maximize their chances of getting elected.

[6] See R. Barlow, "Efficiency Aspects of Local School Expenditures," *Journal of Political Economy*, vol. 78, pp. 1028–1040, September/October 1968; J. Barr and O. Davis, "An Elementary Political and Economic Theory of the Expenditures of Local Governments," *Southern Economic Journal*, vol. 33, pp. 149–165, October 1966; T. C. Bergstrom and R. D. Goodman, "Private Demands for Public Goods," *American Economic Review*, vol. 63, pp. 280–296, June 1973; T. Borcherdig and R. Deacon, "The Demand for the Services of Non-Federal Governments," *American Economic Review*, vol. 62, pp. 891–901, December 1972.

THE ECONOMICS OF THE VOTING RULE

In the analysis of the two-party system in the preceding section, we implicitly assumed that the winning candidate must receive more votes than the other candidate, or more than 50 percent of the votes. The voting rule in that situation was, therefore, a simple majority; and, indeed, most issues which confront student clubs and other civic and governmental bodies are determined by the simple-majority voting rule. However, not all collective decisions are made on the basis of that rule, *nor is it necessarily desirable that they be made on that basis.* Some collective decisions are of such trivial importance that we allow a committee or club officer to make them; the potential costs which will be borne by people in this group because of "wrong" decisions or because of higher dues or taxes that are imposed can be so small that it is uneconomical for the group to take the time and trouble to put the issue to debate and vote. Furthermore, less-than-majority voting rules are frequently employed to elect political leaders. Richard Nixon was elected president in 1968 with only 43 percent of the popular vote, and no government in England since 1945 has had a majority of the popular vote.[7]

On the other hand, we require much more than a simple majority to settle other issues. For example, in murder cases juries are required to reach unanimous agreement on the verdict concerning the defendants. The Constitution requires that amendments receive the support of two-thirds of the members of Congress and two-thirds of the state legislatures. In these instances, misguided collective decisions are thought to be very costly. Requiring that people incur the cost of achieving a two-thirds majority can, therefore, be justified. Regardless, the specific voting rule which is used for various policy areas or categories can minimize the combined total of (1) the

[7] Since 1870, only two-thirds of all American presidents have been elected with a majority of the popular vote. The less-than-majority votes have occurred primarily because of minor third-party votes and the closeness of the Democratic and Republican candidates.

"decisions costs" involved in developing the necessary agreement among voters and (2) the "external costs" which collective decisions may impose on people in the form of misguided policies and additional taxes to pay for the governmental programs. Because the decision and external costs will be different for different policy areas, different voting rules can be justified.[8]

The voting rule followed by government is important because it will be influential in determining the size and scope of governmental activities. A voting rule which requires very few people to agree on, for example, budgetary proposals will generally mean a large scope and size of government. With such a voting rule, small and different groups of people can make budgetary proposals, vote for and pass them, and, in that way, expand the scope of governmental activities. Conversely, a voting rule which requires unanimous agreement among voters is likely to mean that very few things will be agreed to and will be done by government. There are simply very few issues on which *everyone* agrees, particularly when a large number of people are involved.[9] In addition, the costs of trying to bring everyone into agreement on many issues will be prohibitively high. If everyone's vote is critically important to the passage of legislation, as it is when unanimity is the voting rule, everyone is in a strategic bargaining position. Everyone can attempt to bargain for special treatment; anyone who does not get his or her way can effectively veto the proposed legislation. Voting rules which require close to unanimity can also encourage people in small groups to bargain for special favors, increasing the decision costs and overall costs of the government activity and reducing the likelihood that it will be passed.

Consequently, those who are interested in restricting the scope of government are often in favor of increasing the required majority for passage of legislation. If this is done, fewer issues will receive the necessary number of votes for passage. Conversely, those people who are interested in seeing the scope and size of government increased are often in favor of replacing the simple-majority rule, so frequently employed, with less-than-majority rule. Delegating legislative responsibilities to committees which are composed of members with special interests in particular types of legislation is one means of circumventing the simple-majority voting rule and increasing the role of government.

Regardless, the important point of this section is that although the intent of government may be to represent people's collective interest, which interests and to what extent those interests are represented are dependent upon the voting rule that is used. Further, the voting rule which is used depends upon the potential costs which collective decisions can impose on people through taxes and faulty policy and on the costs of people reaching agreement. Careful selection of the voting rule can minimize the costs of collective decisions.

THE POLITICAL DEFICIENCIES OF DEMOCRACY

Democracy as a means of making governmental decisions has a number of favorable attributes to recommend it. It tends to disperse the decision-making power among a large number of people, and this dispersion reduces the tendency of government to respond to the changing whims, fancies, and interests of any one person or small group of persons. In this way, democracy provides some protection for individual liberties and for the market system against the encroachment of government. Also, democracy provides political candidates with some (but limited) incentive to seek out the interests of their constituencies and to represent them. To the extent that there is

[8] For a diagrammatical exposition of voting-rule determination, see James M. Buchanan and Gordon Tullock, *The Calculus of Consent: Logical Foundations of Constitutional Democracy* (Ann Arbor: University of Michigan Press, 1962), chap. 6; or Robert L. Bish, *The Public Economy of Metropolitan Areas* (Chicago: Markham Publishing Co., 1971).

[9] Notice that unanimity is often required of juries, but juries are composed of a relatively small number of people who are in close contact with one another. In a small group bargaining costs are much lower than they are in a large group. Therefore, a unanimous voting rule can work more effectively in small groups.

competition among candidates for votes, candidates are induced to reveal what they are willing to do for various groups of the electorate, as opposed to just what *they* want to do for themselves. However, the democratic system, like the market, has deficiencies; and as the framers of the Constitution recognized, these deficiencies are functionally related to the size and scope of governmental activities.

In this section, we discuss the deficiencies of democracy as a form of government; and before we proceed, a word of caution is in order. If there are deficiencies and, consequently, costs from government activity (and there surely are), it does not follow that government should not be used for certain activities or that it should be replaced by another social organizer. There very commonly are costs involved in the use of the market process, also; these costs have been pointed out in a number of preceding chapters. What we must do in structuring social order is to measure the costs in one area against the costs in the other and choose the social organizer which is most efficient for the particular problem at hand. In order to make this decision on a sound and rational basis, we have to carefully consider any externalities or other defects in the private market on the one hand and the various problems which lead to inefficiency in government on the other. As we suggested before, we must listen to *both* opera singers and choose the one who has fewer defects. The situation is much like an engineer choosing between a diesel engine and a steam engine. He knows that neither is perfectly efficient, and for some purposes one works better than the other. The fact that neither is perfect is no argument for not making a choice, but it is an argument for care and careful calculations.

The Problem of Single Quantities of Public Goods

Public goods tend to benefit all persons within the community; and of necessity the government tends to buy a single quantity of any public good. When you buy something like ice cream in the private marketplace, you can decide how much of the good you want. You can adjust the quantity you consume to your individual preferences and your ability to pay for the good, and you can choose that quantity which is "efficient" to you. On the other hand, if you club together with your neighbors to purchase some public service, you have to accept the quantity of that public service which is decided upon by the collective decision process. As we have mentioned before, the outcome of that process is dependent upon your and your neighbors' preferences and the voting rule which is used.

Consider the police department in your town. It may be that you would prefer to pay somewhat higher taxes and have a larger police force with the hope of a concomitant lower crime rate, whereas your neighbors prefer a lower tax rate, a smaller police force, and a higher crime rate. If it were possible to purchase police services efficiently in the private market, you could each have your personal optimum quantity of police services. Since it must be purchased publicly, you have to reach some compromise. The compromise inflicts costs upon you in the sense that it *may* not be your individual optimum quantity of police protection. We say "may" because you may be a part of the "median voter group" whose preferences determine the political outcomes; the cost that we are attempting to highlight is imposed on those who happen to be outside the median voter group.

In the case of pure public goods, people on balance can still be better off because of the decision that is made collectively; they receive the benefits of a service which cannot be had in any other way. However, the single-quantity problem becomes more significant when the government extends its activities to services which can be provided, although imperfectly, through the market. For example, people in a given area are required to pay taxes in different amounts to receive the same basic type of public education that everyone else receives. Although there are good arguments for public provision of education, the point is that an individual's demand for education does not have much effect on the kind and quantity of education that is received. As a general rule, special treat-

TABLE 21·1 HYPOTHETICAL SCHEDULE OF BENEFITS AND COSTS OF A PUBLIC PARK FOR A FIVE-PERSON COMMUNITY

Individuals (1)	Dollar Value of Benefits to Each Person (2)	Tax Levied On Each Person (3)	Net Benefit (+) or Net Cost (−) [(2) − (3)] (4)	Vote For or Against (5)
A	$200	$100	+$100	For
B	150	100	+ 50	For
C	125	100	+ 25	For
D	50	100	− 50	Against
E	25	100	− 75	Against
Total	$550	$500		

ment for different people is not permitted. There are exceptions, of course, but these exceptions are frequently illegal and frowned upon.

The Problem of the Simple-Majority Voting Rule

Democratic decisions made on the basis of any majority voting rule less than unanimity can result in some people being made better off at the expense of others. Because the expense of the government activity is spread over all taxpayers, the majority voting for the project can impose an *external* cost on the minority. To see this point, consider a democratic community composed, for simplicity, of only five people; and assume that all persons in the community can benefit from a proposed public park in the middle of town but that they differ in the benefits that they receive. Assume also that the total cost of the park, which is $500, is divided evenly over the five people; that is, a tax of $100 is levied on each person. The relevant values of the benefits and tax shares are contained in Table 21·1. In the case of this particular project, the total benefits ($550) exceed the total cost ($500), and the measure will pass by a vote of three to two, with A, B, and C voting for the project. However, the majority imposes a net cost (benefits minus costs) of $50 and $75 on D and E, respectively.

Alternatively, the distribution of the benefits can be so arranged that while the total cost of the project will exceed the total benefits, still the project can pass. In Table 21·2 we have provided an illustration of this prospect. Again we assume that the proposed project is a park that costs $500 and that the cost is shared equally by the five people. Suppose, however, that the benefits are distributed as they are in column 2 of the table. Individuals A, B, and C receive more benefits from the project than their individual shares of the cost, and they will form the necessary majority to pass the project, even though the project cannot be justified on the basis of the relationship between the *total* costs ($500) and *total* benefits ($430).

Further, if different measures are put to different votes in this community, different majorities can emerge to pass all the measures, even though the total cost of all measures exceeds their total benefits to the voters. If the measures are considered at one time, they can all be defeated. Consider the costs and benefits to the five people on three proposed projects—a park, road, and school—in Table 21·3. If the park is put to a vote by itself, it will receive the majority support of A, B, and C. In a similar way, the road project will pass with a majority composed of A, C, and E; and the school will pass, if considered separately, with the supporting majority of C, D, and E. However, if all the projects are considered as a package, they will be defeated; the total cost of all projects ($3,500) is greater than the total benefits ($2,910)

TABLE 21·2 ALTERNATIVE SCHEDULE OF BENEFITS AND COSTS OF A PUBLIC PARK FOR A FIVE-PERSON COMMUNITY

Individuals (1)	Dollar Value of Benefits to Each Person (2)	Tax Levied on Each Person (3)	Net Benefit (+) or Net Cost (−) [(2) − (3)] (4)	Vote For or Against (5)
A	$140	$100	+$ 40	For
B	130	100	+ 20	For
C	110	100	+ 10	For
D	50	100	− 50	Against
E	0	100	− 100	Against
Total	$430	$500		

to all five people. Voters A, B, and D will vote against the package of the three projects (see column 4).

Granted there are many measures which are presented for a vote of the democratic government for which the total benefits to all people exceed the total costs. In addition, the voters in our hypothetical community can engage in *logrolling*—that is, vote trading—and defeat some of the projects even though they are considered separately. For instance, A can agree to vote against the park if D will vote against the school, resulting in the defeat of both measures.[10] Our purpose in this section, however, has been to demonstrate that the democratic process can produce results which are inefficient in cost-benefit terms. Further, the government may take on an activity in order to alleviate the problem of external costs generated by the market; however, in the process of trying to reduce externalities, it can impose net external costs of its own on people because of the voting rule and the way the cost of the project is shared.

[10] For an extended discussion of the advantages and disadvantages of logrolling as a political reality, see Appendix B to this chapter.

The Problem of Political Ignorance

We now turn to the information problem, which in some ways is the most severe problem for democratic systems. It is unfortunate but true that the

TABLE 21·3 SCHEDULES OF BENEFITS AND COSTS OF A PARK, ROAD, AND SCHOOL FOR A FIVE-PERSON COMMUNITY

	Park (1)			Road (2)			School (3)			Total, 3 Projects (4)		
Individuals	Benefit	Cost	Vote	Benefit	Cost	Vote	Benefit	Cost	Vote	Benefit	Cost	Vote
A	$120	$100	For	$250	$ 200	For	$ 50	$ 400	Against	$ 420	$ 700	Against
B	120	100	For	50	200	Against	50	400	Against	220	700	Against
C	120	100	For	250	200	For	500	400	For	870	700	For
D	50	100	Against	50	200	Against	500	400	For	600	700	Against
E	50	100	Against	250	200	For	500	400	For	800	700	For
Total	$460	$500		$850	$1,000		$1,600	$2,000		$2,910	$3,500	

typical voter, unless he or she pursues politics as a hobby, is not very well informed about political issues or candidates for whom he or she votes. People are continually being told that it is their duty to be well informed on public issues, and perhaps it is. However, as a matter of fact, the welfare of individuals is not perceptibly influenced by how little or how much they, by themselves, know about public issues.

No doubt the members of your class are way above the national average in their enthusiasm for and understanding of politics and political issues. Nevertheless, we suggest a simple classroom experiment that will stress the point that we wish to make. Ask everyone in class to write down the name of their member of Congress from memory. Then, ask them to write down the name of the person the congressman ran against in the last election, and check names. We are reasonably confident that less than half the class will be able to correctly give both names. Even then, we doubt that the people who can give the name of their congressman have anything more than a vague idea as to how their congressman has voted over the last year on the major issues that have been considered in Congress. Indeed, one of the authors has undertaken a survey of the political knowledge of junior and senior college students. When asked to state how the senators from their state voted on what the *Congressional Quarterly Weekly* considered to be the major bills passed or defeated by Congress in the previous year and a half, the students, most of whom had taken a significant amount of economics, political science, and sociology, could do no better than would be expected from guessing.[11] These results are consistent with the findings of other studies. For example, Donald Stokes and Warren Miller found that a majority of voters do not know which party controls Congress.[12] Also, public opinion polls indicate that most voters greatly underestimate the cost of such programs as social security to them. For example, Edgar Browning estimates that the typical voter is aware of only 17 percent of the actual cost of the social security system to him.[13] This situation is partly the result of the complicated and purposefully disguised way in which the taxes are collected.

Why is it that voters are so unintelligent about politics? In recent years the economics of information has been a major field of interest for most economists; let us apply the analysis here. Suppose that you are considering buying a new car. This is an important decision for most people. Although it is not clear that the time most people spend on their investigations of cars is "socially optimal" in a strict economic sense, it is reasonably clear that they spend a modest amount of time on the problem. They will look at advertisements, visit a number of car dealers, look at cars the dealers have, and talk to the salespersons. Further, most potential buyers will test-drive one or more cars before they buy. Many purchasers, however, do not stop with the test-drive. They ask the advice of friends and take note of their friends' experiences with different models of automobiles. A few consumers will go so far as to read specialized magazines on automobiles.

These are the ways people go about buying cars *now*. Let us suppose, however, there is an institutional change: every five years you purchase a new car, but you are not permitted to make the choice of the car. A government bureau allocates Chevrolets, Fords, Chryslers, Toyotas, etc., among buyers, and you simply are required to pay whatever is the market price of the car, turn in your old car, and receive the new one. Under these circumstances, it seems very doubtful that you will put very much time and effort into careful study of the characteristics of the car before you get it. The energy would be wasted, because learning which is the best car for you will not affect the car you receive. Indeed, there is a negative payoff to becoming informed about cars

[11] Richard B. McKenzie, "Political Ignorance: An Empirical Assessment of Educational Remedies," *Frontiers of Economics* (Blacksburg, Va.: University Publications, 1977).

[12] Donald E. Stokes and Warren E. Miller, "Party Government and the Saliency of Congress," *Public Opinion Quarterly*, vol 26, pp. 531–546, Winter 1962.

[13] Edgar Browning, "Why the Social Insurance Budget Is Too Large in a Democracy," *Economic Inquiry*, vol. 13, pp. 373–388, September 1974.

under the assumed circumstances. If you become well informed about cars, your first choice may not be allotted to you by the government. Thus, you are likely to be disappointed in the one you do receive. Besides, you have to incur the cost of the study, which has no bearing on the car you receive.

What does all of this have to do with politics? The answer is that your relationship to the government is similar to getting the car without choosing it. The decision as to which party will govern the United States or what policy will be adopted is sometimes of relatively little importance to the individual, particularly if the positions of the two parties are very similar. On the other hand, the final decision may be of considerable importance. The individual has to keep in mind, however, that his own vote will have little or no effect on the election or the adoption of government policy. We do not know how you and/or your parents voted in the last election, but consider what would have happened if you and they had voted the other way. Unless it was an extraordinary and unusual election, the answer is, nothing! The total number of votes for the winner and loser would have been slightly different, but the same person or party would have won. In short, in terms of the expected benefits of becoming politically well informed, a great many people are unable to justify incurring the cost of acquiring very much information on political candidates and issues. The same people who spend a considerable amount of time to decide which car they will buy will typically spend very little time determining with much precision the political position of the candidates for whom they vote: they will, to a large degree, remain politically ignorant.[14]

Granted, it is quite possible that if voters as a group are well informed on what government proposes to do and on the implications of proposed policies, more "correct" decisions can possibly be made by government, the overall efficiency of the social system can be improved, and the welfare of almost everyone can be enhanced. In this sense, political intelligence is a public good which benefits people when it is provided. However, as we have indicated before, people in very large groups have very little incentive to contribute, on a voluntary basis, anything toward the production of the public good. The reason is simply that their individual contribution, which is their vote and is the only contribution over which they have any control, will have very little effect. The argument of this section is an application of the public goods argument that we have repeated in different contexts throughout the book (see Chapters 5, 6, 18, and 19, in particular). The problem with the public good of political intelligence is that in order for people to remain politically free, they must retain the right to determine for whom and on what basis they will vote. The efficiency of government will partially reflect the kinds and amounts of information which the electorate seeks to rationally obtain. Fortunately or unfortunately, they will frequently make up their minds on the basis of the "impressions" they receive from newspaper headlines and TV commercials.[15] The analysis of this section provides a plausible explanation for the important role given to "image makers" in political campaigns.

Education is a solution which is offered by many people who are concerned about the political intelligence of the general population; and it may be the only practical solution. However, having taken course work in political science, economics, or other subjects, a student must have an incentive to retain what he or she has learned and to employ these newly acquired analytical methods in evaluating candidates and issues. The public goods argument we have presented raises questions as to whether or not indi-

[14] To determine the payoff from acquiring political information, the benefits of acquiring the information must be discounted by the very low probability that an individual's vote will determine the outcome of the election and must then be subtracted from the cost of acquiring the information. For further study on this topic, see Anthony Downs, *An Economic Theory of Democracy* (New York: Harper and Row, 1957), chaps. 11–13; and Gordon Tullock, *Toward a Mathematics of Politics* (Ann Arbor: University of Michigan Press, 1967), chaps. 7–9.

[15] It is not completely clear that greater political intelligence on the part of people will actually improve the efficiency of government. With the additional information, people may learn how to better use government as a means of pursuing their own private ends, as many already do.

viduals have the necessary incentive to incur the implied costs of using what they have learned.[16] The lack of political intelligence on the part of voters was a problem which the framers of the Constitution recognized; they tried to surmount it, in part, by devising a representative government. They also believed that so long as government remained small, the number of issues that voters will have to consider will remain small and within the bounds of their comprehension and the time they are likely to spend on analyzing political issues. They were concerned about the growth of government because it implied a growth in the number and complexity of issues with which voters will have to deal. By choice or historical accident, we now have very large governmental units. The problem of ensuring that government operates efficiently is compounded by the complexity of its current tasks and by the lack of incentive which voters have to check on what the government is or is not doing.

The Problem of Special-Interest Groups

The problem of political ignorance of voters is especially acute when the benefits of government programs are spread more or less evenly over all voters and the benefits to each person are relatively small. However, the benefits are not always spread evenly, and the benefits to subgroups of voters—"special-interest groups"—are often substantial. These groups can include farmers, particular labor unions, and civil servants; and members of each of these groups will have more rational motives for acquiring information with respect to their own private interests than will society as a whole. For example, members of the general voting public may have little or no incentive to learn about the consequences of particular farm programs. However, individual farmers, because their incomes are directly affected, have a substantial motive to learn about those consequences and to speak with their congressmen or congresswomen about their interests when they have a chance. Civil servants have significant reason to keep abreast of proposed pay increases and fringe benefits. Lockheed and General Dynamics have a private interest in the military budget and how it is being handled in Congress.

[16] This line of argument is developed more fully in Richard B. McKenzie, "Politics, Learning, and Public Goods Literacy," *Frontiers of Economics* (Blacksburg, Va.: University Publications, 1976).

On the one hand, special-interest groups have an incentive to know what their representatives do that affects them; on the other hand, the general public will typically be ill informed about politics. Knowing this, representatives have a distorted incentive to cater to the wishes of special-interest groups. Therefore, the governmental budgets and law books can become burdened, as they have to some extent, with programs designed, not to serve some "public interest," but rather to serve the interests of special groups which are politically important. Indeed, the "public (or general) interest" may only infrequently carry much weight in practical politics.

DECENTRALIZATION AND COMPETITIVE GOVERNMENTS

The power which an individual producer has over the customers is dependent upon the number of competitors he or she confronts, that is, the number of close and viable substitute goods and services to which the customers can turn. A producer who is the only producer of a good with no close substitutes—who is a monopolist—can raise the price of a product with little concern that the customers will move to other producers. On the other hand, a producer who is one of a number of producers of a good knows that any attempt on his or her part to independently raise the price (or lower the quality) of the product will cause the customers to move not only to distant products, but also to other producers of the same or a very similar product; but such a producer knows that any price increase will result in a sharp reduction in the quantity of the good that will be sold. Further, to avoid being undersold, the individual producer must do what is possible to keep production costs down as low as possible. In these ways, competition constrains the behavior of private producers; it keeps the price down and production efficiency up from what they would be in the absence of competition.

These are basic points which we developed in detail in our discussion of markets in Chapters 7 and 10. They are also points which the framers of the Constitution had in mind when they set up the American system of government—or, more precisely, system of governments. James Madison wrote,

> The accumulation of all powers . . . in the same hands, whether of one, a few, or many, and whether hereditary, self-appointed, or elective, must justly be pronounced the very definition of tyranny.[17]

Recognizing the control which a division of powers and responsibilities among different governmental units (like states, counties, and towns) would have on government, Madison also wrote,

> In a single republic, all the power surrendered by the people is submitted to the administration of a single government; and the usurpations are guarded against by a division of the government into distinct and separate departments. In the compound republic of America, the power surrendered by the people is first divided between two distinct governments, and then the portion allotted to each subdivided among distinct and separate departments. Hence a double security arises to the rights of people. The different governments will control each other, at the same time each will be controlled by itself.[18]

In short, the framers of the Constitution intended to establish a system of competing governments. Under this system, governments will be controlled by people's votes and people's ability to move among governments. If one governmental unit like a city raises its "tax price" for the services which it renders (or attempts to lower the quality of those services), people can move to other, competing governmental units. The government that raises its tax price will lose a portion of its tax base. Granted, many people are resistant to moving because of an independent tax increase and, consequently, governments, even in the republican system that was established, do have a measure of "monopoly power"; however, the founding fathers were attempting to introduce at least a modest amount of "competitive control" into their system of government.[19]

There are several good arguments often heard for extending the scope of any governmental unit to cover the responsibilities which are held by several units. For instance, it is frequently argued that local governments, especially those in metropolitan areas, should consolidate in order that their garbage, road, and sewage services can be offered on a large scale and on a lower cost basis. In other words, there are "economies of scale" in the provision of governmental services just as there are in many private industries. Further, the benefits of services offered in one governmental unit are often "external" to that unit; they "spill over" into jurisdictions of surrounding governments. The government that provides the benefits is unable to tax the people outside its jurisdiction for the benefits they receive. For example, people who work in downtown San Francisco but live outside the city benefit from the garbage pickup and road maintenance which is paid for by the city of San Francisco; the beneficiaries do not have to bear their share of the tax cost of the services. By consolidating several governmental units into one large unit, the benefits are "internalized"; the people who benefit are taxed.

Consolidation of governmental activities, however, can be a mixed blessing. James Madison would be very much concerned that consolidation movements will tend to reduce the benefits of competitive governments and will, therefore, increase the control which any one government has

[17] James Madison, "The Social Foundations," p. 124.

[18] Ibid. pp. 124–125.

[19] For an extended discussion of this thesis, see Robert L. Bish and Vincent Ostrom, *Understanding Urban Government: Metropolitan Reform Reconsidered* (Washington: American Enterprise Institute for Public Policy Research, 1973); and Vincent Ostrom, *The Political Theory of a Compound Republic: A Reconstruction of the Logical Foundations of American Democracy as Presented by The Federalist* (Blacksburg, Va.: Center for Study of Public Choice, 1971).

over its residents. Larger governmental units will reduce the number and variety of alternative government forms which are open to people, and they will increase the cost which individuals will have to incur in moving to an alternative governmental form. Consolidation, in other words, can increase the monopoly power of any government. If we can assume that politicians and government employees are interested only in pursuing the "public interest," no harm may be done by consolidation. However, if the people who run governments have private interests of their own, a government with greater monopolistic power can be used as a means by which they can pursue their interests. Although the potential for greater efficiency may exist through consolidation of governments, the actual efficiency of government may be reduced as the cost of the larger government is raised, the quantity of services provided is reduced, and the efficiency benefits of government are absorbed by politicians and bureaucrats in terms of higher salaries, better working conditions, and less work. The available data, indeed, suggest that there is a direct relationship between the size of governmental units and the cost of their services.[20] The data are not conclusive; however, they and the competitive-government argument indicate that proposals to consolidate governmental units or special programs like welfare services should be examined very carefully. These facts raise the question of whether or not we should expect behavior from people in the public sector any different from what we expect from private entrepreneurs in private markets.

[20] For a short review of several studies, see Bish and Ostrom, *Understanding Urban Government*, chaps. 4 and 6. For more details on the underlying argument, see Delores T. Martin and Richard B. McKenzie, "Bureaucratic Profits, Migration Costs, and the Consolidation of Local Governments," *Public Choice*, vol. 23, pp. 95–100, Fall 1975.

SUMMARY AND EXTENSIONS

In this chapter we have applied the cost-benefit analysis used in our discussion of private markets to politics; in this way we have developed elementary economic models of problems of democracy. (These models are more fully developed in the appendices.) The picture of the politician that we have drawn indicates that each is attempting to be elected and not necessarily that he or she is attempting to maximize the "public interest." We think this is realistic and, in particular, that politicians who are attempting to get elected are more likely to be elected than politicians who disregard that goal. Barry Goldwater and George McGovern, the respective 1964 and 1972 losing presidential candidates have demonstrated the fate of politicians who have strong policy ideals and who attempt to persuade the voters of the truth of these ideals. Enoch Powell is a British example. Although all three have been able to get a good deal of national attention, none has risen to the goal he sought. Johnson and Nixon in the United States and Callihan and Heath in Great Britain are far better examples of the type of people who reach the top, and we doubt that anyone will claim that they were primarily motivated by devotion to a particular consistent set of policies. It is true that they normally talked in terms of the public good, but, watching them over time, we have seen that the policies they favored changed, depending on where political support might have been found.

The last several pages of the chapter have probably impressed you as a criticism of democracy. That is the way they impress us, too. Democracy depends upon a set of politicians who make actual decisions, but the system attempts to control these politicians by making their continued employment subject to the will of the voters. If voters are rational (or to the extent that they are), they will be well informed on issues which affect them directly and not very well informed on issues which affect the general population. The political maneuvering of politicians in search of votes will tend to reflect this distorted distribution of information. To say that this is, as it is, a weakness of democracy is not to say that some other form of government is better. Indeed, the common nondemocratic form of government—the dictatorship—has immense defects of its own. Earlier we talked about the choice between government and market provision of various services. The defects of the market process are fairly well known; the defects of the governmental process we have been discussing here are not so well known. Nevertheless, they should be taken into account. Again, we should listen to both opera singers before we make our decision. In Chapter 22 we continue analysis of government by dealing more specifically with the bureaucratic delivery system of governments.

QUESTIONS TO PONDER

1 In their studies of politics, many people have assumed that the aim of politicians has been to maximize achievement of those goals which are in the "public interest." In this chapter, the authors have assumed that politicians aim to maximize their "private interest." What does the change in the assumption at this basic theoretical level do to the case for government? To the likely acceptable scope of government?

2 Assuming that the objective of government is not to give people what they want, what is it? Discuss your suggestions with your classmates and see if there is much agreement. Why do you suppose that this assumption—that the objective of government is not simply to give people what they want—has been so widely made?

3 Do you think it desirable that the government characteristically adopt policies which are approximately those of the median voter? Why or why not?

4 As a student you face certain required courses and certain elective courses. Do you put as much time and energy into finding out in advance about the quality and significance of the required courses as of the electives? Why? What does this have to do with the subject of this chapter?

5 It is sometimes thought that making a rational decision requires perfect information. Would it be rational to acquire perfect information about politics? Would it be possible?

6 "Revenue sharing" is the governmental process by which the federal government collects taxes and distributes the collected funds to states according to a predetermined formula. The system of revenue sharing does not change the tax base (people's incomes) from which the taxes are collected; it merely means that the federal government is now charged with collecting taxes that were once collected by state and local governments. Given the discussion in the text concerning the monopolistic power of centralized governments, what effect will revenue sharing have on total taxes collected? Why would states be interested in having the federal government collect their taxes?

RECOMMENDED READINGS

Bish, Robert L.: *The Public Economy of Metropolitan Areas* (Chicago: Markham Publishing Co., 1971), chaps. 1–4.

Downs, Anthony: *An Economic Theory of Democracy* (New York: Harper and Row, 1957), chaps. 1 and 11–13.

Ostrom, Vincent: *The Political Theory of a Compound Republic: A Reconstruction of the Logical Foundations of American Democracy as Presented in The Federalist* (Blacksburg, Va.: Center for Study of Public Choice, 1971), chaps. 1–5.

APPENDIX A: A MORE COMPLEX POLITICAL MODEL

From the analysis of this chapter we can conclude that skillful politicians will adopt political positions which are close to the preferences of the median voter. However, you should understand that the model we employed was very simple, involving only one issue and two parties. Indeed, the conclusion which we have just restated applies only to a two-party system. In this appendix we introduce complications to our model and show that in a three-party election which involves two issues, the candidates will, if they start with political positions which are closely similar on two issues, move apart. We cannot say just how far apart candidates will be in a three-party election, but we do not expect them to be as close as two candidates will be in an election involving only two parties.

To illustrate, consider Figure 21A·1. In this figure we show two possible issues, expenditures on police and on fire fighters, on which the three candidates, X, Y, and Z, can take a political stand. The possible expenditures on police are on the horizontal axis, and the possible expenditures on fire fighters are on the vertical axis. Assume that voters are evenly distributed within the figure, that the three candidates take very similar positions initially at X, Y, and Z in the center of the graph, and that this means they divide the votes among themselves. Candidate X takes all the votes bounded by the area $0abc$, candidate Y takes all the votes in the area bounded by the area $bcdef$, and candidate Z takes all the votes in the area bounded by $abfg$. They divide the votes in this way simply because the voters in those respective areas are closer to the candidates in the area than they are to either of the others. Notice that at their initial positions each candidate has an incentive to move away from the center of the figure: this is because each candidate can, by moving away, in-

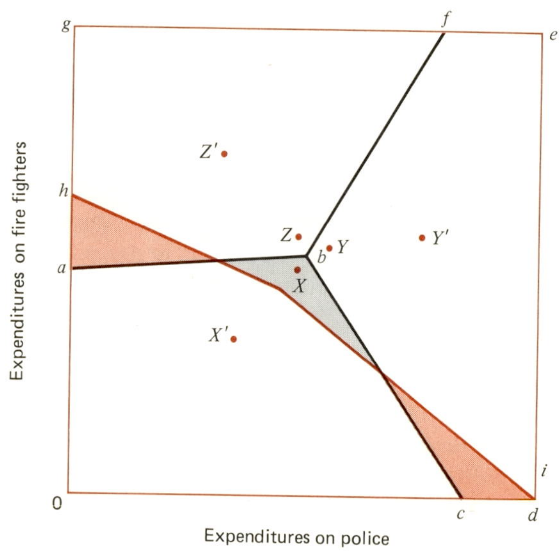

FIG. 21A·1 If the three candidates initially assume similar political positions, like X, Y, and Z in Figure 21A·1, they can each benefit by moving away from the center. Candidate X, for example, can move to X' and increase the area which represents the votes he receives.

crease his or her vote total and, thereby, increase his or her chances of winning the election.

If, for example, candidate X moves away from the center to a position like X', he or she may lose some votes in the center of the distribution. This is because some of the people who would have voted for the candidate at X now find their political position closer to one of the other candidates. On the other hand, by moving away from the center, candidate X takes a political position which is now closer to the positions of voters who were initially closer to Y and Z. The graph illustrates that by moving away candidate X gains more votes than he loses. The people who will now vote for him are in the area bounded by $0hid$. Notice that the total area that he adds to his political support (shaded orange) is greater than the area that he loses (shaded gray). Similarly, Y and Z have an incentive to move away from the center: they know that by doing so they can increase their chances of being elected and offset the gains that would have otherwise been made by candidate X. Consequently, we might anticipate that the three candidates will end up at political positions something like X', Y', and Z'.

Thus, in a two-party system, one anticipates that the parties would be very close together and, in a system of three or more parties, there would be considerable differences between them. This is what we observe in the real world. In those European countries in which there are more than two parties, the differences between the parties are usually considerably greater than in the two-party system.

One thing can be said for certain about a system of three or more parties: it requires a great deal more skill on the part of the party leaders, and mistakes are much easier to make. In a two-party system, there is a simple operational rule for the politician: Go find out what the other party is doing and take a position very close to it in the popular direction. With a three-party system, there is no such rule. Difficult decisions must be made, and frequent errors are to be expected.

APPENDIX B: LOGROLLING AS A FORM OF POLITICAL EXCHANGE

The word *logrolling* is an unusual word. Its meaning, however, is really very simple: *Logrolling is vote trading.* One member of Congress, for example, will agree to vote for something that another wants in return for his or her vote on another issue. Logrolling is also very common in any democratic political system; indeed, in most democracies it dominates the policy selection process, although it is frequently concealed from public view. In this appendix we consider the advantages and disadvantages of logrolling as a form of "political market activity."

Implicit and Explicit Logrolling

Logrolling is usually classified as either *explicit* or *implicit.* It can either be a clearly defined trade of votes by two politicians, in which case it is explicit logrolling, or it can be implied by the way the legislation is proposed, in which case it is implicit logrolling. For instance, measures which different politicians favor can be incorporated in one piece of congressional legislation and voted on at one time. By voting for the whole legislative package, the members of Congress have voted on the measure favored by the others; therefore, although difficult to detect, an exchange of votes has effectively taken place.

Regardless of whether or not it is implicit or explicit, logrolling occurs because most laws have differential effects: they affect some people more than others. Any proposal to change the tax laws will have more effect on some citizens than on others. Even changes in the criminal law usually have differential effects in a society. Under the circumstances, logrolling is not obviously undesirable in all cases. Suppose that all government acts are decided upon by direct majority vote. Further, suppose that there is a project which would benefit some city, say Denver, very greatly and which would have a relatively modest cost to the national taxpayers. The total benefit received by people in Denver may exceed the cost of the project. However, if the project were paid for by a national tax, the proposal to governmentally fund the project would most assuredly lose in the absence of logrolling. There can be many other projects in other areas of the country which would suffer a similar fate if implicit or explicit logrolling were forbidden. To illustrate the problems more carefully, we can consider cases of logrolling.

Implicit logrolling: the interstate highway system

In Congress logrolling is fairly open and aboveboard. It is true that the bulk of the negotiations take place in committees, cloakrooms, and congressional offices, but there is no particular secret as to what is going on. Suppose, then, that we are 20 years in the past and President Eisenhower has decided that an interstate highway system should be built in order to improve the ease of automobile travel. It is to be paid for (as indeed it was) by a tax on the gasoline consumed by all drivers—those who drive on the interstates and those who do not.

Under these circumstances, any given community can be better off if it has one of the interstates running through it, but it must also pay for interstates built in other parts of the country. One would anticipate, then, that the congressional delegation from Utah would, on the whole, be in favor of interstates in Utah and, to some extent, those outside; but, generally speaking, they would not be interested in taxing the inhabitants of Utah to build interstates in Oklahoma. This problem was met by Eisenhower by implicit logrolling rather than explicit logrolling. He made up a package of interstates so designed that it benefited a majority of constituencies. The individual member of Congress, instead of having to make up his or her own bargains with people, could look at the whole collection and decide whether he or she would vote for it or not. Note that this does not in any real sense eliminate logrolling: it simply obscures it. At any rate, the interstate highway system passed *as a package.* Presidential candidates also try to get elected through developing the same type of "package" in the form of their platforms and position papers.

In a way, the clearest example of implicit logrolling will be found in some referenda on local improvements in the United States. Sometimes these referenda involve a large project of one sort or another. The voters in Montgomery County, Virginia (where Tullock lives) have just voted down a proposal for a new courthouse. Often, however, the referendum proposal is a collection of different projects like those in Table 21 · 3, which have no great relation to each other except that it is thought that, if they are all grouped together, a majority of the population will favor them, whereas there would be a majority against any individual one. This kind of referendum is frequently used in school financing.

Explicit logrolling: an oceanography laboratory

Explicit logrolling is more visible but also a little more complicated to develop. Suppose that the congressional delegation from Mississippi is interested in having the National Oceanography Laboratory moved to southern Mississippi, as in fact it is. It goes to the delegation from Nevada and offers to support some irrigation projects there in return for its support for Mississippi. It also approaches, let us say, the delegation from Oregon, which is interested in a flood control project in Oregon, and agrees to vote for that in return for support. By making a number of such trades with Texas, New York, etc., eventually the Mississippi delegation gets a majority of members willing to push for the establishment of the oceanographic laboratory in Mississippi. The other states are engaged in soliciting by similar methods, and we may find that the flood control project in Oregon and the irrigation project in Nevada will go through.

Note that there is no reason in this type of logrolling why the coalition that votes for the oceanographic laboratory in Mississippi should be the same coalition of states as that which voted for the irrigation project in Nevada. Mississippi will vote for the irrigation project in Nevada because that is the trade, but Nevada probably has at least some states in its winning coalition which are different from the states backing Mississippi.

When is Logrolling Desirable?

If logrolling can clearly create benefits for the society, it can also cause harm. Consider a very simple society of nine voters who confront a large collection of measures, each of which will be paid for by a tax of $1 per head and each of which will confer benefits exclusively upon one of the nine. Policy A, for example, will cost a total of $9 in the form of a $1 tax on each voter, but it will confer upon voter A a benefit worth $15. Clearly, we would, on the whole, prefer that projects like this go through, although we might object to its distributional consequences. Normally we would anticipate that the voters, if confronted only with this bill, would vote 8 to 1 against it; but with logrolling, assuming there were similar projects for other voters, it would get through as part of a package. The end product would clearly be an improvement in the state of society.

Consider another project which, like our first one, involves a cost of $1 to each of our nine citizens and confers upon voter A a benefit of only $2. Here there is a net cost of $7 to society as a whole. We would not want this bill to get through. As a matter of fact, it would not get through under logrolling because the voter could not afford to vote for four other bills, each of which would cost him $1 apiece, in return for four other people voting for his bill. This would lead to a loss for him of $3 net, and hence he would not attempt to logroll the issue through.

So far, logrolling has worked very well; unfortunately, there is an intermediate class of issues where it works badly. Suppose that the return to voter A of a bill (which, once again, costs $1 apiece to every one of the nine taxpayers) is $7. He would be willing to trade a favorable vote on four other issues for four votes on his issue. This would net him $2 on the entire deal. Society as a whole, however, would have been paying $9 for something which was worth only $7. In this case, logrolling reduces the efficiency of government.

22

The Political Economy of Bureaucracy

The General Accounting Office has found that it costs the government nearly twice as much as it costs private insurance carriers to process each Medicare claim because federal employees get paid more and do less work.

The government also is slower in paying claims than the less-costly private firms, the GAO said. . . .

The government disagreed with the GAO's conclusions.

Stuart Auerbach[1]

PREVIEW OF CHAPTER

Central question

How can we explain the behavior of government bureaucracies?

Major objectives

1 To compare and contrast the incentive systems within private and public bureaucracies
2 To develop theories of the behavior of government bureaucracies
3 To propose a means of increasing the efficiency of government bureaucracies

1 Private bureaucracies tend to operate more efficiently than public bureauc-

[1] Stuart Auerbach, "GAO Faults U.S. Health Claim Costs," *Washington Post*, Oct. 28, 1975, pp. A1 and A14.

racies because private bureaucrats have a relatively straightforward and easily measured goal—profit maximization—and because private bureaucracies are induced to a greater degree to operate efficiently by the forces of competition in private markets. Public bureaucracies typically have complex objectives which are not easily measured.

2 Public bureaucracies tend to be overly large because the supervising legislators often do not know the true cost of providing many government services and because bureaucrats typically benefit personally by an expansion of the bureaucracy.

3 One way of increasing the efficiency of public bureaucracies is to increase the number of bureaucracies which can provide any given public service. In this way, competition can be introduced into the provision of public services.

In a democracy, voters have direct, but limited, control over their elected representatives. However, elected representatives account for a relatively minor portion of the total governmental work force. Below the elected representatives of the people, there are a large number of employees. Some we call *civil servants;* some are members of the armed forces. For simplicity, these people will be called the "bureaucracy" from now on. In the past, all of them were appointed by elected officials, but now a very large number of them are selected by a relatively impersonal system using examinations or based on selection by people who are not themselves either elected by the people or directly appointed by elected politicians. In general, it is very difficult to fire them for inefficiency, laziness, or simple stupidity.[2]

In theory, the government structure is one in which direct representatives of the people give detailed orders, which are then carried out by an elaborate hierarchical body of nonelected civil servants. Directly below the president is a layer of cabinet and subcabinet officers who are appointed by the president. These officials are supposed to transmit orders from Congress and the president to the permanent civil servants and high-ranking officers who are below them; and the permanent civil servants and officers, in turn, are arranged in a large number of grades in hierarchical order, with the higher-ranking ones giving orders to junior officers and so on down the line. At the bottom, the policy determined at the top, theoretically speaking, is carried out. Of course, the transmission of orders through the bureaucratic hierarchy from the top to the bottom rarely works as smoothly or efficiently as may be suggested here, and explaining why it does not is the purpose of this chapter.

Ultimately, the performance of government bureaucracy must be evaluated in terms of its viable alternatives. Private production of goods is one of those alternatives; consequently, we begin our analysis of government bureaucracy by reviewing the incentive system within the bureaucracy of private companies. This review will provide us with a standard of comparison and basis for understanding the relative efficiency of government bureaucracy. We conclude the chapter with suggestions as to how government bureaucracy can be induced to work more efficiently.

THE PRIVATE BUREAUCRACIES OF LARGE CORPORATIONS

Many large corporations, such as General Motors and AT&T, have more employees than governments of many countries. Indeed, these corpora-

[2] There is less difficulty in the military services than in the civil branch. Nevertheless, even in the military services the number of people who are booted out is quite small.

tions are often bigger than major departments of the federal government. None of them, of course, is as large as the federal government taken as a whole.

The structure of a corporate bureaucracy and that of the government bureaucracy are similar because the corporation itself has a democratic structure. In every corporation is a body of voters, called *stockholders,* who elect a group of officials, called the *board of directors,* who in turn appoint various subordinate officials with the same kind of hierarchical structure we observe in government. Private corporations use the right to fire officials and workers as an incentive to attain minimum performance standards. The existence of labor unions does severely impede many of them from firing people at the bottom level, however.

Further, one has only to talk to a few civil servants and a few officials of corporations about their daily routine to realize that many of the internal activities, like paperwork, of these large structures are very similar. There is the same internal atmosphere and the same kind of combination of intrigue and back-stabbing, on the one hand, and cooperation, on the other, that one observes in the government hierarchy. Indeed, one of the principal students of private government bureaucracy, William A. Niskanen, remarked that, "Sociologically, the corporate bureaucracy and the government bureaucracy are identical."[3] This is true despite the great differences between the two in their respective goals, the one political and the other economic, but this is not because there are any differences in the people or in their interrelationship with each other at the personal or social level.

The corporate bureaucracy, however, typically works more efficiently than government bureaucracy. The reason is not that there is anything inherent in the organization of the corporation but the simple fact that the corporation pursues a simple incentive system: *profit.* Furthermore, for this simple objective there is a rather good (although not perfect) measure in the form of the accountants' profit and loss statements.

The stockholders are typically as ill informed about the detailed functioning of their company as the voters are about that of the government. (See Chapter 21 for a detailed discussion of voter ignorance.) Further, for most of the stockholders, this ignorance is perfectly rational in the same way that it is for voters in national politics. The average stockholder will not be able to improve the "quality" of his vote, and raise his own wealth, by becoming well informed about the corporation to a large enough degree to offset the cost of obtaining this information.

It has to be emphasized here, however, that we are talking about the average stockholder. The number of votes in a corporation depends on the number of shares a stockholder holds. Thus, it is not at all infrequent in even very large corporations that there are individual stockholders who hold enough stock for them to have rational motives for acquiring significant amounts of information on the detailed performance of their corporations. Very commonly, such large stockholders will have themselves elected to the board of directors. Since their principal interest in the corporation is to increase the value of their stock, they act as good proxies for the remainder of the stockholders. However, though this is a frequent phenomenon, it is not universal. The stockholders' interest in the corporation is very simple: they want to make money. They are interested in their dividends (periodic payments based on the level of corporate earnings) and in the market price of the stock.[4]

The stockholders, then, do not have to devote a substantial amount of time to obtaining the relatively simple information which they need to "cast an intelligent vote" when it comes time to elect corporate officials. Indeed, their control in this respect is so obvious that a corporation which is

[3] Mont Pelerin meeting, Rockford, Ill., 1971. William A. Niskanen, Jr., has written *Bureaucracy and Representative Government* (Chicago: Aldine-Atherton, 1971).

[4] Shares are sold in stock markets like the New York Stock Exchange. If a corporation is profitable, the demand for and the price of the stock will rise. Stockholders' benefits are equal to the difference between the purchase price and the price at which they can sell their stock.

doing badly normally changes its management internally without waiting for the next stockholders' election. If it does not, and the low profits of the corporation are the result of poor management, the danger of being replaced by "corporation raiders" is high.

Corporate raiders are specialized entrepreneurs who look for corporations which do not seem to be managed in a profit-maximizing way. They buy stock in such corporations—usually quite a bit of it—and undertake to change the management. The change in the management normally does not involve a "proxy fight"[5]; but if worst comes to worst, corporate raiders are sometimes willing to go to that extreme. Usually the existing management realizes its position is bad and gracefully bows out of the picture. The corporate raider then installs a new management which, if the raider has not made a mistake, is able to increase the profits, with the result that the value of the stock goes up. The corporate raider sells the stock at a profit and proceeds to look for another corporation which is not profit-maximizing.

All of this should not be taken to mean that the stockholder control over the board of directors and higher management is perfect. It is not—but some control is present. *The reason is not that the stockholder has more power than the voter in politics or is more intelligent, but that the stockholder has a very simple objective, and it happens to be relatively easy for him to find out whether the corporation is carrying out this objective. The voter, on the other hand, normally has very complicated objectives for government, and it is very hard for such a voter to find out whether the government is achieving those objectives.* Under the circumstances, it is not surprising that the same person will produce much more knowledge about the relevant performance of a corporation than about the performance of a democratically run nation-state.

[5] A stockholder can generally delegate his voting rights to someone else, known as a "proxy." A "proxy fight" for voting control of the corporation typically develops between management and some stockholder who wants to replace present management with this stockholder's own managers. If the stockholder does not have enough votes to do this by himself, he can solicit the proxy votes of other stockholders.

For much the same reasons, the corporate top management is better able to control its subordinates than the government is. For the remainder of this chapter, we will primarily be concerned with the government bureaucracy; but, as we have said before, sociologically, government bureaucracy is not greatly different in strategic respects from private bureaucracies.

We must not exaggerate, of course. There are inefficiencies in corporations. It is possible for the higher and lower management, to some extent, to pursue nonprofit goals, such as expansion of their departments, rather than profit for the stockholders. This is particularly true in companies that would be very highly profitable in any event, with the result that the stockholder gets a large return and does not realize that he could have received a larger one. But there are limits to what managers can do in this respect. If the company's products do not sell, or even if the profit dips, the management is in danger.

Because most corporations function in markets where there are some competitors, the drive toward profit is reinforced. Efficiency will lead to profits, and efficiency is necessary in a competitive market. General Motors knows that Toyota exists and that its customers can switch to Toyota at any time if that automobile company gives consumers a better deal. In fact, the stockholders can, if they like, sell their General Motors stock and buy stock in Toyota.

"VOTING WITH ONE'S FEET"

Competition among democratic governments is not as strong as is usual in the market, but it is not nonexistent. Although voter-citizens do not have stock to sell in government, they can, in the aggregate, apply pressure on governments by moving to the jurisdictions of other governments—they can "vote with their feet." Consider the area around most large cities. There are a large number of suburbs, each of which may be chosen by residents of the metropolitan area as a place to live or, in some cases, to set up a business. These suburbs may offer different combinations of taxes and services. There will be wealthy suburbs with high taxes and superb schools, and there will be other suburbs that offer "economy-class service" in most public activities and "economy-class taxes" as well.[6]

Thus, the individual, who in this case we can call a "customer" as well as a citizen, is faced with a number of alternatives when he or she thinks of where to live or set up a business and can make a choice among them. These communities are, in a limited sense, in competition with larger governmental units. People generally find it more difficult (i.e., costly) to move among states than among local governments, and they find it even more difficult to move among nations. The moving expense and cultural barriers are typically greater as the size of the governmental unit becomes larger. Still, there are people who move from state to state and from one nation to another because of their feelings about the different governments. These people affect the tax bases (that is, for example, the income from which taxes can be drawn) of the different governments and, in that way, put pressure on governments to serve the "consumers'" interest.

We tend to think that businessmen, if given an opportunity, will seek to restrict competition by cartel or monopoly organization. Since there is no reason to believe that bureaucrats are significantly different from businessmen, we may reasonably expect that they will resist the kind of competition we have described above and will attempt to establish governmental cartels or monopolistic organizations, too. In recent years there has been a strong drive to consolidate governmental units. School districts, for example, are now about seven times as large on the average as they were in 1950. There is also a drive to consolidate the local suburbs around the major cities into so-called "metro" governments and to make the federal government responsible for welfare and other social service programs.

As we explained in Chapter 21, the arguments offered for this consolidation are, for example, improvements in efficiency, the elimination of duplication, and economies of scale. Businessmen, when organizing cartels, seldom say that they are doing it simply for profit and normally argue that, somehow or other, it is for the benefit of the customers. Thus, we should be skeptical of this kind of argument, whether it comes from a bureaucrat in General Motors or a bureaucrat in the Chicago municipal government. *It is possible that a consolidation will indeed lead to greater efficiency and lower costs, but it is also possible that it is simply a cartel arrangement intended to improve the well-being of the government employees.*

In this case, empirical tests can be used to determine whether or not consolidation increases or reduces government efficiency. In the particular case of school consolidation, the empirical tests are fairly decisive. There is no improvement in efficiency; indeed, the students seem, if anything, to be learning less and there is a considerable increase in cost. The salaries, and in particular the salaries of the administrators, go up with consolidation and there is no evidence of any countervailing efficiency. With respect to the consolidation of cities in metro organizations, data are a little harder to come by because, as a matter of fact, consolidation has not been undertaken in very many places and most of the statistical studies are fairly recent. It does appear, however, that the resulting effect is a rise in government cost of services without any improvement, and perhaps with a deterioration, of services. The same general conclusion can be drawn for police services and fire protection.[7]

Greater inefficiency is what we would expect in the private, nonpolitical marketplace from cartel arrangements. We would anticipate that if Ford, Chrysler, and General Motors were permitted to get together and form a consolidated automobile company, we would end up paying much more for

[6] However, see, Robert L. Bish, *The Public Economy of Metropolitan Areas* (Chicago: Markham Publishing Co., 1971).

[7] Robert L. Bish and Vincent Ostrom, *Understanding Urban Government: Metropolitan Reform Reconsidered* (Washington: American Enterprise Institute for Public Policy Research, 1973), especially chaps. 4 and 6. Bish and Ostrom review a number of studies in these chapters.

our transportation. This is the reason for antitrust laws. (See Chapter 10.) It is not surprising that government officials tend to behave the same way as officials of corporations, because, as we have said before, they are very similar people. The difference is simply that the corporation executive organizing a monopoly finds it necessary to transfer a large part of the profit to the stockholders of the corporation, while the government executive organizing a monopoly can use it for raising his or her salary and those of fellow workers and increasing their fringe benefits.

PUBLIC BUREAUCRACIES

Let us now turn to public bureaucracies. In our study of public bureaucracies, the main theme is simply that bureaucrats are like other people. If bureaucrats are ordinary people, they are to some extent rational and will make most (although not all) of their decisions in terms of what benefits them and not necessarily in terms of what benefits society as a whole. Like other people, they may occasionally sacrifice their own well-being to some extent for the greater good, but we should not count upon this to control their day-to-day activities.

A business operator, if carrying on a business in an environment which is reasonably competitive and lacking severe externalities, will normally make a decision which is more or less in accord with the well-being of consumers (see Chapter 7). But this is not because this executive is consciously aiming to serve the "public good." He is simply attempting to make as much money as possible, and makes the most money by doing what is in the interest of consumers. We assume that the bureaucrat will also do what is in the social interest *if* the constraints to which he is subject are such that the official's personal interest is maximized by pursuing the social interest.

Motives of Bureaucrats

Our theory of bureaucracy aims at the design of constraints which will lead to a similarity between the bureaucrats' self-interest and the interest of society. Before producing improved institutional designs, however, we must study what does happen in a bureaucracy. To begin, let us consider the motivation of the bureaucrats. Bureaucrats, like everyone else, are presumably attempting to improve their own utility. Their utility, again like everyone else's, is partly based upon their immediate ability to consume various goods and services and partly on their appreciation of good things happening to other people. In other words, they are partly selfish and partly interested in benefiting others.

The assumption that the business operator is trying to maximize money income turns out to work rather well, although seldom perfectly in the private sector. In the case of the bureaucracy, we would like to make a somewhat similar assumption. We can begin by listing those things which are of primary concern to a bureaucrat: the salary, the conditions of work in the sense of office size and furniture (strictly apportioned according to rank in most bureaucracies), job security, and retirement benefits, public respect, and reputation. In addition to these self-regarding values, let us assume that the bureaucrat also is interested in the public good and consciously wants to accomplish something in the job.

We can easily think of cases in which the public and private motives would be in clear conflict. James Smith, for example, is up for promotion to department head, but Mary Brown is the best person for the job. It is dubious that Smith will bring his relative capabilities to the attention of his superiors. On the other hand, we can easily find cases where Smith, for purely selfish reasons, will be motivated to do something which is desirable from the standpoint of society. Consider again the example of Smith and Brown, but assume that Smith is in fact abler than Brown. Under these circumstances, his selfish motives will point in the same direction as his public-interest motive.

One of the advantages of the simple profit-maximizing assumption in business is that it permits us to assume a single objective which the business person attempts to maximize and it permits us to make predictions. If we consider the business person as maximizing his or her utility, which means maximizing something other than profit, we no longer have as easy a problem. It is difficult to predict exactly what the person will maximize. This is because the business person can maximize different things, such as personal income, respect in the profession, or other aspects of the office. In general, economists have given up on attempting to deal with such a complex objective function, and they assume a simple, single goal—profit. The loss in accuracy in this model of business behavior is compensated by the predictive capability of the model. The same can be said for the theories of bureaucracy we present.

Size Maximization of Bureaucracies

Is there a single goal, similar to profit, we can use for government bureaucracies? The answer is, unfortunately, no, if we want to be completely accurate. Different bureaucrats tend to maximize different collections of "goods." But it is true that if we confine ourselves to the type of bureaucracy that is found in most Western countries, there are two reasonable approximations which are frequently employed. These approximations are "size maximization" and "waste maximization," and we consider them in that order.

As a general rule, bureaucrats will find that their possibilities for promotion increase; that their power, influence, and public respect improve; and that even the physical conditions of their offices will improve, if the bureaucracy in which they work expands. This proposition is fairly general. Almost any bureaucrat gains at least something if the whole bureaucracy expands, in terms of service it provides. Each gains more, however, if his or her particular ministry expands, and more yet if the particular subdivision in which he or she is employed expands.

Note, however, that we have confined this to *most* bureaucracies in *modern Western democracies.* It is not necessarily true of all bureaucracies, and it is not necessarily true of bureaucracies in other areas. Further, there is one important limitation on profit maximization which also applies to size maximization for bureaucracies: in general, people do not like hard work.

Consider several government bureaucrats who are ordered to do research on, let us say, methods for breaking up the OPEC oil cartel. Presumably, the bureaucrats are interested in cheaper gasoline, but they are apt to give more weight to the opportunity to expand the size of their offices and hence increase the probability of their promotion, prestige, etc. However, it is by no means certain that they will work terribly hard to achieve either of these goals. In an extreme case, these bureaucrats will waste time and not accomplish their official duties. The time they do devote to work will be devoted to an effort to expand their offices with no concern at all for their ostensible object. In the more normal case, although they may not engage in very hard work, nevertheless they will devote a good deal of attention both to seeking methods of breaking OPEC and to the objective of using the project to expand their offices.

For simplicity, let us assume that the bureaucrats are solely attempting to maximize the size of their particular bureaucracies, while we leave aside their desire to consume leisure. Economists have gone a long way with the very simple goal of profit maximization for business people, and if we cannot get as far with our equally simple assumed goal for bureaucracies, we can make some progress.

We must begin by pointing out that one way of increasing the size of one's bureaucracy is to do a good enough job so that people want more. No doubt the Postal Service would be handling a good deal more mail if it performed more efficiently. Whether its total budget would be larger or smaller is not obvious, of course. It depends on the elasticity of demand for mail services. Regardless of the actual elasticity of demand for the services of the Postal Service, undeniably there are many cases in which individual bureaucrats, whose only motive is to expand the size of their bureaucracy, will try to improve efficiency and provide good service.

An Analysis of Bureaucratic Expansion

Let us look at size maximization of bureaucracy a little more carefully. Consider some government activity, say police protection. For simplicity, assume it is produced at constant marginal cost, as shown by the horizontal line MC on Figure 22 · 1. There is some public demand for police protection, and this demand, D_1, is downward sloping. It is the legislature acting for the citizenry which "demands" the police services.

The usual way of organizing the police is to set up a series of regional monopolies, with all the police in Richmond, Virginia, for example, being supplied by one organization. This police force in Richmond has its own decision-making process and its own goals, which are not necessarily any more similar to the goals of the legislature than General Motors' objectives are to the goals of its customers. If it were somehow possible to purchase police service competitively at a constant price of P_1 for each unit of police service, the optimum amount of police service would be Q_2, at which the price (or marginal cost) equals the marginal benefit of the last unit of police service. The total cost equals $P_1 \times Q_2$ (or the area $0P_1AQ_2$), and there is a consumer surplus generated for the citizenry shown by the triangular area P_1P_3A. However, if police service must be purchased from a profit-maximizing monopoly, production will occur where the marginal cost of the last unit produced equals the marginal benefit of it.[8] This equality occurs at quantity Q_1 (or point E). At that production level, the monopolist makes a profit equal to the rectangular area bounded by P_1P_2ED: it receives a total revenue of $P_2 \times Q_1$ (or the rectangle $0P_2EQ_1$) and incurs a total cost of $P_1 \times Q_1$ (or the rectangle $0P_1DQ_1$). (P_1 is the cost of each unit produced; therefore, $P_1 \times Q_1$ is the cost of all Q_1 units.) With the monopolized production level, there is still some consumer surplus—equal to the triangular area P_2P_3E—left for consumers; but, clearly, consumers are worse off under monopolized production than under competitive market conditions: consumers have the benefits of fewer units of police protection and pay a higher price for the units they receive.

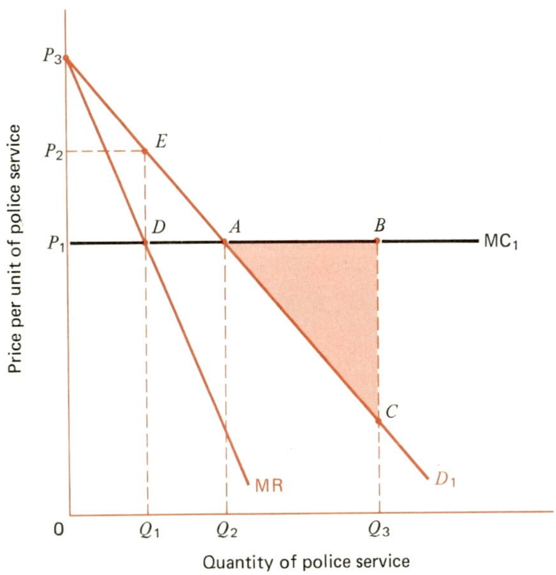

FIG. 22 · 1 Given the demand curve for police service, D_1, and the marginal cost curve of providing that service, MC_1, the optimum quantity of police service is Q_2. However, a monopolistic police bureaucracy interested in maximizing bureau profits will supply only Q_1 and will sell that quantity at a tax price of P_2. The monopolistic police bureaucracy interested in maximizing its size will expand the quantity of police service provided to the limit of Q_3.

Let us now make our model more realistic and assume that the individuals cannot purchase police services as individuals but must use a government agency which has a demand for police services derived from the demands of the individual citizens. The supplier realistically is still a monopoly—there is only one police force in Richmond, Virginia. Assume that the police attempt to maximize the size of their bureaucracy. What is the likely outcome? First, we have one buyer

[8] See Chapter 10 for a review of the profit-maximizing condition for a monopolist.

against one seller (what is called a "bilateral monopoly"); and because the different bargaining strategies can be taken by buyer and seller, it is usually difficult for economists to indicate the outcome of the bargaining process. Let us begin, however, by inquiring what will happen if one or the other of the two parties has everything his own way. Suppose, for example, that the legislature is in complete control of the situation and has a perfect knowledge of the actual cost of producing police services. Under these circumstances, they can have the same solution as is obtained by competition. They can force the police to produce Q_2 units of service and pay them P_1 for each of those units.

However, suppose the police have all the information on their side, which in this case means that they are able to conceal their cost from the legislature. They can misrepresent to the legislature the cost of providing various amounts of police services, and the legislature will not be able to discover the truth. This leads to a most extraordinary outcome. The police will provide at the limit Q_3 units of police services and charge a total amount equal to $P_1 \times Q_3$ (or the rectangle $0P_1BQ_3$). Note that this means that for the additional police services—those units between Q_2 and Q_3—the police are charging more than people collectively think they are worth, and there is a net social waste shown by the orange-shaded triangle. They are able to get away with this, however, because the size of the shaded triangle, ABC, is the same as P_1P_3A. By extending police service to Q_3, the bureau has squeezed out the entire consumer surplus, but it has "spent" the surplus on providing additional police services.

How do we reach this conclusion? First, note that the police department is not profit-maximizing, i.e., it is not possible for the policemen simply to pocket any profit they make. The police administrators benefit, however, in various ways by the expansion in the size of the force. Since we are currently assuming that they are perfectly exploiting the demand, the police maximize size and their own benefits by this socially wasteful expansion.

The situation outlined above is the result which could be expected if the bureaucracy worked hard at expanding its budget and was able to exploit the full monopoly gains from the legislature. At Q_3, the taxpayers will be completely indifferent between having the existing police force and having no police at all with much lower taxes. For this reason it seems dubious that any existing bureaucracy will actually expand all the way to Q_3 but will achieve some size short of Q_3.

Waste Maximization of Bureaucracies

Instead of maximizing the amount of service which the bureau offers, the bureaucrats with monopoly power can choose to maximize their waste for any *given* quantity of service they choose to provide. For example, they can increase their salaries, the pleasantness of their working conditions, and the number of people with whom they can share a given amount of work. All of these changes result in an increase in the cost of providing a given amount of service, and in Figure 22·2 we show how far the bureau can go in increasing the cost of (or budget for) their service. The marginal cost curve, MC_1, is the minimum cost of providing additional units of police protection, if the police have to offer their service at the minimum cost; the optimum quantity of police protection is, therefore, Q_1, the same as in Figure 22·1. However, if it is possible for police to "pad" their costs of operation, claiming that they are necessary for an efficient police force, the marginal cost curve can be moved up to a limit of MC_2 in Figure 22·2. The total budget of the bureau is, at this limit, $P_2 \times Q_2$. The "revealed" marginal cost of each unit of police service, MC_2, between Q_1 and Q_2 is greater than the marginal benefit, indicated by the demand curve. However, so long as the loss in welfare shown by the shaded triangle ABC is less than the perceived consumer surplus triangle P_2P_3A, the total benefits of the police protection are greater than the total cost. By moving their cost curve all the way to MC_2, the bureaucrats extract all consumer surplus and make the buying agency or public indifferent between having the police force or not

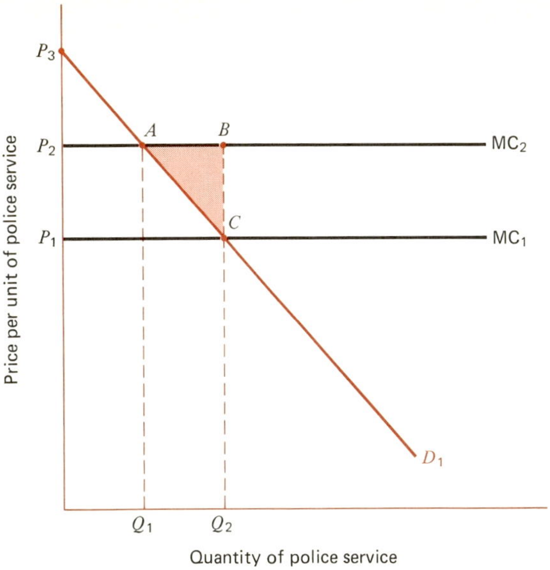

FIG. 22·2 Given the demand for police service, D_1, and the marginal cost of providing police service, if that service is provided efficiently, MC_1, the optimum quantity of police service is Q_2. However, the monopolistic police bureaucracy, interested in maximizing its waste by inflating its costs, will give the impression that the marginal (and average) cost of police service is MC_2. It will supply Q_2 units of police service at a tax price of P_2 per unit.

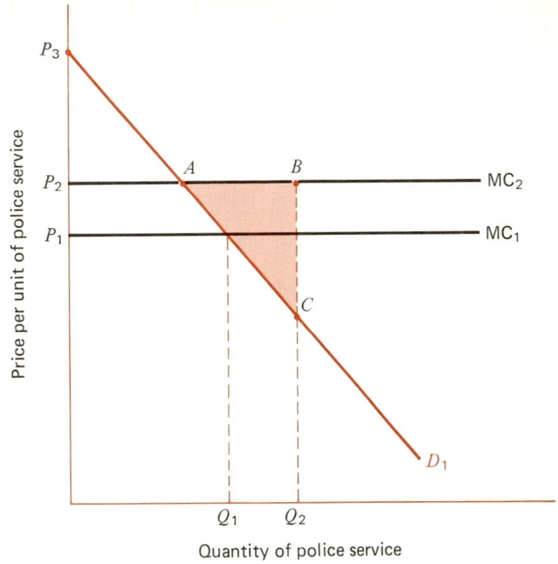

FIG. 22·3 As opposed to expanding the size of the bureaucracy to its limit in terms of size of output or in terms of the average cost of each unit provided, the monopolistic bureaucracy can choose to increase the number of units of police service provided *and* increase the average cost of each unit of service provided. However, to the extent the average cost of service is raised, the size of the bureaucracy in terms of quantity of service provided must be restricted, and vice versa.

having it, as is true in the size-maximization model developed above.

Most bureaus very likely combine the objective of size maximization with waste maximization: they try to expand both the size and scope of their bureau and the funds they receive for each unit of service provided. However, on the margin they have to make trade-offs in achieving both objectives. When they expand the size of their bureaucracy, they must forgo an expansion in the funds they receive per unit of service provided. The reason is that there is only so much consumer surplus for them to extract. One possible combination of size and budget maximization is illustrated in Figure 22·3. The bureau in this case chooses to expand the size of its bureau from the optimum quantity of Q_1 to Q_2; having done this, they can only expand the funds they can receive per unit to MC_2. The shaded triangle is again equal to the triangular area above the marginal cost curve MC_2 and below the demand curve.

Bureaucrats, Leisure, and Efficiency

Obviously there are a number of reasons why bureaucrats would not usually be able to reach this goal. First, and obviously, the legislature or purchaser of the services from the bureaucracy has at least some information about the production function of the bureaucracy; hence, it is not subject to what we might call "complete" exploitation. Secondly, the members of the bureaucracy (as we have mentioned above) want, among other things, leisure. Therefore, they may not do the hard work necessary to exploit the legislature to the theoretical maximum.

Ironically, the desire for leisure (what we normally call laziness) has a net benefit for society. Suppose that the individuals in the bureaucracy work only hard enough to get 80 percent of what they could get if they worked devotedly to achieve their goal. This would mean that the cost line MC in Figure 22·1 would be adjusted upward to indicate that you have to hire 25 percent more policemen to get a given amount of protection. This would be disadvantageous from the standpoint of the taxpayer-citizen. On the other hand, the bureaucracy would not get all the welfare triangle by negotiating with the legislature; it would leave 20 percent of it to the citizen. The result would be that the citizens would in fact get some net benefit from the service. If the police were energetic and hard-working in both policing and exploiting the legislature, on the other hand, the consumer surplus would be entirely consumed in "efficiently" producing police services which are not worth their cost. The citizen-taxpayer is better off with lazy servants than with diligent ones here, but this is because diligent ones will use their diligence to extract surplus value from the taxpayer as well as to police efficiently.

THE DEMAND FOR BUREAUCRACIES

Let us return to the question of whether the bureaucracy actually can extort the entire area under the demand curve from the legislature. This is the classic monopoly-against-monopsony problem, and economists normally say it is unsolvable. There are good reasons, however, for believing that the bureau (the monopoly) will be able to "exploit," to some extent, the legislature (or Congress) which funds the bureau. The bureaucracy will have a good idea of the legislative demand for its services simply because the legislative demand for services is essentially derived from the voters' demand. The bureaucracy has access to the newspapers, television, and public opinion polls of its own, and therefore frequently has a reasonably good idea of what the popular demands for its services are. The legislature is not able to keep its demand curve a secret.

These factors are strengthened by two special characteristics of governmental demand. First, most government services are demanded by pressure groups—the farmers, for example. (Indeed, bureaucracies often act as an in-house lobbying organization for the special-interest groups.) Such pressure groups are normally intimately connected with the bureaucracy which will carry out the policy in their area, the Department of Agriculture in this case. The Department of Agriculture, then, is very well informed as to the political pressures which can be brought to bear upon Congress and the president for agricultural expansion. Secondly, a major part of the demand for bureaucratic services comes not from the people who will receive those services, but from the people who will be paid to deliver them. The bureaucrat who works for the Department of Agriculture or the police officer who works for the city is, after all, also a voter. In voting, the police officer and family have two demands for their particular bureaucracy's service: (1) they, like other citizens, gain indirectly whatever public benefits the service generates for the country, and (2) they gain privately.[9] The bureaucrats, then, are part of the demand for their own services, and a particularly important part. They combine very good information about their bureaus with strong motivation.

If the bureaucracy has an excellent idea of the demand for the service by the government cabinet, the government has great difficulty determining the minimum cost. In general, the only source of such information is the bureaucracy,

[9] Of course, this assumes that the payment to them is higher than their opportunity cost, but this does not seem to be a particularly radical assumption in most modern governments. At the time this book was under preparation, the city of New York, as a result of a fiscal crisis, was talking of firing 10,000 police officers. The police officers' union prepared and circulated to tourists a pamphlet entitled "Scare City," warning against the dangers of visiting New York City if the police force was reduced. Of course, this was an effort to manipulate the demand for their own services.

and the monopoly bureaucracy, like any monopoly, has little or no incentive to reveal possible cost savings. If budget cuts are imposed when cost savings are revealed, the bureaucracy has an incentive to maximize its cost instead of attempting to do the best job it can under the circumstances.

This kind of behavior is perfectly normal with bureaucracies, and, in general, members of Congress have found it difficult to prevent. William Niskanen, whose book *Bureaucracy and Representative Government* develops the size-maximizing principle with great rigor,[10] has spent most of his life as an economist employed by the Department of Defense. Immediately after writing his book, he moved to a higher-level agency, the Office of Management and Budget, which is the general control agency of the United States government. A part of his new job was to control government costs. In both places, he found that it was impossible for him to outmaneuver the bureaucrats. They simply knew more about their particular fields than he did. Since leaving the government, he has done some empirical work on the problem. This empirical work is difficult to undertake because bureaucrats do not provide very much information which is really useful in judging their efficiency. Nevertheless, his studies show that bureaucracies are draining substantially all the consumer surplus.[11]

Bernard Sobin, in testimony on behalf of the United States Postal Service before the Postal Rate Commission in 1975, has provided us with insight into the way the Postal Service works as a bureaucracy and argues for postal rate and fee increases.[12] Sobin was an economist who had been working for the government for practically his entire career and for the Postal Service for five years, and he seems to have a low opinion of the efficiency of the Postal Service. For example, in the appendix on delivery of magazines to his 200 pages-plus testimony, he calculates that employees of private magazine delivery companies work 8 hours a day as opposed to 4.5 hours for Postal Service employees. Making a few other comparisons, he calculates that Postal Service carriers, performing exactly the same duties as the private companies already in the business, will deliver 525 magazines per day, whereas the private personnel will deliver 875.[13] To repeat, this is the argument used by Sobin, who was at the time General Manager of the Rate Economics Division, Office of Rates, Rates and Classification Department, United States Postal Service, and who was asking for an increase in postal rates. He was making a common appeal of bureaucracies: We will do better if we are given more money.

[10] William A. Niskanen, Jr., *Bureaucracy and Representative Government* (Chicago: Aldine-Atherton, 1971).

[11] William A. Niskanen, Jr., "Bureaucracy and the Interests of Bureaucrats" (paper presented at Universities–National Bureau Committee for Economic Research Conference on Economic Analysis of Political Behavior, Boston, Apr. 11, 1975).

[12] Direct Testimony of Bernard Sobin on behalf of the United States Postal Service, before the Postal Rate Commission, 1975.

[13] Ibid., Appendix A, pp. 9–10.

SOLUTIONS TO THE PROBLEMS OF BUREAUCRACY

What can be done about the inefficiency of government bureaucracies? The first suggestion obviously is an attempt to develop managerial expertise at the congressional level, and the development of techniques for measuring the costs and benefits of programs. It should be noted, however, that cost-benefit analysis itself will not necessarily lead to any great improvements. What is needed is some way of lowering the bargaining potential of the monopoly bureaus, not improving information about them, even though improving information will help.

In the marketplace, we do not try to figure out the costs of companies from whom we buy goods and services. All we do is compare the prices and products offered by different sellers and choose the one that is best from our standpoint. Of course, a monopoly of any kind, private or public, makes this task hard. Is there some way by which Congress could have the same ability to select the lowest price from among several offers rather than trying to determine the operating efficiency of any given bureaucracy? The answer, fortunately, is that in many cases it is possible and it will improve government efficiency.

Although most government services are produced under monopoly conditions, there are a certain number of them which are produced with some degree of competition. It is very hard to get measures of efficiency in any government case, but something can be done. Studies show that the least efficient bureaus are those which have the greatest monopoly power. Next in inefficiency come the bureaus where, although the individual bureau has a monopoly over the activity in one geographic area, there are several different bureaus operating in different areas, and hence the legislature can at least compare costs.[14] The police forces, which are organized as a series of local monopolies rather than a national service, are one of many examples.

More efficient yet are those government bureaus which carry out some service that is also available from private companies. This is rather rare but not totally unknown. Waste removal in the United States, for example, is sometimes a government activity and sometimes is carried out by private companies. So far as we can tell, the government bureaus that act in this area, although not as efficient as the private companies (higher prices and poorer service), are nevertheless markedly more efficient than government bureaus which do not face a threat of private competition. We suppose it will not be particularly surprising that government bureaus, even when nonprivate alternatives are available, are rarely as efficient as their private counterparts. The question of the efficiency of private industry in monopolistic situations is not an issue here, since no one, so far as we know (aside from the monopolists themselves), regards this as a desirable organization of the economy.

The reason for this is simple. Consider Figure 22·1. As we learned in Chapter 10, when the degree of competition increases, the individual enterprise faces a demand curve which becomes progressively flatter. In other words, if one company protected by a high tariff has a monopoly on automobile production in some country, the company's demand curve is the country's demand curve for automobiles in total. If there are two companies, each individual company faces a demand curve that is markedly flatter because the individual who is thinking of whether or not to buy a Ford now also has the alternative of buying a Chevrolet. Similarly with a bureaucracy, the more alternative sources of a service, the more competition, the flatter the demand curve for the services of each bureau, and hence, the more bureaucracy is forced to produce close to the optimum output and more production efficiency.

Are there ways we can introduce competition into bureaucracy? The answer is, fortunately, yes there are. Indeed, it should be fairly easy. The first step is to stop enacting cartel legislation for government bureaus. Most "efficiency" studies of government have attempted to root out competition, which, in the government area, is called *duplication*. The proposal often made is to eliminate alternative sources of a government service to the consolidation of several agencies into one. Using the same line of reasoning, the same types of efficiency studies of the automobile industry might recommend the consolidation of General Motors, Ford, Chrysler, and American Motors, and a lot of odd foreigners like British Leyland, Fiat, Volkswagen, and Toyota, into one large auto cartel. This recommendation has never seriously been made for the automobile industry; indeed, the most frequently heard recommendation is that the large automobile firms be broken up into separate and competing companies. On the assumption that employees of government and private companies have the same basic motivation in their jobs, the proposal may be considered reasonable for government bureaucracy.

In the United States, highways are usually built

[14] For research on the relationship between the "market structure" of bureaus and governments, see Thomas E. Borcherding, ed., *Budgets and Bureaucrats: Sources of Government Growth* (Durham, N.C.: Duke University Press, 1977); William Niskanen and Mickey Levy, "Cities and Schools: A Case for Community Government in California," working paper no. 14 (Berkeley: Graduate School of Public Policy, University of California, 1974); Delores T. Martin and Richard E. Wagner, "The Institutional Framework for Municipal Incorporations: An Economic Analysis of Local Agency Formation Commissions in California," working paper (Blacksburg, Va.: Center for Study of Public Choice, Virginia Polytechnic Institute and State University, 1976).

by private companies. Normally, however, their repair and maintenance is done by monopolistic government enterprises. There seems to be no reason except historical precedent for this pattern of behavior. The switch to competitive provision of maintenance, as well as highway construction, can possibly improve efficiency in the provision of safe highways.

One way, then, to increase the competitiveness of government services is simply to contract them out. A great many government services are contracted out in various places in the world. The entire line of public utilities—telephone, telegraph, radio and television transmission, water supply, sewage removal, electricity, and gas—is sometimes provided privately and sometimes publicly. Usually private companies in these lines are given some kind of government-guaranteed monopoly, which sharply reduces their efficiency; but this is not always true, and places where these services are produced competitively can be found.

There are also many other activities which governments perform which can be performed by private agencies on contract. Fire protection is, in general, a government activity. In the state of Arizona, however, a private fire protection industry has developed. These private fire protection companies enter into contracts with the smaller cities to provide them with fire protection, but they also offer their services to individual citizens in rural areas. Comparative studies seem to show that these private fire protection companies provide a given amount of fire protection for about half the cost of public fire departments serving similar communities.[15]

Use of the private market is not the only means of introducing competition to bureaucracies. It is quite possible to retain bureaucratic control *and* competition. First, simply dividing up the area served by a bureaucracy into a number of small areas with separate budgets can help. It will be particularly helpful if Congress makes a habit of changing the geographic scope of the various small bureaucracies handling, for example, police protection. If, for example, a lieutenant in charge of the Fifth Precinct seems to have done better last year than the lieutenant in charge of the neighboring Fourth Precinct, one might remove 15 percent of the Fourth Precinct, add it on to the Fifth, promote the lieutenant of the Fifth to captain, and reduce the lieutenant of the Fourth Precinct to sergeant. We anticipate that in the following year there would be a good deal of very hard thought on methods of improving efficiency by the captain and the sergeant. Perhaps the 15 percent would be shifted back at the end of the next year.

Competition of this sort is seldom formal, but in practice a good deal of it occurs. As we mentioned above, "efficiency" committees periodically look over the federal government in order to eliminate what they call duplication and what may often be more accurately described as competition. The fact that they always find a good deal of it is evidence that some competition sneaks into the government, in spite of the efforts of the "efficiency experts."

The head of one particular bureau comes to the conclusion that he can expand his bureau by taking over some of the activities of some other bureau. He makes a proposal to that effect, either to Congress or to his superiors in the executive branch. Normally at this point, the bureau whose activities he wishes to usurp (or at least infringe upon) begins complaining about duplication; but, characteristically, it also makes some efficiency improvements in the area where the outside entrepreneur is threatening. Needless to say, the areas where this "duplication" occurs are the areas where the efficiency is highest, because bureaucrats are compelled to take into account the possibility of simply being eliminated in some later budget revision.[16]

As an example of competitive bureaucratic behavior, the Department of Transportation,

[15] Roger S. Ahlbrandt, Jr., *Municipal Fire Protection Services: Comparison of Alternative Organization Forms*, Sage Professional Papers in Administrative and Policy Studies, 03–002 (Beverly Hills, Calif.: Sage Publications, 1973).

[16] As Samuel Johnson put it, "When a man knows he's to be hanged the following morning, it concentrates his mind wonderfully."

which sounds like a fairly peaceful organization, played an important military role in Vietnam. The Navy had a doctrinal rule against use of ships of less than 100 feet in length. With the development of the war in Vietnam, use of boats on rivers and very close to shore became necessary, and the Navy insisted on 100-foot gunboats. A bureaucratic entrepreneur in the Coast Guard (a subsidiary of the Department of Transportation) saw an opportunity to increase his budget. As a result, a large collection of Coast Guardsmen was removed from their normal duties and sent to Vietnam, where they piloted small boats (called "swift boats") up and down rivers. Since the budget of the Coast Guard was appropriately increased, they were able to hire more people and more high-ranking officers.

The Navy was a little slow at catching on, but as of now they have a major program on "riverine war," and one can predict that in the future the Navy will be equipped with boats less than 100 feet in length in competition with the Coast Guard. Of course, they are attempting to get the Coast Guard permanently removed from this role, and the Coast Guard is objecting.

SUMMARY AND EXTENSIONS

The theme of this chapter has been that people with monopolistic market positions will tend to exploit their positions. This is generally accepted as being true for private entrepreneurs; we believe that it is also applicable to government bureaucrats. Empirical studies of government uphold this point of view. If government bureaus do not have competitors inside or outside government, they are in a relatively strong bargaining position with respect to their funding agent—i.e., the legislature or Congress. Being the only producer of a service, the bureau can curtail its service and deny the benefits of its service to people; in this way, the bureau can increase the price that is paid for its services. The funding agent is also dependent solely upon the monopoly bureau for its data on the cost of the bureau's service; the funding agent does not have alternative producers of the service to whom it can turn for the information needed to make a comparative cost analysis. Using its monopoly position, the bureau can extend the amount and scope of its service beyond the optimum production level at which the marginal social benefit of the last unit produced is equal to actual marginal cost of production. Alternatively, the bureau can allow its costs to creep upward beyond their minimum level, causing additional increases in the bureau's budget. Either way, like the private monopolist, the monopoly bureau will operate inefficiently.

In this chapter we have suggested that in many cases government bureaucracy can be encouraged to operate more efficiently than it presently does. The general solution is to introduce competition into government bureaucracy. This means that, where possible, there should be alternative sources of any good or service provided by government. In attempting to maximize their size or their budgets, bureaus will then have to compete with other bureaus by offering their services at lower tax-prices or by increasing the quality of their service for any given tax-price. As in the case of private markets (Chapter 7), competition can induce bureaus to reveal, within limits, what they will do and not just what they want to do. This is not the only solution for the problems of bureaucracy, but it is, perhaps, a step in the right direction.

QUESTIONS TO PONDER

1 The authors have assumed in this chapter that government bureaucrats attempt to maximize the size and budget of their bureaucracy. Can you think of additional goals of bureaucrats?

2 What effect does competition have on the slope of an individual firm's demand curve? Why? What effect does a change in the slope of a producer's demand curve have to do with economic efficiency? What do your answers have to do with the problem of government bureaucracy?

3 "Competition forces producers to reveal what they are willing to do at the limit and not just what they want to do." How does this statement apply to government bureaucracy and the facility with which Congress can control it?

4 Would you expect government bureaucracies to be more efficient at the state, local, or federal level? Cite arguments used in the chapter.

5 Write down a list of all the services government provides which you can think of. Which of these services *must* the government provide through its own bureaucracies? Which of these services can be provided through competitive contracts as government buildings are presently provided?

RECOMMENDED READINGS

Bish, Robert L., and Vincent Ostrom: *Understanding Urban Government: Metropolitan Reform Reconsidered* (Washington, D.C.: American Enterprise Institute for Public Policy Research, 1973).

Stockfish, J. A.: *The Political Economy of Bureaucracy* (New York: General Learning Press, 1972).

Tullock, Gordon: *The Politics of Bureaucracy* (Washington, D.C.: Public Affairs Press 1965).

Part Nine
Macroeconomics: Money and Inflation

Do changes in the quantity of money matter? . . . There is massive historical evidence that they do. *Every economic recession but one in the U.S. in the past century has been preceded by a decline in the rate of growth of the quantity of money.* And the sharper the decline, the more serious the subsequent recession—though this tendency is far from uniform.

Milton Friedman
Dollars and Deficits: Inflation, Monetary Policy, and the Balance of Payments (Englewood Cliffs, N.J.: Prentice-Hall, Inc., 1968), p. 165.

In the next several chapters, we seek to describe and explain the performance of the United States economy and its major subdivisions. Accordingly, we begin a study of a branch of economics called *macroeconomics.* More specifically, our purpose in this part is to explain the role which the quantity of money plays in determining the overall performance of the economy. To achieve this objective we define and evaluate in Chapter 23 measures of the "macroeconomy": (1) Gross National Product, which is a measure of how much is produced annually in the United States, (2) the unemployment rate, and (3) price indexes, such as the Consumer Price Index, which measure inflation. In Chapter 24 we discuss the meaning of money and explain how money is created through the banking system and controlled by the Federal Reserve, the central bank in the United States. We also describe in Chapter 25 how a change in the amount of money in the hands of consumers and businesses affects the economy's production of goods and services, the unemployment rate, and, most important for this section of the book, the rate of inflation. Further, we discuss how and to what extent the macroeconomic variables of production, unemployment, and inflation are interrelated—how, for example, the rate of inflation affects the level of unemployment in the short and long run. In Chapter 27 we evaluate the distributional effects of inflation; that is, we consider the question of who gains and who loses from a general increase in prices; in this way we try to explain the long period of high rates of inflation in the United States.

23

The Macroeconomy and Measurements of General Economic Activity

"But 'glory' doesn't mean 'a nice knock-down argument,'" Alice objected.
"When I use a word," Humpty Dumpty said in a rather scornful tone, "it means just what I choose it to mean–neither more nor less."
"The question is," said Alice, "whether you can *make words mean so many different things."*
"The question is," said Humpty Dumpty, "which is to be a master—that's all."
Lewis Carroll[1]

PREVIEW OF CHAPTER

Central question

What are the primary ways of measuring overall economic activity in the United States economy?

Major objectives

1 To introduce the subject of *macroeconomics*
2 To define and evaluate *Gross National Product* as a measure of total production of goods and services in the United States
3 To define and evaluate the *Consumer Price Index* and the *Wholesale Price Index* as means of measuring inflation or the general rise or fall of prices

[1] Lewis Carroll, *Through the Looking Glass and What Alice Found There*. A number of modern sources are available.

Major conclusions

1 Macroeconomics is a branch of economics which involves the study of national production, unemployment, and inflation. It involves the study of what is happening in the economy generally, not with what is happening in particular markets.

2 Although they may be our best measures of national production, unemployment, inflation, Gross National Product, the unemployment rate, and the Consumer and Wholesale Price Indexes are deficient in several respects. These deficiencies should be kept in mind when using these measures as means of evaluating the performance of the economy.

Important terms and concepts

Microeconomics	Civilian labor force
Macroeconomics	Unemployment rate
Gross National Product	Consumer Price Index
Employed	Wholesale Price Index
Unemployed	GNP Deflator

When economists measure, explain, and predict the performance of markets for very specific products like bicycles and hand calculators, they are dealing in the area of *microeconomics.* As the term *micro* (as in *micro*scope) suggests, *micro*-economics involves the analysis of those small divisions, like individual markets, which exist within the entire economic system. The first twenty-two chapters in this book have used microeconomic analysis to interpret events in the marketplace, the political arena, and even personal-choice situations.

Economists are also interested in measuring, explaining, and predicting the performance of the economic system as a whole and the performance of its broad subdivisions. One such subdivision is the total market value of the output of all firms that produce consumer goods for households or capital goods for businesses. The branch of economics that deals with these large subdivisions is called *macroeconomics.* Instead of concentrating attention on individual markets, economists involved in macroeconomic analysis concentrate on the total (or aggregate) market value of many different goods and services. A relevant question in macroeconomics is not how many bicycles or hand calculators are sold, but how many goods consumers have purchased *in total* or how much *all* producers have spent on new plants and equipment. Whereas *micro*economics is concerned with the price of a particular good in a particular market, *macro*economics is concerned with the "price level" (or average of all prices) of very broad categories of goods and services. When dealing with labor issues, *micro*economists focus on the wage rate and the number of people employed and unemployed in specific labor markets, like the market for plumbers or aerospace engineers. *Macro*economists, on the other hand, study such issues as the total incomes of all laborers and the total number of people employed and unemployed throughout the economy. In short, macroeconomics involves the study of national production, unemployment, and inflation. For these reasons, macroeconomics is often and, perhaps, more descriptively referred to as "aggregate economics."

Our primary purpose in the next several chapters is to develop an understanding of many past and present government policies. Fifteen years ago economists were generally (but, of course, not totally) agreed on what policies the government should follow to reach "satisfactory levels" of national production, employment, and inflation. However, after years of high rates of inflation and unemployment in the United

States and elsewhere, economists are no longer agreed as they once were that government, constrained by the dictates of political realities, can follow the desired policy course to achieve the goals of low unemployment, low rates of inflation, and high rates of economic growth. Many economists now suggest that government policy has increased the rates of unemployment and inflation and that the country would have been better off if the government had done nothing. Other economists forcibly argue that in order to accomplish the task of reducing unemployment and inflation, government needs more direct controls over the economy; in short, that it needs to engage in national economic planning. *National economic planning* generally means centralized and detailed control of large sectors of the economy by government. Its basic purpose is to ensure that the demands for goods are matched with adequate supplies at noninflationary prices and that those who want jobs can find them. How and to what extent the government can improve the economic performance of the economy through its policies is the question which is at the core of the remaining chapters in the book. For now, in order to analyze the program that the government has followed, we must start with definitions and analysis of the fundamental macroeconomic variables upon which many government decisions are made. These variables are (1) *Gross National Product,* a measure of national production; (2) the *unemployment rate;* and (3) price indexes, like the *Consumer Price Index,* which is a measure of the change in the price level.

GROSS NATIONAL PRODUCT: A MEANS OF MEASURING THE NATION'S PRODUCTION

There are three basic reasons for measuring the nation's total production of goods and services. First, economists want to test their theories of how the macroeconomy operates against real-world data. Second, using these theories, economists and government officials can seek to develop policies which will raise the nation's production level. With statistical data, economists can evaluate the country's economic progress over a period of years and the quantitative impact of government policy on production and people's incomes.

Third, business people who must plan for future production are interested in data on what is happening generally in the economy. They understand that the level of production in the economy taken as a whole will affect their sales. Automobile producers, for example, realize that the number of cars they sell depends upon the productivity of and income earned by people in other industries. If production is down elsewhere, people will earn less and have less money to spend on automobiles. With data on recent and current economic activity, business people can estimate, although with imprecision, how much they should produce in the future to meet market demand and can better determine their future needs for raw materials and labor.

For these reasons, any measurement of the nation's economic activity does more than just record what has transpired in the economy in the past; it also influences public opinion and government and business policies. If the data show that prices have been rising at an unacceptably high rate, the availability of the data can create popular dissatisfaction which can influence future government policies. The data will also increase the information flow to businesses; and, to that extent, they will change the response which businesses make to changes in economic conditions. In short, data measuring economic activity will not have a neutral effect on the economy. The methods used in collecting data are, therefore, important. For these reasons, economist Kenneth Boulding has written,

> The Gross National Product is one of the great inventions of the twentieth century, probably almost as significant as the automobile and not quite so significant as TV. The effect of physical inventions is obvious, but social inventions like GNP change the world almost as much.[2]

[2] Kenneth E. Boulding, "Fun and Games with the Gross National Product: The Role of Misleading Indications in Social Policy," in Harold W. Helfish, Jr., ed., *The Environmental Crisis* (New Haven, Conn.: Yale University Press, 1970).

The Meaning of Gross National Product

There are many ways of measuring the nation's general level of economic activity. However, the measure which is most often used in developing government policies and most often cited in newspapers and television news programs is called the *Gross National Product.*

Gross National Product (or just GNP) is the current market value of all final goods and services produced in the economy.

Normally, Gross National Product figures are given for the full calendar year, but data are also compiled for each "quarter" or three-month period. In Table 23 · 1, we give the Gross National Product figure for 1976 along with figures on the different amounts of goods and services produced and purchased by consumers, investors, and the government. The table shows that during 1976 the United States economy produced $1692.4 billion (or nearly $1.7 trillion) worth of goods and services. Of this total, over $1078 billion of the goods and services were purchased by consumers; this amount is called "personal consumption expenditures." Over $241 billion of the GNP figure was purchased by businesses in the form of plant and equipment and additions to inventories and by households in the form of new houses. This is "gross private domestic investment." The table also shows that in 1976 government at all levels (federal, state, and local) bought a little over $365 billion of the nation's total production of goods and services. In addition, the table shows that we exported goods worth $6.9 billion *more* than we imported. This is the "net exports of goods and services."[3]

TABLE 23 · 1 GROSS NATIONAL PRODUCT FOR 1976

Gross National Product:	$1692.4 billion
Personal consumption expenditures	$1078.6 billion
Gross private domestic investment	$ 241.2 billion
Government purchases of goods and services	$ 365.8 billion
Net exports (exports minus imports)	$ 6.9 billion

NOTE: The principal subdivisions of GNP indicated in the table are further broken down into smaller expenditure categories. For these details, see the source of the table.

SOURCE: *Economic Report of the President,* 1977, p. 187.

When added together, these four major expenditure categories equal Gross National Product. Because the amount the different groups of buyers spend on goods and services equals the amount received by producers, the expenditures of all groups must equal the market value of the goods produced:

$$\text{Dollars spent} = \text{dollars received} = \text{dollar value of output} = \text{GNP}$$

By looking at Figure 23·1, which contains a plotting of GNP figures from 1929 to 1976, we can assess the economic progress of the country over a period of years. We can see, for example, that the Great Depression of the 1930s, as the name implies, was, relatively speaking, a significant blow to economic activity. Further, we can observe the growth of national production since the Second World War. With further study, economists can attempt to draw cause-and-effect relationships between business and government policies on the one hand and national production (as measured by GNP) on the other.

[3] The GNP statistics record the "net exports of goods and services." The goods imported into the United States are counted in one of the other subdivisions of the table. When the imports are consumer goods like clothing and are ultimately purchased by consumers, they are considered additions to "personal consumption expenditures." However, imports are not a part of the total production of the United States. They are the output of some foreign country and should be subtracted from any statistic which purports to measure economic activity in the United States. On the other hand, exports from the United States are part of the country's total productive activity and should be added to the GNP figures. The Department of Commerce, which compiles the figures, chooses to add to GNP the net amount of exports minus imports. This procedure has the same effect on GNP as adding in the value of United States exports and subtracting United States imports.

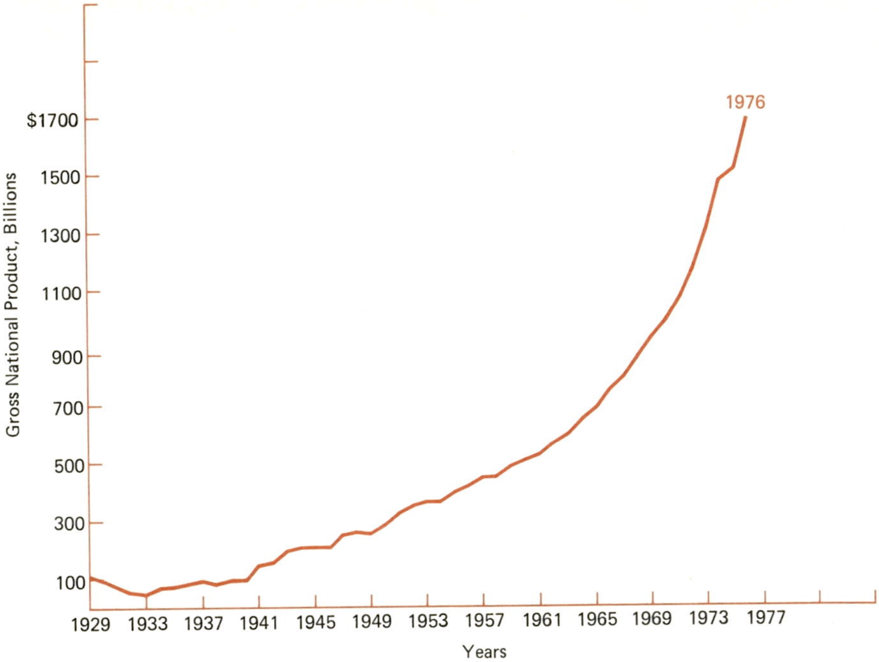

FIG. 23 · 1 Gross National Product has increased significantly over the past four or five decades. However, the upward movement in the growth path has been irregular. (SOURCE: *Economic Report of the President*, 1971 and 1977.)

Certain words in the definition of Gross National Product need to be stressed. First, GNP is often viewed as a measure of that elusive concept called "social welfare"; however, you should be ever mindful that GNP measures the economy's production of goods and services in terms of *current market prices.* To the extent that market prices are defective in indicating the intrinsic worth of various goods and services, GNP, as a measure of social welfare, is also defective.

Second, GNP includes the market values of only *final* goods and services; it does not try to measure the dollar value of *all* transactions in the country. For instance, GNP does not include the value of "intermediate goods." *Intermediate* goods are goods which are used in the production of other goods. If intermediate goods are included in the determination of GNP, the total value of productive activity will be overstated, because intermediate goods will be counted more than once. The value of the intermediate goods will be counted when they are sold to be used in production of other goods and again when the final products of which they are a part are sold.

To illustrate, consider the case of wheat, flour, and bread. Wheat is an intermediate good which is used to make flour; flour is also an intermediate good which is sold to bakers to make bread. If a given quantity of wheat, flour, and bread sell in the market for the amounts indicated below and we add all three market transactions, our measure of economic activity will be $600:

Selling price of the wheat to the miller	$100
Selling price of the flour to the baker	200
Selling price of the bread to the consumer	300
Total of all three transactions	$600

However, in adding these three market transactions, we count the value of the wheat three times, since it is a part of the value of the flour and, consequently, a part of the value of the bread. Because the value of the bread includes the value of the wheat and the flour, the total productive activity in this sector of the economy can be measured by the market value of the *final* product, the bread.

Further, if we compute GNP by adding the market values of all transactions, GNP will change not only with actual changes in production but also with changes in the structures of industries. For example, initially, as we discussed in our illustration, wheat farming, milling, and baking are three separate businesses. If we add the total value of the three transactions, our measure of economic activity will be $600. However, if these three businesses decide to consolidate into one firm, the intermediate market transactions are eliminated. The farmer and miller merely ship their products to another department within the single firm and no market value is attached to what they do. As the result of a change in the organization of this business, our measure of economic activity will fall from $600 to $300, which is the value of the bread sold to consumers.

Deficiencies of Gross National Product

Gross National Product is probably the best measure we have of the overall productive activity of the United States economy; however, the figure that is provided is not, by any means, a perfect measure. The purpose of this section is to briefly describe the deficiencies and limitations of GNP as an economic indicator (or measure of economic activity).

Nonmarket production Aside from a couple of exceptions, Gross National Product includes only a dollar evaluation of the goods and services which are bought and sold in the market.[4] It does not include an evaluation of the productive activity in which people engage in their homes for themselves, their family, and their friends. For instance, GNP includes the price paid for the meat, potatoes, and lettuce which people use in the preparation of their dinners. However, it does not measure the productive activity of the family members who prepare the meal. On the other hand, it does include the full purchase price of meals eaten at restaurants. Similarly, GNP does not encompass the value of the lawn upkeep and home repair services which we provide for ourselves.

Two reasons are given for the exclusion of nonmarket productive activity. First, it is very difficult to put a value on the services we provide for ourselves, since the quality of those services varies so greatly from person to person. Since estimates of the value of such services have to be very rough, they are just excluded. Second, it is difficult to draw the line between which nonmarket activities should be included and which should not. What forms of housework do we include? Do we include washing the dishes, taking out the garbage, and washing clothes? Should we include brushing our teeth, since such services when performed by a dentist are included?

Because nonmarket productive activity is excluded, GNP figures taken over a period of time can give a distorted view of changes in people's welfare. For example, during the Great Depression, the GNP fell from a high of $103.1 billion in 1929 to a low of $55.6 billion in 1933. People on the average were much worse off in 1933 than they were in 1929. However, total production, when one includes both market and nonmarket activity, did not fall by as much as GNP indicated for two reasons. First, prices of goods fell significantly.[5] In addition, people who were unemployed were able to do more things to maintain their households for themselves. More people grew bigger gardens and did more of their own repair work around the house than they did before the downturn in economic activity. This increase in home-related productive activity was not included

[4] The Commerce Department assigns a value to the farm products which farmers grow and consume themselves. It also imputes a value for the rental value of homes which are occupied by owners. Both of these imputations are added to personal consumption expenditures.

[5] We will say more about the problem of prices below.

in the GNP figures. This does not mean that people were able to compensate fully for their reduced money incomes; it means only that they were able to partially offset the adverse effects of the depression of the 1930s.

Leisure time GNP includes the production of goods and services; it does not include the value which we place on our leisure time. In this century the length of the workweek (the average number of hours worked by each laborer per week) has gradually decreased from about 60 hours per week at the turn of the century to about 36 hours per week in 1976. This means that workers have more hours of leisure time. It also means that if people still worked "on the job" the same number of hours per week that they once did, the total value of the country's production would be much greater than it is under present circumstances.

Production of "bads" The economy produces "goods" which people want, and the value of these goods and services are included in our calculation of Gross National Product. However, in the process of producing goods and services, the economy also produces "bads," things which people would rather not have and which detract from the quality of life. In the process of producing steel, for example, the environment around steel mills is often polluted. Modern industrial societies are also burdened with the problems of solid waste disposal. The "negative value" of these "bads," however, is not subtracted from Gross National Product. Indeed, if a water pollution problem is created in the process of the production of a good and people take measures to clean up the water, the cleanup, because it involves the production and purchase of pollution control and cleanup equipment, can increase the value of the Gross National Product.

Prices of goods and services Gross National Product figures of different years are computed in terms of prices of each year. If prices go up over time, the GNP will reflect those price increases. GNP figures for different years, measured in current-dollar terms, will exaggerate the actual change in the total production of goods and services.

To illustrate the problem with changing prices, consider Table 23·2. Column 1 of the table presents the current-dollar value of GNP for selected years between 1929 and 1976. Seeing the substantial difference between GNP in 1929 and 1976, one may conclude that production in the United States in 1976 was almost 17 times the production level of the economy in 1929. One may also conclude that output fell by 50 percent between 1929 and 1933 and that output rose by more than 70 percent in the 6 years between 1970 and 1976. However, much of what is perceived as changes in production reflects changes in the prices of goods and services. Although prices fell significantly between 1929 and 1933, prices have historically risen. In the first half of the 1970s, prices of most goods and services increased at rates that were much greater than the rates in any other period since World War II.

To eliminate the distorting influence of price changes, the Department of Commerce "adjusts" GNP measured in current-dollar terms by dividing the GNP figure of each year by a price index, called the *GNP Deflator*. This price index is a measure of the prices in one year relative to the prices of another year. For example, if prices in 1976 were 25 percent greater than they were in 1972 and 1972 is the "base year," meaning that its prices are used as the standard of comparison and its index value is, therefore, 1.00, the price index for 1976 will be 1.25. Again, this index figure is intended to indicate that prices in 1976 were 125 percent of what they were in the base year, 1972. To adjust for this price increase, the GNP figure for 1976 measured in the prices of that year (as recorded in column 1 of Table 23·2) is divided by 1.25. If this type of adjustment is made for all other years, the production in all years is measured in terms of the prices of the base year; this is given in column 2 of Table 23·2. Any change in the adjusted or *constant-dollar GNP,* as it is called, then reflects changes in production, not changes in prices. The GNP figures in columns 1 and 2 in Table 23·2 are computed as in Table 23 · 3. The Ps and Qs represent sets of prices and

TABLE 23·2 GROSS NATIONAL PRODUCT: 1929–1976

Year	GNP Measured in Current Dollars (billions) (1)	GNP Measured in Constant 1972 Dollars (billions) (2)	Population of U.S. (millions) (3)	Per Capita GNP Measured in Constant 1972 Dollars [(2) ÷ (3)] (4)
1929	$ 103.4	$ 314.7	121.7	$2586
1933	55.8	222.1	125.6	1768
1940	100.0	343.6	132.1	2601
1950	286.2	533.5	152.3	3503
1960	506.0	736.8	180.7	4077
1970	982.4	1075.3	204.9	5248
1972	1171.1	1171.1	208.8	5609
1973	1306.6	1235.0	210.4	5870
1974	1413.2	1214.0	211.9	5729
1975	1516.3	1191.7	213.5	5582
1976	1692.4	1265.0	215.1	5881

SOURCE: *Economic Report of the President*, 1977, pp. 187, 188, and 217.

quantities of the different goods and services, respectively. The subscript indicates the year.

Notice that the computed values of GNP in column 1 vary with *both changes in price and changes in quantity*. If prices are held *constant* with the use of P_{72} for all years, as in column 2, the computed value of GNP in constant-dollar terms varies *only with changes in the quantity* of goods and services produced, not with price. Because prices in 1972 were higher than in previous years, the constant-dollar GNP figures before 1972 increase over what they are in column 1. Since prices in 1976 were higher than in 1972, the constant-dollar GNP figure for 1976 is lower than its current dollar value.

TABLE 23·3 METHOD OF COMPUTING CURRENT-DOLLAR AND CONSTANT-DOLLAR GNP

Year	GNP Measured in Current Prices (1)	GNP Measured in Constant 1972 Prices (2)
1929	$P_{29} \times Q_{29}$	$P_{72} \times Q_{29}$
1933	$P_{33} \times Q_{33}$	$P_{72} \times Q_{33}$
1940	$P_{40} \times Q_{40}$	$P_{72} \times Q_{40}$
1950	$P_{50} \times Q_{50}$	$P_{72} \times Q_{50}$
1960	$P_{60} \times Q_{60}$	$P_{72} \times Q_{60}$
1970	$P_{70} \times Q_{70}$	$P_{72} \times Q_{70}$
1972	$P_{72} \times Q_{72}$	$P_{72} \times Q_{72}$
1973	$P_{73} \times Q_{73}$	$P_{72} \times Q_{73}$
1974	$P_{74} \times Q_{74}$	$P_{72} \times Q_{74}$
1975	$P_{75} \times Q_{75}$	$P_{72} \times Q_{75}$
1976	$P_{76} \times Q_{76}$	$P_{72} \times Q_{76}$

NOTE: P = price; Q = quantity.

The *absolute* value of the figures in column 2 of Table 23·2 is meaningless. What is important is the *relative* value of these figures. These constant-dollar figures show that production in the United States was indeed greater in 1976 than in 1929. The comparison of the constant-dollar figures reveals that the 1976 output level was slightly more than four times the output level of 1929. In addition, column 2 reveals that between 1929 and 1933 total production of goods and services fell by approximately 30 percent and that between 1970 and 1976 output grew in the United States but only by 17.6 percent. The table shows that output fell by 3.5 percent between 1973 and

1975, indicating the worst recession (or downturn in economic activity) in the United States since World War II.

Population growth Gross National Product, measured in constant dollars, can grow over time, but still, on average, people may not be markedly better off. This is because the population of the country can grow, partially or totally, offsetting the growth in GNP. To determine what is happening to the level of production per person or "per capita," the GNP figures measured in constant 1972-dollar terms must be divided by the nation's population of each year. This procedure gives us the per capita GNP figures in column 4 of Table 23 · 2. The figures in this column reveal that, on a per capita basis, the production of goods and services in the United States increased by 2.3 times between 1929 and 1976. GNP on a total basis quadrupled.

Quality of goods and services GNP provides an estimate of the market value of goods and services, but over a period of time prices will not necessarily reflect changes in the quality of goods.[6] For instance, the price of a good like the hand calculator may go down while the quality of the good goes up. On the other hand, the price increase of a good or service may not fully represent the quality improvements. Further, a nation's production can shift from consumer goods in peacetime to war equipment in times of war. In the sense that war goods can be used to restrict the aggression of foreign enemies, war goods are productive; however, their production also means that fewer other consumer goods will be produced. GNP may, therefore, remain constant or even go up in time of war,[7] but this does not mean that people on the average are as well or better off than they once were. Some people may be better off because they find that the demand for war materials has increased the demand for and price of their professional services; many others who pay higher taxes to finance the war will be worse off.

[6] Prices reflect only the relative *marginal* values of goods (or the values of the last units consumed). They do not indicate the value of *inframarginal* units of a good (or all the units consumed up to the last one).

[7] Production did go up in the United States during World War II and the Vietnam war.

Other Measures of General Economic Activity

Gross National Product includes the current value of all goods and services produced in the economy which are defined to be "final." This means that GNP includes capital goods (plant and equipment) which are purchased by businesses to *replace* plant and equipment that have been worn out. Because some plants and pieces of equipment wear out (or depreciate) each year, GNP overstates the actual increase in total goods and services which are available for, say, consumption and production of other goods. To more accurately represent the "net" increase in the goods available for consumption and production during a given year, the Department of Commerce subtracts the value of worn-out plant and equipment (called *capital consumption* or *depreciation allowance*) from the Gross National Product figure. This adjusted measure is appropriately called *Net National Product* (NNP).

GNP − capital consumption allowance = NNP

Because the depreciation allowance has been subtracted out, Net National Product includes the current market value of all final goods which are produced in the economy and are either used by consumers and governments or are added to the total capital stock of businesses. The value of Net National Product for selected years is recorded in Table 23 · 4. Net National Product is usually equal to between 91 and 92 percent of Gross National Product, and it rises and falls in relation to it. Therefore, Gross National Product and Net National Product figures are equally good measures for indicating the *changes* in production over time.

When people produce goods and services, they generate income. This is so because what they call *income* is really a measure of their contribution to the production of goods and services. Since production must be ultimately attributed to

TABLE 23·4 GROSS NATIONAL PRODUCT, NET NATIONAL PRODUCT, AND DISPOSABLE INCOME MEASURED IN CURRENT DOLLARS: 1929–1976

Year	Gross National Product (billions) (1)	Net National Product (billions) (2)	Disposable Personal Income (billions) (3)	Per Capita Disposable Personal Income (4)
1929	$ 103.4	$ 93.7	$ 82.3	$ 676
1933	55.8	48.3	45.5	362
1940	100.0	91.0	75.2	569
1950	286.2	262.3	205.5	1349
1960	506.0	458.3	349.4	1933
1970	982.4	891.6	685.9	3347
1976	1692.4	1512.7	1181.8	5494

SOURCE: *Economic Report of the President*, 1977.

someone (like laborers, managers, or owners of capital assets), all people's contribution to production must add to the value of the goods they produced. For instance, if $100 worth of goods is produced, the people who produce the goods must earn $100 in income. The $100 worth of output must be attributable to someone. For this reason, economists equate the value of production with income. However, people do not receive all that they earn; they do not take home in pay the total value of their incomes. This is so primarily because taxes are deducted directly and indirectly from their incomes. What people take home and can use in the purchase of goods and services is what economists refer to as *disposable income*. People's disposable income represents what they have after taxes to spend, and this measure of economic activity is, perhaps, the best measure of what we think of as people's welfare. Figures on disposable income on a total and a per capita basis are also included in columns 3 and 4 of Table 23·4. This table shows that in 1976 people had a disposable income of $1182 billion, which equals approximately 70 percent of the Gross National Product for that year. In 1929, disposable income represented approximately 80 percent of GNP. The primary differences between 1929 and 1974 are that taxes were higher in 1976 than in 1929 and many more people in 1976 got a part or all of their disposable income from government "transfer payments" (like social security and welfare or government unemployment). The disposable income figures included in Table 23·4 must be adjusted for price changes and population growth before they can accurately reflect changes in consumer purchasing power. (More details are given on the way disposable income and other aggregate income measures are derived in the appendix to this chapter.)

THE UNEMPLOYMENT RATE

In general terms, the unemployment rate is a measure of the percent of the nation's labor force out of work. The data are compiled monthly by the Bureau of Labor Statistics, and Table 23·5 gives the average monthly unemployment rate for selected years from 1950 to 1976. It shows, for example, that the unemployment rate was 5.3 percent in 1950. Two decades later the average monthly unemployment rate was 4.9 percent; however, by 1975 the rate had risen to 8.5 percent; and in 1976, it was down to 7.7 percent.

TABLE 23 · 5 NUMBER OF PEOPLE EMPLOYED AND UNEMPLOYED, AND THE UNEMPLOYMENT RATE: 1950 TO 1976

Year	Number of People Counted as "Employed" (millions) (1)	Number of People Counted as Unemployed (millions) (2)	Civilian Labor Force (millions) [(1) + (2)] (3)	Unemployment Rate (percent) [(2) ÷ (3)] (4)
1950	58.9	3.3	62.2	5.3
1955	62.2	2.9	65.0	4.4
1960	65.8	3.9	69.6	5.5
1965	71.1	3.4	74.4	4.5
1970	78.6	4.1	82.7	4.9
1975	84.8	7.8	92.6	8.5
1976	87.5	7.3	94.8	7.7

SOURCE: *Economic Report of the President,* 1977, pp. 218 and 220.

Evaluating Unemployment Statistics

Like Gross National Product figures, the unemployment rate is used by the press, the public, politicians, and government officials as an indicator of present economic activity and the degree to which established public policy goals are being achieved. An increase in the unemployment rate is construed by almost everyone as a sign of worsening economic activity and of the increasing hardship which a segment of the population, those who are unemployed, is having to bear because of the general state of the economy. An increase in the measured unemployment rate can not only mean that more people are out of work, but can possibly induce some businesses to curtail their production plans, causing more workers to be laid off in anticipation of lower consumer incomes and reduced consumer demand for goods and services. An increase in the rate also can be a major political advantage for opposition candidates in election years. For example, in his election campaign President Carter scored "political points" with the unemployed, unions, and many worker groups by stressing the "high" unemployment rates which, by historical standards, existed in 1976 and by stressing the apparent failure of the Ford administration to bring the unemployment rate down to a "reasonable level." Very likely, the unusually high unemployment rate at the time was a key factor in Carter's narrow election victory.

In evaluating the state of the economy or in assessing the political positions of political candidates by way of the unemployment rate, we should reflect on what Humpty Dumpty said to Alice in Lewis Carroll's *Through the Looking Glass,* "When I use a word, it means just what I choose it to mean—neither more nor less."[8] Similarly, the unemployment rate should be interpreted in the light of what the Bureau of Labor Statistics chooses it to mean. The unemployment rate is computed from very precise definitions of "employed" and "unemployed" persons, and to understand the meaning of the rate, we must know these definitions.

Stated rigorously,

The unemployment rate is the ratio of the number of people estimated to be unemployed to the number of people estimated to be in the Civilian Labor Force,

or

[8] Lewis Carroll, *Through the Looking Glass.*

$$\text{Unemployment rate} = \frac{\text{number unemployed}}{\text{Civilian Labor Force}}$$

The Civilian Labor Force consists of all nonmilitary persons who are counted as unemployed or employed,[9] or

$$\text{Civilian Labor Force} = \text{number unemployed} + \text{number employed}$$

The unemployment rate can therefore be rewritten as

$$\text{Unemployment rate} = \frac{\text{number unemployed}}{\text{number unemployed} + \text{number employed}}$$

The definitions of employed and unemployed persons are given below. Basically, the only people who can be counted as "employed" or "unemployed" are those who are 16 years of age and older and who are not a part of the "institutional population" of the country, that is, who are not inmates of penal and mental institutions and homes for the aged, infirm, and needy. According to the Bureau of Labor Statistics, "Persons under 16 years of age are excluded from coverage in the survey [on which the unemployment rate is based] because child labor laws, compulsory school attendance, and general social customs prevent most of these children in the United States from working."[10]

Employed Persons

Subject to the restrictions indicated above, employed persons include:

1 All persons who, during the week that the survey is taken, did any work at all for pay or who worked at least 15 hours for no pay in a family-operated business.

2 All persons who were not working during the survey week, but who had jobs or businesses from which they were temporarily absent because of illness, bad weather, vacation, strikes, or a number of personal reasons.

Those persons who work in or around their homes doing things for themselves or who work for charitable or religious organizations are specifically excluded from employed or unemployed categories and, therefore, from the Civilian Labor Force.

Unemployed Persons

Unemployed persons include:

1 All persons who did not work at all during the survey week but who were looking for work and who were available for work

2 All persons who, although they may not have worked or have looked for work during the survey week, made an effort to find work, such as to fill out an application, in the past four weeks and who were waiting for the results of their efforts

3 All persons (*a*) who were waiting to be called back to a job from which they had been laid off, (*b*) who were waiting to report to a new job within the next 30 days, or (*c*) who would have been looking for work if they had not been sick

Not in the Labor Force

Classified as "not in the labor force" are all persons who neither are classified as employed or unemployed nor are in the military. This group includes people who are under 16 years of age or who are in school full time, those who are homemakers, those who are unable to work, those who are retired, those who do less than 15 hours of unpaid work for their family business, those who are seasonal workers and who are idle because it is "off season" for them, and those who are scheduled to report to a new job in *more* than 30 days.

Sample Survey

The statistics on the weekly average number of people employed and unemployed from which the

[9] The total labor force is equal to the Civilian Labor Force plus the members of the armed forces of the United States.

[10] Bureau of Labor Statistics, U.S. Department of Labor, *BLS Handbook on Methods for Surveys and Studies*, Bulletin 1711 (Washington: U.S. Government Printing Office, 1971), p. 8.

unemployment rate is computed are included along with the unemployment rate in Table 23·5. The statistics are gathered from a sample survey of approximately 55,000 housing units. These housing units are located in 923 counties and cities scattered throughout the 50 states and the District of Columbia. They include about 105,000 people who are 16 years of age or older. In gathering the data, the Bureau of Labor Statistics relies on people's voluntary cooperation in answering a series of questions which will enable the Bureau to classify them as employed, unemployed, or not a part of the labor force. Each household selected is interviewed for four consecutive months, then dropped for eight months, and then interviewed for four more months.

The households surveyed are a representative sample of all households in the country. From the sample data, the Bureau is then able to estimate the number of people employed and unemployed in the country. These are the figures given in Table 23·5.

The Deficiencies of Unemployment Statistics

Like any survey, the employment and unemployment data rely on the professionalism of the survey workers to administer the surveys properly and on the integrity of the interviewees to respond correctly. To the extent that survey workers may not follow the established procedures—that is, they ask their questions in different ways and put different emphasis on different questions—or the procedures are changed, the results of the survey can be distorted, and the distortion can vary from month to month, changing the unemployment rate. Further, to the extent that those who are interviewed feel reluctant to reveal their true employment status, the results of the survey will be distorted and will not reveal the true employment-unemployment picture of the country. In short, small changes in month-to-month unemployment rates may indeed mirror the changes in people's employment opportunities, but they may also mirror errors and institutional changes which artificially change the number of people who are counted as unemployed.

Can the unemployment rate be reduced to zero? Given the way the statistics are gathered, the answer is no. As we have already suggested, in our present society and economy, some people are unemployable because they do not have the skills to be paid the minimum wage rate for even the most menial jobs; there are many others who think that they deserve a higher-paying job than those that are offered and who continue to search for the jobs they want. Also, there are people who are unemployed and who should not be counted as a part of the labor force according to BLS definitions but who are unwilling to admit to the survey workers that they have stopped looking for a job. If they admit that they have given up looking for work, they may suffer a loss of self-respect and/or perceive that their unemployment payments will be terminated.

Consider this example of how a change in the law can affect the computed unemployment rate. In the early 1960s people who were not working but who received government assistance from such programs as Aid to Families with Dependent Children and Food Stamps were not required to look for work and were not counted as unemployed unless they were actively looking for work on a voluntary basis. In the late 1960s, the law was changed and families who received such government aid were required to register and look for work and accept job training unless it was impossible for them to do so. Furthermore, the definition of the unemployed was changed to include those people who had registered for work and training under several government programs. According to Kenneth Clarkson and Roger Miners, this meant that more than 2 million people were counted as unemployed in 1976 that would not have been counted 10 years earlier.[11] They also argue that 90 percent or more of these people were "unemployable," meaning that they did not

[11] Kenneth W. Clarkson and Roger E. Miners, *Inflated Unemployment Statistics: The Effects of Welfare Work Registration Requirements* (Coral Gables, Fla.: Law and Economics Center, University of Miami School of Law, 1977).

have the skills necessary to be profitably hired at prevailing wage rates. Clarkson and Miners conclude that although the "official unemployment rate" was 7.7 percent for the first nine months of 1976, the "corrected rate," computed after taking out the people who were forced to register for work but were unemployable, was 5.3 percent, which was not very far removed from the average unemployment rate for the previous 20 years. The authors of the study contend that the change in the "rules of the game" explains the peculiar situation in 1976 which showed a high unemployment rate in a period in which a relatively high percentage of the working-age population (56 percent) had jobs.

Finally, in a dynamic economy there will always be people who are in the process of changing jobs. Among these people there will be some who are caught in the survey who expect to report to a "new job within 30 days." These people will be classified as "unemployed." One of the authors, McKenzie, was a part of the sample survey in the period July–October of 1966. He had just finished his master's degree at the University of Maryland in July and had a contract to start teaching at a college in Virginia on September 1, 1966. When he was interviewed in July, he was not looking for work and did not want to work. Accordingly, he was classified as "not a part of the labor force." In August, however, even though he still was not looking for work and did not want to work, he was scheduled to report to work within 30 days. Using the definitions of the Bureau of Labor Statistics, in August he was counted as part of the Civilian Labor Force and as unemployed. In September, he was counted as employed.

For these reasons, almost all economists agree that the unemployment rate, as it is presently defined, cannot be reduced below 3 percent. Many argue that the rate cannot realistically be pushed below 4 percent, and others contend that unless institutional changes are made, like the elimination of the minimum wage law and union barriers to entry into various unionized labor markets, the unemployment rate will not fall very much below 5 percent for a long period of time.

The unemployment statistics are also deficient in that they fail to clearly indicate the hardship which a significant number of people have to bear. Anyone who has worked for any amount of time for pay during the survey week is counted as employed. This means that even people who have worked for only 5 or 10 hours and who want to work more are counted in the same category as persons who worked for 40 hours during the survey week. If the automobile industry, for example, cuts production by reducing the number of days and hours which each employee can work, the unemployment rate is unaffected. In short, the unemployment rate alone does not reveal the percentage of people who are "underemployed."

INFLATION AND PRICE INDEXES

By definition,

inflation is the general rise in the level of prices over a period of time

Inflation must be distinguished from a rise in the price of one particular good or in the prices of a small group of goods. The rise in the price of one particular product, like bread, can occur at the same time that the price of some other product, like meat, falls. In this event, the price *level* of all goods has not necessarily risen, although there has been a change in the relative prices of goods. Inflation occurs when the rise in the prices of many goods and services is not offset by decreases in the prices of other goods. In other words, it occurs when the *price level, meaning the weighted average of all prices, rises.*

The Bureau of Labor Statistics computes changes in the rate of inflation (that is, the percentage increase in the level of prices) in three principal ways: (1) the Consumer Price Index, (2) the Wholesale Price Index, and (3) the GNP Deflator. Because these price indices are developed for different sets of products and for different purposes, we discuss each separately.

Consumer Price Index

The Consumer Price Index is the most often cited measure of price increases or price decreases (rare occurrences in recent decades) of the things consumers buy and, for this reason, it is frequently referred to as the *Cost of Living Index.* Table 23·6 gives the figures for the Consumer Price Index (CPI) for selected years from 1929 to 1976. You should note that the Consumer Price Index does not, however, represent the cost of living for everyone. The index is designed only to represent the price increases of a specified collection of goods which tend to be bought in significant quantities by urban wage earners and clerical workers.[12] The index is based on family budget studies of people who work in cities, such as craftsmen, factory supervisors, carpenters, and salespeople. The index is, therefore, not necessarily representative of the cost of living of professional or technical workers who work in cities or of any people who live and work in rural areas. On the other hand, the index does provide a reasonably accurate picture of the price changes of the approximately 400 items included in the so-called "market basket." This market basket includes most items which urban wage earners and clerical workers buy, such as food, clothing, automobiles, homes, house furnishings, household supplies, fuel, drugs, and recreational goods; fees to doctors, lawyers, and beauty shops; rent, repair costs, transportation fares, public utility rates, and taxes associated with the purchase of a good and its continued ownership.

[12] The official name of the index is the Consumer Price Index for Urban Wage Earners and Clerical Workers.

TABLE 23·6 CONSUMER PRICE INDEX AND WHOLESALE PRICE INDEX: 1929 TO 1976

Year	Consumer Price Index (1)	Wholesale Price Index (2)
1929	51.3	49.1
1938	38.8	34.0
1940	42.0	40.5
1950	72.1	81.8
1960	88.7	94.9
1967	100.0	100.0
1970	116.3	110.4
1974	147.7	160.1
1975	161.2	174.9
1976 (November)	173.8	185.6

SOURCE: *Economic Report of the President,* 1977, pp. 241 and 247.

The necessary data on prices are obtained principally by survey workers in 56 areas of the country who visit each month nearly 18,000 stores and service establishments where urban wage earners and clerical workers tend to shop. Using very detailed specifications for the products in the "market basket," the survey workers record the prices of the products and services which, when weighted by their importance in people's purchases, go into the establishment of the "cost of the market basket."

The Consumer Price Index is simply the ratio of the cost of the market basket in any year to the cost of the market basket in the base year.

If, for example, the base year is 1967, the Consumer Price Index for 1978 will be equal to

$$\text{Consumer Price Index} = \frac{\text{cost of market basket in 1978}}{\text{cost of market basket in 1967}} \times 100$$

The index figures in Table 23·6 were obtained by dividing the cost of the market baskets of each of the represented years by the cost of the market basket in 1967 and multiplying that quotient by 100. The index for 1967 is, of course, equal to 100, since it is equal to the cost of the market basket for that year divided by the cost of the same basket of goods, which is 1 multiplied by 100. Because prices were lower in years prior to 1967, the indices for those years are less than 100. Because prices have been higher in years since 1967, the indices for all years since 1967 are greater than 100. From the table we can see that the cost of the market basket (or the *cost of living*, as it is called) increased by 73.8 percent from the end of 1967 to November 1976. Prices fell by around 25 percent between 1929 and 1933 (a fall which, as we said earlier, is reflected in the values of the current-dollar GNP), and they rose by about 49 percent between 1970 and 1976.[13] The rate of price increase between 1975 and 1976, as indicated by the Consumer Price Index, was a little less than 8 percent.

Wholesale Price Index

The Wholesale Price Index is a measure of the price changes of more than 2500 commodities which are sold in large quantities in *nonretail* markets, that is, what are called "primary" or "wholesale" markets. Among those commodities are included eggs, live poultry, cotton products, hides, coal, electric power, rubber and rubber products, lumber, plumbing fixtures, and electrical machinery. The index figures which are given in column 2 of Table 23·6 are obtained by dividing the (weighted) cost of the wholesale commodities in each year by the (weighted) cost of the wholesale commodities of the base year, which happens to be 1967, and by multiplying the quotient by 100. Again, the wholesale price index for 1978 is

$$\text{Wholesale Price Index} = \frac{\text{cost of commodities in 1978}}{\text{cost of commodities in 1967}} \times 100$$

The table reveals that the prices of wholesale commodities rose by 74.9 percent between 1967 and 1975. They rose by 58 percent between 1970 and 1975 and by 9 percent, as was the case for consumer prices, between 1974 and 1975.

[13] To compute the percentage increase in prices between any two years, simply divide the index of the later year by the index of the earlier year. To obtain the 49 percent increase in prices between 1970 and 1976, we divided the index for 1976, which is 173.8, by the index of 1970, which is 116.3:

$$\frac{173.8}{116.3} = 1.49$$

GNP Deflator

The GNP Deflator, although infrequently cited, is another price index which is broader in the goods and services it covers than either the Consumer Price Index or the Wholesale Price Index. It includes both retail and wholesale commodities. It is this index that is used to adjust (or "deflate") current-dollar GNP for price changes. When current-dollar GNP figures are divided by the GNP deflator, the result is constant-dollar GNP measured in terms of the prices of the base year used for the index.

SUMMARY AND EXTENSIONS

The Gross National Product, the unemployment rate, and the Consumer and Wholesale Price Indexes are measures of the economic performance of the United States economy in terms of national production, the percent of the work force without jobs, and the level and rate of price increases. However, this chapter has attempted to indicate that these measures will always be rough approximations of the variables which are being measured. The methods used for determining Gross National Product dictate that much productive activity in the economy will remain unmeasured; we simply do not have a reasonable means of putting a monetary value on the goods and services which we produce for ourselves. Because of their cost, surveys of the employment status of people and of prices of goods and services cannot be all-inclusive. The Bureau of Labor

Statistics cannot bear the cost of interviewing every potential worker in the United States every month, and we cannot hope to record monthly the prices of the millions of goods and services which are produced in the economy. Nor is this necessary. The Bureau has settled on sample surveys; and it has very precise means of categorizing people's employment position and of recording the prices of goods that are included in the sample. Precise definitions are necessary; otherwise, no one will know what is being measured.

As rough as they are, statistics like those we have discussed can influence the performance of the economy. As we have mentioned, changes in the flows to businesses of information concerning the economy can alter the decisions which businesses make with regard to future production plans. The dissemination of the data can arouse the emotions of the public. If the statistics "look bad," politicians may feel compelled "to do something," to demonstrate their concern for economic conditions even though their response may be inadequately planned, ill-timed, and, perhaps, unwarranted. Unless we understand the meaning of the statistics—their sample base, limitations, and deficiencies—the figures reported in the press can become our masters, as Humpty Dumpty suggests. People who are unaware of how an *unemployed person* is defined by the Bureau of Labor Statistics may fail to understand why the government does not try to reduce the unemployment rate to zero. They may continue to expect more of government than government can possibly deliver.

On the other hand, measures of macroeconomic activity have been designed to provide the government with a statistical base for making policy decisions. The purpose of the next several chapters is to explain how government monetary, tax, and expenditure policies influence the overall performance of the economy.

QUESTIONS TO PONDER

1 Are the absolute current-dollar GNP figures meaningful?

2 Using the definitions of *employed, unemployed,* and *not a member of the labor force,* classify each of the following:

- **a** A person who works 20 hours a week for no pay in a family-owned drugstore
- **b** A person who works 10 hours a week for a charitable organization
- **c** A person who works 6 hours a week for pay
- **d** A person who is out on strike
- **e** A person in the steel industry who has been laid off because of a strike in the automobile industry
- **f** A person who expects to report back to work within 10 days
- **g** A person who is not working but who expects to report to a new job within 60 days
- **h** A person who is not working but who expects to report to a new job within 15 days
- **i** A full-time college student
- **j** A person out of work because he is sick
- **k** A person 15 years old who works 30 hours a week for pay

I A person 17 years old who works 14 hours a week on his family's farm

3 Using the data in question 2, determine the unemployment rate.

4 Since the Consumer Price Index is computed for the purchases of urban wage earners and clerical workers, what is the value of the index for the teacher who works in a rural area?

5 Do small month-to-month changes in the unemployment rate and Consumer and Wholesale Price Indexes mean very much? Why? How may the party represented in the presidency interpret those changes? How may the opposition party interpret them?

6 Do people have sufficient incentive to learn about the limitations and deficiencies of economic statistics? Given your answer, how may the statistics be used by politicians?

RECOMMENDED READINGS

For more details on the procedures used in computing the unemployment rate, the Consumer and Wholesale Price Indexes, and other measures of economic activity, see:

Handbook of Methods, bulletin 1711 (Washington: U.S. Government Printing Office, 1971).

For the most current data on GNP, the unemployment rate, and the price indices, as well as more details on these data and other measures of economic activity, consult one of the following excellent sources:

Survey of Current Business (published monthly)
Federal Reserve Bulletin (published monthly)
Economic Report of the President (published annually in February)

APPENDIX: RELATIONSHIP OF GROSS NATIONAL PRODUCT AND FOUR MEASURES OF ECONOMIC ACTIVITY

Gross National Product is the current market value of all final goods and services produced in the economy. The market value of final goods and services is equal to the total number of dollars paid for those goods by consumers, businesses, and governments. In this appendix we consider other frequently cited measures of overall economic activity. They are (1) Net National Product, (2) National Income, (3) Personal Income, and (4) Disposable Income.

Net National Product

In Table 23A·1 we have recorded the Gross National Product figure for 1976 and have shown the way in which Net National Product is computed. As we have indicated in this chapter, Net National Product is Gross National Product minus "capital consumption allowance" (that is, the depreciation of plant and equipment). Net National Product, however, is not directly equal to the payments actually received by people. To obtain some better indication of how much people have to spend and, therefore, how much of the Gross National Product people can buy, several adjustments—subtractions and additions—must be made to Net National Product.

National Income

A measure of economic activity cited less frequently than GNP is *National Income.*

National Income is the total cost of the goods and services which are included in Net National Product. It is, therefore, total payments made to owners of productive resources, like laborers and owners of land and capital, for the use of those resources.

Indirect business taxes, like federal excise taxes on liquor and local property taxes, are paid to

TABLE 23A·1 RELATION OF GROSS NATIONAL PRODUCT, NET NATIONAL PRODUCT, NATIONAL INCOME, PERSONAL INCOME, AND DISPOSABLE INCOME, 1976* *(in billions)*

Gross National Product			$1692.4
Less:	Capital consumption allowances	$ 179.8	
Equals:	Net National Product		1512.7
Less:	Indirect business taxes	149.7	
	Business transfers	7.1	
	Statistical discrepancy	7.6	
Plus:	Subsidies less current surplus of government enterprises	1.2	
Equals:	National Income		1349.4
Less:	Corporate profits	118.7	
	Net interest	82.1	
	Contributions for social insurance	122.8	
Plus:	Government transfers to persons	184.2	
	Personal interest income	123.1	
	Dividends	35.1	
	Business transfer payments	7.1	
Equals:	Personal Income		1375.4
Less:	Personal tax payments	193.6	
Equals:	Disposable Income		1181.8
	Personal outlays	1104.0	
	Personal saving	77.8	

SOURCE: *Economic Report of the President*, 1977, pp. 206, 207, and 212.

governments and, although they are included in the calculation of Net National Product, are not considered to be a payment to a resource owner. Therefore, indirect business taxes are deducted from Net National Product in Table 23A·1 to obtain National Income. (As can be seen in the table, a couple of other minor adjustments are made.)

Personal Income

Personal Income is that part of gross national income which is paid to individuals as opposed to businesses.

To obtain Personal Income, deduct from National Income corporate profits and interest payments which do not go directly to individuals and social security taxes. Then add to National Income the interest income, government transfers, corporate dividend payments, and business transfer payments received by individuals. Personal Income is the figure which emerges. The arbitrary nature of the accounting system is clearly revealed in the way in which Personal Income is computed. Social security taxes are deducted from National Income to obtain Personal Income. However, personal income taxes are not deducted. No good reason has been presented for including one form of taxation and omitting another form.

Disposable Income

Disposable Income is Personal Income minus personal income tax payments.

It is the best measure of the total amount of money which people have to spend (or "dispose of") as they see fit. In 1976 Disposable Income equaled about 70 percent of Gross National Product, or about 80 percent of Net National Product. Of the nearly $1.2 trillion in Disposable Income people had in 1976, $1104 billion was spent by consumers. About $78 billion (or 7 percent of Disposable Income) was saved.

24

The Meaning and Creation of Money

For one thing, money is a contract—the freest, most gorgeous contract of them all. Money is somebody else's promise to pay, to give me what I want, when I want it. What a magnificent conception! . . . Whatever else history may ultimately record of the Western bourgeoisie, this honor most certainly must be accorded them: They perfected modern money, which is a contract with parties unknown for the future delivery of pleasures undecided upon.

David Bazelon[1]

PREVIEW OF CHAPTER

Central question

What is *money* and how is it created?

Major objectives

1 To define money
2 To explain how the *money stock* is measured
3 To explain why money has value
4 To show how money is moved through the banking system when checks are written
5 To explain how money is created through the banking system
6 To show how changes in the *money stock* affect the price level in the country and, consequently, the value of money

[1] David T. Bazelon, *The Paper Economy* (New York: Vintage Books, 1965), p. 73.

Major conclusions

1 Money is a medium of exchange and a store of purchasing power.

2 There are two predominantly cited measures of the United States money stock. They are called M_1 and M_2. M_1 includes currency and *demand deposits.* M_2 includes M_1 plus saving account deposits at commercial banks and "small" certificates of deposits.

3 Money does not have value because of any kind of "gold backing"; rather it has value because of people's confidence in its general acceptability.

4 When a check is written by one person to another, the demand deposit of the person writing the check falls while the demand deposit of the person receiving the check increases. Further, the bank of the person who writes the check loses *reserve deposits;* the bank of the person who receives the deposit gains reserve deposits. The total money stock in the country, however, remains the same.

5 When commercial banks make loans, they create money.

6 The ability of banks to create money is restricted by the *reserve requirement.*

7 Under normal conditions, an increase in the money stock will lead to an increase in the price level.

Important terms and concepts

Money
Medium of exchange
Store of purchasing power
Liquidity
Money stock
M_1
M_2
Reserve deposits
Reserve requirement (or ratio)
Total reserves
Required reserves
Excess reserves
Equation of exchange

Take a dollar bill from your wallet and compare it with a piece of notebook paper. On one side, the dollar bill has, among other things, a picture of George Washington, the signature of the Secretary of the Treasury, the words "The United States of America" written in bold letters, and a lot of fancy engraving. On the back there are the memorable words "annuit cœptis; novus ordo seclorum" surrounding a one-eyed pyramid. On the other hand, the piece of notebook paper has a few holes in it and a number of blue lines on it. Although the notebook paper is more easily torn than the dollar bill, it is several times larger and can be used for writing down class notes.

You may not think your dollar bill is very valuable, but you are likely to be more concerned about losing it than losing a piece of plain paper. Have you ever wondered why the dollar bill has any value at all to you—why, for example, you are willing to buy a wallet to protect it? Have you ever wondered what gives the dollar its value? Do you know how dollar bills are created, or, for that matter, why the dollar bill is considered to be *money* and the piece of notebook paper is not? Have you ever wondered what form the money in your bank account takes or what you are actually giving when you give someone a check? Have you ever wondered how banks can make loans to people at the same time you and other people are drawing out their deposits?

Have you ever wondered what *money* is? If you have ever wondered any of these things, this chapter should be of interest to you. Its purpose is to unravel some of the "mysteries" of money, to describe how money is created and how the creation process is controlled. Although you will find that the subject of money is not as mysterious as it seems, the effects which money has on any national economy are sufficiently mysterious to occupy the time of a great many economists. This is why we treat the subject of money in detail in this and the following chapter.

THE MEANING OF MONEY

Money is a social phenomenon which has developed in different forms in different cultures. In the United States, we think of money in terms of dollars. In Great Britain, money is the pound sterling; in France, it is the franc. At other times and in other places, money has been or is thought to be silver, cigarettes, beads, or seashells. Today, in some parts of Tanzania in Africa, the monetary unit is the cow or bull, and cattle are used in exchange as we use dollar bills.[2] In all its different forms,

money is both a readily acceptable means of making payment (or "medium of exchange") and a financial asset—a form of saving—which represents a store of readily usable purchasing power.

Money can be either traded to obtain the things we want or held until we decide we want to use it in trade. This is the essence of money.

In a barter economy—which uses no money—goods trade for goods and people are paid for their labor with the goods they and others produce. In barter, the buyer must find a seller who not only has the goods the buyer wants but also wants the goods that the buyer has to offer in trade. For instance, the person who has turkeys to sell and wants pigs must find someone who has pigs to sell and wants to buy turkeys. The person who is paid in corn for his work must then trade this corn with people who are paid in terms of the many other goods and services that he or she wants. Needless to say, trade in a barter economy is very complicated, time-consuming, and costly.

When money is used as a medium of exchange, it facilitates trade and contributes to national production. If money is readily accepted by others, people with money need only to find the things they want to buy and then use their money to buy them. Those who receive money in exchange for what they sell can in turn use it to buy the things they want. The cost (time and effort) of searching for trades that will be mutually beneficial is reduced. People are then free to use the time that they would otherwise have used to search for a trading partner in the production of goods and services. In this indirect way, money contributes to national production. If money is for some reason withdrawn from an economy, we expect people will spend much more time consummating trades and less time producing goods, and the country's production will fall. This is what happened in Germany in the years following World War I and World War II. During these two periods, national output fell dramatically, in part because the German currency lost its acceptability among the German people, and rose again only after the government instituted a new currency in the economy.

As a store of purchasing power, money provides its owner with *liquidity*. This means that the owner of money can quickly and inexpensively transform his financial asset, money, into other assets like furniture, a loaf of bread, or even stock in a corporation. In other words, he can trade his money for what he wants. Other financial assets, such as corporate bonds, cannot be as easily converted into other assets. If a person owns a bond and wants a car, typically he must sell the bond for money and use the money he receives to buy the car. The transactions that these steps require can take time and can involve a fee which is paid to the agent or brokerage house that sells the bond. Corporate bonds are assets which are more liquid than a house, which may take several weeks to sell, but they are far less liquid than money. To be a good means of storing purchasing power,

[2] For an interesting discussion of the use of cattle as money in Tanzania, see Thomas R. Ireland and Jack L. Rutner, *Principles of Macroeconomics and Money* (Hinsdale, Ill.: The Dryden Press, 1973), pp. 171–173.

however, money's value—that is, how much it will buy—must be reasonably stable. If prices rise rapidly, the purchasing power of stored money will deteriorate very rapidly and then people will be resistant to holding onto it. They will use the money they have to buy goods and services, like gold, jewels, and stocks, *now* as opposed to later when it will take more dollars to buy them.

THE MONEY STOCK

Aside from dollar bills and coins, which we think of as money, there are several other financial assets that provide their owner with mediums of exchange and stores of purchasing power. Another *liquid* asset (or an asset which can be readily used as purchasing power) is demand deposits, money in your checking account at your bank that is payable on demand or when you write a check. Next in terms of liquid assets are saving account deposits and "certificates of deposit," which are similar to government saving bonds but which are issued by banks. With these varied forms of purchasing power, how do we measure the amount of money that is in the economy at any point in time? What, in other words, constitutes the "money stock"? The answer to that question is not as simple as it may seem, because the issue is still subject to much debate among economists. Different groups of economists define the money stock in different ways, and how one calculates the total amount of money in the economy changes with changes in the definition of the money stock.

However, in spite of the debate, two measures of the money stock are used prominently in economic literature and financial sections of newspapers and magazines.[3] They are called M_1 and M_2. M_1 is made up of

1 The public's holdings of currency (paper bills and coins) plus

2 The public's total demand deposits at commercial banks

TABLE 24·1 MEASURES OF THE MONEY STOCK FOR JANUARY 1977 *(billions of dollars)*

	M_1 (1)	M_2 (2)
Currency (paper bills and coins)	81.3	81.3
Demand deposits	232.3	232.3
Saving deposits and "small" certificates of deposit	. . . .	431.8
Totals	313.6	745.4

SOURCE: *Federal Reserve Bulletin*, March 1977, A14.

Using this measure, the money stock was $313.6 billion in January 1977 (see Table 24·1). Of this total, $81.3 billion (26 percent) was in currency and $232.3 billion (74 percent) was in demand deposits.

The second frequently cited measure of the money stock, M_2, includes

1 M_1 plus

2 People's saving account balances at commercial banks and holdings of "small" (less than $100,000) certificates of deposits

Using this measure, the money stock in January 1977 was $745.4 billion, as shown in Table 24·1. This is more than twice the size of M_1.

M_1 and M_2, as measures of the amount of money in the economy, reflect the two basic economic functions which we have noted that money serves: a medium of exchange and a store of purchasing power. M_1 is composed of only those types of money which are used directly in trades (coin, paper bills, and demand deposits). Although we make many purchases with bills and coins, we complete most of our major transactions, like mortgage payments and the purchase of new cars, by writing checks against our bank accounts, i.e., by drawing down our demand

[3] There are actually five measures of the money stock reported in the *Federal Reserve Bulletin*: M_1 through M_5. The *Federal Reserve Bulletin* is published once a month and, in addition to carrying measures of the money stock, contains many general statistics on the state of the economy.

deposits. M_1, therefore emphasizes the medium-of-exchange role of money.

On the other hand, M_2, as a measure of the money stock, stresses the fact that money serves as a store of readily usable purchasing power. When paper bills, coins, and demand deposits are not being actively used in exchanges (or as mediums of exchange) they are being held as a store of purchasing power; for this reason they are also included in M_2. In addition, however, people store purchasing power in their saving accounts and in small certificates of deposits. This is the reason these forms of "money" are included in M_2.[4]

Economists are interested in statistically evaluating theories of how the stock of money in the country affects prices, national production, and unemployment. (In following chapters, we will develop these theories in detail.) The measure of the money stock which is used in these statistical studies will depend, in part, upon how the researcher perceives money. Those economists who view money as being mainly that which is *held* as opposed to that which is *traded* will use M_2 in their studies. Those who view money primarily as that which is *traded* will use M_1.

THE VALUE OF MONEY

Why are people willing to trade things of value for nicely engraved pieces of paper? For that matter, why are they willing to trade the goods and services they have to sell for checks? The receipt of checks ultimately means that their bank balance will increase. The "dollars" that they receive when given a check do not even remotely resemble the engraved "green stuff" that we normally think of as dollars; the dollars that people have on deposit with their banks are simply figures on the bank's accounting records (like the bank statements you receive), nothing more nor less. When people's demand deposits rise, banks adjust these figures upward; and the figures are not green, nor do the banks have a green dollar bill in their vaults for every dollar of demand deposits they have. The \$232 billion of demand deposits reported for January 1977 in Table 24·1 is the total of the bank account balances of individuals and nonbank corporations throughout the country. In short, it is a calculation on a piece of paper. The deposits are, nonetheless, money in the sense that they have all the essential characteristics of dollar bills: they are used as means of making payment and are financial assets which represent stored purchasing power.

Again, why do people accept dollars in exchange for goods and services? The answer cannot be that dollar bills have intrinsic value; dollars in bank accounts obviously cannot have any intrinsic value—they are figures on paper. The paper that is used for printing dollar bills is tough and relatively expensive, as far as paper goes, but the value (purchasing power) of the dollar is far greater than the value of the paper that is used. Further, the value of the dollar is not based on some form of "gold backing": there is no such thing. At one time, the government was required to hold \$0.25 in gold for every dollar outstanding. In this sense, the dollar was "backed" by gold. Even then, however, the gold did not determine the value of money, for how can \$0.25 in gold give a dollar bill a dollar's worth of value? The answer is simply that it can't, and the so-called "gold backing" did not give money value.

Contrary to popular belief, the government no longer holds gold in Fort Knox to "back" the dollar. Just consider the possibility of Fort Knox blowing up tomorrow. Or suppose the newspapers report tomorrow that they have found that there is no gold in Fort Knox and that the elaborate defenses around Fort Knox were merely instituted to give the *impression* that they had gold in the vault. Would you give away your dollars because you would assume them to be worthless? Probably not.

From the standpoint of the population as a whole, it is difficult to explain why people hold

[4] The reason for additional measures of the money stock, M_3 through M_5, is that people store purchasing power in other forms, like "large" certificates of deposits and saving accounts at thrift institutions like saving and loan banks and credit unions. M_3, M_4, and M_5 are viewed as "broader" measures of the money stock, since they include additional stores of purchasing power.

dollars; but, from the standpoint of any one individual, trades of goods for dollars, or vice versa, are very sensible. People can always unload the dollars they receive on someone else.

Dollars have value simply because people have confidence that others will accept them, and other people accept dollars because they know that you and others will accept them.

The value of money is all a matter of people's confidence in its general acceptability.

This was also true of gold and silver coins when they were used as money. Although gold and silver do have intrinsic value in the sense that they can be used for making ornaments, they would be worth much less if it were not for their value as money. The only reason that they were valued as much as they were is that people were willing to accept them fairly readily and easily in exchange. Money is an interesting commodity because its value to any one person depends upon its value to everyone. This is true whether we are talking about a "commodity money" like gold, which has value in itself, or an engraved piece of paper.

All of this may seem a little like magic, but the fact remains that confidence in its general acceptability is the "stuff" that money is made of. The fact that there is the message, "This note is legal tender for all debts public and private," on the front of dollar bills gives the bills some commercial value; but, in the final analysis, the value of money depends on an unwritten social agreement that it is valuable, and this agreement makes money valuable.

THE BANKING SYSTEM

As we have seen, demand deposits which people hold in banks are an important component of the money stock. Therefore, the banking system is an integral part of the monetary system of any economy. The two most significant parts of the United States banking system are (1) commercial banks and (2) the Federal Reserve System. We briefly discuss each below.

Commercial Banks

Commercial banks are privately owned businesses. For our purposes, the two most important functions of commercial banks are (1) they hold deposits for individuals and firms, and (2) they make loans to people who are willing and able to meet the interest payments and repay the amount of the loan.

Today there are nearly 14,000 commercial banks in the United States. The operations of these banks are closely supervised by state banking commissions, when they are chartered by the states, and by the Federal Reserve System, when they are chartered by the federal government. Commercial banks are generally told how much money must be invested in them by their owners, what types of loans they can make and to whom they can make them, what types and amounts of securities they can buy, and the minimum reserves in the form of deposits in other banks and vault cash they must have. The various regulatory agencies enforce their regulations by periodic unannounced examinations of the accounting records of commercial banks.

More than 5,000 of the nation's banks belong to the Federal Reserve System. These are mainly federally chartered banks, which are required to be members. However, because most of the larger banks in the country are members of the Federal Reserve System, about 80 percent of the demand deposits in all commercial banks are held in banks which are members of the Federal Reserve. For this reason, we now turn to a description of the "Fed," as the system is often called.

The Federal Reserve System

The Federal Reserve System, created by an act of Congress in 1913, is made up of twelve Federal Reserve District Banks scattered throughout the country. Figure 24·1 reveals the scope of the district which each Federal Reserve Bank serves. For example, if you live in the Far West, you are in district 12, the district of the Federal Reserve Bank of San Francisco. This district covers the states of Alaska, Hawaii, Washington, Oregon, California,

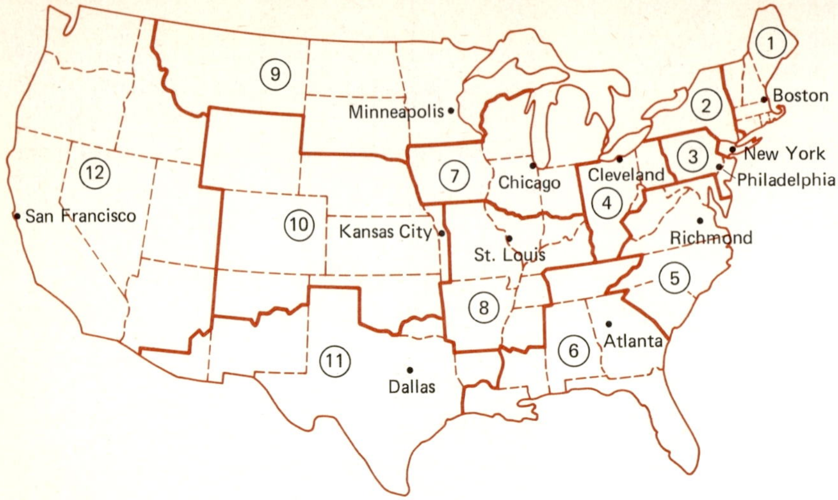

FIG. 24·1 The twelve Federal Reserve Districts.

Idaho, Nevada, Utah, and most of Arizona. Each district bank has one or more branch offices, and each branch office serves a part of the entire district.

The Federal Reserve System is headed by a seven-member Board of Governors; each member is nominated for the position by the president and confirmed by the Senate. Each governor is appointed for a term of 14 years. The chairman of the Board of Governors is Arthur Burns. Like the chairman of any collective organization, his power is limited. However, Arthur Burns is still one of the most influential people in the country when it comes to determining economic policy. At the district level, each Reserve Bank is supervised by a board of directors made up of representatives from its district. This board appoints a president for the Reserve Bank.

The primary function of the Fed is to establish and conduct the nation's *monetary policy.*

Monetary policy is the general name applied to governmental measures aimed at increasing or decreasing the money stock (M_1 or M_2).[5]

Its primary purpose is to affect the country's level of production and rates of unemployment and inflation. The major monetary policy decisions are made by the Federal Reserve's Boad of Governors and a group called the Federal Open Market Committee. The Federal Open Market Committee is composed of the seven members of the Board of Governors plus five of the twelve presidents of the Reserve Banks. The president of the Federal Reserve Bank of New York is always a member of the Open Market Committee; the other four positions on the committee for Reserve Bank presidents are rotated among the remaining eleven presidents.

[5] *Monetary policy* is often contrasted with the *fiscal policy* of a government. Fiscal policy includes all government actions designed to regulate tax levels and rates and levels of government expenditures. Fiscal policy is the subject of Chaps. 28 through 31.

Originally, the Federal Reserve System was established to disperse the decision-making power over monetary policy among the twelve Reserve Banks; and, for this reason, the individual Reserve Banks have, on paper, the power to set the rate of interest (called the "discount rate") which Reserve Banks charge on loans which they make to member banks. However, the Board of Governors operating out of Washington has the authority to review the decisions made at each of the Reserve Banks, and in practice the discount rate is set by the Board of Governors.

The Federal Open Market Committee meets about once every three weeks, and at these meetings the monetary policy of the Fed is reviewed. That is, the Open Market Committee determines whether or not the money stock should be increased or decreased, by how much, and what actions will be taken to achieve the established objectives. As we will see later, these decisions are implemented by ordering the manager of the so-called "open market account" to buy or sell government bonds on the free and open bond market. These purchases or sales result in changes in the money stock. Before charting the prescribed course of action for the manager of the open market account, those in attendance review the state of the economy in terms of such measures as GNP, the unemployment rate, Consumer and Wholesale Price Indexes, and the money stock and consider projections of what will happen to unemployment, prices, national production, and related matters in the near future.

The Federal Reserve System is the central bank of the United States. As the central bank, the Fed is a bank to bankers, meaning that the Reserve Banks provide many of the same services to commercial (or privately owned) banks that commercial banks provide for their depositors. The Reserve Banks hold the reserve accounts of commercial banks in their districts, make loans to those which are members of the Federal Reserve System, and provide them with currency when they need it. For instance, if a bank needs more currency to meet demand deposit withdrawals, it can call the Reserve Bank (or one of Fed's branch offices) and order more. The commercial bank pays for the currency with an appropriate reduction in its reserve deposit held at the Reserve Bank. In addition, the Federal Reserve Banks provide check clearing services for banks; checks are funneled to the Fed, sorted, and distributed to the different banks.[6]

Finally, as we have noted above, not all commercial banks are members of the Federal Reserve System. Therefore, not all banks can get loans directly from the Fed; on the other hand, nonmember banks can obtain for a small fee other services, like check clearing, which the Fed offers members.

CHECKS AND THE TRANSFER OF MONEY

When you write a check, you know that eventually your bank balance will fall while the balance of the person or firm to whom you write the check will rise. But how does the money "move" from one bank to another? Actually, nothing that is tangible ever moves; figures on the books of banks are adjusted to account for the check. To see this, we will have to look at some simplified bank records called "T accounts." These accounting statements get their names from their appearance: as in Figure 24·2, they take the form of a T. The two sides of the T represent the two sides of an accounting statement, called a "balance sheet." For our purposes, we can think of the accounts of a bank as being divided into two broad categories, assets and liabilities. Briefly, the asset accounts include all properties of the bank, and the liability accounts include all claims which nonowners have against the bank. Entries into asset accounts are recorded on the left-hand side of the T account, and entries into liability accounts are recorded on the right-hand side. As

[6] The Fed is not the only source of check clearing services. A number of large commercial banks provide check clearing services for other banks. Therefore, a check you write may be channeled through a Federal Reserve Bank, as we discuss below, or it may be channeled through another commercial bank which provides check clearing services.

"balance sheet" implies, the two sides of the T account must balance; this results because there is, given standard bookkeeping techniques, an equal asset entry for every liability entry.[7]

Having identified the essential features of the bookkeeping system that we will employ, let us suppose that you write a check for $10 to your university's bookstore, and let us describe the resulting bookkeeping entries in terms of Figure 24·2. When the bookstore deposits the check, its demand deposit goes up, as you might expect. This demand deposit or checking account is a legal claim which your bookstore has against its bank, which we assume is First and Merchants National Bank; therefore, we have classified the increase in the bookstore's deposit as a liability of First and Merchants and have entered $10 in the name of the bookstore on the right-hand side of First and Merchant's balance sheet. This is entry *a*.

How is the money which has just been received from your university's bookstore collected? There are several ways, but the simplest is for First and Merchants to send the check to the Federal Reserve. Indeed, because it has received a deposit from your bookstore, First and Merchants can receive an increase in its reserve deposit in the Federal Reserve. This is how the money is ultimately transferred. The reserve deposit of First and Merchants rises (entry *b*) while the reserve deposit of your bank, Northwestern National, against which the check is written, falls (entry *c*). While First and Merchants' reserve deposit is a liability to the Fed, it is an asset on the accounting records of First and Merchants. For these reasons, the check which you write to the bookstore results in an increase in First and Merchants' reserve deposit on the records of the Federal Reserve (entry *b*) and an increase in the assets of First and Merchants on their own bookkeeping records (entry *e*).

Once the appropriate entries are made on the

[7] Actually, the balance sheet includes an additional set of accounts called "capital accounts," which represent the claims of the owners against the assets. Therefore, there can be combinations of entries other than the one we have indicated. However, we will leave those complications to courses in accounting.

First and Merchants National Bank

Assets	*Liabilities*
Reserve deposit + $10 (entry *e*)	University bookstore's demand deposit + $10 (entry *a*)

Federal Reserve Bank

Assets	*Liabilities*
	First and Merchants + $10 reserve deposit (entry *b*)
	Northwestern National Reserve deposit − $10 (entry *c*)

Northwestern National Bank

Assets	*Liabilities*
Reserve deposit − $10 (entry *f*)	Your demand deposit − $10 (entry *d*)

FIG. 24·2 Bookkeeping entries resulting from a $10 check which you write to the university's bookstore.

accounting records of the Federal Reserve, the check is sent out, along with others that have come in, to your bank, which, for example, we assume is the Northwestern National Bank. It is only when the check reaches your bank, which may be as many as three or four days after you wrote it, that your account balance is reduced. This is indicated in Northwestern's balance sheet entry d. Because your bank's deposits are down by $10, its reserve deposit with the Federal Reserve must also fall by $10, since, as we indicated above, reserve deposits of banks must rise and fall with the deposits they hold for people like you. The decrease in the reserve deposit of the Northwestern National Bank is indicated by entry c, and it is recorded in its own asset accounts (entry f).

We suspect that you did not imagine that a simple check could create so many bookkeeping entries. But it can, and several important points should be remembered. First, the check causes your bank balance to fall and the balance of the bookstore to rise (entries d and a). Second, the check causes an adjustment in the Fed's reserve deposits of the two commercial banks: the reserve deposit of your bank goes down while the reserve deposit of the bookstore's bank goes up (entries c and b). Third, the reserve deposits in the Federal Reserve are not the same "money" as the deposits which you or your bookstore have; they are what we have called *reserves* or *bookkeeping deposits* which are *based* on the amount of demand deposits which banks have in total. These "reserves" are not money because they are not used directly in trades; the demand deposits are the money that is traded for goods and services. When a bank's demand deposits which are held for the public go up or down, its reserve deposits go up or down, respectively. Fourth, reserve deposits are assets of banks; in exactly what sense they are assets will become clear in the next section. For now, we note that any check you write causes the assets of your bank to fall and the assets of another bank to rise (entries e and f). This statement assumes that the person who writes the check and the person who receives the check have accounts in different banks. If both parties have accounts with the same bank, one person's deposit goes up while the other's goes down. The *total* deposits of the bank remain the same: the bank's reserve deposit, therefore, does not have to be adjusted. Fifth, and most important, when you or anyone else writes a check, the money stock in the country does not change; it is simply moved from one account to another.

THE CREATION OF MONEY

Gold is no longer used to any significant extent as money. However, when gold was used as money, someone had to mine the gold ore from the ground, to smelt the gold from the ore, and to mold the gold into coins. Regardless of exactly how it was done, gold money was "created" in a way that is not markedly different from the process of producing jewelry. Manufacturing plants, whether owned by private companies or by the government, were involved; and the amount of gold in the ground and the cost of getting it out were the principal determinants of how much money was "created." In this section we explain how money is created in modern economies.

A General Introduction

We no longer use gold as money, but still the type of money that we do use must be "created" or "produced" by someone or some institution.

Today, in industrial countries like the United States, money is created principally through the commercial banking system. Banks create money, and they create money every time they make a loan.

How do they do it? They certainly do not do it by loaning out someone else's money; that would mean that the money that is already in existence was being *transferred* from one person to another. Rather, banks create money by writing checks to or increasing the deposits of borrowers. To illustrate, let us assume again that you have an account with Northwestern National and that you negotiate a loan with the bank for $5000 to buy a new car. Further, let us assume that you ask the bank to make the loan by writing out a check to the car dealer. The loan agreement is completed when you sign the necessary papers and the bank writes and gives you the check to deliver to the car dealer. When the car dealer *accepts* the $5000 check and deposits it in the company's account, money is created!

How? you ask again. Very simply. The bank creates it! The bank officer with whom you are talking takes out a blank check form, writes in the name of the car dealer, fills in "$5000" (or any other amount), and signs his name to the check. The essential characteristic of money is that it is generally accepted in the trade of goods and services. So long as the car dealer is willing *to accept* the check and other people are willing *to accept* checks which he writes on his account, something has been created which has *general acceptability*. We call this something *money*. Granted, there are no smelting furnaces involved, but banks do have some very nice buildings (plants) and a number of bank officers and clerical assistants (production workers) who keep track of how much money they have and can create.

Banks are restricted in how much money they can create; they cannot create an unlimited amount. Legally, the amount of money a bank can create depends upon the amount of deposits it holds for its customers. The greater the amount of customer deposits it has, the greater the amount it can loan and the greater the amount of money it can create.

In addition to the amount of a bank's deposits, the money-creating capability of banks is further restricted by the *reserve requirement.*

The reserve requirement is that portion of a bank's total reserve deposits which cannot be loaned and must be held on deposit with the Federal Reserve or in cash in the bank's vaults.

As we saw in Figure 24·2, a commercial bank receives an increase to its reserve deposit with the Federal Reserve. Each deposit that a commercial bank receives from customers causes an increase in its reserve deposit at the Fed. When you ask for a loan, the reserve account is the account against which your bank writes its check. Therefore, the bank's reserve deposit decreases when the bank makes a loan. However, the bank is not permitted to loan out the entire amount of its reserve deposit; it must hold onto a portion. That portion is the *reserve requirement.* The reserve requirement is expressed as a percent of the bank's total demand deposits. For example, if the reserve requirement is 15 percent, the bank must have reserves in its reserve deposit with the Fed or in the form of cash in its vaults equal to at least 15 percent of its demand deposits. This means the bank can make loans *equal to* 85 percent of its demand deposits. (Note the use of "equal to"; this does not mean the bank actually loans out 85 percent of its demand deposits.[8]) The reserves held by a bank that are over and above what it is required to hold are called *excess reserves:*

Total reserves = required (or legal) reserves + excess reserves

Excess reserves = total reserves − required reserves

How much the bank can loan out—that is, how much money it can create—is therefore dependent upon its excess reserves, which is dependent upon the reserve requirement: the excess reserves and money-creating capability of a bank go up when the reserve requirement goes down, and they go down when the reserve requirement goes up. This relationship is illustrated in the following schedule:

Reserve Requirement (percent)	Loans Can Be Equal to This Percentage of Demand Deposits (percent)
10	90
15	85
17	83
20	80

[8] Actually, a commercial bank makes loans from its reserves, as we have said, but the reserves are not the same as the bank's demand deposits; the bank's reserves are bookkeeping contrivances.

Using this table, you can see that a bank with a total demand deposit of $10 million and a reserve requirement of 10 percent can make loans up to $9 million (90 percent × $10 million). On the other hand, when the reserve requirement is 17 percent, the bank can make loans of only up to $8.3 million (83 percent × $10 million). We stress again that the bank's ability to create money moves with its ability to make loans.

T Accounts and Money Creation

Let us consider the money creation process more carefully. Start again with the assumption that a bank, called Bank A, has total customer deposits of $10 million and a reserve deposit of an equal amount. As we begin, the accounts of Bank A and the Federal Reserve look like what is shown in Step I of Figure 24·3.

Again, assume that the reserve requirement is 20 percent. Bank A can loan out 80 percent of its $10 million in reserves; that is, it can loan out as much as $8 million. The initial accounting position of Bank A is revealed in Step I of Figure 24·3. Further, let us assume that Bank A makes the loan via a check to someone who buys goods from someone else who has an account with Bank B. What are the consequences of the loan on the amount of money in the economy? First, we note that the check that Bank A writes results in an increase in Bank B's total customer deposits. Bank A's loan, therefore, at this point results in an increase in our definition of the money stock discussed earlier. This change is indicated in the balance sheet of Bank B in Step II of Figure 24·3 (entry a). Second, Bank B can now receive a reserve deposit of its own equal to $8 million with the Federal Reserve Bank; this change is recorded as entry b. Third, the check that ends up as a deposit in Bank B is drawn against the reserve deposit of Bank A. In a manner similar to the way your account changes when you write a check on it, the reserve deposit of Bank A falls from $10 million in Step I to $2 million ($10 million − $8 million) in Step II (entry c). Fourth, the assets of Bank A are rearranged because of the loan that is made. Bank A's total loan assets increase by $8 million (entry d), and its reserve deposit decreases to $2 million (entry e). Fifth, Bank B records in its own records the increase in its reserve deposit assets of $8 million (entry f).

Interestingly, the total of all banks' demand deposits has risen from $10 million in Step I, when only the demand deposits of Bank A could be counted, to total demand deposits of $18 million ($10 million of demand deposits in Bank A plus $8 million of demand deposits in Bank B) in Step II.

As a consequence of the loan, the total money stock has increased; it is for this reason that economists say banks create money when they extend loans.

However, notice that the money-creating potential of the banking system does not stop with Bank A's loan. Bank B now has newly acquired reserves of $8 million, and it can, like Bank A, loan out 80 percent of its additional reserves. It can make loans up to $6.4 million (80 percent of $8 million). A loan of this magnitude can end up as a deposit in another bank, like Bank C, as we have illustrated in Step III of the figure. Because of Bank B's loan, total demand deposits in the banking system rise to $24.4 million ($10 million in Bank A + $8 million in Bank B + $6.4 million in Bank C). Again, the money supply increases because of a loan made by a bank. The appropriate adjustments to the accounts of Banks A, B, and C and the Federal Reserve Bank are shown in the T accounts of Step III of Figure 24 · 3: the accounts of Bank A remain the same because it has done nothing in this step. However, the total demand deposits of Bank C rise (entry g). The reserve deposit of Bank B decreases by $6.4 million in its own records and in the records of the Federal Reserve (entries h and i). The loan account of Bank B rises by $6.4 million (entry j), and the reserve deposit of Bank C increases in its own accounts and in the Federal Reserve's accounts by $6.4 million (entries k and l).

Bank C can now extend loans based on its newly acquired demand and reserve deposits. Like Banks A and B, Bank C can loan out 80 per-

Step I

Bank A

Assets	*Liabilities*
Reserve deposits: $10 million	Total deposits: $10 million

Federal Reserve Bank

Assets	*Liabilities*
(Offsetting asset entry explained in Chap. 25)	Reserve deposit of Bank A: $10 million

Step II

Bank A

Assets	*Liabilities*
Reserve deposit: $2 million (entry *e*) Loans: $8 million (entry *d*)	Total deposits: $10 million

Bank B

Assets	*Liabilities*
Reserve deposit: $8 million (entry *f*)	Total deposits: + $8 million (entry *a*)

Federal Reserve Bank

Assets	*Liabilities*
(Offsetting asset entry explained in Chap. 25)	Reserve deposit of Bank A: $2 million (entry *c*) Reserve deposit of Bank B: + $8 million (entry *b*)

Step III

Bank A

Assets	*Liabilities*
Reserve deposit: $2 million Loans: $8 million	Total demand deposit: $10 million

Bank B

Assets	*Liabilities*
Reserve deposit: $1.6 million (entry *h*) Loans: $6.4 million (entry *j*)	Total demand deposits: + $8 million

Bank C

Assets	*Liabilities*
Reserve deposit: $6.4 million (entry *k*)	Total demand deposits: $6.4 million (entry *g*)

Federal Reserve Bank

Assets	*Liabilities*
Offsetting entry explained in Chap. 25)	Reserve deposit of Bank A: $2 million Reserve deposit of Bank B: $1.6 million (entry *i*) Reserve deposit of Bank C: $6.4 million (entry *l*)

FIG. 24·3 Money creation through the banking system.

cent of its reserve. The bank that receives an increase in its demand deposits because of Bank C's loans can increase its loans. As successive banks extend loans up to the legal maximum dictated by the reserve requirement, the money stock expands. However, the money stock will not rise indefinitely; there is a limit to the size of the increase in the money stock. As indicated by the steps in Figure 24 · 3, each successive bank in the chain of events which we have been discussing is able to loan out less than the one before it; each successive bank is able to add progressively less to the total money stock. Given the reserve requirement of 20 percent and the initial excess reserves of $8 million, we could add to our table the adjustments that will occur in the banking system as successive banks make loans and others receive additional deposits, and we could then see how much additional money can be created in the entire banking system. This can be done by adding together the additional deposits of n banks. Fortunately, there is a simpler way of computing the maximum total increase in the money stock.[9]

$$\text{Maximum increase in money stock} = \text{Bank A's excess reserves} \times \frac{1}{\text{reserve requirement}}$$

The maximum increase works out to be $40 million, because

$$\text{Maximum increase in money stock} = \$8\text{ million} \times \frac{1}{0.20} = \$40\text{ million}$$

The total money stock will then be $40 million plus $10 million of demand deposits in Bank A plus whatever other currency is held by the public plus other demand deposits held throughout the banking system. Regardless, once all banks have extended their loans to the legal maximum, the money stock cannot expand further without a change in the reserves held by banks or a change in the reserve requirement. In Chapter 25 we explain how the Federal Reserve can change reserves and the reserve requirement to either increase or decrease the money stock.

[9] This formula can be mathematically derived.

Difficulties in the Money Creation Process

The foregoing discussion of how money is created in the banking system has been based on several assumptions which have facilitated discussion and have allowed us to describe the broad outlines of the money creation process. However, you should be aware that the money creation process does not work as smoothly as the above discussion may suggest. Banks are beset with problems of managing their asset and liability accounts which do not always permit them to keep their loans up to the legal maximum. For instance, we have pointed out that loans reduce bank reserves and increase the money stock. It is also true that when people pay off their loans, they increase the reserves of banks. Furthermore, when loans are repaid, the money stock is reduced, since the checks are written against people's demand deposits. A bank is continually receiving payments on loans outstanding. Because it earns its income from the loans it has outstanding, a bank will attempt to reloan the funds it receives in loan payments as quickly as possible. However, a bank's loan payments and loan requests will not always be regular and will not always run together. At times, the loan payments a bank receives will be greater than the requests it receives for loans. During these times, the bank will have excess reserves; it will not have as many loans outstanding as it can have; it will not have created as much money as it can create. To the extent that all banks have problems of this kind and have excess reserves, the total money stock will not be as great as it can be—it will not be at the maximum, as computed by the formula.

Further, the analysis above has been developed on the assumption that all bank loans end up as demand deposits in banks. That is, the loans of Banks A, B, etc., become deposits of other banks. This may not always be the case; part of the money created by banks may end up as currency held in the pockets of the public. Although currency is money, it is not the type of money which permits banks to claim reserve deposits. It is not, therefore, the type of money on which additional loans can be made. To the extent that bank loans end up as currency, the ability of banks to expand loans and increase the money stock is reduced.

For instance, suppose that the person who received the $8 million check indirectly from Bank A deposited $7.5 million but took $500,000 in currency, for example, in $100 bills. Bank B then would have received only $7.5 million in additional demand deposits and $7.5 million in reserves with the Federal Reserve. Bank B could have then made additional loans only up to $6 million ($7.5 million × 0.80) instead of $6.4 million. Bank C would have received a smaller deposit and would also not have been able to loan as much. In short, any money that is created and held as currency reduces the ability of the banking system to expand the money stock. Because of currency holdings, the maximum increase in the money stock will be less than we computed using the formula. One final point should be noted. In general, the public's willingness to hold money in the form of currency and demand deposits will influence the overall level of the money stock. If, for some reason, the public decides to reduce its demand deposits and increase its holdings of currency, banks will have lower reserves and will not be able to make as many loans. Because banks will be unable to create as much money, the money stock will fall without other compensating changes to be discussed in the next chapter. Similarly, if the public reduces its currency holdings by depositing the currency in its demand accounts, bank reserves will rise. Banks can therefore increase the amount of loans they make, thereby increasing the money stock.

The Purpose of the Reserve Requirement

Many students are inclined to look upon the reserve requirement as a means of ensuring that banks have some "money" on account with the Federal Reserve to meet the public's withdrawals from their demand deposits. As is true of so many other things in economics, appearance is deceiving.

The reserve requirement has nothing to do with maintaining the financial soundness of the banking system or of ensuring that banks can meet withdrawals on demand. The purpose of the reserve requirement is simply to restrict the amount of money which banks can create.

Banks *must* have the required reserves on account; if they want "security" against customer withdrawals, they must have reserves which exceed their required reserves. As our discussion has shown, banks do not really loan out other people's money when they make loans. Reserve deposits on which loans are based and demand deposits are totally different phenomena, as indicated by the separate figures on the different accounts of banks. The reserve deposits are calculated based on a bank's demand deposits, but they are not the same thing. If demand and reserve deposits were the same thing, banks could not create money; a bank loan would then constitute a *transfer* of money from a bank depositor to a borrower. As the system works, however, loans are made from the bank's reserve deposit, a separate bookkeeping phenomenon from the bank's demand deposit.

THE MONEY STOCK, THE VALUE OF MONEY, AND THE EQUATION OF EXCHANGE

The exchange value of anything is measured by what can be gotten for it in trade. Consequently, the exchange value, or just value, of money is what money will buy. The value of the dollar is not 29 cents or some such figure, because very few people would trade a dollar for 29 cents. The value of a dollar must be measured by any other good or services which a dollar will buy. For example, if a dollar will buy a quarter-pound hamburger at the local McDonald's restaurant, the exchange value of the dollar is one quarter-pound hamburger.

What determines the value of the dollar? In general, the value of the dollar depends upon the supply of dollars relative to the supply of the goods and services which people have to sell. If the supply of dollars that people can and are willing to offer in exchange for goods goes up relative to the quantity of goods being bought on the market, the value of the dollar will go down. As goods rise in price, what the dollar will buy goes down; therefore, the value of the dollar falls. Since people typically spend more dollars when they have more dollars, an increase in the money stock is normally associated with an increase in the number of dollars being spent and a decrease in the value of the dollar.

This relationship between the money stock and the value of the dollar has been observed throughout history. In the time of Alexander the Great, gold was the currency metal. When Alexander conquered the Persian Empire and took its capital, Persepolis, he found an immense hoard of gold which the Persian emperors had been accumulating for generations. Not surprisingly, Alexander spent the gold partly on his army and partly on improving his own living standard. As a result, prices all over the Greek world rose quite sharply. The Greeks did not fully understand the phenomenon, but it can be explained simply. The supply of money suddenly became greater relative to the supply of other goods and services, and so many people wanted to spend the increased number of gold pieces in their possession that the competitive bidding for goods and services pushed the prices of goods up and the value of gold, the money, down.

Alexander's extravagance in promptly spending his gold is not the only case in history in which there has been inflation in a metallic currency. The development of gold and silver mines by the Spanish in the newly discovered American continents led to an increase in the supply of gold and silver in Europe and a subsequent fall in its value. The fall in the value of gold and silver was reflected in a rise in the price of everything else. The California Gold Rush had much the same effect throughout the world. There was a sharp increase in the supply of gold, and hence a fall in its value. The most recent example of a gold-backed inflation occurred between 1890 and 1910. In this case, it was not the discovery of new gold mines. but the development of an improved process for extracting gold from ore, the cyanide flotation process, which increased the supply of gold and decreased its value.

Today, the monetary system is substantially different, but the same relationship between the money stock and the price level is the same. The German government financed the First World War by printing marks, the German currency. This dramatic rise in the money stock caused prices to soar; in 1923, prices in Germany were one trillion times as great as their prewar level, a rate of inflation that has not been seen since. The value of German money diminished so rapidly that people were no longer willing to accept it in trade or to hold onto what they had. Germany in 1923 became a "moneyless" economy, and economic activity largely collapsed. In recent years, governments in several South American countries, Italy, and Great Britain have essentially printed more money than the economy could absorb without spiraling rates of inflation. At one time in the 1960s, the annual rate of inflation in Brazil was over 150 percent. The money stock in the United States in the late 1960s and early 1970s has also been increased at rates much faster than the rates of two decades earlier. The consequence was higher rates of inflation and greater decreases in the value of the dollar than had been observed two decades before.

Economists have a simple formula which summarizes the relationship between the money stock and the price level, as measured by, for example, the Consumer Price Index. It is called "the equation of exchange" and is expressed

$$MV = PO = Y$$

where M = money stock
V = velocity of money, that is, average number of times each dollar is used
P = index of the price level, like Consumer Price Index or GNP Deflator
O = total output of goods and services in economy in physical terms
Y = monetary value of country's production of goods and services (as measured by, say, GNP)

Expressed in words, this equation says that the money stock (M) multiplied by the average number of times each dollar is used (V) equals the prices of goods and services (P) multiplied by the quantity of goods and services produced (O), which is equal to the monetary evaluation of the country's production (Y). On one level, the equation says simply that the value of people's expenditures (MV) must be equal to the value of what people buy (PO). On a quite different level, the "equation of exchange" relates changes in the money stock to changes in the price level. If V is held constant, an increase in the money stock, M, on the left-hand side of the equation must result in an increase in either P or O on the right-hand side of the equation. If the economy is at full employment of its resources—that is, if we are producing all of O that can be produced—an increase in M must be fully reflected in an increase in the price level, P.

Granted, V, the average number of times dollars are used, may not remain constant when the money stock is raised. Indeed, there is reason to believe that it will rise when the money stock is increased. The increase in the money stock can lead to inflation, which means that money is losing its value. Under these conditions, people will very probably spend the money they get more rapidly, increasing the rate by which money turns over, V. Further, the nation's output level may not be at full employment. In this case, an increase in the money stock will not necessarily be fully mirrored in the price level; it can be reflected in an increase in both P and O. Still, economists expect prices to rise with an increase in the money stock. The very special conditions under which this will not happen will be explained in Chapters 29 and 30. For now, in the following chapter, we will use the framework of the equation of exchange to discuss what is called *monetary policy* in what will amount to a discussion of how the Federal Reserve's ability to control the money stock also gives it partial control over the price level, the level of national production (GNP), and employment.

SUMMARY AND EXTENSIONS

Money is a medium of exchange which facilitates trade; it also takes the form of financial assets which can be held and easily used to buy goods and services. In both respects money is productive. It reduces the time which people need to spend searching out mutually beneficial trades and increases the amount of time which they have to produce goods and services. People who hold money in the form of either currency, demand deposits, or savings deposits benefit from the *liquidity* that money provides. There must be benefits to holding money because there is a cost to holding it. When people hold money, they give up the goods and services which money can buy. The benefits of holding money must be greater than or at least equal to the benefits of the goods and services that money can buy.

Modern paper or bank money has value simply because it is used as money. People are willing to accept and to hold money because they have confidence that others will accept this money at some future point in time. However, an important point of this chapter is that modern money is relatively easy to produce. The amount of money that can be created is not constrained by, for example, the amount of gold below the earth's crust. Modern money is figuratively created with the stroke of a pen by governments and commercial banks, supported by their central banks; the central bank of the United States is called the Federal Reserve System.

There is a temptation for a government to "run the printing presses" to produce the money that it wants, and modern monetary history reveals that many governments have succumbed to the temptation. The result has been a continuing increase in the money stocks of various countries and a continuing increase in the price levels of various world economies, that is, inflation. One of the most pressing problems in monetary economies is how to control the money stock—that is, how to control government tendency to increase it. This is no simple problem. We examine its origin and possible solutions in the next two chapters.

QUESTIONS TO PONDER

1 Suppose that you are the head of government in a country that is involved in a war that is very unpopular and that you have a choice of paying for the cost of the war either through increasing the taxes that people are required to pay or by printing more money. Which policy option would you take? What would be the consequences of your action?

2 Dollar bills have rather elaborate engraving on them to avoid counterfeiting. Why? Why are there laws against counterfeiting? If dollar bills could be easily duplicated, for example, with the aid of an office duplicator, what would happen to the money stock? What would happen to the nation's level of production and prices? What would happen to the value of the dollar? Would the dollar continue as a form of money?

3 Why are S&H Green Stamps not included in any of the official definitions of the money stock?

4 Suppose that you receive a $15 check from a friend who has an account in another bank in another part of the state. Using T-accounts and assuming that you deposit the check in your account, show the bookkeeping entries that will be made on the accounts of your bank, your friend's bank, and the Federal Reserve. Because of the check you receive, what happens to the money stock? What happens to the ability of your bank and your friend's bank to make loans?

5 Suppose that your bank has a total deposit of $20 million, the reserve requirement is 10 percent, and your bank has already made loans worth $5 million. How much in additional loans can your bank make to people who want to borrow?

6 If the reserve requirement is 100 percent, will banks be able to make loans? Will banks be willing to handle the public's demand deposits?

7 Suppose that we reestablish gold and silver coins as the medium of exchange in the United States. Under such a metallic monetary system, would there be periods of inflation and deflation? Suppose dimes are made of silver, and the amount of silver in a dime varies from coin to coin. Which coins would tend to be used in trade?

RECOMMENDED READINGS

Friedman, Milton: *Dollars and Deficits: Inflation, Monetary Policy, and the Balance of Payments* (Englewood Cliffs, N.J.: Prentice-Hall, Inc., 1968), chaps. 2–4 and 10.

Ireland, Thomas R., and Jack L. Rutner: *Principles of Macroeconomics and Money* (Hinsdale, Ill.: The Dryden Press, 1973), chap. 9.

McCulloch, J. Huston: *Money and Inflation: A Monetarist Approach* (New York: Academic Press, 1975), chaps. 1–3.

Ritter, Lawrence S., and William L. Silber: *Money* (New York: Basic Books, Inc., 1973), chaps. 1–3.

25

The Federal Reserve's Control of the Money Stock and the Causes of Inflation and Deflation

PREVIEW OF CHAPTER

Central question

How does the Federal Reserve control the money stock?

Major objectives

1 To explain how the Federal Reserve controls the money stock
2 To emphasize the limits of the Federal Reserve's ability to control the money stock
3 To explain how Federal Reserve actions can affect the price level and the rate of inflation and deflation in the economy

Major conclusions

1 The Federal Reserve has three fundamental ways of controlling the money stock. They are (*a*) control of the reserve requirement, (*b*) control over loans to member banks, and (*c*) the purchase and sale of government bonds.
2 The Federal Reserve can increase the money stock by (*a*) *reducing* the reserve requirement, (*b*) *increasing* loans to member banks, and (*c*) *purchasing* government bonds.

3. The Federal Reserve can reduce the money stock by (*a*) *increasing* the reserve requirement, (*b*) *decreasing* loans made to member banks, and (*c*) *selling* government bonds.
4. Under conditions of full or nearly full employment of resources in the economy, any action of the Federal Reserve which increases the money stock will lead to an increase in the price level. Any action of the Federal Reserve which reduces the money stock will lead to a reduction in the price level. Therefore, Federal Reserve policy can be a cause of inflation or deflation. However, a Federal Reserve action may be taken to accommodate political pressure from Congress. The purpose of this pressure may be to get the Federal Reserve to reduce market interest rates and/or the level of unemployment.

Important terms and concepts

Open market operations
Discount rate
Deflation

The amount of money that banks can create is dependent upon the reserves that banks have and upon the reserve requirement. That is one of the central points of the last chapter. In this chapter, we explain how the Federal Reserve can control bank reserves and the reserve requirement and how and to what extent the "Fed" (as the Federal Reserve is called) can, thereby, control the money stock.

By showing that the Fed has controls over the money stock, we do not mean to suggest that the Fed can control the money stock precisely. In several respects, the controls that the Fed has over money stock are similar to the controls that the climatologist has over the weather. The climatologist knows that by seeding clouds and planting rows of trees in certain areas, the weather can be affected. However, he also knows that there are many natural forces which are constantly changing; therefore he is never quite sure what the weather will be. Similarly, because of the many forces that are constantly changing in the banking system, when the Federal Reserve manipulates one of its monetary controls, it cannot always be sure exactly what will happen to the money stock. It may know the *range* within which change occurs, but not the exact amount of the change. As we noted in Chapter 24, a change in the money stock will affect a country's price level, and the Fed controls the money stock. However, the Fed will not always know very precisely what effect its actions will have on the price level. The Fed may know the directional movement of prices, but there can be significant variance in the extent of the price movement. We will see why in this chapter and in Chapter 26.

THE FEDERAL RESERVE'S CONTROL OVER THE MONEY STOCK

The Federal Reserve exercises control over the money stock through (1) the reserve requirement, (2) loans which the Fed makes to commercial banks, and (3) the Fed's purchases or sales of government bonds. These tools of control are discussed separately in this section.

The Reserve Requirement

As we explained in Chapter 24, the reserve requirement is that portion of a bank's total reserves that a bank cannot loan to borrowers. Since reserves are generated from demand deposits, the

TABLE 25·1 RESERVE REQUIREMENTS IN EFFECT ON DEMAND DEPOSITS OF MEMBER BANKS: FEBRUARY 28, 1977

Demand Deposits	Reserve Requirement
0– $2 million	7 percent
$2– $10 million	9.5
$10–$100 million	11.75
$100–$400 million	12.75
Over $400 million	16.25

SOURCE: *Federal Reserve Bulletin*, March 1977, A9.

reserve requirement is expressed as a percentage of the bank's demand deposits. That is, the reserves of a bank, which include the bank's deposit at the Fed and the currency in the bank's vaults, can be no lower than a certain percentage of the bank's demand deposits. Actually, the reserve requirement is not *one* figure, but a set of figures which apply to different levels of demand deposits. This is illustrated in Table 25·1, which gives the reserve requirement for each level of deposits. As of the end of February 1977, banks were required to hold 7 percent of their first $2 million in demand deposits in required reserves; they were required to hold 9.5 percent of the next $8 million of demand deposits in required reserves; and so on up the scale. Using Table 25·1, a bank with $350 million in demand deposits would have been required to have minimum reserves of $43.3 million.[1] The average reserve requirement, expressed as a percent of demand deposits ($44/$350), equals 12.3 percent.

To consider the effects of changes in the reserve requirement on the money stock, suppose that banks have loaned all that they can, given the reserve requirement. If the reserve requirement (or, more precisely, the reserve requirement schedule) is reduced, banks will be able to make more loans—that is, they can create more money. As banks increase their loans, the money stock rises. The additional loans end up as bank deposits or currency (as in Chapter 24), both of which are money and can be used like the money that was in existence before the reserve requirement was lowered.

On the other hand, an increase in the reserve requirement means that banks must hold larger reserves relative to their demand deposits. To increase their reserve deposits, banks must make fewer loans. Just as an increase in bank loans means an increase in the money stock, a decrease in bank loans means a decrease in money stock. If people pay off their loans by "drawing down" their demand deposits and banks cannot reloan the acquired reserves, the money stock must fall. The ratio of reserves held by banks to demand deposits rises to the new required level.

We know from this analysis that a decrease in the reserve requirement tends to increase the money stock and an increase in the reserve requirement tends to decrease the money stock. However, it is very difficult for the Fed to calculate by how much the money stock will actually change given a change in the reserve requirement, and it is hard for the Fed to determine when the money stock will change. The Fed may lower the reserve requirement, but many banks may not want or be able to expand their loans immediately. At the time that the reserve requirement is lowered, forces may be at work in the economy that lead banks to hold reserves which are in excess of what they are required to hold. Suppose, for instance, that banks expect interest rates to rise in the near future. Instead of increasing their loans immediately at the present relatively low interest rates, many banks may wait until interest rates rise. Alternatively, when the Fed increases the reserve requirement, many banks may have all the reserves they need to meet the new higher reserve requirements. Therefore, many banks will not have to contract their loans immediately; others may. At different times, the banking system, confronted with different market forces, will respond differently to an increase in the reserve requirement. In predicting the effects of a given change in the reserve requirement, sophisticated statis-

[1] This figure is calculated by multiplying the first $2 million in demand deposits times 0.07, the next $8 million by 0.095, the next $90 million by 0.1175, and the next $250 million by 0.1275, and by adding the products.

tical procedures—called "econometric model building"—can be used to increase the accuracy of the predictions; however, the point of this discussion is to suggest that those predictions will not always be accurate. The Fed will then have to take measures to correct for the "excessive" change in the money stock, a change which is either too large or too small.

Loans to Member Banks

The Federal Reserve can increase the reserves of member banks by making loans to them. Individuals and businesses borrow from commercial banks. Similarly, a commercial bank, which is a member of the Federal Reserve System, can borrow from the Federal Reserve Bank that serves its region. The commercial bank commits itself to an IOU to the Federal Reserve Bank and receives in return an increase in its reserve deposit. This type of transaction is illustrated by the two T-accounts in Figure 25·1. Suppose that Northwestern National wants to borrow $1 million in reserves from the Federal Reserve Bank of San Francisco. It can do this by calling the Reserve Bank. Provided the Reserve Bank agrees to the loan, Northwestern effectively commits itself to paying the loan back and receives a $1 million increase in its reserves. The loan is a liability to Northwestern (entry *a*) and, because an interest payment is collected on it, an asset to the Federal Reserve Bank (entry *b*). On the other hand, the reserve deposit that is acquired is an asset to Northwestern (entry *c*) and a liability to the Federal Reserve (entry *d*).

The commercial bank, Northwestern, can then use its reserves to make additional loans to the public, on which it earns its interest income, or to ensure that it has sufficient reserves to meet the reserve requirement. In the former case, the loans result directly in an increase in the money stock (just like all other loans). In the latter case, the bank will not have to reduce its outstanding loans in the event that its reserves are below what they should be to meet the reserve requirement. For example, suppose that Northwestern National has demand deposits of $10 million and reserves of $1 million. If the reserve requirement is 20 percent, Northwestern has $1 million fewer reserves than it needs to meet the reserve requirement. It can get the needed reserves by reducing the loans it has outstanding. This procedure, however, will reduce the money stock. By borrowing the $1 million in reserves from the Fed, Northwestern can avoid reducing its loans to the public and can avoid contributing to a reduction in the money stock. Therefore, because a bank has acquired a loan from the Fed, the money stock is greater than it would otherwise have been: the Fed's loan to a member bank either increases the money stock directly or keeps the money stock from falling.

Banks can borrow from the Fed for very short periods of time: two or three weeks, and often for much shorter periods than that. When they pay back their loans, they reduce their reserves. Consequently, when they pay off their loans to the

Northwestern National Bank

Assets	*Liabilities*
Reserve deposit + $1 million (entry *c*)	Loans from Federal Reserve + $1 million (entry *a*)

Federal Reserve Bank of San Francisco

Assets	*Liabilities*
Loans to member banks + $1 million (entry *b*)	Reserve deposit of Northwestern + $1 million (entry *d*)

FIG. 25·1 A Federal Reserve loan to Northwestern National Bank.

Fed, banks have fewer reserves to loan and can create less money. However, to the extent that some banks are borrowing from the Fed at the same time other banks are paying off their loans, loans by the Federal Reserve are a source of reserves to the banking system and increase the money-creating potential of banks. At times, the net borrowing of commercial banks has exceeded $1 billion; however, banks' total loans from the Fed totaled only $44 million in April 1976. This figure represented about 0.1 percent of the $34 billion in bank reserves at the time.

Where does the Fed get the reserves that it loans to commercial banks? The Fed creates them! It simply accepts the bank's IOU and increases the bank's reserve deposits. These are all straightforward accounting procedures, and the Fed can create the reserves because only bookkeeping entries are involved. The commercial bank can then use those newly created reserves to make loans—to create money.

The Federal Reserve can control the money stock by controlling the amount of loans that it makes to member banks in two principal ways. First, it can simply refuse to grant the loans, since borrowing from the Fed is considered a *privilege* rather than a *right* of membership. Second, the Fed can affect the amount of bank borrowing by changing the interest rate—called the "discount rate"—which it charges on loans to member banks. A decrease in this discount rate will encourage bank borrowing, since it makes those loans less costly. An increase in the discount rate will discourage banks from borrowing, since the loans are then more costly. Either way, the important point is that the money stock in the country is affected by the amount of loans which the Federal Reserve makes to member banks: an increase in those loans will tend to increase the money stock; a decrease in those loans will tend to decrease the money stock.

Open Market Operations

By far the most important tool of monetary control which the Fed has is its "open market operations." Simply stated,

open market operations are the purchases and sales of United States government bonds[2] by the Federal Reserve.

The conclusions to be drawn from an analysis of the Fed's open market operations are (1) that the purchase of government securities by the Fed will increase bank reserves and the money stock, and (2) that the sale of government securities by the Fed will decrease bank reserves and the money stock.

Consider the Fed's purchase of a $1 million government bond that is initially owned by a private citizen or firm. When the Fed decides to purchase a government bond, the manager of the system's open market account, who works out of the Federal Reserve Bank of New York, asks various people (primarily major dealers in the government securities market) for their selling price on the bonds that they hold. Suppose the Fed agrees to pay $1 million for the government bond. The bond will be delivered to the Federal Reserve and the Federal Reserve will issue a check for $1 million to the appropriate person or firm. The check will eventually end up as a demand deposit in some bank. At the moment it does, the money stock, which includes demand deposits, rises. The bank that receives the new demand deposit can then claim an increase in its own reserve deposit with the Federal Reserve.

The appropriate entries in the accounting records of Northwestern National Bank, which we assume gets the deposit, and the Federal Reserve Bank are indicated in the T accounts in Figure 25 · 2. The Federal Reserve's bond holdings, which are an asset, increase (entry *a*), and there is an offsetting increase in its liabilities in the form of an increase in the reserve deposits of Northwestern National (entry *b*). Similarly, Northwestern National has an increase in demand deposits (entry *c*) and an increase in its reserve deposit account (entry *d*). Northwestern can now increase its loans up to the limit dictated by the reserve requirement. In short, Northwestern can create

[2] United States government bonds are long-term debt obligations of the federal government.

Northwestern National Bank		Federal Reserve Bank	
Assets	*Liabilities*	*Assets*	*Liabilities*
Reserve deposit + $1 million (entry *d*)	Demand deposit + $1 million (entry *c*)	Holdings of U.S. Government Securities + $1 million (entry *a*)	Reserve deposit of of Northwestern National + $1 million (entry *b*)

FIG. 25·2 The purchase of a government bond by the Federal Reserve.

money, and the money expansion process can proceed through the banking system in the way that we described in Chapter 24.

Where does the Fed get the "money" to buy bonds? Again, the answer to that question is simple. It creates it! So long as people are willing to accept checks written by the Federal Reserve in exchange for their bonds, and so long as banks are willing to accept the checks as a basis for demand deposits, that which the Federal Reserve creates to buy the bonds is money.

On the other hand, the Federal Reserve can just as easily reduce the money stock. It does this by selling one of the approximately $100 billion worth of government securities that it has. If the Fed sells a government bond, it gives the bond to someone in exchange for a check. Because the check is written, the demand deposit of someone or some firm will fall and therefore the reserves of its bank will fall. However, the Fed does not increase the reserves of any other bank or the demand deposits of anyone else with the "money" represented by the check it has accepted in exchange for the government bond. It figuratively "destroys" or "burns" the money that it is given; to explain this less dramatically, the money simply goes out of existence.

The appropriate bookkeeping entries for this transaction are illustrated in Figure 25·3. Assuming that the check which is used to pay for the bond is written by someone who has an account with Northwestern, the demand deposits of Northwestern will fall by the amount of the purchase price of the bond, which we assume, in this case, is $1 million (entry *a*). The reserve deposit of Northwestern will then also fall by $1 million (entry *b*). The Federal Reserve has lost an asset in the form of the bond (entry *c*) and dispensed with

Northwestern National Bank		Federal Reserve Bank	
Assets	*Liabilities*	*Assets*	*Liabilities*
Reserve deposit − $1 million (entry *b*)	Demand deposit − $1 million (entry *a*)	Holdings of U.S. Government Securities − $1 million (entry *c*)	Reserve deposit of Northwestern − $1 million (entry *d*)

FIG. 25·3 The sale of a government bond by the Federal Reserve.

a liability in the form of a decrease in the reserve deposit of Northwestern National (entry d). Assuming that Northwestern was loaned up to the legal maximum before the Fed's sale of the bond, Northwestern must reduce its loans to build its reserves back up to the legal requirement. In this way, the money stock decreases further.

Summary of Controls

If the Federal Reserve wants to increase the money stock, it can take any combination of the following actions:

1 It can *reduce* the reserve requirement.
2 It can *increase* the loans which it makes to member banks.
3 It can *buy* government securities on the open market.

On the other hand, if the Federal Reserve wants to decrease the money stock, it can take any combination of the following actions (which are easy to remember since they are the opposite of the actions taken to increase the money stock):

4 It can *increase* the reserve requirement.
5 It can *decrease* the loans which it makes to member banks.
6 It can *sell* the government securities which it holds.

When the Fed takes any of the first three policy actions and the money stock rises faster than it has in the immediate past, it is said to follow an "expansionary" or "loose" monetary policy course. When it takes any of the last three policy actions and the money stock decreases or grows at a significantly lower rate than it has in the immediate past, the Fed is said to be following a "contractionary" or "tight" monetary policy course. These are the types of policy decisions which the Federal Open Market Committee attempts to chart in its meetings.

The Fed has very powerful controls over the money stock; however, the difficulty of controlling the money stock within narrow limits must be recognized. For example, when the Fed attempts to increase the money stock, it must realize that banks may not loan out all their excess reserves, and that, in any event, it takes time for the money expansion process to work its way through the banking system. Further, at the same time that the Fed is attempting to increase the reserves of banks, the public may be increasing its holdings of currency and reducing its holdings of demand deposits. As we studied in the preceding chapter, a movement of dollars from demand deposits to currency reduces the reserves of banks and their ability to create money. Also, the public may be moving its dollar holdings from demand deposits to saving accounts, changing the composition of the money stock. In addition, the federal government has demand deposits in the Fed and in various commercial banks around the country. At times it may be moving its deposits from commercial banks to the Federal Reserve. Such a movement of government deposits reduces the reserves of the commercial banks (because they now have fewer demand deposits), an action which, in turn, reduces the ability of commercial banks to make loans, that is, to create money. In short, the actions of the Fed to *increase* the money stock may simply offset forces in the banking system which are tending to reduce the money stock. Indeed, the Fed often buys government securities (or reduces the reserve requirement or increases the loans to member banks) to keep the money stock from falling rather than to increase it. The Fed confronts similar difficulties when it attempts to conduct a contractionary monetary policy.

THE "CAUSES" OF INFLATION

We have now learned how the Federal Reserve changes the money stock to conduct monetary policy. The end goal of monetary policy is not, however, simply to change the money stock. Rather, it is to influence the country's levels of production, employment, and prices. The primary purpose of this section is to explain the connection between the monetary policy conducted by the Fed and the rate of inflation and, thereby, to discuss the causes of inflation. To see the connection between monetary policy and inflation, we must briefly review a portion of the analysis from Chapter 24.

In Chapter 24 we learned that, everything else being held constant, an increase in the money stock will lead to an increase in the price level. In a similar way, a continuous increase in the money stock, everything else being held constant, will lead to a continuous increase in the price level. In other words, an increase in the money stock will lead to inflation. This can best be seen in terms of the equation of exchange, which we discussed in the previous chapter:

$$MV = PO$$

where M = money stock
V = velocity of money (or average number of times each dollar is used in trade)
P = price level
O = nation's output of goods and services

Assuming that velocity, V, and output, O, remain constant, an increase in M on the left-hand side of the equation must lead to a proportional increase in P on the right-hand side of the equation. This must happen if the two sides of the equation are to remain equal. Another more intuitive explanation for the increase in P is that if people have more money to spend and they continue to spend the money they have at the same rate (that is, if V is constant), there will be a greater number of dollars chasing after the given quantity of goods and services, and the prices of those goods and services will be pushed up by competition.

Granted, the country's output of goods and services does not always remain constant when the money stock is increased. Indeed, if there is unemployment in the economy, an increase in the money stock can lead to higher prices, and higher prices can be the inducement employers need to hire more workers and expand production. Under these conditions, an increase in the money stock will not lead to an equal percentage increase in the price level. The effect of the growth in the money stock will be split between an increase in the price level, P, and an increase in production, O. The point of the discussion in Chapter 24, however, was to emphasize the linkage between the money stock and the price level, not to demonstrate that the linkage is one-to-one, i.e., a 1 percent increase in the price level for every 1 percent increase in the money stock.

The equation of exchange enables us to draw other insights about the relationship between production, the money stock, and the price level. For example, suppose that the nation's production level, O, is continuously expanding as the result of increases in people's productivity. If the money stock and velocity remain constant in the face of increases in O, the price level, P, must fall; this is necessary to ensure that PO remains equal to MV. In order for the price level not to fall when production is rising, M or V or both must rise. In other words, during times of rising production levels, increases in the money stock can lead to a stable price level. There will be general inflation only when the money stock and/or velocity grows at a faster rate than the level of production rises. Alternatively, if production *falls* while velocity remains constant and the money stock rises, again we have the familiar problem of too many dollars chasing after too few goods, and prices will rise.

The equation of exchange also reveals that if the money stock is held constant, an increase in velocity, V, can cause a rise in price. That is, assuming that M remains constant, an increase in V on the left-hand side of the equation must lead to an increase in P (price level) and/or O (output) on the right-hand side of the equation. Of course, from what we have said, it follows that prices can rise because of a rise in both M and V.

What causes inflation? Following the analysis above, inflation is attributable to increases in velocity and/or "excessive" increases in the money stock. This explanation does not cover all the causes of inflation, nor is it intended to; but it does focus attention on two very important variables. Increases in velocity are not likely to be the cause of *long periods* of continuous price increases. Increases in velocity occur because people are using their money more rapidly and therefore holding onto lower and lower money balances. There are institutional constraints, such as regular pay periods, which determine the amount of money people must hold; and, although the velocity can adjust upward, there are limits to how far and how fast velocity can increase. There are, therefore, limits to how much inflation can be "caused" by upward adjustments in velocity.

Increases in the money stock have been explained to be a cause of inflation. However, our explanation cannot stop at this level of analysis. We have learned in this chapter that the Fed has controls over the money stock and that, if it increases the money stock, higher prices can result. Therefore, inflation can be attributed to the Fed's monetary policy. That is, the Fed may at times increase the money stock by more than is warranted, given the country's level of production. This explanation, however, is not always complete. Monetary policy is not created in a vacuum; it is a product of forces which are operating on the Federal Reserve and of the fact that the Fed is usually concerned about more than one objective at a time. It has been trying to reduce both inflation *and* unemployment.

To see the problems that the Fed faces in conducting monetary policy, suppose that at the same time that the Fed is concerned about inflation, the federal government spends more than it collects in taxes. By spending more than it collects in taxes, the federal government runs a budgetary deficit and must borrow the difference between its tax revenues and its expenditures. It raises the needed funds by selling bonds in the bond market; this causes the demand for borrowed funds to rise. The increase in the market demand for borrowed funds will tend to raise the interest rates which businesses, individuals, and governmental units at all levels have to pay. In such instances, important members of the House Banking Committee and the administration will often accuse the Federal Reserve of conducting an unreasonably tight monetary policy, and the evidence they give to support their claim is that interest rates are rising. As a result, they say people are being burdened with exorbitant interest rates on the purchase of new housing and that governments at all levels are being burdened with higher interest payments on the funds they borrow for school construction, road improvements, and the like. All this tends to be attributed to the "unreasonable" monetary policy course conducted by the Fed. Frequently, members of Congress will threaten to revise the charter of the Fed in order to make it more responsive to the concerns of the public. Given this kind of political pressure, the Fed has, in times when the federal government is borrowing heavily, entered the market as a buyer of bonds. The Fed's purpose is to keep interest rates down. However, as we pointed out earlier, purchases of bonds by the Fed lead to increases in the money stock. This in turn leads to higher price levels. Is the Fed responsible for the inflation? In a sense it is, since the Fed did yield to the pressures exerted by Congress and the administration. Looking at the Fed's position more sympathetically, however, inflation may be attributed to those who bring pressure to bear on the Fed to do something about the "high" interest rates.

The Fed may also recognize that many union wage settlements cannot be supported by current market conditions; that is, it may conclude that wage increases will result in significant unemployment because the wage rates will be above the equilibrium wage rates. The Fed may also recognize that it will be pressured by the administration and Congress to do something to alleviate the unemployment problem which will result from the "excessive" wage increases. If it does anything, the Fed must increase the rate of growth in the money stock; but, by doing so, it will contribute to inflation. However, businesses can then justify hiring more workers at the higher wage rates. Again, in this case, one can lay the blame for the inflation on the Federal Reserve, since it allowed the money stock to grow at a faster pace. On the other hand, the Fed may reasonably argue that it was "forced" by the realities of political life to take the actions that it did.

THE INDEPENDENCE OF THE FEDERAL RESERVE

Theoretically, the Federal Reserve is an independent agency. It does not have to seek the advice or the consent of the administration or the Congress for the policies that it pursues. Actually, it has only to *inform* the Congress of what it plans to do in the near future. However, the Congress has always retained the power to change the charter of the Federal Reserve and, thereby, to change the degree of independence that it has. In trying to protect its independence by catering to administrative and congressional political pressures, the Fed has effectively given up much of the independence that it has. From about 1972, the Federal Reserve has with unusual vigor resisted political pressures from many corners of the Democratic and Republican parties to conduct a more expansionary monetary policy. Its resistance was, no doubt, fortified by the unusually high rates of inflation experienced in the United States in the early years of the 1970s. If, however, history contains any lessons, we cannot be sure that this new resistance will hold for very long.

THE "CAUSES" OF DEFLATION

Deflation is the opposite of inflation: it is a general decrease in the level of prices in a country.

What causes deflation? We have already described one possibility in our discussion of the causes of inflation. Assuming that the money stock and velocity remain constant, deflation can occur when the production of goods and services increases. Refer back to the equation of exchange,

$$MV = PO$$

If M and V remain constant, their product, MV, remains constant. It also follows that the product of P and O on the right-hand side of the equation must also remain constant. If the country's production, O, increases, it follows that P must fall to keep PO constant and equal to MV. It also follows that deflation can occur if the production of goods and services rises faster than the money stock. In both of these cases, if output increases relative to the increase in the money stock, the dollars in existence will be chasing after relatively more goods. The prices of goods and services should therefore fall.

Deflation can also result from a decrease in the money stock and/or a decrease in the velocity of money. A decrease in either of these variables on the left-hand side of the equation of exchange must be offset by a decrease in either prices or production on the right-hand side. For example, generally we expect prices to fall when the money stock falls. The decrease in the money stock, assuming everything else in the equation of exchange is held constant, will mean that fewer dollars will chase after goods and services. This general decrease in demand for the country's output will lead to lower prices as producers compete to attract the dollars that are being spent. Unless the costs of production fall along with the prices businesses charge, unemployment of resources, including people, will be a consequence of a decrease in the money stock. With lower prices on the products they sell and constant wages paid to workers, businesses can no longer afford or justify hiring as many workers. Wages may possibly adjust downward during times of deflation; but typically they will not adjust as rapidly as is needed, and unemployment emerges in times of deflation. How much unemployment emerges in times of deflation depends upon how much and how fast the money stock is reduced and how rapidly the prices of products and resources are able to adjust downward.

Although inflation has been the general rule throughout history, deflations have occurred on a number of occasions in a number of countries. Generally, periods of deflation have occurred after wars. During wartime, countries often increase the money stock as a means of financing their war-related expenditures, and prices in these countries have increased with the growth in the money stock. After wars, countries have attempted to reduce prices and bring them in line with prewar prices by reducing the money stock. The result has been deflation. After the Napoleonic wars, England underwent a lengthy period of mild deflation; and the same thing happened in the United States after the Civil War. There was also a significant drop in prices in the 1920–21 recession that occurred in the United States following World War I. The deflations in all these instances were brought about by a reduction in the money stock.

SUMMARY AND EXTENSIONS

A purpose of this chapter has been to introduce the methods that the Federal Reserve can employ to increase or decrease the money stock. The specific actions which the Fed can take to expand or contract the money stock have been listed. More important, a purpose of this chapter has been to develop the connection between the monetary policy of the Federal Reserve and inflation. Drawing this connection requires that we understand the policy tools of the Fed and the impact that a change in the money stock has on the price level. In demonstrating the effects of monetary policy on prices, the "equation of exchange," $MV = PO$, was used.

These are all technical matters; and although the Federal Reserve is theoretically an independent monetary agency, you should never overlook the political setting in which monetary policy must be conducted. The Fed can simply be pressured into taking monetary actions which it knows at the time are contrary to its long-run policy objectives. Aside from that, policy actions of the Federal Reserve have occasionally been misguided. For instance, we have mentioned that at times the Fed has attempted to keep interest rates "low" to accommodate new debt issues of the Treasury. The result has been that the Fed has bought bonds, and the consequence of that has been an increase in the rate of growth in the money stock and higher rates of inflation. As we will study in some detail in the next chapter and in Chapter 31, an increase in the rate of inflation can lead to higher interest rates. A short explanation is that creditors—people who are willing to loan their money or buy bonds—will require a higher rate of interest to compensate for the expected depreciation of the dollars that they will receive as interest payments. The policy course of trying to keep interest rates low can, therefore, be self-defeating, because interest rates will tend to rise with the ensuing higher rate of inflation.

In evaluating monetary policy, it should be kept in mind that the policy course of the Fed is determined by a committee, the Federal Open Market Committee. At the Committee's meetings, some very informative presentations are made by the members of the staff of the Board of Governors; however, there is often a great deal of rambling discussion and irrelevant comments and questions. In addition, although the Committee bases its decisions on the most up-to-date data, these data are often inadequate and conflicting on exactly what is happening in the economy; and in the past not all board members have been fully adept in the monetary matters with which they have to deal.[3] In short, we should not be overly impressed by the fact that a group of men[4] with impressive credentials

[3] For a discussion of open market strategy as developed in the Open Market Committee in the 1950s and early 1960s, see Jack M. Guttentag, "The Strategy of Open Market Operations," *Quarterly Journal of Economics*, vol. 80, pp. 1–30, February 1966.

[4] There are no women on the Board of Governors at this writing.

has been meeting in Washington to handle our country's monetary policy, and we should not be surprised that these policy decisions are at times faulty and inconsistent. With these points in mind, we turn to a description of the costs and benefits of inflation in the next chapter.

QUESTIONS TO PONDER

1 Suppose that people decide to withdraw more money than usual from their demand deposits and that they take their withdrawals in the form of currency. What effect would this shift in the form of money held by the public do to the ability of banks to make loans? What effect would it have on the money stock?

2 What actions can the Fed take to increase the money stock? What actions can the Fed take to offset the effects of greater currency holdings on the part of the public? Based on your answers to the above questions, does it follow that, when the Fed is in the market buying bonds, it is always attempting to increase the money stock?

3 What is the relationship between people's willingness to hold money in currency and demand deposits and the velocity of money (the average number of times that each dollar is used)? What is the relationship between the rate of interest and people's willingness to hold money? Based on your answers to above questions, what is the relationship between the interest rate and the velocity of money?

4 The Federal Reserve conducts monetary policy in part through the purchase and sale of government bonds. Would it make any difference if, when engaging in open market operations, the Federal Reserve bought and sold the bonds of private companies instead of government bonds?

5 Suppose that all power groups, like large unions, large corporations, and governmental units, pushed up prices in the economy and held them there, and that this meant a dramatic rise in the price of almost everything. Assume that the money stock was held constant. What would be the effects in the economy? Explain your answer in terms of the equation of exchange.

6 If the central bank of a country controls the money stock and continually increases the money stock at rates that will cause high rates of inflation, what can be done to control the central bank? Suppose that the central bank is merely responding to political pressures. How then can the central bank be controlled?

RECOMMENDED READINGS

Friedman, Milton: *Dollars and Deficits: Inflation, Monetary Policy, and the Balance of Payments* (Englewood Cliffs, N.J.: Prentice-Hall, Inc., 1968), chaps. 1, 4–6.

McCulloch, J. Huston: *Money and Inflation: A Monetarist Approach* (New York: Academic Press, 1975), chaps. 1 and 2.

Morley, Samuel A.: *The Economics of Inflation* (Hinsdale, Ill.: The Dryden Press, Inc., 1971).

Ritter, Lawrence S., and William L. Silber: *Money*, 2d ed. (New York: Basic Books, Inc., 1973), chaps. 2, 3, 5, 6, and 8–11.

26

The Costs and Benefits of Inflation

In a full-employment situation money creation is strictly equivalent to taxation: Normal methods of taxation can be supplanted by the government's money creation, which . . . will cause inflation and a tax on people's average cash balances.

Roger Miller
Raburn Williams[1]

PREVIEW OF CHAPTER

Central question

Who gains and who loses from inflation?

Major objective

To identify those who benefit and those who lose because of inflation.

Major conclusions

1 The major groups of losers from inflation are (*a*) holders of demand and saving deposits, (*b*) creditors, (*c*) bond buyers, and (*d*) taxpayers.

2 The major groups of gainers from inflation are (*a*) debtors, (*b*) certain groups of businesses and workers who are able to adjust their prices and wages upward faster than the general rise in prices, and (*c*) government.

3 The redistributional effects of inflation arise primarily from inflation being unanticipated or unexpected.

[1] Roger Leroy Miller and Raburn M. Williams, *The Economics of National Issues* (San Francisco: Canfield Press, 1972), p. 114.

4 Money creation by government can be a hidden tax on the public. An increase in the rate of money creation can lead to a higher, unanticipated rate of inflation and to greater government tax collection. Government tax collections go up in times of inflation primarily because of the progressive income tax rate system that is generally employed.

The costs of inflation are widely recognized and often exaggerated. Although wages tend to rise at faster rates during periods of rapid inflation, many people consider the cost of inflation equivalent to the reduction in the purchasing power of their money incomes. They often fail to see that their wages rise as fast as they do as a result of the rise in prices. In this way, the "costs of inflation" are exaggerated; and for this reason, reference to the "benefits of inflation" in the title of this chapter may puzzle many readers. This reference should not be nearly so puzzling when this chapter is completed. As the title suggests, our purpose is to explore who gains and who loses during inflationary times. We start our exploration with a relatively simple proposition: if no one benefited and everyone, including the government, was injured from inflation, the political opposition to inflation would probably be overwhelming. However, as we will see, governments and segments of the population benefit from inflation. For this reason, inflation is difficult to stop once it is started. We begin with a discussion of the costs of inflation and then proceed to the benefits of inflation, indicating the incentives which governments have to inflate prices.

THE COSTS OF INFLATION

The extent of the costs imposed on people by inflation depends primarily upon two factors: (1) whether the rate of inflation is anticipated or unanticipated, and (2) what the exact rate of inflation is. Let us begin our discussion with the adverse effects of a rate of inflation which people did not anticipate. This is the type of inflation which characterized the United States economy in the decade between the mid-1960s and mid-1970s.

Throughout the 1950s and the early years of the 1960s, the United States inflation rate oscillated between 1 and 3 percentage points. People were accustomed to modest price increases. When prices started to rise by 4 and 5 percent during the late 1960s, and then by more than 10 percent in the early 1970s, many people were caught off guard and understandably upset by the unexpected changes. There were a few demonstrations by grocery shoppers against escalating prices at grocery stores in the beginning phases of the inflationary spiral. The "exorbitant" 5 percent rate of inflation was a major issue in Richard Nixon's 1968 campaign for the presidency. In August of 1971 because of the public concern over inflation and his own concern for his reelection chances, President Nixon imposed a wage and price freeze on practically all goods and services. This occurred at a time when prices were rising at an annual rate of about 3.5 percent. From the vantage point of the mid-1970s, the rate of inflation at the time of the price freeze must be considered relatively modest.

Losses Suffered by Holders of Cash Balances

Unanticipated inflation of the sort experienced in the United States in the late 1960s imposes costs on people who have financial assets which are measured in dollars and which require future payments in the then current dollars. That statement is quite a mouthful, but it has a relatively simple message. It says that people who have dollars in their pockets or demand and saving accounts in their banks will lose if unanticipated inflation occurs. The value of those dollars that are held will go down, and the people who hold them will lose if a sudden increase in prices occurs. If people anticipate a high rate of inflation, they will purchase many goods and services at the prevailing lower prices before prices suddenly rise. One might argue that people who hold onto dollar assets are wagering a bet that the benefits of holding onto dollars will exceed the cost that may be suffered in the event that prices rise unexpectedly. However, that position does not change the fact that people lose from unanticipated inflation, and one must question whether or not people should be expected to wager such bets.

Losses Suffered by Institutional Creditors

Institutional creditors, like banks and insurance companies, who make loans to people during noninflationary times also lose from unanticipated inflation. For example, assume a bank makes a loan for $30,000 to someone who agrees to pay back the loan at the end of a year with a rate of interest equal to 6 percent. The bank receives $31,800 [$30,000 + (1.06 × $30,000)] at the termination date of the loan. If prices rise unexpectedly by 10 percent during the following year, the real value (what the dollars will buy) of the dollars that the creditor receives in payment are worth less than the dollars that he loaned: the $31,800 payment received is actually worth $28,900 in terms of the price level at the time the loan was made. That is to say, the creditor could have taken the $30,000 that he loaned and bought land or some other real good and have watched its price rise along with prices of other goods and services. If the price of the asset had risen by 10 percent, which is also the rate of inflation, the asset would be worth $33,000 [$30,000 + (1.10 × $30,000)]. The purchasing power of the $33,000 will be no greater than the purchasing power of the $30,000 loaned one year earlier. The bank will not have gained anything, but it will not have lost anything either, as it would have in making a loan.

If the inflation rate is anticipated, banks and other creditors can demand a higher rate of interest on money they loan out to compensate themselves for the lost purchasing power of the dollars that are paid back in inflationary times. This is what tends to happen in periods of inflation; and it is, therefore, no surprise that we usually observe higher rates of interest when the rate of inflation goes higher. According to this analysis, instead of being a cause of inflation, high interest rates tend to be a consequence of inflation.

Losses Suffered by Individual Bond Buyers

People who buy government saving bonds and corporate bonds are creditors just like banks. They "buy" bonds, but in a true sense they *loan* money to either the government or some corporation. They expect to be paid an interest return at regular intervals, and they expect to receive the principal (that is, the face value of the bond) at the "maturity date" (that is, when the loan must be repaid). The interest payments and principal are normally stated in dollar terms. An unanticipated increase in the rate of inflation can mean that people who hold these kinds of financial assets lose in terms of an unexpected drop in the purchasing power of the money they receive from their interest payments and the principal. As in the case of the bank creditors above, individuals can protect themselves against *anticipated* inflation. Unless they receive an interest rate which compensates them for the expected rate of inflation, they can (and will tend to) withhold their funds from the bond market and buy real assets like real estate, gold, and furniture.

Losses Due to Market Imperfections and Institutional Barriers

Inflation means that prices *in general* are on the rise. It does not necessarily follow that *all* prices are rising by the same percentage. In fact, some prices may not be rising at all.

Some prices tend to change rather rapidly and smoothly, reflecting changes in market forces, one of which is the quantity and velocity of money. The prices of agricultural commodities, like wheat and beef, which are determined principally in what may be characterized as an "auction market," tend to mirror changes in market conditions with reasonable rapidity. The prices of many other goods take time to adjust upward. Generally, this is a consequence of the way things are done in the market. For instance, there may be a long lag between the time an order is placed and when the product itself is delivered. Much work in many industries may be done under contracts which specify the number of dollars to be paid at the time of delivery. This is descriptive of the conditions under which commercial airplanes, heavy electrical equipment, and many buildings are constructed and sold. Unanticipated inflation can mean cost increases for the producers and narrower than expected profit margins, in addition to the fact that the value of the dollars that are paid are worth less because of the inflation.

The different rates of price increases for different goods can result in differences in the rate of increases in the wages of different worker groups. As we studied in Chapter 14, the wages paid to workers are dependent upon the prices that can be charged for the products produced. Therefore, if the prices of different products rise at different rates, the then wages must follow at different rates. Furthermore, the wages of certain worker groups are tied to contracts which extend over a period of one or more years. In short, the wages of some workers may rise as fast as prices, in which case no harm is done; the wages of other workers may lag behind the price increase. These latter workers will suffer a loss until they can adjust their contracts to account for the higher rate of inflation.

Not all reductions in the purchasing power of people's wages can be attributed to inflation. In any dynamic economy, there will always be groups of workers whose real wages are on the decline because of special market forces. Special market forces include a decrease in the demand for the good a particular group of workers produces or an increase in the supply of workers in a particular employment group. (See Chapters 14 and 15 for a thorough review of these points.) The increase in the number of people receiving doctoral degrees to teach in many areas at the college level meant that the *relative* salaries of these groups of workers fell. The rate of inflation experienced in the country over the past decade made the downward adjustment in the real wages of these groups of professionals more certain and rapid. The downward adjustment has occurred as the allotted salary increases for many educators have increased by less than prices have increased. In short, inflation can mean temporary losses in purchasing power for some groups. However, the loss in purchasing power of the wages of other groups may be more attributable to their competitively weak market position than to inflation.

Losses to Taxpayers

Almost every income earner is hurt by inflation because of the way the income tax system is structured. We have discussed the problem of the "inflation tax" in Chapter 18 (see, especially, Table 18·7); and, therefore, our treatment of the problem can be brief here. Most tax systems are arranged so that they take a higher percentage of a person's earned *money* income as his or her *money* income rises. This means that even if the Jones's money income rises with inflation—that is, their purchasing power remains constant—the government will take a greater percentage of their money income in the form of taxes. The purchasing power of the Jones's after-tax money income is less than before the inflation.

In Table 18·7 of Chapter 18 we provided a more detailed example of what could happen. We assumed that the rate of inflation was 10 percent and that the Joneses, a family of three, had a 10 percent increase in money income and a zero percent increase in real income. Given the tax structure, the Jones's tax payments rose from $1985 to $2323. Although the Joneses actually had more after-tax dollars to spend, those extra dollars did not make up for the loss in purchasing power of all dollars received in money wages. In fact, we showed that, measured in 1975 prices, the real purchasing power of the Jones's after-tax income fell from $13,015 to $12,888 during the inflationary period.

General Losses from Inflation

The general loss in the purchasing power of the dollar during inflationary times can cause people to hold fewer dollars and more real assets, such as land, houses, and business inventories. Many of these assets will be simply held and not used, in the same way and for the same reasons that money was just held. Because people hold onto real goods and resources, inflation can, therefore, mean that fewer resources are available for production and fewer goods are available for purchase. To the extent that this occurs, people will have lower incomes. There will be, in other words, losses spread throughout the economy; and because there are fewer goods and services available, these losses will be reflected in even higher prices for goods and services.

Inflation can also lead to an "overheating" of the economy. If businesses foresee a higher rate of inflation in the future and want to avoid paying higher prices, they can build up their inventory stock in the present. At some point, having accumulated more inventories than they need, businesses will cut back on their orders for goods. Then production will fall, leading to unemployment. The lost income of the unemployed workers is a cost of inflation. More will be said on these matters in Chapters 30 and 31.

In periods of modest rates of anticipated inflation, creditors can adjust their interest rates in such a way that they are compensated for the decreased value of the dollars they receive in repayment of loans. Furthermore, workers can increase their wage demands to offset the effects of inflation. However, during periods of very high inflation rates, sometimes called "hyperinflation," the rate at which the value of the dollar deteriorates can be so great that people are no longer willing to accept and hold dollars in trade for goods and services. Acting rationally, people may decide to spend the dollars they receive as fast as they can to avoid incurring significant economic losses. According to some theories, hyperinflation can lead to a moneyless economy and a return to the barter system. In the barter system, as we learned earlier, more resources will have to be devoted to searching out mutually beneficial trades; fewer resources will be available for production. The production level of the economy can fall significantly. As we pointed out before, barter was more prevalent in Germany after the First World War; hyperinflation has had some of the same effects in other places and in other times.

THE BENEFITS OF INFLATION

When someone loses from an unanticipated increase in prices, someone else typically benefits at the expense of the loser. The obvious exception is when inflation contributes to a downturn in total production in the economy. However, at the risk of being somewhat repetitious, we outline below the categories of people who tend to gain in inflationary times. As we will see, the benefits (like the costs) of inflation emerge to a large extent because the inflation is unanticipated by all people or is unevenly anticipated by different groups. When one group of people correctly anticipates an upward surge in prices and other groups do not, the group that anticipates the inflation will frequently gain at the expense of all others. The group that correctly anticipates a higher inflation rate can buy at relatively low prices before the higher inflationary rate begins and sell later at much higher prices. This point brings to light one of the problems countries face when inflationary spirals appear to be recurrent possibilities: people then tend to devote resources to trying to anticipate inflation in order that they may be among the gainers. Having made these introductory remarks, the categories of people who gain from inflation can be considered separately.

Gains to Debtors

Probably the largest single group of people to gain from inflationary periods are those who are *debtors*—that is, people who owe money *at the time the inflation begins.* The largest subgroup in this category includes people who have purchased homes under mortgage agreements and who have not yet paid off their mortgages. This subgroup represents a significant part of the population, since this is the way most single-family dwellings are financed. Homeowners benefit to the extent that the real value of their mortgages shrinks. From another perspective, the person who has a mortgage during inflationary periods is paying back dollars which are worth progressively less than the dollars that were borrowed.

To see how this works, consider a person who has purchased a house for $30,000 in 1959, putting $1000 down and taking out a mortgage for $29,000 at 6 percent interest. Today, the dollar can purchase less than half of what it could back in 1959. This means that the person's mortgage, although still in the same number of dollars, is really worth much less to the creditor (usually the bank that holds the mortgage). Furthermore, it is possible that this person's house can be sold in 1976 for something in the neighborhood of $60,000, not because it is worth more in real terms than it was back in 1959, but because the price of housing has risen in line with the prices of everything else. The real asset, the house, has held its value relative to other goods as the value of the dollar has decreased; the dollar asset, the mortgage, held by the mortgage company shrank. The debtor, in this case, gains at the expense of the creditor.

We cannot necessarily deduce, however, that the homeowner who has gained so much on his home mortgage has, *on balance*, gained from inflation. The homeowner may also have some dollar assets of his own. For example, suppose he purchased a government bond at 3 percent interest in 1964. Shrinkage of the bond's value due to inflation (a cost) can partially, if not totally, offset the shrinkage in the real value of the home mortgage.

Gains to Certain Groups of Businesses and Workers

We mentioned in the section on the costs of inflation that not all prices adjust upward in times of inflation. Institutional barriers to wage and price adjustments, such as production procedures and labor contracts, can mean that some people's wages and some product prices will rise more rapidly than others. We explained that the people who were unable to adjust their prices or wages as rapidly as others tend to incur costs because of inflation. By the same token, those people who are able to adjust their wages and prices more rapidly than others can receive temporary benefits from unanticipated inflation. Statistics reveal that in the early phases of a new and higher rate of inflation, business profits tend to rise, meaning that often product prices tend to rise faster than wages. In this case, entrepreneurs gain from inflation at the expense of workers who, perhaps, have less opportunity to figure out what the future inflation rate will be before it starts and to incorporate the anticipated higher rate of inflation into their wage demands.

Gains to Government

Those who are responsible for increasing the money stock and contributing to inflation tend to benefit from inflation. This is true whether money is made of gold or of paper. The reader may recall from an earlier chapter that the discovery of gold in California in the middle of the nineteenth century led to general, worldwide inflation. Clearly, the gold miners benefited from the gold they produced and sold. However, their benefits were limited to the difference between the cost of mining the gold and the price the gold commanded at the time they sold it. Their benefits, in other words, were equal to the profits on gold mining.[2] To the extent that gold mining increased the demand for resources, like shovels and pans, which go into gold mining, the benefits from the production of money spread to these resource owners; and we might also note that the benefits were received by the bartenders and prostitutes who followed the gold miners west.

Who paid for the benefits received by the gold miners? The answer is that part of the cost was shared among all the people who held gold at the

[2] It should be noted that not all gold miners benefited from the inflation. Many found that their costs of production exceeded the value of the gold, which had fallen in the inflationary times.

time. The new supply of gold—money—reduced the value of the gold already held. Also, people who had to compete with gold miners for resources had to pay higher prices for them; they, in a sense, bore a part of the costs.

Because gold is much more difficult and expensive to produce than paper money, the profits from producing new paper money can be much greater. This advantage has been used by a number of countries, particularly in wartime. New paper money can be produced by governments in two ways. First, the government can increase the money stock directly by either printing more dollar bills or, using appropriate bookkeeping entries, raising the bank balance that the government holds with the Federal Reserve. The government can then use this newly created money to buy the resources it needs to carry out established policy. For example, the government can use the new dollars to build more roads or military bases. How can the government do this so simply? So long as people are willing to accept dollar bills or the checks the federal government draws on its Federal Reserve account, the "stuff" the government prints or adds to its bank balance is money. In this instance, government benefits from the increase in the money stock and the inflation that ensues; more precisely, we might say that the politicians and government workers and the people who are on the receiving end of government programs benefit from the inflation. The losers are the people who have dollar assets and those who have to pay higher prices for goods and services because fewer resources are available for nongovernment uses.

The United States federal government does not now use this direct approach to increase the money stock. Instead, it can increase the money stock in a second, more circuitous manner: it can run a budgetary deficit and borrow the difference between its tax receipts and its expenditures. How does the government borrow? By issuing bonds. The Federal Reserve can then buy government bonds in the bond market, a process which creates the money which the public needs to buy the new issues of government bonds. The Fed by law does not have to accommodate or concede to the wishes of the federal Treasury. However, as we noted in Chapter 25, the Fed is often under political pressure to keep interest rates from rising, and if this pressure is great enough, the Federal Reserve will enter the market as a buyer of bonds when the federal government enters as a seller.

Regardless of the Fed's motivation, when the Fed accommodates the Treasury and buys federally issued bonds, the money stock is increased. The effect on prices is virtually the same as that which occurs when the federal government prints more dollar bills. The government gains at the expense of all people who hold onto financial assets denominated in dollars. The government gains further at the expense of taxpayers, who have to pay a higher percentage of their *real* income to the government in the form of taxes.

MONEY CREATION AS A METHOD OF TAXATION

Money creation is a means by which government can potentially redistribute resources from private to public uses. Money creation increases directly or indirectly the purchasing power of government and inflates prices. Taxes also redistribute purchasing power from the public to the government; for this reason, money creation can be considered a form of disguised taxation. This type of tax system is particularly objectionable to most economists. Through inflation the cost of government programs is distributed rather haphazardly among people. In addition, the way in which the "taxes" are collected is obscured from public scrutiny by the rather complex mechanism by which money is created. Finally, the "taxes" that are collected are never approved by Congress; therefore, it is difficult to hold elected representatives responsible for them. On the other hand, inflation can be a "desirable" tax system for politicians who want to vote for public programs without voting for compensating taxes. It is also a "desirable" tax system for government workers who want to expand the scope and size of their programs and for beneficiaries of government programs who have their relative welfare improved by this disguised form of taxation and the expanded government programs.

SUMMARY AND EXTENSIONS: SOLUTIONS TO THE REDISTRIBUTIONAL EFFECTS OF INFLATION

The general picture that emerges from our examination of inflation is that many individuals are hurt by it, particularly those who are creditors with long-term loans outstanding. Others, however, undeniably benefit from inflation, particularly debtors and the government. Further, once inflation has been under way for a time, it becomes hard to stop it without causing harm to a number of people who have made sensible adjustments to existing economic conditions. To illustrate the harmful effects that can result from stopping inflation, consider the case of the home buyer who takes on a mortgage at a high rate of interest. He accepts the high rate of interest on the assumption that inflation will continue and that he can pay the interest on the loan with depreciated dollars in the future. If the rate of inflation is reduced, the homeowner will be caught with high mortgage payments to be paid with dollars that do not depreciate as rapidly as expected. *The economic and ethical question which arises when considering the problem of inflation is whether or not people should be expected to cope with changes in the rate of increase in the price level which are beyond their control.* Using the jargon of previous chapters, monetary stability is a public good, a benefit to the general population, which can be produced by government. The problem that confronts monetary economics is one of finding ways to induce government—politicians and bureaucrats—to produce monetary stability.

Problems with inflation arise principally when the inflationary rate is unanticipated and when it is so high that people are no longer willing to accept dollars in general commerce. If the inflation is anticipated, however, as we have indicated in this chapter, people can make adjustments in the financial and real assets which they hold and in the wages which they demand for their labor. If inflation is expected, creditors can require higher rates of interest for the funds they have to loan, and laborers can incorporate the expected price increases into the calculation of their labor contracts. In general, any institutional barriers which prevent price and wage adjustments can be changed to accommodate the need to adjust prices and wages on a regular basis. There need not be in cases of expected inflation a redistribution of income from creditor to debtor and from employee to employer (or vice versa). There can still be costs associated with expected inflation, but the point is that one way of reducing many of the redistributional effects of inflation is to keep the rate of price increases sufficiently steady so that people can reasonably expect a similar rate of price increase in the future.

There is one redistributional effect of inflation which requires congressional action to correct. This is the movement of purchasing power from private citizens to the government, resulting from higher tax rates which are applied to the progressively higher *money* incomes which people tend to receive during inflationary periods. Presently, social security payments to retired people are adjusted upward along with price increases. Indeed, the pay of members of Congress now rises along with prices. These methods of adjusting to inflation suggest a solution to the "inflation tax." The tax rates which people pay on their money incomes can be adjusted downward to offset the increases in their money incomes. The purpose of the tax rate adjustment would be to ensure that inflation does not increase the *real* tax collections of government without a specific act of Congress. This is an idea, called "tax indexing," which is being employed in Canada and several European countries.

QUESTIONS TO PONDER

1 During the last few years, what effect has inflation had on your real income position? List the gains and losses that you have experienced, and indicate the net effect of inflation.

2 In this chapter we have considered the question of who gains and who loses from *inflation*. Determine who gains and who loses from *deflation*.

3 Why does *anticipated* inflation have effects on the distribution of incomes different from the effects of *unanticipated* inflation?

4 If all people *perfectly* anticipated the rate of inflation and could *perfectly* adjust their prices and wages to the anticipated rate of inflation, would there be any harm done by inflation?

5 The government presently increases the money stock via the Fed's purchase of government bonds. Would there be different effects on the economy if the government printed up dollar bills and dumped them out of airplanes?

6 Do you think inflation can be stopped? Explain.

RECOMMENDED READING

Tatom, John A.: "The Welfare Cost of Inflation," *Federal Reserve Bank of St. Louis Review,* November 1976, pp. 9–21.

Part Ten
Macroeconomics: Unemployment and National Income

Can the United States have high-employment prosperity without inflation? For some time, the American people have been asked to tune in tomorrow and find out; but the last episode of the serial has not yet been produced. In no period during the past forty years has the American economy been free of excessive unemployment *and* inflationary tendencies simultaneously. Nor has any other industrial nation found the happy combination. Hitting the dual target of high utilization and essential price stability remains the most serious unsolved problem of stabilization policy throughout the Western world.

Arthur Okun
The Political Economy of Prosperity (New York: W. W. Norton and Company, Inc., 1970), p. 100.

In this part of the book, the emphasis of our analysis shifts from the social problem of inflation to the social problem of unemployment. In Chapter 27 we reconsider the definition of unemployment and discuss several types of unemployment. Beginning in Chapter 28 and extending through Chapter 31, we consider the causes and proposed cures for what is called *cyclical* unemployment—that unemployment which rises and falls with changes in the overall demand in the economy for goods and services. In doing this we draw with greater precision the relationship between the rate of inflation and unemployment, and between the level of unemployment and the level of national production (as measured by GNP) and income. We conclude our discussion of macroeconomics in Chapter 32 with an analysis of the arguments for and against national economic planning.

27

The Meaning and Causes of Unemployment

In this country, as in others, the central government has gradually assumed political responsibility for the overall performance of the economy. Today the electorate does not fatalistically accept business cycles, unemployment, and inflation as acts of nature. Incumbent administrations and opposition candidates are expected to do something about them. Presidents are judged by their economic statistics.

James Tobin[1]

PREVIEW OF CHAPTER

Central question

What are the causes of unemployment?

Major objectives

1 To distinguish several types of unemployment

2 To outline several causes of unemployment

Major conclusions

1 There are three categories of unemployment: *frictional, structural,* and *cyclical. Frictional unemployment* is short-term unemployment that is due, for example, to shifts in consumer, business, and government demand among products. *Structural unemployment* arises because of major (struc-

[1] James Tobin, *The New Economics One Decade Older* (Princeton, N.J.: Princeton University Press, 1974), p. 71.

tural) changes in the economy, like the introduction of a new technology for supplying energy. It is the type of unemployment which may force workers to retrain before they can become employed again. *Cyclical unemployment* emerges when there is a general decrease (as opposed to a shift) in demand by the government, consumers, and businesses. (Cyclical unemployment will be treated extensively in Chapters 28 through 31.)

2 Unemployment can be present for any one of the following reasons: (*a*) the rationality of "job search," (*b*) government restrictions on labor mobility, (*c*) union and business restrictions on labor mobility, and (*d*) unemployment relief benefits which induce people to remain out of work longer than they otherwise would have.

Important terms and concepts

Frictional unemployment
Structural unemployment
Cyclical unemployment

We have defined macroeconomics as the study of the overall level of prices, production, and employment in the economy. In the last several chapters we explored the connection between the money stock and the price level and briefly discussed the relationship between prices and unemployment. In this and the next five chapters we focus on the social and economic problem of unemployment, its causes and possible remedies. This chapter is specifically concerned with defining several categories of unemployment recognized by economists. These categories are (1) *frictional unemployment*, (2) *structural unemployment*, and (3) *cyclical unemployment*. More important, we delineate several possible causes of so-called *frictional* and *structural* unemployment, emphasizing that given people's incomes and restrictions on the mobility of workers among different labor markets, some people's unemployment is rational and to be expected. Several of the points we make in this chapter require that we review the analysis of earlier chapters.

THE MEANING AND TYPES OF UNEMPLOYMENT

In 1976 approximately 55 percent of all persons 16 years old and older had jobs outside the home. This means that the rest, 45 percent, did not. Defining "unemployment" very broadly, one could say that 45 percent of the working-age population was "unemployed." Although unusual, this concept of the unemployment rate draws attention to a question which is too easily ignored: What are we trying to communicate when we talk about "unemployment" or the "unemployment rate"? There is no easy way to answer this question because different people want to communicate different images of the economy. Further, the concept of unemployment has evolved in economic analysis with few people giving serious thought to what unemployment is at a conceptual (as opposed to definitional) level. However, we will suggest answers which may be agreeable to many and may reflect the views of the people who compute *the* official unemployment rate.

We will discuss two ways to interpret unemployment statistics. First, in a limited sense, the unemployment rate is a "negative" measure of what is happening in the economy; it describes what is wrong with the economic position in which one segment of the population finds itself. For this reason, the concept of the unemployment rate does not include everyone who does not have a job. There are many people in the segment of the working-age population who do not have "regular" jobs but who are unperturbed by that fact. Within the range of their realistic life expectations, they are reasonably pleased with what they are doing. For example, there are homemakers and students who are not "working" in the normal sense of that term—but who are satisfied with what they *are* doing relative to what they think they *could* or should be doing. A student may give up school and take a "regular" job if someone offers him a $20,000 annual salary to do so; but that option is not usually within the range of a student's realistic expectations. *Given his opportunities and expectations,* on the other hand, he is content to be a student. To include the average college student in any unemployment figures would be misleading.

From this point of view, the unemployment rate is a conceptual indication of the percentage of the people who are out of work and are dissatisfied with what they are doing, given their employment opportunities. In designing a workable measure of the unemployment rate (that is, a rate that can be compiled each period), the Bureau of Labor Statistics has had to develop largely arbitrary definitions of what constitutes an employed ("satisfied") or unemployed ("dissatisfied") person. As we explained in Chapter 23, people under 16 are not even classified as a part of the labor force and are, therefore, not even given a chance to express their satisfaction with regard to their economic position. Further, people who are working are assumed to be "satisfied," whereas people who are not working but say they would like jobs better than those being offered them are assumed to be dissatisfied." We must draw this conclusion because a person can turn down a job that he considers unacceptable, remain out of work, and be counted as one of the unemployed by a survey worker of the Bureau of Labor Statistics who may interview him. Regardless of the measurement problems, when we discuss the unemployed in this and the following chapters, we will, in one sense, be referring to a group of people who are not working and are dissatisfied with their economic positions and who believe that their dissatisfaction is due to factors beyond their control.

The concept of unemployment can be interpreted in a second way: as an economic variable to be manipulated through the design of appropriate government policy. As James Tobin suggests in the quotation heading this chapter, the federal government has gradually assumed responsibility for maintaining "full employment" of the labor force. This responsibility was explicitly delegated to the administration by Congress in the "Employment Act of 1946," and it has been reaffirmed in the "Full Employment and Balanced Growth Act of 1976" (also called the "Humphrey-Hawkins Bill"). Although the Humphrey-Hawkins Bill is still before Congress at this writing, it provides us with a very good example of the type of policy position often considered by Congress and endorsed by the Carter administration. Senator Hubert Humphrey, a sponsor of the bill, has said of this bill:

> There is nothing radical in the Full Employment and Balanced Growth Act. Put in its simplest terms, it says that the overriding responsibility of the Federal Government is to pursue the budgetary and monetary tools that have long been at hand to achieve and sustain the economic conditions that will provide everyone who wants to work with the opportunity for meaningful employment at fair wages, while maintaining an adequate check against inflation. And it fleshes out its mandate with a time frame, procedures and a numerical goal to do so.[2]

This particular bill would require the federal government to reduce the unemployment rate for adults to 3 percent within four years after the bill is enacted. Regardless of whether or not the bill is ever passed, the principle in the bill requires the government to follow certain policy courses. To reduce unemployment, the federal government is required to use monetary policy (of the kind discussed in Chapter 25) and fiscal policy (of the kind to be discussed in Chapter 30) to increase the country's demand for goods and services and, thereby, employment. This particular bill requires that the government become the "employer of

[2] Hubert H. Humphrey, "Humphrey View on S.50," *Public Interest Economics Review*, September 1976, p. 3.

last resort," providing public service–type jobs for those people who cannot find employment at a "fair wage" in the private sector of the economy. If the government decides to affect the level of employment in the country, it must have *a target* at which it can direct public policy and by which it can judge the relative effectiveness of different public policies. The concept of unemployment is that target.

Presumably, the purpose of a public employment policy is to improve people's employment opportunities. In order to achieve this goal, the variable to be manipulated, the unemployment rate, should then be a measure of that portion of the population whose employment can be improved by public policy. As we learned in Chapter 23, the unemployment rate, as it is computed, is deficient as a means of determining how many people have an unsatisfactory employment position. For instance, people who are temporarily out of work because they are in the process of changing jobs (that is, are scheduled to report to a new and possibly better job within 30 days) are counted as a part of the unemployment statistics. Many consider the inclusion of this group in the unemployment statistics inappropriate. However, the unemployment rate can still be a rough approximation of how public policy is working. Regardless, this view of the concept of unemployment presumes that the unemployment has causes which can be remedied by government action.

Three types of unemployment are distinguished at the conceptual level, although they are difficult to distinguish in unemployment statistics. They are as follows:

1 *Frictional unemployment.* This type of unemployment is in part a consequence of short-run shifts in supply of and demand for various goods. It is often called *transitional unemployment* because it is the type of unemployment that emerges in the transition period when, for example, consumers decide to buy less of one good and more of another. This type of unemployment emerged when there was a shift in consumer demand from large to small automobiles and then back when the prices of gasoline went up in the first half of the 1970s and then back down. Generally, this type of unemployment remains for a relatively short period of time, perhaps a few weeks, and it dissipates when workers find new employment opportunities in other industries. However, frictional unemployment can also exist because of short-term adjustment which people must make in response to normal changes in the labor markets, like deaths, retirements, and changes in people's experiences and educational levels.

2 *Structural unemployment.* Structural unemployment is a result of the fundamental structure (or institutional arrangement) of the economy, and its level changes with changes in the economy's basic structure. People are considered "structurally unemployed" while they are in the process of adjusting their work skills to the demands of economic life. Some people, like many unemployed migrant workers, are unable to make the necessary adjustments and remain unemployed; others, like teachers who lose their jobs because of restricted school budgets, remain unemployed only while they retrain for new jobs.

Structural unemployment may also be caused by laws which impose stricter qualifications for certain jobs, laws which ban the production of certain products like fireworks, or laws which impose stricter environmental control standards. Structural unemployment can also emerge as a consequence of substantial changes in programs which are supported by government funds. Many aerospace engineers were structurally unemployed in the late 1960s when the government decided to sharply curtail its manned space exploration efforts. Generally speaking, structural unemployment is distinguished from frictional unemployment by the amount of time required by workers to adjust to changing economic conditions. Structural unemployment requires a longer adjustment period than frictional unemployment. In practice, however, "long" and "short" adjustment periods are never clearly defined, and the terms are often used interchangeably.

3 *Cyclical unemployment.* This is the type of unemployment that emerges as a consequence of downward movements in the level of consumer, business, and/or government demand for practically all goods and services. When people decide, for one reason or another, to buy fewer goods and services and to save more, some workers are no longer needed and are laid off until the overall level of demand picks up again. Cyclical unemployment is the type of unemployment which rises during depressions. In a depression, the production level of almost all industries falls; people's demand for goods and services does not merely shift from one product to another—rather, their demand for almost all products falls. This type of unemployment takes its name from the fact that it tends to appear and dissipate with the irregular up-and-down cyclical swings in nations' production of goods and services (which is measured by Gross National Product).

The causes and proposed cures of cyclical unemployment will be the main focus of Chapters 28–31. In the next section we explain in more detail the possible causes of frictional and structural unemployment.

THE CAUSES OF STRUCTURAL AND FRICTIONAL UNEMPLOYMENT

Structural and frictional unemployment emerge when there are changes in the economy and laborers are required or induced to move from one labor market to another to seek employment. Since we live in an imperfect world in which adaptation to economic changes takes time, economic adjustments are costly. Unfortunately, however, a major portion of the cost of the total adjustment is borne by those who must do the adjusting and remain unemployed while they do so. As we will see in this section, the time it takes workers to make the required adjustments is dependent upon the cost of finding suitable employment, upon restrictions on labor mobility, and upon the income people have to support themselves with while they are out of work. Alexis de Tocqueville, the great French historian of the nineteenth century, was one of the first people to notice a direct relationship between the level of a country's unemployment and the level of the country's income. He observed that relatively wealthy people can afford to be unemployed for a period of time: they can "afford" to be "dissatisfied" with the low-paying jobs that are offered them and wait until better job opportunities appear. People in very impoverished areas of the world must take whatever job they can find to survive; they cannot "afford" to be unemployed for very long. Those who are unemployed frequently die of starvation, as is the case for so many people who live along the southern borders of the Sahara and in southern Ethiopia. In reviewing the causes of unemployment, you should keep in mind that although many unemployed American workers are poor, many are not. Consider, for example, the automobile or steel worker who is at times unemployed. Regardless, even the very poor unemployed American worker typically has a standard of living several times the income of most employed people in underdeveloped areas of the world.

The Rationality of Job Search

Some degree of unemployment is a natural consequence of a free society. This is so partly because people who enter the labor market are not always aware of the employment opportunities available to them. They require time to establish what their employment opportunities are and to select that opportunity which is the best, based on the employment information they are able to collect in their search.

Searching for a job can often be frustrating, aggravating, and demoralizing. The individuals seeking jobs have to incur the cost of assessing (and watching others assess) what their talents and abilities are and how, through training, they can change them. Their problem is complicated by the fact that they have to assess the talents and abilities of their potential competitors in various job markets. They have to try to foresee changes in the supply of and demand for labor in various markets over the course of their working lives and to determine how much upward and lateral mobility they will have in each of several different career choices. Further, when individuals are in the labor market, they are usually concerned about how a job will complement or detract from their other life goals. For example, they will be interested in knowing whether or not they will enjoy those with whom they will have to work and associate, the nature of the community in which they will have to work and live, the respect that they will receive from the general public, and how many sacrifices their families will be forced to make. In summary, the workers who enter the labor market are confronted with a multidimensional problem which is made difficult by the fact that few things are certain. They have to operate on the basis of very rough probabilities, and the more carefully they research all these factors, the more time they spend unemployed and, consequently, the more costly their job search becomes.

A careful job search is costly; however, people can also incur a significant cost if they make a mistake in choosing their employment. If they find their job situation disagreeable and resign or if they are fired because their employer is dissatisfied with what they are doing, they have to incur the cost of searching for another job. On the other hand, if they fail to find the highest-paying or most satisfying job they could have obtained, they have to incur the opportunity cost of having a lower-paying job for many years. If they had searched for a job more carefully in the beginning, these types of costs could have been avoided.

Rational persons in the labor market will weigh the *expected* costs of job search against the *expected* benefits (as revealed in their demand curve). They can be expected to seek some optimal level of job search. As we learned in the first half of this book, the optimal level of doing anything like undertaking job search will be the point at which the marginal benefit of the last unit of job search is equal to the marginal cost of it. Since searching for a job involves time, all that we have said leads to the conclusion that there is some rationally determined level of unemployment, and that rational level will be different for different people. So long as there are costs and benefits to searching out jobs, the unemployment rate will not be zero. However, we expect the actual, rationally determined level of unemployment to vary with the magnitude of the costs and benefits of searching for a job. The *greater* the benefits of job search, the *greater* the unemployment, and vice versa. The *greater* the cost of job search, the *lower* the unemployment, and vice versa.

Social and Governmental Restrictions on Labor Market Mobility

Unemployment is often caused by restrictions on the movement of labor into and among labor markets. Many of these restrictions are socially determined. For example, a country's elderly, its youth, and its black workers may be unemployed because of unwritten social rules which mitigate against their employment. Alternatively, many people have family ties to a region which keep them from moving to areas of the country where jobs are more plentiful. In addition to social or cultural barriers to labor market mobility, government regulations can act as barriers. Perhaps the most clear-cut example of governmentally inspired barriers is the group of laws in effect in advanced countries prohibiting or stringently controlling the immigration of people from poorer parts of the world in search of a job. These restrictions can increase the number of people who remain unemployed in all countries. The foreign laborers who legally or illegally enter the United States, for example, can indirectly increase the rationally determined level of measured unemployment of some Americans. A greater supply of foreign laborers can reduce the wages of all laborers in United States markets into which the immigrants move. At the lower wage, many American workers will then find the cost of remaining unemployed and, perhaps, searching for a job longer than otherwise. This should lead to an increase in the time spent on job search by some Americans and an increase in their unemployment.

One government restriction on the labor market undeniably generates a fairly significant amount of unemployment: the minimum wage law. As we studied in Chapter 15, the minimum wage law says, in essence, that if a worker's labor is not worth the current minimum wage, it is illegal for him or her to be hired. If the minimum wage law is sufficiently high to effectively raise the wage rate of some workers, it will bar employment for some workers whose productivity is low. This is so because the demand for labor is downward sloping. (See Chapter 14 for a review.) Low-productivity workers barred by the minimum wage are generally new entrants into the labor market who have not yet acquired needed work skills or not yet developed a reputation for hard and productive work. The minimum wage law is, therefore, particularly hard on teenagers and has been cited as a particularly oppressive law for black teenagers.

There are other groups, however, who have difficulty with the minimum wage. People who are only intermittently in the labor force may find it difficult to get jobs because their productivity is so low that no one is willing to pay them the minimum wage, and hence they are not readily employed while the minimum wage is in existence. People who are compelled to change from one job to another are also apt to be hurt by the minimum wage law. The minimum wage makes it legally impossible for new labor market entrants to offer to work for low money wages in return for receiving on-the-job training which will increase their incomes later.

There are a number of other governmental restrictions which are designed to increase employment. The effect of many of these restrictions, however, is to reduce some existing employment opportunities. The most obvious of these laws is the 40-hour workweek law passed during the 1930s. The idea behind the law was to spread the given number of work-hours per week over a larger number of people by restricting the total employment of any one person to 40 hours per week. By compelling the employer to pay time-and-a-half for each hour over 40 that a person works in one week the proponents of the bill hoped to reduce the total hours worked per week by each employee. This restriction has accomplished its purpose, but it has also had the effect of increasing the number of workers who "moonlight," that is, take a second job. Many people who would like to work more than 40 hours a week but whose employers do not think their labor is worth the required time-and-a-half simply get a second, part-time job. Approximately one-fifth of the American labor force takes a second job. Some companies have effectively circumvented this labor market restriction by trading work forces. That is to say, when the workers of two companies reach the 40-hour limit, the workers of one company will go to work for the other company, and vice versa. The two companies can then legally avoid paying time-and-a-half for the extra labor. To the extent that the actions of these employers and employees are costly, the 40-hour workweek rule contributes to inefficiency. The law also encourages employers to hire only those workers to whom they feel they can justifiably pay time-and-a-half overtime when extra labor is needed during peak production periods. This rule may increase the employment opportunities of the more productive; however, it will tend to reduce the employment opportunities of workers who are relatively unproductive.

Employment opportunities can also be reduced by governmentally imposed employee health standards and occupational safety standards for various industries. These standards tend to increase the cost of hiring people; to the extent that this is the case, the standards will lead to a reduction in the number of people hired. Wherever possible, businesses will substitute capital equipment (such as automated machines) for labor, reducing employment opportunities in the process. In Chapter 16 we suggested that the improved housing standards for migrant workers reduced their employment opportunities; the argument concerning the effects of health and safety standards in other industries follows the same line of analysis. When employers are held responsible for employees' job-related injuries, the cost of hiring workers again rises, and fewer workers will be demanded. Employers will tend to hire those workers who have the lowest risk of being injured. These laws tend to reduce the employment opportunities of accident-prone workers. All that we have said here is not meant to suggest that these laws are "bad," using that term in a broad sense. On the contrary, we mean only to suggest the unemployment consequences of such laws. In the final analysis, people may wish to trade some employment opportunities for additional job security which may come with government control of various aspects of labor markets.

Union and Business Restrictions on Labor Market Mobility

Unions can reduce employment opportunities in two basic ways. First, if a union excludes some workers from membership, it excludes them from having the chance to be employed in jobs which, according to a contract between employer and the union, must be done by union members. For example, in order to do plumbing work on many construction projects, a person must be a member of the union that has contracted with the builder binding the builder to employ only union workers. Second, a union can use its monopoly power to raise the wages of an industry's workers. If the union-determined wage rate is raised, the employer will hire fewer workers. The result of the higher-than-free-market wage is a reduction in employment opportunities. If the employers can pay a lower wage, they can lower the price of their final product. A lower price on the final product increases the volume of sales of the final product and, thereby, increases the number of jobs available to workers.

As indicated here, unions can reduce employment opportunities. This does not mean that all workers excluded from employment in the unionized industries will necessarily be unemployed in the sense that they do not have a job. Many workers excluded from work in the unionized sector of the economy can get a job in the nonunionized sector. This means, however, that because of unions, there will be more people who seek jobs in the nonunionized sector, and the wages paid in that sector will fall. The fall in nonunion wages reduces the cost of being unemployed and increases the likelihood of people deciding to search for longer periods of time for a job. This line of reasoning is especially applicable to people who want to become the second income earner within a family. These people, unsatisfied with the wages that are paid in the jobs that they have been offered, can be supported while they search for better-paying jobs. Still, while the second income earner searches for a job, he or she is counted as unemployed.

The pay which union scales require employers to maintain is often very rigid. In other words, employers are unable to reduce the wage rates they pay during times of slack demand for their products. Employers, therefore, must respond to a fall in demand for their final products by changing the number of workers they hire. Because of the prevalent seniority rules in unionized industries, new workers with relatively low seniority are laid off first in times of slack demand. This does not mean, however, that joining a union is not a good idea for a young worker. If wages paid to union members are well above wages that can be earned in nonunionized markets, it can be worth a young worker's time to take a job in a unionized industry even though realizing that, for a number of years, he or she will be laid off when there is a reduced volume in the company's business. On the other hand, one can expect that in the latter part of one's life one will acquire enough seniority to work steadily.

Where seniority rules exist in a unionized industry, there may be unemployment among younger workers who have chosen, quite deliberately, intermittent employment for a number of years with the idea of eventually having steady employment at a high wage. Although this type of unemployment is inefficient, it does not necessarily impose suffering on the workers who are unemployed. The young workers "lose" when they are unemployed, but they may believe that they will be compensated with higher-than-free-market wages when they work.

We explained in Chapter 15 that a *monopsonistic* employer is a dominant employer in a given labor market which, thereby, can significantly affect the market wage rate by changing its demand for labor. By reducing its demand for labor, the monopsonistic employer can reduce the wage rate that it has to pay its workers and can increase its profits by doing so. This profit-maximizing behavior on the part of the monopsonist, however, represents a barrier to employment for some workers. Because the monopsonist hires fewer workers than would have been hired in a competitive market, some workers remain unemployed or are forced to seek employment in markets not controlled by the monopsonist. The wages in these nonmonopsonistic markets will be lower than they otherwise would have been; some workers will, accordingly, rationally decide to remain unemployed and continue to seek higher-paying jobs.

Unemployment Relief as an Inducement to Unemployment

We indicated above that an individual who is seeking a job for one reason or another will be well advised to spend at least some time looking over the market and not to simply grab the first job that is available. How long should one look for a new job? Clearly, the answer to this question is partially affected by one's resources. If someone (the federal government, for example) is paying one a high percentage of what one would have made if one were employed, one may be well advised to look around very carefully.

Many unemployed workers are impoverished because they are unable to find work for a long period of time and because they have no significant source of income other than their unemployment compensation. Eleven million people in the United States in 1976 lived in families with incomes below the poverty line because they were unable to find work during the entire year or were "unemployed 15 weeks or more." This group of people accounted for approximately 42 percent of the total 25.9 million people who were officially classified as poor in 1976.[3] On the other hand, not all unemployed workers are impoverished, and some (although we do not know how many) are able to treat the period of time they are unemployed as a vacation. Some of these workers pick up their unemployment checks in the state where they vacation. In 1976 a CBS television program, "60 Minutes," interviewed a number of unemployed workers who were on vacation in Florida and receiving their unemployment checks there. One of the several people whom they interviewed was a young golf professional whose work in the North as a teaching pro lasted from late spring to early fall. During the winter he was unemployed and went to Florida, where he could continue to practice his golf game while receiving unemployment compensation. When discussing the difficulties of the Austrian hotel industry during the 1975 general depression in Europe, the London *Economist* said, "Hotels and pensions were full but the visitors—many of them Germans holidaying on unemployment pay—economized rigidly, buying beer at the corner store and drinking water with meals."[4] No doubt these German tourists were interested in a job which would permit them to take vacations in greater luxury, but it is equally certain that, while they were on vacation in Austria, they were not vigorously looking for a job in Germany.

By listing the possible income sources which an unemployed worker has, we do not mean to suggest that every unemployed worker leads the "life of Riley" while unemployed. Most lead lives which are far removed from the life of the vacationer. We mean to indicate only that the unemployment compensation can, for some people, be the small added advantage which will induce some people to remain unemployed longer than they would otherwise. The actual benefits which an unemployed worker can receive while unemployed are not very large. In 1976 the maximum payment for an unemployed worker was $103 a week, and the whole amount is nontaxable. In addition to this income, many unemployed workers apply for and receive the benefits of the food stamp program. The amount of the subsidy under the food stamp program depends upon the size of the family and the amount of assets the family has. In addition, the unemployment compensa-

[3] "2.5 Million More Americans in Poverty: Nation's Poor Now Number 25.88 Million, Census Bureau Says," *Washington Post*, Sept. 26, 1976, p. 1.

[4] "Just Before the Wave Breaks," *The Economist*, Oct. 11, 1975, p. 58.

tion can be income which is added to the income earned by other members of the family.

England provides us with a particularly striking illustration of how unemployment compensation can affect the unemployment rate. From 1945 to 1966, the unemployment rate in England was less than 1 percent. During this period the government compensation for the unemployed Englishman was so low that a significant percentage of the unemployed in England did not bother to pick up their checks. In 1966, the unemployment compensation was sharply raised. To the surprise of many Englishmen, the unemployment rate rose dramatically and has remained about twice its highest pre-1966 level ever since. A part of this rise is simply due to the fact that a larger percentage of the people already unemployed registered with the unemployment commission in order to be eligible for the higher unemployment compensation. Since the English unemployment rate is computed with reference to the number of *registered* unemployed workers, the unemployment rate rose with the increase in the number of people registering. In addition, however, the higher unemployment compensation induced people to remain unemployed for a longer period of time.

This experience has led to a debate in England between those who believe that the greater unemployment compensation served to increase unemployment and those who argue that the observed relationship between the greater unemployment compensation and the higher unemployment rate was a coincidence and can be explained by other factors. However, the experience has led the government to experiment with a new method for providing unemployment relief. The English are experimenting with paying people who become unemployed, not an income of so much per week until they find a job, but a flat payment which is based on the probable number of weeks of unemployment times the established payment rate. This payment is made when the person becomes unemployed and can be kept even if the person is reemployed the following day. On the other hand, if it turns out that the person has great difficulty in getting a job and is unemployed for a much longer time than the payment covers, he or she is in trouble. Although this method provides an incentive to unemployed people to get jobs, it does raise the question of whether or not and to what extent the unemployed should be called upon to run the risk of having no governmental relief in the event suitable employment cannot be found by the time the expected payment period ends. Further, this new system provides an incentive for people who know that they can find another job with relative ease to seek ways of being laid off or fired. Needless to say, the results of this "social experimentation" are not complete at this writing.

SUMMARY AND EXTENSIONS

In this chapter we have defined and explained several causes of *frictional* and *structural* unemployment. It follows that, given any reasonable measure of the unemployment rate, there is some rationally determined level of unemployment below which the economy cannot be pushed. Several factors, such as the rationality of job search, governmental and union restrictions on labor movements among different markets, and unemployment compensation, lead to some level of unemployment called the "natural rate of unemployment." This terminology is misleading in the sense that it may suggest that this is all that can be expected of a market economy operating "naturally." However, we stress that several of the causes of unemployment can be affected to some extent by both governmental and union policy. Much unemployment is "natural" or "inevitable" only to the extent that the government is unable or unwilling to take appropriate policy action, such as to reduce the minimum wage.

In the final analysis, the design of government policy must realistically consider the political constraints of a democratic form of government. Since there are many more people who benefit from the minimum wage laws than there are people who are harmed by them, and since there are many people who fail to understand the adverse effects of such laws, we doubt that minimum wage laws will ever be removed from the books. Further, there is always a question of equity when we consider the problems of unemployment and what should be done about them. It may be true that people are induced to become unemployed and to remain unemployed longer than they would otherwise because of the unemployment compensation payments made by government. However, should we not be willing to trade a little efficiency in the operation of the market in order to alleviate the hardship which many people experience? Should the government not impose safety standards in places of work in spite of the fact that some unemployment may emerge? These are some very tough questions which economics cannot answer. On the other hand, economics can tentatively suggest the possible trade-offs which must be made when public policy is formulated.

QUESTIONS TO PONDER

1 Although people usually overlook them, there are actually many potential jobs around at very low pay. Make up a list of things that you would be willing to pay someone 50 cents a day to do, if labor at that price were available. How many "unemployed" people would be willing to work for that wage rate? Should people who refuse to work for that wage rate be classified as unemployed? How much would you have to offer to get most of the things on your list done? Why are you willing to do many of those things for yourself?

2 Many students have part-time jobs while they are in college. Suppose that, in an effort to aid these students, Congress passed a law providing a minimum wage of $5 per hour for anyone in college. What would be the effect on unemployment?

3 Let us suppose that the present unemployment pay for most people, after adjustment for taxes, leaves the unemployed with a take-home income of about 70 percent of what they would have earned if employed. Assume that if we lowered the rate to 60 percent, unemployment would be cut by one-third, and if we raised it to 80 percent of the normal income, unemployment would be increased by one-third over the present level. Would either of these changes seem sensible to you? Why or why not?

4 Currently, after a period of 26 weeks unemployment benefits run out. One of the responses of democratic legislatures to sizable unemployment is to extend the period a person is eligible for unemployment compensation. What effect do these extensions have on the unemployment rate? Explain the logic that you used in arriving at your answer.

5 Currently, the government spends approximately $20 billion per year on unemployment compensation. Professor Robert Z. Aliber of the University of

Chicago proposes that the government take a portion of this amount and pay employers for increasing their employment in times of high unemployment. The amount to be paid for each additional worker hired would be determined by competitive bidding among employers; that is, employers would make bids to the government to hire so many workers for so much in the way of a government "unemployment grant," and the government would take those bids which, given the funds it has for the purpose, would maximize the additional employment opportunities for people. What effect would this have on the unemployment rate? What effect would this scheme have on the incentive of employers to fire workers and bid for the government funds?

RECOMMENDED READINGS

Galbraith, John Kenneth: *The New Industrial State* (Boston: Houghton Mifflin Company, 1967), chaps. 21, 22, and 33.

Smith, Robert Stewardt: *The Occupational, Safety, and Health Act: Its Goals and Its Achievements* (Washington, D.C.: American Enterprise Institute for Public Policy Research, 1976).

28

The "New Economics" of Unemployment and the National Income Level: An Introduction

Revolutions occur infrequently in the United States. Or else, when these uprisings happen, there are few observers sufficiently alert to recognize them. Relative unobtrusiveness is only one reason that the "new" economics is so remarkable; with hardly a shot fired, it was named an "economic" revolution in its own time.

E. Ray Canterberry[1]

PREVIEW OF CHAPTER

Central question

Who is John Maynard Keynes, and what are the essential characteristics of his theory of how the national income and employment levels are determined?

Major objectives

1 To explain the importance of the work of John Maynard Keynes in the history of economic thought

2 To develop in an elementary way the essential characteristics of what has

[1] E. Ray Canterberry, *Economics on a New Frontier* (Belmont, Calif.: Wadsworth Publishing Company, Inc., 1968), p. i.

come to be known as the "Keynesian model of income and employment determination"

3 To compare Keynesian economics with theories of income and employment determination that were prevalently held by economists at the time Keynes developed his theories

Major conclusions

1 John Maynard Keynes is primarily remembered today for his theories of income and employment determination that were developed in *The General Theory of Employment, Interest, and Money.* This book was published in 1936 and reflects Keynes's interest in developing a theory which explained the Great Depression, a long period of high unemployment and low production levels.

2 Before Keynes, economists attributed unemployment to normal shifts in the supplies of and demands for products and to rigidities in wage rates paid to labor, that is, to labor market obstacles which prevented the wage rate from seeking its equilibrium rate. Unemployment could also be due to such factors as changes in the money stock which effect the price level and, therefore, the *real wage rate* paid to labor and the quantity of labor supplied and demanded in the market.

3 Keynes argued that unemployment could be due to the failure of consumers and businesses to buy all the goods produced in the economy. That is, if businesses and consumers fail to buy all that is produced in the economy, firms will have to lay off people, reducing national production and increasing unemployment.

4 In the Keynesian model of income determination, the conditions for equilibrium in the macroeconomy can be stated in two ways: first, the macroeconomy is in equilibrium when the aggregate (or total) demand for all goods and services in the economy is exactly equal to the aggregate (or total) supply of all goods in the economy. Second, when government is left out of the analysis, the macroeconomy is in equilibrium when the level of *saving* undertaken by households and firms exactly equals the level of *investment* expenditures (i.e., the purchase of plant and equipment).

5 In the Keynesian model the equilibrium income level may or may not be the full-employment income level.

6 A way of solving the unemployment problem in the Keynesian system is for government to increase aggregate demand in the economy either by increasing its own expenditures on goods and services like roads and schools or by lowering taxes which people have to pay.

Important terms and concepts

Classical economists
Real wage rate
Circular flow of income
Saving
Investment
Equilibrium income level

No single individual has had more profound influence on the direction of modern economic thought than John Maynard Keynes. Keynes (1883–1946) was an erudite British professor of economics who wrote principally in the area of monetary and international economics and who advised heads of state in Great Britain and the United States on economic policy. During his lifetime, he was able to accumulate a sizable fortune speculating in (that is, buying and selling) currencies in the foreign exchange market, and he died Lord Keynes.

Keynes's career was distinguished, but his reputation today rests primarily upon a book he published in 1936, *The General Theory of Employment, Interest, and Money*.[2] In that work Keynes waged a frontal attack on the conventional explanation for unemployment, a theory which he attributed to the so-called "classical economists." By "classical economists" Keynes meant, generally speaking, those economists who tended to think about problems of unemployment in terms of the type of supply and demand analysis of individual labor markets we employed in the first half of this book. These economists explained most unemployment by focusing on the "structural" and "frictional" obstacles in individual markets which prevent the wage rate from falling and bringing the number of people who want to work in line with the number of jobs available. As we pointed out in the preceding chapter, these obstacles may include union resistance to wage reductions, minimum wage laws, and unemployment compensation.

In the sense that these traditional theories of unemployment deal with specific labor markets, they were, and still are, considered to be "partial equilibrium theories." That is, these theories do not attempt to bring together the analysis of different markets under the umbrella of one general theory of unemployment. Keynes, on the other hand, formulated a theory of unemployment which transcended individual labor markets and dealt with the economy as a whole. His was truly a theory of the macroeconomy.

Keynes wrote *The General Theory* during the depth of the Great Depression, a period of very low production levels, high unemployment, and falling prices and wages. The classical theories, as he perceived them, were unable to explain the persistence of high unemployment rates throughout the entire economy. Keynes sought to break with tradition in an effort to explain the events of his day. He hit upon the relatively simple notion that unemployment is, in part, a consequence of the inability or unwillingness of consumers and businesses in the aggregate to buy enough in the marketplace to keep all people who are willing to work employed. Because he integrated his model of insufficient total or aggregate demand with theories of the supply of and demand for money and how interest rates are determined, he considered his work a "general theory."

Falling wages and prices may eventually bring about full employment; but, as Keynes wrote, "In the long run, we are all dead." He was concerned with the welfare of people during the period (which may not be short) in which the pricing system adjusts toward equilibrium. He set his sights on policy recommendations which, although they may have few lasting effects, will alleviate the *short-term problems*—that is, economic conditions of very low production and very high unemployment similar to those which existed during the Depression of the 1930s. His basic policy recommendation was that during periods of heavy unemployment in the private sector of the economy, the government should add stimulus to the economy by spending more than it collects in taxes. In other words, the government should purposefully run *budgetary deficits*.[3] Before Keynes, the prevailing political philosophy centered around the view that government must balance its budget—that is, government must spend no more than it collects in taxes.

[2] John Maynard Keynes, *The General Theory of Employment, Interest, and Money* (New York: Harcourt, Brace, and World, Inc., 1936).

[3] A budgetary deficit is an excess of expenditures over tax receipts. If the government collects $350 billion in taxes but spends $395 billion, the deficit is $45 billion.

Given this view, Keynes's policy recommendation was considered radical by many, and his analysis has been referred to as the "new economics" of unemployment. Viewing Keynes's ideas in the 1970s, however, his analysis of the cause and cure of unemployment has become "old hat."

Over the past four decades, Keynes's *General Theory* has been interpreted, reinterpreted, refined, and extended. The questions "What did Keynes really say?" and "What did the interpreters of Keynes say that Keynes said?" have formed the basis of a plethora of doctoral dissertations and journal articles in economics. During the 1960s the Keynesian prescription for dealing with unemployment became accepted doctrine for most economists and reasonable governmental policy for most politicians. Now, after several years of high unemployment and high inflation rates, accompanied by large budgetary deficits, the faith of many economists in the Keynesian model has been shaken. In the 1930s Keynes faced and sought to deal with the problems of high unemployment and *falling* prices; but the high rates of inflation and unemployment are a combination which Keynesian analysis was not designed to handle. Many economists are in search of an alternative approach to the problems of unemployment that will fit the conditions of the 1970s and 1980s. Some believe the answer is a variation on the basic Keynesian model; others have virtually abandoned the Keynesian approach, adopting in its place the "monetarists' model" of unemployment and inflation. In some respects, these latter economists have returned to a more sophisticated version of explanations for unemployment that had strong professional acceptability during the first third of this century, completing the circle, in a limited way, to the time before Keynes. The study of Keynesian economics, however, is still important because the study of it will help us understand what has taken place in the economy over the last fifty years and evaluate government policy adopted in the recent past and present.

In this and the following three chapters we plan to cover macroeconomic theory, past and present. We begin by briefly considering several theories of unemployment prominent before the "Keynesian revolution" with an eye to putting that revolution in historical perspective. Then we develop the basic Keynesian model of unemployment, not as Keynes himself developed it, but as his followers have. In Chapter 29 we extend and state more precisely the basic model developed here. We explain in Chapter 30 the logic behind the Keynesian solutions to the problems of unemployment. Chapter 31 deals with the monetarist model of unemployment and inflation and compares the Keynesian and monetarist models.

As Keynes wrote, "The Theory of Economics does not furnish a body of settled conclusions immediately applicable to policy. It is a method rather than a doctrine, an apparatus of the mind, a technique of thinking which helps its possessor draw correct conclusions."[4] We will see in this section on unemployment that the competing theories have led to conflicting advice as to appropriate economic policy. Many years will go by before the debate is really, if ever, settled; we cannot, therefore, pretend to offer settled conclusions here. In the interim, government policy must go on, and we can only outline the framework which economists use to think about unemployment and inflation and, in that way, isolate the points of contention in observed governmental actions.

BEFORE KEYNES

The economic problems of the Great Depression were some of the most severe that people have had to face. Many economists turned their attention to these problems, and several prior to Keynes developed theories to explain what they saw. In fairness, a number of economists who wrote about unemployment in the pre-1936 era made many of the same policy recommendations that Keynes did. They argued that in times of heavy unemployment, the government should purposefully run budgetary deficits, that is, spend more than it collects in taxes, and in that way stimulate the economy and create jobs. Their

[4] John Maynard Keynes, op. cit.

theories, perhaps, were not as precisely developed as Keynes's; nonetheless, their conclusions were identical to Keynes's. For instance, Jacob Viner and Frank Knight, two economists whom Keynes would have probably included in the "classical school," argued for deficits also. Viner said, "When business activity is declining, or is stagnant and at a low level, reduced taxation, and budget deficits are, from the point of view of the national economy as a whole, sound policy rather than unsound."[5] Frank Knight also wrote, "As far as I know, economists are completely agreed that the Government should spend as much and tax as little as possible at a time like this—using the expenditure to do the most good in itself and also to point toward relieving the depression."[6]

To these and other economists, *The General Theory* was nothing new, and they may have been surprised to find later that the book had become the manifesto for the "new economics." However, in order for an idea to become widely accepted, it must be presented and promoted in an attractive way. For this reason the significance of Keynes probably lies more in how he said what he did and how he attracted professional and public attention than in the complete originality of what he said.

Still, many economists of the 1930s were hard pressed to explain the Great Depression, and *The General Theory* provided a relatively simple and straighforward explanation. We now turn to the development of several explanations of unemployment held before the appearance of *The General Theory*.

The Basic Classical Model

In discussing the problems of unemployment, the classical economists assumed that the number of workers that employers are willing to hire is inversely related to the *real* wage rate: if the real wage rate rises, the number of available jobs falls, and vice versa. As you will recall, the *real* wage equals the purchasing power of the *nominal* or *money* wage rate (i.e., the number of dollars a person earns per hour or day). Because the general price level determines how much a given money wage will buy, the real wage can be expressed as the ratio W/P, where W is the *money* wage and P is an index (like the Consumer Price Index) representing the general price level, or

$$\text{Real wage} = \frac{\text{money wage}}{\text{price index}} = \frac{W}{P}$$

Notice that the real wage, W/P, will rise with an increase in the money wage, W, and will fall with an increase in the price level, P.

In our previous discussions of labor markets (Chapters 14 and 15), we talked in terms of an inverse relationship between the *money* wage and the quantity of labor demanded by employers. We were able to talk in these terms because we assumed that the price level is constant, which means that a change in the money wage will cause a proportional change in the real wage. In this section, dealing with the macroeconomic problems of inflation (increases in the price level) and unemployment, we are no longer able to hold to the assumption of constant prices and must, therefore, introduce the real wage as a ratio (that is, W/P).

In addition to assuming that the number of workers demanded is inversely related to the real wage rate, the classical economists also assumed a direct relationship between the real wage and the number of laborers willing to work. The supply and demand curves for our representative labor market are D_1 and S_1 in Figure 28 · 1. As we studied earlier, the equilibrium real wage rate for a competitive market will tend to move toward the intersection of the two curves, or toward point a. At that real wage $(W/P)_2$, everyone willing to work (Q_3) can find a job; in this limited sense, the competitive market processes tend toward "full employment." If there are unemployed workers, that means there are some people on the market willing to work who cannot find work at the going real wage: the market is not in equilibrium; the real wage is above the intersection of supply and demand. This is true of any real wage above

[5] As quoted in J. Ronnie Davis, *The New Economics and the Old Economists* (Ames: Iowa State University Press, 1971), p. 40.

[6] Ibid., p. 16.

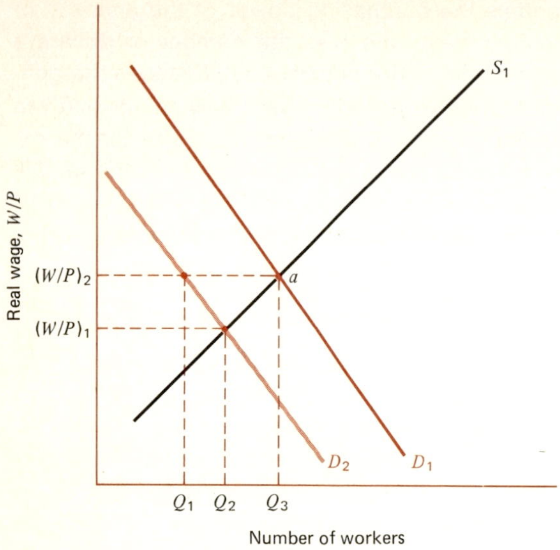

FIG. 28·1 With the supply and demand for labor curves positioned at S_1 and D_1, full employment will be achieved at a real wage rate of $(W/P)_2$. However, if for some reason the demand for labor in this market falls to D_2, the number of workers willing to work (Q_3) will initially exceed the number demanded (Q_1). Until the real wage rate adjusts downward to $(W/P)_1$, some unemployment will exist.

$(W/P)_2$: the number of workers supplied (shown by the supply curve) will, for any real wage above $(W/P)_2$, be greater than the quantity demanded (shown by the demand curve).

Even in a competitive market, unemployment can emerge temporarily as a consequence of changes in supply and demand. Some unemployment will remain as long as the real wage is in the *process* of adjusting toward the new equilibrium level. For instance, suppose that the demand for labor in Figure 28·1 falls from D_1 to D_2 as the result of a switch in consumer buying habits from the product the workers in this market produce to some other product. Regardless of the reason for the drop in demand, the market will be jarred out of equilibrium and into a state of disequilibrium (a state in which the number of workers demanded and the number supplied are not equal): the quantity of labor that employers demand at the initial real wage rate, $(W/P)_2$, will fall to Q_1 while the number of people willing to work remains at Q_3; initially, the unemployed will be the people willing to work who are now unable to work ($Q_3 - Q_1$). In a free and perfectly competitive market, the real wage, along with the money wage, may fall very quickly, eliminating the gap between the number of jobs available and the number of people seeking them. However, in the world as we know it, markets never work that smoothly. The adjustment process requires time—days or even months or years—and during this period, some people are unemployed.

An increase in the supply of labor—that is, the number of people willing to work—can have a similar effect on unemployment—again, for a temporary period. In this case, the quantity of people willing to work at the initial market wage will exceed the number of jobs available. However, if the real wage adjusts downward in a competitive manner, that gap is closed; but, as before, during the period of "transition" from one equilibrium to the next, unemployment exists.

Some of the increase in unemployment which caught the newspaper headlines during the early and mid-1970s was a consequence of the growth in the number of women wanting to enter the labor market. This growth in what is called the "labor force participation rate of women" created a disequilibrium in labor markets and resulted in some unemployment among women who wanted to work and men who then had to compete with a greater number of women for the available jobs. As time goes by, we expect some of this type of transitional unemployment to be reduced as the *real* wage rate falls to accommodate the greater supply of labor and/or the growth in the demand for labor catches up with the increase in supply.

According to classical economists, if unemployment persists beyond some unspecified "transitional" period, it is due to "obstructions" in the labor market which keep the real wage rate from falling. For instance, if the money wage is held at W_2 in Figure 28·2 by union contract while the price level remains at P_1 (real wage W_2/P_1), unemployment will persist and will equal the difference

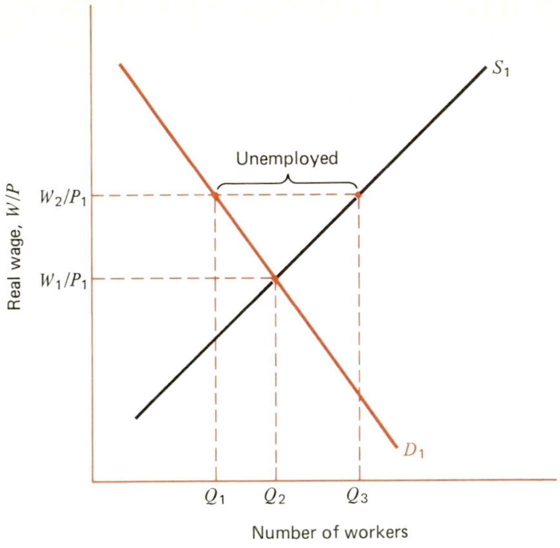

FIG. 28·2 In a free competitive market, the real wage will settle at W_1/P_1. However, if unions, for example, hold the money wage at W_2, the real wage will be above equilibrium and there will be unemployed workers equal to the difference between Q_1 and Q_3.

between Q_3 and Q_1. The government can solve the unemployment problem by increasing the money stock and, along with that, the general price level. (See Chapter 25 for a review of the connection between the money stock and the price level.) With an increase in the price level, the real wage (W/P) will fall, assuming, of course, that the money wage rate remains constant. However, if unions, in an attempt to keep their real wage above equilibrium, are able to negotiate perpetual wage increases, a government policy intent on pushing the real wage rate toward equilibrium requires a continual increase in the price level (inflation). If money wages and prices rise together and the real wage remains above equilibrium, unemployment will persist. Economists before Keynes reasoned that we would always have some unemployment because of normal adjustments in the market and because there are forces in the market which prevent the real wage from adjusting to its equilibrium level.

Agricultural Theories

Economic life has always proceeded irregularly; there have always been good years and bad years, as measured, for example, by Gross National Product. At a time when a large segment of the population was tied to farming, the ups and downs in economies were frequently caused by weather. Bad growing conditions affected not only farmers but also merchants who made their living by buying from and selling to farmers. Changes in the weather would alter farm production and, thereby, the income level and the distribution of income. The changes in the community's income level and distribution would cause shifts in the demand for various goods and, along with that, shifts in demand for various types of labor. The new supply and demand conditions required labor markets to adjust their wage rates and caused transitional unemployment of the type discussed above.

Because agriculture was so dominant in the economic lives of people in the eighteenth and nineteenth centuries, scientists looked to natural causes for an explanation of economic fluctuations. In the last half of the nineteenth century, the "sunspot theory" was a prominent explanation for changes in economic activity. It was formulated because observers noticed a high correlation between the occurrence of sunspots and poor growing seasons and, therefore, fluctuations in economic activity. The theory is being revived to explain droughts in sections of the United States in the 1970s. Today, however, agriculture is less prominent in our nation's production, and causes other than sunspots must be sought for observed unemployment levels.

A Theory of "General Glut"

With the development of commerce and industry, people began to realize that there are ups and downs in the economy which do not seem to be connected to agriculture. This led to an early and very naïve group of theories which go by the name "general glut." A number of merchants, observing that there would be periods in which business was bad in all lines of merchandise and that they could not dispose of their goods at the usual prices and in the usual volume, decided that the problem was "overproduction": there had been too much production of all the various goods, and hence there was a "glut" of all goods. This, in turn, was the general cause of unemployment.

This theory may appear to be highly unsophisticated from today's standpoint. Today, we produce at a level which is four or five times greater than the level which proponents of this theory considered to be overproduction. The theory was attacked almost immediately on theoretical grounds by Jean Baptiste Say, a French economist of the late eighteenth and early nineteenth centuries. Say argued that in a barter economy, the production of one good for sale represented at the same time the demand for some other good. This is so simply because the production of one good is a means of gaining the purchasing power to acquire others: we produce more than we want to consume in order that we may trade with others to acquire what we want and do not produce. This led to the formulation of what is known as Say's law: The supply of one good, in effect, creates its own demand. An increase in total quantity of a good produced means that people demand more of other goods; this occurs because they are producing the good so that they can trade it for others. At times, the wrong goods may be produced for sale, or goods may be produced in the wrong quantities, causing changes in the relative prices of goods, changes in the supplies of and demands for various types of labor, and transitional adjustments in employment. However, there need not be a "general glut" in the sense that there is insufficient demand for *all* goods and services.

Monetary Theories

In a barter economy, Say's law is essentially a correct answer to the theory of the general glut. However, Say hinted that the introduction of money into the system can create difficulties in applying his line of reasoning. Specifically, if, while supplying goods on the market, people hold the money they receive from the sale of goods for use in future transactions or for the purposes of security or speculation, the supply of all goods can be greater than the demand for all goods. If a person sells the product of his labor for $100 and does not spend the $100, $100 worth of other goods will be left on the market. In this sense and for the period of time that people hold the money and in that sense demand money balances, there can be overproduction and cause for reduction in economic activity.

Other monetary theories of fluctuations in economic activity focused on the structure of the banking system and the contraction of the money supply during times of "runs" on banks. During the eighteenth and nineteenth centuries, the money stock consisted of gold, silver coins, and paper money. Paper money was printed by banks, and for this reason it acquired the name "bank notes." If a customer took one of these pieces of paper into a bank and demanded payment, he could receive gold coins. Because banks made money from expanding their loans via bank note issues, there was the ever-present temptation to overextend these issues—to create too much money. This was because bank notes were easy to print.

Periodically during the nineteenth century, some bank would get into financial trouble in the sense that it could not immediately meet the demands of its depositors for gold. (It would go "bankrupt.") This might have been because of bad management or because of loans that were not repaid. In any event, because banks, themselves, held deposits in other banks, the financial problems of any one bank could spread throughout the banking system. The bank, under pressure, would withdraw its deposits from other banks to pay off its customers. Seeing the run on one bank, the customers of other banks would lose confidence in the security of their deposits; they, too, would try to withdraw their deposits. Banks never held (and still do not hold) sufficient reserves to meet the demands of their depositors in times of widespread "runs" or "panics." As a consequence, there would be a cumulative process by which all banks within a city, or, perhaps, even a country, collapsed at virtually the same time, causing a dramatic decrease in the money supply and a decrease in the prices of goods and services. (Remember the quantity equation, $MV = PO$. With V held constant by the institutional constraints, a decrease in M on the left-hand side of the equation must lead to a decrease in P or O on the right-hand side of the equation. The classical economist argued that a decrease in M would have an immediate impact on P.)

During times of widespread bank failures, businesses will find that the real value of their financial obligations has risen. Unable to cope with the greater financial pressures, many businesses will go bankrupt. These bankruptcies alone will lead to disruptions in the flow of economic activity. Furthermore, the dramatic decrease in prices will lead to an *increase* in the real wage (W/P) of workers, causing a decrease in the quantity of labor demanded and the emergence of unemployment. (Consider Figure 28·2; the numerator, W, will remain constant while the denominator, P, will fall, resulting in a higher W/P.) Given unemployment and a competitive labor market, the nominal wage and real wage will eventually fall back towards equilibrium. However, during the period while the banking system collapses and the money supply contracts, unemployment will persist. Therefore, a collapse of the banking system will cause the same type of transitional unemployment we discussed in connection with a decrease in the demand for particular goods and an increase in the supply of labor. It was essentially the type of reasoning outlined here that prompted Irving Fisher, a classical economist whom we have quoted before, to suggest that depressions and booms are merely a consequence of "the dance of the dollar."

The instability of the banking system during the nineteenth century was undesirable and the system was in need of reform. This is the historical setting out of which the Federal Reserve System sprang. The Fed's primary purpose was initially to ensure that the banking system, through the availability of credit at the Fed, had an "elastic money supply." This is still an important function of the Federal Reserve. In times of runs on banks, banks can obtain all the currency they need to satisfy the demands of their depositors. Through squelching bank runs and preventing the collapse of the banking system, the Fed is designed to prevent major deflationary periods and the problems of unemployment and recession we have discussed.

The monetary interpretation of recessions has been carried over to the period following the formation of the Federal Reserve, except that this time the government and the Fed are the source of the contraction of the money supply. For instance, World War I was financed by all belligerents (including the United States) in part by expansion of the money supply. The Fed aided this process in the United States by making its discount windows and credit readily available to banks. The expansion of the money supply at home and abroad led inevitably to inflation. For reasons that are obscure, the Federal Reserve Board permitted the inflationary climate to continue through 1919. Then, in 1920, it cracked down hard, reducing significantly the growth in the money stock. This resulted not only in an end to the inflation and a substantial deflation, but to one of the sharpest—albeit one of the shortest—depressions in American history. Unemployment grew out of governmental-Fed policy in the same way that runs on banks in the past caused decreases in the money stock. A similar explanation has been given for the Great Depression. According to these monetary theorists, the Great Depression emerged as a result of a collapse of the banking system and of a drastic (one-third) reduction in the money stock. The Fed did nothing to stop the drop in the money stock and, according to the proponents of this monetary theory, encouraged the drop in the money stock by failing to make credit available to banks. Prices fell precipitously, the real wage rates rose, and unemployment was prevalent.

THE ESSENTIALS OF THE KEYNESIAN PERSPECTIVE

Thomas Kuhn, a philosopher who has written extensively on the development of science, has hypothesized that science advances in two distinct ways.[7] The first and usual procedure is what he calls "normal science," by which new discoveries are made and a gradual improvement in knowledge takes place. This procedure is relatively methodical and orderly. Occasionally, however, something which Kuhn calls a "paradigm change" occurs. This involves a radical change in the basic "paradigm" or view of the world that is held by the scientists in some particular field. For example, Newton worked a paradigm change in physics, and later Einstein and the quantum physicists brought about others. In the history of economic thought, one abrupt change in the general view of the nature of the world came with the work of Stanley Jevons (1835–1882), who directed economists' attention to the concepts of *marginal* benefits and *marginal* costs and marginal conditions of "optimum behavior."

Although other economists shared many of the same ideas independently, Keynes is responsible for working a paradigm change in economists' view of recessions and unemployment. As opposed to taking the labor supply and demand curves, like those used above, as his frame of reference, Keynes focused on the interrelationship between the overall or national income level (and, therefore, employment, since the two variables are closely related) and *aggregate* (meaning total) demand for goods and services.

Circular Flow of Income

To see the interconnection between the national income level and aggregate demand in the simplest of terms possible, let us envision an economy in which government is absent. (This is a highly unrealistic assumption, but it does allow us to develop basic ideas; government will be brought into the analysis at a later point.) Further, let us divide private economic activity into two broad categories, the *consumption* of goods by household members and the *production* of goods by firms. This assumed division is illustrated in Figure 28·3 by the two boxes, "Households" and "Firms."

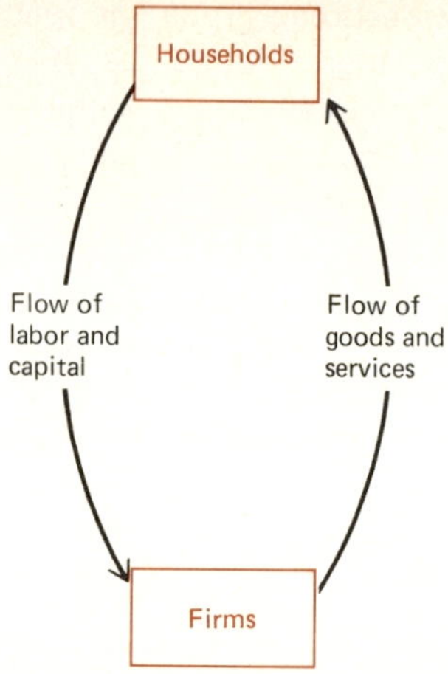

FIG. 28·3 If the macroeconomy is viewed as being composed of two sectors, households and firms, resources like labor and capital can be viewed as flowing from the households to the firms (left-hand arrow), and goods and services can be viewed as flowing from firms to households (right-hand arrow). In a barter economy, the resources are traded for the goods and services that are produced.

In this model, households perform two roles: first, they supply resources such as labor and capital to the firms; this role is described by the arrow on the left side of the diagram pointing toward the square labeled "Firms." Second, "Householders" buy and consume the goods and services produced by the firms; the flow of these goods from the firms to the householders is described by the black arrow on the right side of the diagram, pointing toward the "Household" square. Similarly, firms perform two distinguishable roles: they buy labor from households and sell their products back to the households.

[7] Thomas S. Kuhn, *The Structure of Scientific Revolutions*, 2d ed. (Chicago: University of Chicago Press, 1970).

In a barter economy, the two arrows would describe the simplicity of the system: resources go to firms which, in turn, supply goods back to households in exchange for the resources used. However, in a monetary economy, the system is not so simple. Resources are supplied to firms in exchange for money (wages). Individuals or households use the money obtained from the sale of labor or capital to buy goods and services from the firms. These implied monetary flows are added to our basic diagram in Figure 28·4 via orange arrows pointing in the opposite direction from the flow of goods and services on the right-hand side and the flow of resources on the left-hand side. The complete diagram illustrates what is called the "circular flow of income."

The money received by households (the outerflow on the left-hand side of Figure 28·4) mirrors the household earnings; it is a reflection of the contribution of household members to the production of goods and services within the firms. If

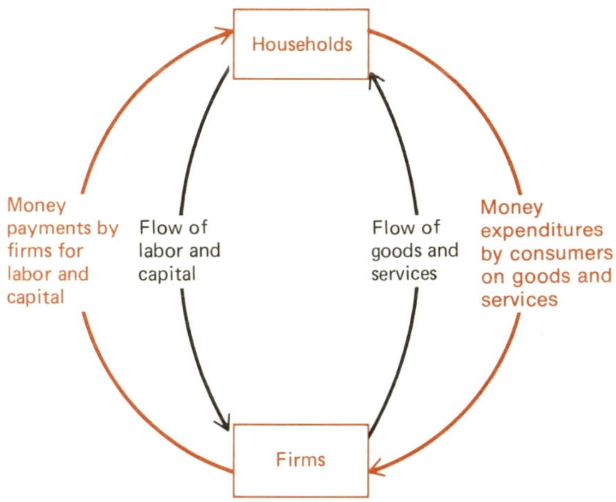

FIG. 28·4 In the world of today, resources and goods and services trade for money. The orange arrow on the left-hand side represents the money payments which firms make to households for the resources the households provide, and the orange arrow on the right-hand side represents the money payments by households on goods and services produced in the firms.

$100 worth of goods and services is produced by all firms, the aggregate earnings of households (or national income) must likewise equal $100. This is so simply because the full value of anything which is produced must ultimately be attributed to someone and, in that sense, earned by a member of a household. This is because someone will want to claim the $100 which is the value of the goods and services. Although people's take-home pay is generally less than their earnings, on a conceptual level, income (or earnings) and the value of what is produced are equal.[8] In short

$$O = Y$$

where O stands for national output and Y stands for national income. Therefore, national output and income can be used, as we do use them, interchangeably in future discussion.

With this model in mind, we can see that the ability of firms to sell their products is dependent upon households' willingness to buy what is produced. On the other hand, the propensity (tendency) of householders to buy what is produced is positively influenced, among other things, by the income they earn. Since firms' production plans determine the income earned by households, those same production plans have an influence on how much householders buy or how much firms sell. If firms do not produce, householders do not have the purchasing power to buy goods and services. In a similar manner, we may conclude that the employment opportunities of people and the income they earn are, in part, determined by the aggregate buying decisions of householders. If households in the aggregate refuse to buy goods and services, there is no basis for employment or pay checks.

It follows that if all households' take-home pay equals their income and householders spend all

[8] Students, at times, become concerned over whether or not the market value of goods produced is determined prior to the time the income is distributed and whether the income distributed is determined before the market places a value on what is produced. Actually, income and the market value of output are determined simultaneously. That is, at the moment that the market places a value on goods which have been produced, the incomes of laborers, landlords, entrepreneurs, etc., are determined.

they receive on firms' output, all this output will be purchased. Since income is equal to the value of the output, households have the opportunity to buy all that has been produced. If firms fail to pay householders all they earn, or if households fail to spend what they earn on the goods produced by firms in their country, problems emerge: households will have insufficient income to buy what has been produced and/or firms will not be able to sell all that they have produced. If firms keep producing at, say, a full-employment level—that is, at that point where everyone who wants a job can find one—and households continue to spend less than they earn, all goods will not be taken off the market, unwanted inventories (or unsold goods) will pile up, and, to alleviate the accumulating inventory problem, firms will cut back on production. This, in turn, leads to a reduction in household income (since less is produced and fewer people are needed to produce the lower output) and, to the extent that consumption is influenced by people's total income, to a reduction in consumer expenditures. The accumulating process can mean that fewer goods and services are produced and less labor and fewer other resources are required in the production process. The result is unemployment.

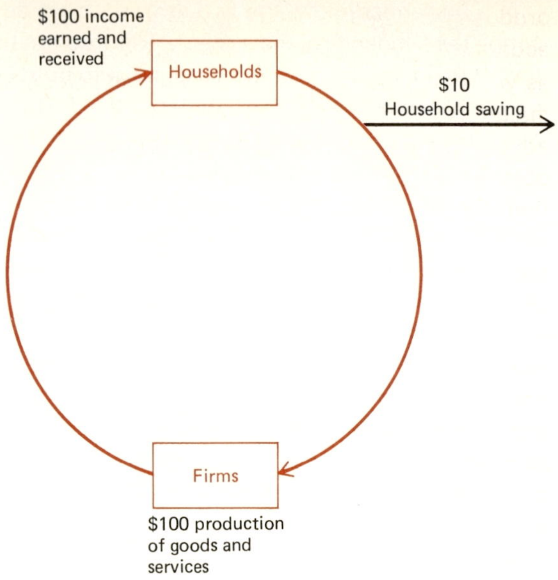

FIG. 28·5 If households have a tendency to save $10 of each $100 in money income they earn, they will buy only $90 of the $100 of goods and services that are produced. If firms continue to produce at the level of $100 each production period, unwanted inventories will pile up, and at some point production will be curtailed and unemployment will rise.

Savings

To see these points more clearly, let us turn to Figure 28·5. We have simplified this figure by taking out the inside arrows—they will get in our way, and, besides, they mirror the money flows. Suppose that firms pay householders an amount which equals their full income and that the households have a propensity to save a portion of their earnings. This saving is described as a *leakage* or *outflow* from the circular flow and is appropriately illustrated by the black arrow on the right side of the figure pointing outward. Imagine that firms produce $100 worth of goods and householders receive the equivalent, $100, as income but are inclined to save 10 percent. The households will save $10 and spend $90. The firms will sell only $90 of what they have produced and will have $10 of unwanted inventories on hand. If the firms continue to produce at a level of $100 and the households continue to save $10, business inventories will mount by $10 each time $100 of goods is produced. At some point, with inventories mounting, the firms will try to bring their production levels in line with sales. However, when they do this, they reduce employment and household income, an action which, in turn, has a dampening influence on household savings and also reduces consumer expenditures in the aggregate. The result can be that firms, after reducing production during one time period, have to reduce it still further. For example, if households earn $100 and spend $90 and if producers reduce production to $90, people in the aggregate may reduce their saving rate from $10 to $7, but they will be spending only $83 ($90 of income minus $7 of saving). Goods will continue to go unsold.

At this point you may ask, "Why don't prices fall to take care of the surplus of goods and services produced?" The Keynesian model of the macroeconomy generally assumes constant prices; and, as you can imagine, this assumption has been a major focus of controversy between those who adhere to the Keynesian paradigm and those who object to it. We can sidestep this point of contention for the moment by merely stating the rationale for the assumption of constant prices. There are two points which Keynesians make in defense of the constant-price assumption. First, the model is intent on demonstrating that *during the short run*—a period in which prices may exhibit a degree of "rigidity," if not complete inflexibility—adjustments in economic activity may take place as much or more in terms of output as in terms of price. There is, in other words, a presumption that income can adjust downward faster than prices.

Second, as prices fall, wages and other payments to resource owners (households) must fall, suggesting that although a given number of dollars will buy more in the marketplace, there is less money income to go around. Therefore, lower prices may not stimulate greater sales because people have less money income to purchase these goods. Eventually, prices and wages may fall to the point where consumers are induced to buy more of what is produced. A simultaneous drop in both wages and prices can eventually induce greater consumption through the impact of price reductions on people's bank account balances. As prices fall, the purchasing power of bank account deposits rises. There is a so-called "wealth effect." Because people may feel wealthier at lower price levels, they may spend more. The hypothesis is certainly in line with the rest of the Keynesian model of the economy. However, again, the Keynesian model is designed to illuminate the problems of the adjustment process in the short run. Wages and prices *take time* to fall, and during that period of time, production can fall along with employment. Remember the practical concern expressed in Keynes's statement, "In the long run we are all dead." The economic system may eventually work itself out, but that notion is not likely to have much appeal to people unemployed during the weeks and months, or even years, of the adjustment process.

Investment

The damaging effects of saving can be partially, if not fully, offset by investment spending. (By "investment" we do not mean here or anywhere in following chapters the purchase of stocks and bonds by individuals; rather, we mean the purchase of capital goods like plant and equipment by firms.) For instance, in Figure 28·6, we have added investment spending as a component of *aggregate* demand (i.e., total spending). If this investment inflow into the circular flow is equal to the saving outflow, all the goods produced are purchased. The firms produce $100 of goods and services; the households buy $90 and save $10; the firms themselves buy the remaining $10 of goods produced which are capital goods (plant and equipment) and, perhaps, planned additions to inventories. The aggregate demand of con-

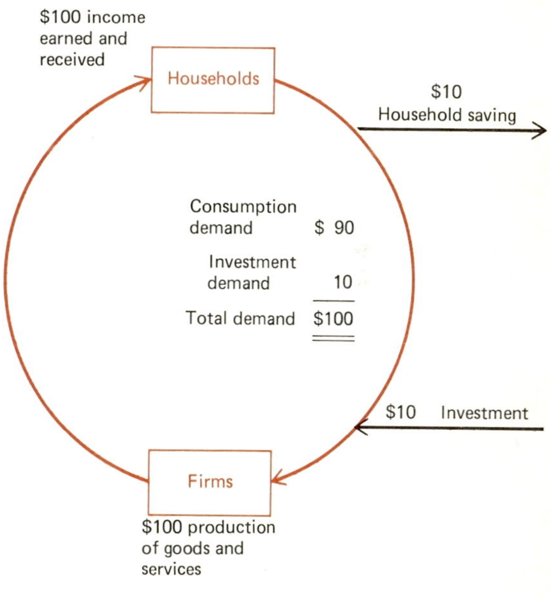

FIG. 28·6 When the saving outflow is exactly equal to the investment (purchase of plant and equipment) inflow, the macroeconomy is in equilibrium. This means that the total or aggregate demand for goods in the economy by all sectors is exactly equal to the quantity of goods being produced. There is, therefore, no reason for firms to expand or contract production.

sumers and investors (AD) is exactly equal to the income and output level (Y) of $100. The system is in a state of *equilibrium;* there is no reason for the firms to produce either more or less than they are producing. Note that the condition for equilibrium is aggregate demand equals national income or output (or aggregate supply), or

$$\text{AD} = Y$$

Since aggregate demand is made up of consumption C and investment I,

$$\text{AD} = C + I$$

and since income (Y) is made up of consumption expenditures (C) and saving (S), which is what can be done with income in this model,

$$Y = C + S$$

We know that equilibrium occurs when

$$C + I = C + S$$

or, if the equation is reduced, when

$$I = S$$

We observe in the circular-flow diagram, Figure 28·6, that the investment inflow ($10) is indeed equal to the saving outflow ($10), and the output or income level does not change.

If the system is at the "full-employment income level" initially, it will tend to stay there so long as the investment and saving levels remain constant. However, discrepancies in the saving and investment levels can arise, causing adjustment in the aggregate income and employment levels. For instance, if saving is $15 while investment is $5, households and investors will spend a total of $90 ($85 in consumption and $5 in investment). Ten dollars of goods will go unsold, calling for a reduction in production and employment.

The Relevance of Interest Rates: The Classical View

Is there a mechanism for bringing the level of saving into equality with investment? Classical economists argued that there is. Saving is a means by which people can earn a return in the form of interest. People will vary the amount they save with the interest rate: if the interest rate rises, more will be saved, and vice versa. On the other hand, investment (the purchase of capital equipment) will increase as the rate of interest decreases, and vice versa. The explanation is relatively simple. At lower rates of interest, firms are able to justify investing in capital projects which yield lower rates of return. At a 15 percent interest rate, firms can justify investing only in those projects which yield a greater rate of return than 15 percent. (Obviously, they want to earn at least as much as it costs to borrow the money for the investment expenditure.) At a 10 percent interest rate, they can invest not only in capital projects with greater than 15 percent rates of return, but also in projects which yield anything between 10 and 15 percent.

In Figure 28·7 we have placed "interest rate"

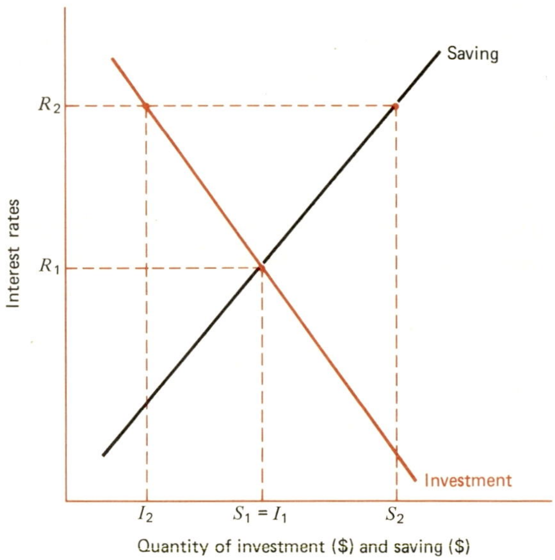

FIG. 28·7 The classical economists assumed that the interest rate would adjust to maintain an equality between saving and investment. However, Keynes argued that the interest rate can be held above the equilibrium rate to a rate such as R_2, in which case the level of saving exceeds the level of investment expenditures.

on the vertical axis and "saving" and "investment," both measured in dollars, on the horizontal axis. Given the construction of the graph, we can draw the investment function as a downward sloping curve; it indicates the inverse relationship between the level of investment and the interest rate. The curve representing the direct relationship between saving and the interest rate is upward sloping. People are induced to save more (and consume less) as the interest rate rises. (Note: We are able to put both investment and saving on the horizontal axis because they are both dollar figures which vary with the interest rate.)

Classical economists argued that in a competitive market the interest rate moves toward the intersection of saving and investment functions, R_1. If the interest rate is below that level, investor demand for funds is greater than the amount being made available through saving. The interest rate rises, causing investors to cut back on their investment plans and households to save more. In a similar competitive process, if the interest rate is above R_1, firms want to borrow less than people want to save. The interest rate falls to R_1. At R_1, notice that the level of saving and that of investment are equal. In terms of Figure 28 · 6 (the last circular-flow diagram used), the economy is the equilibrium. Furthermore, the classical economists argued that, unless there are "obstacles" in the labor market, the wage rate (and the prices of other resources) will adjust to bring about full employment of resources. The economy will, therefore, move toward a full-employment income level, and also to the equilibrium income level.

Keynesian Objections to the Classical Interest Rate Theory

Keynesian economists object to this line of reasoning on two grounds; both concern the "speed" with which the pricing system may be counted on to adjust to economic conditions like a gap between saving and investment. First, they emphasize the resistance of labor to downward movements in wage rates. The resistance of labor to wage reductions can keep the wage above equilibrium and can create temporary but still major unemployment problems. Second, they argue that forces other than the demand for investment and the supply of savings determine the interest rate.

More specifically, they argue that people, in addition to wanting to loan a part of their savings to investors, want to hold a part of their income in the form of cash or bank balances for three reasons: (1) to carry out expected day-to-day transactions (the "transaction demand for money"), (2) to have some reserve for unexpected purchases or emergencies (the "precautionary demand for money"), and (3) to speculate on what the future interest rate will be (the "speculative demand for money"). The last motive for holding money is the only one which requires additional explanation. If people expect the interest rate to go up in the near future, they will want to hold larger than usual money balances. If they loan their money or buy a bond now, it will be tied down to a low rate of interest. If they hold onto their money, and if they are right in their expectations, they will be able to loan what they have at a higher rate of interest. While they are holding onto their funds, they are neither consuming nor loaning their funds to others for them to use. Further, because of such speculation, the interest rate is held up above its equilibrium rate, R_1, in Figure 28 · 7. If the interest rate settles, for instance, at R_2 and is held there by speculation, the level of saving, S_2, will be greater than the level of investment, I_1.

Referring to Figure 28 · 8, we can visualize the impact of this discrepancy on the income level. As in the example used earlier, investment is given at $5 while saving is set at $15. (These conditions, you must remember, are set to reflect the gap between saving and investment at an interest rate of R_2 in Figure 28 · 7.) Given this gap, consumers will buy $85 of goods and services ($100 in income minus $15 in saving) and investors will buy $5. The aggregate or total demand is, therefore, $90. Further, the total spending falls $10 short of the value of goods and services produced, $100. With the investment inflow failing to offset the saving outflow, producers will eventu-

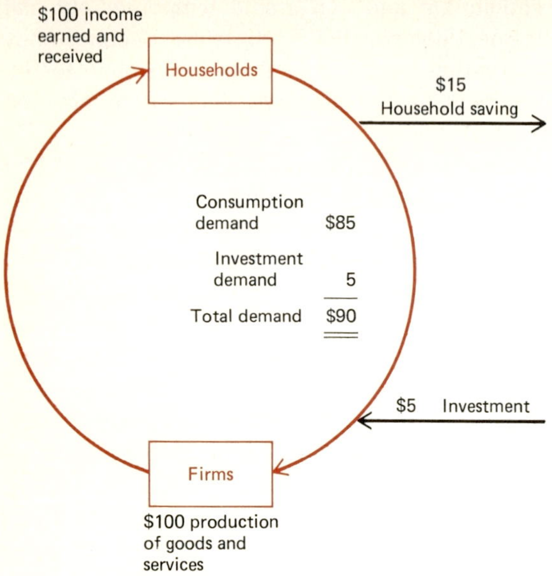

FIG. 28·8 When household saving ($15) is greater than investment expenditures ($5), the aggregate demand ($90) is less than the level of production in the firms ($100), unwanted inventories in the firms will build up, and production will eventually be cut back, leading to a lower national income level and a higher unemployment level.

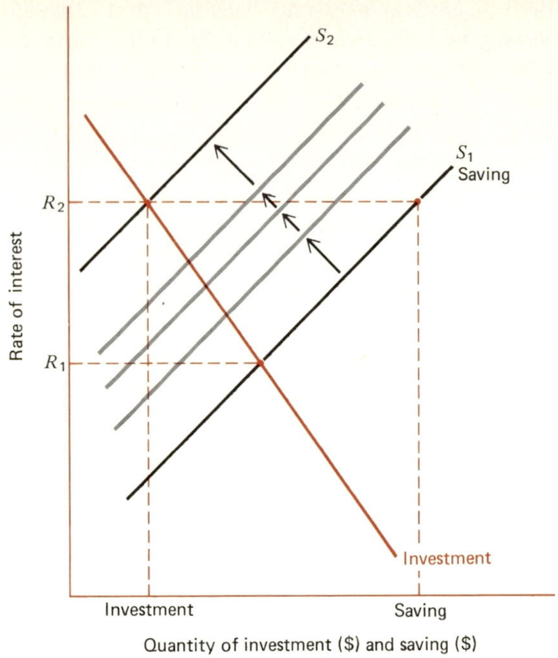

FIG. 28·9 In the classical system, the interest rate adjusts downward toward R_1 to eliminate any discrepancy between the levels of saving and investment. In the Keynesian system the saving function (the upward sloping curve) adjusts backward, as income falls, until the level of saving is brought into equality with the level of investment. In both systems the macroeconomy is in equilibrium when saving and investment are equal.

ally cut back on production in order to bring it in line with sales. This can mean, as before, an accumulating downward spiral in production, income, and employment. With reduced production, fewer workers are needed and household incomes fall. This leads to a reduction in consumption level and a further cutback in production and employment.

The downward spiral, however, will not continue unabated. If investment remains constant as saving and income fall, at some income level saving and investment will become equal. The income level at which saving and investment are equal is the "equilibrium income level." In terms of Figure 28·9, the saving curve will shift to the left as income decreases, and there is some shift in the saving curve (and therefore some decrease in income) which will bring the actual level of saving into equality with investment at an interest rate of R_2. This is true when the saving curve has moved from S_1 all the way to S_2. A new equilibrium is established with saving equal to investment in terms of this graph and in terms of the circular-flow charts which we have used. However, notice that in the process of moving toward that equilibrium the national income level must fall and unemployment emerges. Classical economists argued that the saving curve would not shift because the interest rate would adjust downward rapidly enough to bring about equality between saving and investment. The contrast between the classical and Keynesian models of the private economy is clear: in the classical model, interest rate adjustments are made to eliminate discrepancies between saving and investment; whereas in the Keynesian model, income adjustments alleviate the discrepancies.

In the long run, the interest rate usually adjusts downward in the Keynesian system also. This can occur as people adjust their expectations of future interest rates. If people believe that increasing unemployment and a falling national production level will cause interest rates to fall, rather than holding onto their money they will want to loan it at the present relatively high interest rates. In trying to loan their money on the current market, people will effect a reduction in current interest rates, thus stimulating investment and the total demand for goods and services and increasing the need for more workers. Furthermore, in the long run, wages and prices may fall far enough to bring about additional increases in consumer investment expenditures and additional reductions in unemployment. In the meantime, however, unemployment can be a significant social problem. The Keynesian prescription for government *fiscal* (meaning taxing and spending) action is directed at solving the *short-run* unemployment problems. Keynes was fully aware that his policy recommendations would not begin to solve long-run unemployment problems which emerge and remain for decades.

SUMMARY AND EXTENSIONS

The primary purpose of this chapter has been to briefly discuss the Keynesian explanation for periods of depressed output levels and high unemployment rates. In terms of the circular-flow model that we have used, that explanation focuses on the potential discrepancy between saving and investment. In the Keynesian model, with everything else equal, the national income level will fall and unemployment will emerge when the level of investment expenditures *is less* than the level of saving. On the other hand, the national income level will rise and unemployment will fall when investment expenditures *exceed* the level of saving.

In order that you may understand the meaning of the Keynesian revolution, we have set this theory in the context of its historical predecessors. The solution to an unemployment problem from the point of view of the classical model is to speed up the informational flow to workers who may be transitionally unemployed and to reduce the restrictions on wage movements and labor flows, such as minimum wage laws, union shops, and some forms of labor market discrimination, such as racial and sexual discrimination. Keynes and his followers have largely accepted these types of labor market restrictions as a part of the political reality, assuming that there is little that can be done about them in the short run. These economists have looked for other means of correcting unemployment problems. The Keynesian solution for unemployment problems is to effect an increase in the aggregate demand for goods and services. In terms of the model employed in this chapter and in terms of its more precise version to be developed in Chapter 29, this general conclusion means that either investment demand must be increased or people's inclination to save must be reduced. The latter alternative requires that consumption expenditures of households be increased. As we will see in Chapter 30, government can increase the national income level and reduce unemployment by (1) increasing government expenditures while holding taxes constant or (2) reducing taxes while holding expenditures constant. The first option available to government directly increases aggregate demand. If taxes are reduced, people have more take-home pay and can be expected to spend more, increasing the overall level of demand. The purpose of the following chapter is to develop the Keynesian model with more precision and to explore these policy conclusions in more detail.

QUESTIONS TO PONDER

1 Given the classical model of unemployment that is summarized in Figures 28·1 and 28·2, what will happen to employment if there is a rapid rise in the price level? What will happen to the money wage rate? The real wage rate?

2 Suppose that investment increases. What will happen to the level of income in the classical system? In the Keynesian system?

3 The graph below depicts the saving and investment schedules as a function of the interest rate. Suppose that the interest rate is held above equilibrium at R_2, as can be the case in the Keynesian model. If income falls, as it is supposed to in the Keynesian model, what will happen to the saving function in this graph? Why?

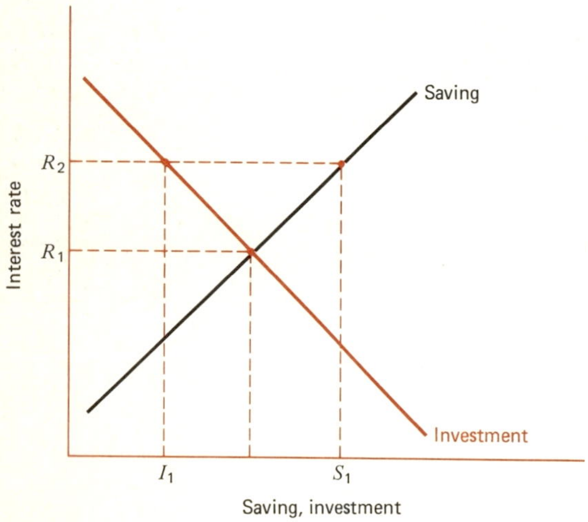

4 Given the information in the graph above, assume that the interest rate is not held rigidly at R_2 but falls very slowly when saving exceeds investment. Will the income level fall by as much in this case as when the interest rate is held rigidly at R_2? Explain your answer in terms of a graph like the one above and Figure 28·6.

RECOMMENDED READINGS

Harris, Seymour E.: *Economics of the Kennedy Years and a Look Ahead* (New York: Harper & Row, Publishers, Inc., 1964).

Heller, Walter W.: *New Dimensions of Political Economy* (New York: W. W. Norton and Company, Inc., 1967).

Okun, Arthur M.: *The Political Economy of Prosperity* (New York: W. W. Norton and Company, Inc., 1970).

Tobin, James: *The New Economics One Decade Older* (Princeton, N.J.: Princeton University Press, 1974).

29

The "New Economics": A Refinement of the Basic Model

It is too early to say, but it does not now appear an extravagant statement, that Keynes may in the end rival Adam Smith in his influence on the economic thinking and governmental policy of his time and age. Both lived at profound turning points in the evolution of the economic order. Both were products of their times. Yet both were also powerful agents in giving direction to the unfolding process of instructional change.

Alvin Hansen[1]

PREVIEW OF CHAPTER

Central question

How are the national income and employment levels determined in the Keynesian model of the macroeconomy?

Major objectives

1 To explain how the equilibrium income and employment levels are determined in two ways: (*a*) the saving-investment approach and (*b*) the aggregate demand approach

2 To demonstrate what can cause *business cycles* (ups and downs in economic activity)

[1] Alvin H. Hansen, "The General Theory," reprinted in M. G. Mueller, ed., *Readings in Macroeconomics*, 2d ed. (New York: Holt, Rinehart and Winston, Inc., 1971), p. 23.

3 To develop the concept of the *multiplier,* which relates small changes in consumption and investment demand to larger changes in the national income and production levels
4 To provide a Keynesian explanation for the Great Depression of the 1930s
5 To discuss the policy problem of the apparent trade-off between reducing the rate of inflation and unemployment in the economy

Major conclusions

1 Using the saving-investment approach to national income determination, equilibrium in national income and employment will be established where the level of saving equals the level of investment.
2 Using the aggregate demand approach, equilibrium in national income and employment will be established where the aggregate (or total) demand for goods and services equals the level of production or income in the economy. (At this equilibrium income level saving will also equal investment.)
3 Investment spending by firms can go up or down as the result of changes in such factors as the rate of interest which firms pay on money they borrow to buy new plant and equipment. A decrease in the rate of interest will lead to an increase in the level of investment and, therefore, to an increase in the national income and employment levels. The converse is also true. In the Keynesian model of the national economy, each interest rate is associated with a specific national income level.
4 The national income level will change by some multiple of any change in aggregate demand. An increase in investment demand, for example, will lead to an increase in the national income level which is greater than the increase in the investment demand.
5 The *multiplier* is equal to the reciprocal of the *marginal propensity to save.*
6 According to the Keynesian model of income determination, the Great Depression was caused by decreases in consumption and investment demand for goods and services produced in the economy.
7 Keynesian analysis presumes that there is a trade-off between reducing the level of unemployment and inflation: the rate of unemployment can be reduced only at the cost of the economy enduring a higher rate of inflation, and vice versa. One policy problem for government officials is, therefore, to determine the combination of unemployment and inflation which is "socially most desirable" (or "least undesirable").

Important terms and concepts

Investment
Marginal propensity to save
Marginal propensity to consume
Equilibrium income level
Aggregate demand
Multiplier
Business cycle

The development of the circular-flow model of the macroeconomy in the preceding chapter is a useful means of introducing the essential elements of Keynesian economics. The model provides us with a broad picture of the economy. However, much was left unsaid. "Equilibrium income level" and the relation between national income and saving or consumer expenditures were only sketchily described in our analysis. Furthermore, we have not given a very clear explanation of *how much* the national income level will rise or fall with changes in investment and consumer (household) demand; we have demonstrated only the directional rise or fall in national income when saving and investment are unequal.

Being able to predict the directional movement in national income is important; however, Keynes and Keynesian economists have made additional contributions to the study of macroeconomics. The purpose of this chapter is to add an element of precision to the line of analysis introduced in Chapter 28. We do this in two ways: first, we develop the concepts of the "saving and investment functions," which are instrumental in describing how the "equilibrium national income level" is established. Second, we develop the concept of the "consumption function," which enables us to describe national income from the perspective of equality between national output and aggregate demand. In short, we provide two approaches to answering the question, "How are the national income and employment levels determined?" In this chapter we explicitly exclude government from our analysis; however, in the next chapter we introduce government to our model and consider the policy question, "What can the government do to remedy problems of high unemployment and low production levels in the economy?" As we will see, the basic model which we develop here will be important in our understanding of government actions over the past twenty or thirty years.

THE KEYNESIAN PERSPECTIVE: INVESTMENT-SAVING APPROACH

In Chapter 28, several important conclusions were presented: (1) If the rate of saving during any given period of time is greater than the level of investment expenditure, the aggregate demand for goods and services by households for consumer goods and by firms for capital goods will be less than the production level. Firms will not be able to sell all that they have produced, inventories will pile up, and firms will eventually have to cut back on production in order to bring their output back into line with sales. When production is curtailed, the national income level will fall: less is produced and, accordingly, total earnings (also called aggregate or national income) must be less. (2) On the other hand, if the opposite condition exists, if investment expenditure is greater than the flow of saving out of the circular flow, the aggregate demand for all goods and services will exceed the quantity of goods and services being produced. Production is then less than sales, and inventories will dwindle. If there are workers and other resources which are unemployed in the economy, firms can and will expand production. In this way, the national income level will rise.

(3) Finally, we concluded that when saving and investment are equal, there is no reason for firms in the aggregate to either expand or contract production. Therefore, as long as saving and investment remain equal, the income flow in the economy will remain constant: the macroeconomy will be in "equilibrium." These points are the fundamentals of Keynesian analysis. To extend the discussion, we must state the underlying assumptions more carefully and recognize more explicitly the specific influence which a number of economic variables has on saving and investment and, thereby, on the national income level and employment.

Investment

The expenditures of businesses on plant and equipment (that is, investment) are related to such variables as the market interest rate, the national income level, the expectations of businessmen and women regarding the profitability of future production, the discovery of new ways of producing goods and the development of new goods, and the tax policies of government. As we argued in Chapter 28, investment expenditures are likely to be inversely related to market interest rates; that is, investment will rise with a decrease in interest rates paid on borrowed money and will fall with increases in market interest rates. There are at least two possible explanations for this theoretical and observed relationship. First, some investment projects (expenditures on capital goods) are more profitable than others; and since firms borrow the money to make the investment and pay an interest rate on the money they borrow, more investment projects will be economically justified at low rates of interest than at high ones. At low rates, firms can justify borrowing more funds to expand their plant and equipment. Second, a current rise in market interest rates can persuade some firms to postpone their investments until a later date when it is hoped that interest rates may be lower.[2]

The level of business investment tends to increase or decrease along with the level of national income. During prosperous periods when national income is up and on the rise, businesses have more profits and more funds from internal sources to invest. Many businesses will expand their plants to meet the rising demand for their products. Furthermore, entrepreneurs frequently project present business conditions into the future. The confidence which investors have in the future profitability of production often rises in prosperous times and often falls during more depressed economic periods. Therefore, investment can be expected to rise and fall with investor confidence and current economic conditions (like the production and employment levels) because current purchases of plant and equipment can only be used in production in future time periods.

The general level of investment can be significantly affected by the introduction of new technology. The development of the automobile continues to stimulate considerable investment in roads, service stations, tourist facilities, and assembly lines to produce new and modified automobiles and their component parts, such as emission control systems. Future developments in the technology of solar and wind energy will inevitably affect the level and distribution of investment expenditures. Government tax policies determine the profitability of current investment in many ways; an increase in business taxes can generally be expected to have a dampening effect on investment because business will then have less after-tax income to devote to new plant and equipment, and vice versa.

While recognizing the many determinants of investments, let us begin the development of our more complicated version of the Keynesian model by assuming that all the economic forces which influence investment are given and that investment does not vary with income—it remains constant over the relevant income range. This is one of those assumptions which is made simply to allow the discussion to begin at an elementary level. Later in this chapter and in Chapter 30, the assumption will be dropped, and we will consider the effect which a change in interest rates or tax policy can have on the level of investment expenditures and the national income level. For now, with the assumption of a constant investment level, the "investment function," as the assumed relationship between income and investment is called, can be described as a horizontal line in Figure 29·1*a*. The horizontal axis of this graph measures national income; investment and saving levels are scaled along the vertical axis. In this illustration, we assume that the investment is constant at I_1, or $400 billion.

Saving

The level of saving is influenced by many variables: the interest rates which people can receive from buying and holding onto government and corporate bonds and saving accounts, personal income levels, income tax policies, job security, expected rate of inflation, age distribution in the population, and, in general, people's inclination to buy goods and services currently (since saving is defined as that portion of people's disposable income which is not spent currently). High interest rates on various types of securities and savings accounts increase the relative price of cur-

[2] On the other hand, if a present increase in interest rates causes firms to believe that interest rates will go even higher in the future, firms will not wait to invest.

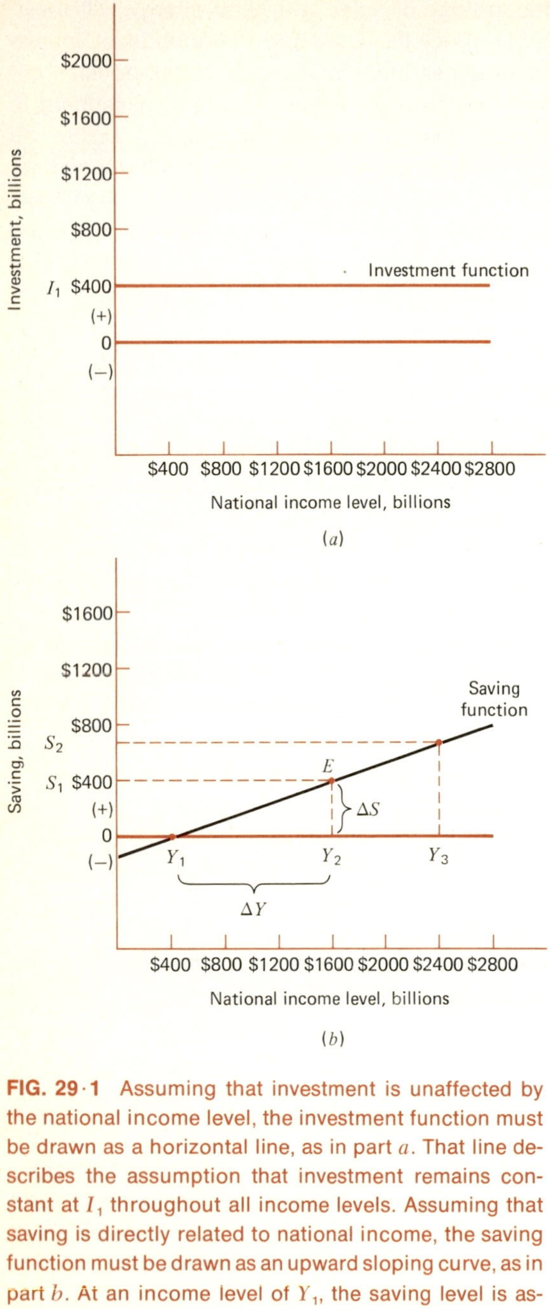

FIG. 29·1 Assuming that investment is unaffected by the national income level, the investment function must be drawn as a horizontal line, as in part *a*. That line describes the assumption that investment remains constant at I_1 throughout all income levels. Assuming that saving is directly related to national income, the saving function must be drawn as an upward sloping curve, as in part *b*. At an income level of Y_1, the saving level is assumed to be zero; however, at a national income level of Y_2, saving is S_1. At an even higher national income level, saving is still higher, S_2.

rent consumption. This is so because people then have to give up more income and, thereby, consumer goods in the future. People will tend to contract their current consumption expenditures, to save their current incomes, and to postpone spending until a later date.

Increases in personal incomes can cause people to buy more of all goods, and one of these goods is security. This "good" can be purchased by adding to one's savings—by increasing one's financial reserves for less advantageous times. Personal and corporate income taxes largely determine the take-home pay of workers and the after-tax profits of firms; in this way, taxes indirectly influence the ability and willingness of people to save and the ability and willingness of corporations to invest and pay dividends. An altogether reasonable hypothesis, which has been confirmed by actual experience, is that saving will rise and fall inversely with taxes: that is, as taxes rise, saving falls, and vice versa.

Expectations about future inflation rates and income levels will also influence current saving levels. If people expect prices to rise sharply in the future, they will tend to buy more (and save less) currently to avoid relatively higher future prices. If people expect to experience significant drops in their future incomes, they are likely to save more now in order to build up the needed cash reserves to carry them through the expected "lean" weeks or months.

Again, to keep the discussion simple, we assume that all the nonincome variables which influence the level of saving are given. However, unlike our assumption with regard to investment, we explicitly assume, as did Keynes, that saving is a direct function of the national income level. That is, people in the aggregate have a tendency to save a portion of any increase in their income. This assumed tendency is known as the *marginal propensity to save* (MPS) and can be defined as a ratio:

$$\text{MPS} = \frac{\Delta S}{\Delta Y}$$

where MPS has already been defined; "ΔS" represents a change in the saving level, and "ΔY"

stands for the change in income. In less mathematical terms,

the marginal propensity to save is the portion of any change in total income which people will save in the aggregate (expressed as a percentage).

To illustrate, if the marginal propensity to save is 10 percent (MPS = $^1/_{10}$), this means that people as a group are inclined to change their level of saving by 10 percent of any increase or decrease in their total income. If their incomes rise by $100, people will be inclined to save $10 more (10 percent of $100). The converse is also true; a $100 decrease in aggregate income will lead to a $10 reduction in the saving level. It also follows that the higher the MPS, the greater the increase in saving with any given increase in national income, and vice versa.

The upward sloping curve in Figure 29 · 1*b* describes the assumed direct relationship between saving and income: it is called the "saving function." The saving function, as we have drawn it, incorporates the assumption that there is some income level at which people save nothing in the aggregate: this income level is Y_1. This income level is descriptive of the United States economy during several years in the 1930s when Americans *as a whole* saved nothing. At income levels lower than Y_1, people engage in "negative saving"—also called "dissaving"; this means that people are, in the net, withdrawing funds from their saving accounts in order to meet their obligations.

At income levels higher than Y_1, the saving level is positive—that is, people are adding to their financial assets, which include savings accounts and stocks and bonds. For instance, at an income level of Y_2, people save a total of $400 billion (or S_1) and at Y_3 the saving level is $666 billion (or S_2). Regardless of the particular income and saving levels, the upward sloping curve reflects the fundamental assumption that income and saving are positively correlated.

Geometry teaches that the slope of any curve like this saving function is equal to the opposite side divided by the adjacent side of the triangle Y_1Y_2E, or $\Delta S/\Delta Y$, which, as you will recall, is equal to the marginal propensity to save:

$$\text{Slope of saving function} = \frac{\Delta S}{\Delta Y} = \text{MPS}$$

Since ΔS is substantially less than ΔY, the MPS is assumed to be much less than 1. Or, in other words, people are assumed to save a minor fraction of any change in income, an assumption which is intuitively plausible and has been empirically verified.

The Equilibrium Income Level

Given the information summarized in the saving and investment functions, both of which are now included in Figure 29 · 2*a*, we are in a position to explain why the economy will move toward an "equilibrium income level" of Y_2 (or $1600 billion). We can do this best by considering the condition of the economy at other income levels. For example, suppose that firms are producing an output and generating income of Y_3, $2400 billion. Investment will be at its assumed constant level of I_1. However, saving will be at a level of S_2, which, as can be seen, is greater than investment: rather than purchasing all Y_3 goods, people are saving a portion of their income, causing a "contractionary gap" between saving and investment. Investment does not make up for the lack of consumer spending which is reflected in household savings. At an income level of Y_3 firms will produce more than they sell; they will pile up unplanned additions to their inventories and at some point will have an incentive to cut back on production, which causes a reduction in aggregate income. The reduction in aggregate income leads to a reduction in saving; and, as can be seen in Figure 29 · 2*a*, a movement back from Y_3 toward Y_2 will close (contract) the gap between saving and investment. At Y_2 saving is equal to investment. What consumers are not buying is being bought by investors (i.e., businesses) who want capital goods. Once at Y_2, firms may try to expand production. If they do, saving will increase and the gap between saving and investment will re-

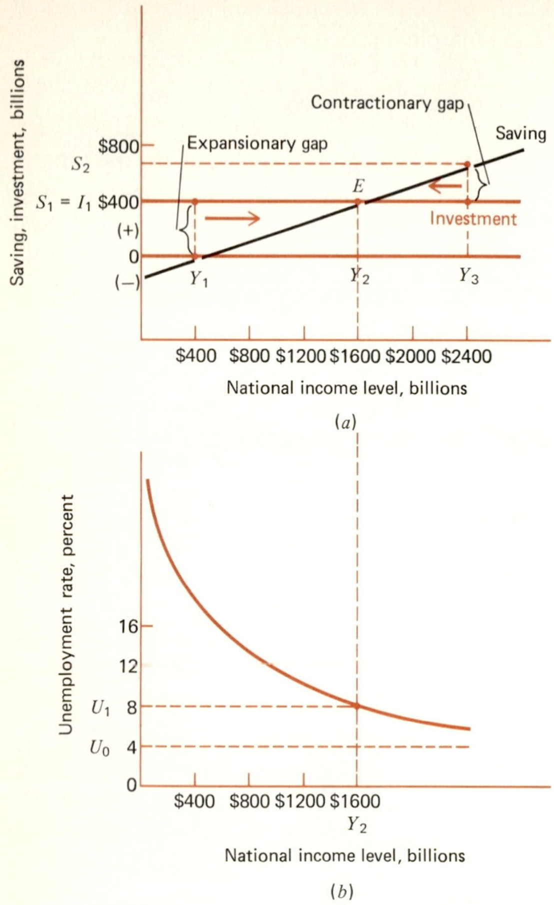

FIG. 29·2 The equilibrium national income level is Y_2, or $1600 billion. At national income levels above Y_2, saving is greater than investment and the national income level will fall; at national income levels lower than Y_2, investment is greater than saving and the national income level will rise.

emerge, giving the firms cause to move back toward Y_2.

If the economy is below Y_2, say at Y_1, we can show that firms in the aggregate will have an incentive to expand production and, in the process, expand household incomes. At Y_1, saving is zero, investment is I_1. Consumers are spending all they earn, which is equal to the value of the goods being produced. Still, firms want to buy additional capital goods, as indicated by the I_1 investment level. In short, the aggregate demand of households and investors at Y_1 is greater than the level of production: there is, in this case, an "expansionary gap" between saving and investment. To satisfy this excess demand, firms must produce more. In the process, they increase household income; and, assuming a positive marginal propensity to save, the level of saving will rise with increases in income. With investment remaining constant and saving increasing, saving and investment must at some point become equal. Again, this occurs at a national income level of Y_2, or $1600 billion.

We have therefore illustrated a basic point in Keynesian economics: that point is that there is some income level toward which the economy will gravitate and, once there, at which it will tend to remain so long as conditions in this model (the saving and investment functions) do not change. This income level may or may not be the full-employment income level. In part b of the figure, we have illustrated the technical relationship between the unemployment rate and the national income level. As more goods and services are produced, more resources, including workers, are needed in production; *the unemployment rate, therefore, falls as income rises.* The equilibrium income level of Y_2 corresponds to an unemployment rate of U_1, which is above the minimum unemployment rate which can be achieved, U_0. (See Chapter 23 for an explanation of why the unemployment rate, as it is presently computed, cannot be expected to fall to zero.) This conclusion that an *equilibrium income level* can exist with unemployment stands in marked contrast to the deduction of the classical economist, which is that the national income level will move toward the minimum unemployment rate. In classical theory, if the economy exhibits unemployment above that minimum rate, the national income level will rise and unemployment will fall as the result of a reduction in wage rates. The Keynesians, on the other hand, stress that the economy may not be at full employment because households may be saving too much (or householders may be consuming too little) or that firms may not invest enough to induce sufficient production to achieve full employment.

THE KEYNESIAN PERSPECTIVE: AGGREGATE DEMAND APPROACH

We can often improve our understanding of complicated ideas by considering them from different points of view. For this reason, we provide here an alternative way of describing equilibrium in national income. In the preceding section, we noted that when the equilibrium income level is achieved, saving (the *outflow*) is equal to investment (the *inflow*).

Saving = investment

In Chapter 28, we found that when this equality holds, the aggregate demand for all goods and services is exactly equal to the national output (or aggregate supply) of all goods and services. That is, we found that equilibrium in the national income level is achieved when firms in the aggregate sell exactly what they have produced, or when

Aggregate demand = national output

This condition for equilibrium is intuitively plausible since when firms sell exactly what they produce, they have no reason to either expand or contract their production levels.

The two equilibrium conditions stated above are mathematically consistent. From earlier discussion, we know that national income (Y) is a mirror image of national output (O); national income is simply a reflection of what is produced in the economy, and without production there is no income. Further, in our simple model, from which government has been excluded, households can do only two things with the income they earn: they can use it for consumption (C) or saving (S). Therefore,

$$Y = C + S$$

If saving is equal to investment ($S = I$), we can rewrite the equation above to read

$$Y = C + I$$

Since national income and output measure the same thing, and since consumption and investment demands make up aggregate demand in our model, the equation above means that when saving and investment are equal, aggregate demand (AD) is equal to national output: as we said, in equilibrium, what is produced by firms is bought either by consumers in the form of consumption expenditures or by businesses in the form of investment expenditures. Stated mathematically,

$$\text{AD} = C + I = O = C + S = Y$$

where AD = aggregate demand (the summation of consumption and investment expenditures)
C = consumption expenditures
I = investment expenditures
O = national output
S = saving (that part of aggregate income not spent by consumers)
Y = national income

We can, therefore, discuss the forces which determine the equilibrium national income level by concentrating attention on the forces which determine aggregate demand. This is the approach which Keynes himself emphasized.

Keynes developed his theory of income determination from two relatively simple propositions:

First, he argued that the level of national income (Y) in the economy is dependent upon the level of aggregate demand (AD). That is, how much is produced and, therefore, earned in the economy is dependent upon how much households and firms in the aggregate want to buy (or demand).

$$Y = f(\text{AD}) = f(C + I)$$

Second, he contended, as we have demonstrated above, that the equilibrium income level will be established where aggregate demand is equal to national income, or where

$$\text{AD} = C + I = Y$$

We consider the question of how the national income level is established by considering the forces which determine the level of consumption demand (C) and the level of investment demand (I). This approach requires that we introduce the concept of the "consumption function," to which we now turn.

Consumption

The consumption expenditures (or demand) of households are, like saving, influenced by a number of variables. Among these variables are the interest rate which people receive on their saving, the expected rate of inflation, income taxes, and the national income level. Interest rates are likely to be inversely related to consumption expenditures: as the interest rate rises, people will be inclined to save more and to borrow less to buy things like furniture and cars. Inflation affects consumption because if people expect the rate of inflation to rise in the future, they are likely to buy more now than they otherwise would in order to avoid paying higher prices in the future. If income taxes rise, people are expected to reduce their consumption expenditures because they will have less after-tax income to spend. Finally, an increase in the national income level is likely to lead to an increase in the consumption expenditures of households simply because people will then be able to satisfy more of their unfilled wants.

Although Keynes recognized that consumption demand is related to a number of variables, he paid special attention to the relationship between national income and consumption demand. This relationship is called the *consumption function.* Stated more formally,

the consumption function is the assumed relationship between the national income level and the consumption expenditures of households.

This relationship can be characterized as a set of four intuitively plausible assumptions (called the "consumption function assumptions"). They are:

1 As income rises, consumption expenditures will rise.

2 As income rises, consumption expenditures will not rise as much as income. That is, people will not spend all of any increase in their income; they will save a part of the increase. This inclination of consumers to spend a fraction of any increase in their income is called the *marginal propensity to consume* (MPC) and can, like the marginal propensity to save, be expressed as a ratio:

$$\text{MPC} = \Delta C/\Delta Y$$

where ΔC is the change in consumption and ΔY is the change in income. In nonmathematical terms,

the MPC is the percentage of any change in income which consumers are inclined to spend.

If the MPC is \$.90 (MPC = $^9/_{10}$), this means that consumers are inclined to spend 90 percent of any change in their income: if national income rises by \$100, consumption expenditures will rise by \$90. The converse is also true.

(You may have noticed that the marginal propensity to consume and the marginal propensity to save, developed in the previous section, are complementary concepts. Indeed, what consumers don't spend of any increase in income, they must save. Remember: $Y = C + S$. Therefore, if the marginal propensity to save is 0.10, the marginal propensity to consume must be 0.90 because MPC + MPS = 1.*)

3 There is some national income level, albeit a very low level, at which consumers will spend all that they earn. At some very low income level, consumers may be simply unable to afford the luxury of saving, that is, to postpone consumption until some future date; they must use what they earn currently for subsistence.

4 There are national income levels—which are lower than the income level described in paragraph 3—at which consumers spend more than they earn currently. If people's income levels are

* (Notice that $\Delta Y = \Delta C + \Delta S$, that MPC = $\Delta C/\Delta Y$, and that MPS = $\Delta S/\Delta Y$. If we divide both sides of the first equation by ΔY,

$$\frac{\Delta Y}{\Delta Y} = \frac{\Delta C}{\Delta Y} + \frac{\Delta S}{\Delta Y}$$

which can be translated to read 1 = MPC + MPS.

seriously depressed for a short period of time, they will draw down their savings accounts in order to meet their current obligations and for subsistence. If people are spending more than they are currently earning, this means that they are buying more goods than are being currently produced. (Remember that income and output are always equal.) The only way firms can sell more than they are currently producing is by reducing their inventories. Consequently, consumption expenditures cannot exceed income indefinitely: firms will eventually run out of inventories to sell.

The upward sloping curve labeled "consumption function" in Figure 29·3 graphically depicts these four assumptions. It therefore describes the relationship between the national income level and the consumption expenditures of households. At a national income level of $400 billion ($Y_1$), the consumption level is also $400 billion ($C_1$). This is the income level at which people spend all that they earn. However, at a higher income level, $1600 billion ($Y_2$), the consumption level is also higher, $1200. Notice that the increase in consumption expenditures ($800 billion, or ΔC) is not as great as the increase in national income ($1200 billion, or ΔY) that caused the rise in consumption. This means, as we assumed above, that the marginal propensity to consume (MPC $= \Delta C/\Delta Y$) is less than 1. Indeed, in the case of this particular curve, the MPC is 2/3:

$$\text{MPC} = \frac{\Delta C}{\Delta Y}$$

therefore,

$$\text{MPC} = \frac{\$800}{\$1200} = \frac{2}{3}$$

Figure 29·3 also reveals that at all national income levels above $400 billion (or Y_1), consumers in the aggregate are saving some part of their incomes. Every point on the line in the figure which extends out of the origin at an angle of 45° is at an equal distance from each axis. Therefore, the vertical distance between Y_2 on the horizontal axis and point a, which is on the 45° line, is equal to

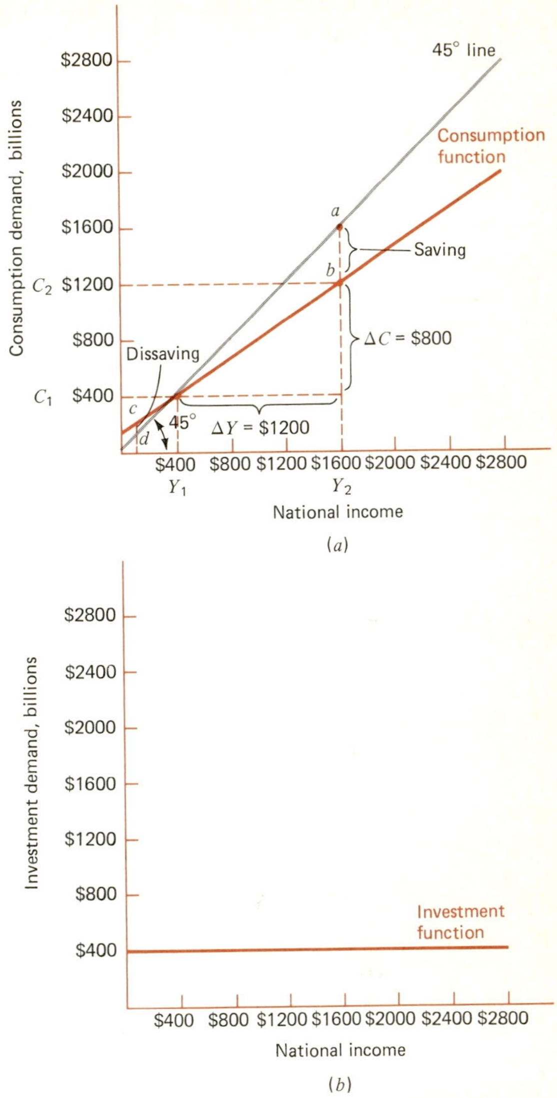

FIG. 29·3 Assuming that consumption expenditures of households are directly related to national income, the consumption function is drawn as the black upward sloping line. At Y_1 consumers are spending all that they earn; there is no saving. At higher national income levels, consumption is higher, but it is not as great as national income and there is saving. For example, at a national income level of $1600 billion, the consumption level is $1200 ($Y_2b$) and the saving level is $400 billion ($ab$). Dissaving occurs at income levels below Y_1.

the national income level at Y_2; it is equal to $1600 billion. If consumers are spending $1200 at an income level of Y_2, they must be saving the rest; they must be saving $400 billion ($Y_2 - C_2 =$ $1600 billion − $1200 billion). This level of saving is represented in the figure by the vertical distance between points a and b. At higher national income levels, the vertical gap between the consumption function and the 45° line is larger; in other words, the level of saving at those higher income levels is greater. This is in line with our previous discussion which assumed that the level of consumer saving is directly related to national income (see Figure 29 · 1a).

At national income levels below Y_1, notice that the consumption function is above the 45° line. Since the vertical distance between the horizontal axis and the 45° line equals the national income level, the level of consumption at any of the income levels below Y_1 is greater than the national income level: consumers are spending more than they are earning. In that area of the graph, consumers are engaging in "negative saving" or "dissaving" in the sense that they are drawing down their saving accounts. The dissaving is the vertical distance between the 45° line and the consumption function. For example, at a national income level of $100 billion, the level of dissaving is $100 billion, or the vertical distance between points c and d in the graph. It follows that since consumers are spending more than they earn at any one of these low income levels, they must be buying more than is currently being produced; businesses must be drawing down their inventories to meet a part of consumer demand.

Investment

In our simplified model of the macroeconomy, investment is the only other component of aggregate demand. (Remember: AD $= C + I$.) However, we fully discussed investment demand in the previous section, and we have nothing to add here. As before, we recognize that investment expenditures are influenced by many factors, but we continue to assume, for the time being, that investment is at a level which is given and does not vary with national income. We can, therefore, describe the investment function as a horizontal line as in Figure 29 · 3b (which is a replication of Figure 29 · 1a).

Equilibrium in National Income

A basic proposition underpinning Keynesian analysis is that equilibrium in national income and employment will be established where aggregate demand is equal to national income (or output). In our model, aggregate demand is composed of consumption and investment expenditures. Therefore, to describe the equilibrium income level graphically, we must add the consumption function of Figure 29 · 3a and the investment function of Figure 29 · 3b to get the "aggregate demand function." This is what we have done in Figure 29·4a. The line labeled $C + I$ in that figure is the aggregate demand function: it is the summation of the consumption function (which is also drawn in the figure and labeled C) and the investment function. The investment demand is represented as the vertical difference between the consumption function C and the aggregate demand function $C + I$. You may notice that this difference is exactly equal to the figure of $400 billion of investment demand in Figure 29·3b.

Given the aggregate demand in Figure 29·4, we can deduce that the equilibrium national income level is $1600 billion, that is, where the $C + I$ curve crosses the 45° line. At that income level (Y_2), consumers buy $1200 billion of the goods that are produced (that is, their consumption demand is C_1) and firms buy $400 billion of plant and equipment. Therefore, aggregate demand is equal to $1600 billion:

AD $= C + I$

Therefore,

AD = $1200 billion + $400 billion
= $1600 billion

Aggregate demand is equal to the national income level,

AD = $1600 billion = Y

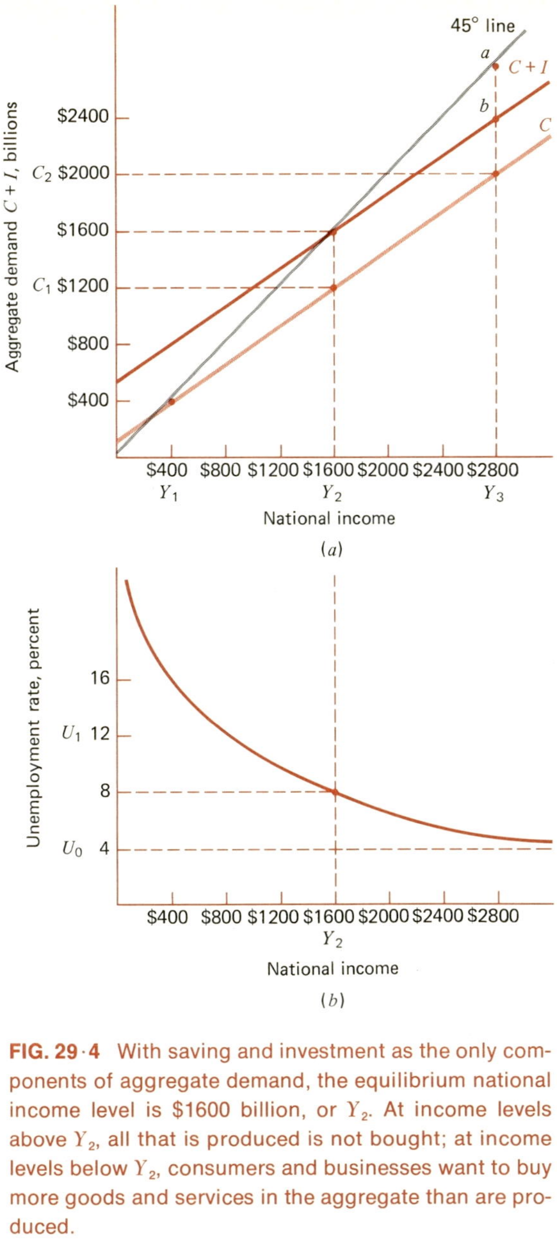

FIG. 29·4 With saving and investment as the only components of aggregate demand, the equilibrium national income level is $1600 billion, or Y_2. At income levels above Y_2, all that is produced is not bought; at income levels below Y_2, consumers and businesses want to buy more goods and services in the aggregate than are produced.

which means that consumers and firms are buying all that is being produced.

If the national income level is not $1600 billion, it will move toward that level. For instance, suppose that the national income level is $2800 billion. At that income level, consumers in the aggregate will buy $2000 billion of goods and services (C_2); businesses will buy $400 billion. Aggregate demand by consumers and firms will therefore be $2400 billion,

$$\text{AD} = \$2000 \text{ billion} + \$400 \text{ billion} = \$2400 \text{ billion}$$

which means that more is being produced ($2800 billion) than is being purchased ($2400 billion). So long as firms continue to produce $2800 billion and to sell $2400 billion, unwanted inventories will pile up. (The vertical distance between points a and b in the figure represents $400 billion of unwanted inventories. The total vertical distance between the horizontal axis and point a is equal to the national income level of $2800 billion. Of this total, $2400 billion, or up to point b, is bought by either consumers or firms; the remainder, $a - b$, is therefore equal to what is not sold and is added to inventories.)

Instead of continually adding goods to their inventories, firms will, at some point, reduce their production levels. When they do, the national income level will fall, and consumer expenditures will fall as national income falls. However, they will not fall by as much as national income falls. It follows that if national income is greater than aggregate demand at the start, and if national income and consumption demand fall but national income falls by more than consumption falls, at some point both the total demand for goods and services ($C + I$) and national income (Y) must become equal. This equality is achieved, as stated above, at a national income level of $1600 billion ($Y_2$). At Y_2, firms are selling exactly what they are producing, and there is no reason for them to either expand or contract production. Therefore, if the national income level is at any point above Y_2, more is being produced than is being sold (as revealed by the gap between the $C + I$ and the 45° line), and the national income level will fall (as firms cut back on production) toward Y_2.

In addition, if the national income level is below Y_2, it will expand toward Y_2. Suppose that firms in the aggregate generate only $400 billion in national income (that is, produce $400 billion of goods and services). At that income level, Y_1, in Figure 29·4*a*, consumers are inclined to spend \$400 billion; businesses are also inclined to spend \$400 billion on capital goods. Obviously the aggregate demand of households and firms exceeds the quantity of goods firms produce:

$$\begin{aligned} \text{AD} &= C + I \\ &= \$400 \text{ billion} + \$400 \text{ billion} \\ &= \$800 \text{ billion} \end{aligned}$$

In order to satisfy that level of aggregate demand, firms will have to draw down their inventories and/or expand production. At some point they are likely to choose the latter course of action, that is, increase their production levels to meet demand. When they expand production, more national income is generated, and this leads to a rise in consumption. Since initially demand is greater than production and production (or national income) rises by more than consumption expenditures, producers at some point will be able to meet the demand for what they produce. Again, they will be able to do this at a national income level of \$1600 billion, or Y_2. We note that Y_2 is the same as the equilibrium income level described by the saving-investment approach in Figure 29·2. This is because at Y_2 in Figure 29·4, saving is equal to investment. The vertical distance between C and $C + I$ is the investment level (\$400 billion). The vertical distance between c on the consumption function and d on the 45° line is equal to the saving level (\$400 billion) at a national income level of Y_2. Therefore,

$$S = \$400 \text{ billion} = I$$

Figures 29·2*a* and 29·4*a* are mirror images of the same Keynesian model, with each figure emphasizing a different aspect of the model.

Because there are forces which cause the national income level to move toward Y_2 when either less than or more than that amount of goods is being produced, Y_2 is the *equilibrium* income level. As shown in Figure 29·4*b*, a national income level of Y_2 is consistent with an unemployment rate of 8 percent, which is above the minimum unemployment rate which can be achieved if more is produced. But, before more is produced, firms and consumers must be inclined to buy more. It is in this sense that Keynesian analysis leads to the conclusion that the national income and employment levels are dependent upon the level of aggregate demand in the economy.

As we have stressed before, in the classical model, unemployment is a consequence of labor market obstructions; in the Keynesian system, unemployment is caused by insufficient demand by all sectors of the economy.

CHANGES IN AGGREGATE DEMAND

In the Keynesian system, just as the levels of investment and consumption (or saving) determine the national income level, changes in the levels of investment and consumption (or saving) will change the equilibrium income level toward which the economy will move. In this section we discuss the effect which changes in investment and consumption have on the national income level.

Changes in Investment

Investment decisions can change because of changes in any of the forces mentioned earlier which influence the profitability of investment: interest rates on borrowed funds, expectations regarding the profitability of future production, tax policies, the national income level, and the development of new technologies. If any one of these variables changes, the level of investment will change and, as we will see, so will the national income level. Consider the assumed inverse relationship between the market interest rate and the level of investment discussed above and depicted by the solid downward sloping curve in Figure 29·5. Assuming that the interest rate is initially r_3 in that figure, the level of investment will be I_1. This level of investment corresponds to the level of investment, I_1, in Figure 29·5; to a national income level of Y_2 in Figure 29·6; and to an unemployment rate of U_2 in part c of Figure 29·6. It follows that since investment depends upon the interest rate, the rate of r_1 is related to specific in-

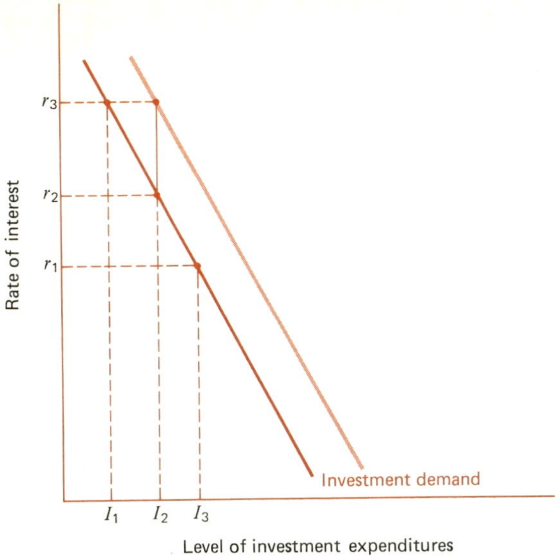

FIG. 29·5 Investment is inversely related to the rate of interest which firms have to pay on money they borrow to buy plant and equipment. This means that if the rate of interest falls from r_3 to r_2, the level of investment will rise from I_1 to I_2. An outward shift in the investment demand curve from I_1 to I_2, with the interest rate remaining constant at r_3, will also cause the level of investment to rise from I_1 to I_2.

come and unemployment levels. Notice that the minimum level of unemployment (U_0 in part c, "full employment") will not be achieved until the level of investment reaches a much higher level, say I_3. This means, for example, that the interest rate must fall to r_1.

If the interest rate falls to r_2 in Figure 29·5, the level of investment will rise to I_2. With the greater level of investment, the aggregate demand function in Figure 29·6a rises to $C + I_2$, and the investment function of Figure 29·6b rises to I_2. At the initial income level, Y_2, the aggregate demand, $C + I_2$, is greater than the level of saving. This can be seen in parts a and b of the figure. In simple terms, firms face a greater demand for goods and services than their current production schedules

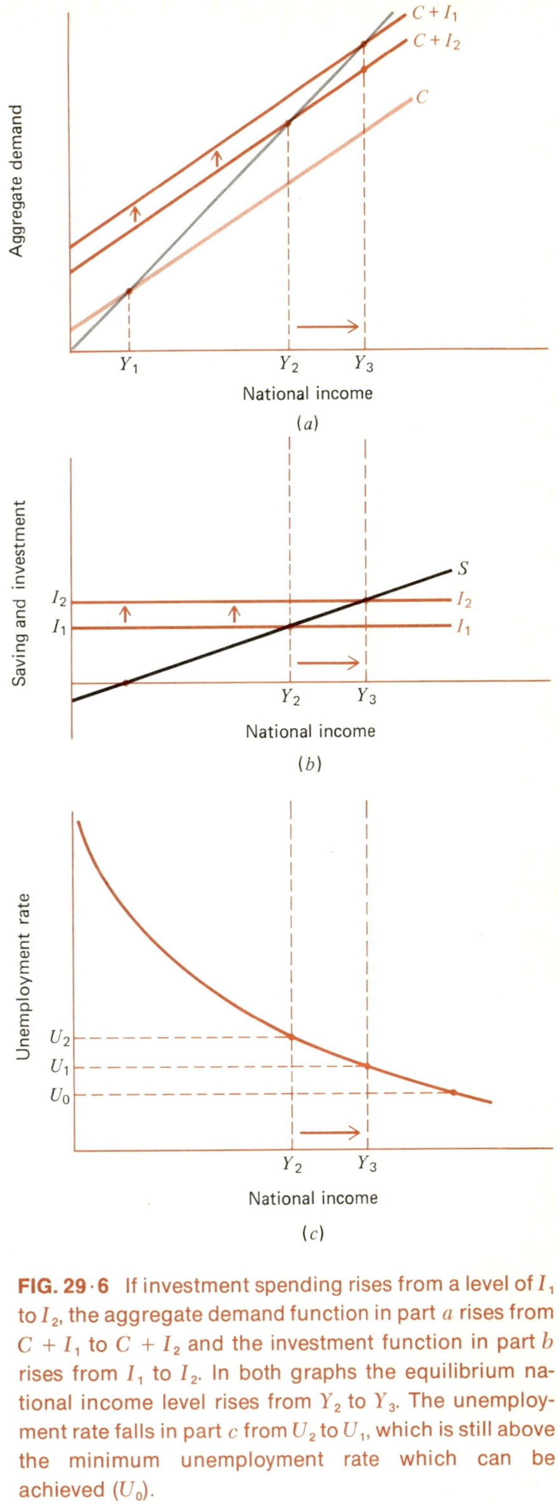

FIG. 29·6 If investment spending rises from a level of I_1 to I_2, the aggregate demand function in part a rises from $C + I_1$ to $C + I_2$ and the investment function in part b rises from I_1 to I_2. In both graphs the equilibrium national income level rises from Y_2 to Y_3. The unemployment rate falls in part c from U_2 to U_1, which is still above the minimum unemployment rate which can be achieved (U_0).

can satisfy. Given the lower unemployment rate of U_1, more workers are employed and more production can be expected. The incomes of households rise, and they save more; the economy moves toward the new equilibrium income level of Y_3, at which saving and investment are once again equal. As can be seen in the figures, an interest rate of r_2 is consistent with the lower unemployment rate of U_1, still above the irreducible minimum.

An increase in the investment demand curve in Figure 29·5 can have an effect similar to a reduction in the interest rate. If the investment demand curve of Figure 29·5 rises from the lower curve to the higher curve and the interest rate remains constant at r_3, the level of investment will rise from I_1 to I_2 and the income level will rise again from Y_2 to Y_3. This shift in the curve can be the consequence of an increase in the expected profitability of investment or, perhaps, more fundamentally, from an increase in the productivity of capital goods, or a reduction in the property taxes on business assets.

It should go without saying that a reduction in the level of investment expenditures (say from I_2 to I_1 in Figure 29·6) will have the exactly opposite effect of the rises detailed above: the national income level will fall and the unemployment rate will rise. A reduction in the level of investment can be brought about by an increase in the interest rate or a downward shift in the investment function of Figure 29·5.

The Multiplier

In the process of moving toward the new equilibrium a peculiar phenomenon occurs. Investment increases in Figure 29·6 by the difference between I_2 and I_1, but the national income level increases by a great deal more, $Y_3 - Y_2$ (ΔY). In fact, the increase in income is *three times* the increase in investment. How can this occur? The answer to that question involves one of the most significant contributions of Keynesian analysis—the concept of the *multiplier*. Simply stated, the multiplier is the ratio of the change in income to the change in aggregate demand that stimulated the change in income: or

$$m = \frac{\Delta Y}{\Delta \text{AD}} \quad (1)$$

where m stands for the multiplier, ΔY for the change in income, and ΔAD for the change in aggregate demand, which, in the example above, is simply the change in investment demand. We emphasize, however, that the concept of the multiplier is applicable to any change in aggregate demand—to consumer or government spending as well as to investment expenditures. By rearranging this ratio, we can see that the multiplier relates the change in income (ΔY) to the change in aggregate demand (ΔAD) in a precise mathematical way:

$$\Delta Y = m\ \Delta \text{AD} \quad (2)$$

We can derive the multiplier (m) by following an elementary line of reasoning. We know that at the initial equilibrium income level of Y_2, saving and investment are equal. Saving and investment must again be equal after the new equilibrium income level (Y_3) is attained. Therefore, any increase in investment which causes firms to produce more must eventually be matched by an increase in saving. If investment goes up by \$10 billion, causing a movement away from equilibrium, a new equilibrium will not be reached until saving has risen by \$10 billion. If the marginal propensity to save is one-third (which is a hypothetical figure we have been using), people will be inclined to save one-third of any change in income. Alternatively, income will rise by three times the change in saving. Consequently, if saving must rise by \$10 billion in order to make saving and investment equal once again, income must rise by \$30 billion. The multiplier ($m = \Delta Y/\Delta$AD) is equal to 3 (m = \$30/\$10 = 3). We can derive the multiplier with much more precision in the following way:

We know that the necessary condition for equilibrium is

$$S = I \quad (3)$$

If investment changes, saving must change by an equal amount, so

$$\Delta S = \Delta I \quad (4)$$

We also know that ΔS is related to the changed income through the marginal propensity to save:

$$\Delta S = \text{MPS}\ \Delta Y \qquad \left(\text{since MPS} = \frac{\Delta S}{\Delta Y}\right) \tag{5}$$

Since ΔS and ΔI must be equal, we can substitute ΔI for ΔS in the above formula to get

$$I = \text{MPS}\ \Delta Y \tag{6}$$

The equation can be rearranged to read

$$\frac{1}{\text{MPS}} = \frac{\Delta Y}{\Delta I} \tag{7}$$

Since m is equal to $\Delta Y/\Delta$AD (from equation 2) and the change in investment is equivalent to the change in aggregate demand, in our simple model the multiplier is equal to the reciprocal of the marginal propensity to save of

$$m = \frac{1}{\text{MPS}} \tag{8}$$

$$\left(\text{or} \qquad m = \frac{1}{\text{slope of the outflow curve}}\right)†$$

(Since the MPS is equal to the slope of the outflow curve, the multiplier is equal to the reciprocal of that slope.) With a marginal propensity to save equal to one-third, which is equal to the slope of the saving function in Figure 29·6, the multiplier is

$$m = \frac{1}{1/3} = 3 \tag{9}$$

This multiplier of 3 simply means that the national income level will rise by three times the change in investment demand (as is the case in this example) or by three times the change in any component of aggregate demand, whether it be consumer demand for goods and services or, as we will discuss in the next chapter, government demand for the goods and services.

The reason for the multiple impact of a change in investment demand can be easily understood in terms of a concrete example. Businesses buy more plant and equipment (I_2 instead of I_1) during each time period. These purchases result in more production and greater income for the suppliers of the investment goods (construction workers and the owners of firms making heavy equipment, for example). With their greater incomes, these suppliers will increase their personal consumption expenditures on such goods as automobiles and refrigerators. The producers of automobiles and refrigerators will then have more income to spend on groceries and clothes. In this way, an increase in demand for capital goods will affect incomes spread throughout the economy.

There is, however, a limit to how much a permanent increase in investment will raise income. As the income level rises, people in the aggregate save more, and eventually the saving level will reach the new higher level of investment, at which point equilibrium will again be attained.

Before we consider the effects of changes in investment, note that the size of the multiplier and, therefore, the potential change in the national income level are critically related to the value of the marginal propensity to save (or the slope of the outflow curve).[3] Consider the following values for the MPS and the associated multiplier:

$$\text{MPS} = 2/5 \qquad m = \frac{1}{2/5} = 2.5$$

$$\text{MPS} = 1/2 \qquad m = \frac{1}{1/2} = 2$$

$$\text{MPS} = 3/5 \qquad m = \frac{1}{3/5} = 1.66$$

All the marginal propensity to save figures are much higher in these illustrations than they are ever likely to be in the real world. However, they can be used as a means of showing the relationship between the MPS and the multiplier. As the marginal propensity to save rises, the value of the multiplier falls. Since the multiplier determines

† Since MPC + MPS = 1 (see footnote*), MPS = 1 − MPC. Therefore, we can rewrite the formula for the multiplier m = 1/MPS to read

$$m = \frac{1}{1 - \text{MPC}}$$

[3] Again, since MPC + MPS = 1, we can say that the value of the multiplier is related to the marginal propensity to *consume*, which is the slope of the consumption function.

just how much income rises with an increase in investment (remember, $\Delta Y = m\ \Delta\text{AD}$), we can conclude that the higher the MPS, the smaller the change in income with any change in investment. A corollary proposition is also true: If a country's marginal propensity to save is very small, say 0.05, it takes only a very small change in aggregate demand to cause a sharp change in the nation's income level. Remember that the multiplier operates on any change in aggregate demand; a decrease in investment can have a multiplier effect in the same way that an increase can. If investment falls for any of a number of reasons, the income level will fall by some multiple of the fall in investment, and unemployment will rise.

Change in Consumption or Saving

For many people saving is a virtue. It demonstrates that the individual is trying responsibly to take care of expected and unexpected future needs. However, on an aggregate level and within the confines of the Keynesian model of income determination, saving can have detrimental effects on income and unemployment levels. To see this, suppose again that we are at an initial equilibrium level of Y_2 in parts a and b and an unemployment rate of U_1 in part c of Figure 29·7. The aggregate demand function is initially $C_1 + I$ in part a, and the saving function is initially S_1 in part b. Further, suppose that people become more concerned about being thrifty; they decide, in the aggregate, to save more because they anticipate a recession in the future and want to set aside more in their saving accounts for those "lean" days.

The saving function in part b of Figure 29·7 shifts upward to S_2, reflecting the greater saving level at each level of income. This shift in the saving function is reflected in the downward shift in the consumption function in part a. At the initial income level of Y_2, the level of saving will exceed investment (part b). Similarly, national production exceeds aggregate demand (part a). Firms will not be selling all that they produce; their inventories will pile up; and they will seek to bring production into line with sales by laying off workers. Unemployment rises (indicated in part c) as the income level falls. As income falls, the

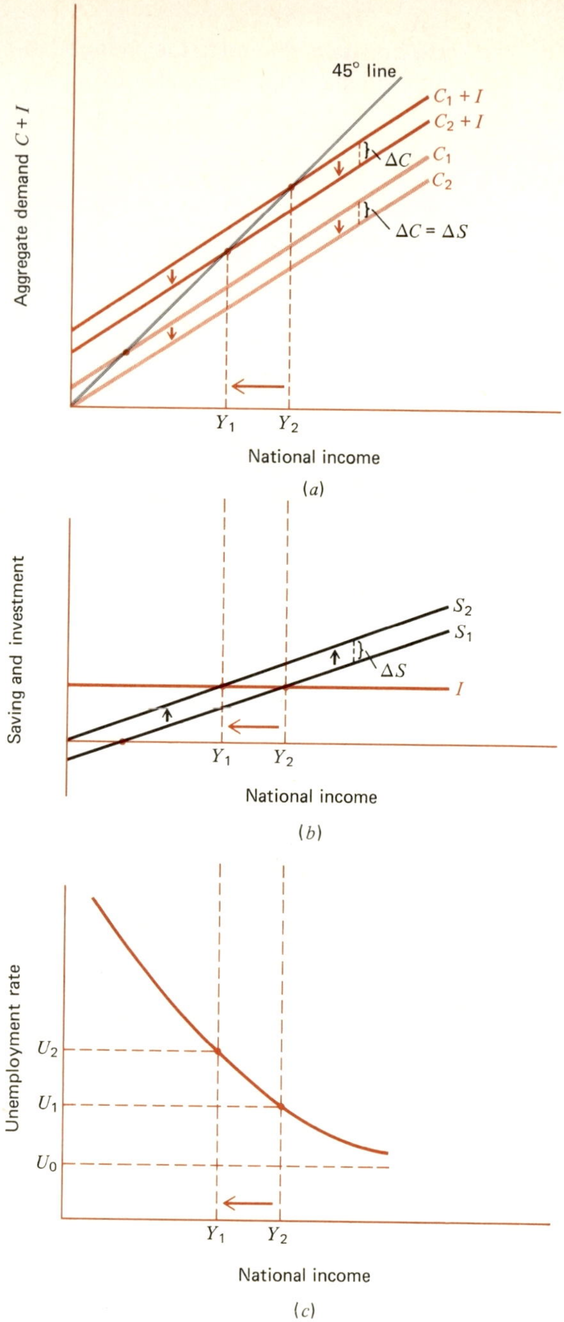

FIG. 29·7 An increase in the level of saving will cause the saving function in part b to shift upward from S_1 to S_2. This increase in saving will be reflected in a decrease in the consumption function in part a from C_1 to C_2 and an equal decrease in the aggregate demand curve from $C_1 + I$ to $C_2 + I$. The result is a decrease in the national income level from Y_2 to Y_1 and an increase in the unemployment rate from U_1 to U_2.

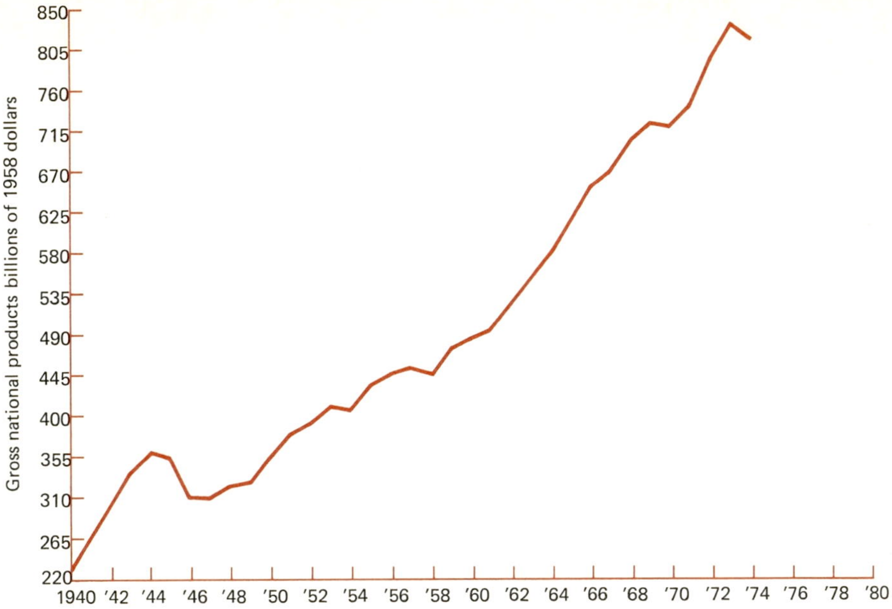

FIG. 29 · 8 Growth in the output of goods and services in the United States, as measured by real GNP, has been irregular during the last several decades.

amount people save also falls, bringing saving back in line with investment. At the lower income level of Y_1, saving and investment are once again equal; aggregate demand is also once again equal to national income. However, the movement toward greater thrift has created unemployment and a lower income level for the country as a whole. Furthermore, at the new equilibrium people are not able to save any more than they were able to save at the higher initial income level of Y_2. For this reason, Keynesians argue that efforts to save can be counterproductive in the short run. People's aggregate income level will fall.

The income level falls for the simple reason that people will consume less when they try to save more; so there will be a lower level of production. An increase in saving, through its effects on consumption, should have the same multiplying effect on the income level as would an equivalent drop in investment. In Figure 29 · 7, saving rises by the vertical distance between the two saving functions, S_1 and S_2; however, the income level falls by a greater amount—three times as much, to be precise. The multiplier is 3; this is because the slope of the saving function (and, therefore, the MPS) is still $1/3$, as before.

It follows from this analysis that a *decrease* in saving or an *increase* in consumption demand will have a positive multiplying effect on the economy, whereas a *decrease* in investment will have a negative effect. These results are consistent because the multiplier effect moves in the same direction as the change in *aggregate demand.*

THE KEYNESIAN EXPLANATION FOR THE BUSINESS CYCLE

Over a long period of time, economic activity usually proceeds in a very irregular manner, as illustrated in Figure 29 · 8 by the historical data for *real* Gross National Product (one means of measuring the national output). Within these data for 1940–1975 there is evidence of a gradual upward movement in the level of overall economic activity. This long-term movement is called the *trend.* However, there are irregular movements within

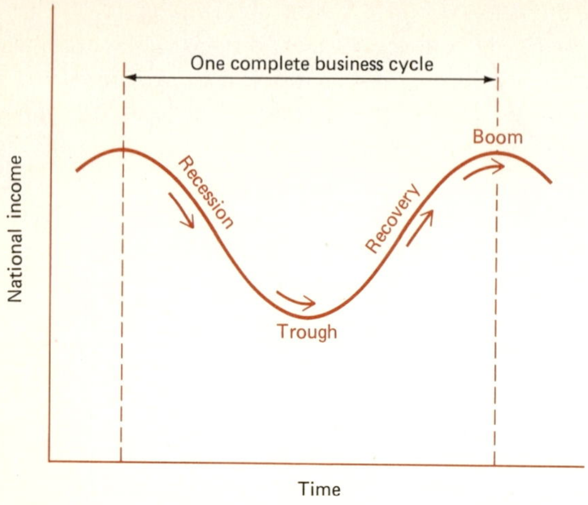

FIG. 29·9 One complete business cycle is made up of four phases: recession, trough, recovery, and boom.

this trend. These movements, which may last for several years, are called *business cycles.* In our amplified illustration of one of these cycles in Figure 29·9, we have identified the four phases of the cycle: "recession," "trough," "recovery," and "boom," which is sometimes called "prosperity." A recession is a downward movement in economic activity, including national income and employment. In the Keynesian paradigm, the recession can be initiated by a drop in either investment or consumption expenditures. Because of the multiplier effect, the income level will fall further than the decrease in expenditures that initiated the downward spiral. The recession may be even more prolonged and severe than the simple multiplier process indicates. A drop in income may also have negative effects on other investment projects. Since the aggregate income level falls during a recession, businesses may decide that some planned investment projects are no longer wise and should be postponed, if not canceled. This further reduction in investment causes a greater decrease in national income than could be computed by considering only the multiplying effect of the initial decrease in investment.

The economy need not spiral downward endlessly. After all, people do need to buy many things in the way of appliances, clothing, and transportation, even though these purchases may be significantly curtailed during the recession. Once the economy hits bottom, it may remain there for a period of time. This is the "trough." However, new technological innovations, changes in consumer and business expectations, etc., can cause an increase in aggregate demand. Then the multiplier process will work its effect on the economy in an upward direction. Once the economy begins to "pick up steam" more and more investment projects will look profitable, and there can be an accumulative upward movement ("recovery") until the economy moves close to full employment of resources and the labor force. This is called the "boom" phase or, alternatively, the "prosperity" phase. In this phase, businesses may become overly optimistic and overproduce and overinvest. If excess capacity develops, firms will reduce their investment spending, setting the stage for the next recession. As we will see in the next chapter, the Keynesian model of macroeconomic activity provides an argument for government adoption of certain budgetary policies to dampen the swings, both the ups and downs, of the business cycles. In this chapter, we merely wish to demonstrate the way in which Keynesian framework can be used to explain the cyclical behavior of the economy.

THE GREAT DEPRESSION: A KEYNESIAN EXPLANATION

In 1929 the United States began sliding into the worst depression in its history. In that year Gross National Product totaled $103 billion. In 1933, at the bottom of the Great Depression, GNP had fallen to $56 billion. During this 4-year period, the prices of practically everything fell sharply, and after adjusting for price reductions, the country's *measured* output level had fallen by 31 percent.[4]

[4] We emphasize that the country's *measured* output level fell by 31 percent because, as the depression got worse, people began to do more and more things for themselves, such as planting gardens. As we studied in Chapter 23, these nonmarket productive activities do not enter into the computation of the Gross National Product. The country's total production of market and nonmarket goods actually fell by less than 31 percent, but it is impossible to say how much less.

The unemployment rate had risen to 25 percent of the civilian labor force. Many more were working only part time; although underemployed, they were not counted in the official unemployment statistics. The level of private business investment fell from $16 billion in 1929 to a little over $1 billion in 1933, and, as a consequence, the country was wearing out its plant and equipment faster than these were being replaced. At the peak of the stock market boom in 1929, the total dollar value of stocks listed on the New York Stock Exchange was $90 billion; at the bottom of the stock market collapse, the market value of these stocks was $15 billion, a decline in value of 83 percent in 3 years.

What caused it all? Keynesian economists point to the decrease in demand, particularly investment demand, which began to emerge in the last half of the 1920s. They contend that in the first half of the 1920s the demand for plant and equipment was bolstered by several important factors. First, World War I had left much of the industrial and agricultural productive capacity of Europe in ruin. Therefore, European countries looked to the United States for many of the capital goods, consumer products, and agricultural commodities which they needed. This specific foreign demand for United States goods not only contributed to greater production in the facilities already built but also fostered the expansion of plant and equipment in order that the greater demand could be met. Second, United States concentration on the production of war-related goods during the late 1910s left a backlog of demands by Americans for new and improved housing and for consumer goods of all kinds after the war. Many industries had to retool to meet the shifts in domestic demand and to expand their productive capacity. Third, during the 1920s the use of the automobile expanded considerably and new products such as the radio, electric stove, and refrigerator were introduced and accepted as a part of the American way of life. These new and expanding domestic industries created a greater demand for even more capital goods during much of the decade. Fourth, people were caught up in a wave of optimism. Many people began to base their consumption expenditures on the belief that the stock market would continue to rise to ever greater heights, and businesses, ignoring the underlying economic conditions which were beginning to turn sour, continued in the latter half of the 1920s to make their investment decisions on the presumption of continued growth in demand and profit.

Beginning in the middle of the decade, the productive capacity of many industries caught up with the backlog of consumer demand. In some industries the productive capacity had obviously been overextended. As is indicated in Table 29·1 below, the construction of housing units reached a peak of 937,000 units in 1925; by 1929 construction had fallen to 509,000, a drop of 46 percent. Until 1928 the decline in residential construction was more than offset by the rise in nonresidential construction; however, there was a significant decline in *total* construction in 1929.[5] Purchases of

[5] Dudley Dillard, *Economic Development of the North Atlantic Community* (Englewood Cliffs, N.J.: Prentice-Hall, Inc., 1967), p. 577.

TABLE 29 · 1 URBAN RESIDENTIAL CONSTRUCTION, 1920–1929

Year	Dwelling Units	Year	Dwelling Units
1920	247,000	1925	937,000
1921	449,000	1926	849,000
1922	716,000	1927	810,000
1923	871,000	1928	753,000
1924	893,000	1929	509,000

SOURCE: U.S. Bureau of the Census, *Historical Statistics of the United States*, p. 393.

automobiles and electrical appliances had similar declines. By the middle of the decade, most European industries had rebuilt and were able to satisfy domestic demands for consumer products and capital goods. Brokerage houses and banks, riding the wave of excessive speculation in stocks and bonds, had expanded their facilities during most of the decade; by the late 1920s, it was clear that they had overexpanded.

All of these underlying economic trends caused a significant drop in investment demand during the late 1920s. If productive capacity has caught up with consumer demand, there is no need for further investment. Further, there is no need for investment in plant and equipment which produce other capital goods. As discussed in this chapter, a reduction in investment demand will lead to a reduction in production, lower incomes, and, accordingly, further reductions in consumption. A lower level of consumption expenditures can lead to a further reduction in investment, and the cumulative (multiplier) process can proceed downward into something on the order of the Great Depression.

The stock market collapse did not cause the Great Depression; the drastic fall of stock prices from their inflated levels merely reflected a sudden and pervasive recognition on the part of investors that the boom of the twenties was over. The sudden collapse, however, contributed to a worsening of what would have been a severe recession anyway. The Great Crash, as it is called, dramatically shattered business confidence and, in this way, caused a further decline in business investment. It also substantially reduced the financial wealth of many people. To rebuild the security they had lost, people had to earnestly try to save more in what were already hard economic times. Furthermore, many people who had money to buy consumer goods were resistant to do so because of the fear that the depression would eventually spread to them. This reduced the aggregate demand and contributed to the downward spiral. In addition to these movements in expenditures and reduction changes, many banks collapsed and a sharp reduction in the money supply and the demand for goods based on credit occurred. Given all the forces at work, we can wonder why the Depression was not more severe than it was.

THE TRADE-OFF BETWEEN INFLATION AND UNEMPLOYMENT

The Keynesian model was originally designed to deal with the problem of unemployment, not inflation. Unemployment was a more important problem during the 1930s, 1940s, and 1950s, when the model was developed and refined. However, inflation (increasing price levels) became a serious social problem in the United States in the last half of the 1960s. Although the problems of inflation are difficult to integrate fully into their model, Keynesians have argued that as aggregate demand pushes the economy toward full employment, the rate of inflation becomes progressively higher. This relationship is described by the downward sloping curve known as the "Phillips curve," named for the person who first developed it. This curve is illustrated in Figure 29·10. It

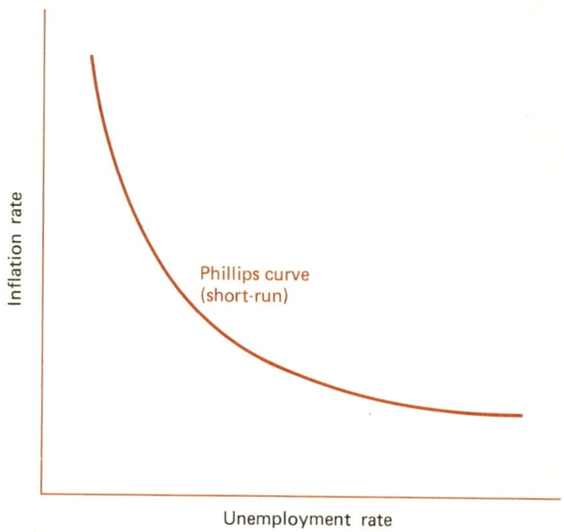

FIG. 29·10 The Phillips curve illustrates the presumed trade-off between the achievement of full employment and stable prices. The curve shows that a reduction in the unemployment rate can be achieved only at the expense of a higher rate of inflation, and vice versa.

shows that as the rate of unemployment falls, the rate of inflation increases, and vice versa.

Several explanations have been offered for this observed relationship. First, as the level of unemployment falls, unions acquire greater bargaining power and are able to negotiate higher wages.[6] Because of higher consumer demand, businesses are able to pass higher wage costs along to consumers in the form of higher prices. To offset the adverse effect of these price increases, unions and other employee groups may seek even higher wages. This is called a "wage-price spiral." Second, any general increase in aggregate demand is not necessarily spread evenly throughout the economy. Inevitably, some sectors will reach full employment before others, and some geographical and economic areas, such as the ghettos of large metropolitan areas and the depressed sections of Appalachia, may never feel the employment effects of a general increase in demand. However, excess demand in certain sectors can cause prices to rise, and these price increases will spread to other sectors via the interdependency of the economy. For example, a general increase in aggregate demand can mean a disproportionate increase in the demand for steel. A "bottleneck" may develop in steel as the demand for steel extends to the industry's production capacity. As a consequence, prices may rise in the steel sector, purely as a market phenomenon; these price increases become cost increases for the automobile and electrical appliance industries. The price increase of transportation can mean further cost increases for additional industries.

Third, generally speaking, not all the labor that is unemployed during any period of time is equally productive. As the recovery phase of the cycle begins, businesses will tend first to hire those workers who are most efficient. Less efficient, less skilled, or less predictable workers tend to be hired during the latter stages of the recovery. By virtue of the lower productivity of the less skilled workers, their employment causes the cost of production to rise. These costs are passed through to consumers in the form of higher prices. When the economy reaches virtually full employment, any excess demand which exists will be reflected in higher prices.

Regardless of the explanation for the Phillips curve, there is, in the short run, a presumed trade-off between unemployment and inflation. There are, therefore, two problems for government: (1) to devise an appropriate policy to deal with the problems of unemployment and inflation, and (2) to choose the most "socially desirable" combination of unemployment and inflation—that is, the appropriate combination on the Phillips curve. We turn to the development of these issues in Chapter 30. In Chapter 31, we present a "monetarists'" model of macroeconomic activity, which suggests that trade-off between inflation and unemployment is descriptive of a much shorter period of time than may be implied in the Keynesian model. In more direct terms, an increase in the rate of inflation may *temporarily* lead to a reduction in unemployment; in the long run, however, unemployment will reemerge at a higher rate of inflation.

[6] Fewer workers looking for work mean there are fewer workers who can take over union jobs in the event of a strike. Further, since sales are up during the boom phase of the cycle, a strike is more costly to employers.

SUMMARY AND EXTENSIONS

The more sophisticated model of the Keynesian perspective developed in this chapter has provided a convincing explanation for business cycles for many economists and policy makers. Business cycles are defined as the intermittent swings between rising and falling levels of national income and employment opportunities. A decrease in the national income level may be initiated by a decrease in investment demand or an increase in saving. The effect of such decreases is magnified by what is called the "multiplier effect." For instance, a drop in investment will lead to cumulative reductions in people's income, a drop in their level of consumption, and, as a consequence, further drops in production and income. Increased investment demand and a reduction in saving will have a multiplier effect in the opposite direction. In this chapter we derived the multiplier as being equal to the reciprocal of the slope of the outflow curve; in a model with saving as the only outflow, the multiplier is equal to the reciprocal of the marginal propensity to save ($m = 1/\text{MPS}$).

To alleviate the persistence of unemployment, classical economists recommend the elimination of labor market restrictions, such as minimum wage laws and union power to resist wage reductions. The Keynesian model, on the other hand, suggests that unemployment problems may be reduced by appropriate reductions in the level of saving and, therefore, increased consumption and/or appropriate increases in investment demand. As we will see in the following chapter, through its tax and expenditure policies, the government can take an active role in directing the economy toward the full-employment income level. The government can increase its own demand for goods and services while holding taxes constant, or it can reduce personal and corporate income taxes. Reduction of personal taxes increases people's disposable income and leads to an increase in consumer demand. A decrease in corporate income taxes will increase after-tax profits for corporations which can be used for investment. The lower tax rates will also increase the rate of return on investment, increasing the investment demand (as in Figure 29·3) and the national income level. Furthermore, as is true with any change in investment demand, higher levels of consumption and increased government and investment demands will have a multiplying effect in the national economy. In short, to achieve a given increase in the national income level, the government need only increase its own expenditures by a fraction of the desired change in national income.

QUESTIONS TO PONDER

1 Suppose that the marginal propensity to save is $1/5$, that the level of consumption expenditures increases by $15 at each income level, and that investment expenditures increase by $10; what will be the amount and direction of the change in national income? What will happen to the unemployment rate?

2 Given the following MPSs and changes in investment, compute the multiplier and the change in national income:

MPS	Multiplier	ΔI	ΔY
$1/10$	________	+$10	________
$1/15$	________	−$20	________
$3/100$	________	+ $5	________

3 Suppose that the level of saving rises by $10 at the same time that the level of investment increases by $10. What will happen to the national income level?

4 In the graph on page 539 we have drawn the saving function which was used in this chapter. However, we have also drawn the investment function as an upward sloping curve; the implied assumption is that investment is a direct function of the national income level. That is, as the income increases, so does investment, and vice versa. Given this information, suppose that the level of saving increases at each and every income level. What will happen to the national income level and the unemployment rate? What will happen to the actual level of saving due to the upward shift in the saving function? Explain the sequence of events that would lead to the answers you have given to the above questions.

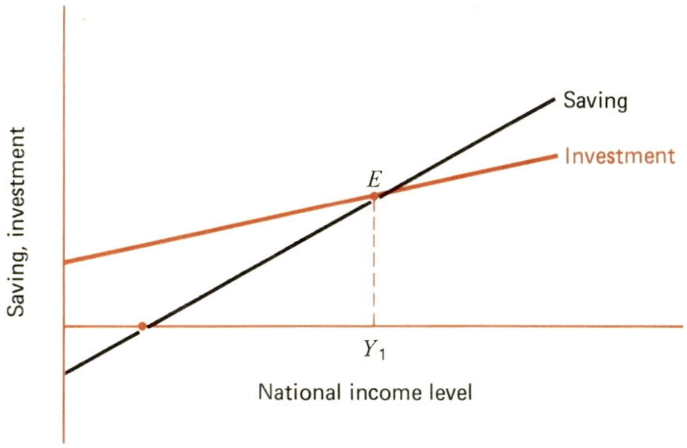

RECOMMENDED READINGS

Dillard, Dudley: *Economic Development of the North Atlantic Community* (Englewood Cliffs, N.J.: Prentice-Hall, Inc., 1967), chaps. 31 and 32.

Galbraith, John Kenneth: *The Great Crash; 1929* (Boston: Houghton Mifflin Company, 1955).

(See also the "Recommended Readings" for Chapter 28.)

30

The "New Economics" and Government Policy

To hit the fiscal brakes . . . when unemployment and economic slack are still legion and inflation is ebbing would be fiscally irresponsible. "Fiscal responsibility" is not synonymous with "fiscal restraint." Rather, it calls for an intelligent fitting of tax and spending positions to the needs of the economy.

Walter Heller[1]

PREVIEW OF CHAPTER

Central question

What fiscal policy actions should the government take to raise national production, reduce unemployment, and stabilize prices?

Major objectives

1. To introduce government into the Keynesian model of the macroeconomy
2. To explain how government can employ *fiscal policy* to achieve the goals of full employment and stabilize prices
3. To explain how government fiscal policy can affect business investment and why there is controversy over the effectiveness of fiscal policy
4. To develop the arguments for and against deficit spending by the government
5. To explain why politicians may find Keynesian economics an attractive theory for the formulation of government policy and why Keynesian solutions for reducing unemployment may be overused

[1] Walter W. Heller, "Ford's Budget and the Economy," *Wall Street Journal*, Feb. 5, 1976, p. 18.

6 To reveal the effects which increases in the money stock have on the national income level in the Keynesian model

Major conclusions

1 Government can increase aggregate demand and, thereby, the national level by (*a*) increasing government spending while holding taxes constant or (*b*) reducing taxes while holding government spending constant. In short, to raise the national income level and to reduce unemployment, the government should run a budgetary deficit.

2 To reduce inflation, government can reduce aggregate demand by (*a*) reducing government spending while it holds taxes constant or (*b*) increasing taxes while it holds government spending constant. In short, the government should run a budgetary surplus.

3 In the Keynesian model, increases or decreases in government spending or taxes have multiplier effects on the national income level. Therefore, to raise the national income level, the government needs only to raise its expenditures or to reduce taxes by some fraction of the desired increase in national income.

4 An increase in government spending of a certain amount will have a greater effect on the national income than a tax reduction of an equal amount. Alternatively, in order to achieve a given increase in the national income level, the government must reduce taxes by more than it increases government spending; it must run a larger budgetary deficit when it reduces taxes than when it increases government spending.

5 The national debt does not have to be paid off; it can be refunded. That is, when a portion of the national debt must be paid off, the government can issue new bonds to acquire the funds which are needed to pay off the debt that has matured.

6 When government borrows money to cover a deficit that may be caused by, say, an increase in government spending, the market interest rate may rise and businesses may reduce the investment spending they plan to undertake. The reduction in business investment can partially offset the effects which the increase in government spending has on the national income level.

7 Deficit spending has political benefits for representatives who wish to be reelected. If politicians can run budgetary deficits, this means that they can increase expenditures for public goods, from which their constituencies benefit, without asking their constituencies to pay for those goods in terms of higher taxes. Politicians can, at times, be expected to vote for larger budgetary deficits than may be justified, given national goals of full employment and stable prices.

8 In the Keynesian model, an increase in the money stock will lead to (*a*) a reduction in the interest rate; thereby, (*b*) an increase in business investment; thereby, (*c*) an increase in aggregate demand; and, thereby, (*d*) an increase in the national income level.

Important term

Fiscal policy

In the preceding two chapters we developed the basic Keynesian model of income and employment determination. This model showed that changes in total demand for goods and services, through the multiplier process, caused changes in national income and total employment. We also saw that the economy may settle at an income level which is not the full-employment level and that if the economy moves away from full employment, there are not, necessarily, natural forces in the short run that can move the economy back to full prosperity and employment.

In this chapter we extend the Keynesian model by introducing government tax and spending policies. According to this more complete model, the government can add the corrective forces which are absent in the private sector. Specifically, the government can move the economy out of a recession by running budgetary deficits—that is, by spending *more* than it collects in taxes. It can reduce inflationary pressures during periods of prosperity by incurring budgetary surpluses—that is, by spending *less* than it collects in taxes.

In the Keynesian model, economic stability at the full-employment income level is a *public good* which (like all other public goods) requires collective governmental action to attain. If the economy is in the midst of a recession, the income level can be increased if *all* investors increase their expenditures on plant and equipment or if *all* consumers reduce their saving levels. However, as we have repeatedly noted in this text, each household or firm in the context of a large group (like the economy) has little private incentive to contribute to the production of a public good like economic stability or the achievement of full employment. Each household or firm is too small to make a significant contribution to that end or too small to realize any substantial benefits from its own actions. Therefore, investors and consumers do not develop their spending plans on the basis of the "common interest," but rather by comparing the private costs and benefits of their own individual situations. All tend to become "free riders." Government action is, therefore, necessary to produce economic stability for essentially the same reason it is necessary in the production of national defense. Using this line of argument, much of our government's economic policy over the past two decades has been formulated with Keynesian theory in mind, giving us some real-world situations to analyze. In the concluding section of this chapter we'll look at how Keynesian macroeconomic analysis has been used by political leaders during the 1960s and 1970s and examine some problems which reveal the limitations of the "new economics."

THE GOVERNMENT AND THE CIRCULAR FLOW

In Chapter 28 we defined the *circular flow* as the flow of expenditures by households on goods produced by firms and the flow of money payments (wages, interest, and dividends) made by firms to households. We demonstrated that if households receive in total payments from firms an amount equal to their earnings and if they spend all that they earn on goods produced by firms, income flow remains constant—the macroeconomy is in "equilibrium." Saving, however, constitutes a leakage from the circular flow; and unless saving is offset by investment, the national income level will change. If saving is greater than investment, the income level will fall. If the opposite is true, the income level will rise, provided, of course, that there are unemployed resources that can be used in production. In this chapter, we introduce government into the analysis. The introduction of government makes the analysis less simplistic but more descriptive of the world as we know it.

Government Taxes and Expenditures

Government taxes are one means of diverting a part of consumer purchasing power away from the circular flow.[2] Taxes may reenter the circular

[2] Corporate income taxes and property taxes also divert funds from businesses and their stockholders from the circular flow to the government. In order to keep the analysis as simple as possible, we shall mention but sidestep these forms of taxation. This simplification does not affect the general line of the argument nor the conclusions drawn.

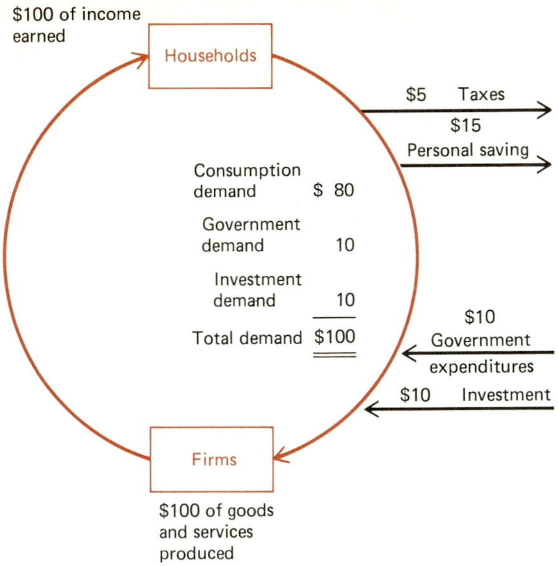

FIG. 30·1 When government is introduced into the circular-flow model, equilibrium in national income will occur when the sum of the outflows, saving and taxes, is exactly equal to the sum of the inflows, investment and government expenditures. This is the case when taxes are $5, saving is $15, government expenditures are $10, and investment is $10.

flow in the form of government expenditures; however, at the moment taxes are extracted by the government, they have essentially the same effect on the circular flow as personal savings, which we discussed in Chapter 28. For this reason, we describe the tax outflow in Figure 30·1 as an arrow pointing out of the circular-flow diagram. Government expenditures on goods and services (such as on defense hardware, buildings, and roads) produced in the private sector, on the other hand, constitute an inflow to the economy: they represent sales of firms which are not direct purchases of households. Given their similarity in this respect to business purchases of capital equipment, we have described government expenditures as an arrow pointing toward the circular flow, just like investment.

Equilibrium

Once governmental action is introduced into the analysis, it is no longer enough to have saving and investment equal in order to have equilibrium. Rather,

the sum of the outflows (saving and taxes) must equal the sum of the inflows (investment and government expenditures).

If this condition holds, the national income level will remain at one constant level. This situation is illustrated in Figure 30·1. Here, assume again that $100 worth of goods and services is produced. The households earn this amount; however, they pay $5 in taxes and choose to save $15. Government expenditures are $10 and investment is $10. Therefore, the consumption demand of households is $80 [$100 − ($5 + $15)]; the demand for goods and services coming from businesses and government totals $20 ($10 + $10). The aggregate demand is $100 ($80 + $20). All the goods produced are sold to investors, consumers, or government. There is no reason for firms either to expand or to lower production.

For this more complicated model, the conditions for equilibrium in national income can be stated formally. Aggregate demand (AD) is now composed of three expenditure categories: consumption (C), investment (I), and government spending (G), or stated algebraically,

$$\text{AD} = C + I + G$$

Similarly, there are now three things which people can do with the income (Y) that they earn: they can spend it (C), they can save it (S), and they can pay taxes (T); therefore,

$$Y = C + S + T$$

In equilibrium, we know from Chapter 29 that aggregate demand must equal national income,

$$\text{AD} = Y$$

or

$$Y = C + I + G$$

In our circular-flow example, this condition is

met. There are \$100 of goods and services produced and, therefore, \$100 of income earned. Of this amount, consumers in the aggregate buy \$80, firms buy \$10 in the form of investment goods, and the government buys \$10:

$$Y = \$100 = \$80 + \$10 + \$10 = \text{AD}$$

On the other hand, if aggregate demand equals national income, we know that

$$C + I + G = C + S + T$$

which reduces to

$$I + G = S + T$$

In terms of the circular-flow model, this condition simply means that in equilibrium

Inflows = outflows

which is the case in our example

\$10 + \$10 = \$15 + \$5

In our circular-flow illustration, saving is greater than investment. This may be bothersome because in the no-government model of the economy, studied in Chapter 28, if saving is greater than investment, the income level will fall and unemployment will rise. However, here we can see that the income level is stable because of the offsetting force of government. Government expenditure exceeds taxes by the same amount (\$5). The government runs a *budgetary deficit* (which is the amount by which its expenditures exceed tax revenues) in this example, but in doing so, it keeps the national income level from falling.

According to the Keynesian paradigm, the public (and, perhaps, hidden) benefits of the budgetary deficit can be assessed by comparing the stable equilibrium income level and the lower income level to which the economy will fall if the deficit does not exist. If taxes and government expenditures both equal \$10 (that is, the budget is balanced because the government's inflows and outflows are equal), consumption demand will be \$75 [\$100 − (\$10 in taxes + \$15 in saving)] and total demand, \$95 (\$75 in consumption + \$20 in government expenditures and investment). Not all the \$100 worth of goods and services will be sold; therefore, firms will have a reason to cut back on production. The national income level will spiral downward in a multiplying process of lower consumption, lower incomes, and further reductions in income and consumption.

If resources are unemployed at an income level of \$100, the government can take action to raise that income level. It can reduce taxes; or it can increase expenditures on roads, schools, hospitals, or military hardware; *or* it can reduce taxes and increase expenditures at the same time. Regardless, the Keynesian prescription is to run a budgetary deficit, or if the budget is already in deficit, as it is in our illustration, to run a larger deficit. To see this clearly, suppose that the government increases its expenditures by \$5 to \$15. The quantitative changes are recorded in Figure 30·2. The consumption demand is still \$80. However, with the increase in government spending, the economy's aggregate demand rises to \$105. Consum-

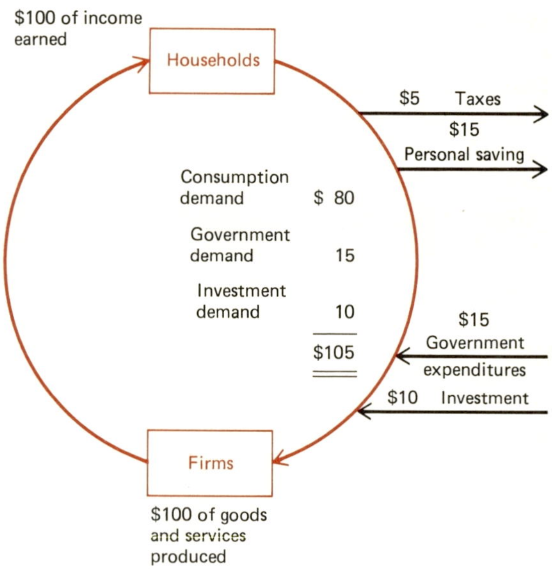

FIG. 30·2 When the sum of the inflows is greater than the sum of the outflows, the aggregate demand in the economy will be greater than the national income. The national income level will rise if resources, capital and workers, are initially unemployed.

ers, investors, and government independently demand more than is being produced; therefore, firms have an incentive to raise their production levels. Increased production means higher income levels and greater consumption. Increased consumption induces firms to produce even more goods and services and generate more income. In this way, the national income level moves up.

On the other hand, the economy is moving toward a new equilibrium income level. As income rises, saving rises and, because income tax rates are tied to people's income levels, taxes also rise. If incomes rise from \$100 to \$110, saving will very likely rise from \$15 to, say, \$16 and taxes will rise from \$5 to, say, \$5.25. Once the sum of saving and taxes equals the new, higher level of investment and government expenditures (\$25), a new equilibrium income level will be achieved. Virtually the same increase in national income can be achieved by reducing tax rates and, thereby, tax payments at the initial income level. The major difference is that when taxes are reduced, people may elect to save a portion of their tax reduction. A \$5 reduction in taxes may mean a \$1 increase in saving, in which case the total of the two outflows, saving and taxes, does not fall by \$5, but by \$4. Therefore, an increase in government expenditures will tend to have a greater effect on the national income level than an equal decrease in taxes. (Can you show this in a diagram similar to Figure 30·2?)

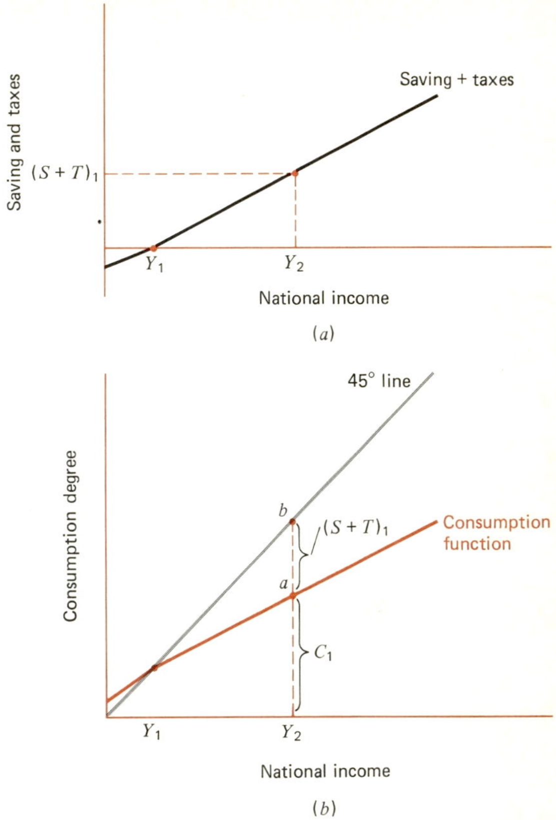

FIG. 30·3 Saving and taxes are both related to the national income level. These two outflows can, therefore, be described as the upward sloping line in the figure. The slope of this function is steeper than the saving function used in previous figures. The consumption function is still drawn upward sloping; however, the vertical distance between the consumption function and the 45° line is the combined total of saving and taxes at each national income level. The slope of the consumption function is lower than the consumption function of earlier figures.

A MORE PRECISE STATEMENT OF GOVERNMENT IN THE KEYNESIAN MODEL

To illustrate these conclusions with more precision, let us employ graphs (similar to ones used in Chapter 29) that relate the various inflows, outflows, and spending categories of the circular-flow diagram to the national income level. In our model economy, tax payments and saving are directly influenced by the national income level; as the income level rises, people save more and, beyond some minimum income level, they also are required to pay more in taxes. This functional relationship is described in Figure 30 · 3*a*. At an income level of Y_1, the levels of saving and taxes paid are both assumed to be zero. However, at a higher income level, say Y_2, the sum of saving and investment is positive and equal to $S + T$. At even higher national income levels, the sum of these two outflows is even greater. However, you should keep in mind that the taxes which are collected reduce the saving outflow; in other words, the two outflows are not independent of one another.

The effect which the additional outflow in the form of taxes has on the consumption function, derived in Chapter 29, is illustrated in part *b* of Figure 30·3. The consumption function in that figure has a slightly lower slope than the one we used in Chapter 29, reflecting the fact that when taxes are drawn from national income, the consumer expenditures at each national income level fall because people have less *disposable* income to spend. At a national income level of Y_2, total consumer expenditures are C_1 in part *b*, which is less than would have been the case if it were not for the tax outflow. The saving and tax level at that income level is equal to the vertical distance between the consumption function at Y_2 (point *a*) and the 45° line (point *b*). The $(S + T)_1$ in part *b* is the same as the $(S + T)_1$ in part *a* of Figure 30 · 3.

Congressional appropriations and, thereby, government spending may be influenced by the national income level; however, to keep the analysis as simple as possible, let us assume that government expenditures, along with investment expenditures, do not change with respect to national income. The curves illustrating the assumed relationship between the national income and government and investment expenditures are, therefore, horizontal lines, as in Figure 30·4*a* and *b*. Adding these two curves results in another higher horizontal curve like the one in part *c* of Figure 30·4. As the income level changes, the sum of government and investment expenditures does not change.

The Equilibrium Income Level

In Figure 30·5*b* we have combined the saving-taxes curve (outflows) of Figure 30 · 3*c* with the government spending–investment (inflow) curve of Figure 30 · 4*c*. We have also combined the new consumption function in Figure 30·3*d* with the government spending–investment curve of Figure 30·4*c* to obtain a new aggregate demand curve labeled $C + I + G$ in Figure 30·5*a*. With these two graphs we are able to illustrate equilibrium in national income. From our previous discussions, we know that national income will be in equilibrium where the outflows equal the inflows or, alternatively, where aggregate demand equals national income or output. These conditions are both met at an income level of Y_2 in Figure 30 · 5, parts *a* and *b*. At higher or lower national income levels,

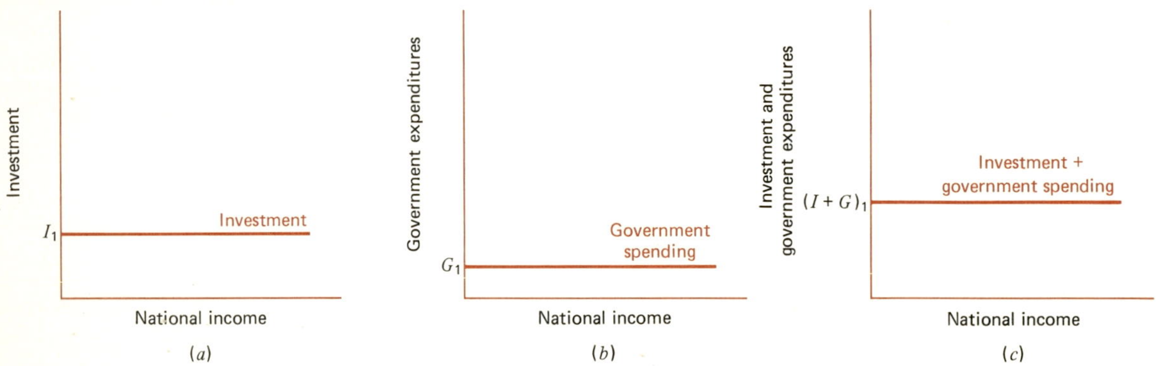

FIG. 30·4 Investment and government spending are both assumed to be unaffected by the national income level. Therefore, the investment and government spending functions are drawn as horizontal lines as in parts *a* and *b*. The combined total of investment and government spending at each income level is represented by another higher horizontal line in part *c*.

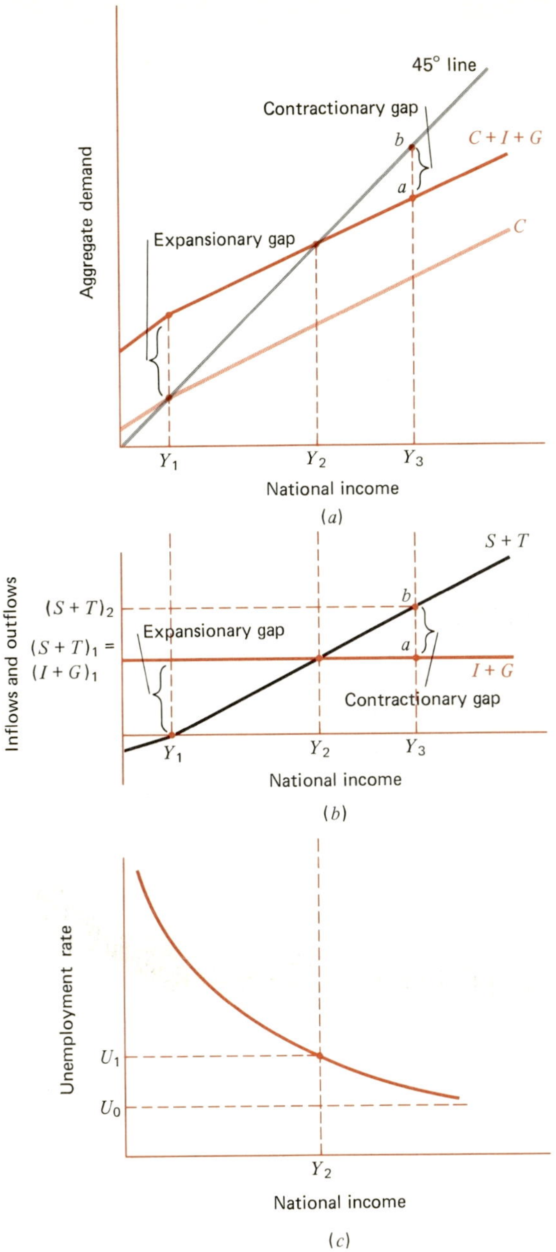

FIG. 30·5 Equilibrium in the national income level is achieved at Y_2. At higher national income levels, national output is greater than aggregate demand (part *a*) and the saving and tax outflows exceed the investment and government spending inflows (part *b*): there is a "contractionary gap" between what is produced and what is demanded by business, consumers, and government, and the economy will move down toward Y_2. At national income levels below Y_2, aggregate demand exceeds national output (part *a*) and the investment and government spending inflows exceed the saving and tax outflows (part *b*): there is an "expansionary gap" between what is produced and what business, consumers, and government want, and the national income will move up toward Y_2.

there will be cause for firms to either cut back or expand production. For instance, at an income level of Y_3, the level of outflows [saving plus taxes, $(S + T)_2$] is greater than the level of inflow [investment plus government expenditures, $(I + G)_1$] in part *b*; there is a "contractionary gap" equal to the vertical distance between points *a* and *b* in parts *a* and *b* of the figure. Firms are not selling all they produce and have an incentive to reduce production. As a result, the income level contracts toward Y_2, along with saving and taxes.

On the other side of equilibrium, Y_2, the level of investment and government expenditure is greater than the level of saving and taxes; here, there is an "expansionary gap." Firms are producing less than people want and so have an incentive to raise their production plans. As they do, they increase the national income level and increase the outflows of saving and taxes. Eventually, the outflows match the inflows. This occurs at Y_2, as stated before. At that income level

Outflows = inflows

$$S + T = I + G$$

and

Aggregate demand = national income

$$C + I + G = C + S + T$$

Still, the unemployment rate (U_1) is above the minimum rate, as indicated in Figure 30·5*c*.

Changes in Government Expenditures

If the government increases its expenditures while it holds taxes constant, it runs a budgetary deficit and in so doing changes the national income level. Figure 30·6 illustrates the impact of an increase in government expenditure and, by

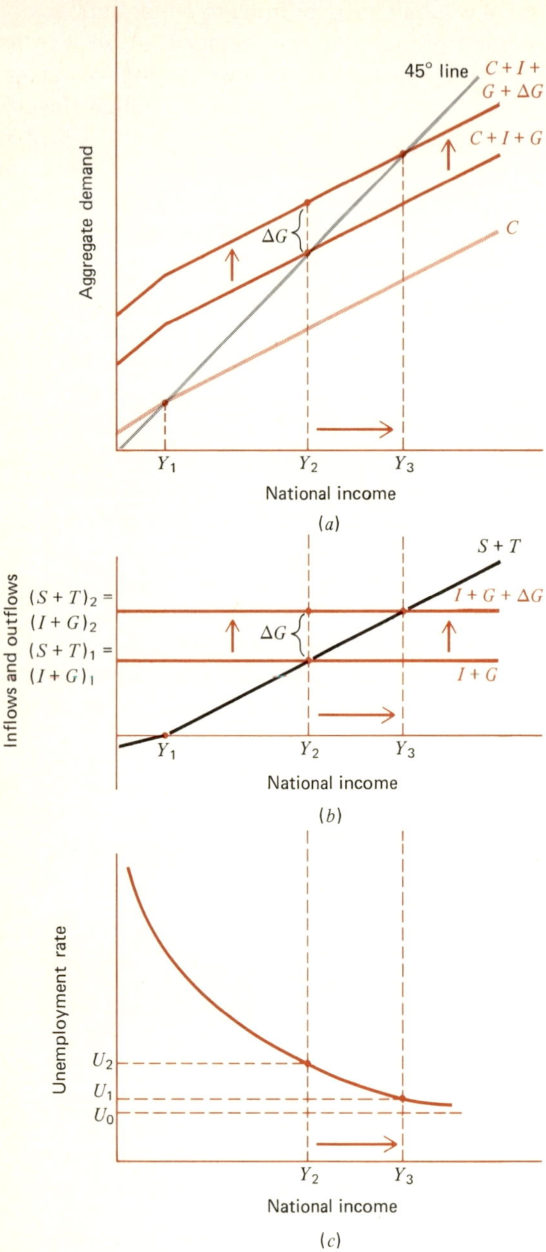

FIG. 30·6 An increase in government spending by ΔG will move the aggregate demand curve in part a up to $C + I + G + \Delta G$ and the inflow curve in part b up to $I + G + \Delta G$ in part b. The national income level moves from Y_2 up to Y_3.

inference, a budgetary deficit. With an increase in government expenditures, equal to ΔG, the aggregate demand curve, $C + I + G$, shifts upward to $C + I + G + \Delta G$ in part a of Figure 30·6. This shift is mirrored in part b by an upward shift in the inflow curve from $I + G$ to $I + G + \Delta G$. At the initial income level of Y_2, an expansionary gap is now present: total inflows are now greater than total outflows: businesses are not producing enough to satisfy the total demand. As businesses produce more, the income level rises along with saving and tax outflows. The economy reaches a new equilibrium at Y_3, at which point the outflows and inflows on the one hand and aggregate demand and national income on the other are once again equal.

Notice, however, that the change in national income, $Y_3 - Y_2$, is greater than the change in government expenditure, ΔG, which initiated the rise in economic activity. The change in income is greater because of the multiplier effect of the government's action. The government spends more, causing more production and higher incomes. Having higher incomes, consumers spend more. This, in turn, causes a rise in production, a further rise in income, and a further rise in consumption expenditures. The spiraling process comes to an end when the increase in saving and tax outflows equals the increase in government expenditures. In short, using the Keynesian model to evaluate the impact of more government spending, the increase in income will be some multiple, greater than 1, of the change in government spending (ΔG). Since the change in national income equals the multiplier times the change in aggregate demand, or

since

$\Delta Y = m\,\Delta \text{AD}$ (from Chapter 29)

and

$\Delta \text{AD} = \Delta G$

then

$\Delta Y = m\,\Delta G$

where ΔY = change in national income level
m = multiplier

ΔAD = change in aggregate demand
ΔG = change in government expenditures

With the tax outflow added to the outflow of saving, the multiplier is not quite as large as it was in examples used in Chapter 29. As we have explained before, this is because taxes, like saving, drain off purchasing power when the income level rises, and it is through the expenditures of people and firms that the multiplier process is fueled. Therefore, the multiplier is less. Actually, as we mentioned before in discussing the multiplier, the multiplier is equal to the reciprocal of the slope of the outflow curve:

$$m = \frac{1}{\text{slope of outflow curve}}$$

The slope of that curve in Figure 30·6*b* is steeper when the tax outflow is added to saving; therefore, the reciprocal of that slope (that is, the multiplier) is lower.

If government decreases its expenditures and keeps taxes constant, a budgetary surplus will emerge. The decrease in government spending will have the effect of decreasing total demand and the national income level. If some resources are unemployed initially and the government spends less, firms will produce less, people will receive less income and consume less, etc. The income level moves cumulatively downward by some multiple of the decrease in government expenditures; unemployment rises. In this case the government's spending policy causes (or contributes to) a recession in the economy.

Fiscal policy is the tax and expenditure actions of government which are directed at achieving full employment of the labor force and stable prices.

As opposed to intentionally causing a recession, which is implied in the above example of reduced government spending, the government may use fiscal policy to reduce the rate of inflation. Suppose, for instance, that initially the flow of government expenditures and investment into the economy adds up to $(I + G)_1$ in Figure 30·7. The equilibrium income level is Y_1, where the outflow and inflow curves intersect. However, notice in

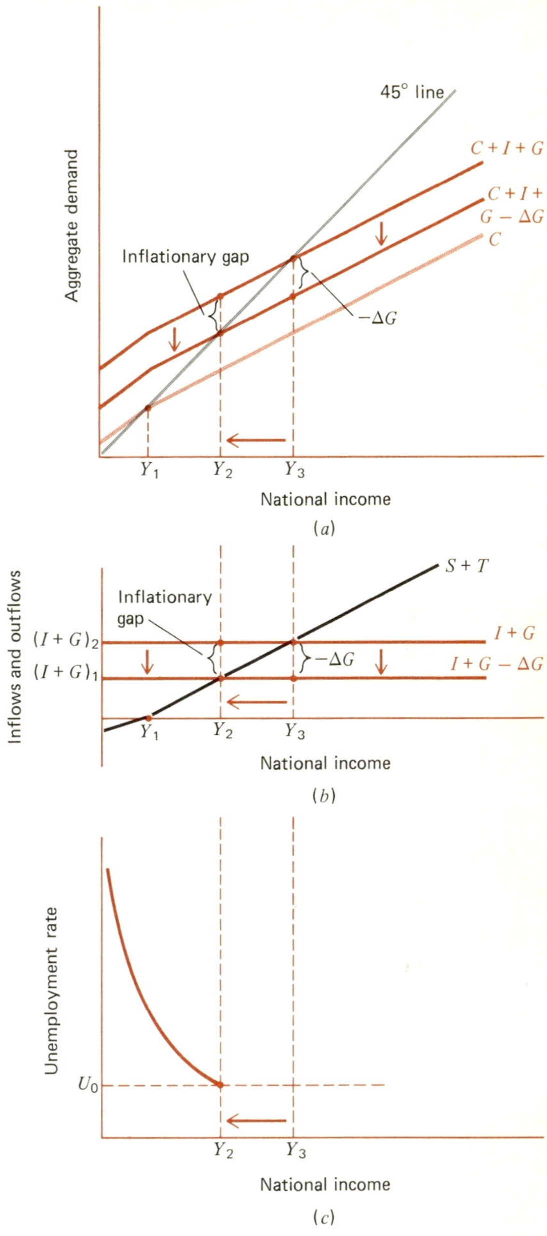

FIG. 30·7 Inflation can be caused by the aggregate demand exceeding national output when the labor force is fully employed. By reducing its own expenditures by ΔG, the government can reduce aggregate demand to $C + I + G - \Delta G$ and can move the economy away from the inflationary equilibrium income level of Y_3 to a noninflationary income level of Y_2.

part c of the figure that the economy reaches the minimal unemployment rate of U_0 at a much lower income level, Y_2. The economy simply does not have sufficient labor to produce an output level of Y_3. On the other hand, the demand in the economy is attempting to push production to that level. There is an "inflationary gap" between what is demanded (point b in part a) and what at the limit can be produced, Y_2 (or point a), and the consequence of the excess demand should be inflation. The government can eliminate these inflationary pressures by reducing its own expenditures and, thereby, reducing aggregate demand in part a to $C + I + G - \Delta G$ and the aggregate inflow curve in part b to $(I + G)$. The equilibrium income level will then be the full-employment level.

Changes in Taxes

If government holds its expenditures constant and lowers taxes, a budgetary deficit will emerge. On the other hand, an increase in taxes will result in a budgetary surplus. As we will see in this section, these surpluses and deficits induced by tax changes will have effects on national income that are similar to those generated by government expenditure changes.

If people's saving habits are unaffected by the taxes they pay, a reduction in taxes equal to ΔT will cause a downward shift in the outflow $(S + T)$ curve in Figure 30·8b to the curve labeled $S + T - \Delta T$, and the new equilibrium income level will be Y_4. However, we may expect some modest upward adjustment in saving with a tax reduction, particularly if the tax cut is a relatively large one. In this event, the tax cut is partially offset by an increase in saving. As opposed to the $S + T$ curve shifting to $S + T - \Delta T$, it may move only part of the way, to $S + T - \Delta T + \Delta S$. Aggregate demand in part a of the figure rises by ΔC, which is equal to the reduction in taxes minus the increase in saving.[3]

The national income level rises only to Y_3. The unemployment level falls from U_2 to U_1, not to the minimum.

A tax increase will, of course, reduce people's disposable income: it will reduce their level of saving and also their level of consumption. Lower consumption means lower production and lower incomes. As with a reduction in government expenditures, the intent of a tax increase is usually to reduce inflationary pressures which arise because the aggregate demand from all sectors exceeds the ability of the economy to produce goods and services. When the demand for all goods and services is lowered, there is less competition for the available resources and less reason for prices to rise.

A Comparison of Tax and Expenditure Changes

Keynesian analysis leads to two important conclusions. First, an increase in government expenditures will have the same *directional* effect on national income as a reduction in taxes. Increases in expenditures and reductions in taxes lead to greater national income levels; decreases in government expenditures and increases in taxes retard inflationary pressures or lead to lower national income levels.

Second, an increase in government expenditures of a given amount will have a greater effect in terms of the change in national income than an equal reduction in taxes, and conversely. For instance, suppose that the multiplier equals 3 and that the government increases expenditures on a permanent basis by $10 billion. The change in the national income level will be $30 billion (the multiplier times the change in demand). On the other hand, a $10 billion reduction in taxes will not all be spent by consumers. Some of the reduction

[3] The reduction in taxes represents an increase in disposable income for taxpayers. Taxpayers will spend a portion of this increase in disposable income, and that portion may be roughly measured by the marginal propensity to consume (MPC). Therefore, $\Delta C = \text{MPC}(-\Delta T)$. If the MPC is $9/10$ and taxes are reduced by $30 billion, consumption expenditures will rise by $27 billion; the remaining portion of the tax cut, $3 billion, will be saved.

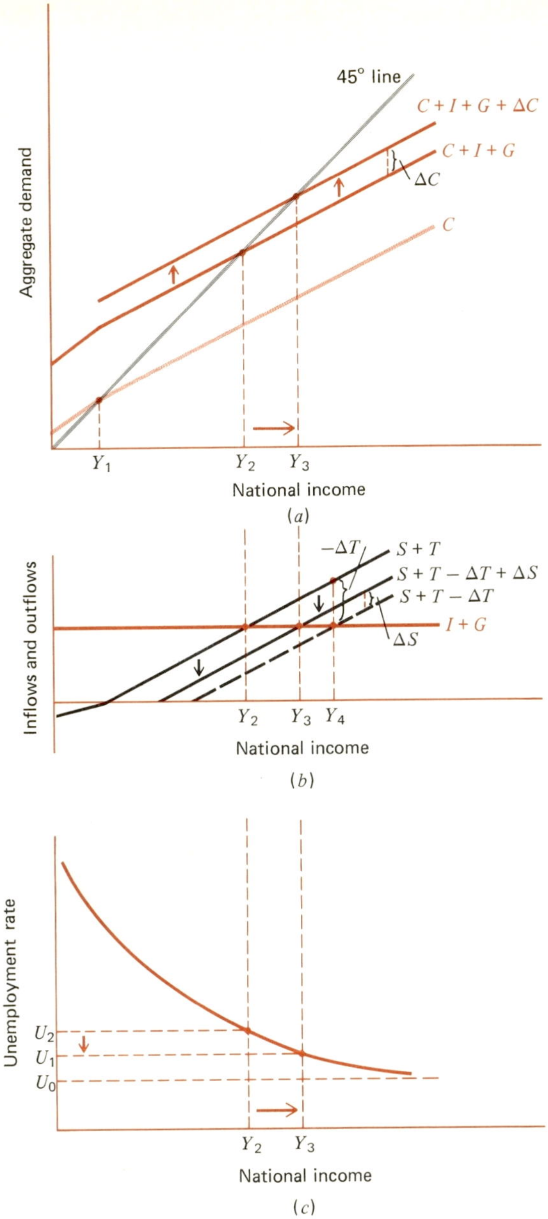

FIG. 30·8 A reduction in taxes increases consumption expenditures and the aggregate demand function in part a to $C + I + G + \Delta C$. The outflow curve in part b shifts downward by the difference between the reduction in taxes and the increase in saving which is caused by lower taxes. In both parts a and b, the equilibrium national income level moves up from Y_2 to Y_3; and in part c the unemployment rate falls from U_2 to U_1.

will go into saving. If saving goes up by $1 billion when taxes go down by $10 billion, consumption expenditures rise by only $9 billion. Because it is the increase in consumer expenditures (not the tax reduction, per se) which initiates the multiplier process, the change in income will accordingly be $27 billion (the multiplier times the increase in consumer demand). Another way of stating the same conclusion is that if the government wants to increase the national income level by some amount which equals the difference between the current income level and the full-employment income level, the government will have to reduce taxes by more than it will have to increase government expenditures.

When President John F. Kennedy took office in 1960, the economy was in a mild recession, and he had pledged that he would "get the economy moving again." He and his economic advisors concluded that the way to move the economy out of the recession was to reduce taxes by approximately $12 billion. Given the greater potential effect of an increase in expenditures, why did Kennedy choose to reduce taxes? Political considerations probably played an important role in the selection of the fiscal policy to be followed. Before Kennedy, a number of presidents had run budgetary deficits, but these deficits, it was claimed, were incurred "accidentally" or to finance wars. The earlier government deficits had been equated with "fiscal irresponsibility," because, supposedly, the deficits imposed burdens on further generations and, if continued, would lead to national bankruptcy. No president had proposed to intentionally run a budgetary deficit in order to stimulate the economy. To increase government expenditures would have created fears not only of national financial ruin for many but also of a government that was becoming too big and intruding too far into the private economy. Although the measure was controversial, the tax cut was politically more acceptable to the public and to Kennedy, who knew that he would be up for reelection in 1964.

There was, however, a more technical reason for the choice of the tax cut. Kennedy's economic advisors argued that the tax rates were, at that time, simply too high to achieve full employment in the economy. They argued that if the economy ever got on the road to recovery and the national income level started rising, tax revenues would rise to such a high level that people would have too little to spend to push the economy to the full-employment income level. Kennedy's economists argued that this drain on personal purchasing power would be reduced by a reduction in tax rates, that people would at all points in the recovery have more to spend and would spend more at all points in the recovery, and that without the tax cut, the economy would stop moving upward at some point prior to full employment. There is, unfortunately, a continuing debate over whether or not the tax cut had the positive effect on national income that was expected.

KEYNESIAN ECONOMICS AND THE BUSINESS CYCLE

As we have studied, in the recession phase of the business cycle, the Keynesian prescription for impeding the downward movement in income and employment is for the government to reduce taxes and/or increase its level of spending and let the multiplier process start to work. The government cannot, however, completely eliminate all ups and downs in economic activity through its fiscal (tax and spending) policies. First, before fiscal action can be taken, the government must first recognize that a recession is under way, and this may take several months, given the lack of speed with which some economic data are collected. Additionally, the data are likely to be mixed in the beginning phase of a recession. Some figures, like the number of houses started in the previous month, will show a decline in economic activity; others, like new orders for heavy industrial equipment, may indicate that the economy is still moving upward on its own steam. Government policy makers may not be able to come to an immediate conclusion to recommend added government stimulus to the economy.

Second, after policy makers have concluded that a recession is under way, they will have to convince Congress that additional appropriations to increase government demand for goods and services or tax cuts for businesses and households are in order. Because members of Congress themselves have to be convinced of the appropriateness and desirability of specific policy recommendations, particularly since they may wish to bargain for extra benefits for the districts they represent, an additional lag transpires before any fiscal action is actually taken. It took 16 months for the Kennedy tax cut package to go through Congress; of course, given increased acceptability of Keynesian economics, lags of this sort have been reduced.

If a tax cut is approved by Congress, the stimulative influence will be felt almost immediately as people's take-home pay increases. On the other hand, an increase in government expenditures works its way more slowly through the economy. New contracts for roads must be negotiated and surveys made. All in all, the economy can be well on its way to the bottom of a cycle before the appropriate fiscal action is taken and its effects are evident. If a stimulus designed to combat a recession is added late in the recovery phase of the business cycle, it can add to inflationary pressures as the economy approaches the boom phase. In a world of perfect information, appropriate actions may be taken at appropriate times. However, fiscal policies must be formulated in the political arena. The constraints of that arena mean that policy actions may be taken at inappropriate times, exacerbating the cycle.

Furthermore, Congress may use the Keynesian prescriptions for dealing with unemployment for pursuing their own private ends. For example, increases in expenditures and reductions in taxes may be made to develop political support for members of Congress, and these actions may be taken sporadically, thus making the business cycle effects worse or generating a "political business cycle"—one which moves in accord with elections.

THE INFLUENCE OF GOVERNMENT DEFICITS ON INVESTMENT

If the government spends more than it collects in taxes and intends to keep the money stock constant, it must borrow the difference between its expenditures and taxes.[4] Government does this by selling bonds in the bond market (which is something like the stock market) to lenders. The buyers of the bonds loan their money to the government for a specified period of time and at a specified interest rate. Keynesians argue that during periods of recession, the federal government borrows funds which would otherwise remain idle—that is, funds that would not be used to finance other business investment projects, for state and local government expenditures, or for consumer purchases. Keynesians feel that in a recession people tend to hold onto their money balances in fear that current loans to businesses are unsafe and in anticipation that interest rates will rise in the future. To the extent that this is the case, the foregoing analysis of the impact of fiscal policy is correct. However, if government borrows funds which would otherwise be used by someone else, market interest rates will rise and the impact of fiscal policy is reduced. Federal government expenditures may rise; but because of the higher interest rates, the increase in government spending may be either partially or totally offset by a decrease in private business ventures and a decrease in state and local government expenditures. If private investment falls at the same time and by the same amount as government expenditures increase, there is no change in aggregate demand. There is, therefore, no multiplier effect —no subsequent increase in the national income level. On the other hand, if investment falls by $7 billion when government expenditures increase by $10 billion, the net change in aggregate demand is $3 billion. The multiplier process will work through this $3 billion net change in aggregate demand, but not by the $10 billion increase in government expenditures.

In the 1960s and 1970s the effectiveness of fiscal policies has been the subject of significant controversy among economists and government policy makers. Economists who speak from the Keynesian perspective argue that stimulative action on the part of the federal government will not be offset by reductions in other aggregate demand components, such as private investment, state and local government expenditures, and consumer purchases. They have statistical studies which support their view that an increase in federal government expenditure will increase national income by two or three times.

Economists who generally adhere to the monetarists' view of the macroeconomy (which we develop in detail in the following chapter) argue that if the federal government increases expenditures and has to borrow in the bond market, it will "crowd out" other potential borrowers. Therefore, any stimulative effect of the government's expenditures will be offset by reductions in private investment, consumer expenditures, and expenditures by state and local governments. The monetarists also have statistical studies which support their position. These studies show that an increase in spending by the federal government can be expected to have a stimulative effect on the economy for, at most, a period of 6 months. Even then, monetarists claim that this temporary increase in the national income level will not be greater than one-half the amount of the increase in government spending. For example, a $30 billion increase in government spending, accompanied by an equal amount of borrowing, will raise the national income level no more than $15 billion, not by two or three times $30 billion, which is implied by the Keynesian multiplier process. According to the monetarists, this is the best that can be expected. The effect, in fact, may be virtually nil.

The debate is a truly important one. The political acceptability of the Keynesian motive for deficit spending is clearly related to the impact which the spending has on the economy. A small effect generally means few back-home benefits to politicians and the possibility that they will be charged with "fiscal irresponsibility." A small multiplier effect can also mean continued unemployment and economic hardship for many people.

[4] Given its constitutional powers to print and coin money, the government can spend more than it receives in taxes by merely increasing the money stock. (See Chapter 25 for a discussion of how the money stock can be increased.)

TABLE 30 · 1 U.S. FEDERAL GOVERNMENT DEBT (IN BILLIONS OF DOLLARS)

End of Year	Total Gross Public Debt (in Current Dollars) (1)	Debt Held by Government Agencies and Federal Reserve Banks (in Current Dollars) (2)	Debt Held by Private Investors (in Current Dollars) (3)	Debt Held by Private Investors (in 1972 Dollars*) (4)
1939	41.9	8.6	33.4	
1946	259.1	50.8	208.3	472.8
1955	280.8	83.8	207.1	339.9
1961	296.2	81.4	214.8	310.0
1962	303.5	84.0	219.5	311.1
1963	309.3	88.9	220.5	308.0
1964	317.9	95.4	222.5	306.1
1965	320.9	100.5	220.5	296.7
1966	329.3	110.2	219.2	285.6
1967	344.7	122.2	222.4	281.4
1968	358.0	139.5	228.5	276.7
1969	368.2	146.2	222.0	256.0
1970	389.2	159.2	229.9	251.6
1971	424.1	176.2	247.9	258.2
1972	449.3	186.8	262.5	262.5
1973	469.9	208.1	261.7	247.1
1974	492.7	221.7	271.0	233.2
1975	576.6	226.2	350.4	275.4
1976	653.5	244.1	409.4	306.0

* Figures in this column were obtained by dividing column 3 by the GNP deflator, a broad price index.
SOURCE: *The Economic Report of the President*, 1977.

DEFICIT SPENDING AND THE POLITICAL BIAS OF KEYNESIAN ECONOMICS

Before the rise of Keynesianism, the dominant political philosophy of government spending was that the government *should* strive to restrict its expenditures to the level of its tax receipts. In other words, the government should try to balance its budget. Among politicians and a substantial majority of the general public, deficit spending was explicitly equated with "fiscal irresponsibility." The principal argument undergirding this budgetary norm (or philosophy) was that the federal government is like an individual household. It cannot continually incur budgetary deficits without running the risk of bankruptcy. Further, because it was thought that the debt would have to be paid back at some point, deficit spending was believed to be a burden to future generations. The growth in the federal government debt, revealed in column 1 of Table 30 · 1, was, and still is, horrifying to people who hold to the balanced budget philosophy.

Arguments for and against Deficit Spending

Keynesian economics has substantially weakened the balanced budget fiscal norm with several strategic counterarguments. First, they argue that during periods of slack demand and high unemployment, there are no present or future costs associated with deficit spending; on the contrary, because of deficits, more people are able to work, more income is generated, and more is produced by people and equipment. These resources would otherwise remain idle; and since the real cost of any government action must be measured against what is forgone, it follows that the real cost of running a deficit during a recession is (virtually) zero.[5]

Furthermore, to the extent that deficit spending during a recession builds more roads, schools, and national parks, and/or to the extent that it encourages private investment, future generations actually benefit from present deficits. They will have more capital assets (or goods) to use in the production of the goods and services they want; their incomes will be higher because of the past government deficits. Future generations may have to meet the required interest payments on the debt, but they will also have higher incomes with which to meet those payments. Besides, to the extent the interest is paid to United States citizens, the payments do not represent a loss of resources of goods and services *to the country* as a whole. Because we effectively owe the debt to ourselves, we pay the interest to ourselves, or so the argument goes.

On the other hand, during times of full employment, a government deficit does impose a cost on the private sector simply because there are then no idle resources. During full employment, deficits cause resources to be diverted from private uses to government uses. The cost of the deficit can be measured by what is given up in the private sector. Therefore, most Keynesians argue that deficit spending is an appropriate policy only during periods of unemployment.

As explained earlier, the monetarists argue that deficit spending, except possibly during times of *severe* recessions, tends to reduce private investment. Indeed, economists such as Milton Friedman have argued that one dollar of deficit means one dollar less in private investment and/or consumer expenditures. There is, in other words, a cost. Keynesians counter with statistical studies which support their position that although private investment may be affected, government deficits do not *fully* offset private investment demand. There are some net benefits remaining. The monetarists, of course, have statistical studies which contradict the studies of the Keynesians. Needless to say, this debate will not be settled at the academic level any time soon. However, because of the persuasiveness of the Keynesian argument, many more politicians now than in the late 1950s reject the balanced budget norm for government policy.

The second counterargument to the balanced budget philosophy has to do with the comparison made between a household and the government as economic units. Because their lives are limited, members of each household must make arrangements to pay off their debts either before death or through an estate after death. However, the debt of *all* households combined can grow over time as the ability of households collectively to pay interest and to pay back the debt increases. As some households are paying off their debts, they can also incur new debts. Many people who are in the process of paying off a car loan are at the same time buying furniture on installment credit. Furthermore, some households can increase their total indebtedness by more than other households reduce theirs. As people's incomes grow over time, their ability to handle debt increases, and many people take advantage of the opportunity they have. Thus, the total debt of all households can increase, even though each household must still be responsible for paying off each of its IOUs. This is what has happened in a rather dramatic way since World War II in the United States and in most industrial countries. In 1946 consumer debt in the United States totaled $8 billion; by 1974 total consumer debt had risen to $190 billion. The aggregate debt of all corporations has also increased dramatically, from $93 billion in 1946 to $1.3 trillion in 1974. Even after allowing

[5] Keynesians do acknowledge that there may be costs associated with the management of the federal debt; however, these administrative costs are generally considered to be of little importance.

for the effects of inflation, the increase in consumer and corporate debt has been substantial. If members of households and corporations, individually and collectively, can increase their total indebtedness over time, why not allow the government to do so as well—at least within limits?

The life of government is not limited as are the lives of individuals; it has a perpetual life (at least, almost). Government, therefore, does not necessarily have to make arrangements to pay off its debt. Granted, government bonds carry maturity dates (dates on which the bondholders are repaid the amounts loaned to the government); however, the government can *refund* the debt—it can issue new bonds and use the funds collected to pay off the debt which has come due. In this way the government perpetuates the existence of the national debt in the same way that all households perpetuate the existence of the *total* consumer debt.

The major constraint on the government's ability to expand its debt is the willingness of people to buy government bonds. This depends upon the stability of the government and how much of their incomes people are willing to devote to saving. If the life of the government is uncertain, that is, if it is in jeopardy of being overthrown like governments in so many countries in other parts of our globe, people will be reluctant to loan their money to the government. However, even stable governments must find means of encouraging people to devote a portion of their incomes to government bonds. The government does this by paying interest on the money it borrows. So long as the government is willing to pay the going market interest rate and can assure buyers of bonds that it has the tax base from which to draw the interest payment, government bonds will be as attractive, if not more attractive, than the bonds of private businesses. United States government bonds are, in fact, more attractive to many investors than bonds of most corporations, as evidenced by the lower interest rate the federal government has to pay. Besides, the argument is that through deficit spending the government can raise the national income level and, therefore, the tax revenues of government, part or all of which can be used to pay the interest on any newly created government debt.

Furthermore, although the total federal government debt has been rising, as indicated in column 1 of Table 30·1, the government has borrowed much of this debt from itself. This is shown by the portion of the federal debt held by government agencies and the Federal Reserve System. (See column 2 of Table 30·1.) With regard to the portion of the debt held by government agencies, such as the Social Security Administration and the highway trust fund, the government is effectively "borrowing" and using current tax collections. It collects taxes and then loans the money to itself for its current expenditures. The Federal Reserve, in order to buy government securities, newly creates the money for the purchase and simply "monetizes" that portion of the debt. (See Chapter 25.) In this latter case, new money is printed to cover government expenditures. These two portions of the debt do not necessarily mean that the government will go bankrupt, since the government owes these portions of the debt to itself. Printing new money, however, can lead to higher prices; and new government debt, through its impact on inflation, can lead to instability of the government.

When we consider that portion of the total government debt held by private individuals, such as government savings bonds and other larger bonds held by banks, we observe that its *real value* has been decreasing over the past three decades. In column 4 we have computed the portion of the government debt held by the private investor adjusted for the rise in prices between 1946 and 1976. Given these figures, we note that the real value of the privately held debt (measured in constant 1972 prices) decreased from $472 billion in 1946 to $233 billion in 1974. Between 1974 and 1976, the real value of this portion of the debt rose from $233 to $306 billion. However, in real terms and over the long run, this portion of the debt is being "retired" or "paid off" via inflation: this happens because prices have been rising at a faster rate than the federal debt.

The monetarists, on the other hand, argue that deficit spending leads to greater rates of inflation. They draw their conclusion from the following line of reasoning. The federal government enters the bond market as a borrower (i.e., it offers bonds to investors to obtain money for government programs). This offering, because it increases the demand for loanable funds, puts upward pressure on interest rates. In order to prevent a rise in interest rates, the Federal Reserve Bank "accommodates" the Treasury by entering the bond market as a buyer of government securities. The purchases of securities by the Fed increases the money stock, a development which (through the quantity theory of money) leads to higher prices. Inflation, according to monetarists, is a disguised means by which government imposes a tax on people, and it is a kind of tax which, although the public may not be able to understand it, is the consequence of an expansion of government programs. In terms of Table 30·1, column 4, the disguised tax is equal to the reduction in the real value of the privately held public debt. In other words, through inflation, private bondholders have been forced to give up a portion of their wealth as surely as if the government had imposed a tax on that wealth.

The Political Bias of Keynesian Economics

When Keynes wrote *The General Theory*, economic policy in Britain was largely formulated by a small group of intellectually gifted men. In the development of his arguments Keynes assumed a continuation of this state of affairs. Roy Harrod, Keynes's biographer, described Keynes's predilection toward economic policy in this manner:

> We have seen that he [Keynes] was strongly imbued with what I have called the presuppositions of Harvey Road. One of the presuppositions may perhaps be summarized in the idea that the government of Britain was and would continue to be in the hands of an intellectual aristocracy using the methods of persuasion.[6]

Keynes was interested in providing a theoretical model for the formulation of "good" economic policy; in doing so, he and others who have followed him assumed that given "good" policy recommendations, "good" men will do "good" things. Keynes did not assume that policy would be formulated by politicians in Washington and Whitehall (the seat of English government), who, although not necessarily "bad" men, would have to pay attention to being elected and reelected and would have to compete for voter support.

James Buchanan and Richard Wagner argue that politicians in general display a natural tendency to vote for spending programs and to vote against tax legislation to pay for expenditures.[7] Government expenditures benefit many people, and to the extent that they benefit a politician's constituency, such expenditures increase his or her political support. On the other hand, taxes impose costs on political constituencies and tend to reduce the support for politicians who vote for them.

If politicians accept the fiscal rule that government budgets must be balanced, they will tend to vote for government expenditures only so long as the marginal political support generated from them is greater than the political support lost from raising taxes. However, if the balanced budget imperative is broken, politicians are given the opportunity to spend more than the government collects in taxes. They are given the opportunity to boost their political support by voting for government expenditures without incurring the political damage that a compensating tax increase may bring. Given the present acceptance of Keynesian economics, even politicians who are ideologically opposed to deficits will be pushed by their political competitors to accept deficits, or at least to accept greater deficits than they would otherwise.

In times of inflation, the government should reduce aggregate demand by running budgetary surpluses. However, politicians have an understandable aversion to voting for budget surpluses even during periods of inflation. In order for a

[6] Roy F. Harrod, *The Life of John Maynard Keynes* (London: Macmillan Company, 1951), pp. 192–193.

[7] James M. Buchanan and Richard E. Wagner, *Democracy in Deficit: The Destructive Legacy of Lord Keynes* (New York: Academic Press, 1977).

surplus to develop, politicians must vote for taxes which are not offset by expenditure programs or for expenditure reductions which are not offset by tax reductions. Surpluses will result in a net loss of political support. In summary, a breakdown in the balanced budget fiscal norm should, by itself, lead to greater deficits than necessary during periods of recession and to lower surpluses (and even deficits) during periods of excessive demand and inflation.

In the process of generating political support for politicians, deficits may lead to inflation; however, these effects are very indirect. For the typical voter to understand that government deficits contribute to inflation, the voter must understand a good deal of macroeconomic theory. He or she must have an incentive not only to learn the theory, but also to employ this knowledge in evaluating the behavior of politicians. A politically and economically astute electorate can be instrumental in the development of sound economic policy by Congress; however, we indicated in our study of the democratic-political process (Chapter 21) that the payoff to the typical voter for undertaking such an analysis of government policy can be very, very small. The typical voter may, therefore, remain largely ignorant of the indirect and detrimental effects of deficits. The voters may judge their representative solely in terms of the representative's ability to "bring home the bacon" for their district. Besides, the voters of any one district may reason that government expenditures in their district are too small in total to materially aggravate the inflationary problem of the economy as a whole.

Since voters are more likely to be aware of the direct benefits of deficit spending than of the indirect inflationary effects of deficits, politicians are more likely to favor deficit spending than they would if the health of the economy were their sole concern. Furthermore, since voters are more likely to be aware of the excess tax burden of budget surpluses than of the indirect benefits which budget surpluses have on dampening inflation, politicians have reason to resist proposals for budgetary surpluses as a means of reducing inflation. Buchanan and Wagner argue that in Keynesian economics there is a built-in political bias for deficits and against surpluses when economic policy is determined through democratic processes. They also argue that acceptance of the Keynesian paradigm will also lead to the political acceptance of greater rates of inflation.

Their theory at this time has not been rigorously tested. However, the public's generally low level of economic literacy has been documented over the past two decades by the Joint Council on Economic Education and other people concerned with economic education. In addition, the experience of the United States over the last decade tends to support the plausibility of the Buchanan-Wagner argument. Since 1961 when the Keynesian paradigm was accepted by the Kennedy administration as a basis for policy, the United States government has had only one year (1969) in which its budget was not in deficit. During many of these years, the economy has experienced rates of inflation several times higher than the rates of the 1950s when government fiscal policy was largely, but by no means entirely, directed toward balancing the budget. In 1966 President Johnson rejected the advice of his economic advisors to fight inflation by raising taxes. He refused on the grounds that a tax increase would exacerbate the growing political opposition to the Vietnam war. These tendencies toward deficits and away from tax increases in inflationary times, of course, may change if voters change their attitudes toward deficit spending. There has been some evidence in recent years that voters are becoming less convinced that government can manage the economy in the way envisioned by Keynes and his intellectually gifted associates. Buchanan and Wagner suggest that if the balanced budget fiscal norm is reintroduced, it will not necessarily be because people have come to doubt the validity of the Keynesian theory, but because the policy of the balanced budget introduces an element of political discipline into the determination of economic policy. In other words, the need for such discipline *may* become more important to the economic health of the country than the benefits of deficit spending outlined by the Keynesian analysis.

MONEY IN THE KEYNESIAN SYSTEM

During the Great Depression, many banks failed and many others went to the brink of bankruptcy. Banks were hit hard from both sides of their balance sheets: some borrowers were unable to pay back their loans; and some depositors, skeptical of the solvency of their banks, withdrew their deposits. The banks' predicament was made more difficult by the attitude of the Federal Reserve. The Fed was established in order to ensure that banks could borrow needed reserves whenever their bank customers made heavy withdrawals. However, during the 1930s the Fed severely discouraged banks from borrowing at the discount window; thus many banks failed simply because they were unable to obtain necessary reserves from the Fed. After this experience, banks became very cautious about their loans policies and began to increase their reserve deposits with the Federal Reserve and other banks. When in the 1930s the Fed attempted to increase the money supply, banks held onto a part of the newly created reserves for their own protection. They simply wanted insurance against the prospect of future recessions and bank panics. Many economists now interpret events in the banking industry during the 1930s in this way.

However, Keynes and other economists of his era saw the situation in another light. To them, the buildup in excess reserves in combination with very low interest rates during the 1930s demonstrated that during a severe depression, people have a highly (if not perfectly) "elastic demand for money." In other words, at very low interest rates, banks will hold onto whatever reserves they can and people will hold onto whatever money is created by the Federal Reserve. The money simply will not be spent, and without an increase in spending, the economy will remain depressed with low incomes and high unemployment. Given this analysis, Keynes and his followers argued that monetary policy would not alleviate the depression. They argued that the only way to stimulate the economy would be for the government to take fiscal action of the sort explained in this chapter: to increase expenditures or to reduce taxes. According to Keynesian analysis of the macroeconomy, fiscal policy is not only useful but an absolute necessity at certain times.

Almost all economists now recognize that monetary policy is a useful means of fighting recessions. The Federal Reserve can increase the money supply by any one of the three ways developed in Chapter 25: (1) reducing the discount rate, (2) reducing the reserve requirement, and (3) buying government securities on the open market. Any one of these actions will increase the reserves which banks have, thereby increasing the loan capacity of banks. To the extent that the banking industry is competitive, the interest rate on loans will fall.[8] With a drop in the interest rate, people will borrow and invest more. Through the process discussed in Chapter 29, the increase in investment will have a multiplying effect on the level of income. Employment will rise along with production and income. This sequence of events is accepted by practically all Keynesians. However, debate continues over the *relative* effectiveness of "fiscal" and "monetary" policy during the various phases in the business cycle.

[8] Assuming that the interest rate was initially at equilibrium, the injection of new reserves into the banking industry means that the supply of loanable funds will exceed the demand at the initial interest rate. To attract new borrowers, banks must lower the interest rate they charge.

SUMMARY AND EXTENSIONS

The Keynesian prescription for dealing with an economy experiencing unacceptably high unemployment is to increase the demand for goods and services. This can be achieved through an increase in government expenditures or a reduction in taxes. Both policy actions will work to increase the level of purchases and hence national income. Either way, the government must stand ready to incur budgetary deficits. In times of excessive demand and inflation, the government can reduce the level of demand and inflation by either increasing taxes or reducing its own expenditures; that is, the government can run a budgetary surplus.

The same basic effects can be obtained by appropriate increases or decreases in the money supply. An increase in the money supply will tend to lower interest rates and encourage investment; a decrease in the money supply will tend to have the opposite effect. Although Keynesian economics is associated closely with fiscal policy, modern Keynesians argue that monetary and fiscal actions can be taken separately or together to solve problems of unemployment and inflation.

As we will see in more detail in the following chapter, there is considerable debate at present among economists over the appropriateness of the Keynesian model for directing economic policy. Setting this debate aside, we have indicated that the acceptance of Keynesian budgetary prescriptions may introduce a political bias toward greater deficits and lower surpluses than economic conditions warrant. How do we structure the political process in order that we may expect "good" or "appropriate" economic policy to emerge from it? If we reject the balanced budget as a controlling device on politics, with what do we replace it? These are the types of questions which may be of greater concern to economists, policy makers, and voters in the future.

QUESTIONS TO PONDER

1 Will an increase in government expenditures of $10 billion have the same effect on the national income level as a decrease in taxes of $10 billion? Explain.

2 In the Keynesian system, will a decrease in the money supply reduce or increase the national income level? Logically explain the steps that lead you to your conclusion.

3 If a $10 billion increase in government expenditures causes a $10 billion decrease in investment expenditures, what will happen to national income?

4 Given the Keynesian reliance on the Phillips curve (see Chapter 29), what effect will a reduction in taxes have on the rate of inflation?

5 In past years, Congress has passed an "investment tax credit." Through this legislation, if businesses invest in new plant and equipment, they are permitted to reduce their tax payments to the government by, say, 7 percent of the value of that plant and equipment purchased during the year. If a business spends $100,000 on equipment, it can reduce its tax payment by $7,000. Using the Keynesian model of income and employment determination, explain the possible effect of this legislation.

6 In the authors' view there is a political tendency toward budgetary deficits built into the Keynesian system. Explain that political tendency.

RECOMMENDED READINGS

See the "Recommended Readings" section at the end of Chapter 28.

31

THE "MONETARISTS'" VIEW OF UNEMPLOYMENT AND INFLATION

My position regarding the cause of inflation and high market interest rates is that they both stem from the same source—an excessive trend rate of expansion of the nation's money stock. Monetary policy, therefore, can contribute to solving both of these problems over a period of a few years by fostering a noninflationary rate of growth of the money supply.

Darryl Francis[1]

PREVIEW OF CHAPTER

Central question

From the perspective of the monetarists, what are the causes of unemployment and inflation, and how can these social problems be remedied?

Major objectives

1 To explain, from the perspective of the monetarists, why changes in the rate of growth in the money stock affect prices, unemployment, national income, and interest rates

2 To explain why the monetarists believe that fiscal policy has virtually no effect in relieving problems of unemployment, inflation, and low national production levels

[1] Darryl R. Francis, "The Role of Monetary Policy in Dealing with Inflation and High Interest Rates," *Federal Reserve Bank of St. Louis Review*, August 1974, p. 2.

3 To show why there is considerable controversy among economists and government officials over appropriate fiscal and monetary policy

Major conclusions

1 From the point of view of the monetarists, the primary cause of recessions and periods of high inflation is abrupt changes in the rate of growth of the money stock.

2 Increases in the rate of growth in the money stock will lead to unanticipated increases in the rate of inflation, to a temporary reduction in the real wages paid to workers, and to a temporary decrease in unemployment. However, in the long run, people will begin to anticipate the new rate of inflation and to work their expectations into their wage demands. Once money wages start to rise, the level of unemployment will rise back to a level that is dictated by labor market obstacles like minimum wage laws. There is no long-run trade-off between unemployment and inflation, as might be presumed from observation of the Phillips curve.

3 Decreases in the rate of growth in the money stock will lead to an unanticipated reduction in the rate of inflation, a temporary increase in the real wages paid to workers, and a temporary increase in the unemployment rate. However, in the long run, money wage rates will not rise as fast, the real-wage rate received by workers will fall, and unemployment will fall back to the level dictated by such labor market obstacles as minimum wage laws.

4 An increase in the anticipated rate of inflation will lead to an increase in the demand for loanable funds and a decrease in the supply of loanable funds. The result will be a rise in the market interest rate. The contrary will also hold: a reduction in the anticipated rate of inflation will lead to lower interest rates. In the monetarists' model of the macroeconomy, high rates of inflation cause high rates of interest, and not vice versa.

5 In the monetarists' model, deficit spending by the government means that the demand for loanable funds and market interest rates increase. The higher interest rates mean that business will invest less when the government runs a budgetary deficit. Indeed, the monetarists argue that the decrease in business investment spending will (virtually) offset the increase in government spending that may have been intended to stimulate the economy. Therefore, deficit spending by the government has little or no effect on the national income and employment levels.

In our development and analysis of the Keynesian model of the macroeconomy, we contrasted at times the views of Keynesian economists with some opposing theories of inflation and unemployment. Most of these ideas have been developed by economists loosely grouped together under the name "monetarists." Our purpose in this chapter is to analyze this interpretation of the macroeconomy, which is based on changes in the money stock. You should realize that individual monetarists do not always agree on the particulars of the way the macroeconomy should be modeled. Our intent in this chapter is to outline the broad theoretical framework within which most monetarists' models can be placed.

We noted that when Keynes developed his *Gen-*

eral Theory, the Depression was at its worst. Modern industrial nations were faced with falling prices and high unemployment, and government spending seemed to be a good tonic for restoring economic stability. Since the 1930s, Keynes's theories have been adopted by legislators for the development of fiscal policies. In the past two decades, however, the United States economy has been subject to problems different from those found in the 1930s, and the Keynesian prescriptions have not solved them. Since the mid-1960s, we've been faced with high rates of inflation, reaching a high of 12 percent in 1974, which have been accompanied by high rates of unemployment. You'll recall that Keynesian economics predicts a drop in unemployment with an increase in inflation and budgetary deficits. The disparity which has apparently existed between Keynesian predictions and economic realities has provoked many economists to search for another model of the macroeconomy. The most significant model has been proposed by the monetarists, and we will study it in detail in the sections that follow.

The monetarists are economists who argue that the root cause of most cyclical swings in unemployment and inflation can be traced to abrupt changes in the rate of growth of the money stock; that without changes in the money stock, fiscal policy will have only limited influence in solving short-term problems of unemployment and inflation. They believe that, as Darryl Francis, former President of the Federal Reserve Bank of St. Louis, suggests in our opening quotation, past problems of inflation, high interest rates, and cyclical unemployment can be solved through steady control of the monetary throttle.

THE MONETARISTS' VIEW OF UNEMPLOYMENT

In developing their theory of the macroeconomy, the monetarists borrow heavily from microeconomics; they begin with basic propositions of consumer and market behavior developed in the first half of this book. The monetarists analyze macro problems in the tradition employed prior to Keynes. For instance, as we have briefly discussed before, they view the long-term problems of unemployment as a consequence of "obstacles" in various labor markets which prevent real wage rates from falling to their equilibrium levels (that point at which the number of workers demanded by employers equals the number of workers willing to work). These obstacles may be minimum wage laws or union contracts. They may be restrictions on labor mobility, such as lack of information, or customs which prevent (or retard) wage reductions for nonunion workers. (See Chapter 27.)

To review this part of the monetarists' model graphically, consider Figure 31·1. The demand for labor is inversely related to the real wage rate (W/P); the supply of labor is directly related to the real wage rate (W/P). Hence, we have normal slopes for the supply and demand curves in Figure 31·1. If the real wage rate is restricted from falling below $(W/P)_2$, the number of workers

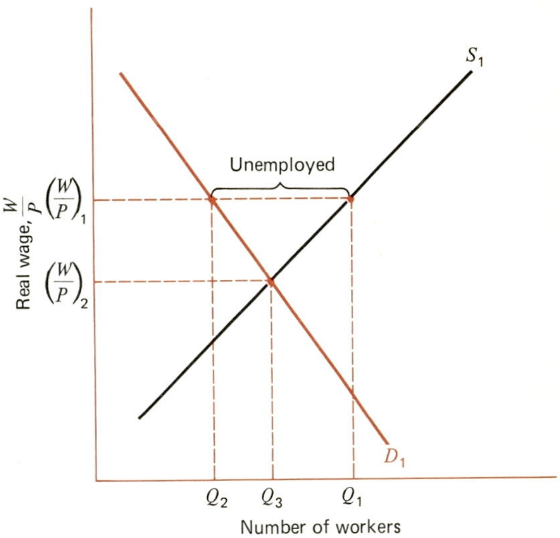

FIG. 31·1 Assuming that the demand for labor is downward sloping, the supply of labor is upward sloping, and the real wage rate is $(W/P)_2$, the number of unemployed workers in this and similarly situated labor markets equals $Q_3 - Q_1$ workers. An increase in the price level, while the money wage rate remains constant, will cause the real wage and the number of unemployed workers to fall.

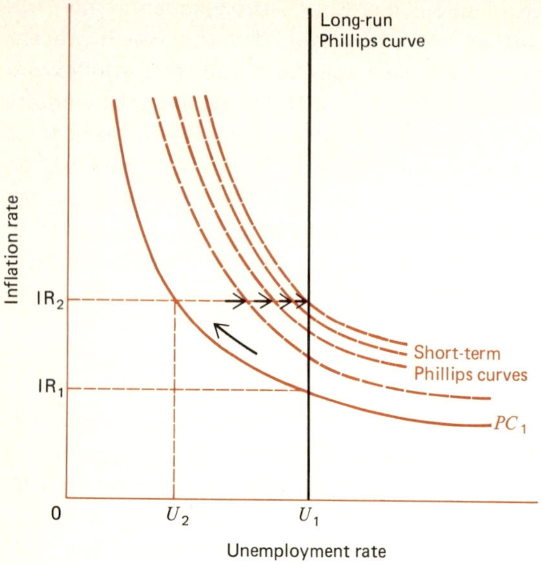

FIG. 31·2 An unemployment rate of U_2 can be caused by such factors as unions holding the real wage rate up above equilibrium. The rate of unemployment can be temporarily reduced by an unexpected increase in the price level. However, in the long run money wages will catch up with the higher prices, and the level of unemployment will rise toward U_2.

willing to work will be Q_3; however, only Q_1 workers will be hired. The difference between Q_3 and Q_1 is the number of people unemployed. So long as the money wage rate and the price level remain constant, or so long as the money wage rate and the price level increase at the same rate, the real wage remains constant, and a $Q_3 - Q_1$ level of unemployment persists. This long-term level of unemployment can be translated into a long-term unemployment rate equal to U_2 in Figure 31·2. Assuming that prices and wages are rising at the same rate, this unemployment rate is consistent with an inflation rate of IR_1 in Figure 31·2. Both IR_1 and U_2 are on the same short-term Phillips curve, PC_1. The Phillips curve was first discussed in Chapter 29; succinctly, it describes the presumed trade-off between inflation and unemployment. A Phillips curve of PC_1 in Figure 31·2 suggests that a lower unemployment rate can be achieved only at the cost of a higher inflation rate.

If the rate of inflation increases and employers realize that prices are rising faster than employee wages before employees do, the real wage will fall and a larger number of workers will be employed. Employers will move down their demand curve for labor, and the gap between the number of workers willing to work and the number hired will close. In this way, the increase in the rate of inflation parallels a reduction in the unemployment rate. This is why the trade-off between inflation and unemployment is observed in short-run Phillips curves.

Eventually, however, workers will see that their *real wage* rates are falling. Unions, for example, will bargain for higher wage increases. In competitive labor markets, where the demand for labor rises because of rising prices of final products, wages will begin to rise at faster rates. Eventually, the previous structure of real wage rates will reestablish itself. However, the previous unemployment (U_1) will reemerge at a higher rate of inflation.

In terms of Figure 31·2, the increase in the rate of inflation causes, in the short run, a movement up and along the Phillips curve PC_1 to an unemployment rate of U_2 and an inflation rate of IR_2. As workers' expectations of price increases change, the Phillips curve shifts out and to the right. With the inflation rate at IR_2, the unemployment rate gradually increases to U_1, back from U_2. *In the long run, according to monetarist theory, the Phillips curve is vertical. There is no trade-off between unemployment and inflation.* If the unemployment rate is to remain below U_2, prices will have to increase at progressively higher rates, forcing workers to play "catch up" in their wage demands. Even then, as time passes, workers may begin to anticipate that the rate of inflation will rise to progressively higher levels as a matter of course and they will demand escalating wage increases to keep their real wage rates constant.

A reduction in the rate of inflation relative to the rate of increase in wages will have the opposite effect. When it is unexpected, a reduction in the rate of inflation will cause the real wage to rise. (The numerator, W, of the fraction W/P rises more rapidly than the denominator, P.) An increase in the real wage, in terms of Figure 31 · 1, causes the gap between the number of workers on the market and the number hired to grow. The economy will move down and to the right along a short-run Phillips curve. The rate of inflation is down while the rate of employment is up. However, these movements are temporary. In the long run, an increase in the number of unemployed will cause the rate of increase in money wages to fall. As a result, the real wage will decrease and employers will demand more workers. The unemployment rate will move back toward U_1 at a lower rate of inflation.

This then is the crux of the monetarists' position on unemployment: In the long run, the choice is between some unemployment and some inflation or the same level of unemployment at a higher rate of inflation. There is no long-term trade-off between unemployment and inflation as described in Keynesian analysis.

The monetarists have observed the economic trends of the past few decades and have accumulated information to support their claim that the Phillips curve is not stable over the long run and that the trade-off between unemployment and inflation is only temporary. Many of these studies are quite sophisticated; however, the type of information which supports their argument is recorded in Figure 31 · 3. Each point in the graph shows the combinations of inflation and average unemployment rates that have been experienced from 1953 to 1975. In that chart the unemployment rate in the United States has clustered around an average of 4.9 percent; the rate of inflation, on the other hand, has moved progressively higher since the early 1960s. The monetarists argue that the unemployment rate of 4.9 percent results from structural obstacles in labor markets, causing some people to be employed, and from transitional movements of labor among markets. Decreases in the level of unemployment are due to short-run unexpected increases in the rate of inflation.

To sum up, a reduced rate of inflation may lead to more unemployment in the short run, but in the long run the unemployment rate will return to its "natural rate." The way to reduce this "natural rate" is to eliminate labor market obstacles and to speed up the movement of unemployed labor among labor markets, a solution which lies in neither fiscal nor monetary policy. This is a dramatically different conclusion from that which is reached by many Keynesians.

THE MONETARISTS' VIEW OF INFLATION

Monetarists argue that temporary changes in the level of unemployment and resulting changes in the national income level are linked to variations in the rate of inflation. A higher rate of inflation leads, temporarily, to a lower level of unemployment and vice versa. The monetarists feel that the rate of inflation is directly related to the growth in the money stock, which, as developed in earlier chapters, can be summarized in the equation of exchange,

$$MV = PO = Y$$

where M = money supply
V = velocity (or turnover rate) of money
P = an index of price level
O = number of transactions
Y = national income level

To see the link between changes in the money supply and changes in unemployment, we must step back and consider an individual's demand for money.

The Demand for Money Balances

To monetarists, money is one among many assets, such as goods and securities (i.e., stocks and bonds), which people wish to hold for the services the assets provide. Television sets give people pleasure directly; securities yield income; and money enables people to carry out their expected and unexpected day-to-day transactions. Money is an asset which permits people to bridge the gap

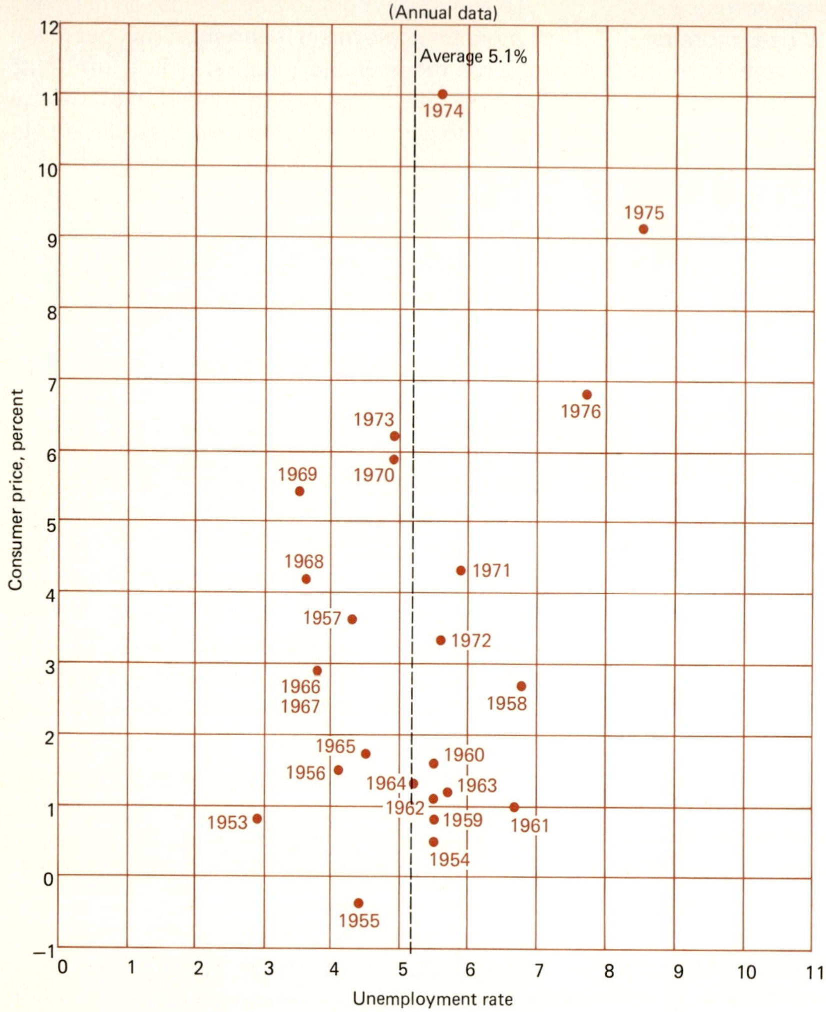

FIG. 31 · 3 The unemployment rate has averaged 5.1 percent between 1953 and 1976. During periods of high inflation rates, the unemployment rate has fallen below 4 percent for only short periods of time, suggesting that the Phillips curve may, as illustrated in Figure 31 · 2, shift to the right in inflationary periods.

between their money receipts (usually in the form of payroll checks) and their money expenditures. Whatever their wealth, people will seek some optimum combination of real goods, securities, and money balances in their bank accounts. Their demand for money balances is, therefore, dependent upon the benefits received from holding money relative to the benefits of holding other assets. The demand for money, in the monetarists' model, is subject to five principal factors: (1) the price level, (2) personal wealth, (3) institutional factors, (4) rate of interest, and (5) expected rate of inflation.

1 Price level—If prices go up, people will need to hold greater money balances to carry out the same number of expected and unexpected transactions. Consequently, the demand for money balances increases or decreases with corresponding increases or decreases in the price level.

2 Personal wealth—A person's demand for money is directly related to his wealth. When people hold money, they forgo the use of other assets, including clothes and cars. Since the rich can hold onto a great deal of money without forgoing these other goods more easily than can the poor, we should expect the rich to hold a greater proportion of their assets in the form of money balances than the poor do. As a person's wealth increases over time, he can be expected to hold (demand) a proportionately greater money balance. Because a country's collective wealth grows slowly, total wealth will have little influence in the short run, on the total demand for money. Over the long run, however, the demand for money will increase as the result of an increase in people's wealth.

3 Institutional factors—People's demand for money also depends on the rate at which they are paid and on the rate at which they pay for goods and services; it depends upon the facility with which they can get credit and the penalty they may have to pay if they are unable to pay their bills on time. People who are paid once a month will tend to hold, on the average, larger money balances than people who are paid weekly. People who are paid monthly must carry a money balance at the first of the month sufficient to carry them to the end of the month; people who are paid on a weekly basis need only a balance sufficient to get them through a week. In addition, people who have easy access to credit require lower money balances than people who are less able to obtain credit. The people who can obtain credit can use it to see themselves through any unforeseen, increased need for money. All of these factors relate to the way payments are made. Payment patterns can change, but only over a period of years.

4 Rate of interest—When money is held in money balances, it does not earn interest. Remember, by money balances we do not mean stocks and bonds; rather we mean cash, demand deposits, and (to the monetarists) saving deposits. Interest payments on bonds are the *opportunity cost* of holding money balances in the form of cash and demand deposits,[2] and people can, therefore, be expected to vary their demand for money inversely with changes in the interest rate. This behavior is consistent with the law of demand. When the interest rate rises, the opportunity cost of holding money rises. People will substitute bonds for money balances in their wealth holdings; that is, they will demand a lower money balance and more securities. Theoretically, the interest rate should have an effect on people's demand for money. From their empirical studies of the demand for money, however, most monetarists have concluded that the effect is "very slight"—so slight that the influence of interest rates on money demand has a minimal influence on people's demand for money balances.

5 Expected rate of inflation—If the rate of inflation increases and people expect it to continue to increase, the cost of holding wealth in the form of money balances goes up. Because people will have to pay more for goods and services as time goes on, expected increases in the rate of inflation should lead to a lower demand for money in the present; people will use the money balances they have to buy goods and services currently.

An Increase in the Supply of Money

How does an increase in the supply of money affect prices? If the money supply increases through actions taken by the Federal Reserve, people as a group will have more money in their money balances than they need, given stable levels of institutional payment patterns, the price level, people's wealth, interest rates, and the expected rate of inflation. They will use this excess money to buy bonds and goods and services.

[2] Remember that the cost or, more precisely, the opportunity cost, of undertaking an action is the value of the best opportunity forgone. See Chap. 3.

What are the effects of those expenditures? A greater demand for bonds will cause the market interest rate to fall, increasing investment. An increase in the demand for goods and services by businesses and consumers should lead to an increase in the price level. It is this increase in the price level which, as noted before, leads to greater employment and a higher income level. Eventually, however, wages will begin to rise, pushing real wage rates back to their "normal" level and the unemployment rate back to its "normal" level—at a higher price level.

The price level is generally on the rise because the money stock is constantly growing. If the Federal Reserve increases the *rate* of growth in the money stock, the rate of inflation, in the manner described above, will increase. The monetarists argue that the rate of inflation will eventually be higher than the rate of growth in the money stock: a 6 percent rate of growth in the money stock may produce a rate of inflation of 7 or 8 percent. The explanation for this is reasonably straightforward: as the rate of inflation increases, the value of money held in currency or bank accounts falls at progressively higher rates, and the cost of holding onto money becomes greater. Consequently, in the face of inflation, people will hold fewer dollars in their bank accounts. Instead, they will buy more goods, such as real estate, which have the potential to increase in value over time. As people increase their purchases, dollars will turn over faster (at a higher velocity); the price level will rise not only because more dollars are being used, but also because the dollars in existence will be used with greater frequency.

A Decrease in the Money Stock

If the money stock contracts, people will have fewer dollars to hold, and, given their other assets, they may have fewer dollars in their money balances than they want or need. To build up their money balances to the "proper" level, some will convert (sell) a portion of their financial assets, such as bonds. Others will refrain from buying cars, furniture, etc. Fewer dollars will chase after goods and services. In order to sell their products, manufacturers will reduce their prices. In this way, a decrease in the money stock will lead to a lower price level.

A decrease in the *rate* of growth in the money stock will mean fewer dollars coming onto the market; upward pressure on prices will be diminished and the rate of inflation will fall. Since prices are no longer rising as fast as they once were, people's expectations about future inflation adjust downward, the cost of holding money is not as great, and people can justify holding a larger portion of their assets in money balances. Therefore, in the face of a falling rate of inflation, the velocity of money will fall.

In the monetarists' model, the short-run velocity of money is not constant; it is, however, directly related to the rate of inflation. As the rate of inflation rises, the velocity of money rises, and vice versa. This stable relationship is observed simply because of the effect which the rate of inflation has on the rationality of holding money.

From Money Growth to Unemployment

We have now considered the full sequence of events which follows an increase in the rate of growth in the money stock and leads to a temporary reduction in the unemployment rate. The following is a summary of that sequence. The Federal Reserve increases the rate of growth in the money stock. For example, it may buy more government securities on the open market. Because more money has been put into circulation and people must hold greater balances, people will seek a new optimum combination of money balances, real goods, and securities in their wealth portfolios. This means that they buy more real goods directly and more securities, including bonds. The greater demand for bonds will mean lower market rates of interest. Lower interest rates will increase investment. Increased investment and consumer expenditures will mean greater demands for goods and services and higher prices. Higher prices will lead to reductions in the real wage rates paid to labor, a greater quantity of labor demanded, and greater output. The end result of this sequence of events is lower *short-run* employment.

However, when workers begin to expect price increases, they will demand higher wages as compensation for the higher cost of living. The real wage rate will rise to its previous level, moving employers up their labor demand curves, meaning that fewer workers will be demanded. Employment will again fall, and with it, the national income level falls. A higher rate of inflation, generated by the higher rate of growth in the money stock, now accompanies the old "normal" unemployment rate.

The sequence of events emanating from a decrease in the rate of growth in the money stock is exactly opposite. The rate of inflation diminishes, leading to a temporary increase in unemployment. This is because the real wage rises, causing employers to demand fewer workers. In the long run, however, the unemployment rate will return to the "normal" rate. This is because greater unemployment will lead to smaller increases in money wages and to a drop in the real wage. Still, although no permanent decreases in unemployment have been achieved, the rate of inflation will be lower.

The monetarists, therefore, argue that if people can endure a temporary increase in the level of unemployment (perhaps lasting three or four years), the rate of inflation can be lowered by reducing the rate of growth in the money stock. Once at the new employment equilibrium, business cycles can be moderated, but not eliminated, by a steady, say 4 percent, rate of growth in the money stock. A steady growth in the money stock will lead to a steady rate of inflation and to a steady unemployment rate. In the monetarists' view, it is primarily the unpredictable ups and downs in the growth rate of money which lead to ups and downs in inflation and unemployment rates.

The Historical Evidence

To support their theory, monetarists point to many statistical studies which show a relationship between growth in the money stock and the rate of inflation. In a notable historical study written by Milton Friedman and Anna Schwartz, *A Monetary History of the United States 1867–1960*,[3] the authors conclude that every major business downturn in United States history has been a consequence of a contraction in the money stock; every period of rapid increase in prices has been accompanied by an equally rapid increase in the money stock. Modern monetarists point to charts like the one illustrated in Figure 31·4, which contains the recent record of money growth rates, inflation rates, unemployment rates, and growth in real output as measured by real GNP. Notice the growth path of the money stock at the top of the page, part *a* of the graph. Then drop down to the next tier, part *b*, and notice the course of prices between 1952 and 1974. Even to the most unsophisticated observer, the similarities in these two growth paths are most striking. Monetarists recognize that the relationship between the two curves is not perfect, but the tendency of the two variables to move together is readily apparent.

The chart indicates that during the 1950s the rate of growth in the money stock was, on the average, 1.8 percent. During that same period of time, the rate of increase in the general price index was also 1.8 percent. Early in the 1960s, the rate of increase in the money stock almost doubled to 3.4 percent. The rate of inflation followed suit, with a short time lag, to an average of 3.7 percent. In the late 1960s, the rate of growth in the money stock once again rose, this time to an average annual rate of 6 percent, and in the early 1970s it rose to 6.8 percent. The rate of inflation first rose to 5.3 percent in the late 1960s, then to 9 percent in the 1972–74 period. By 1975, the inflation rate had reached over 12 percent. This is the worst peacetime inflation the United States has experienced.

United States recessions are shown in parts *c* and *d* of Figure 31 · 4, which record the movement of real output and the unemployment rate. (The periods of recession are indicated by the shaded areas of the chart.) As can be seen in part *a*, each of the indicated recessions is preceded or accompanied by a drop in the rate of growth in the money supply. This drop in the growth rate is revealed as a reduction in the slope of the growth

[3] Milton Friedman and Anna J. Schwartz, *A Monetary History of the United States, 1867–1960* (Princeton, N.J.: Princeton University Press, 1963).

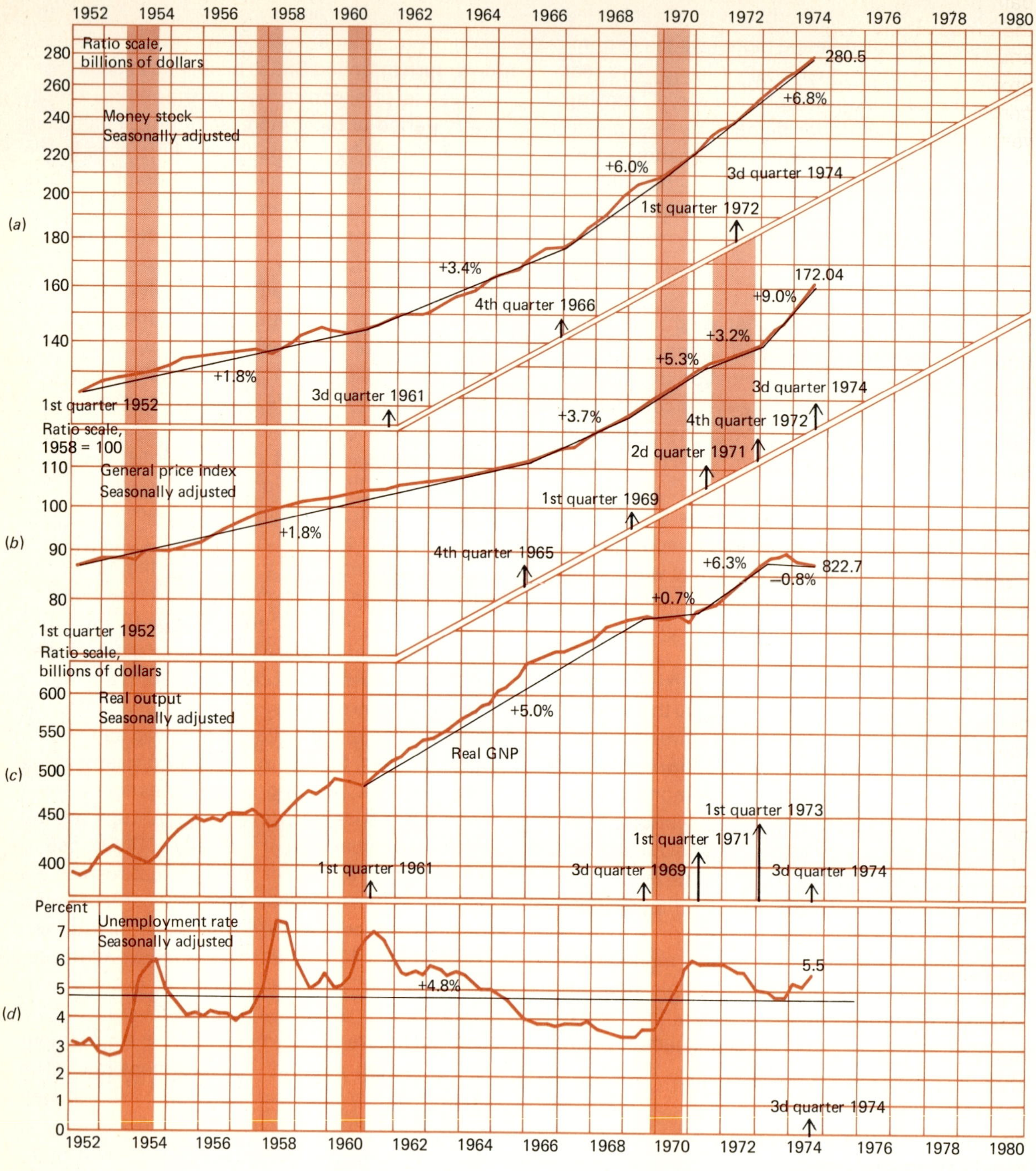

FIG. 31·4 As illustrated in parts a and b, the growth path in the money stock is generally followed by the growth in the general price level. The shaded areas in part c reveal periods of recession. These periods were typically preceded and accompanied by periods of decreases in the rate of growth in the money stock. As expected, the unemployment rate in part d goes up in recessions and falls during other periods.

path of the money stock. Monetarists argue that the drops in real output which occurred in 1960 and 1970 were a consequence of the drop in the growth in the money stock from something over 6 percent to practically zero in the last part of these years.

THE MONETARISTS' VIEW OF HIGH INTEREST RATES

In the Keynesian model, an increase in the growth rate of the money stock leads to a reduction in interest rates, and vice versa. As the money stock grows, more funds will be made available for loans, pushing the interest rate downward. Monetarists concur, but argue that any decrease in interest rates will be a temporary phenomenon—that eventually interest rates will rise. In other words, in the long run, greater growth in the money stock will lead to higher interest rates.

Why will this be true? Many people who have money to loan will refuse to do so at current low interest rates because the initial interest rates do not compensate them for the higher rate of inflation. For example, if a lender can receive only 5 percent, the money that is paid back by the borrower is worth less in purchasing power than the money that is loaned. Besides, the funds can be invested in real assets, like goods and land, whose nominal values are rising at 7 percent. Therefore, unless interest rates rise, lenders will withhold their funds from loan markets and invest them in real estate, land, etc., whose monetary values are rising and whose real values, at least, tend to remain constant.

Because of the higher rate of inflation, the demand for money will fall. Private individuals, businesses, and governments will speed up their purchases of goods and services to avoid the future cost increases that inflation entails. Many individuals will buy cars and appliances now in order to avoid paying higher prices when the new models come out. Businesses will increase their current investment in plants and equipment, and governments will build schools and roads to avoid higher construction costs in the future. To accomplish these goals, individuals, businesses, and governments will want to borrow greater sums in the money market.

Because loanable funds will be in lower supply (people being unwilling to lend money at low interest rates) yet in greater demand, market interest rates will by pushed upward. Hence, monetarists conclude that greater growth in the money stock and higher inflation rates should be accompanied by higher rates of interest on consumer and business loans and on government and corporate bonds. People may pay higher interest rates for the money they borrow, but part of their interest payment is effectively returned to them in the form of price increases on the assets they are currently able to buy. To illustrate, during a period of double-digit inflation, a business may have to pay an initial charge of 15 percent or more for the money that it borrows to buy raw materials needed in the production of consumer goods. It can justify paying a very high interest rate for such a loan because it knows that the price of the final goods it produces with these materials will rise over time. It can use a part of the price increase on its good to meet the interest payments. In short, the "nominal" or market rate of interest (that rate which firms or people pay on loans) is made up of two basic components: (1) the "real" rate of interest, which reflects the rate of return on real capital goods, and (2) the rate of inflation, or

$$\text{Market interest rate} = \text{real interest rate} + \text{rate of inflation}$$

Therefore, during periods of high rates of inflation, high market interest rates do not necessarily discourage investment. The monetarists contend that the way to reduce market interest rates is to reduce the rate of inflation, which, in turn, means to control the growth of the money stock. So, as we said at the first of this chapter, monetarists relate problems of inflation, unemployment, and interest rates to a problem of control of the money stock.

THE MONETARISTS' VIEW OF GOVERNMENT DEFICITS

In Chapter 30 we introduced the monetarists' view of deficit spending, which is an integral component of Keynesian analysis. Here we merely restate the monetarists' position in terms of the equation of exchange,

$$MV = PO = Y$$

If government deficit spending raises the national income level, Y, as the Keynesians suggest, it follows that the other side of the equation, MV, must also rise. If the money stock M is held constant, velocity V must rise when the government runs a deficit. Indeed, Keynesians do argue that velocity rises because the government borrows (through issuance of bonds) and then puts into active use the money that people would otherwise have held in idle money balances. The turnover rate of money therefore rises. On the other hand, monetarists contend that velocity is primarily determined by the expected rate of inflation, institutional payment habits, and people's wealth. Payment habits and people's wealth show little variation in the short run, and velocity changes with a change in the rate of inflation, which is due to a change in the growth rate of money. Therefore, government deficits do not materially affect the national income level, or so the monetarists argue.

True, monetarists do recognize that the velocity of money is a reflection of people's willingness to hold money balances and that their willingness to hold money balances is inversely related to market interest rates: people can see that deficit spending on the part of government puts upward pressure on interest rates (more demand chases after the same amount of money). The higher the interest rates, the lower the money balances people will hold, and hence the greater the velocity. Theoretically, in the monetarists' model, government deficits can induce people to hold less money—increasing velocity—and can lead to a higher national income level. However, from statistical studies, monetarists conclude that the effect of interest rates on velocity is not sufficiently great to make deficit spending an important national policy measure.

After the 1964 tax cut, the government ran a deficit and the national income level went up while the unemployment rate went down. Keynesians contend that the deficit led directly to the increase in the national income level. The monetarists contend, on the other hand, that the effect of the deficit, if any, was very indirect. The federal deficit led to greater borrowing by the Treasury, a greater overall demand for loanable funds, and upward pressure on interest rates. According to the monetarists, the increase in national income occurred only because the Fed, in an attempt to keep interest rates down, expanded the money stock at a faster rate than it had in previous years. In other words, fiscal policy has a significant short-run effect on unemployment, national income, and inflation only to the extent that it "forces" the Federal Reserve to change the rate of growth in the money stock.

SUMMARY AND EXTENSIONS

In the monetarists' model, money is not the only thing that matters in determining the national income level, the unemployment rate, and the inflation rate. Growth in technology, union power, people's wealth, and other factors also have long-term effects on the macroeconomy. However, money is a very important variable in the monetarists' model. The rate of growth in the money stock is the prime determinant of the inflation rate. Changes in the growth rate of money will cause cyclical swings in unemployment and inflation rates. In this sense, monetary policy matters greatly and fiscal policy matters very little.

One of the main distinctions between the Keynesian and monetarist models of the macroeconomy is that the Keynesian model provides a strong argument for government intervention and control of the economy, whereas the monetarist model provides a strong argument against government control, except, of course, for control over the money stock (which is the primary responsibility of the Federal Reserve). The Keynesians argue that government manipulation of the budget and the money stock can foster a more stable economy that fully employs the nation's available manpower. The monetarists, on the other hand, contend that the federal government's manipulation of its budget, taken by itself, will have no lasting effect on the overall employment level. Any increase in the rate of growth in the money stock will lead only to temporary reductions in unemployment and to greater inflation rates. In the long run, the unemployment rate will return to a level determined only by the "obstacles" which create rigidities in the real wage rates of various labor markets. In short, the long-run solution to problems of unemployment is the elimination of as many of these obstacles as possible.

QUESTIONS TO PONDER

1 Given the monetarists' model of the macroeconomy, why will an increase in the growth rate of the money stock fail to permanently reduce unemployment?

2 What actions would a president of the United States who holds to the monetarists' model take to increase the chance of being reelected next year? Of being reelected four years from now? If a president could be reelected for more than one term, would this change the choices?

3 Imagine you have overheard the following: "Given the equation of exchange, $MV = PQ = Y$, deficit spending alone can increase Y. This can occur because the deficit will increase the price level; this in turn will lead to an increase in V." Given the monetarists' model, what is wrong with this statement?

4 In earlier chapters, we presented arguments that suggest that the democratic process provides voters with few incentives to become politically intelligent. How does the debate between the Keynesians and the monetarists affect the willingness of voters to become politically intelligent?

RECOMMENDED READINGS

Friedman, Milton: *Dollars and Deficits: Inflation, Monetary Policy, and the Balance of Payments* (Englewood Cliffs, N.J.: Prentice-Hall, Inc., 1968), chaps. 1–8.

Ireland, Thomas R., and Jack L. Rutner: *Principles of Macroeconomics and Money* (Hinsdale, Ill.: The Dryden Press, 1973), chaps. 14–16 and 18.

McCulloch, J. Huston: *Money and Inflation: A Monetarist Approach* (New York: Academic Press, 1975).

32

NATIONAL ECONOMIC PLANNING

Planning will not usher in any more socialism or any more corporate domination than we already have. It will not abolish the Bill of Rights or private property. But will provide a new framework for urgently debating competing visions of the future. That will shake us up much more than anything the detractors of planning have feared in their more feverish moments.

Myron Sharpe[1]

The effect of people's agreeing that there must be central planning, without agreeing on the ends, will be rather as if a group of people were to commit themselves to take a journey without agreeing where they want to go: with the result that they may all have to take a journey which most do not want at all.

Friedrich Hayek[2]

PREVIEW OF CHAPTER

Central question

What are the major issues in the debate over *national economic planning?*

Major objectives

1. To define and outline the various forms which national economic planning can take
2. To develop the case for and the case against national economic planning

[1] Myron E. Sharpe, "Reply to a Critic of Planning," *Challenge*, July/August 1975, p. 5.

[2] Friedrich A. Hayek, *The Road to Serfdom* (Chicago: University of Chicago Press, 1944), p. 62.

Major conclusions

1. Planning is the process of thinking through the future, establishing objectives, and making things happen that would not otherwise happen—desirably, in accordance with established objectives. National economic planning involves the coordination of various government policies and programs and the coordination of the various public and private sectors of the economy to accomplish national goals.
2. National planning can take many forms; however, almost all forms can be grouped into three categories: (*a*) *decorative planning,* (*b*) *indicative planning,* and (*c*) *imperative planning.*
3. The case for national economic planning is fundamentally an itemized listing of the failures of the market system which we have studied throughout this book. The case against national economic planning is founded on the argument that planning an entire national economy, like the United States, is simply too complicated for any group of intelligent and highly dedicated people to accomplish effectively.

Important terms and concepts

National economic planning
Decorative planning
Indicative planning
Imperative planning

Our study of economics has been far-ranging. In the first half of this book we learned about the market—its deficiencies and its ability to adjust to changes in production and consumption through the pricing system. In the latter half, we concentrated on the public sector—on how, why, and to what extent the government may accomplish democratically established national goals. In many essential respects, our study has been a study in comparative economic systems; it has been a study of two at times complementary and at times competing ways of organizing the economic life of the country, the market and the government. While recognizing that almost all societies will have a private (or market) sector and a public (or government) sector, we have repeatedly raised these questions: To what extent can governmental action (or interference in the market) be expected to improve people's welfare? More directly, how much government or how much market do we need or should we have as a nation? Where do we draw the line between the public and the private sector?

In this concluding chapter, these basic questions remain with us and are drawn into sharper focus. Here we consider the growing debate over national economic planning in the United States. The issue is no ordinary one, for it concerns the way of economic life for the country. People's emotions on the issue run deep because national planning, in most of its various forms, proposes a fundamental shift of the decision-making powers regarding the economy from the private to the public sector. The advocates of national planning see in their proposal a better, more reasoned institutional setting for the development of specific governmental programs. They see it as a means of giving to the market guidance which it would not otherwise have. The opponents of national planning, on the other hand, see in it the potential for marked erosion of individual liberties. They also contend that national planning assigns to the government tasks which it simply cannot accomplish.

These are the broad dimensions of the debate. In this chapter we will explore in some depth the specific arguments frequently made for and against national planning. As we will see, the issue of national planning forces us to draw on our understanding of macroeconomics and the way in which markets and governments work to accomplish individual and social goals. However, we will also see that one's appraisal of national planning hinges in large measure on philosophical and ideological considerations, such as how one views the importance of individual goals in relation to social goals. We begin by considering planning as it relates to individuals. With this background, we discuss what is generally meant by national planning and the different forms which such planning can take.

THE NATURE AND FORMS OF PLANNING

The word "planning" does not have a standard definition. Different people use the term for dramatically different purposes. For this reason, the definition that we give is a suggestion for outlining the dimensions of the concept.

In a broad sense, planning is the process of thinking about the future, of establishing objectives, and of making things happen that would not otherwise happen—desirably, in accordance with the established objectives.

At the individual level, we all make at least some plans for the future, if only for short periods of time, and we usually advise other people to plan their future activities rather than simply to do things without much thought. Because well-developed plans can increase our money and nonmoney incomes, we are usually on the lookout for some means of improving our plans. So our plans are generally not fixed. Situations change, and we allow for this prospect in our plans. Indeed, we do not usually produce a single plan but develop what amounts to a series of plans. We "plan" to do A if M, N, and O happen; B if X, Y, and Z happen; and C if M, Z, and O happen. In practice, we do not make a complete list of all the things that could conceivably happen and then make a plan for all of them because there are simply too many "conceivable things." The investment (in time and energy) that would be required would be astronomical; the future will pass us by as we calculate.

Still, while remembering that "the best laid schemes of mice and men go oft astray," most of us do give some thought to what we should do in the future. This kind of planning, however, is more accurately described as thinking about future actions and responses rather than as making up a formal plan. The whole process of individual planning is made manageable because the goals of the plan are internally derived from the values of the individual or in consultation with a relatively small number of people with similar tastes and preferences, such as the family. This planning, in other words, does not require a collective decision-making process of the magnitude required by the U.S. Congress, representing the entire population of the country.

For individuals and small groups, planning is desirable and to be expected in a world in which present actions influence our future situations. There is no debate about planning here. The debate is over whether or not the concept of planning which is so commonly employed at the individual and small-group level can be employed with tolerably efficient results at the national level or even at the level of a region of a country. This is the substantive issue of this chapter; but before we can approach that complex question, we must recognize that planning at the national level can take different forms with different degrees of governmental control of the economy. First, we briefly characterize three forms which national planning can take and has taken around the world. We call them (1) *decorative planning,* (2) *indicative planning,* and (3) *imperative planning* (sometimes called *coercive planning*). These three forms of planning lie on a continuum that runs from zero governmental planning in the economy to a completely planned economy.

Decorative Planning

"Decorative planning" is so named because it is designed to give the impression that the government is actually involved in national planning. In short, it is a form of "window dressing." Various people think that having a yearly or a 5-year plan is something in and of itself that the government should do. Accordingly, a purely decorative plan is developed. This plan, however, has no effect on anything that happens in the future except that it may form the basis of further planning of the same sort.

Another kind of planning that is largely decorative generates academic and political discussion over what the government should or should not do, while little is actually done to ensure that the goals of the plan are achieved. Most Scandinavian countries have this kind of "plan," and in a way this kind of plan can be found in the annual report of the Council of Economic Advisors and in many other documents produced by government agencies. In these reports goals for the economy are set forth but very little is done to see that the goals are accomplished. One reason given is that no one has the authority to do anything. Aside from the fact that decorative plans give the appearance that the government is doing what it should be doing, this kind of plan is relatively useless.

Indicative Planning

Indicative planning is a form of planning which is more influential in determining the economic path a country takes than is decorative planning. Indicative planning is so named because the plan attempts to project (indicate) what the various sectors of the economy will be doing in the relatively near future. This term, and the process itself, were both pioneered in France, although some scholars of planning have maintained that what the French actually have is decorative planning.

The primary purpose of indicative planning is to increase the amount of information which businesses, government, and consumers have on what other groups in the economy plan to do in the future. This objective is accomplished by bringing together representatives from major industry groups, unions, and government for the purpose of discussing and formulating the broad objectives for the plan that is to be devised. For example, a list of high-priority programs may be developed and sent to the president for consideration. The actual targets for the plan, such as the desired or planned growth rate for Gross National Product, the unemployment rate, and consumer and government spending, may then be proposed by a cabinet-level committee and may finally be submitted to the Congress for its approval.

At the same time that specific targets are being developed, the government collects information on what all groups in the economy plan to do during the next year or the next 5 years. This information is then distributed to the different economic groups. On the basis of this information, the various groups may adjust their own plan and this new information, contained in revised individual plans, is assembled and distributed by government. The government can use its monetary and fiscal policy tools to ensure that the targets of the plan are achieved.

The guiding principle underlying indicative planning is simple and appealing: If business executives, union leaders, and government officials will openly discuss their individual tentative plans for the future, all will have better information on which to base their own final plans, some risk in undertaking investment will be reduced, and the demands of competing power groups can be settled before they develop into a wage-price spiral. For example, if business managers know how much money consumers will have to spend, how much other businesses will invest, and what the government will do to supplement the expenditures of the private sector, they will be more confident about being able to sell their products and may feel secure enough to invest more. If unions know beforehand the rate of inflation and the profit margins which businesses intend to achieve, they can better decide what their wage demands should be.

Indicative planning is more reasonable in theory than in practice. There are several problems with it which the French, with over 30 years of experience, have not been able to resolve completely. First, businesses are often reluctant to reveal what they actually intend to do in the future. Such revelations are important pieces of information that they want to conceal from their competitors. Second, after the plan is devised, consumers, government, and businesses often make further adjustments to the plan; and, obviously, by definition, these adjustments are not included in the plan. In other words, the plan may not accurately foretell what people really intend to do.

Third, and most important, it is very difficult for firms to predict what they will do in the future. There are many contingencies to consider, and each of the firms that is involved in the indicative planning process may reveal only one of the many contingency plans that it has. The plan the firm actually follows may only remotely resemble the plan that it announces to the planning authorities. If the national plan is founded upon the announced plans of various economic groups and any of these announced plans change, the national plan will be in error and can mislead people in making their individual plans. Such errors can be transmitted, through the national plan, to the rest of the economy. For instance, suppose the automobile industry announces that it plans to produce 12 million cars during the next year but it actually produces only 9 million because of new competition from imported cars. The steel industry, however, has probably adjusted its production capacity to produce 12 million cars. Needless to say, the steel industry will have excess capacity. If many miscalculations of this kind are made in formulating the national plan, people will simply ignore it and adjust to circumstances as they would if there were no plan. The plan then becomes decorative, and many advocates of planning may then press the government to take actions to ensure that national plans are adhered to. Proponents of planning often take the position, "Well, of course, if they don't carry out the plan, it will be necessary to force them." If the plan must be followed "or else," the planning process retains only the pretense of being voluntary. It takes on the character of imperative or, more to the point, coercive planning, to which we now turn.

Imperative Planning

All forms of planning involve the establishment of national objectives; however, imperative planning has an additional feature which makes it markedly different. Imperative planning uses the coercive powers of government or economic inducements conceived by government to ensure that the national plan is followed. Government coercion and economic inducements appear on the surface to be vastly different methods of achieving the same end. However, in both cases it is the government's objectives, not the individual's or business firm's objectives, that are sought. The hoped-for outcome does not emerge from the economic interplay of individuals; rather, the interplay is "guided" by goals that are externally derived from the economic system. As Herbert Stein has written, "If the government in the process of carrying out a national plan can make a private citizen an offer he cannot refuse, it can exercise coercion."[3]

How extensively government coercive powers are used varies from one planned economy to another. The government can take over the entire economy, but this is not necessary. Ludwig von Mises refers to the planned economy as the "Hindenburg pattern."[4] Under the Hindenburg system, private firms and individuals continued to own various industries and other forms of private property, but the basic economic decisions were made by the government bureaucracy, including the legislature and planning bodies, and were communicated to the owners as binding laws, regulations, or orders to produce certain things in certain ways. The details of the way in which this type of planning is carried out can also vary. In Germany, between the 1920s and 1941–42, the scope of the regulations and orders handed down to private owners steadily expanded, until, for all intents and purposes, the German economy in the

[3] Herbert Stein, *Economic Planning and the Improvement of Economic Policy* (Washington, D.C.: American Enterprise Institute for Public Policy Research, 1975), p. 25.

[4] Ludwig von Mises, *Human Action: A Treatise on Economics* [Chicago: Henry Regnery Company, 1966 (originally published 1944)], p. 717.

early part of World War II was as fully planned and controlled as was the Soviet economy. The plant managers in Germany, however, were still nominally appointed by stockholders rather than by the planning authorities.

Imperative planning need not be as extensive and as "coercive" as the planning that occurred in the period between World Wars I and II. An imperative plan can rely on fiscal and monetary policy tools like those we studied in previous chapters. For example, if the government wants to reduce inflationary pressures in the economy, it can increase its tax collections or reduce expenditures, or it can restrict the rate of growth in the money stock. Imperative planning can also involve the use of coordinated programs for pollution control, wage and price controls—and a means by which wages and prices can be adjusted upward—tariffs and quotas on imported goods, and selective direct subsidies embodied in reduced taxes or low-interest-rate loans for encouraging or discouraging consumer and investment spending at various points in the business cycle. All these techniques of social control can be coordinated with increases in government expenditures on such public goods as roads, public parks, housing, education, research on developing new energy sources and exploiting the energy sources that we have, medical care, and public service jobs for people who cannot find employment in the private sector of the economy.

Many of these techniques of carrying out social goals have at various times been employed in the United States. As we have mentioned before, the "investment tax credit" and excise taxes on consumer products have been adjusted to change the level and distribution of consumer spending. Sweden has altered the flow of investment spending over the business cycle by permitting firms to place untaxed profits in a special government account during periods of excess demand and inflation. The firms can then withdraw their funds, still untaxed, during periods of recession, falling national production, and rising unemployment. The proponents of planning and advocates of imperative planning propose that these types of policies be coordinated with many other government control measures. The argument is that without a coordinated national plan, the left hand of government will not know what the right hand is doing, and neither will know what the overall objectives of government policy are. Coercion or inducements are thought to be needed because people, acting in the context of the very large group of producers and consumers, have no incentive to follow an indicative plan. (See Chapter 6 for a review of individuals' behavior in the context of large and small groups.)

THE CASE FOR NATIONAL ECONOMIC PLANNING

The case for national economic planning is founded primarily upon the contention that the market economy has failed to achieve many established social goals and to provide for the needs of certain segments of the population, such as the poor and the elderly. The market economy, in other words, needs guidance from the government. Further, governmental programs that have been devised in the past to deal with various social problems have been inadequate and uncoordinated. Therefore, the economy needs a "grand design" which may be included in a national plan and which takes into account democratically established, national social objectives. Finally, proponents of national planning argue that a national plan can in fact be made to work—that it can improve upon the efficiency of the market economy. Having said this, we now turn to specific arguments for national planning.

The Failure of the Market Economy

The advocates of national economic planning contend that the failures of the United States economy are clearly revealed in economic statistics. In 1976, the unemployment rate was 7.9 percent while the rate of inflation was still in the neighborhood of 6 percent. United States industries had been using only between 70 and 75 percent of their productive capacity. The difference between actual Gross National Product and what the economy could have produced if it had been producing at full employment of resources was between $150 billion and $200 billion in 1976. Leon Keyserling, who was chairman of the Council of Economic Advisors under President Truman, has computed the deficiencies of the United States economy in more dramatic terms:

From the start of 1953 through the end of 1974, the long-term retreat from full employment and full production caused us to forfeit more than 2.6 trillion dollars (measured in 1974 dollars) of total output and enjoyment of goods and services; under the present tax structure we have forfeited enough public revenues at all levels of government to enable us to make an additional 760 billion of public outlays to service the starved priorities of domestic public needs; and we have lost more than 54 million man-years of employment opportunity. If the larger economy performs no better from now through 1980—and nothing more seems in prospect without vast changes in national economic policies and programs under planning—we will forfeit during 1975–80 more than 1.2 trillion 1974 dollars of total output and another 460 billion of needed public outlays, and forfeit 16.5 million man-years of employment opportunities.[5]

The Full Employment and Balanced Growth Act of 1976 proposes that the United States engage in national economic planning. It makes its case for national planning in this way:

The Congress finds that the Nation has suffered substantial and increasing unemployment and underemployment, over prolonged periods of time, imposing numerous economic and social costs. Such costs include the following:

1 The Nation is deprived of the full supply of goods and services, the full utilization of labor and capital resources, and the related increase in individual income and well-being that would exist under conditions of genuine full employment.

2 Insufficient production is available to meet pressing national priorities.

3 Workers are deprived of the job security, income, skill development, and productivity necessary to maintain and advance their standard of living.

4 Business and industry are deprived of the production, sales, capital flow, and productivity necessary to maintain adequate profits, create jobs, and contribute to meeting society's economic needs.

5 The Nation is exposed to social, psychological, and physiological costs and traumas, including disruption of family life, loss of individual dignity and self-respect, and the proliferation of physical and psychological illnesses, drug addiction, crime, and social conflict.

6 Federal, state, and local government economic activity is undermined as government budget deficits occur because tax revenues fall and expenditures rise for unemployment compensation, public assistance, and other recession-related services in the areas of criminal justice, drug addiction, and physical and mental health.

The Congress further finds:

1 High unemployment often increases inflation by diminishing labor training and skills, underutilizing capital resources, reducing the rate of productivity advance, increasing unit labor costs, reducing the general supply of goods and services and thereby generating cost-push inflation. In addition, modern inflation has been due in large measure to errors in national economic policy, including erratic monetary policy, inadequate energy and food policies, and ineffective policies to maintain competition in the private sector.

2 Although necessary for sound economic policy, aggregate monetary and fiscal policies are inadequate by themselves to achieve full employment production and to restrain inflation. Such policies must be supplemented by more direct private and public measures to create employment and reduce inflation.

3 Genuine full employment has not often been achieved, in part, because explicit short- and long-term national economic goals and priorities have not been established by the President, the Congress, and the Federal Reserve. Moreover, public and private economic policies have not been organized and coordinated to achieve national goals and priorities.

4 Increasing job opportunities and full em-

[5] Leon H. Keyserling, "For a Full Employment Act by 1976," *Challenge*, July/August 1975, pp. 22–23.

ployment make a major contribution to the abolition of discrimination based upon sex, age, race, color, religion, national origin, and other important factors.

The Congress further finds that an effective full employment and balanced growth policy should (1) be based on the development of explicit economic goals and policies involving the President, the Congress, and the Federal Reserve, as well as state and local governments, with full use of the resources and ingenuity of the private sector of the economy, and (2) include programs specifically designed to reduce high unemployment due to recessions, and to structural unemployment within regional areas and among particular labor force groups.

The Congress further finds that full employment and balanced growth are important national requirements that will promote the economic security and well-being of all citizens.[6]

The Causes of Market Failure

The advocates of national economic planning cite several causes of market failure, a number of which we have discussed in the last ten chapters. One cause they include is insufficient private demand. That is, the social problem of unemployment is caused by insufficient private demand for goods and services; consumers and businesses are unwilling to buy all the goods and services which the nation's industries can and will produce when all resources are fully and efficiently employed. Government must, therefore, supplement demand in the private sector by adjusting its monetary and fiscal policies. This is the Keynesian argument developed in Chapters 28 to 30.

Although proponents of national planning usually do not dispute basic Keynesian theory, they are critical of Keynesian economics' "overemphasis" on the management of aggregate demand. They contend that government policy objectives ought to be broadened to include not only management of *aggregate demand* but management of *aggregate supply* as well. In other words, just as insufficient demand in the economy can lead to a recession, there may also be times in which there are insufficient supplies of various resources and goods and services which can also lead to production bottlenecks and recessions and, perhaps, to recession and inflation. According to this argument, the inability of the market economy to properly satisfy public demand for goods and services is illustrated by the fact that, at times in the past, gasoline, natural gas, steel, and transportation facilities have been in short supply. Proponents of national planning also believe that the failure of the government to pay attention to the management of the supply side of the market has led to more union strikes than are necessary. If union leaders can be brought into the development of the national plan, they will see what kind of wage rates and fringe benefits they can reasonably request, and conflicts between union and management will be averted before contracts run out.

Another explanation given for the failure of the market is that the many autonomous economic units in the country do not attempt to coordinate their individual plans with the plans of all other producers and consumers. The result may be either surplus production, leading to a recession, or shortages of various goods and services, setting the stage for inflationary spirals. To illustrate, the firm planning to expand the number of motel rooms it has in a given geographical area, such as a stretch of seacoast, may not know that other firms are also planning to expand the number of rooms in their motels. As a result of all firms expanding their rooms, all may suffer financial losses. Alternatively, one steel producer may not know that all other steel producers will be expanding their production capacity at the time that it expands its production capacity. The result is that the steel industry generates excess capacity, resources go unused and are wasted, and unemployment emerges. These are the results in this and all similar situations because resources have been misdirected to the expansion of the productive capacity of an industry which needs no fur-

[6] U.S. Congress, House, Committee of the Whole House on the State of the Union, *Full Employment and Balanced Growth Act of 1976*, Report No. 94-1165, 94th Cong. 2d Sess., 1976, pp. 29–34. The text of the bill can also be found in *Challenge* (May/June 1976), pp. 56–68.

ther expansion. Leontief has stated the point with a little more bite:

In regard to increasing steel production, we have many steel companies that officially are not permitted to confer with each other [because of anti-trust laws], though, of course, they do. If additional steel-producing capacity is called for, each of the steel companies decides how much to build without formally or publicly taking into account what the others will do. The result of this method is a hit or miss performance. Of course, if the steel companies overbuild, it's their funeral; they'll bear the losses or even go bankrupt. That's pure competition. It's a very expensive way of attaining equilibrium—equilibrium through bankruptcies.[7]

Looking at the matter this way, national planning can enhance the planning process undertaken by individuals and firms. As Myron Sharpe has commented,

The idea [of national planning] is not to abolish private planning but to give it a better chance to succeed. Private planning is disrupted by inflation, unemployment and shortages. Anyone who thinks well of private planning ought to welcome efforts to achieve a stable economy within which private planning can be more successful.[8]

According to the supporters of national planning, the failures of the economy cannot be laid completely in the lap of market capitalism. A signigicant portion of the social problems we have experienced can be traced to faulty and uncoordinated government policy. Senator Hubert Humphrey, the Senate sponsor of the Full Employment and Balanced Growth Act of 1976, commented as follows on the disarray into which government policy, uncoordinated by a national plan, has fallen:

We don't have any economic impact statement for governmental decisions. The government goes willy-nilly making decisions of consequence. There was no estimate of the economic impact of the Occupational Safety Act. . . . I happen to be for the occupational safety program, but what were its economic implications? No, . . . The manner in which we are presently utilizing government resources and government agencies is a haphazard, helter-skelter enterprise.[9]

Government planning, in other words, is seen by its advocates to be a constraint on the various government agencies as well as on market participants. The goals established by the planning process will serve to coordinate government policy throughout all its branches. The conclusion then drawn is that the more consistent government economic policy is, the less the government will interfere with the workings of the private market economy.

The Large Corporations

Undergirding the case for a free, unplanned market economy is the assumption that consumers determine what they want and that producers respond passively to consumer demand; in other words, production satisfies demand, not the other way around. John Kenneth Galbraith, a noted and widely read economist, argues, on the other hand, that the modern economy, which he calls "the new industrial state," is dominated by large corporations, some of which produce as much as many of the world's less developed countries. In other words, the ordering has been reversed: the large corporations determine what is in their interest to produce and manipulate demand through advertising techniques which compel consumers to buy what is produced.[10] That is to say, consumers do not buy Chevrolets because of some innate desire for that type of au-

[7] Wassily Leontief, *National Economic Planning: Right or Wrong for the U.S.?* AEI Round Table Discussion held April 1, 1976 (Washington, D.C.: American Enterprise Institute for Public Policy Research, 1976), pp. 36–37.

[8] Myron E. Sharpe, "A Reply to a Critic of Planning," *Challenge*, July/August 1975, p. 3.

[9] As quoted by Murray Weidenbaum in "The Case For and Against National Economic Planning," *Challenge*, March/April 1976, p. 35.

[10] See John Kenneth Galbraith, *The New Industrial State* (Boston: Houghton Mifflin Co., 1967), or *Economics and the Public Purpose* (Boston: Houghton Mifflin Co., 1973).

tomobile or because they really do need a new car, but rather because General Motors has led consumers to believe that the Chevrolet is the type of automobile they should have, and also because General Motors has persuaded the consumer that a new car is somehow essential for his well-being. In Galbraith's view, the economy is already being managed, or planned, but the objectives are not national objectives; they are objectives which reflect the private interests of the major corporations in the country. National planning is a means, according to Galbraith and many others, of replacing the narrow objectives of large corporations with national social objectives. It is also a means of managing the corporations that now manage parts of the economy and do a very bad job of it.

The Establishment of Collective Goals

In an unplanned economy, people have, by their actions, something to say about what will happen in their personal lives; but they are unable to have much at all to say about the overall direction of the economic system of which they are a part. Proponents of national planning believe that through the establishment of collective goals, *national planning gives people a voice in what happens to the economic system.* The planning process may involve coercion, in the sense that sanctions are imposed on people who fail to adhere to the dictates of the national plan, but this is necessary in order to ensure that people will abide by the plan. The theory of large groups developed in Chapter 6 is applicable to this part of the proponents' case. In the context of a large group, people feel insignificant, and their actions may have an insignificant effect on the attainment of the common goals expressed in any national plan. Adherence to the plan, on the other hand, imposes costs on people. Before people can be made to incur these costs, they must be given an incentive in the form of a government sanction or reward.

Proponents of national planning believe that the influence of the government in the planned economy need not be construed as authoritarian. The goals of the plan and the techniques used to carry it out can be the product of the democratic system. Myron Sharpe recognizes the role which coercion can play in the planning process but argues that there is no reason to be alarmed:

> Let us not beat around the bush. Whenever the government passes a tax law, prohibits the dumping of toxic chemicals into a stream, or puts up a stop sign at a street intersection, these arrangements are coercive. Sanctions apply to those who ignore them. But the coercion here is accepted voluntarily, if reluctantly, because we elected the representatives who passed the laws. Suppose the next Democratic presidential candidate (or, farfetched fable, Republican candidate) proposes to set up an Economic Planning Board in the White House responsible for making a sector-by-sector analysis of the economy and for proposing tax and credit policies to help these sectors—say energy production and consumption—balance better than they do now. Suppose that the candidate proposes that the Joint Economic Committee be empowered to hold hearings on such proposals and recommends to Congress (or not, as it sees fit) the legislation needed to enable the President to carry out the proposed program. Suppose further that the voters elect the said candidate. The resulting planning will be no more coercive than the batch of disparate and incoherent proposals which are normally made in the absence of planning. But the results are likely to be a good deal more effective.[11]

The question which Sharpe fails to address in his remarks is whether or not the majority which elects this hypothetical candidate will be imposing its will on the rest of the population. As we will discuss in the following section, the opponents of planning see in this process a means by which the majority of voters in the country are given broader and more "tyrannical" powers over those who do not agree with them than they now have.

[11] Sharpe, "A Reply to a Critic of Planning," p. 4.

THE CASE AGAINST NATIONAL ECONOMIC PLANNING

One's view of national economic planning is strongly influenced by one's view of the way society is organized. Those who favor national planning tend to take a "holistic" view of society, meaning that they tend to attribute to society a strength and vitality which is separate from and more powerful than the total strength of the individuals who compose it. Society is a force which shapes the behavior of individuals, and not the other way around. It is perfectly consistent for people with this point of view to promote the concept of the "public interest" and to want to control that which they believe is in control of the behavior of individuals.

The opponents of national planning, on the other hand, tend to see society as a composite of individuals, each with interests of his or her own and each interacting in a highly complex web of personal and economic relationships with all other people. According to this view, society is a "composite" rather than a "whole." The perspective of the "individualistic" view of society is represented in Adam Smith's summary statement from *The Theory of Moral Sentiments:*

> The man of systems [which was the eighteenth-century term for national planner] . . . seems to imagine that he can arrange the different members of a great society with as much ease as the hand arranges the different pieces upon the chessboard; he does not consider that the pieces upon the chessboard have no other principle of motion besides that which the hand impresses upon them; but that, in the great chessboard of human society every single piece has a principle of motion of its own, altogether different from that which the legislator might choose to impress upon it.[12]

To the individualist, society is that which "emerges" from the behavior of individually motivated people; it is not that which is "planned" by some omniscient and omnipotent being. To talk about a "planned society" from this perspective is a contradiction in terms, because society takes its existence from behavior which is not and cannot be centrally directed. The values or goals which must be taken into account are those of the individual. To express one's individuality, one must have the freedom to do so. This, according to the opponents of national planning, is what the market system provides. The planned economy must deny basic economic freedoms to one extent or another. With this introduction, consider several points frequently stated by persons opposed to national planning.

Social Goals and Economic Freedom

A national plan presupposes some set of "social" or "national" goals which the plan is intended to accomplish. The opponents of national planning argue, however, that these social goals cannot be expected to fall like manna from heaven; rather, they will emerge from the political process, in which there can be dramatic differences among people as to what the social goals of the country should be. If these goals are expressed in very broad terms—such as, "Our goals are to reduce unemployment and inflation and improve the environment and the quality of life for all"—they will attract the political support of the great majority of people. On the other hand, the very vagueness of such goals leaves substantial room for interpretations. Different people will see different policy courses emanating from the same set of broad social goals. Agreement over what methods the country should actually use to attain its accepted goals has been merely postponed until a later date. Sooner or later policy decisions must be made.

If there were only one way to achieve a broadly stated national objective, the problem of collective decision making would not arise. However, as the last several chapters have made clear, there are many different ways to achieve a reduction in unemployment and inflation. There are even more ways to improve the environment or the quality of people's lives. There are many different policy courses from which the government can choose, and all people *do not* receive the same benefits or incur the same costs when the government imple-

[12] Adam Smith, *The Theory of Moral Sentiments*, E. G. West edition (New Rochelle, N.Y.: Arlington House, 1969), pp. 342–343.

ments a particular policy course. For example, a program designed to increase employment through an increase in military spending will have a different set of direct beneficiaries from those of a program designed to increase employment by an increase in highway construction expenditures. The "quality of life" can be improved by increasing the availability of medical care, increasing the size and diversity of city and national parks, rebuilding inner-city areas, subsidizing mass transit, and in many other ways. In each case, the benefits will be distributed differently. The costs of such programs are also unevenly distributed, depending upon the method chosen to finance them.

Interest groups who are affected by what the government does can be expected to work to have their own interests adopted as the national interest. If national economic planning is in effect, special interests will have an added incentive to see to it that their goals are taken into account when the plan is drawn up. In this way, national economic planning, according to its opponents, will increase the range of questions to be settled politically and, therefore, the influence of special-interest groups. In other words, opponents of planning fear that national goals will be set by "special interests," acting in the context of power politics—not by objective "truth" standards. These opponents of planning believe that people in the political arena tend to seek their own interests, even though the politicians' private interests may be shrouded in the rhetoric of the public interest.

Opponents of national planning also feel that it will be difficult to change the national plan in response to changing economic conditions. For example, suppose the price of some strategic imported good, like oil, suddenly increases for reasons which are beyond the control of those who are in charge of the plan. The result will be that parts of the plan will then be inappropriate.

To increase the flexibility of the planning process, the authority to change government policy can be delegated to a "planning board." The opponents of national planning often charge that such boards concentrate considerable political power in the hands of a very few people who may not be able to acquire the information necessary to make the decisions required of them. When mistakes are made by the planning board, those mistakes can impose significant costs on people. The advocates of planning, on the other hand, contend that the mistakes of planners will be far fewer in number than the mistakes of the market system.

Finally, if people differ over what the nation's planning objectives should be, and if only one set of national objectives is established for the plan, the national goals which are selected will be imposed on people who disagree with them. To the opponents of national planning, this means that government coercion must be used to make the plan workable. Myron Sharpe, quoted earlier, contends that so long as policies are formulated in the context of a democratic process, no coercion is involved (or, at least, that planning does not increase the use of government coercive powers). The opponents of national planning see in planning an extension of the scope of government and, by definition, an increase in the use of government coercion. They argue that even "persuasive controls," which is what economic inducements are sometimes called, are a subtle form of government coercion. Warren Nutter, an economist at the University of Virginia, writes:

> "Persuasive controls" are said to be noncoercive because they merely convey special benefits to firms that conform to the plan. The instruments available for "persuasion" will vary with the powers exercised by the government in question, but it takes little imagination to realize that the distinction between persuasion and coercion is a fine one, and that it vanishes completely when a firm's survival comes to depend on accepting persuasive enticements. It is also clear that such a system of controls would be administered only by discretionary authority with full powers to decide, case by case, whether firms merit the privileges being dispensed. Just as the power to tax is the power to destroy, so the power to "persuade" is the power to coerce.[13]

[13] G. Warren Nutter, *Central Economic Planning: The Visible Hand* (Washington, D.C.: American Enterprise Institute for Public Policy Research, 1976), p. 9.

Echoing the same theme with a different emphasis, Henry Hazlitt writes,

> The second basic error of government planners is their failure to point out that the real question being raised is not: plan or no plan? but whose plan? For when it is government that lays down the master plan, the plans of all the rest of us must be either set aside or subordinated. "Planning" means coercion.
>
> The more sophisticated Planners . . . disavow any such intentions. They do not favor "coercive" planning, they say, but only "indicative" planning. . . . Says the new Initiative Committee for National Economic Planning: "The planning office would not set specific goals for General Motors, General Electric, General Foods or any other individual firm. But it would indicate the number of cars, the number of generators and the quantity of frozen foods we are likely to require in, say, five years, and it would try to induce the relevant industries to act accordingly."
>
> But suppose GM or GE preferred its own estimates or guesses to those of the bureaucrats? Ah, then, we begin to get hints of coercion: "The inducements would be laws, as specific as necessary, or taxes, subsidies and environmental problems."[14]

"Informational Overload"

The economy of the United States, or any other country, for that matter, is an extremely complex web of economic relationships. Consider the complexity of the economic relationships involved in producing automobiles. Several thousand parts go into the production of an automobile, and these parts are obtained from many different sources. Some are obtained from the automobile manufacturers themselves, but many other parts come from other firms which specialize in supplying automobile parts. Each of these parts is made of several, if not many, different resource inputs. Additionally, each resource can be the result of a production process which also uses a number of resources. For example, production of the steel used in a car requires resource inputs of iron ore, coal, various pieces of capital equipment, and several kinds of labor. The coal is produced with the resources of land, labor, and capital such as mining equipment. The coal mining equipment, such as the power diggers, is produced from many different parts and resources. The cars and trucks which are the final product are also used, for instance, in the production of steel, of coal, and of the coal mining equipment. The full complexity of the automobile manufacturing process has, of course, not been fully developed. We have not considered how the several types of paints, plastics, and rubber that are used in cars get produced and delivered to automobile plants. Further, we have not mentioned the fact that different people like different types of cars with different levels of comfort, different colors, and different degrees of maneuverability, among other things. Each type of car requires different combinations of parts, which require different resource inputs.

Taken by itself, the production of automobiles is a difficult planning problem. It is so difficult that a firm like General Motors does not try to plan all aspects of the entire production process. General Motors plans its internal production operations, but it has found it too complex to plan all the various activities of all its suppliers of parts and resources. The opponents of national planning ask, given the millions of final and intermediate goods produced in the United States, is it possible for a national planning board or the Congress or the administration, or all of them together, to plan a significant portion of the economic life of the country? Is it possible for them to plan even a significant fraction of all production processes, taking into account possible changes in consumer tastes? Friedrich Hayek, who has written extensively in opposition to national planning, argues that the human mind is simply too feeble to handle all the information that must be absorbed by the national planners:

> The point which is so important is the basic fact that it is impossible for any man to survey more

[14] Henry Hazlitt, "Planning Disaster," *Challenge*, July/August 1975, pp. 45–46.

than a limited field, to be aware of the urgency of more than a limited number of needs. Whether his interests center around his own physical needs or whether he takes a warm interest in the welfare of every human being he knows, the end about which he can be concerned will always be an infinitesimal fraction of the needs of all men.

This is the fundamental fact on which the whole philosophy of individualism is based. . . . From this the individualist concludes that the individuals should be allowed, within defined limits, to follow their own values and preferences rather than somebody else's; that within these spheres the individual's system of ends should be supreme and not subject to any dictation by others.

This view does not, of course, exclude the recognition of social ends, or rather of a coincidence of individual ends which makes it advisable for men to combine for their pursuit. But it limits such common action to the instances where individual views coincide; what are called "social ends" are for it merely identical ends of many individuals—or ends to the achievement of which individuals are willing to contribute in return for the assistance they receive in the satisfaction of their own desires. Common action is thus limited to the fields where people agree on common ends.[15]

In short, national planning imposes an "informational overload" on the people who are supposed to do the planning; it assigns to them a task which, by virtue of their limited mental capacity and the enormity of the information they must handle, they cannot possibly accomplish in a way which is *more* satisfactory than the market system's. According to those opposed to planning, the market system works because each person or firm which is involved in the production of a good or one of its parts handles a relatively small amount of information. Much of the information that people need to effectively operate in a market is summarized in the price of the goods they sell and the prices they pay for the resources and parts which they use in production. When these prices—or information flows—change, market participants know how and in what direction they must change their production plans. The market is, contrary to the advocates of planning, a relatively efficient means of coordinating the national economy. Exactly how the market coordinates the economic activity of so many market participants has been discussed in earlier chapters, especially Chapter 7.

In support of their contention that planning is "too complex," its critics point to the experiences of other countries. Often, national plans are not completed before they are due to be put in effect. Five-year plans may not be completed until after their effective period; annual plans may not be completed until the year is half over; and monthly plans may not appear until the month is almost through. In such cases, Warren Nutter writes, "The question naturally arises whether the plan is egg or chicken—whether performance derives from plan or plan from performance."[16]

The Soviets, for example, did not complete their 5-year plan for 1970–75 until 1972. It was published in the late spring of 1972, and that summer there was a substantial crop failure in the Soviet Union. As a result, the 1970–75 plan was obsolete by the fall of 1972. In 1965 in England, the newly elected Labour Party government decided that the country needed a national plan, and it organized a special ministry to work it out and apply it. The ministry took a year to produce a 5-year program. Because of balance of payments problems and recession, the plan was abandoned 9 months after it was adopted. The opponents of planning argue that national plans are often abandoned or incompletely implemented because too many things can go wrong in a dynamic economy. The possibility of a breakdown of a national plan is particularly strong in an economy which, through international trade, is subject to economic forces that originate beyond the boundaries of the economy.

"The Road to Serfdom"

As individuals, we adjust our plans and behavior to account for expected and unexpected

[15] Friedrich A. Hayek, *The Road to Serfdom* (Chicago: University of Chicago Press, 1944), pp. 59–60.

[16] Nutter, *Central Economic Planning*, p. 6.

changes. The adjustments that we make, however, are self-imposed and are consistent with things which we want to do. To the extent that this is true, our plans are not dictated by others and we all share a modicum of personal freedom.

As we have indicated, the opponents of national planning argue that planning will lead to misallocation of resources, further rounds of inflation, recessions, and a worsening of the social ills which planning is designed to cure. They fear that, if the plan fails to achieve its stated social goals, its developers will conclude, not that the plan has been badly designed, but that the planners have had inadequate control over people's behavior. The threat which the opponents of planning see is that planners will be given progressively stronger controls over people's behavior, and personal freedom will diminish. If this happens, collective goals rather than individual goals will determine the type of society we have.

For years the government has attempted to control monetary and fiscal policies in order to achieve full employment and price stability. The advocates of planning now contend that these controls are inadequate to achieve the stated goals and that they need additional controls like those mentioned earlier in this chapter. According to the opponents of national planning, those in charge of conducting the nation's monetary and fiscal policy have been unwilling to accept the fact that policy, given the constraints of the democratic process, has been poorly conducted. Giving government policy makers additional controls over the economy will not, by itself, increase the efficiency with which government policy is conducted; it will, on the other hand, force the country to take one additional step down what Friedrich Hayek calls "the road to serfdom" and toward a state in which government bureaucracy has more and more to say about what people can and will do.

The Bureaucratic Maze

As we have noted earlier, John Kenneth Galbraith argues that public demand is being controlled by the large corporations. Therefore, he contends planning is necessary to redirect the use of resources away from serving the private interests of corporations to serving the public interest. The opponents of planning reply that Galbraith's argument assumes that the government bureaucrats who conduct the planning process are more concerned about the public interest than their counterparts in private industry.

Planning opponents fear that government bureaucrats will use national planning as a means of increasing the budgets of their bureaus and their own salaries, reducing the amount of work they do, and imposing their values on others. In this way, the benefits of national economic planning would be absorbed by the inefficient operation of the bureaucracy. In short, the opponents of planning ask, "How do we control the planners?" Theoretically, the public has control over bureaucracy through the political process; but does the public have any more control over government bureaucracies than it does over corporations by exercising its option not to buy what the corporations have to sell in the market? GM is a large corporation, but individuals who dislike GM's products, advertising techniques, or management can buy their cars from other manufacturers. Opponents of planning recognize the imperfections of consumer control over private companies, but they contend that their control of private firms is far greater than their political control over government bureaucracies.

SUMMARY AND EXTENSIONS

The debate over national economic planning has been rekindled by the Full Employment and Balanced Growth Act of 1976, and we do not expect the debate to subside. Indeed, we expect it to intensify as specific planning objectives for national planning are hammered out in Congress. It is, therefore, all the more important that the central issues in the debate be kept in mind. In this chapter we have developed the major points of the case for planning. Briefly, those points are:

1 The unguided market economy has failed to achieve full employment, price stability, and an adequate production of goods and services which benefit the general population. National planning will provide the market economy with the guidance that it needs.

2 Large corporations are now in control of large segments of the market economy and are planning their individual segments to suit their own private interests. The plans of these corporations need to be controlled by a national plan that will coordinate the activities of all segments of the economy in accord with national goals.

3 Through national planning and the political process individual citizens will have limited, but still some, influence over the direction the national economy will take in the future.

The case against planning includes the following major points.

1 National planning requires that national objectives be established and be substituted in many instances for the objectives of individuals. National planning, therefore, means that in many instances the will of the majority will supplant the will of individuals and that individual freedoms will accordingly be lost.

2 Detailed national planning cannot work because it ultimately means that the planners will be required to absorb much more information about how production should be organized than they can possibly absorb. The result will be that national planning will not work in any meaningful sense. At worst, national planning will compound the social problems which the planning process is designed to correct. The market system is not perfect, but it will do a better job of producing what the public (as opposed to the planners) wants than will a planning system.

3 The national planning process will be run by government bureaucrats who, like their counterparts in private industry, have their own private interests. They will tend to use their position to further their own interests and to impose their will on the rest of the population.

Our discussion of the pros and cons of national planning has, of necessity, been brief and incomplete. We know that there are arguments that have not been developed here, but the arguments we have presented capture the areas of strongest disagreement between those who oppose and those who favor national planning. The reader should remember that the two sides are not always this far apart. Much of the disagreement centers on the question of how much national planning can be efficiently organized by government. Be that as it is, the broad outlines of the debate have been presented here. We anticipate that the country at some point in the future will embark on the process of national planning. This social experiment should prove interesting to anyone who has watched the debate: it should give us some indication of who is right. We suspect, however, that regardless of the outcome, both sides will claim victory.

QUESTIONS TO PONDER

1 As an experiment, make up plans now for next week and the week after that. Make your plans as detailed as possible and try to carry out your plans. At the end of each week, evaluate how well you were able to follow your plan for the week. At that time, ask yourself whether or not following the plan was always a good idea. Was making your plans as detailed as you did worth the time and trouble? Additionally, is the accuracy of your plans a function of how far in the future they are applicable? Why? Does your experiment suggest anything about the benefits and difficulties of planning a significant portion of a national economy?

2 National plans are almost always adjusted to changing events. Indeed, the final plan constructed for a planning period may have little resemblance to the initial plan. Does this mean that the planning process itself is of little value? Explain.

3 The adoption of a national planning process in the United States will surely increase the demand for and wages of economists. However, there are still economists who oppose national planning. How would you explain their position?

4 In *The Road to Serfdom,* Friedrich Hayek argues that the public sector should be restricted to doing those things over which there is broad public agreement, such as providing a court system. Does this mean that national planning should not be the responsibility of government? Does the heterogeneity of the population have anything to do with the general acceptance of national planning?

5 Monetarists tend to argue that fiscal policy and monetary policy have little long-run effect on the level of national income and employment. As a general rule, would you expect monetarists to be for or against national planning? Would you expect Keynesians to be for or against national planning? Explain.

6 Those in favor of planning often argue that monetary and fiscal policy tools are effective but inadequate tools for dealing with the problems of national planning. Why?

7 Give your reaction to the following statement: "If planning is good for consumers and businesses, it must be good for the country."

8 Take a look at several of the articles on national planning in the Recommended Readings section of this chapter. Write down a list of arguments for and against national planning that were not considered in this chapter. Having done that, what is your overall position on national planning?

RECOMMENDED READINGS

Galbraith, John Kenneth, et al.: "The Case For and Against National Economic Planning." *Challenge,* March/April 1976, pp. 30–38.

———: *The New Industrial State* (Boston: Houghton Mifflin Co., 1967), esp. chaps. 18–24.

Hayek, Friedrich A.: *Individualism and Economic Order* (Chicago: The University of Chicago Press, 1948), esp. chaps. 7–9.

———: *The Road to Serfdom* (Chicago: The University of Chicago Press, 1944), esp. chaps. 3–7.

Hazlitt, Henry: "Planning Disaster," *Challenge*, July/August 1975, pp. 44–46.

Keyserling, Leon H.: "For a Full Employment Act by 1976," *Challenge*, July/August 1975, pp. 20–25.

Komiya, Ryutaro: "Economic Planning in Japan," *Challenge*, March/April 1975, pp. 9–20.

"The New Humphrey-Hawkins Bill." Interview with Hubert H. Humphrey, *Challenge*, May/June 1976, pp. 21–29.

Nutter, G. Warren: *Central Economic Planning: The Visible Hand* (Washington, D.C.: American Enterprise Institute for Public Policy Research, 1976).

Sharpe, Myron E.: "Reply to a Critic of Planning," *Challenge*, July/August 1975, pp. 3–5.

Stein, Herbert: *Economic Planning and the Improvement of Economic Policy* (Washington, D.C.: American Enterprise Institute for Public Policy Research, 1975).

Glossary

The definitions provided in this section are not meant to be complete. For full discussions of the terms or concepts, see the page indicated in each definition in this section.

Absolute advantage The greater efficiency which one person (or country) has in the production of a commodity. See page 287.

Acreage allotment The number of acres a given farmer is permitted to use for a given crop, such as tobacco. See page 156.

Administered prices Prices set by internal decisions of firms, not by the external forces of market competition. See page 191.

Aggregate demand The summation of all demands of various sections in the economy. AD $= C + I + G$. See page 523.

Appreciation of the dollar An increase in the value of a dollar; in international exchange, a reduction in the dollar price of another national currency. Example: A change in the exchange rate from £1 = \$1.80 to £1 = \$1.50. See page 304.

Average cost The total cost divided by the quantity produced. See page 213.

Balance of payments deficit The difference between the payments and receipts of one country to all other countries when payments exceed receipts; conceptually, the shortage that exists between the quantity of foreign currencies demanded and supplied when the exchange rate is held down *below* the equilibrium rate. See page 307.

Balance of payments surplus The difference between the payments and receipts of one country to all other countries when receipts exceed payments; conceptually, the surplus that exists between the quantity of foreign currencies demanded and supplied when the exchange rate is *above* the equilibrium rate. See page 307.

Balance of trade The difference between a country's exports and imports. See page 288.

Barter system Transactions involving the exchange of goods. See page 302.

Behavioral determinist Social theorists who believe that a person's behavior is determined by his or her genetic makeup and the environmental and social forces around the person. See page 28.

Black market Transactions involving exchanges of goods at some price or in some quantity differing from that set by law. See page 200.

Budgetary deficit The amount by which government expenditures exceed government revenue. See page 544.

Business cycle The irregular up and down movement around the growth trend of the economy; that portion of economic movement composed of a recession, trough, recovery, and boom. See page 533.

Cartel An organization of producers whose economic purpose is to restrict supply, divide the market, and raise price. See page 168.

Cash transfers Aid to the poor given in money. Example: welfare payments. See page 374.

Caveat emptor "Let the consumer beware." Legal rule which means that the consumer bears full responsibility for his or her purchases. See page 228.

Caveat venditor "Let the seller beware." Legal rule which means that the seller bears full responsibility for what he or she sells. See page 229.

Choice A selection from among alternatives when not all alternatives may be chosen. See page 20.

Circular flow of income The exchange of goods and services and labor and capital between households and firms; the movement of money payments to firms from households and then back to households in the form of earned income. See page 506.

Civilian Labor Force The total number of people classified as employed and unemployed. See page 436.

Common interest theory of group behavior Considers all groups as having been organized to pursue the common interest of the group members; a holistic approach to the study of group behavior. See page 94.

Communal property right A condition in which everyone has the right to use a resource, good, and service with no one having the right to exclude anyone else. See page 84.

Comparative advantage The relatively greater efficiency which a person (or country) has in the production of a commodity. See page 287.

Competition The regulating force which keeps profit to a minimum and pushes production toward the lowest possible cost level. The process by which market rivals attempt in various ways to outdo or avoid being outdone by other market rivals. See pages 112 and 114.

Competitor One producer among many who sells essentially the same good or a closely related good. Example: Producer of hand calculators. See page 44.

Complementary goods Goods which, when one of the goods is used, the other is also. Example: Cream and coffee. See page 47.

Consumer equilibrium Used to describe the consumer in a stable state in which the ratios of marginal utilities to their prices of various goods are equal: $MU_a/P_a = MU_b/P_b \ldots MU_n/P_n$. See page 34.

Consumer Price Index The ratio of the cost of a defined market basket of goods sold in retail markets in any year to the cost of the same market basket in some base year. See page 439.

Cost The value placed on the most favored alternative not taken when a choice is made. See page 20.

Currency reserves Foreign currencies held to meet balance of payments deficits. See page 311.

Currency swaps The trades of currencies between nations for the purpose of increasing each country's international reserves. See page 312.

Cyclical unemployment Unemployment as a result of an economic downtrend. See page 489.

Decision costs Costs incurred in the process of making choices among alternative proposals. Example: Time involved in convincing all persons of the correctness of a proposal. See page 392.

Decorative planning The process by which government gives the false impression it is engaging in national economic planning. See page 576.

Deflation A decline in the price level. See page 471.

Demand curve A collection of points which are downward sloping to the right demonstrating the inverse relation between price and quantity demanded of a good, everything else constant. See page 37.

Demand for labor The assumed inverse relation between the wage rate and the quantity of labor employers will hire, everything else equal. See page 247.

Depreciation of the dollar Reduction in the value of the dollar; in international finance, an increase in the dollar price of another national currency. Example: A change in the exchange rate from £1 = \$1.80 to £1 = \$2.00. See page 304.

Difference principle A concept advanced by John Rawls stating that justice requires that the income of lower-income people be maximized. See page 369.

Discount rate The interest rate which the Federal Reserve charges on its loans to commercial banks. See page 451.

Disposable income The money people actually have to spend. See page 434.

Economic theory of group behavior Considers the group to be a collection of independently motivated individuals who organize voluntarily to pursue their common interest only in small groups; an individualistic approach to the study of group behavior. See page 95.

Economic theory of regulation Regulation that results because firms have a demand to be protected from the forces of competition by government. See page 221.

Economics A discipline which can be described as a way of studying human behavior in the context of social interaction. See page 13.

Economies of scale The characteristic of being able to reduce costs at higher levels of output by increasing all resource inputs. See page 213.

Efficiency range The limits within which production in real-world markets will normally take place; the range between the equilibriums of perfect competition and pure monopoly. See page 168.

Elastic demand An increase in price which results in a decrease in total consumer expenditures, and vice versa; $E_d = \% \Delta Q / \% \Delta P > 1$. See page 41.

Elasticity coefficient The ratio of the percentage change in quantity demanded to the percentage change in the price, or $E_d = \% \Delta Q / \% \Delta P$. See page 42.

Employed People who have jobs. For specifics, see page 436.

Equation of exchange $MV = PO$. See page 459.

Equilibrium A market state in which quantity supplied equals quantity demanded. See page 124.

Equilibrium The national income level at which aggregate demand equals aggregate supply; the national income level at which withdrawals equal injections. See page 512.

Equilibrium quantity The amount at which the quantity supplied equals quantity demanded. In a competitive market, the output level at the intersection of the supply and demand curves. In a monopolistic market, the output level at which marginal cost equals marginal revenue. See page 122.

Equilibrium price The price at which quantity supplied equals quantity demanded. In a competitive market, the price at the intersection of the market; in a monopolistic market, the price on the demand curve above the point at which marginal cost equals marginal benefit. See page 122.

Equilibrium wage rate The wage rate at which quantity demanded of labor equals quantity of labor supplied. See page 251.

Expected benefit The increase in satisfaction which the individual anticipates for a given choice; the raw benefits discounted by the probability of the benefits actually being received. See page 22.

Expected cost The cost which the individual anticipates for a given choice; the raw costs discounted by the probability of the costs being incurred. Example: Cost of committing a crime and being punished. See page 22.

Expected values The raw costs or benefits discounted by the probability of their being realized. See page 24.

Excess reserves Total reserves minus required reserves; reserves which can be loaned. See page 454.

Explicit cost An out-of-the-pocket expenditure. Example: Expenditure on this book. See page 55.

Explicit logrolling A clearly defined trade of votes between two politicians. Example: One representative agrees to vote for a dam in another representative's district in return for a vote on a sewer system in his district. See page 404.

External benefit The economic gain some third party acquires from a transaction between two other parties. See page 230.

External cost The loss some third party endures as a by-product of a transaction between two other parties. See page 232.

Externalities The positive or negative effects which exchanges have on people not participating in a transaction. See page 345.

Federal Reserve System The central bank in the United States created by Congress in 1913 for the purpose of controlling the money stock and regulating banks. See page 449.

Final goods Goods which have reached their finished market form. See page 429.

Fiscal policy The tax and expenditure actions of the government to achieve the goals of full employment, price stability, and economic growth. See page 549.

Fixed exchange rate system System under which the international exchange rate is set by government. See page 309.

Floating exchange rate system System under which the international exchange rate is determined by the free movement of supply and demand for foreign currencies. See page 309.

Free ride The attempt of an individual to gain benefits with no cost to himself. See page 25.

Free trade Exchanges free of government restrictions. See page 293.

Frictional unemployment Short-term unemployment due to shifts in market demand. Example: Unemployment due to a temporary decrease in the demand for bicycles. See page 488.

GNP deflator A price index which covers a broad range of retail goods and services and wholesale commodities and is used to compute real or constant dollar GNP figures. See page 440.

Gold reserves Gold held to meet balance of payments deficit under a fixed exchange rate system. See page 310.

Gross National Product The current market value of all final goods and services produced in the economy during the calendar year. See page 428.

Human capital Those skills and knowledge which an individual acquires. Example: College education. See pages 254 and 255.

Imperative planning The process by which government uses its powers to ensure that the goals of a national plan are realized. See page 578.

Implicit cost Hidden cost; not an out-of-the-pocket expenditure; typically, an opportunity forgone. Example: The income forgone when one goes to college. See page 55.

Implicit logrolling Implied trade of votes by the way legislation is proposed. Example: Design of interstate highway system proposal in 1950s. See page 404.

Income A measure of people's contributions to the production of goods and services. See page 433.

Income redistribution The channeling of income from one group in society to another. See page 377.

Indicative planning The process by which projections of future economic activity are made in order to give consumers and businesses a better, more informed basis for making economic decisions. See page 577.

In-kind transfers Aid to the poor which is tied to specific commodities. Example: Food stamps. See page 371.

Inelastic demand An increase in price results in an increase in total consumer expenditures, and vice versa; $E_d = \% \Delta Q / \% \Delta P < 1$. See page 41.

Inferior good Good for which demand decreases as income rises. Example: Beans or potatoes in low-income neighborhoods. See page 46.

Inflation A rise in the overall level of prices over a period of time. See page 438.

Intermediate goods Goods used in the production of other goods. See page 429.

International exchange rate The price of a national currency in terms of another national currency. Example: £1 = $1.80. See page 303.

International Monetary Fund An international agency founded for the purpose of providing countries with greater reserves. See pages 311 and 312.

Investment The purchase of capital goods. See page 509.

Internalizing externalities The process of inducing the one who generates social costs to consider them in his or her actions. See page 89.

Law of demand Everything else held constant, the assumed inverse relation between the price of a good and the quantity of the good consumers are willing and able to buy. (People will buy more at lower prices than at higher prices.) See page 34.

Law of diminishing returns If additional units of one input are applied to a *fixed* amount of another input, there is a point beyond which the *additional* output begins to diminish. See page 60.

Liquidity The ease with which a financial asset can be converted to purchasing power. See page 446.

Liquidity problem Insufficient reserves to fill a persistent deficit in the balance of payments. See page 310.

Logrolling Vote trading. See page 403.

Luxury goods Goods for which demand increases at a rate greater than the increase in incomes. Example: Yachts. See page 46.

Macroeconomics That portion of economics dealing with large subdivisions of economic activity or with the entire economy. See page 426.

Marginal cost The additional cost incurred from producing one additional unit of a good, activity, or service. See page 59

Marginal cost of labor The additional cost of an additional unit of labor. See page 267.

Marginal product (of labor) The additional output acquired from an additional unit of input (labor). See page 61.

Marginal propensity to consume The percent of any increase in income which is spent: MPC $= \Delta C / \Delta Y$. See page 524.

Marginal propensity to save The percent of any increase in income which is saved: MPS = $\Delta S/\Delta Y$. See page 520.

Marginal revenue The increase in total revenue acquired from selling one additional unit of output. See page 171.

Marginal utility The additional satisfaction received from one additional unit of a good consumed. See page 34.

Market Any arrangement by which people exchange goods and services. Example: Farmer's market. See page 7.

Market demand The horizontal summation of individual demands for private goods. See page 39.

Market supply curve The horizontal summation of individual supply curves. See page 68. (*See* Supply curve.)

Marketing quota A restriction on the amount of a good an individual producer (e.g., farmer) can legally sell. See page 157.

Market shortage The condition in which quantity demanded exceeds quantity supplied; exists only when price is below the equilibrium price. See page 123.

Market surplus The market condition in which quantity demanded is less than quantity supplied; exists only when price is above the equilibrium price. See page 121.

Median family income That income for a family which is at the midpoint of the income distribution. See page 360.

Median voter group The people who represent the center of the distribution of political viewpoints. See page 390.

Medium of exchange Money; anything which can be used to carry out transactions and can avoid the use of barter (goods trading for goods). See page 446.

Microeconomics That portion of economics dealing with the economic behavior of individuals, firms, and specific markets. See page 426.

Minimum wage rate The wage rate below which employers may not legally hire employees. See page 256.

Money wage rate The number of dollars earned per unit of time. See page 251.

Monetary policy Government measures aimed at increasing or decreasing the money stock (M_1 or M_2) for the purpose of affecting employment, interest rates, or the rate of inflation in the country. See page 450.

Money A readily acceptable means of making payment (or "medium of exchange") and a financial asset—a form of saving—which represents a store of readily usable purchasing power. See page 446.

Money cost What is paid in money for some good or service. See page 20.

Money stock Total quantity of money in circulation measured as M_1 and M_2. M_1 = currency + demand deposits; $M_2 = M_1$ + saving account balances at commercial banks and small certificates of deposits. See page 447.

Monopolistic competition A market structure in which there are a number of producers who sell similar but differentiated products. See page 168.

Monopoly (pure) A market in which there is only one producer of a good and there are no close substitutes for that good. See page 167.

Monopsony (pure) The sole *buyer* of some good or service. See page 264.

Multiplier The ratio of the change in national income to the change in aggregate demand that stimulated the change in income: $m = \Delta Y/\Delta ad$; m = 1/MPS = 1/1 − MPC. See page 530.

National economic planning The process by which national economic goals are established and actions are taken to ensure that the goals are realized. See page 427.

National income The total payments made to owners of productive resources.

Natural monopoly A firm whose average and marginal costs decline within the range of the market demand for the product. See pages 214 and 215.

Negative income tax A government supplement to the income of low-income people; the difference between some governmentally guaranteed minimum income level and the actual income earned. See page 375.

Net National Product Gross National Product less capital consumption allowances (depreciation). See page 443.

Normal good Good for which market demand increases when consumer income rises. Example: clothes. See page 46.

Normative economics The subjective aspects of economics. Example: Deals with "what ought to be." See page 11.

Oligopoly A market structure in which there are a few major competitors selling an identical or differentiated product. See page 168.

Open market operations The purchases or sales of governmental bonds by the Federal Reserve.

Opportunity cost The most highly valued alternative forgone when choice is made. Example: The value of some activity that you would have undertaken in lieu of reading this book. See page 20.

Opportunity set Range of alternatives open to choice. See page 28.

Perfect competition A market structure in which there are numerous producers no one of which produces a significant portion of the total market output and in which there is complete freedom of entry and exit from the market. See page 118.

Personal income That part of national income which is paid to individuals. See page 443.

Planning The process of establishing objectives for the future and of taking action to ensure that the objectives are realized. See page 576.

Positive economics The objective, scientific aspect of economics. Example: deals with "what is." See page 11.

Poverty income level The amount of income below which the government judges one to be poor. See page 361.

Present value The value of future costs in today's terms. See page 23.

Price What a person gives up for each unit of goods or services purchased. See page 38.

Price-cost squeeze A condition in which the producer is caught between rising costs and a declining or stable price for his product. See page 151.

Price elasticity of demand The responsiveness of consumers to a change in price: $E_d = \%\Delta Q/\%\Delta P$. See page 41.

Private good (pure) A good whose benefits are exclusively received by the person who has possession of it. Example: An ice cream cone. See page 24.

Private property rights The right of individuals to possess resources or goods and to exclude others from their use.

Progressive tax system Tax structure under which the tax rate varies directly with income. Example: Federal income tax system. See page 332.

Property rights The permissible limits to the use of resources, goods, and services. See page 77.

Proportional tax system Tax structure under which the tax rate remains constant over all income levels. See page 332.

Public interest theory of regulation Regulation is necessary to overcome free-market problems of externalities and monopoly power. See page 218.

Public good A good whose benefits are shared by the relevant group if the good is provided or consumed by any one person; the receipt of benefits by one person does not deny those benefits to anyone else. Example: National defense, police protection, environmental quality. See page 24.

Quota A quantitative restriction on imports or exports. See page 291.

Rational behavior Actions which are logical and in one's best interests. Basic assumptions: One (1) knows what he or she wants, (2) is able to order his or her wants, and (3) is able to act consistently upon the wants that are ordered. See pages 17, 26, and 27.

Real-wage rate The ratio of the money wage to the price index; the purchasing power of the money wage rate. See page 501.

Recession A downward movement in economic activity. See page 534.

Regressive tax system Tax structure under which the tax rate varies inversely with income. Example: Sales tax. See page 332.

Rent controls Government restrictions on payments to landlords for use of apartments, houses, and business. See page 202.

Required reserves Reserve ratio times a bank's demand deposits; the deposit in the Federal Reserve plus vault cash which a bank must have. See page 454.

Reserve deposit The balance of a commercial bank's deposit in the Federal Reserve. See page 453.

Reserve requirement (or ratio) That portion of a bank's total reserve deposit which cannot be loaned and must be on deposit with the Federal Reserve or in cash in a bank's vault.

Revenue sharing Federal grants given to the states local governments to use as they see fit. See page 325.

Saving That portion of income which is not spent. See page 508.

Short-run equilibrium The price-quantity combination in existence until producers can expand their operations or other market conditions change. See page 129.

Social contract An agreed-on compact which stipulates limits of individual behavior; a set of behavioral rules. See Chapter 5.

Social cost The costs imposed on others not a party to a transaction; often called third-party or spillover effects of a transaction. See page 89.

Social order The various ways people interact to obtain what they want. See page 7.

Special drawing rights An accounting creation of the International Monetary Fund which can be used to meet balance of payments deficits. See page 312.

Spillover A by-product of one individual's behavior which affects others. See page 24.

Soil bank program A government program initiated in 1956 which paid farmers to hold a portion of their land out of production. See page 157.

State property rights The condition in which the state may exclude someone from using resources, goods, or services. See page 86.

Structural unemployment Long-term unemployment due to basic institutional conditions in the economy. Example: Unemployment due to unions and minimum wage laws. See page 488.

Substitute products Goods which may be used in place of each other. Example: Coffee and tea, or Coke and Pepsi. See page 47.

Sunk costs Those costs incurred because of past choices. See page 67.

Supply curve The collection of points indicating the units of a good that will be produced at each price; generally, the assumed direct relation between the price and the quantity of a good producers are willing to offer on the market, everything else held constant. See page 62.

Supply of labor The assumed direct relation between the wage rate and the quantity of labor workers will offer, everything else constant. See page 250.

T accounts Simplified accounting statements with assets under the left wing of the T and liabilities under the right side of the T. See page 451.

Tariff A tax on imported goods. See page 291.

Theory A model of how the physical and social world is put together. See page 9.

Total labor force The civilian labor force plus the armed forces. See page 436.

Unemployed People who do not work but who want to work. For specifics, see page 436.

Unemployment rate The ratio of the number of people classified as unemployed to the number of people in the civilian labor force. See page 435.

Union Organization of labor designed to raise wages and improve working conditions. Example: AFL-CIO. See page 273.

Unitary elastic demand When a price change results in no change in total expenditures or when $E_d = \%\Delta Q/\%\Delta P = 1.0$. See page 41.

User charge A price firms must pay per unit of each resource used on pollution emitted. See page 354.

Usury laws Laws designed to restrict interest rates which may be charged on loaned money. See page 203.

Util The economist's name for a unit of satisfaction. See page 35.

Utility Satisfaction. See page 17.

Velocity of money The rate at which money is used and reused: $V = PO/M$ OR $V = Y/M$ where V is velocity, P is the price level, O is output, M is the money stock, and Y is the national income level. See page 565.

Voting rule The degree of agreement necessary for a legislative proposal to pass. Example: Simple majority. See page 392.

White market The legal exchange of goods. Example: Proposed legal sale of coupons distributed to ration gasoline. See page 202.

Wholesale Price Index The ratio of the cost of a defined set of commodities sold in large quantities in nonretail markets in any year to the cost of the same commodities in some base year. See page 440.

Index